Introduction to SQL,

Fourth Edition

Introduction to SQL, Fourth Edition

Mastering the Relational Database Language

20th Anniversary Edition

Rick F. van der Lans

Translated by Diane Cools

✦✦ Addison-Wesley

Upper Saddle River, NJ • Boston • Indianapolis • San Francisco
New York • Toronto • Montreal • London • Munich • Paris • Madrid
Cape Town • Sydney • Tokyo • Singapore • Mexico City

Many of the designations used by manufacturers and sellers to distinguish their products are claimed as trademarks. Where those designations appear in this book, and the publisher was aware of a trademark claim, the designations have been printed with initial capital letters or in all capitals.

The author and publisher have taken care in the preparation of this book, but make no expressed or implied warranty of any kind and assume no responsibility for errors or omissions. No liability is assumed for incidental or consequential damages in connection with or arising out of the use of the information or programs contained herein.

The publisher offers excellent discounts on this book when ordered in quantity for bulk purchases or special sales, which may include electronic versions and/or custom covers and content particular to your business, training goals, marketing focus, and branding interests. For more information, please contact:

> U.S. Corporate and Government Sales
> (800) 382-3419
> corpsales@pearsontechgroup.com

For sales outside the United States please contact:

> International Sales
> international@pearsoned.com

This Book Is Safari Enabled

The Safari® Enabled icon on the cover of your favorite technology book means the book is available through Safari Bookshelf. When you buy this book, you get free access to the online edition for 45 days. Safari Bookshelf is an electronic reference library that lets you easily search thousands of technical books, find code samples, download chapters, and access technical information whenever and wherever you need it.

To gain 45-day Safari Enabled access to this book:

- Go to http://www.awprofessional.com/safarienabled
- Complete the brief registration form
- Enter the coupon code 1AHY-IN3H-VX7Z-Q2HE-GICS

If you have difficulty registering on Safari Bookshelf or accessing the online edition, please e-mail customer-service@safaribooksonline.com.

Visit us on the Web: www.awprofessional.com

Library of Congress Cataloging-in-Publication Data

Lans, Rick F. van der.
  [SQL leerboek. English]
  Introduction to SQL : mastering the relational database language / Rick F. van der Lans. — 4th ed.
    p. cm.
  ISBN 0-321-30596-5 (pbk. : alk. paper) 1. SQL (Computer program language) I. Title.
  QA76.73.S67L3613 2006
  005.13'3—dc22
                              2006021135

ISBN 0-321-30596-5

Text printed in the United States on recycled paper at R. R. Donnelley in Crawfordsville, Indiana.

First printing, September 2006

Dedicated to Diane

Contents

V Procedural Database Objects   803

About the Author

Rick F. van der Lans is an independent consultant, author, and lecturer specializing in database technology, SQL, and data warehousing. He is managing director of R20/ Consultancy. He has been a member of the Dutch ISO committee responsible for developing the SQL standard. For the past 20 years, he has taught SQL classes to thousands of attendees. His popular books, including *Introduction to SQL* and *The SQL Guide to Oracle*, have been translated into various languages and have sold more than 100,000 copies.

Rick is an internationally acclaimed lecturer. Throughout has career, he has lectured in many European countries, South America, USA, and Australia. You can contact Rick via email at sql@r20.nl.

Preface

Introduction

SQL was, is, and will stay for the foreseeable future the database language for relational database servers such as IBM DB2, Microsoft SQL Server, MySQL, Oracle, Progress, Sybase Adaptive Server, and dozens of others. This book contains a complete and detailed description of *SQL* (Structured Query Language). It should be seen primarily as a textbook in the active sense. After reading this book, you should be familiar with all the statements, the features, and some idiosyncrasies of SQL, and you should be able to use SQL efficiently and effectively.

SQL supports a small but very powerful set of statements for manipulating, managing, and protecting data stored in a database. This power has resulted in its tremendous popularity. In the early 1980s, there were only 10 to 20 SQL database servers, but today this number is at least multiplied by four. Almost every database server supports SQL or a dialect of the language. Currently, SQL products are available for every kind of computer, from a small handheld computer to a large server, and for every operating system, including Microsoft Windows and many UNIX variations. An official international standard for SQL was introduced in 1987. This has developed into what Michael Stonebraker, an authority in the field of databases, once expressed as *intergalactic dataspeak*.

Topics

This book is completely devoted to SQL. Every aspect of the language is discussed thoroughly and critically. These aspects, among others, include the following:

- Querying data (joins, functions, and subqueries)
- Updating data
- Creating tables and views
- Specifying primary and foreign keys and other integrity constraints
- Using indexes
- Considering data security

- Developing stored procedures and triggers
- Developing programs with embedded SQL and ODBC
- Working with transactions
- Optimizing statements
- Dealing with object relational concepts, such as subtables, references, sets, and user-defined data types
- Using the catalog

Which SQL Dialect?

Many SQL products are available on the market today. All these implementations of SQL resemble each other closely, but, unfortunately, differences do exist between them. Some do not support all the SQL statements, and others do not have all the features of a specific SQL statement. In some cases, identical statements can even return different results by different products.

The question then becomes, which SQL dialect is described in this book? To make the book as practical as possible, we describe the SQL statements and features supported by most of the dominant SQL products. This increases the practical value of this book. After reading this book, you can work with any SQL product. In other words, the focus is not so much on DB2, Oracle, or MySQL, and not even on the international standards for SQL; instead, it is on *common SQL*—SQL as implemented by most products.

For Whom Is This Book Intended?

We recommend this SQL book to those who want to use the full power of SQL effectively and efficiently in practice. This book is, therefore, suitable for the following groups of people:

- **Students** in higher education, including those in technical colleges, polytechnics, universities, and sixth-form colleges
- **Developers** who develop or intend to develop applications with the help of an SQL product
- **Designers**, **analysts**, and **consultants** who have to deal, directly or indirectly, with SQL or another relational database language and want to know its features and limitations
- **Home students** who are interested in SQL in particular or relational databases in general
- **Users** who have the authority to use SQL to query the database of the company or institute for which they are working

A Practical Book

This book should be seen primarily as a *textbook* in the active sense, and less as a reference work. To this end, it contains many examples and exercises (with answers). Do not ignore the exercises. Experience shows that you will learn the language more thoroughly and more quickly by practicing often and doing many exercises.

Practicing with MySQL

One of the best-known SQL database servers is a product called *MySQL*. In this book, we assume that you will use MySQL to do the examples and the exercises. MySQL has been chosen because of its popularity and because its SQL dialect includes extensive functionality and shows much similarity to the international standard for SQL.

We advise you to install MySQL and practice as many exercises as possible with the help of MySQL. Executing SQL statements and studying the results is still the best way to master this powerful language. Later in this book, we describe how to install the product.

What Is on the CD-ROM?

The CD-ROM included in this book contains MySQL, of course. The version included on the CD-ROM has no functional limitations; it has the same functionality as the commercial version.

The version included is Version 5.0.7 for Windows. You can also download this product free of charge for many other platforms, including Linux, Sun Solaris, FreeBSD, MAC OS, HP-UX, IBM AIX, and Novell NetWare from the Web site www.mysql.com. You can even choose which version you would like to use.

A useful tool called WinSQL is also included on the CD-ROM, which makes working with MySQL easier. It is at least worth the effort to try these products.

This Book's Web Site

When you leaf through the book, you will find numerous SQL statements. Sometimes these are examples and sometimes they are answers to questions. After you install MySQL, you can run through these statements to see whether they work and see their effect. You could type in all the statements again like a real Spartan, but you can also make life easy for yourself by downloading all the statements from the Internet. A special Web site for this book, www.r20.nl, includes all the SQL statements.

The SQL statements have been placed deliberately on this Web site and not on the CD-ROM included in the book because it is easier to change them, if needed. It also makes it possible to add alternative solutions.

You can use the Web site for other aspects as well:

- For MySQL, an installation process and instructions are included. When you install MySQL under Windows, you will find useful tips on the Web site. The installation process of the example database is also explained there.
- If an error is found in the book, a rectification will be placed on the Web site.
- Reader comments that could be of interest to others will also be placed on the Web site.
- We even will consider making additional chapters available on the Web site in the future.

Therefore, keep an eye on this Web site.

Prerequisite Knowledge

Some general knowledge of programming languages and database servers is required.

The History of This Book

It was 1984, and the database world was under the spell of a revolution. SQL had started its triumphal procession. Vendors such as IBM and Oracle had introduced the commercial versions of their SQL database servers, and the marketing machine went at full speed. The market reacted positively to this rise of first-generation SQL database servers. Many organizations decided to buy such a database server and gradually phase out their existing products.

My employer at that time had decided to get involved in this tumult as well. It also wanted to make money with this new database language, and the plan was to start organizing SQL courses. Because of my background knowledge, I was charged with this task. That SQL would become such a success and that my agreement to present the courses would have far-reaching consequences, personally as well as professionally, was never in my mind.

After studying SQL closely, I started to develop the material for the course. After teaching SQL for two years with great pleasure, I got an idea to write a book about SQL. It would have to be a book that would be completely dedicated to this language, with its many possibilities and idiosyncrasies.

After producing gallons of blood, sweat, and tears, I completed the first Dutch edition in 1986, entitled *Het SQL Leerboek*. Barely before the book was published, I was asked to write an English version. That book was published in 1987, and in that language it was the first book completely devoted to SQL. After that, a German and Italian version appeared. Obviously, there was a need for information about SQL. Everyone wanted to learn about SQL, but there was not much information available.

Because SQL was still young, development was fast. Statements were added, extended, and improved. New implementations became available, new application areas were discovered, and new versions of the SQL standard appeared. Soon a new edition of the book had to be written. And there was more to come. The book you have in your hands right now is already the fourth edition of the English version. And it will not be the last because SQL has gloriously won the revolution in the database world, and there is no competition in sight on the horizon.

The Fourth Edition

This book is a completely revised fourth edition of *Introduction to SQL*. The previous edition was also seriously revised, so why a completely revised edition now? The explanation is simple: Once again, SQL has changed dramatically. However, not many statements have been added this time; the changes are more in the details. The language has been adjusted at several places, so the way in which certain statements are explained had to change.

And Finally . . .

Writing this book was not a solo project. Many people have contributed to this or previous editions of this book. I would like to use this preface to thank them for their help, contribution, ideas, comments on the contents, mental support, and patience.

I am grateful to the MySQL organization for providing the software. I think this product is invaluable for anyone who wants to learn SQL. The best way to learn a language is still to work with it!

It does not matter how many times a writer reads through his own work; editors remain indispensable. A writer does not read what he has written, but what he thinks he has written. In this respect, writing is like programming. That is why I owe a great deal to the following people for making critical comments and giving very helpful advice: Marc van Cappellen, Ian Cargill, Corine Cools, Richard van Dijk, Rose Endres, Wim Frederiks, Andrea Gray, Ed Jedeloo, Josien van der Laan, Oda van der Lans, Deborah Leendertse, Onno de Maar, Andrea Maurino, Sandor Nieuwenhuijs, Henk Schreij, Dave Slayton, Aad Speksnijder, Nok van Veen, and David van der Waaij. They all have read this manuscript (or parts of it), or the manuscript of a previous edition, a translation of it, or an adjusted version.

I would also like to thank the thousands of students across the world whom I have taught SQL over the past years. Their comments and recommendations have been invaluable in revising this book. In addition, a large number of readers of the previous edition responded to my request to send comments and suggestions. I want to thank them for the trouble they took to put these in writing.

For the first and second editions, Diane Cools did much of the typing and corrected many errors. I am still grateful for that because working with WordStar Version 1 on a

PC/XT without a hard disk looked like a luxury then. I would like to thank her again for her work on this new edition. As an editor, she made this book readable to others. For a writer, it is also reassuring to know that there is someone who, especially in difficult times, keeps stimulating and motivating you. Thanks, Diane!

Finally, again I would like to ask readers to send comments, opinions, ideas, and suggestions concerning the contents of the book to sql@r20.nl stating "Introduction to SQL." Many thanks in anticipation of your cooperation.

Rick F. van der Lans
Den Haag, The Netherlands, June 2006

I | Introduction

SQL is a compact and powerful language for working with databases. Despite this compactness, it cannot be described simply in a few chapters. We would do the language no justice then. Vendors of SQL products have made it even more complicated by implementing different SQL dialects. For a structured explanation, we start this book with a number of introductory chapters that form the first part.

In Chapter 1, "Introduction to SQL," we provide an overall description of SQL, give the background and history of SQL, and outline several application areas of the language. We also describe a number of concepts in the relational model (the theory behind SQL).

This book contains many examples and exercises. So that you do not have to learn a new database for each example, we use the same database for most of these examples and exercises. This database contains the basis for the administration of an international tennis league. Chapter 2, "The Tennis Club Sample Database," describes the structure of this database. Look closely at this before you begin the exercises.

We strongly recommend that you use MySQL when doing the exercises. For this, you must install the software and the example database. Chapter 3, "Installing the Software," describes how to do that. For several related aspects, we refer you to the Web site of the book.

This part closes with Chapter 4, "SQL in a Nutshell," in which all the important SQL statements are reviewed. After reading this part, you should have both a general idea of what SQL offers as a language and an overall impression of what is discussed in the book.

Introduction to SQL

1.1 Introduction

In this chapter, we provide a general description of SQL, give the background and history of SQL, and discuss several applications areas of the language. We also cover basic subjects, such as the database and database server. SQL is based on the theory of the *relational model*. To use SQL, some knowledge of this model is invaluable. Therefore, in Section 1.3, we describe the relational model. In Section 1.4, we briefly describe what SQL is, what can be done with the language, and how it differs from other languages (such as Java, Visual Basic, or Pascal). Section 1.6 is devoted to the history of SQL. Although SQL is thought of as a very modern language, it has a history dating back to 1972. SQL has been implemented in many products and has a monopoly position in the world of database languages. In Section 1.9 we outline the most important current standards for SQL, and in Section 1.10, we give a brief outline of the most important SQL products.

This first chapter closes with a description of the structure of the book. Each chapter is summarized in a few sentences.

1.2 Database, Database Server, and Database Language

Structured Query Language (SQL) is a database language used for formulating statements that are processed by a database server. This sentence contains three important concepts: *database*, *database server*, and *database language*. We begin with an explanation of each of these terms.

What is a *database*? In this book, we use a definition that is derived from Chris J. Date's definition; see [Date 95]:

> A database consists of some collection of persistent data that is used by the application systems of some given enterprise, and that is managed by a database management system.

Card index files do not, therefore, constitute a database. On the other hand, the large files of banks, insurance companies, telephone companies, or the state transport department can be considered databases. These databases contain data about addresses, account balances, car registration plates, weights of vehicles, and so on. For example, the company you work for probably has its own computers, and these are used to store salary-related data.

Data in a database becomes useful only if something is done with it. According to the definition, data in the database is managed by a separate programming system. We call this system a *database server* or *database-management system* (DBMS). MySQL is such a database server. A database server enables users to process data stored in a database. Without a database server, it is impossible to look at data, or to update or delete obsolete data, in the database. The database server alone knows where and how data is stored. A definition of a database server is given in [ELMA03] by R. Elmasri:

> A database server is a collection of programs that enables users to create and maintain a database.

A database server never changes or deletes the data in a database by itself. Someone or something has to give the command for this to happen. Examples of commands that a user could give to the database server are "delete all data about the vehicle with the registration plate number DR-12-DP" or "give the names of all the companies that haven't paid the invoices of last March." However, users cannot communicate with the database server directly. Commands are given to a database server with the help of an application. An application is always between the user and the database server. Section 1.4 discusses this subject.

The definition of the term *database* also contains the word *persistent*. This means that data in a database remains there permanently, until it is changed or deleted explicitly. If you store new data in a database and the database server sends the message back that the storage operation was successful, you can be sure that the data will still be there tomorrow (even if you switch off your computer). This is unlike the data that we store in the internal memory of a computer. If the computer is switched off, that data is lost forever; it is, therefore, not persistent.

Commands are given to a database server with the help of special languages called *database languages*. Commands, also known as statements, which are formulated according to the rules of the database language, are entered by users using special software and are processed by the database server. Every database server, from whichever manufacturer, possesses a database language. Some systems support more than one. All these languages are different, which makes it possible to divide them into groups. The *relational database languages* form one of these groups. An example of such a language is SQL.

How does a database server store data in a database? A database server uses neither a chest of drawers nor a filing cabinet to hold information; instead, computers work with storage media such as tapes, floppy disks, and magnetic and optical disks. The manner in which a database server stores information on these media is very complex and technical, and it is not explained in detail in this book. In fact, it is not required to have this technical knowledge because one of the most important tasks of a database server is to offer *data independence*. This means that users do not need to know how or where data is stored: To users, a database is simply a large reservoir of information. Storage methods are also completely independent of the database language being used. In a way, this resembles the process of checking luggage at an airport. It is none of our business where and how the airline stores our luggage; the only thing we are interested in is whether the luggage is at our destination upon arrival.

Another important task of a database server is to maintain the *integrity* of the data stored in a database. This means, first, that the database server has to make sure that database data always satisfies the rules that apply in the real world. Consider, for example, the case of an employee who is allowed to work for one department only. It should never be possible, in a database managed by a database server, for that particular employee to be registered as working for two or more departments. Second, integrity means that two different pieces of database data do not contradict one another. This is also known as *data consistency*. (As an example, in one place in a database, Mr. Johnson might be recorded as being born on August 4, 1964, and in another place he might be given a birth date of December 14, 1946. These two pieces of data are obviously inconsistent.) Each database server is designed to recognize statements that can be used to specify *constraints*. After these rules are entered, the database server takes care of their implementation.

1.3 The Relational Model

SQL is based on a formal and mathematical theory. This theory, which consists of a set of concepts and definitions, is called the *relational model*. The relational model was defined by E. F. Codd in 1970, when he was employed by IBM. He introduced the relational model in the almost legendary article entitled "A Relational Model of Data for Large Shared Data Banks"; see [CODD70]. This relational model provides a theoretical basis for database languages. It consists of a small number of simple concepts for recording data in a database, together with a number of operators to manipulate the data. These concepts and operators are principally borrowed from *set theory* and *predicate logic*. Later, in 1979, Codd presented his ideas for an improved version of the model; see [CODD79] and [CODD90].

The relational model has served as an example for the development of various database languages, including QUEL (see [STON86]), SQUARE (see [BOYC73a]), and, of course, SQL. These database languages are based on the concepts and ideas of that relational model and are therefore called *relational database languages*; SQL is an example. The rest of this part concentrates on the following terms used in the relational model, which appear extensively in this book:

- Table
- Column
- Row
- Constraint or integrity constraint
- Primary key
- Candidate key

- Alternate key
- Foreign key or referential key

Please note that this is not a complete list of all the terms used by the relational model. Most of these terms are discussed in detail in Part III, "Creating Database Objects." For more extensive descriptions, see [CODD90] and [DATE95].

1.3.1 Table, Column, and Row

Data can be stored in a relational database in only one format, and that is in *tables*. The official name for a table is actually *relation*, and the term *relational model* stems from this name. We have chosen to use the term *table* because that is the word used in SQL.

Informally, a table is a set of *rows*, with each row consisting of a set of *values*. All the rows in a certain table have the same number of values. Figure 1.1 shows an example of a table called the PLAYERS table. This table contains data about five players who are members of a tennis club.

Figure 1.1   *The concepts value, row, column, and table*

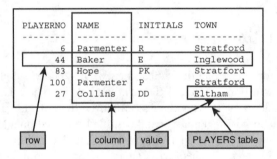

This PLAYERS table has five *rows*, one for each player. A row with values can be considered as a set of data elements that belong together. For example, in this table, the first row consists of the values 6, Parmenter, R, and Stratford. This information tells us that there is a player with number 6, that his last name is Parmenter and his initial is R, and that he lives in the town Stratford.

PLAYERNO, NAME, INITIALS, and TOWN are the names of the *columns* in the table. The PLAYERNO column contains the values 6, 44, 83, 100, and 27. This set of values is also known as the *population* of the PLAYERNO column. Each row has a value for each column. Therefore, in the first row there is a value for the PLAYERNO column and a value for the NAME column, and so on.

A table has two special properties:

- The intersection of a row and a column can consist of only one value, an *atomic value*. An atomic value is an indivisible unit. The database server can deal with such a value only in its entirety.
- The rows in a table have no specific order. One should not think in terms of the first row, the last three rows, or the next row. The contents of a table should actually be considered a *set* of rows in the true sense of the word.

1.3.2 Constraints

In the first section of this chapter, we described the integrity of the data stored in tables, the database data. The contents of a table must satisfy certain rules, the so-called *integrity constraints* (integrity rules). Two examples of integrity constraints are: The player number of a player may not be negative, and two different players may not have the same player number. Integrity constraints can be compared to road signs. They also indicate what is allowed and what is not allowed.

Integrity constraints should be enforced by a relational database server. Each time a table is updated, the database server has to check whether the new data satisfies the relevant integrity constraints. This is a task of the database server. The integrity constraints must be specified first so that they are known to the database server.

Integrity constraints can have several forms. Because some are used so frequently, they have been assigned special names, such as primary key, candidate key, alternate key, and foreign key. The analogy with the road signs (as shown in Figure 1.2) applies here as well. Special symbols have been invented for road signs that are frequently used, and they also were given names, such as a right-of-way sign or a stop sign. We explain those named integrity constraints in the following sections.

Figure 1.2 *Integrity constraints are the road signs of a database*

1.3.3 Primary Key

The *primary key* of a table is a column (or a combination of columns) that is used as a unique identification of rows in that table. In other words, two different rows in a table may never have the same value in their primary key, and for every row in the table, the primary key must always have one value. The PLAYERNO column in the PLAYERS table is the primary key for this table. Two players, therefore, may never have the same number, and there may never be a player without a number.

We come across primary keys everywhere. For example, the table in which a bank stores data about bank accounts will have the column bank account number as primary key. And when we create a table in which different cars are registered, the license plate will be the primary key, as shown in Figure 1.3.

Figure 1.3   *License plate as possible primary key*

1.3.4 Candidate Key

Some tables contain more than one column (or combination of columns) that can act as a primary key. These columns all possess the uniqueness property of a primary key and are called *candidate keys*. However, only one is designated as the primary key. Therefore, a table always has at least one candidate key.

If we assume that passport numbers are also included in the PLAYERS table, that column will be used as candidate key because passport numbers are unique. Two players can never have the same passport number. This column could also be designated as the primary key.

1.3.5 Alternate Key

A candidate key that is not the primary key of a table is called an *alternate key*. Zero or more alternate keys can be defined for a specific table. The term *candidate key* is a general term for all primary and alternate keys. Because PLAYERNO is already the primary key of the PLAYERS table, LEAGUENO is an alternate key.

1.3.6 Foreign Key

A *foreign key* is a column (or combination of columns) in a table in which the population is a subset of the population of the primary key of a table. (This does not have to be another table.) Foreign keys are sometimes called referential keys.

Imagine that, in addition to the PLAYERS table, there is a TEAMS table; see Figure 1.4. The TEAMNO column is called the primary key of this table. The PLAYERNO column in this table represents the captain of each particular team. This has to be an existing player number, one that is found in the PLAYERS table. The population of this column represents a subset of the population of the PLAYERNO column in the PLAYERS table. PLAYERNO in the TEAMS table is called a foreign key.

Now you can see that we can combine two tables. We do this by including the PLAYERNO column in the TEAMS table, thus establishing a link with the PLAYERNO column in the PLAYERS table.

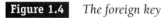

Figure 1.4   *The foreign key*

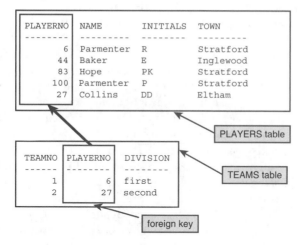

1.4 What Is SQL?

As already stated, SQL is a *relational database language*. Among other things, the language consists of statements to insert, update, delete, query, and protect data. The following is a list of statements that can be formulated with SQL:

- Insert the address of a new employee.
- Delete all the stock data for product ABC.
- Show the address of employee Johnson.
- Show the sales figures of shoes for every region and for every month.
- Show how many products have been sold in London the last three months.
- Make sure that Mr. Johnson cannot see the salary data any longer.

SQL has already been implemented by many vendors as the database language for their database server. For example, IBM, MySQL, and Oracle are all vendors of SQL products. Thus, SQL is not the name of a certain product that has been brought onto the market by one particular vendor. Although SQL is not a database server, in this book, SQL is considered, for simplicity, to be a database server as well as a language. Of course, wherever necessary, a distinction is drawn.

We call SQL a relational database language because it is associated with data that has been defined according to the rules of the relational model. (However, we must note that on particular points, the theory and SQL differ; see [CODD90].) Because SQL is a relational database language, for a long time, it has been grouped with the declarative or nonprocedural database languages. By *declarative* and *nonprocedural*, we mean that users (with the help of statements) have to specify only *which* data elements they want, not *how* they must be accessed one by one. Well-known languages such as C, C++, Java, PHP, Pascal, and Visual Basic are examples of procedural languages.

Nowadays, however, SQL can no longer be called a pure declarative language. Since the early 1990s, many vendors have added procedural extensions to SQL. These make it possible to create procedural database objects such as *triggers* and *stored procedures*; see Part V, "Procedural Database Objects." Traditional statements such as IF-THEN-ELSE and WHILE-DO have also been added. Although most of the well-known SQL statements are still not procedural by nature, SQL has changed into a hybrid language consisting of procedural and nonprocedural statements. MySQL has also been extended with these procedural database objects.

SQL can be used in two ways. First, SQL can be used *interactively*: For example, a user enters an SQL statement on the spot and the database server processes it immediately. The result is also immediately visible. Interactive SQL is intended for application developers and for end users who want to create reports themselves.

The products that support interactive SQL can be split in two groups: the somewhat old-fashioned products with a terminal-like interface and those with a modern graphical interface. MySQL includes a product with a terminal-like interface that bears the same name as the database server: MYSQL. Figure 1.5 shows what this program looks like. First an SQL statement is entered, and then the result is shown underneath.

Figure 1.5   *An example of the query program called* MYSQL *that specifies the SQL statements interactively*

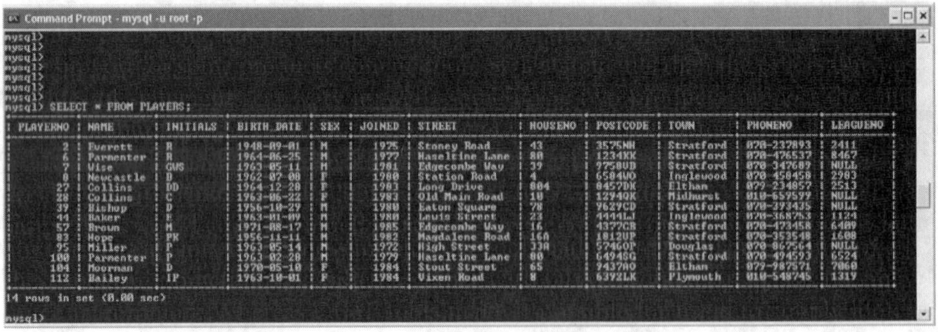

However, products with a more graphical interface are also available for interactive use that are not from MySQL, such as *WinSQL*; see Figure 1.6.

The second way in which SQL can be used is *preprogrammed* SQL. Here, the SQL statements are embedded in an application that is written in another programming language. Results from these statements are not immediately visible to the user but are processed by the *enveloping* application. Preprogrammed SQL appears mainly in applications developed for end users. These end users do not need to learn SQL to access the data, but they work from simple screens and menus designed for their applications. Examples are applications to record customer information and applications to handle stock management. Figure 1.7 contains an example of a screen with fields in which the user can enter the address without any knowledge of SQL. The application behind this screen has been programmed to pass certain SQL statements to the database server. The application, therefore, uses SQL statements to transfer the information that has been entered into the database.

Figure 1.6   *An example of the query program WinSQL*

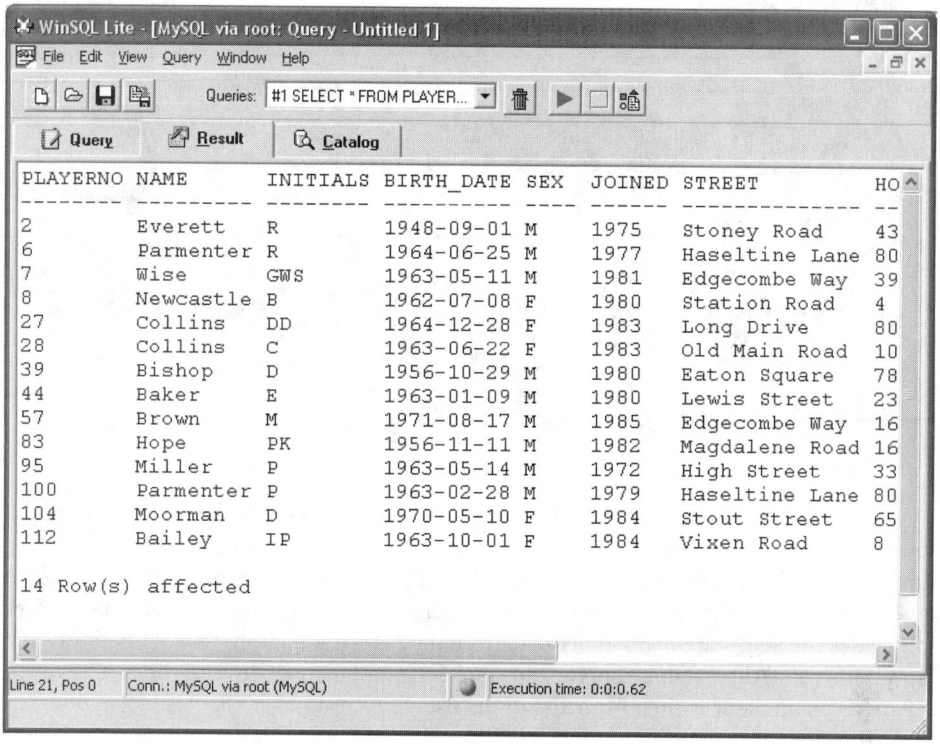

In the early stages of the development of SQL, there was only one method for pre-programmed SQL, called *embedded* SQL. In the 1990s, other methods appeared. The most important is called *Call Level Interface* SQL (CLI SQL). There are many variations of CLI SQL, such as Open Database Connectivity (ODBC) and Java Database Connectivity (JDBC). The most important ones are described in this book. The different methods of preprogrammed SQL are also called the *binding styles*.

The statements and features of interactive and preprogrammed SQL are virtually the same. By this, we mean that most statements that can be entered and processed interactively can also be included (embedded) in an SQL application. Preprogrammed SQL has been extended with a number of statements that are added only to make it possible to merge the SQL statements with the non-SQL statements. In this book, we are primarily engaged in interactive SQL. Preprogrammed SQL is dealt with in Part IV, "Programming with SQL."

Figure 1.7   *SQL is shielded in many applications; users can see only the input fields*

New Recipient - [R20]

Personal Information

Title: | First Name: | Last: |

Company: |

Address1: |

Address2: |

City: | State/Country : | Zip Code: |

Notes: |

Billing: | Misc: |

Connections

| | Country | Area | Local Number | | Extension | |
Fax | | | | x | | Programs... |
Voice: | | | | x | |
Mail | | | Find... |

Send From

Office: Fax   Home: Fax   Away: Fax

Last Values   OK   Cancel

Three important components are involved in the interactive and preprogrammed processing of SQL statements: the user, the application, and the database server; see Figure 1.8. The database server is responsible for storing and accessing data on disk. The application and definitely the user have nothing to do with this. The database server processes the SQL statements that are delivered by the application. In a defined way, the application and the database server can send SQL statements between them. The result of an SQL statement is then returned to the user.

Figure 1.8   *The user, the application, and the database server are pivotal for the processing of SQL*

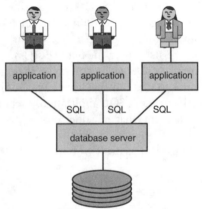

1.5 Several Categories of SQL Applications

SQL is used in a wide range of applications. If SQL is used, it is important to know what kind of application is being developed. For example, does an application execute many simple SQL statements or just a few very complex ones? This can affect how SQL statements should be formulated in the most efficient way, which statements are selected, and how SQL is used. To simplify this discussion, we introduce a hierarchical classification of applications to which we refer, if relevant, in other chapters:

- Application with preprogrammed SQL
  - Input application
    - Online input application
    - Batch input application
  - Batch reporting application
- Application with interactive SQL
  - Query tool
    - Direct SQL
    - Query-By-Example
    - Natural language
  - Business intelligence tool
    - Statistical tool
    - OLAP tool
    - Data mining tool

The first subdivision has to do with whether SQL statements are preprogrammed. This is not the case for products that support SQL interactively. The user determines, directly or indirectly, which SQL statements are created.

The preprogrammed applications are subdivided into input and reporting applications. The *input applications* have two variations: online and batch. An online input application, for example, can be written in Visual Basic and SQL and allows data to be added to a database. This type of application is typically used by many users concurrently, and the preprogrammed SQL statements are relatively simple. Batch input applications read files containing new data and add the data to an existing database. These applications usually run at regular times and require much processing. The SQL statements are again relatively simple.

A batch reporting application generates reports. For example, every Sunday, a report is generated that contains the total sales figures for every region. Every Monday morning, this report is delivered by internal mail to the desk of the manager or is sent to his e-mail address. Many companies use this kind of application. Usually, a batch reporting application contains only a few statements, but these are complex.

The market for applications in which users work interactively with SQL is less well organized. For the first subcategory, the query tools, users must have a knowledge of relational concepts. In the query process, the user works with, among other things, tables, columns, rows, primary keys, and foreign keys.

Within the category of query tools, we can identify three subcategories. In the first category, the users have to type in SQL statements directly. They must be fully acquainted with the grammar of SQL. WinSQL, which we already discussed, is such a program. Figure 1.6 shows what this program looks like. In the middle of the screen there is an SQL statement with the result underneath it.

Query-By-Example (QBE) was designed in the 1970s by Moshé Zloof; see [ZLOO7]. QBE was intended to be a relational database language and, in some ways, to provide an alternative for SQL. Eventually, the language served as a model for an entire family of products, all of which had a comparable interface. It is not necessary for users of QBE to understand the syntax of SQL because SQL statements are automatically generated. Users simply draw tables and fill their conditions and specifications into those tables. QBE has been described as a graphical version of SQL. This is not completely true, but it gives an indication of what QBE is. Figure 1.9 shows what a QBE question looks like.

Figure 1.9   *An example of Query-By-Example*

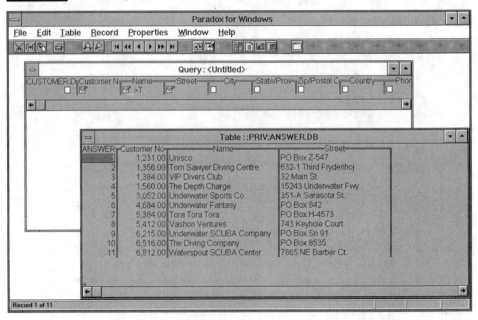

Some vendors have tried to offer users the strength and flexibility of SQL without the necessity of learning the language. This is implemented by a natural language interface that is put on top of SQL, enabling users to define their questions in simple English sentences. Next, these sentences are translated into SQL. The market for this type of products has always been small, but it still is a very interesting category of query tools.

Again, to use these query tools, the user has to understand the principles of a relational database, and this can be too technical for some users. Nevertheless, experts in the field of marketing, logistics, or sales who have no technical background still will want to access the database data. For this purpose, the *business intelligence* tools have been designed. Here, a thick software layer is placed on top of SQL, meaning that neither SQL nor relational concepts are visible.

In this category, the statistical packages are probably the oldest. Products such as SAS and SPSS have been available for a long time. These tools offer their own languages for accessing data in databases and, of course, for performing statistical analysis. Generally, these are specialized and very powerful languages. Behind the scenes, their own statements are translated into SQL statements, if appropriate.

Very popular within the business intelligence tools is the category called *OLAP* tools. OLAP stands for *online analytical processing*, a term introduced by E. F. Codd. These are products designed for users who want to look at their sales, marketing, or production figures from different points of view and at different levels of detail.

Users of OLAP applications do not see the familiar relational interface, which means no "flat" tables or SQL, but work with a so-called *multidimensional interface*. Data is grouped logically within *arrays*, which consist of dimensions, such as region, product, and time. Within a dimension, hierarchies of elements can be built. The element Amsterdam belongs, for example, to the Netherlands, and the Netherlands belongs to Northern Europe. All three elements belong to the dimension called region. Unfortunately, all vendors have their own terminology. *Cube, model, variable,* and *multidimensional table* are all alternative names for *array*.

Figure 1.10   *Three sales regions with their respective sales figures*

	Sales ($)	Plan Sales ($)	Sales (Units)	Sales-Plan	Sales - Plan \<Rank\>	Sales-Plan %Variation	LY Sales ($)	LY Plan Sales ($)	LY Sales-Plan	LY Sales-Plan %Variation
Boston	91,734	128,549	1,118	(36,815)	1	-29%	89,865	81,044	8,821	11%
Portland	89,305	85,866	1,094	3,440	2	4%	82,291	80,295	1,996	2%
Concord	92,82	87,906	1,124	4,918	3	6%	88,987	81,114	7,873	10%

It falls outside the context of this book to give a detailed picture of OLAP, but to give you an idea of what is involved, we have included a simple example. Figure 1.10 contains a number of sales figures per region. There are three sales regions: Boston, Portland, and

Concord. We can see that in the fourth column, the sales figure of Boston is given in brackets. This implies that this number is too low. This is correct because Boston was supposed to achieve $128,549 (see the second column in the table), but achieved only $91,734 (see the first column). This is clearly a long way behind the planned sales. Managers would probably like to know the reason for this and would like to see more detailed figures. To see these figures, all they have to do is click on the word *Boston*; the figures represented in Figure 1.11 then would be shown. Here, the sales figures in Boston are broken down per product. This result shows that not all the products are selling badly—only power drills. Of course, this is not the end of the story, and the user still does not know what is going on, but hopefully this simple example shows the power of OLAP. Without the need to learn SQL, the user can play with data, and that can be very useful. For a more detailed description of OLAP, see [THOM02].

Figure 1.11   *The sales figures of the sales region Boston, split into products*

		Boston						
		Sales ($)	Plan Sales ($)	Sales- Plan	Sales (Units)	Avg Inventory	Turnover (Days)	Sell Through
Power Tools	Power Drill (3/8")	36,283	75,251	(38,968)	330	35	5	100%
	Skill Saw	16,281	15,438	843	181	62	19	80%
	Electric Sander	15,584	14,785	799	312	71	11	70%
	Cordless Drill	23,585	23,074	511	295	60	12	73%
Hand Tools	Handi Screwdriver Set	10,932	10,480	452	365	67	9	91%
	Rachet Kit (74 Piece)	18,787	14,990	3,797	264	65	13	40%
	Adjustable Wrench Set	14,182	13,310	872	355	68	10	85%
	Hammer (28oz.)	8,928	6,073	2,855	273	75	13	92%
Electrical	Romex Wire (3 Strand)	8,184	7,769	415	341	71	10	67%
	Wall Switches (White)	7,584	7,251	333	316	67	11	84%
	Outlets (White)	7,032	6,531	501	293	63	12	43%
	Outlet Box (Single)	8,544	8,225	319	356	68	10	91%
Lawn Products	Lawn Sprinkler	7,744	5,979	1,765	261	70	13	78%
	Garden Hose (75')	8,688	8,293	395	362	69	10	91%
	Lawn Mower (3/4 hp)	6,672	6,375	297	278	68	13	88%
	Delux Leaf Rake	8,640	8,282	358	360	70	9	78%

The last category of business intelligence tools is the *data mining* tools. Incorrectly, these tools are sometimes classified together with OLAP tools to stress that they have much in common. Whereas OLAP tools make it possible for users to simply look at data from different viewpoints and usually present data or summarized data stored in the database, *data mining* tools never present data or a total as a result. Their strength is to find trends and patterns in the data. For example, they can be used to try to find out whether certain products are bought together, what the dominant characteristics are of customers who take out life insurance policies, or what the characteristics are of a product that sells well in a big city. The technology used internally by this kind of tool is primarily based on artificial intelligence. Of course, these tools must also access data to discover trends; therefore, they use SQL. For an introduction to data mining, see [LARO04].

The complexity of the SQL statements generated by statistical, OLAP, and data mining tools can be quite high. This means that much work must be done by the database servers to process these statements.

Undoubtedly, many more categories of tools will appear in the future, but currently these are the dominant ones.

Finally, how tools or applications can locate the database server—or, in other words, how they exchange statements and results—is not discussed in detail in this book. In Part IV, we briefly touch on this topic. For now, you can assume that if an application wants to obtain information from a database server, a special piece of code must be linked with the application. This piece of code is called *middleware* and is (probably) developed by the database server vendor. Such code can be compared to a pilot who boards a ship to guide it into harbor.

1.6 The History of SQL

The history of SQL is closely tied to the history of an IBM project called *System R*. The purpose of this project was to develop an experimental relational database server that bore the same name as the project: System R. This system was built in the IBM research laboratory in San Jose, California. The project was intended to demonstrate that the positive usability features of the relational model could be implemented in a system that satisfied the demands of a modern database server.

A problem that had to be solved in the System R project was that there were no relational database languages. A language called *Sequel* was therefore developed as the database language for System R. The first articles about this language were written by the designers R. F. Boyce and D. D. Chamberlin; see [BOYC73a] and [CHAM76]. During the

Figure 1.12

Don Chamberlin, one of the designers of SQL

project, the language was renamed SQL because the name Sequel was in conflict with an existing trademark. (However, the language is still often pronounced as *sequel*.)

The System R project was carried out in three phases. In the first phase, Phase 0 (from 1974 to 1975), only a part of SQL was implemented. For example, the join (for linking data from various tables) was not implemented yet, and only a single-user version of the system was built. The purpose of this phase was to see whether implementation of such a system was possible. This phase ended successfully; see [ASTR80].

Phase 1 started in 1976. All the program code written for Phase 0 was put aside, and a new start was made. Phase 1 comprised the total system. This meant, among other things, that the multi-user capability and the join were incorporated. The development of Phase 1 took place between 1976 and 1977.

In the final phase, System R was evaluated. The system was installed at various places within IBM and with a large number of major IBM clients. The evaluation took place in 1978 and 1979. The results of this evaluation are described in [CHAM80], as well as in other publications. The System R project was finished in 1979.

The knowledge acquired and the technology developed in these three phases were used to build SQL/DS, which was the first IBM relational database server that was commercially available. In 1981, SQL/DS came onto the market for the operating system DOS/VSE, and in 1983, the VM/CMS version arrived. In that same year, DB2 was announced. Currently, DB2 is available for many operating systems.

IBM has published a great deal about the development of System R, which was happening at a time when relational database servers were being widely talked about at conferences and seminars. Therefore, it is not surprising that other companies also began to build relational systems. Some of them, such as Oracle, implemented SQL as the database language. In the last few years, many SQL products have appeared, and, as a result, SQL is now available for every possible system, large or small. Existing database servers have also been extended to include SQL support.

1.7 From Monolithic via Client/Server to the Internet

Toward the end of the 1980s, an SQL database server could be used in only one architecture: the *monolithic architecture*. In a monolithic architecture, everything runs on the same machine. This machine can be a large mainframe, a small PC, or a midrange computer with an operating system such as UNIX or Windows. Nowadays, there are many more architectures available, of which client/server and Internet are the very popular ones.

The monolithic architecture still exists; see Figure 1.13. With this architecture, the application and the database server run on the same machine. As explained in Section 1.4, the application passes SQL statements to the database server. The database server processes these statements, and the results are returned to the application. Finally, the results are shown to the users. Because both the application and the database server run on the same computer, communication is possible through very fast internal communication lines. In fact, we are dealing here with two processes that communicate internally.

The arrival of cheaper and faster small computers in the 1990s led to the introduction of the *client/server architecture*. There are several subforms of this architecture, but we do not discuss them all here. It is important to realize that in a client/server architecture, the application runs on a different machine than the database server; see Figure 1.14. The machine on which the application runs is called the *client machine*; the other is the *server machine*. This is called working with a *remote database*. Internal communication usually takes place through a local area network (LAN) and occasionally through a wide area network (WAN). A user could start an application on his or her PC in Paris and retrieve data from a database located in Sydney. Communication would then probably take place through a satellite link.

Figure 1.13   *The monolithic architecture*

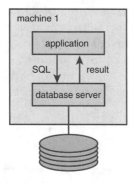

Figure 1.14   *The client/server architecture*

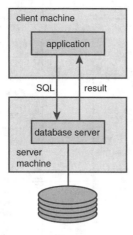

The third architecture is the most recent one: the *Internet architecture*. The essence of this architecture is that the application running in a client/server architecture on the client machine is divided into two parts; see the left part of Figure 1.15. The part that deals with the user, or the user interface, runs on the client machine. The part that communicates with the database server, also called the *application logic*, runs on the server machine. In this book, these two parts are called, respectively, the client and the server application.

There are probably no SQL statements in the *client application*, but statements that call the server application. Languages such as HTML, JavaScript, and VBScript are often used for the client application. The call goes via the Internet or an intranet to the server machine, and the well-known Hypertext Transport Protocol (HTTP) is mostly used for this. The call comes in at a *web server*. The web server acts as a switchboard operator and knows which call has be sent to which server application.

Next, the call arrives at the server application. The server application sends the needed SQL statements to the database server. Many server applications run under the supervision of Java application servers, such as WebLogic from Bea Systems and WebSphere from IBM.

The results of the SQL statements are returned by the database server. In some way, the server application translates this SQL result to an HTML page and returns the page to the web server. And the web server knows, as switchboard operator, the client application to which the HTML answer must be returned

The right part of Figure 1.15 shows a variant of the Internet architecture in which the server application and the database server have also been placed on different server machines.

Figure 1.15   *The Internet architecture*

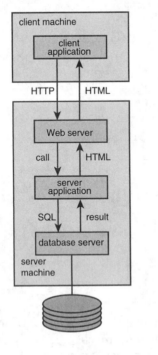
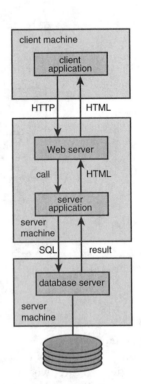

The fact that the database server and the database are remote is completely transparent to the programmer who is responsible for writing the application and the SQL statements. However, it is not irrelevant. With regard to language and efficiency aspects of SQL, it is important to know which architecture is used: monolithic, client/server, or Internet. In this book, we use the first one, but where relevant, we discuss the effect of client/server or Internet.

1.8 Transaction Databases and Data Warehouses

You can use data in a database for any kind of purpose. The first databases were mainly designed for the storage of *operational data*. We illustrate this with two examples. Banks, for example, keep record of all account holders, where they live, and what their balance is. In addition, for every transaction when it took place, the amount and the two account numbers involved are recorded. The bank statements that we receive periodically are probably reports (maybe generated with SQL) of these kinds of transactions. Airline companies have also developed databases that, through the years, have been filled with enormous amounts of operational data. They collect, for example, information about which passenger flew on which flight to which location.

Databases with operational data are developed to record data that is produced at production processes. Such data can be used, for example, to report on and monitor the progress of production processes and possibly to improve them or speed them up. Imagine if all the transactions at the bank were still processed by hand and your account information still kept in one large book. How long would it take for your transaction to be processed? Given the current size of banks, this would no longer be possible. Databases have become indispensable.

We call databases that are principally designed and implemented to store operational data *transaction*, *operational*, or *production* databases. Correspondingly, the matching applications are called *transaction*, *operational*, or *production* applications.

After some time, we started to use databases for other purposes. More data was used to produce reports. For example, how many passengers did we carry from London to Paris during the past few months? Or show the number of products sold per region for this year. Users receive these reports, for example, every Monday morning, either as hard copy on their desk or by e-mail. You will notice in this book that SQL offers many possibilities for creating reports. At first, these reports were created periodically and at times when the processing of the transaction programs was not disturbed, such as on Sunday or in the middle of the night.

More recently, as a result of the arrival of the PC, the requirements of users have increased. First, the demand for online reports increased. Online reports are produced the moment the user asks for it. Second, the need arose for users to create new reports themselves. To minimize the interruption of the transaction databases as much as possible, sepaate databases were built for that purpose. These databases are filled periodically with data stored in transaction databases and are primarily used for online reports. This type of database is called a *data warehouse*.

Bill Inmon defines a data warehouse as follows (see also [GILL96]):

> A data warehouse is a subject oriented, integrated, nonvolatile, and time vari-
> ant collection of data in support of management's decisions.

This definition holds four important concepts. By *subject oriented*, we mean, for example, that all the customer information is stored together and that product information is stored together. The opposite of this is *application oriented*, in which a database contains data that is relevant for a certain application. Customer information can then be stored in two or more databases. This complicates reporting because data for a particular report has to be retrieved from multiple databases.

Briefly, the term *integrated* indicates a consistent encoding of data so that it can be retrieved and combined in an integrated fashion.

A data warehouse is a *nonvolatile* database. When a database is primarily used to generate reports, users definitely do not like it when the contents change constantly. Imagine that two users have to attend a meeting, and, to prepare for this, they both need to query the database to get the sales records for a particular region. Imagine that there are 10 minutes between these two queries. Within those 10 minutes, the database might have changed. At the meeting, the users will come up with different data. To prevent this, a data warehouse is updated periodically, not continuously. New data elements are added each evening or during the weekend.

The *time variance* of a data warehouse is another important aspect. Normally, we try to keep transaction databases as small as possible because the smaller the database, the faster the SQL processing speed. A common way to keep databases small is to delete the old data. The old data can be stored on magnetic tape or optical disk for future use. However, users of data warehouses expect to access historical data. They want to find out, for example, whether the total number of boat tickets to London has changed in the last ten years. Alternatively, they would like to know in what way the weather affects the sales of beer, and for that purpose they want to use the data of the last five years. This means that huge amounts of historical data must be included and that almost all the information is time variant. Therefore, a data warehouse of 1 TB or more in size is not unusual.

Note that when you design a database, you have to determine in advance how it will be used: Will it be a transaction database or a data warehouse? In this book, we make this distinction wherever relevant.

1.9   Standardization of SQL

As mentioned before, each SQL database server has its own dialect. All these dialects resemble each other, but they are not completely identical. They differ in the statements they support, or some products contain more SQL statements than the others; the possibilities of statements can vary as well. Sometimes, two products support the same statement, but then the result of that statement varies from one product to another.

To avoid differences between the many database servers from several vendors, it was decided early that a standard for SQL had to be defined. The idea was that when the database servers would grow too much apart, acceptance by SQL market would diminish. A standard would ensure that an application with SQL statements would be easier to transfer from one database server to another.

In 1983, the International Organization for Standardization (ISO) and the American National Standards Institute (ANSI) started work on the development of an SQL standard. The ISO is the leading internationally oriented normalization and standardization organization, having as its objectives the promotion of international, regional, and national normalization. Many countries have local representatives of the ISO. The ANSI is the American branch of the ISO.

After many meetings and several false starts, the first ANSI edition of the SQL standard appeared in 1986. This is described in the document ANSI X3.135-1986, "Database Language SQL." This *SQL-86 standard* is unofficially called *SQL1*. One year later, the ISO edition, called ISO 9075-1987, "Database Language SQL," was completed; see [ISO87]. This report was developed under the auspices of Technical Committee TC97. The area of activity of TC97 is described as Computing and Information Processing. Its Subcommittee SC21 caused the standard to be developed. This means that the standards of ISO and ANSI for SQL1 or SQL-86 are identical.

SQL1 consists of two levels. Level 2 comprises the complete document, and Level 1 is a subset of Level 2. This implies that not all specifications of SQL1 belong to Level 1. If a vendor claims that its database server complies with the standard, the supporting level must be stated as well. This is done to improve the support and adoption of SQL1. It means that vendors can support the standard in two phases, first Level 1 and then Level 2.

The SQL1 standard is very moderate with respect to integrity. For this reason, it was extended in 1989 by including, among other things, the concepts of primary and foreign keys. This version of the SQL standard is called *SQL89*. The companion ISO document is called, appropriately, ISO 9075:1989, "Database Language SQL with Integrity Enhancements." The ANSI version was completed simultaneously.

Immediately after the completion of SQL1 in 1987, a start was made on the development of a new SQL standard; see [ISO92]. This planned successor to SQL89 was called *SQL2*. This simple name was given because the date of publication was not known at the start. In fact, SQL89 and SQL2 were developed simultaneously. Finally, the successor was published in 1992 and replaced the current standard at that time (SQL89). The new SQL92 standard is an expansion of the SQL1 standard. Many new statements and extensions to existing statements have been added. For a complete description of SQL92, see [DATE97].

Just like SQL1, SQL92 has *levels*. The levels have names instead of numbers: *entry*, *intermediate*, and *full*. Full SQL is the complete standard. Intermediate SQL is, as far as functionality goes, a subset of full SQL, and entry SQL is a subset of intermediate SQL. Entry SQL can roughly be compared to SQL1 Level 2, although with some specifications extended. All the levels together can be seen as the rings of an onion; see Figure 1.16. A ring represents a certain amount of functionality. The bigger the ring, the more functionality is defined within that level. When a ring falls within the other ring, it means that it defines a subset of functionality.

At the time of this writing, many available products support entry SQL92. Some even claim to support intermediate SQL92, but not one product supports full SQL92. Hopefully, the support of the SQL92 levels will improve in the coming years.

Since the publication of SQL92, several additional documents have been added that extend the capabilities of the language. In 1995, *SQL/CLI* (Call Level Interface) was published. Later the name was changed to CLI95. There is more about CLI95 at the end of this section. The following year, *SQL/PSM* (Persistent Stored Modules), or PSM-96, appeared. The most recent addition, PSM96, describes functionality for creating so-called stored procedures. We deal with this concept extensively in Chapter 30, "Stored Procedures." Two years after PSM96, *SQL/OLB* (Object Language Bindings), or OLB-98, was published. This document describes how SQL statements had to be included within the programming language Java.

Figure 1.16   *The various levels of SQL1 and SQL92 represented as rings*

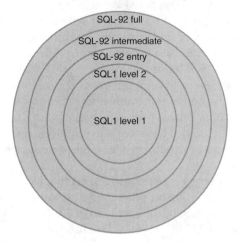

Even before the completion of SQL92, a start was made on the development of its successor: *SQL3*. In 1999, the standard was published and bore the name SQL:1999. To be more in line with the names of other ISO standards, the small line that was used in the names of the previous editions was replaced by a colon. And because of the problems in 2000, it was decided that 1999 would not be shortened to 99. See [GULU99], [MELT01], and [MELT03] for more detailed descriptions of this standard.

When SQL:1999 was completed, it consisted of five parts: SQL/Framework, SQL/Foundation, SQL/CLI, SQL/PSM, and SQL/Bindings. SQL/OLAP, SQL/MED (Management of External Data), SQL/OLB, SQL/Schemata, and SQL/JRT (Routines and Types using the Java Programming Language) and SQL/XML(XML-Related Specifications) were added later, among other things. Thus, the current SQL standard of ISO consists of a series of documents. They all begin with the ISO code 9075. For example, the complete designation of the SQL/Framework is ISO/IEC 9075-1:2003.

Besides the 9075 documents, another group of documents focuses on SQL. The term used for this group is usually *SQL/MM*, short for SQL Multimedia and Application Packages. All these documents bear the ISO code 13249. SQL/MM consists of five parts. SQL/MM Part 1 is the SQL/MM Framework, Part 2 focuses on text retrieval (working with text), Part 3 is dedicated to spatial applications, Part 4 to still images (such as photos), and Part 5 to data mining (looking for trends and patterns in data).

In 2003, a new edition of SQL/Foundation appeared, along with new editions of some other documents, such as SQL/JRT and SQL/Schemata. At this moment, this group of documents can be seen as the most recent version of the international SQL standard. We refer to it by the abbreviation *SQL:2003*.

There were other organizations working on the standardization of SQL, such as The Open Group (then called the X/Open Group) and the SQL Access Group. The first does not get much attention any longer, so we do not discuss it in this book.

In July 1989, a number of mainly American vendors of SQL database servers, among them Informix, Ingres, and Oracle, set up a committee called the *SQL Access Group*. The objective of the SQL Access Group is to define standards for the *interoperability* of SQL applications. This means that SQL applications developed using those specifications are portable between the database servers of the associated vendors, and that a number of different database servers can be simultaneously accessed by these applications. At the end of 1990, the first report of the SQL Access Group was published and defined the syntax of a so-called SQL application interface. The first demonstrations in this field were given in 1991. Eventually, the ISO adopted the resulting document, and it was published under the name SQL/CLI. This document was mentioned earlier.

The most important technology that is derived from the work of the Open SQL Access Group—and, therefore, from SQL/CLI—is ODBC (Open Database Connectivity) from Microsoft. Because ODBC plays a very prominent role when accessing databases and is completely focused on SQL, we have devoted Chapter 28, "Introduction to ODBC," to this subject.

Finally, an organization called the Object Database Management Group (ODMG) is aimed at the creation of standards for object-oriented databases; see [CATT97]. A part of these standards is a declarative language to query and update databases, called Object Query Language (OQL). It is claimed that SQL has served as a foundation for OQL, and, although the languages are not the same, they have a lot in common.

It is correct to say that a lot of time and money has been invested in the standardization of SQL. But is a standard that important? The following are the practical advantages that would accrue if all database servers supported exactly the same standardized database language:

- **Increased portability**—An application could be developed for one database server and could run at another without many changes.

- **Improved interchangeability**—Because database servers speak the same language, they could communicate internally with each other. It also would be simpler for applications to access different databases.

- **Reduced training costs**—Programmers could switch faster from one database server to another because the language would remain the same. It would not be necessary for them to learn a new database language.

- **Extended life span**—Languages that are standardized tend to survive longer, and this consequently also applies to the applications that are written in such languages. COBOL is a good example of this.

1.10   The Market of SQL Database Servers

The language SQL has been implemented in many products in one way or another. SQL database servers are available for every operating system and for every kind of machine, from the smallest cellular phones to the largest multiprocessor machine. Table 1.1 gives the names of the SQL products from various vendors. Some of these products are referred to in this book. For detailed information, we refer you to the vendors, each of which has a Web site where more information can be obtained.

Table 1.1   *Overview of Well-Known SQL Database Servers and Their Vendors*

VENDOR	SQL PRODUCTS
ANTs Software	ANTs Data Server
Apache Software Foundation	Apache Derby
Birdstep Technology	Birdstep RDM Server
Borland	InterBase
Centura Software	SQLBase
Cincom	Supra Server SQL
Computer Associates	CA-Datacom, CA-IDMS
Daffodil Software	Daffodildb
Empress Software	Empress RDBMS
Faircom	c-treeSQL
FileMaker	FileMaker
Firebird	Firebird
FirstSQL	FirstSQL/J
Frontbase	Frontbase
H2 Database Engine	H2 Database Engine
HP	NonStop SQL/MP
Hughes Technologies	Mini SQL (alias mSQL)
HSQLDB	HSQLDB (alias Hypersonic SQL)
IBM	DB2 UDB, Informix Dynamic Server, Informix-SE, RedBrick, Cloudscape JDBMS, UniData (formerly from Ardent Software)

Ingres Corporation	Ingres
InstantDB	InstantDB
InterSystems	Caché
Korea Computer Communications	UniSQL
McKoi	McKoi SQL Database
Micro Focus	XDB
Microsoft	Microsoft SQL Server, Microsoft Access
MySQL	MySQL, MaxDB
NCR	Teradata
Netezza	Netezza Performance Server system
Ocelot Computer Services	Ocelot
Oracle	Oracle 10g, Oracle Rdb, TimesTen Main-Memory Data Manager
Pervasive Software	PSQL
Polyhedra	Polyhedra
PointBase	PointBase Embedded, PointBase Server
PostgreSQL	PostgreSQL
Progress Software	Progress
QuadBase	QuadBase-SQL
RainingData	D3
Siemens	SESAM/SQL-Server, UDS/SQL
Software AG	Adabas D Server
Solid	Solid
StreamBase Systems	StreamBase
Sybase	Sybase Adaptive Server, Sybase Adaptive Server Anywhere, Sybase Adaptive Server IQ
Machine Independent Software Corporation	CQL++
ThinkSQL	ThinkSQL RDBMS
Tigris	Axion
TinySQL	TinySQL
Unify Corporation	Unify Data Server
Upright Database Technology	Mimer SQL Engine

1.11   Which SQL Dialect?

The previous section presented a list of database servers that support SQL. As already indicated in the Preface, all these implementations of SQL resemble each other closely, but, unfortunately, there are differences between them. Even the international SQL standards can be considered as dialects because currently no vendor has implemented them fully. So, different *SQL dialects* exist.

You could ask, which SQL dialect is described in this book? The answer to that question is not simple. We do not use the dialect of one specific product because this book is meant to describe SQL in general. Furthermore, we do not use the dialects of SQL1, SQL92, or SQL:2003 standard because the first one is too "small" and the latter is not yet supported by anyone. We do not even use the MySQL dialect (the product included in the CD-ROM). The situation is more tricky.

To increase its practical value, this book primarily describes the statements and features supported by most of the dominant SQL products. This makes the book generally applicable. After reading this book, you should be able to work with most of the available SQL products. The book is focused on common SQL—SQL as implemented by most products.

What about MySQL? MySQL is supplied with this book—does that mean that all the examples and exercises in this book can be executed with MySQL? Unfortunately, the answer to this question is, no. MySQL has been selected because it is popular, because it is easy to install and available for most modern operating systems, and, foremost, because the SQL dialect is very rich. You can execute most, but not all, of the examples and exercises in this book with this powerful product.

In several places, we use the suitcase symbol to indicate whether certain statements are portable between SQL products and whether MySQL supports them.

> **Portability:** *Here, a recommendation or remark is included concerning the portability of an SQL statement or feature.*

1.12   The Structure of the Book

This chapter concludes with a description of the structure of this book. Because of the large number of chapters in the book, we divided it into sections.

Part I consists of several introductory topics and includes this chapter. Chapter 2, "The Tennis Club Sample Database," contains a detailed description of the database used in most of the examples and exercises. This database is modeled on the administration of a tennis club's competitions. Chapter 4, "SQL in a Nutshell," gives a general overview of SQL. After reading this chapter, you should have a general overview of the capabilities of SQL and a good idea of what awaits you in the rest of this book.

Part II is completely focused on querying and updating tables. It is largely devoted to the SELECT statement. Many examples illustrate all its features. We devote a great deal of space to this SELECT statement because, in practice, this is the statement most often used and because many other statements are based on it. The last chapter in this part describes how existing database data can be updated and deleted, and how new rows can be added to tables.

Part III describes the creation of *database objects*. The term *database object* is the generic name for all objects from which a database is built. For instance, tables; primary, alternate, and foreign keys; indexes; and views are discussed. This part also describes data security.

Part IV deals with programming in SQL. We describe embedded SQL: the development of programs written in languages such as C, COBOL, or Pascal in which SQL statements have been included. Another form in which SQL can be used is with CLIs as ODBC, to which we also devote a chapter. The following concepts are explained in this part: transaction, savepoint, rollback of transactions, isolation level, and repeatable read. And because performance is an important aspect of programming SQL, we devote a chapter to how execution times can be improved by reformulating an SQL statement.

Part V describes stored procedures and triggers. Stored procedures are pieces of code stored in the database that can be called from applications. Triggers are pieces of code as well, but they are invoked by the database server itself, for example, to perform checks or to update data automatically.

Part VI discusses a new subject. In SQL:1999, SQL has been extended with concepts originating in the object-oriented world. These so-called object relational concepts described in this book include subtables, references, sets, and self-defined data types. This part concludes with a short chapter on the future of SQL.

The book ends with a number of appendixes and an index. Appendix A, "Syntax of SQL," contains the definitions of all the SQL statements discussed in the book. Appendix B, "Scalar Functions," describes all the functions that SQL supports. Appendix C, "Bibliography," contains a list of references.

2

The Tennis Club Sample Database

2.1 Introduction

T his chapter describes a database that a tennis club could use to record its players'
progress in a competition. Most of the examples and exercises in this book are based
on this database, so you should study it carefully.

2.2 Description of the Tennis Club

The tennis club was founded in 1970. From the beginning, some administrative data
was stored in a database. This database consists of the following tables:

- PLAYERS
- TEAMS
- MATCHES
- PENALTIES
- COMMITTEE_MEMBERS

The PLAYERS table contains data about players who are members of the club, such
as names, addresses, and dates of birth. Players can join the club only at the first of January of a year. Players cannot join the club in the middle of the year.

The PLAYERS table contains no historical data. Any player giving up membership
disappears from the table. If a player moves, the old address is overwritten with the new
address. In other words, the old address is not retained anywhere.

The tennis club has two types of members: *recreational players* and *competition players*. The first group plays matches only among themselves (that is, no matches against
players from other clubs). The results of these friendly matches are not recorded. Competition players play in teams against other clubs, and the results of these matches are
recorded. Each player, regardless of whether he or she plays competitively, has a unique
number assigned by the club. Each competition player must also be registered with the
tennis league, and this national organization gives each player a unique *league number*.

If a competition player stops playing in the competition and becomes a recreational player, his or her league number correspondingly disappears. Therefore, recreational players have no league number, but they do have a player number.

The club has a number of teams taking part in competitions. The captain of each team and the division in which it is currently competing is recorded. It is not necessary for the captain to have played a match for the team. It is possible for a certain player to be captain of two or more teams at a certain time. Again, no historical data is kept in this table. If a team is promoted or relegated to another division, the record is simply over-written with the new information. The same goes for the captain of the team; when a new captain is appointed, the number of the former captain is overwritten.

A team consists of a number of players. When a team plays against a team from another tennis club, each player of that team plays against a player of the opposing team. (For the sake of simplicity, we assume that matches in which couples play against each other, the so-called doubles and mixes, do not occur.) The team in which the most players win their matches is the winner.

A team does not always consist of the same people, and reserves are sometimes needed when the regular players are sick or on vacation. A player can play matches for several teams. So, when we say "the players of a team," we mean the players who have played at least one match in that team. Again, only players with league numbers are allowed to play official matches.

Each match consists of a number of *sets*. The player who wins the most sets is the winner. Before the match begins, it is agreed how many sets need to be won to win the match. Generally, the match stops after one of the two players has won two or three sets. Possible end results of a tennis match are 2–1 or 2–0 if play continues until one player wins two sets (best of three), or 3–2, 3–1, or 3–0 if three sets need to be won (best of five). A player either wins or loses a match; a draw is not possible. In the MATCHES table, we record for each match separately which player was in the match and for which team he played. In addition, we record how many *sets* the player won and lost. From this, we can conclude whether the player won the match.

Note that the MATCHES table in this book is different in structure, layout, and contents from the MATCHES table in former editions of *Introduction to SQL*.

If a player behaves badly (arrives late, behaves aggressively, or does not show up at all), the league imposes a penalty in the form of a fine. The club pays these fines and records them in a PENALTIES table. If the player continues to play competitively, the record of all his or her penalties remains in this table.

If a player leaves the club, all his or her data in the five tables is destroyed. If the club withdraws a team, all data for that team is removed from the TEAMS and MATCHES tables. If a competition player stops playing matches and becomes a recreational player again, all matches and penalty data is deleted from the relevant tables.

Since January 1, 1990, a COMMITTEE_MEMBERS table has kept information about who is on the committee. There are four positions: chairman, treasurer, secretary, and a general member. On January 1 of each year, a new committee is elected. If a player is on the committee, the beginning and ending dates of his or her committee are recorded. If someone is still active, the end date remains open. Figure 2.1 shows which player was on the committee in which period.

Figure 2.1   *Which player occupied which position on the committee in which period?*

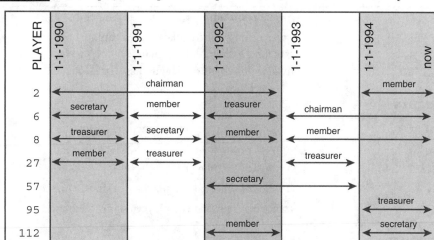

The following is a description of the columns in each of the tables.

PLAYERS

PLAYERNO	Unique player number assigned by the club.
NAME	Surname of the player, without initials.
INITIALS	Initials of the player. No full stops or spaces are used.
BIRTH_DATE	Date on which the player was born.
SEX	Sex of the player: M(ale) or F(emale).
JOINED	Year in which the player joined the club. This value cannot be smaller than 1970, the year in which the club was founded.
STREET	Name of the street on which the player lives.
HOUSENO	Number of the house.
POSTCODE	Post code.
TOWN	Town or city in which the player lives. We assume in this example that place names are unique for town or cities—or, in other words, there can never be two towns with the same name.
PHONENO	Area code followed by a hyphen and then the subscriber's number.
LEAGUENO	League number assigned by the league; a league number is unique.

TEAMS

TEAMNO	Unique team number assigned by the club.
PLAYERNO	Player number of the player who captains the team. In principle, a player may captain several teams.
DIVISION	Division in which the league has placed the team.

MATCHES

MATCHNO	Unique match number assigned by the club
TEAMNO	Number of the team
PLAYERNO	Number of the player
WON	Number of sets that the player won in the match
LOST	Number of sets that the player lost in the match

PENALTIES

PAYMENTNO	Unique number for each penalty the club has paid. This number is assigned by the club.
PLAYERNO	Number of the player who has incurred the penalty.
PAYMENT_DATE	Date on which the penalty was paid. The year of this date should not be earlier than 1970, the year in which the club was founded.
AMOUNT	Amount in dollars incurred for the penalty.

COMMITTEE_MEMBERS

PLAYERNO	The number of the player.
BEGIN_DATE	Date on which the player became an active member of the committee. This date should not be earlier than January 1, 1990, because this is the date on which the club started to record this data.
END_DATE	Date on which the player resigned his position in the committee. This date should not be earlier than the BEGIN_DATE but can be absent.
POSITION	Name of the position.

2.3 The Contents of the Tables

The contents of the tables are shown here. These rows of data form the basis of most of the examples and exercises. Some of the column names in the PLAYERS table have been shortened because of space constraints.

The PLAYERS table:

PLAYERNO	NAME	INIT	BIRTH_DATE	SEX	JOINED	STREET	...
2	Everett	R	1948-09-01	M	1975	Stoney Road	...
6	Parmenter	R	1964-06-25	M	1977	Haseltine Lane	...
7	Wise	GWS	1963-05-11	M	1981	Edgecombe Way	...
8	Newcastle	B	1962-07-08	F	1980	Station Road	...
27	Collins	DD	1964-12-28	F	1983	Long Drive	...
28	Collins	C	1963-06-22	F	1983	Old Main Road	...
39	Bishop	D	1956-10-29	M	1980	Eaton Square	...
44	Baker	E	1963-01-09	M	1980	Lewis Street	...
57	Brown	M	1971-08-17	M	1985	Edgecombe Way	...
83	Hope	PK	1956-11-11	M	1982	Magdalene Road	...
95	Miller	P	1963-05-14	M	1972	High Street	...
100	Parmenter	P	1963-02-28	M	1979	Haseltine Lane	...
104	Moorman	D	1970-05-10	F	1984	Stout Street	...
112	Bailey	IP	1963-10-01	F	1984	Vixen Road	...

The PLAYERS table (continued):

PLAYERNO	...	HOUSENO	POSTCODE	TOWN	PHONENO	LEAGUENO
2	...	43	3575NH	Stratford	070-237893	2411
6	...	80	1234KK	Stratford	070-476537	8467
7	...	39	9758VB	Stratford	070-347689	?
8	...	4	6584RO	Inglewood	070-458458	2983
27	...	804	8457DK	Eltham	079-234857	2513
28	...	10	1294QK	Midhurst	071-659599	?
39	...	78	9629CD	Stratford	070-393435	?
44	...	23	4444LJ	Inglewood	070-368753	1124
57	...	16	4377CB	Stratford	070-473458	6409
83	...	16A	1812UP	Stratford	070-353548	1608
95	...	33A	5746OP	Douglas	070-867564	?
100	...	80	1234KK	Stratford	070-494593	6524
104	...	65	9437AO	Eltham	079-987571	7060
112	...	8	6392LK	Plymouth	010-548745	1319

The TEAMS table:

TEAMNO	PLAYERNO	DIVISION
1	6	first
2	27	second

The MATCHES table:

MATCHNO	TEAMNO	PLAYERNO	WON	LOST
1	1	6	3	1
2	1	6	2	3
3	1	6	3	0
4	1	44	3	2
5	1	83	0	3
6	1	2	1	3
7	1	57	3	0
8	1	8	0	3
9	2	27	3	2
10	2	104	3	2
11	2	112	2	3
12	2	112	1	3
13	2	8	0	3

The PENALTIES table:

PAYMENTNO	PLAYERNO	PAYMENT_DATE	AMOUNT
1	6	1980-12-08	100.00
2	44	1981-05-05	75.00
3	27	1983-09-10	100.00
4	104	1984-12-08	50.00
5	44	1980-12-08	25.00
6	8	1980-12-08	25.00
7	44	1982-12-30	30.00
8	27	1984-11-12	75.00

The COMMITTEE_MEMBERS table:

```
PLAYERNO   BEGIN_DATE   END_DATE     POSITION
--------   ----------   ----------   --------
       2   1990-01-01   1992-12-31   Chairman
       2   1994-01-01   ?            Member
       6   1990-01-01   1990-12-31   Secretary
       6   1991-01-01   1992-12-31   Member
       6   1992-01-01   1993-12-31   Treasurer
       6   1993-01-01   ?            Chairman
       8   1990-01-01   1990-12-31   Treasurer
       8   1991-01-01   1991-12-31   Secretary
       8   1993-01-01   1993-12-31   Member
       8   1994-01-01   ?            Member
      27   1990-01-01   1990-12-31   Member
      27   1991-01-01   1991-12-31   Treasurer
      27   1993-01-01   1993-12-31   Treasurer
      57   1992-01-01   1992-12-31   Secretary
      95   1994-01-01   ?            Treasurer
     112   1992-01-01   1992-12-31   Member
     112   1994-01-01   ?            Secretary
```

2.4 Integrity Constraints

The contents of the tables must, of course, satisfy a number of integrity constraints. Two players, for example, may not have the same player number, and every player number in the PENALTIES table must also appear in the MATCHES table. In this section, we list all the applicable integrity constraints.

A primary key has been defined for each table. The following columns are the primary keys for their respective tables. Figure 2.2 contains a diagram of the database.

A double-headed arrow at the side of a column (or combination of columns) indicates the primary key of a table:

- PLAYERNO of PLAYERS
- TEAMNO of TEAMS
- MATCHNO of MATCHES
- PAYMENTNO of PENALTIES
- PLAYERNO plus BEGIN_DATE of COMMITTEE_MEMBERS

Figure 2.2   *Diagram of the relationships between the tennis club database tables*

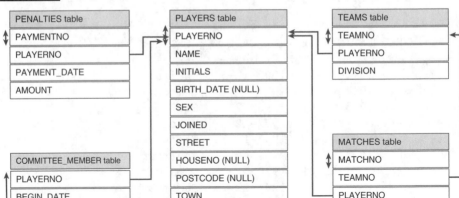

The database also supports a number of alternate keys. For example, the combination PLAYERNO and END_DATE forms an alternate key. This means that two players cannot resign a position in the committee on the same date. The LEAGUENO column is also an alternate key: Two players cannot have the same league number.

The database supports five foreign keys. In Figure 2.2, single-headed arrows show the foreign keys; these run from one table to another. (This notation, in which the arrows point to the primary key, is used in [DATE95] and elsewhere.) The foreign keys are as follows:

- **From TEAMS to PLAYERS**—Each captain of a team is also a player. The set of player numbers from the TEAMS table is a subset of the set of player numbers from the PLAYERS table.

- **From MATCHES to PLAYERS**—Each player who competes for a particular team must appear in the PLAYERS table. The set of player numbers from the MATCHES table is a subset of the set of player numbers from the PLAYERS table.

- **From MATCHES to TEAMS**—Each team that appears in the MATCHES table must also be present in the TEAMS table because a player can compete for only a registered team. The set of team numbers from the MATCHES table is a subset of the set of team numbers from the TEAMS table.

- **From PENALTIES to PLAYERS**—A penalty can be imposed on only players appearing in the PLAYERS table. The set of player numbers from the PENALTIES table is a subset of the set of player numbers from the PLAYERS table.

- **From COMMITTEE_MEMBERS to PLAYERS**—Each player who is or was a member of the committee must also be present in the PLAYERS table. The set of player numbers from the COMMITTEE_MEMBERS table is a subset of the set of player numbers from the PLAYERS table.

The following integrity constraints also hold:

- The year of birth of a player must be earlier than the year in which he or she joined the club.
- The sex of a player should always be an M or an F.
- The year in which the player joined the club should be greater than 1969 because the tennis club was founded in 1970.
- The postcode must always be a code of six characters.
- The division of a team can be nothing but first or second.
- Both the columns WON and LOST must have a value between 0 and 3.
- The payment date should be January 1, 1970, or later.
- Each penalty amount must always be greater than zero.
- The begin date in the COMMITTEE_MEMBERS table should always be later than or equal to January 1, 1990, because the recording of this data was started on that day.
- The end date on which the player ended service as a committee member must always be later than the begin date.

┌─────┐
│ 3 │
└─────┘

Installing the Software

3.1 Introduction

As already mentioned in the preface, we advise you to revisit the examples in this book and to do the exercises. It will definitely improve your knowledge of SQL and pleasure in reading this book.

This chapter describes where to find the required software and the information needed to install all the software necessary. We also indicate how to download the code for the many examples. For practical reasons, we refer frequently to the Web site belonging to this book in this chapter. Here, you can find useful information.

3.2 Installation of MySQL

MySQL is included on the accompanying CD-ROM. With the software, you will find the installation documentation written by the vendor. You can use those documents or, for Windows, follow the step-by-step plan that follows. This detailed plan includes many screen shots for installing MySQL and is, therefore, perhaps easier to understand than the documentation included.

On the CD-ROM, look for the directory called MySQL. This directory contains one file, called `mysql-5.0.7-beta-win32.zip`. Open this zipped file by double-clicking it. Next, a file appears called Setup. Double-click this file to start it. After several seconds, the window in Figure 3.1 appears and the preparations for the installation of MySQL begin. Choose Next in that window. The window in Figure 3.2 appears.

In the window in Figure 3.2, you are asked to select how you want to install MySQL. Select the Complete option. The next question asks whether you are ready for the installation. If so, choose Next; the window in Figure 3.3 appears.

If you are ready for the installation, choose Install. If you want to change something, select Back and change some of the installation parameters. If you select Install, the installation begins and its progress is shown; see Figure 3.4.

Figure 3.1   *Start of the Setup Wizard*

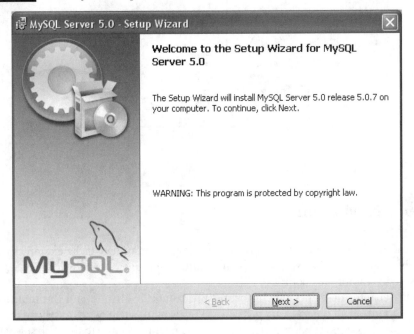

Figure 3.2   *Select a setup type*

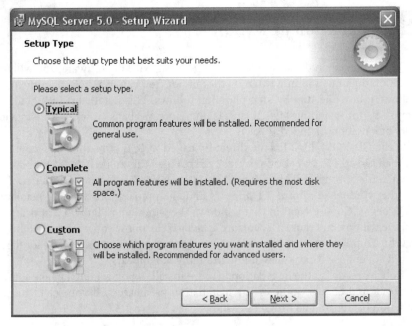

Figure 3.3   *Ready to install MySQL?*

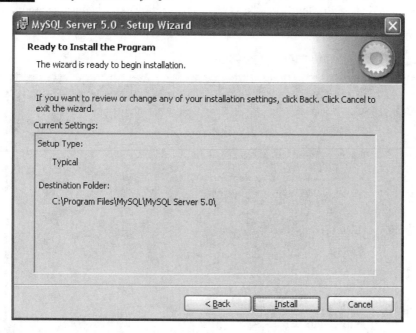

Figure 3.4   *The installation of MySQL in progress*

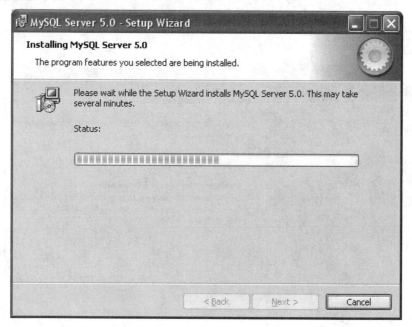

After several seconds, the question presented in Figure 3.5 is shown. Choose Skip Sign-Up in this window and click Next; you can sign up later. The message in Figure 3.6 appears.

Figure 3.5   *Do you want to sign up?*

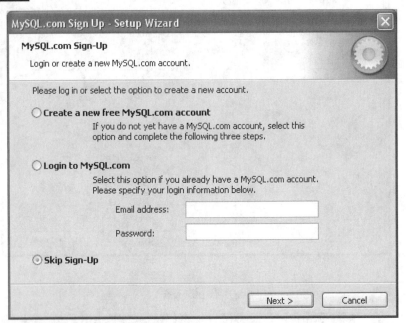

Figure 3.6   *The Setup Wizard is ready*

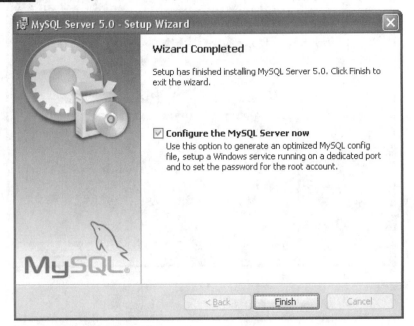

Make sure that in Figure 3.6 the check mark is selected for Configure the MySQL Server now and choose Finish. The window in Figure 3.7 appears. Select Next; the window in Figure 3.8 appears.

Figure 3.7   *Start the configuration of MySQL*

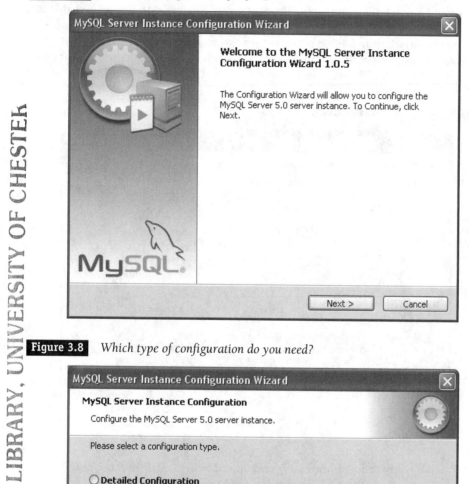

Figure 3.8   *Which type of configuration do you need?*

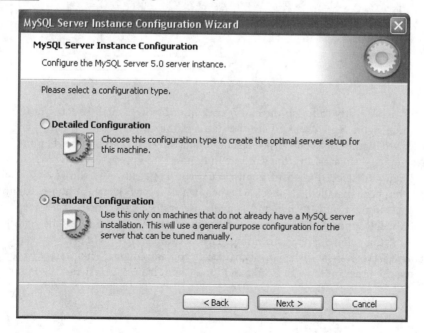

In Figure 3.8, select the option Standard Configuration and then click Next. Later, when you gain the necessary experience and have a thorough knowledge of MySQL, you can always install MySQL again and select Detailed Configuration. After you select Next, the window in Figure 3.9 appears.

In Figure 3.9, choose the option Install As Windows Service and click Next. The window in Figure 3.10 is presented; you must enter the password of the user that has been created by MySQL. The name of this user is root. Of course, you may come up with a password yourself; however, in this book, we assume that you will use root. You must enter this password twice. For security reasons, these passwords are represented as asterisks. Then click Next. The window in Figure 3.11 is displayed.

Figure 3.9   *Install MySQL as a Windows service*

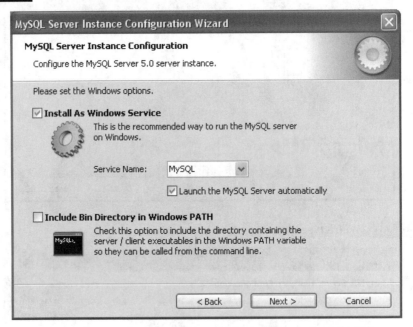

If you are ready to finish the configuration of MySQL, click Execute in the screen shown in Figure 3.11. You will see the status of the configuration process with check marks; see Figure 3.12. This process should take only a few seconds. When the process has completed successfully, the window in Figure 3.13 appears.

When you select Finish in Figure 3.13, you are ready, and the MySQL database server has been installed. To check whether everything works well, choose Administrative Tools in the Control Panel and then choose Services; see Figure 3.14.

If MySQL appears as a service in the list shown in Figure 3.14 (see the eighth row), the MySQL database server is running. The next question is whether you can use the database server—or, in other words, whether you can log on. This is easy to check by starting the program MySQL Command Line Client from the Taskbar; see Figure 3.15.

Figure 3.10   *Give user root his password*

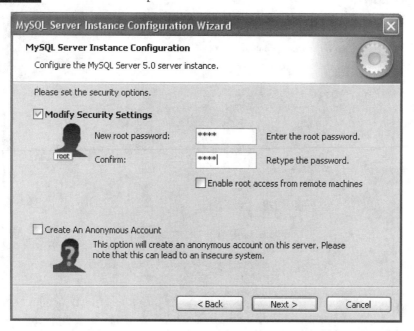

Figure 3.11   *Are you ready to start the configuration?*

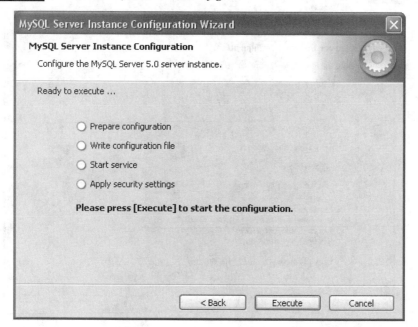

Figure 3.12   *The configuration in process*

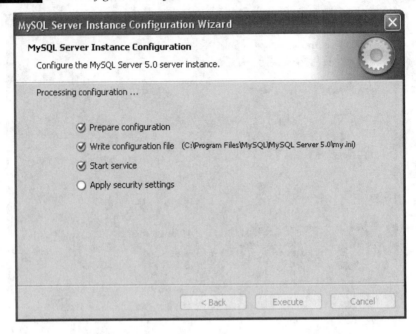

Figure 3.13   *The configuration of MySQL is finished*

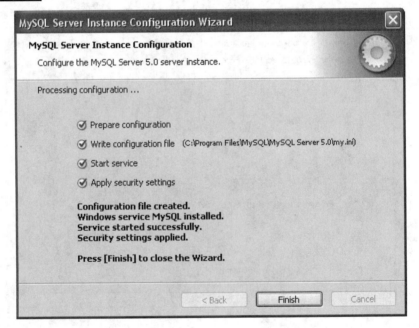

Figure 3.14   *Is MySQL really running?*

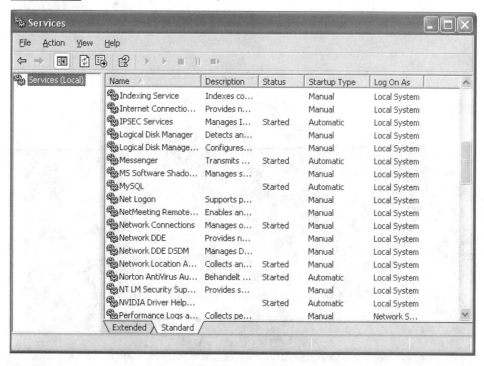

Figure 3.15   *Start the MySQL Command Line Client*

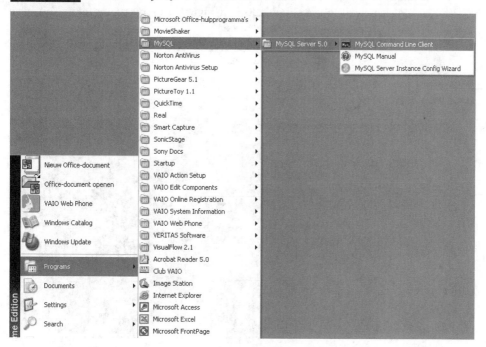

The MySQL Command Line Client asks for the password of the user called root. We assume that it will be root again. Enter **root**. The window in Figure 3.16 appears. In that window, enter the following simple SQL statement (do not forget the semicolon) and press the Enter key:

```
select version();
```

Figure 3.16   *The MySQL Command Line Client needs a password*

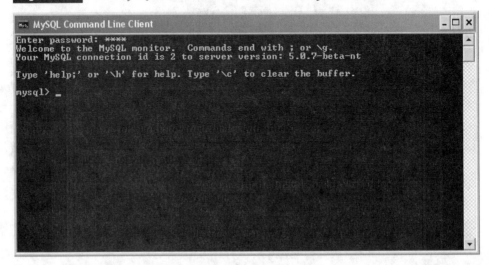

The result is shown is Figure 3.17.

If it all worked well, close the window in Figure 3.17 by typing **exit**. You have installed MySQL correctly—everything works!

We recommend that you install ODBC for MySQL and WinSQL next.

Figure 3.17   *Is everything working well?*

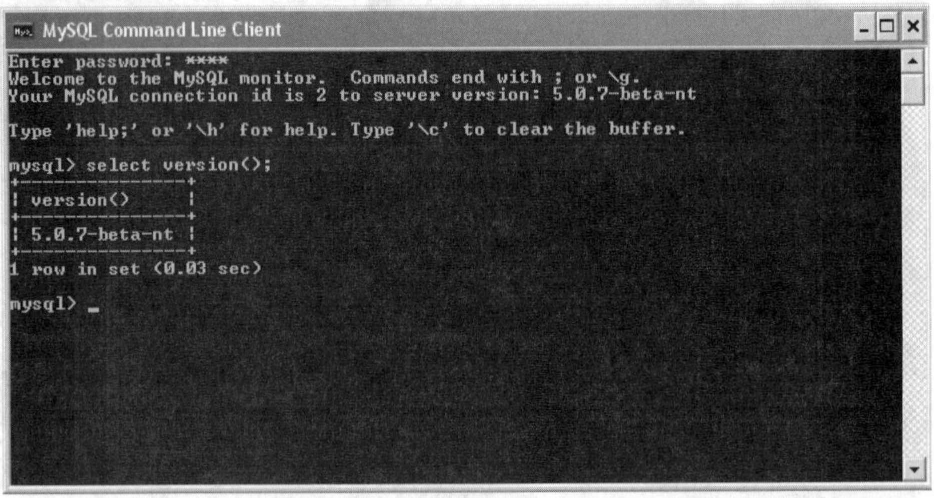

3.3 Installation of ODBC

To access MySQL from WinSQL (and other applications as well), first you must download and install the ODBC driver for MySQL. This is not done automatically when you install MySQL yourself.

Go to the www.mysql.com Web site and look for the MySQL Connector/ODBC for Windows. Select the zipped EXE. After you find it, download it (see Figure 3.18).

If this is Version 3.51, this file is called `mysql-connector-odbc-3.51.12-win32.zip`. After it is downloaded, start the zipped file by double-clicking it from, for example, Windows Explorer. Next, start the program setup in the same way; see Figure 3.19. In this figure, select Next if you are ready to begin. The window in Figure 3.20 appears.

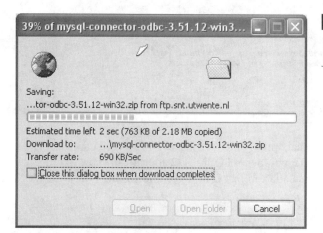

Figure 3.18

Download the ODBC driver for MySQL

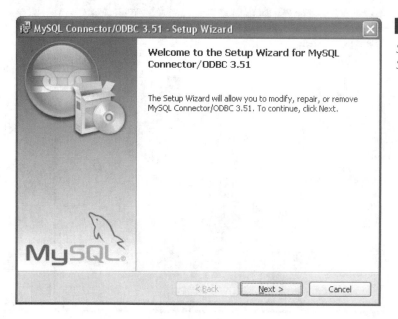

Figure 3.19

Start the Setup Wizard

Figure 3.20   *Select the setup type*

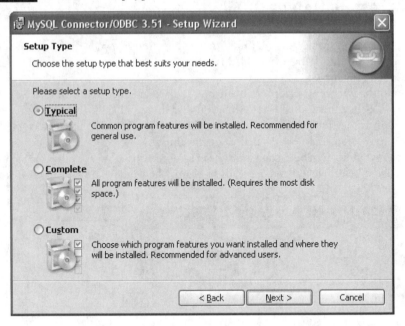

In Figure 3.20, select the Typical option and choose Next. Figure 3.21 appears. Here, select Install and choose Next. The window in Figure 3.22 appears, to show that the features are being installed. If the installation has completed successfully, the window in Figure 3.23 is displayed.

Figure 3.21   *Are you ready to install the ODBC driver?*

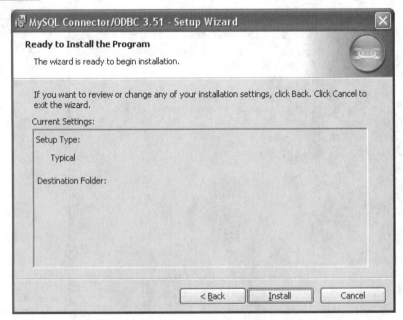

Figure 3.22   *The installation process in progress*

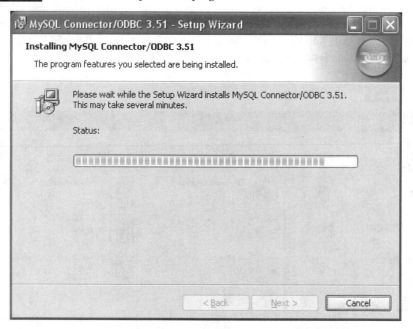

Figure 3.23   *Installation of the ODBC driver is complete*

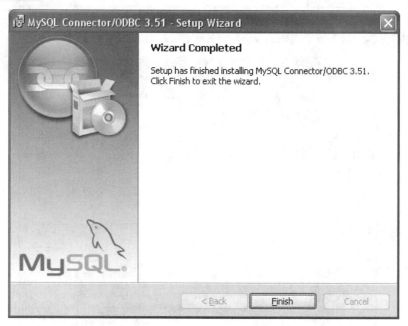

In Figure 3.23, close the window by selecting Finish. We recommend that you check whether the installation was successful. Go to the Taskbar of Windows and select Settings and then Control Panel. Next, start Administrative Tools (see Figure 3.24). In that window, select Data Sources (ODBC) (see Figure 3.25). If the driver of MySQL appears in the list, the installation was successful.

Figure 3.24 *Select the data sources for ODBC*

Figure 3.25 *Is your ODBC driver for MySQL operational?*

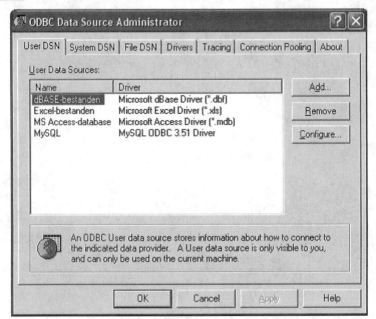

3.4 Installation of WinSQL

The CD-ROM includes a program called WinSQL. This is not a database server but a program with which you can easily enter SQL statements interactively under Windows. It works with most database servers, including MySQL. In this book, we assume, if relevant, that you use WinSQL to process your SQL statements. So again, we strongly recommend that you install this program as well.

On the CD-ROM, look for the directory called WinSQL. This directory contains one file, called WinSQL.zip. Open this zipped file by double-clicking it from, for example, Windows Explorer. Next, start the program Setup in the same way. The window in Figure 3.26 appears, to indicate that the preparations for the installation have started. After a few seconds, the window in Figure 3.27 appears. If you are ready to begin the installation, select Next; the window in Figure 3.28 appears. Select Next in this window, too; see Figure 3.29.

Figure 3.26   *The preparation for the installations of WinSQL have started*

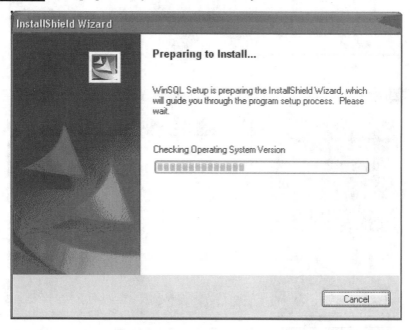

Figure 3.27   *The start of the installation of WinSQL*

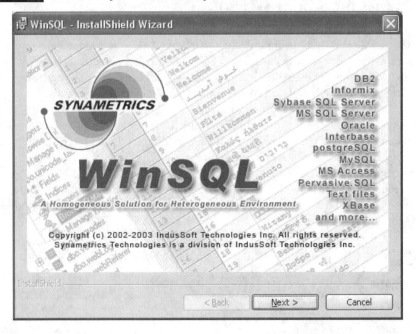

Figure 3.28   *Are you ready to start the installation?*

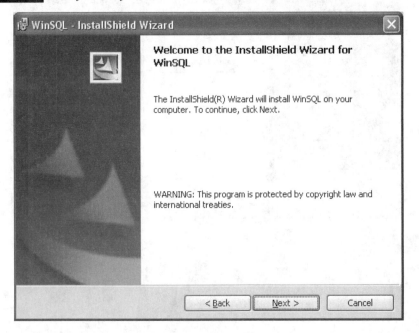

The window in Figure 3.29 shows the license agreement. Read this carefully. If you accept the terms, select I accept the terms in the license agreement. Then select Next. The window in Figure 3.30 appears. Here, enter the fields User Name and Organization, and determine for whom WinSQL must be installed. In this book, we chose Anyone who uses this computer. At the bottom, choose Next; see Figure 3.31 for the result.

Figure 3.29   *Do you accept the license agreement?*

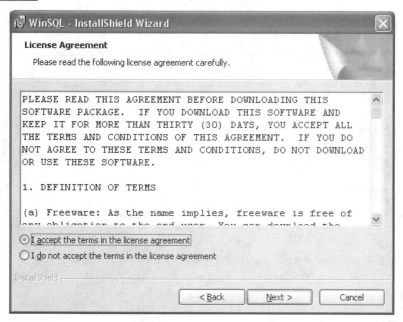

Figure 3.30   *Enter your name and organization*

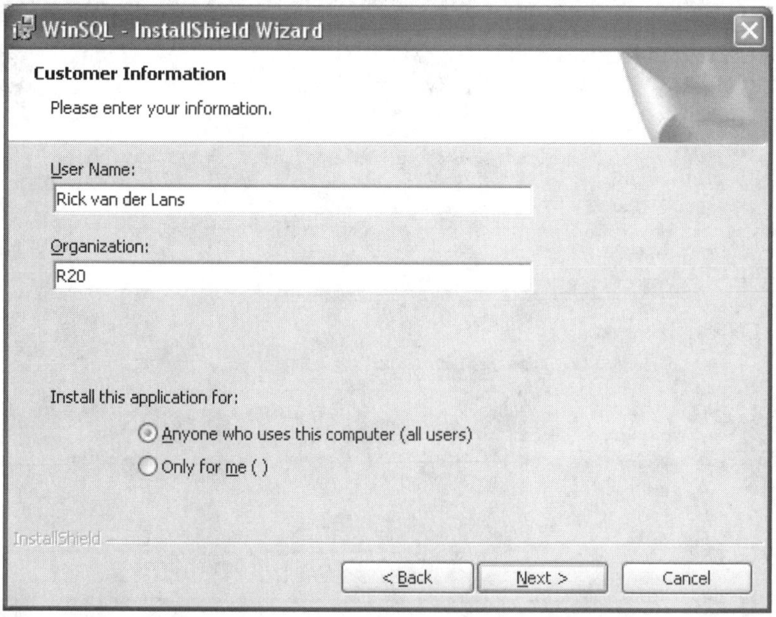

Figure 3.31   *In which directory do you want to install WinSQL?*

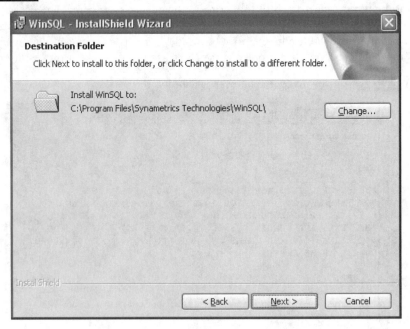

WinSQL proposes a directory in which WinSQL will be installed. If you prefer to use another directory, select Change. Otherwise, continue by clicking Next. The window in Figure 3.32 appears.

Figure 3.32   *Are you ready to install?*

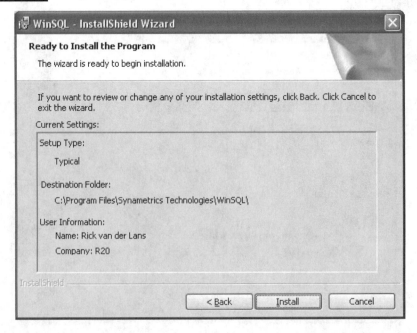

If the installation was successful, the window in Figure 3.34 appears. Select Finish in this window. Because WinSQL is started for the first time, the question displayed in Figure 3.35 appears. Select Yes to display the window in Figure 3.36.

Figure 3.33   *The installation of WinSQL in progress*

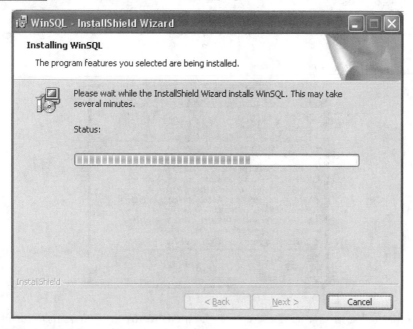

Figure 3.34   *The installation is complete*

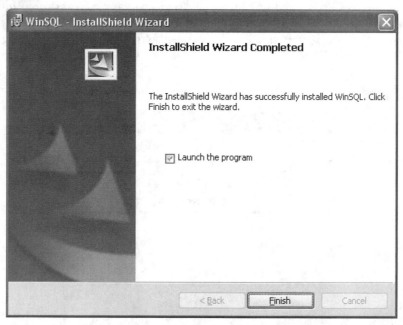

Figure 3.35   *Do you want to register WinSQL?*

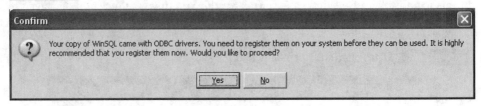

Figure 3.36   *Do you need additional ODBC drivers?*

From the list in Figure 3.36, choose which ODBC drivers you want to install. All the required drivers for MySQL have already been installed, but other database servers might run on your machine as well, and you also want to access them via ODBC. Do not select an unnecessary set of drivers. Click Register; a window such as the one in Figure 3.37 appears. Select OK in this window and close the WinSQL ODBC Installer by clicking Close. WinSQL is started, and a window appears that enables you to log on to MySQL: see Figure 3.38.

Figure 3.37   *Additional ODBC drivers have been installed*

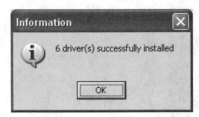

In Figure 3.38, in the fields User ID and Password, type in the name **root** and select Ok. The question shown in Figure 3.39 appears. Plugins are useful for extending the capabilities of WinSQL. Most of these additional capabilities are achieved by querying catalog tables. Choose Yes here; Figure 3.40 appears. In this window, replace all the text in green with this SQL statement (see Figure 3.41):

```
SELECT * FROM MYSQL.USER
```

Figure 3.38   *It is time to log on to MySQL*

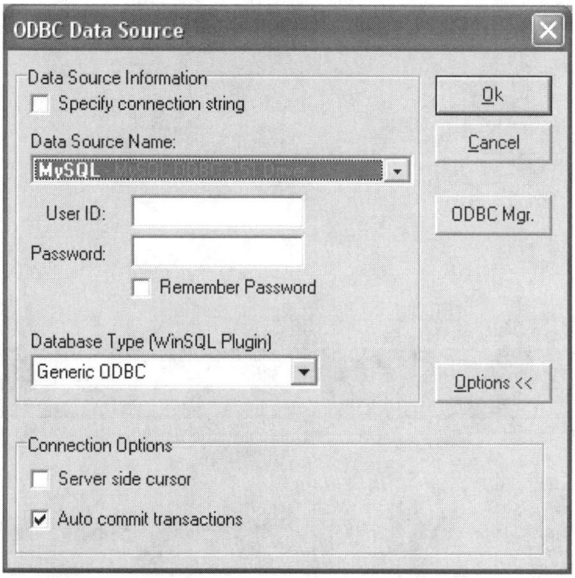

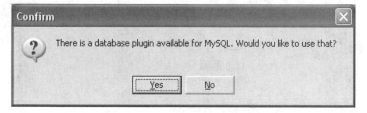

Figure 3.39   *Do you want the database plugin for MySQL?*

Figure 3.40   *WinSQL has started*

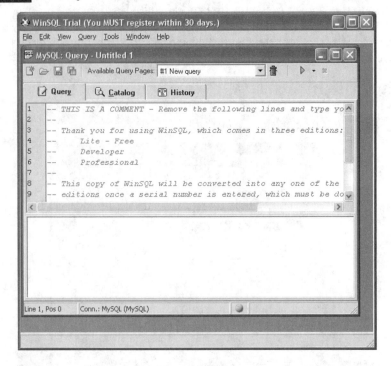

Figure 3.41   *Enter your first SQL statement*

If you entered the entire statement in Figure 3.40, click the green arrow. WinSQL passes the statement to MySQL for processing. WinSQL then presents the result of the SQL statement; see Figure 3.42. The list shown should include the user called root; see the first line in the result.

Figure 3.42   *The SQL statement has processed correctly*

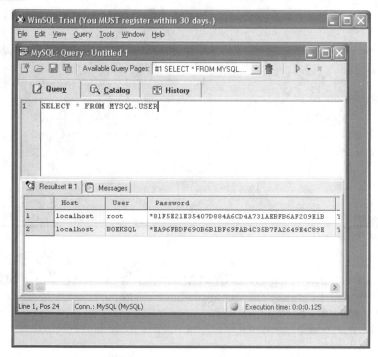

To work comfortably with WinSQL, make sure that some of its properties have been set correctly. For this, select Edit in the menu, followed by Options. Make sure that the Query terminator string setting is a semicolon and that the option Terminators must be on a new line is not selected; see Figure 3.43. The installation of WinSQL then is complete.

Figure 3.43 *Set specific WinSQL properties*

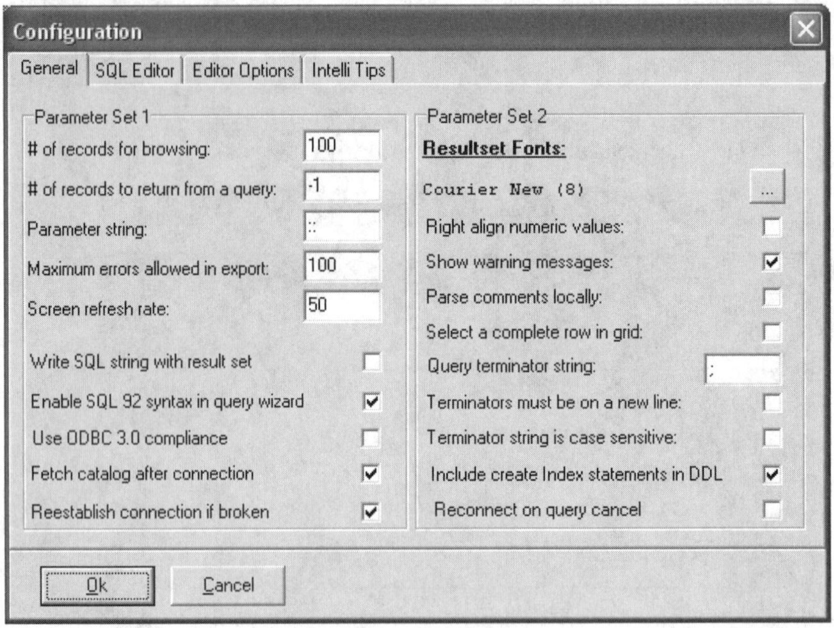

3.5 Downloading SQL Statements from the Web Site

As mentioned in the preface, the accompanying Web site contains all the SQL statements that are used in this book. In this section, we briefly describe how you can download them. This is a good moment to do so because these statements are needed to create the sample database.

The URL of the Web site of this book is www.r20.nl. The statements are stored in simple text files; by cutting and pasting, they can be copied easily to any product. You can open them with any text editor.

A separate file exists for each chapter, as clearly indicated on the Web site. In the file, you will find in front of each SQL statement an identification by which you can search them. For example, Example 7.1 (the first example in Chapter 7, "SELECT Statement: The FROM Clause") has this as identification:

```
Example 7.1:
```
Likewise, in front of Answer 12.6 is this:

```
Answer 12.6:
```
After you have downloaded the SQL statements, you can install the sample database that is used throughout the book. Again, we refer to the Web site of the book: www.r20.nl. There you will find detailed information about how this database can be created and filled. But the next chapter is also quite useful. Without this database, you cannot practice the exercises or answer the questions.

3.6 Ready?

If all things went well, you have now installed MySQL and WinSQL. If you want, you can start to play with SQL. However, the sample database is missing. The next chapter describes how to create that database.

4

SQL in a Nutshell

4.1 Introduction

I n this chapter, we use examples to build up a picture of the capabilities of the SQL
database language. Most SQL statements are discussed briefly. The details and all the
features are described in other chapters. The intention of this chapter is to give you a
feeling of what SQL looks like and what this book covers.

In the first sections, we also explain how to create the sample database. Be sure to
execute the statements from these sections because almost all examples and exercises
in the rest of this book are based upon this database.

> **Portability:** *Not all the statements and features described in this chapter are supported
> by all the SQL products. Especially in the first sections, we include some SQL statements
> that cannot be regarded as common SQL but are specific to MySQL. Those statements
> are explained mainly because readers need to use them to install the example database
> with MySQL.*

4.2 Logging On to the MySQL Database Server

To do anything with SQL (this applies to creating the sample database as well), you must
log on to the database server. Most database servers (including MySQL) require that
users identify themselves before manipulating the data in the database. In other words,
the user has to *log on* by using an application. Identification is done with the help of a
username and a *password*. Therefore, this chapter begins with an explanation of how to
log on to a database server.

First, you need a username. However, to create a user (with a name and password),
it is necessary to log on first—a classical example of a chicken-and-egg problem. To end
this deadlock, most database servers create several users during the installation procedure. Otherwise, it would be impossible to log on after the installation. With MySQL,
one of these SQL users is called root and has an identical password (if you have followed
the installation procedure as described in the previous chapter).

How logging on really takes place depends on the application that you use. We assume that you use WinSQL. In this case, the logon screen looks like Figure 4.1.

Figure 4.1   *The logon screen of WinSQL*

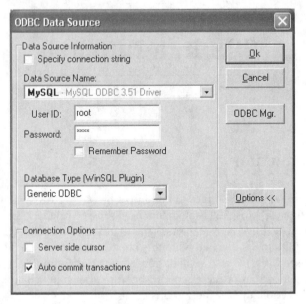

The username is entered in the User ID text box and the password in the Password text box. In both cases, the word you type is **root**. Because of security aspects, the password characters appear as asterisks. Usernames and passwords are case-sensitive, so be sure you type them correctly—not with capitals! After the name and password have been entered, the user can log on and start entering SQL statements.

When you use the application called MYSQL that is included with MySQL, the process of logging on looks different but is still comparable; see Figure 4.2. The code –u stands for *user*, behind which the username (root) is specified followed by the code –p. Next, the application wants to know the password. We explain this in more detail in the next sections.

The Web site contains detailed information about how to log on with different programs.

After you log on successfully with the users that are created during the installation procedure, new users can be introduced and new tables can be created.

4.3 Creating New SQL Users

In Section 1.4, we described the concept of a user. We also mentioned briefly the respective roles of users and applications. A user starts up an application. This application passes SQL statements to the database server that processes them. These SQL statements

Figure 4.2   *Logging on with* MYSQL

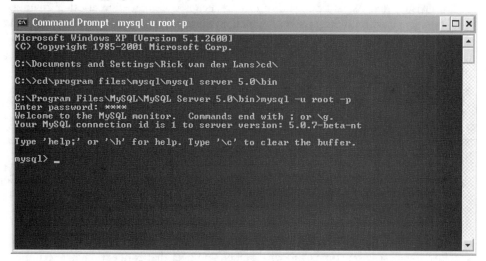

can be entered "live" (interactive SQL) by a user or can be included in the application code (preprogrammed SQL).

Here, a clear distinction should be made between the real, *human* user and the username that he uses to log on. To avoid confusion, we call the latter the *SQL user*.

SQL users can be granted *privileges*. A privilege is a specification indicating what a certain SQL user can or cannot do. For example, one user might be allowed to create new tables, another might be authorized to update existing tables, and a third might be able to only query tables.

The relationship between human users and SQL users can be one-to-one, but that is not required. A human user is allowed to log on under different SQL usernames—and every time he will have other privileges. Additionally, an entire group of human users is allowed to use the same SQL username. They all have the same privileges. Therefore, the relationship between users and SQL users is a many-to-many relationship. You have to decide how you will arrange all this.

So, to log on, you need to have an SQL user. Several SQL users have already been created during the installation procedure, to prevent the chicken-and-egg problem. Therefore, you do not have to create one. However, if you want to create your own SQL users, you can do that with a special SQL statement.

Imagine that you log on with the SQL user called root. Next, you can use the CRE-ATE USER statement to create your own, new SQL users. With this, you assign a new SQL user a name and a password.

Example 4.1: Introduce a new SQL user called BOOKSQL with the password BOOK-SQLPW.

```
CREATE USER 'BOOKSQL'@'localhost' IDENTIFIED BY 'BOOKSQLPW'
```

Explanation: With the specification `'BOOKSQL'@'localhost'`, the name of the new SQL user is created. What `localhost` exactly means is explained in another chapter. The statement ends with the password, which, in this case, is BOOKSQLPW. Be sure that the username, the term `localhost`, and the password are placed between single quotation marks.

> **Portability:** *The CREATE USER statement is not supported by all SQL products. Some use the GRANT statement to create new users. Additionally, for products that do support the CREATE USER statement, differences in syntax exist.*

When an application logs on to a database server with an SQL username, a so-called *connection* starts. A connection should be seen as a unique link between the application and a specific database for the concerned SQL user. This link consists of two parts. The first part bonds the application to the database server; the second bonds the database server to the database. Therefore, when the application logs on, it is connected to the specified database at one time. And what can be sent over that connection is determined by the privileges of the SQL user.

A new SQL user is allowed to log on, but he does not have any other privileges yet. We have to grant those privileges to BOOKSQL first with the GRANT statement.

The features of the GRANT statement are extensive. This statement and related topics are discussed in detail in Chapter 23, "Users and Data Security." However, to put you on your way, the next example contains the statement by which the new SQL user called BOOKSQL is granted enough privileges to create tables and manipulate them afterward.

Example 4.2: Give the SQL user BOOKSQL the privileges to create and manipulate tables.

```
GRANT  ALL PRIVILEGES
ON     *.*
TO     'BOOKSQL'@'localhost'
WITH   GRANT OPTION
```

BOOKSQL can now log on and execute all the statements in the following chapters.

> **Note:** *In the rest of the book, we assume that you log on as user BOOKSQL with the password BOOKSQLPW and that this user has sufficient privileges.*

Portability: *The GRANT statement is supported by most SQL products. However, the syntax to grant users sufficient privileges to create tables looks very different in different products. The GRANT statement just shown, therefore, is specific to MySQL. For example, in DB2, a comparable statement would look like this:*

```
GRANT   DBADM
ON      DATABASE
TO      BOOKSQL
```

4.4 Creating Databases

In Section 1.2, we defined the concept of a database. From this definition, we can derive that a database can be seen as a container for a set of tables. And for SQL, it holds that each table must also be created within an existing database. Therefore, when you want to build tables, you first have to create a database.

Example 4.3: As user BOOKSQL, create a database with the name TENNIS for the tables of the tennis club.

```
CREATE DATABASE TENNIS
```

Explanation: After this CREATE DATABASE statement is processed, the database exists but is still empty.

Portability: *Not all SQL-products support the CREATE DATABASE statement. Some of them have special utilities for creating new databases. Additionally, this statement is not part of any SQL standard. But the products that do support this statement, such as MySQL, use the previous statement.*

4.5 Selecting the Current Database

Most database servers, including MySQL, can offer access to more than one database. When a user has opened a connection with a database server and wants, for example, to create new tables or query existing tables, he must specify the database he wants to work with. This is called the *current database*. There can be only one current database. That means that all SQL statements will be fired at this database.

When no current database has been specified, it is still possible to manipulate tables. In addition, tables from a database other than the current database can also be accessed. For both situations, you must explicitly specify the database in which those tables reside.

To make a specific database current, MySQL supports the USE statement.

Example 4.4: Make TENNIS the current database.

```
USE TENNIS
```

Explanation: This statement can also be used to "jump" from one database to another.

After processing a CREATE DATABASE statement (see the previous section), the created database does *not* automatically become the current database. The USE statement is needed to specify the current database.

No database is current when you log on using the previous technique. Besides the use of the USE statement, there is another way to make a database current. When you log on, you can specify the desired current database:

```
mysql -u BOOKSQL -p TENNIS
```

In the rest of the book, we assume that you log on as user BOOKSQL with the password BOOKSQLPW, that this user has sufficient privileges, and also that the TENNIS database is the current database.

> **Portability:** *Only a few SQL-products support the USE statement. MySQL is one of them. Furthermore, this statement is not part of any SQL standard. The main reason this statement is explained is that readers need to use it constantly to access the data in the MySQL databases. Some products support a CONNECT statement that offers comparable functionality.*

4.6 Creating Tables

Databases in SQL are made up of database objects. The best-known and most important database object is probably the table. The CREATE TABLE statement is used to develop new tables. The next example contains the CREATE TABLE statements that are needed to create the tables from the sample database.

Example 4.5: Create the five tables that form the sample database.

```
CREATE    TABLE PLAYERS
          (PLAYERNO      INTEGER       NOT NULL,
           NAME          CHAR(15)      NOT NULL,
           INITIALS      CHAR(3)       NOT NULL,
           BIRTH_DATE    DATE                   ,
           SEX           CHAR(1)       NOT NULL,
           JOINED        SMALLINT      NOT NULL,
           STREET        VARCHAR(30)   NOT NULL,
           HOUSENO       CHAR(4)                ,
           POSTCODE      CHAR(6)                ,
           TOWN          VARCHAR(30)   NOT NULL,
           PHONENO       CHAR(13)               ,
           LEAGUENO      CHAR(4)                ,
           PRIMARY KEY   (PLAYERNO)             )

CREATE    TABLE TEAMS
          (TEAMNO        INTEGER       NOT NULL,
           PLAYERNO      INTEGER       NOT NULL,
           DIVISION      CHAR(6)       NOT NULL,
           PRIMARY KEY   (TEAMNO)               )

CREATE    TABLE MATCHES
          (MATCHNO       INTEGER       NOT NULL,
           TEAMNO        INTEGER       NOT NULL,
           PLAYERNO      INTEGER       NOT NULL,
           WON           SMALLINT      NOT NULL,
           LOST          SMALLINT      NOT NULL,
           PRIMARY KEY   (MATCHNO)              )

CREATE    TABLE PENALTIES
          (PAYMENTNO     INTEGER       NOT NULL,
           PLAYERNO      INTEGER       NOT NULL,
           PAYMENT_DATE  DATE          NOT NULL,
           AMOUNT        DECIMAL(7,2)  NOT NULL,
           PRIMARY KEY   (PAYMENTNO)            )

CREATE    TABLE COMMITTEE_MEMBERS
          (PLAYERNO      INTEGER       NOT NULL,
           BEGIN_DATE    DATE          NOT NULL,
           END_DATE      DATE                   ,
           POSITION      CHAR(20)               ,
           PRIMARY KEY   (PLAYERNO, BEGIN_DATE))
```

Explanation: SQL does not require the statements to be entered in the exact same way as this. In this book, a certain layout style is used for all SQL statements to make them easier to read. However, for SQL, it does not matter whether everything is written neatly in a row (still separated by spaces or commas, of course) or nicely below each other.

As indicated in Chapter 2, "The Tennis Club Sample Database," several integrity constraints apply for these tables. We excluded most of them here because we do not need them in the first two parts of this book. Chapter 16, "Specifying Integrity Constraints," explains what all the integrity rules look like in SQL.

With a CREATE TABLE statement, several properties are defined, including the name of the table, the columns of the table, and the primary key. The name of the table is specified first: CREATE TABLE PLAYERS. The columns of a table are listed between brackets. For each column name, a data type is specified, as in CHAR, SMALLINT, INTEGER, DECIMAL, or DATE. The data type defines the type of value that may be entered into the column concerned. The next section explains the specification NOT NULL.

Figure 2.2 shows the primary key of the tables, among other things. A primary key of a table is a column (or combination of columns) in which every value can appear only once. By defining the primary key in the PLAYERS table, we indicate that each player number can appear only once in the PLAYERNO column. A primary key is a certain type of integrity constraint. In SQL, primary keys are specified within the CREATE TABLE statement with the words PRIMARY KEY. There are two ways to specify a primary key. Here we make use of only one. After listing all the columns, PRIMARY KEY is specified followed by the column or columns belonging to that primary key. The other way to specify a primary key is discussed in Chapter 16.

It is not always necessary to specify primary keys for a table, but it is important. We explain why in Chapter 16. For now, we advise you to define a primary key for each table you create.

4.7 The *NULL* Value

Columns are filled with values. A value can be, for example, a number, a word, or a date. A special value is the NULL value. The NULL value is comparable with "value unknown" or "value not present." In this book, we represent NULLs in the results of queries with a question mark (?). The PLAYERS table contains several NULL values in the LEAGUENO column (see Section 2.3). This indicates that the player has no league number.

A NULL value must not be confused with the number zero or spaces; it should be seen as a missing value. A NULL value is never equal to another NULL value. So, two NULL values are not equal to each other, but they are also not unequal. If we happened to know whether two NULL values were equal or unequal, we would know *something* about those NULL values. Then, we could not say that the two values were (completely) unknown. We discuss this later in more detail.

In the previous section, you saw that, in the definition of a column, you are allowed to specify NOT NULL. This means that every row of the column *must* be filled. In other words, NULL values are not allowed in a NOT NULL column. For example, each player must have a NAME, but a LEAGUENO is not required.

The term NULL *value* is, in fact, not entirely correct; we should be using the term NULL instead. The reason is that it is not a value, but rather a gap in a table or a signal indicating that the value is missing. However, we employ this term in the book to stay in line with various standards and products.

SQL currently supports just one type of NULL value, with the meaning "value unknown." E. F. Codd, who established the relational model, makes a distinction between two different kinds of NULL values in [CODD90]: "value missing and applicable" and "value missing and inapplicable." SQL does not (yet) make this distinction; therefore, we leave this topic out of consideration in this book.

4.8 Populating Tables with Data

The tables have been created and can now be filled with data. For this, we use INSERT statements.

Example 4.6: Fill all tables from the sample database with data. (See Section 2.3 for a listing of all data.) For the sake of convenience, for each of the tables, only two examples of INSERT statements are given here. At the Web site of the book, you will find all the INSERT statements.

```
INSERT INTO PLAYERS VALUES
    (6, 'Parmenter', 'R', '1964-06-25', 'M', 1977,
    'Haseltine Lane', '80', '1234KK', 'Stratford',
    '070-476537', '8467')

INSERT INTO PLAYERS VALUES
    (7, 'Wise', 'GWS', '1963-05-11', 'M', 1981,
    'Edgecombe Way', '39', '9758VB', 'Stratford',
    '070-347689', NULL)

INSERT INTO TEAMS VALUES (1, 6, 'first')

INSERT INTO TEAMS VALUES (2, 27, 'second')

INSERT INTO MATCHES VALUES (1, 1, 6, 3, 1)
```

```
INSERT INTO MATCHES VALUES (4, 1, 44, 3, 2)

INSERT INTO PENALTIES VALUES (1, 6, '1980-12-08', 100)

INSERT INTO PENALTIES VALUES (2, 44, '1981-05-05', 75)

INSERT INTO COMMITTEE_MEMBERS VALUES
    (6, '1990-1-1', '1990-12-31', 'Secretary')

INSERT INTO COMMITTEE_MEMBERS VALUES
    (6, '1991-1-1', '1992-12-31', 'Member')
```

Explanation: Each statement corresponds to one (new) row in a table. After the term INSERT INTO, the table name is specified; the values that the new row consists of come after VALUES. Each row consists of one or more values. Different kinds of values may be used. For example, there are numeric and alphanumeric values, dates, and times.

Each alphanumeric value, such as Parmenter and Stratford (see the first INSERT statement), must be enclosed in single quotation marks. The (column) values are separated by commas. Because SQL remembers the sequence in which the columns were specified in the CREATE TABLE statement, the system also knows the column to which every value corresponds. For the PLAYERS table, therefore, the first value is PLAYERNO, the second value is NAME, and the last value is LEAGUENO.

Specifying dates and times is somewhat more difficult than specifying numeric and alphanumeric values because certain rules apply. A date such as December 8, 1980, must be specified as: '1980-12-08'. This form of expression, described in detail in Section 5.2.5, turns an alphanumeric value into a correct date. However, the alphanumeric value must be written correctly. A date consists of three components: year, month, and day. The components are separated by hyphens.

In the second INSERT statement, the word NULL is specified as the twelfth value. This enables us to enter a NULL value explicitly. In this case, it means that the league number of player number 7 is unknown.

4.9 Querying Tables

You can use SELECT statements to retrieve data from tables. A number of examples illustrate the diverse features of this statement.

Example 4.7: Get the number, the name, and the date of birth of each player resident in Stratford; sort the result in alphabetical order of name. (Note that *Stratford* starts with an uppercase letter.)

```
SELECT    PLAYERNO, NAME, BIRTH_DATE
FROM      PLAYERS
WHERE     TOWN = 'Stratford'
ORDER BY  NAME
```

The result is:

PLAYERNO	NAME	BIRTH_DATE
39	Bishop	1956-10-29
57	Brown	1971-08-17
2	Everett	1948-09-01
83	Hope	1956-11-11
6	Parmenter	1964-06-25
100	Parmenter	1963-02-28
7	Wise	1963-05-11

Explanation: This SELECT statement should be read as follows: Get the number, name, and date of birth (SELECT PLAYERNO, NAME, BIRTH_DATE) of each player (FROM PLAYERS) resident in Stratford (WHERE TOWN = 'Stratford'); sort the result in alphabetical order of name (ORDER BY NAME). After FROM, you specify which table you want to query. The condition that your requested data must satisfy comes after WHERE. SELECT enables you to choose which columns you want to see. Figure 4.3 tries to illustrate this in a graphical way. And after ORDER BY, specify the column names on which the final result should be sorted.

In this book, we present the result of a SELECT statement somewhat differently from the way SQL does. The "default" layout that we use throughout this book is as follows. First, the width of a column is determined by the width of the data type of the column. Second, the name of a column heading is equal to the name of the column in the SELECT statement. Third, the values in columns with an alphanumeric data type are left-justified, while those in numeric columns are right-justified. Fourth, there are two spaces between two columns. Finally, a NULL value is displayed as a question mark.

Figure 4.2   *An illustration of a SELECT statement*

```
PLAYERNO  NAME        INIT  BIRTH_DATE   STREET           TOWN
--------  ----------  ----  ----------   ---------------  ----------
       2  Everett     R     1948-09-01   Stoney Road      Stratford
       6  Parmenter   R     1964-06-25   Haseltine Lane   Stratford
       7  Wise        GWS   1963-05-11   Edgecombe Way    Stratford
       8  Newcastle   B     1962-07-08   Station Road     Inglewood
      27  Collins     DD    1964-12-28   Long Drive       Eltham
      28  Collins     C     1963-06-22   Old Main Road    Midhurst
      39  Bishop      D     1956-10-29   Eaton Square     Stratford
      44  Baker       E     1963-01-09   Lewis Street     Inglewood
      57  Brown       M     1971-08-17   Edgecombe Way    Stratford
      83  Hope        PK    1956-11-11   Magdalene Road   Stratford
      95  Miller      P     1963-05-14   High Street      Douglas
     100  Permenter   P     1963-02-28   Haseltine Lane   Stratford
     104  Moorman     D     1970-05-10   Stout Street     Eltham
     112  Bailey      IP    1963-10-01   Vixen Road       Plymouth
```

SELECT PLAYERNO, NAME, BIRTH_DATE   WHERE TOWN = 'Stratford'

Example 4.8: Get the number of each player who joined the club after 1980 and is resident in Stratford; order the result by player number.

```
SELECT    PLAYERNO
FROM      PLAYERS
WHERE     JOINED > 1980
AND       TOWN = 'Stratford'
ORDER BY  PLAYERNO
```

The result is:

```
PLAYERNO
--------
       7
      57
      83
```

Explanation: Get the number (SELECT PLAYERNO) of each player (FROM PLAYERS) who joined the club after 1980 (WHERE JOINED > 1980) and is resident in Stratford (AND TOWN = 'Stratford'); sort the result by player number (ORDER BY PLAYERNO).

Example 4.9: Get all the information about each penalty.

```
SELECT    *
FROM      PENALTIES
```

The result is:

```
PAYMENTNO   PLAYERNO   PAYMENT_DATE   AMOUNT
---------   --------   ------------   ------
        1          6   1980-12-08     100.00
        2         44   1981-05-05      75.00
        3         27   1983-09-10     100.00
        4        104   1984-12-08      50.00
        5         44   1980-12-08      25.00
        6          8   1980-12-08      25.00
        7         44   1982-12-30      30.00
        8         27   1984-11-12      75.00
```

Explanation: Get all column values (SELECT *) for each penalty (FROM PENALTIES). This statement returns the entire PENALTIES table. The * character is a shorthand notation for "all columns." In this result, you can also see how dates are presented in this book.

Example 4.10: How much is 33 times 121?

```
SELECT    33 * 121
```

The result is:

```
33 * 121
--------
    3993
```

Explanation: This example shows that a SELECT statement does not always have to retrieve data from tables. It is obvious that they can also be used to perform straightforward calculations. If no tables are specified, the statement returns one row as result. This row contains the answers to the calculations.

> **Portability:** *Several products, such as MySQL and Microsoft SQL Server, allow* SELECT *statements that do not retrieve data from tables. Because this feature is becoming more popular, an explanation is included in this book.*

4.10 Updating and Deleting Rows

Section 4.8 described how to add new rows to a table. This section covers the updating and deleting of existing rows.

A warning in advance: If you execute the statements described in this section, you will change the contents of the database. In the subsequent sections, we assume that the original contents of the database are intact.

The UPDATE statement changes values in rows, and the DELETE statement removes complete rows from a table. Look at examples of both statements.

Example 4.11: Change the amount of each penalty incurred by player 44 to $200.

```
UPDATE    PENALTIES
SET       AMOUNT = 200
WHERE     PLAYERNO = 44
```

Explanation: For each penalty (UPDATE PENALTIES) incurred by player 44 (WHERE PLAYERNO = 44), change the amount to $200 (SET AMOUNT = 200). So, the use of the WHERE clause in the UPDATE statement is equivalent to that of the SELECT statement. It indicates which rows must be changed. After the word SET, the columns that will have a new value are specified. The change executes regardless of the existing value.

Issuing a SELECT statement can show the effect of the change. Before the update, the next SELECT statement:

```
SELECT    PLAYERNO, AMOUNT
FROM      PENALTIES
WHERE     PLAYERNO = 44
```

gave the following result:

```
PLAYERNO  AMOUNT
--------  ------
      44  75.00
      44  25.00
      44  30.00
```

After the change with the UPDATE statement, the result of the previous SELECT statement is different:

```
PLAYERNO  AMOUNT
--------  ------
      44  200.00
      44  200.00
      44  200.00
```

Example 4.12: Remove each penalty for which the amount is greater than $100. (We assume the changed contents of the PENALTIES table.)

```
DELETE
FROM      PENALTIES
WHERE     AMOUNT > 100
```

Explanation: Remove the penalties (DELETE FROM PENALTIES) for which the amount is greater than 100 (WHERE AMOUNT > 100). Again, the use of the WHERE clause is equivalent to that in the SELECT and UPDATE statements.

After this statement, the PENALTIES table looks as follows (seen by issuing a SELECT statement):

```
PAYMENTNO  PLAYERNO  PAYMENT_DATE  AMOUNT
---------  --------  ------------  ------
        1         6  1980-12-08    100.00
        2        44  1981-05-05     75.00
        3        27  1983-09-10    100.00
        4       104  1984-12-08     50.00
        5        44  1980-12-08     25.00
        6         8  1980-12-08     25.00
        7        44  1982-12-30     30.00
        8        27  1984-11-12     75.00
```

4.11 Optimizing Query Processing with Indexes

Now look at how SELECT statements are processed—in other words, how SQL arrives at the correct answer. We illustrate this with the following SELECT statement (note that we assume the original contents of the PENALTIES table):

```
SELECT    *
FROM      PENALTIES
WHERE     AMOUNT = 25
```

To process this statement, SQL scans row by row through the entire PENALTIES table. If the value of AMOUNT equals 25, that row is included in the result. If, as in this example, the table contains only a few rows, SQL can work quickly. However, if a table has thousands of rows and each must be checked, this could take a great deal of time. In such a case, the definition of an *index* can speed up the processing. For now, think of an index created with SQL as similar to the index of a book. In Chapter 20, "Using Indexes," we discuss this topic in more detail.

An index is defined on a column or combination of columns. Here is an example.

Example 4.13: Create an index on the AMOUNT column of the PENALTIES table.

```
CREATE    INDEX PENALTIES_AMOUNT ON
          PENALTIES (AMOUNT)
```

Explanation: This statement defines an index called PENALTIES_AMOUNT for the AMOUNT column in the PENALTIES table.

This index ensures that in the previous example, SQL needs to look at only rows in the database that satisfy the WHERE condition. Therefore, it is quicker to produce an answer. The index PENALTIES_AMOUNT provides direct access to these rows. It is important to bear in mind the following points:

- Indexes are defined to optimize the processing of SELECT statements.
- An index is never explicitly referenced in a SELECT statement; the syntax of SQL does not allow this.
- During the processing of a statement, the database server itself determines whether an existing index will be used.
- An index may be created or deleted at any time.

- When updating, inserting, or deleting rows, SQL also maintains the indexes on the tables concerned. This means that, on one hand, the processing time for SELECT statements is reduced; on the other hand, the processing time for update statements (such as INSERT, UPDATE, and DELETE) can increase.
- An index is also a database object.

A special type of index is the *unique* index. SQL also uses unique indexes to optimize the processing of statements. Unique indexes have another function as well: They guarantee that a particular column or combination of columns contains no duplicate values. A unique index is created by placing the word UNIQUE between the words CREATE and INDEX.

4.12 Views

In a table, rows with data are actually stored. This means that a table occupies a particular amount of storage space; the more rows, the more storage space is required. *Views* are tables visible to users, but they do not occupy any storage space. A view, therefore, can also be referred to as a *virtual* or a *derived* table. A view behaves as though it contains actual rows of data, but, in fact, it contains none.

Example 4.14: Create a view in which the difference between the number of sets won and the number of sets lost are recorded for each match.

```
CREATE    VIEW NUMBER_SETS (MATCHNO, DIFFERENCE) AS
SELECT    MATCHNO, ABS(WON - LOST)
FROM      MATCHES
```

Explanation: The previous statement defines a view with the name NUMBER_SETS. A SELECT statement defines the contents of the view. This view has only two columns: MATCHNO and DIFFERENCE. The value of the second column is determined by subtracting the number of sets lost from the number of sets won. The ABS function makes the value positive. (The precise meaning of ABS is described in Appendix B, "Scalar Functions.")

By using the SELECT statement shown here, you can see the (virtual) contents of the view:

```
SELECT    *
FROM      NUMBER_SETS
```

The result is:

```
MATCHNO   DIFFERENCE
-------   ----------
      1            2
      2            1
      3            3
      4            1
      5            3
      6            2
      7            3
      8            3
      9            1
     10            1
     11            1
     12            2
     13            3
```

The contents of the NUMBER_SETS view are *not* stored in the database but are derived at the moment a SELECT statement (or another statement) is executed. The use of views, therefore, costs nothing extra in storage space because the contents of a view can include only data that is already stored in other tables. Among other things, views can be used to do the following:

- Simplify the use of routine or repetitive statements
- Restructure the way in which tables are seen
- Develop SELECT statements in several steps
- Improve the security of data

Chapter 21, "Views," looks at views more closely.

4.13   Users and Data Security

Data in a database should be protected against incorrect use and misuse. In other words, not everyone should have access to all the data in the database. As already shown in the beginning of this chapter, SQL recognizes the concept of SQL user and privilege. A user has to make himself known by logging on.

That same section also contains an example of granting privileges to users. Here, you can find more examples of the GRANT statement, and we assume that all the SQL users mentioned exist.

Example 4.15: Imagine that the two SQL users DIANE and PAUL have been created. SQL will reject most of their SQL statements as long as they have not been granted privileges. The following three statements give them the required privileges. We assume that a third SQL user (for example, BOOKSQL) grants these privileges.

```
GRANT    SELECT
ON       PLAYERS
TO       DIANE

GRANT    SELECT, UPDATE
ON       PLAYERS
TO       PAUL

GRANT    SELECT, UPDATE
ON       TEAMS
TO       PAUL
```

When PAUL has logged on, he can query the TEAMS table, for example:

```
SELECT   *
FROM     TEAMS
```

SQL gives an error message if DIANE enters the same SELECT statement because she has authority to query the PLAYERS table but not the TEAMS table.

4.14 Deleting Database Objects

For each type of database object for which a CREATE statement exists, there is also a corresponding DROP statement with which the object can be deleted. Here are a few examples:

Example 4.16: Delete the MATCHES table.

```
DROP TABLE MATCHES
```

Example 4.17: Delete the view NUMBER_SETS.

```
DROP VIEW NUMBER_SETS
```

Example 4.18: Delete the PENALTIES_AMOUNT index.

```
DROP INDEX PENALTIES_AMOUNT
```

Example 4.19: Delete the TENNIS database.

```
DROP DATABASE TENNIS
```

All dependent objects are also removed. For example, if the PLAYERS table is deleted, all indexes (which are defined on that table) and all privileges (which are dependent on that table) are automatically removed.

> **Portability:** *All SQL products support the DROP TABLE, DROP VIEW, and DROP INDEX statements. But there does not always exist a DROP statement for every type of database object. For example, MySQL supports a DROP DATABASE, but MaxDB does not.*

4.15 System Parameters

Each database server, including MySQL, has certain settings. When the database server is started, these settings are read and determine its behavior from then on. For example, some settings handle how data must be stored, others affect the processing speed, and still others are related to the system time and date.

These settings are usually called *system parameters* or *system variables*. Each database server has its own set of system parameters; they are not standardized.

Sometimes, it is important to know the value of a certain system parameter. With a simple SELECT statement, its value can be retrieved.

Example 4.20: What is the most recent version of the MySQL database server that we use now?

```
SELECT @@VERSION
```

The result is:

```
@@VERSION
-------------
5.0.7-beta-nt
```

Explanation: In MySQL, the value of the system parameter VERSION is set to the version number. Specifying two "at" symbols before the name of the system parameter returns its value.

Many system parameters, such as the VERSION parameter and the system date, cannot be changed. However, some can be changed, including the SQL_MODE parameter. This parameter affects how certain constructs in the SQL language must be interpreted. To change system parameters, you can use the SET statement.

Example 4.21: Change the value of the SQL_MODE parameter to ANSI.

```
SET SQL_MODE = 'ANSI'
```

Explanation: This change applies only to the present SQL user. In other words, different users can see different values for certain system parameters.

> **Portability:** *As indicated, system parameters are very SQL product-specific. Even the SQL standards do not touch on this topic. Because MySQL is included on the CD-ROM, we decided to describe this concept based on how it has been implemented in MySQL.*

4.16 Grouping of SQL Statements

SQL has many statements. Only a few are described briefly in this chapter. In literature, it is customary to divide that large set of SQL statements into the following groups: DDL, DML, and DCL, and procedural statements.

DDL stands for Data Definition Language. The DDL consists of all the SQL statements that affect the structure of database objects, such as tables, indexes, and views. The CREATE TABLE statement is a clear example of a DDL statement, but so are CREATE INDEX and DROP TABLE.

DML stands for Data Manipulation Language. The SQL statements used to query and change the contents of tables belong to this group. Examples of DML statements are SELECT, UPDATE, DELETE, and INSERT.

DCL stands for Data Control Language. DCL statements relate to the security of data and the revoking of privileges. In this chapter, we have discussed the GRANT statement, but the REVOKE statement is also a DCL statement.

Examples of *procedural statements* are IF-THEN-ELSE and WHILE-DO. These classical statements have been added to SQL to create relatively new database objects, such as triggers and stored procedures.

The names of these groups sometimes assume that SQL consists of several individual languages, but this is incorrect. All SQL statements are part of one language and are grouped for the sake of clarity.

Appendix A, "Syntax of SQL," in which all SQL statements are defined, indicates the group to which an SQL statement belongs.

> **Portability:** *For some SQL products, additional groups of SQL statements are defined beyond those mentioned. We cover them where they are relevant.*

4.17 The Catalog Tables

Most SQL database servers maintain lists of usernames and passwords, and the sequence in which columns in the CREATE TABLE statements have been created (see Section 4.6). However, where is all this data stored? Where does SQL keep track of all these names, passwords, tables, columns, sequence numbers, and so on? Most products have a number of tables for their own use in which this data is stored. These tables are called *catalog tables* or *system tables*, and together they form the *catalog*.

Each catalog table is an "ordinary" table that can be queried using SELECT statements. Querying the catalog tables can have many uses. Three of them are as follows:

- As a *help function* for new users to determine which tables in the database are available and which columns the tables contain
- As a *control function* so that users can see, for example, which indexes, views, and privileges would be deleted if a particular table were dropped
- As a *processing function* for SQL itself when it executes statements (as a help function for SQL)

However, catalog tables *cannot* be accessed using statements such as UPDATE and DELETE. In any case, this is not necessary because the SQL database server maintains these tables itself.

Unfortunately, for each database server, these tables have been designed differently. The tables and columns have different names and a different structure. Sometimes, they are even difficult to access. This is why we have defined several simple views on the catalog tables of MySQL to give you a start.

In the rest of this book, we make use of these simple catalog views, so we recommend that you create these views. On the Web site of this book, you can see the best way to do that. You can adjust these catalog views later, of course. New columns and new catalog views can be added. By studying how these views have been built, it becomes easier to fathom the real catalog tables later.

SQL in a Nutshell 89

Example 4.22: Create the following catalog views. (These views must be created in the sequence specified because of interdependences.)

```
CREATE    OR REPLACE VIEW USERS
          (USER_NAME) AS
SELECT    DISTINCT UPPER(CONCAT('''',USER,'''@''',HOST,''''))
FROM      MYSQL.USER

CREATE    OR REPLACE VIEW TABLES
          (TABLE_CREATOR, TABLE_NAME,
          CREATE_TIMESTAMP, COMMENT) AS
SELECT    UPPER(TABLE_SCHEMA), UPPER(TABLE_NAME),
          CREATE_TIME, TABLE_COMMENT
FROM      INFORMATION_SCHEMA.TABLES
WHERE     TABLE_TYPE IN ('BASE TABLE','TEMPORARY')

CREATE    OR REPLACE VIEW COLUMNS
          (TABLE_CREATOR, TABLE_NAME, COLUMN_NAME,
          COLUMN_NO, DATA_TYPE, CHAR_LENGTH,
          `PRECISION`, SCALE, NULLABLE, COMMENT) AS
SELECT    UPPER(TABLE_SCHEMA), UPPER(TABLE_NAME),
          UPPER(COLUMN_NAME), ORDINAL_POSITION,
          UPPER(DATA_TYPE), CHARACTER_MAXIMUM_LENGTH,
          NUMERIC_PRECISION, NUMERIC_SCALE, IS_NULLABLE,
          COLUMN_COMMENT
FROM      INFORMATION_SCHEMA.COLUMNS

CREATE    OR REPLACE VIEW VIEWS
          (VIEW_CREATOR, VIEW_NAME, CREATE_TIMESTAMP,
          WITHCHECKOPT, IS_UPDATABLE, VIEWFORMULA, COMMENT) AS
SELECT    UPPER(V.TABLE_SCHEMA), UPPER(V.TABLE_NAME),
          T.CREATE_TIME,
          CASE
             WHEN V.CHECK_OPTION = 'None' THEN 'NO'
             WHEN V.CHECK_OPTION = 'Cascaded' THEN 'CASCADED'
             WHEN V.CHECK_OPTION = 'Local' THEN 'LOCAL'
             ELSE 'Yes'
          END, V.IS_UPDATABLE, V.VIEW_DEFINITION, T.TABLE_COMMENT
FROM      INFORMATION_SCHEMA.VIEWS AS V,
          INFORMATION_SCHEMA.TABLES AS T
WHERE     V.TABLE_NAME = T.TABLE_NAME
AND       V.TABLE_SCHEMA = T.TABLE_SCHEMA
```

```
CREATE    OR REPLACE VIEW INDEXES
          (INDEX_CREATOR, INDEX_NAME, CREATE_TIMESTAMP,
          TABLE_CREATOR, TABLE_NAME, UNIQUE_ID, INDEX_TYPE) AS
SELECT    DISTINCT UPPER(I.INDEX_SCHEMA), UPPER(I.INDEX_NAME),
          T.CREATE_TIME, UPPER(I.TABLE_SCHEMA),
          UPPER(I.TABLE_NAME),
          CASE
             WHEN I.NON_UNIQUE = 0 THEN 'YES'
             ELSE 'NO'
          END,
          I.INDEX_TYPE
FROM      INFORMATION_SCHEMA.STATISTICS AS I,
          INFORMATION_SCHEMA.TABLES AS T
WHERE     I.TABLE_NAME = T.TABLE_NAME
AND       I.TABLE_SCHEMA = T.TABLE_SCHEMA


CREATE    OR REPLACE VIEW COLUMNS_IN_INDEX
          (INDEX_CREATOR, INDEX_NAME,
          TABLE_CREATOR, TABLE_NAME, COLUMN_NAME,
          COLUMN_SEQ, ORDERING) AS
SELECT    UPPER(INDEX_SCHEMA), UPPER(INDEX_NAME),
          UPPER(TABLE_SCHEMA), UPPER(TABLE_NAME),
          UPPER(COLUMN_NAME), SEQ_IN_INDEX,
          CASE
             WHEN COLLATION = 'A' THEN 'ASCENDING'
             WHEN COLLATION = 'D' THEN 'DESCENDING'
             ELSE 'OTHER'
          END
FROM      INFORMATION_SCHEMA.STATISTICS


CREATE    OR REPLACE VIEW USER_AUTHS
          (GRANTOR, GRANTEE, PRIVILEGE, WITHGRANTOPT) AS
SELECT    'UNKNOWN', UPPER(GRANTEE), PRIVILEGE_TYPE, IS_GRANTABLE
FROM      INFORMATION_SCHEMA.USER_PRIVILEGES


CREATE    OR REPLACE VIEW DATABASE_AUTHS
          (GRANTOR, GRANTEE, DATABASENAME, PRIVILEGE,
          WITHGRANTOPT) AS
SELECT    'UNKNOWN', UPPER(GRANTEE), UPPER(TABLE_SCHEMA),
          PRIVILEGE_TYPE, IS_GRANTABLE
FROM      INFORMATION_SCHEMA.SCHEMA_PRIVILEGES


CREATE    OR REPLACE VIEW TABLE_AUTHS
          (GRANTOR, GRANTEE, TABLE_CREATOR, TABLE_NAME,
          PRIVILEGE, WITHGRANTOPT) AS
```

```
SELECT    'UNKNOWN', UPPER(GRANTEE), UPPER(TABLE_SCHEMA),
          UPPER(TABLE_NAME), PRIVILEGE_TYPE, IS_GRANTABLE
FROM      INFORMATION_SCHEMA.TABLE_PRIVILEGES

CREATE    OR REPLACE VIEW COLUMN_AUTHS
          (GRANTOR, GRANTEE, TABLE_CREATOR, TABLE_NAME,
          COLUMN_NAME, PRIVILEGE, WITHGRANTOPT) AS
SELECT    'UNKNOWN', UPPER(GRANTEE), UPPER(TABLE_SCHEMA),
          UPPER(TABLE_NAME), UPPER(COLUMN_NAME),
          PRIVILEGE_TYPE, IS_GRANTABLE
FROM      INFORMATION_SCHEMA.COLUMN_PRIVILEGES
```

Table 4.1 lists examples of catalog tables (catalog views, in fact) that are available afterward.

Table 4.1   *Examples of Catalog Views*

TABLE NAME	EXPLANATION
TABLES	Contains for each table, for instance, the date and time on which the table was created and the owner (that is, the user who created the table)
COLUMNS	Contains for each column (belonging to a table or view), for instance, the data type, the table to which the column belongs, whether the NULL value is allowed, and the sequence number of the column in the table
INDEXES	Contains for each index, for instance, the table and the columns on which the index is defined and the manner in which the index is ordered
USERS	Contains for each SQL user the names of the users who were not created during the installation procedure
VIEWS	Contains for each view, for instance, the view definition (the SELECT statement)

The following are a few examples of queries on the catalog tables.

Example 4.23: Get the name, the data type, and the sequence number of each column in the PLAYERS table (which was created in the TENNIS database); order the result by sequence number.

```
SELECT    COLUMN_NAME, DATA_TYPE, COLUMN_NO
FROM      COLUMNS
WHERE     TABLE_NAME = 'PLAYERS'
AND       TABLE_CREATOR = 'TENNIS'
ORDER BY  COLUMN_NO
```

The result is:

COLUMN_NAME	DATA_TYPE	COLUMN_NO
PLAYERNO	INT	1
NAME	CHAR	2
INITIALS	CHAR	3
BIRTH_DATE	DATE	4
SEX	CHAR	5
JOINED	SMALLINT	6
STREET	VARCHAR	7
HOUSENO	CHAR	8
POSTCODE	CHAR	9
TOWN	VARCHAR	10
PHONONO	CHAR	11
LEAGUENO	CHAR	12

Explanation: Get the name, the data type, and the sequence number (SELECT COLUMN_NAME, DATA_TYPE, COLUMN_NO) of each column (FROM COLUMNS) in the PLAYERS table (WHERE TABLE_NAME = 'PLAYERS') that is created in the TENNIS database (AND TABLE_CREATOR = 'TENNIS'); order the result by sequence number (ORDER BY COLUMN_NO).

Example 4.24: Get the names of the indexes defined on the PENALTIES table.

```
SELECT    INDEX_NAME
FROM      INDEXES
WHERE     TABLE_NAME = 'PENALTIES'
AND       TABLE_CREATOR = 'TENNIS'
```

Result (for example):

```
INDEX_NAME
----------------
PRIMARY
PENALTIES_AMOUNT
```

Explanation: The index that is mentioned first, with the name PRIMARY, has been created by SQL because a primary key has been specified on the PLAYERS table. We return to this in Chapter 20. The second index has been created in Example 4.13.

Other chapters describe the effect that particular statements can have on the contents of the catalog tables. In other words, when processing a particular statement leads to a change in the catalog tables, this change is explained. This book therefore discusses the catalog tables as an integral part of SQL.

Portability: *All SQL products support catalog tables. The set of implemented catalog tables differs significantly per product. The columns within tables and the codes within columns are also different.*

4.18 Definitions of SQL Statements

In this book, we use a particular formal notation to indicate precisely the functionality of certain SQL statements. In other words, by using this notation, we can give a definition of an SQL statement. These definitions are clearly indicated by enclosing the text in boxes. To give an idea of what such a definition looks like, the following is part of the definition of the CREATE INDEX statement:

```
<create index statement> ::=
   CREATE [ UNIQUE ] INDEX <index name>
   ON <table name> <column list>

<column list> ::=
   ( <column name> [ { , <column name> }... ] )
```

If you are not familiar with this notation, we advise you to study it before you continue with the next chapters. For this, we refer to Appendix A.

Because the functionality of certain SQL statements is extensive, we do not always show the complete definition in one place, but we extend it step by step. We omit the definitions of the syntactically simple statements. Appendix A includes the complete definitions of all SQL statements.

II Querying and Updating Data

One statement in particular forms the core of SQL and clearly represents the nonprocedural nature of SQL: the SELECT statement. It is the showpiece of SQL. Some vendors even dare to say that they have implemented SQL when they support only this statement.

This statement is used to query data in the tables; the result is always a table. Such a result table can be used as the basis of a report, for example.

This book deals with the SELECT statement in Chapters 5 to 13. Each chapter is devoted to one or two clauses of this statement. Several chapters have been added to explain certain concepts in more detail.

This part concludes with a chapter that describes how to insert, update, and delete data. The features of these statements are strongly based upon those of the SELECT statement, which makes the latter so important to master.

SELECT Statement: Common Elements

5.1 Introduction

This first chapter dealing with the SELECT statement describes a number of common elements that are important to many SQL statements and certainly crucial to the SELECT statement. For those who are familiar with programming languages and other database languages, most of these concepts will look familiar.

We cover, among others, the following common elements:

- Literal
- Expression
- Column specification
- User variable
- System variable
- Case expression
- Scalar function
- Cast expression
- NULL value
- Compound expression
- Aggregation function
- Row expression
- Table expression

5.2 Literals and Their Data Types

Literals have been used in many examples of SQL statements in the previous chapter. A *literal* is a fixed or unchanging value. Literals are used, for example, in conditions for selecting rows in SELECT statements and for specifying the values for a new row in INSERT statements; see Figure 5.1.

Figure 5.1   *Literals in SQL statements*

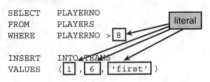

Each literal has a particular *data type*, just like a column in a table. The names of the different types of literals are derived from the names of their respective data types as we use them in the CREATE TABLE statement.

The literals are divided into several main groups: the numeric, the alphanumeric, the temporal, the Boolean, and the hexadecimal literals. They all have their own properties, idiosyncrasies, and limitations. Here, you find the definitions of all literals followed by the descriptions.Each literal always has a *data type*; however, there is not a literal for each data type. All data types (also the one for which no literal exists) are discussed extensively in Chapter 15, "Creating Tables." In that chapter, we describe the CREATE TABLE statement in detail.

```
<literal> ::=
    <numeric literal>        |
    <alphanumeric literal>  |
    <temporal literal>       |
    <boolean literal>        |
    <hexadecimal literal>

<numeric literal> ::=
    <integer literal> |
    <decimal literal> |
    <float literal>

<integer literal> ::= [ + | - ] <whole number>

<decimal literal> ::=
    [ + | - ] <whole number> [ .<whole number> ] |
    [ + | - ] <whole number>.                     |
    [ + | - ] .<whole number>

<float literal> ::=
    <mantissa> { E | e } <exponent>

<alphanumeric literal> ::= <character list>
```

(continued)

```
<temporal literal> ::=
   <date literal>      |
   <time literal>      |
   <timestamp literal>

<date literal> ::= ' <years> - <months> - <days> '

<time literal> ::= ' <hours> : <minutes> [ : <seconds> ] '

<timestamp literal> ::=
   ' <years> - <months> - <days> <space>
     <hours> : <minutes> [ : <seconds> [ . <micro seconds> ] ] '

<hexadecimal literal> ::= X <character list>

<years>           ;
<micro seconds> ::= <whole number>

<months>  ;
<days>    ;
<hours>   ;
<minutes> ;
<seconds> ::= <digit> [ <digit> ]

<boolean literal> ::= TRUE | FALSE

<mantissa> ::= <decimal literal>

<exponent> ::= <integer literal>

<character list> ::= ' [ <character>... ] '

<character>::= <digit> | <letter> | <special character> | ''

<whole number> ::= <digit>...
```

5.2.1 The Integer Literal

SQL has several types of numeric literals. One that is used frequently is the *integer literal*. This is a whole number or integer without a decimal point, possibly preceded by a plus or minus sign. Examples are shown here:

```
   38
  +12
-3404
  -16
```

The following examples are *not* correct integer literals:

```
342.16
 -14E5
   jan
```

5.2.2 The Decimal Literal

The second numeric literal is the *decimal literal*. This is a number with or without a decimal point, possibly preceded by a plus or minus sign. Each integer literal is, by definition, a decimal literal. Examples are as follows:

```
      49
   18.47
   -3400
     -16
 0.83459
    -349
```

The total number of digits is called the *precision*, and the number of digits after the decimal point is the *scale*. The decimal literal `123.45` has a precision of 5 and a scale of 2. The scale of an integer literal is always 0. The maximum range of a decimal literal is measured by the scale and the precision. The precision must be greater than 0, and the scale must be between 0 and the precision. For example, a decimal with a precision of 8 and a scale of 2 is allowed, but not with a precision of 6 and a scale of 8.

In the sample database of the tennis club, only one column has been defined with this data type, and that is AMOUNT in the PENALTIES table.

5.2.3 Float, Real, and Double Literals

A *float literal* is a decimal literal followed by an *exponent*. "Float" is short for "single precision floating point." These are examples of float literals:

```
Float literal  Value
-------------  -----
           49     49
        18.47  18.47
        -34E2  -3400
       0.16E4   1600
         4E-3  0.004
```

5.2.4 The Alphanumeric Literal

An *alphanumeric literal* is a string of zero or more alphanumeric characters enclosed between quotes. The quotation marks are not considered to be part of the literal; they define the beginning and end of the string. The following characters are permitted in an alphanumeric literal:

- All lowercase letters (a to z)
- All uppercase letters (A to Z)
- All digits (0 to 9)
- All remaining characters (such as: ', +, -, ?, =, and _)

Note that an alphanumeric literal can contain quotation marks. For every single quotation mark within an alphanumeric literal, one additional quotation mark is required. Here are some examples of correct alphanumeric literals:

```
Alphanumeric literal  Value
--------------------  -------
'Collins'             Collins
'don''t'              don't
'!?-@'                !?-@
' '
'' ''
'1234'                1234
```

A few examples of incorrect alphanumeric literals follow:

```
'Collins
''tis
' ' '
```

In this section, we assume that the ASCII character set will be used. This simple character set is not sufficient for every application. For example, some applications require the use of special characters, which is why SQL supports the use of other character sets. In Chapter 17, "Character Sets and Collating Sequences," we extensively deal with character sets. The corresponding topic of collating sequences also is discussed there. Collating sequences have to do with the order of characters; for example, should the character æ be placed in front of or after the letter *a*? And is that the case in all languages?

5.2.5 The Date Literal

For working with values related to date and time, SQL supports the *temporal literals*. Here, a distinction is made among date, time, and timestamp literals. These temporal literals are explained in this section and the following sections.

A *date literal*, which consists of a year, a month, and a day, is enclosed in quotes and represents a certain date on the *Gregorian* calendar. The three components are separated by two hyphens. Irrelevant zeroes can be omitted in the last two clauses. Examples are shown here:

```
Date literal  Value
------------  ---------------
'1980-12-08'  8 December 1980
'1991-6-19'   19 June 1991
```

Date literals range from 1 January 0001 to 31 December 9999. The year must always be specified as a four-digit number. Therefore, the year 999 must be represented as 0999. In the months and days component, the irrelevant zeros may be omitted.

Each date literal should also represent a date that exists in reality. Therefore, the date literal '2004-2-31' is not accepted. SQL returns an error message when such a date is used.

5.2.6 The Time Literal

The second temporal literal is the *time literal*, indicating a certain moment of the day. Time literals consist of three components: number of hours, number of minutes, and number of seconds. These three components are separated by colons, and the whole is enclosed in quotation marks. Irrelevant zeros may be omitted. The seconds component may be omitted completely. If that is the case, zero is assumed.

Examples:

```
Time literal  Value
------------  ---------------------------------
'23:59:59'    1 second before midnight
'12:10:00'    10 minutes past 12 in the afternoon
'14:00'       2 o'clock in the afternoon
```

A time literal must be between the points in time 00:00:00 and 24:00:00.

5.2.7 The Timestamp Literal

The *timestamp literal* is the third temporal literal. This literal is a combination of a date literal, a time literal, and an additional component for the microseconds. A timestamp literal, therefore, consists of seven components: years, months, days, hours, minutes, seconds, and possibly microseconds. The first three (that indicate a date) are separated by hyphens, and the next three (that indicate a time) by colons; there is a space between the date and the time, and a decimal point is placed in front of the microseconds.

```
Timestamp literal           Value
-----------------------     --------------------------------
'1980-12-08 23:59:59.59'    1/100 seconds before midnight on
                            8 December 1980
'1991-6-19 12:5:00'         5 minutes past 12 in the
                            afternoon of 19 June 1991
```

All the rules that apply to date and time literals also apply to the timestamp literal. The microseconds can be omitted, which means a zero is assumed. Therefore, when the microseconds component is equal to 8, for example, it does not stand for 8 microseconds, but for 800.000 microseconds. SQL fills the value up to six digits.

5.2.8 The Boolean Literal

The simplest literal is the *Boolean literal* because it can consist of only two possible values: TRUE or FALSE. The numeric value of FALSE is 0 and that of TRUE is 1.

Example 5.1: Get the values of the literals TRUE and FALSE.

```
SELECT TRUE, FALSE
```

Result:

```
TRUE   FALSE
----   -----
   1       0
```

Explanation: The values TRUE and FALSE can be written in lowercase letters.

> **Portability:** *The set of SQL products that supports Boolean literals is still relatively small. MySQL does support them.*

5.2.9 The Hexadecimal Literal

To specify values in a hexadecimal format, SQL has the *hexadecimal literal*. This literal is specified as an alphanumeric literal in front of which the letter *X* is placed. Inside the quotation marks, only the 10 digits and the letters *A* up to *F* can be used. The number of characters must be an even number.

In this book, not much attention is given to this data type and this literal. It is mainly used to store special values in the database, such as figures (in JPG or BMP formats) and movies (in AVI or MPG formats). We restrict ourselves by giving a few examples:

```
Hexadecimal literal   Value
-------------------   --------
X'41'                 A
X'6461746162617365'   database
X'3B'                 ;
```

Exercise 5.1: Specify which of the following literals are correct and which are incorrect; also give the data type of the literal.

```
41.58E-8
JIM
'jim'
'A'14
'!?'
45
```

```
'14E6'
''''''
'1940-01-19'
'1992-31-12'
'1992-1-1'
'3:3:3'
'24:00:01'
'1997-31-12 12:0:0'
X'AA1'
TRUE
```

5.3 Expressions

An *expression* consists of one or more operations, possibly surrounded by brackets, representing one value. Literals, columns, and complex calculations are examples of expressions. Expressions are used, for example, in the SELECT and WHERE clauses of a SELECT statement.

Example 5.2: Get the match number and the difference between sets won and sets lost for each match of which the numbers of sets won equals the number of sets lost plus 2.

```
SELECT    MATCHNO, WON - LOST
FROM      MATCHES
WHERE     WON = LOST + 2
```

Result:

```
MATCHNO  WON - LOST
------   -----------
      1            2
```

Explanation: This SELECT statement consists of several expressions. There are four expressions after the word SELECT: the columns MATCHNO, WON, and LOST, and the calculation WON - LOST. There are also four expressions after the word WHERE: WON, LOST, 2, and LOST + 2.

An expression can be classified in three ways: by data type, by complexity of the value, and by form.

The value of an expression always has, just like literals, a certain data type. Possible data types are the same as for literals—among other things, alphanumeric, numeric, date, time, or timestamp. That is why we can call them, for example, integer, alphanumeric, or date expressions. The following sections describe the various types of expressions individually.

Expressions can also be classified by the complexity of their value. So far, we have discussed only expressions that have one value as result—for example, a number, a word, or a date. These kinds of values are called *scalar values*. That is why all the previous expressions are called *scalar expressions*.

Besides the scalar expressions, SQL supports row expressions and table expressions. The result of a *row expression* is a row consisting of a set of scalar values. This result has a *row value*. Each row expression consists of one or more scalar expressions. If PLAYERNO, 'John', and 10000 are examples of scalar expressions, this is an example of a row expression:

```
(PLAYERNO, 'John', 100 * 50)
```

Imagine that the value of the PLAYERNO column is equal to 1; then the row value of this row expression is (1, 'John', 5000).

The result of a *table expression* is a set of zero, one, or more row expressions. This result is called a *table value*. If (PLAYERNO, 'John', 100 * 50), (PLAYERNO, 'Alex', 5000), and (PLAYERNO, 'Arnold', 1000 / 20) are examples of row expressions, this is an example of a table expression:

```
((PLAYERNO, 'John', 100 * 50),
 (PLAYERNO, 'Alex', 5000),
 (PLAYERNO, 'Arnold', 1000 / 20))
```

Imagine that the values of the three PLAYERNO columns are, respectively, 1, 2, and 3. The table value of this table expression then is equal to ((1, 'John', 5000), (2, 'Alex', 5000), (3, 'Arnold', 50)). Note that these examples of row and table expressions are not correct SQL statements. The way we specify these expressions is dependent on the SQL statements in which they are used. The most popular form of a table expression is the SELECT statement. Each SELECT statement is also a table expression because the result or the value of a SELECT statement is always a table and, therefore, a set of row values.

In Sections 5.15 and 5.16, we discuss row and table expressions, respectively, in more detail.

The third way to classify expressions is on the basis of form. We distinguish between singular and compound expressions. A *singular expression* consists of only one component. Following, in the definition of expression, several possible forms of singular expressions are specified. You have already seen a few examples of it, such as a literal or the name of a column.

When an expression consists of calculations, and thus contains multiple singular expressions, it is called a *compound expression*. Therefore, the expressions 20 * 100 and '2002-12-12' + INTERVAL 2 MONTH are compound.

Table expressions can be compound as well. We can combine the result of two or more table expressions, which leads to one table value. We come back to this in Chapter 6, "SELECT Statements, Table Expressions, and Subqueries."

An example of a compound row expression is (1, 2, 3) + (4, 5, 6). This expression would have the following row value: (5, 7, 9). A new row value is put together from multiple row expressions. Compound row expressions are not (yet) supported in SQL, which is why we do not cover this concept in this book.

```
<expression> ::=
    <scalar expression> |
    <row expression>    |
    <table expression>

<scalar expression> ::=
    <singular scalar expression> |
    <compound scalar expression>

<singular scalar expression> ::=
    <literal>                |
    <column specification>   |
    <user variable>          |
    <system variable>        |
    <cast expression>        |
    <case expression>        |
    NULL                     |
    ( <scalar expression> )  |
    <scalar function>        |
    <aggregation function>   |
    <scalar subquery>

<row expression> ::=
    <singular row expression>

<singular row expression> ::=
    ( <scalar expression> [ { , <scalar expression> }... ] ) |
    <row subquery>

<table expression> ::=
    <singular table expression> |
    <compound table expression>
```

Before discussing expressions and all their different forms, we explain the assignment of names to expressions, followed by the concepts from which scalar expressions are built. Literals have already been described, but column specifications, system variables, case expressions, and functions are among the topics that still need to be discussed.

Exercise 5.2: What is the difference between a literal and an expression?

Exercise 5.3: In which three ways can expressions be classified?

5.4 Assigning Names to Result Columns

When the result of a SELECT statement is determined, SQL must assign a name to each column of the result. If the expression in the SELECT clause consists of only a column name, the column in the result gets that name. We use the next example as a way of illustration.

Example 5.3: Get the number and the division for each team.

```
SELECT    TEAMNO, DIVISION
FROM      TEAMS
```

Result:

```
TEAMNO  DIVISION
------  --------
     1  first
     2  second
```

It is obvious how SQL came up with the names of the result columns in this example. But what will be the name when something else is specified instead of a simple column name? In that case, SQL creates a name. This name can be a serial number, a complete repetition of the entire expression, or completely nothing.

By specifying an alternative name after an expression in a SELECT clause, a name is assigned explicitly to the matching result column. This is sometimes called a *column heading*. This column name is placed in the heading of the result. We recommend specifying a column name when an expression in a SELECT clause is not a simple column name.

Example 5.4: Get for each team the number and the division, and use the full names.

```
SELECT    TEAMNO AS TEAM_NUMBER, DIVISION AS
DIVISION_OF_TEAM
FROM      TEAMS
```

The result is:

```
TEAM_NUMBER  DIVISION_OF_TEAM
-----------  ----------------
          1  first
          2  second
```

Explanation: After the column name, we specify the word AS followed by the name of the result column. The word AS can be omitted.

Example 5.5: For each penalty, get the payment number and the penalty amount in cents.

```
SELECT    PAYMENTNO, AMOUNT * 100 AS CENTS
FROM      PENALTIES
```

The result is:

```
PAYMENTNO  CENTS
---------  -----
        1  10000
        2   7500
        3  10000
        4   5000
        :      :
```

Explanation: When you look at the result, it is clear that the word CENTS has been placed above the second column. If we did not use the column heading in this example, SQL would create a name itself.

By way of illustration, we give another example with somewhat more complex expressions and column headings.

Example 5.6: Get some data from the MATCHES table.

```
SELECT    MATCHNO AS PRIMKEY,
          80 AS EIGHTY,
          WON - LOST AS DIFFERENCE,
          TIME('23:59:59') AS ALMOST_MIDNIGHT,
          'TEXT' AS TEXT
FROM      MATCHES
WHERE     MATCHNO <= 4
```

The result is:

PRIMKEY	EIGHTY	DIFFERENCE	ALMOST_MIDNIGHT	TEXT
1	80	2	23:59:59	TEXT
2	80	-1	23:59:59	TEXT
3	80	3	23:59:59	TEXT
4	80	1	23:59:59	TEXT

In the examples, we specify only column names to make the result easier to read. The names are not mandatory in these examples. In later examples, a column name is actually required; you will see that the column names can be used in other parts of the statement.

So, column headings are defined in the SELECT clause. Chapter 6 describes the order in which the different clauses of a SQL statement are processed. The column headings cannot be used in clauses that are processed before the SELECT clause. Because the SELECT clause is one of the last to be processed, column headings cannot be referenced in most clauses of the SELECT statement, except for the ORDER BY clause.

Example 5.7: For each penalty, get the payment number and the penalty amount in cents, and order the result on that number of cents.

```
SELECT    PAYMENTNO, AMOUNT * 100 AS CENTS
FROM      PENALTIES
ORDER BY CENTS
```

And the result is:

```
PAYEMNTNO   CENTS
---------   -----
        5   2500
        6   2500
        7   3000
        4   5000
        :     :
```

Exercise 5.4: For each match, get the match number and the difference between the number of sets won and the number of sets lost, and name this column DIFFERENCE.

Exercise 5.5: Is the following SELECT statement correct?

```
SELECT    PLAYERNO AS X
FROM      PLAYERS
ORDER BY  X
```

5.5 The Column Specification

A form of the scalar expression that occurs frequently is the *column specification*, which identifies a specific column. A column specification consists of only the name of a column or the name of a column preceded by the name of the table to which the column belongs. Using the table name might be necessary to prevent misunderstandings when statements become more complex. We return to this subject in Section 7.3, in Chapter 7, "SELECT Statement: The FROM Clause."

```
<column specification> ::=
    [ <table specification> . ] <column name>
```

The next two scalar expressions, consisting of column specifications, are both correct: PLAYERNO and PLAYERS.PLAYERNO. When they really refer to the same column, they always have the same value. Placing the table name in front of the column name is called *qualification*.

But what is the value of a column specification? The value of a literal is easy to determine. A literal has no secrets. The value of the literal 381 is 381. However, the value of a column specification cannot be determined just like that. As it happens, the value is fetched from the database when the expression is processed.

In the SELECT statement of Example 5.3, for each team, the values of the column specifications TEAMNO and DIVISION are calculated. Those can be different for each row.

Exercise 5.6: Rewrite the following SELECT statement in such a way that all column names are represented with their complete column specifications.

```
SELECT    PLAYERNO, NAME, INITIALS
FROM      PLAYERS
WHERE     PLAYERNO > 6
ORDER BY NAME
```

Exercise 5.7: What is wrong in the following SELECT statement?

```
SELECT    PLAYERNO.PLAYERNO, NAME, INITIALS
FROM      PLAYERS
WHERE     PLAYERS.PLAYERNO = TEAMS.PLAYERNO
```

5.6 The User Variable and the SET Statement

Portability: *This section discusses user variables and the SET statement with which we can assign values to user variables. Only a few SQL products support this type of variable and this SQL statement. Because the use of both can simplify the explanation of other features, we include them in this book.*

In MySQL, we can use *user variables* within expressions. These variables can be used anywhere scalar expressions are allowed.

It is better to define and initialize a variable before using it. *Defining* means that the user variable is made known to MySQL; *initializing* means that the variable is assigned a value. A variable that has been defined but not initialized has the NULL value.

The special SET statement can be used to define and initialize a variable.

Example 5.8: Create the user variable PLAYERNO and initialize it with the value 7.

```
SET @PLAYERNO = 7
```

Explanation: The @ symbol must always be placed in front of a user variable to distinguish it from a column name. The new value is specified after the assignment operator. This can be any scalar expression, as long as no column specifications occur in it.

The data type of the user variable is derived from the value of the scalar expression. So, in the previous example, that is an integer. The data type of the variable can change later when a new value with another data type is assigned.

A defined user variable, such as PLAYERNO, can be used as a special form of an expression after it has been created in other SQL statements.

Example 5.9: Get the last name, the town, and the postcode of all players with a number less than the value of the PLAYERNO user variable that has just been created.

```
SELECT    NAME, TOWN, POSTCODE
FROM      PLAYERS
WHERE     PLAYERNO < @PLAYERNO
```

The result is:

```
NAME        TOWN        POSTCODE
---------   ---------   --------
Everett     Stratford   3575NH
Parmenter   Stratford   1234KK
```

The value of a user variable can be retrieved by using a simple SELECT statement.

Example 5.10: Find the value of PLAYERNO variable.

```
SELECT    @PLAYERNO
```

The result is:

```
@PLAYERNO
---------
        7
```

We use these variables in this book so that we can explain certain things more easily. Note, however, that the user variable and the SET statement are not a part of standard SQL.

5.7 The System Variable

A simple form of an expression is the *system variable* (also called *special register*). This is a variable that is assigned a value by the database server at the moment that the statement using the variable is executed. Some system variables have a constant value, whereas others can have different values at different times. Every system variable has a data type, such as integer, decimal, or alphanumeric. Table 5.1 lists some system variables supported by several SQL products. For each, we describe the data type and give a brief explanation.

Table 5.1 *Examples of System Variables*

SYSTEM VARIABLE	DATA TYPE	EXPLANATION
CURRENT_DATE	DATE	Actual system date
CURRENT_TIME	TIME	Actual system time
CURRENT_TIMESTAMP	TIMESTAMP	Actual system date and system time
CURRENT_USER	CHAR	Name of the SQL user

At a particular moment in time, the system variables might have the following values:

```
System variable   Value
---------------   ----------
CURRENT_USER      BOOKSQL
CURRENT_DATE      2003-12-08
CURRENT_TIME      17:01:23
```

Example 5.11: Get the privileges from the USER_AUTHS catalog table that have been granted to the current user.

```
SELECT    *
FROM      USER_AUTHS
WHERE     GRANTEE = CURRENT_USER
```

Example 5.12: Show the penalties that have been paid today.

```
SELECT    *
FROM      PENALTIES
WHERE     PAYMENT_DATE = CURRENT_DATE
```

Obviously, this statement has an empty result because your computer clock will undoubtedly show the present date and time, whereas most penalties were incurred before the year 2000.

Portability: *The list of system variables differs considerably per SQL database server. For example, what is called* CURRENT_USER *in some database servers is called* USER *in others.*

Exercise 5.8: Get the database privileges owned by the current user.

Exercise 5.9: Find the numbers of the players who have become committee members today.

5.8 The Case Expression

A special scalar expression is the *case expression*. This expression serves as a kind of IF-THEN-ELSE statement. It can be compared with the SWITCH statement in Java and the CASE statement in Pascal.

```
<case expression> ::=
    CASE <when definition> [ ELSE <scalar expression> ] END

<when definition> ::= <when definition-1> | <when definition-2>

<when definition-1> ::=
    <scalar expression>
    WHEN <scalar expression> THEN <scalar expression>
    [ { WHEN <scalar expression> THEN <scalar expression> } ]...

<when definition-2> ::=
    WHEN <condition> THEN <scalar expression>
    [ { WHEN <condition> THEN <scalar expression> } ]...
```

Each case expression starts with a when definition. Two forms of when definitions exist. We begin with the first one. The easiest way to explain the possibilities of this expression is through a few examples.

Example 5.13: Get the player number, the sex, and the name of each player who joined the club after 1980. The sex must be printed as Female or Male.

```
SELECT    PLAYERNO,
          CASE SEX
              WHEN 'F' THEN 'Female'
              ELSE 'Male' END AS SEX,
          NAME
FROM      PLAYERS
WHERE     JOINED > 1980
```

The result is:

```
PLAYERNO  SEX     NAME
--------  ------  -------
       7  Male    Wise
      27  Female  Collins
      28  Female  Collins
      57  Male    Brown
      83  Male    Hope
     104  Female  Moorman
     112  Female  Bailey
```

Explanation: This construct is equal to the following IF-THEN-ELSE construct:

```
IF SEX = 'F' THEN
    RETURN 'Female'
ELSE
    RETURN 'Male'
ENDIF
```

The data type of the case expression depends on the data types of the expressions that follow the words THEN and ELSE. We can derive a rule from this: The data types of these expressions must all be the same.

As the definition shows, ELSE is not required. The previous case expression could also have been formulated as follows:

```
CASE SEX
    WHEN 'F' THEN 'Female'
    WHEN 'M' THEN 'Male'
END
```

In this case, if ELSE is omitted and the value of the SEX column is not equal to one of the scalar expressions in a when definition (which is not possible), the NULL value is returned.

```
SELECT    PLAYERNO,
          CASE SEX
              WHEN 'F' THEN 'Female' END AS FEMALES,
          NAME
FROM      PLAYERS
WHERE     JOINED > 1980
```

The result is:

```
PLAYERNO  FEMALES  NAME
--------  -------  -------
       7  ?        Wise
      27  Female   Collins
      28  Female   Collins
      57  ?        Brown
      83  ?        Hope
     104  Female   Moorman
     112  Female   Bailey
```

Explanation: A column name is specified to give the second result column a meaningful name.

Many when conditions can be included in a case expression.

```
CASE TOWN
    WHEN 'Stratford' THEN 0
    WHEN 'Plymouth'  THEN 1
    WHEN 'Inglewood' THEN 2
    ELSE 3
END
```

With the case expression, we can create powerful SELECT clauses, especially, if we start to nest case expressions:

```
CASE TOWN
    WHEN 'Stratford' THEN
        CASE BIRTH_DATE
            WHEN '1948-09-01' THEN 'Old Stratforder'
            ELSE 'Young Stratforder' END
    WHEN 'Inglewood' THEN
        CASE BIRTH_DATE
            WHEN '1962-07-08' THEN 'Old Inglewooder'
            ELSE 'Young Inglewooder' END
    ELSE 'Rest' END
```

Example 5.14: Use both case expressions shown above in a SELECT statement.

```
SELECT    PLAYERNO, TOWN, BIRTH_DATE,
          CASE TOWN
              WHEN 'Stratford' THEN 0
              WHEN 'Plymouth'  THEN 1
              WHEN 'Inglewood' THEN 2
              ELSE 3
          END AS P,
          CASE TOWN
              WHEN 'Stratford' THEN
                  CASE BIRTH_DATE
                      WHEN '1948-09-01' THEN 'Old Stratforder'
                      ELSE 'Young Stratforder' END
              WHEN 'Inglewood' THEN
                  CASE BIRTH_DATE
                      WHEN '1962-07-08' THEN 'Old Inglewooder'
                      ELSE 'Young Inglewooder' END
              ELSE 'Rest'
          END AS TYPE
FROM      PLAYERS
```

The result is:

```
PLAYERNO  TOWN        BIRTH_DATE   P  TYPE
--------  ---------   ----------   -  ------------------
       2  Stratford   1948-09-01   0  Old Stratforder
       6  Stratford   1964-06-25   0  Young Stratforder
       7  Stratford   1963-05-11   0  Young Stratforder
       8  Inglewood   1962-07-08   2  Old Inglewooder
      27  Eltham      1964-12-28   3  Rest
      28  Midhurst    1963-06-22   3  Rest
      39  Stratford   1956-10-29   0  Young Stratforder
      44  Inglewood   1963-01-09   2  Young Inglewooder
      57  Stratford   1971-08-17   0  Young Stratforder
      83  Stratford   1956-11-11   0  Young Stratforder
      95  Douglas     1963-05-14   3  Rest
     100  Stratford   1963-02-28   0  Young Stratforder
     104  Eltham      1970-05-10   3  Rest
     112  Plymouth    1963-10-01   1  Rest
```

So far, we have shown only examples of case expressions in which just one condition within the case expression may occur. Here are some examples to show the other form.

Example 5.15: For each player, find the player number, the year in which he joined the club, and an indication of age.

```
SELECT    PLAYERNO, JOINED,
          CASE
              WHEN JOINED < 1980 THEN 'Seniors'
              WHEN JOINED < 1983 THEN 'Juniors'
              ELSE 'Children' END AS AGE_GROUP
FROM      PLAYERS
ORDER BY  JOINED
```

The result is:

```
PLAYERNO   JOINED   AGE_GROUP
--------   ------   ---------
      95     1972   Seniors
       2     1975   Juniors
       6     1977   Seniors
     100     1979   Juniors
       8     1980   Juniors
      39     1980   Juniors
      44     1980   Juniors
       7     1981   Juniors
      83     1982   Juniors
      27     1983   Children
      28     1983   Children
     104     1984   Children
     112     1984   Children
      57     1985   Children
```

Explanation: If the first expression is not true, the next expression is evaluated, then the next, and so on. If none of them is true, the else definition applies.

The advantage of this form of the case expression is that all kinds of conditions can be mixed.

Example 5.16: For each player, find the player number, the year in which he joined the club, the town where he lives, and a classification.

```
SELECT   PLAYERNO, JOINED, TOWN,
         CASE
            WHEN JOINED >= 1980 AND JOINED <= 1982
               THEN 'Seniors'
            WHEN TOWN = 'Eltham'
               THEN 'Elthammers'
            WHEN PLAYERNO < 10
               THEN 'First members'
            ELSE 'Rest' END
FROM     PLAYERS
```

The result is:

```
PLAYERNO   JOINED  TOWN        CASE WHEN ...
--------   ------  ---------   -------------
       2    1975   Stratford   First members
       6    1977   Stratford   First members
       7    1981   Stratford   Seniors
       8    1980   Inglewood   Seniors
      27    1983   Eltham      Elthammers
      28    1983   Midhurst    Rest
      39    1980   Stratford   Seniors
      44    1980   Inglewood   Seniors
      57    1985   Stratford   Rest
      83    1982   Stratford   Seniors
      95    1972   Douglas     Rest
     100    1979   Stratford   Rest
     104    1984   Eltham      Elthammers
     112    1984   Plymouth    Rest
```

Case expressions can be used everywhere scalar expressions are allowed, including in the WHERE and HAVING clauses of the SELECT statement.

Exercise 5.10: Get the number and the division of each team in which the value *first* is written in full as the first division and the value *second* as the second division. If the value of the division is not *first* or *second*, display the value *unknown*.

Exercise 5.11: Imagine that the tennis club has classified all the penalties in three categories. The category *low* contains all the penalties from *0* up to *40*, the category *moderate* contains those between *41* up to *80*, and the category *high* contains all the penalties higher than *80*. Next, find for each penalty the payment number, the amount, and the matching category.

Exercise 5.12: Find the numbers of the penalties belonging to the category *low*. (See the previous exercise.)

5.9 The Scalar Expression Between Brackets

Each scalar expression can be placed between brackets. This does not change anything about the value of the scalar expression. Therefore, the expressions 35 and 'John' are equal to, respectively, (35) and ('John'), but also to ((35)) and (('John')).

Example 5.17: For each player, find the number and the name.

```
SELECT    (PLAYERNO), (((NAME)))
FROM      PLAYERS
```

It is obvious that the number of opening brackets must be equal to the number of closing brackets. The use of brackets is redundant in the previous example. They become useful only when scalar expressions are combined. The next sections give examples of the use of brackets.

5.10 The Scalar Function

Scalar functions are used to perform calculations and transformations. A scalar function has zero, one, or more so-called *parameters*. The value of a scalar function depends on the values of the parameters. Here, we show an example of the UCASE function:

```
UCASE('database')
```

Explanation: UCASE is the name of the scalar function, and the word database is the parameter. UCASE stands for *UpperCASE*. With UCASE('database'), all letters from the word database are replaced by their respective uppercase letter. So, the result (or the value) of this function is equal to 'DATABASE'.

A scalar function is a scalar expression in itself; the parameters of each scalar function are scalar expressions as well.

Portability: *Most of the scalar functions described in this section are supported by most SQL products. However, each product supports its own list of functions.*

SQL has tens of scalar functions. Although we could fill many pages with examples to show their possibilities, we give just a few examples of those functions that are used frequently. Appendix B, "Scalar Functions," describes all the scalar functions in detail.

Example 5.18: Get the payment number and the year of each penalty paid after 1980.

```
SELECT    PAYMENTNO, YEAR(PAYMENT_DATE)
FROM      PENALTIES
WHERE     YEAR(PAYMENT_DATE) > 1980
```

The result is:

```
PAYMENTNO   YEAR(PAYMENT_DATE)
---------   ------------------
        2                 1981
        3                 1983
        4                 1984
        7                 1982
        8                 1984
```

Explanation: The YEAR function fetches the year of any payment date and makes a numeric value out of the year. As already mentioned and as this example shows, scalar functions can be used in, among other things, the SELECT and WHERE clauses. In fact, they can be used everywhere an expression can occur.

Scalar functions can also be *nested*. This means that the result of one function acts as a parameter for the other function. Thus, the expression given next is legal. First, the function MOD(30, 7) is executed, which leads to a result of 2. Next, the value of SQRT(2) is calculated, and that result is passed to the ROUND function. The final answer is 1. In this example, the functions have clearly been nested.

```
ROUND(SQRT(MOD(30, 7)), 0)
```

Example 5.19: For each player whose last name starts with the capital *B*, get the number and the first letter of the first name, followed by a decimal and the last name.

```
SELECT    PLAYERNO,
          CONCAT(CONCAT(LEFT(INITIALS, 1), '. '), NAME)
          AS FULL_NAME
FROM      PLAYERS
WHERE     LEFT(NAME, 1) = 'B'
```

The result is:

```
PLAYERNO   FULL_NAME
--------   ---------
      39   D. Bishop
      44   E. Baker
      57   M. Brown
     112   I. Bailey
```

Explanation: For each player in the PLAYERS table, the first letter of the last name is determined with the LEFT function first `LEFT(NAME, 1)`. When that letter is equal to the capital *B*, the nested function is calculated in the SELECT clause for each. The CONCAT function is used to concatenate two alphanumeric values.

Example 5.20: For each player living in Stratford, get the first name, the last name, and the league number. If the league number is NULL, give the value 1.

```
SELECT    INITIALS, NAME, COALESCE(LEAGUENO, 1)
FROM      PLAYERS
WHERE     Town = 'Stratford'
```

The result is:

```
INITALS   NAME        COALESCE(LEAGUENO, '1')
-------   ---------   -----------------------
R         Everett     2411
R         Parmenter   8467
GWS       Wise        1
D         Bishop      1
M         Brown       6409
PK        Hope        1608
P         Parmenter   6524
```

Explanation: The COALESCE function acts as a kind of IF-THEN-ELSE statement that is used in many programming languages. By using this function as shown, for each row that is printed, the following statement is executed:

```
IF LEAGUENO IS NULL THEN
    RETURN '1'
ELSE
    RETURN LEAGUENO
ENDIF
```

SQL supports many scalar functions for the manipulation of dates and times. Here are several examples.

Example 5.21: For all players with numbers less than 10, get the player number, the name of the day and month on which they were born, and the day's sequence number within the year of the birth date.

```
SELECT    PLAYERNO, DAYNAME(BIRTH_DATE),
          MONTHNAME(BIRTH_DATE), DAYOFYEAR(BIRTH_DATE)
FROM      PLAYERS
WHERE     PLAYERNO < 10
```

The result is:

```
PLAYERNO  DAYNAME(...)   MONTHNAME(...)   DAYOFYEAR(...)
--------  -----------    --------------   --------------
       2  Wednesday      September                   245
       6  Thursday       June                        177
       7  Saturday       May                         131
       8  Sunday         July                        189
```

Explanation: The DAYNAME function determines the day of a date, MONTHNAME determines the month, and DAYOFYEAR calculates what day of the year it is.

Example 5.22: For the players who were born on a Saturday, get the number, the date of birth, and the date that comes 7 days after that date of birth.

```
SELECT    PLAYERNO, BIRTH_DATE, ADDDATE(BIRTH_DATE, 7)
FROM      PLAYERS
WHERE     DAYNAME(BIRTH_DATE) = 'Saturday'
```

The result is:

```
PLAYERNO  BIRTH_DATE  ADDDATE(BIRTH_DATE, 7)
--------  ----------  ----------------------
       7  1963-05-11  1963-05-18
      28  1963-06-22  1963-06-29
```

Example 5.23: Which players have already held a certain position for more than 500 days?

```
SELECT    PLAYERNO, BEGIN_DATE, END_DATE,
          DATEDIFF(END_DATE, BEGIN_DATE)
FROM      COMMITTEE_MEMBERS
WHERE     DATEDIFF(END_DATE, BEGIN_DATE) > 500
OR        (END_DATE IS NULL AND
          DATEDIFF(CURRENT_DATE, BEGIN_DATE) > 500)
ORDER BY  PLAYERNO
```

The result is:

```
PLAYERNO   BEGIN_DATE   END_DATE     DATEDIFF(...)
--------   ----------   ----------   -------------
       2   1990-01-01   1992-12-31            1095
       2   1994-01-01
       6   1991-01-01   1992-12-31             730
       6   1992-01-01   1993-12-31             730
       6   1993-01-01
       8   1994-01-01
      95   1994-01-01
     112   1994-01-01
```

Explanation: The DATEDIFF function calculates the difference in days between two dates or timestamps. The second condition has been added to find those committee members who still hold the position (the ones that have a NULL value as END_DATE). Every day, this statement can have another result, of course.

A more compact formulation for this statement is the following. Now, the statement also calculates the number of days for the committee members who still hold their position.

```
SELECT    PLAYERNO, BEGIN_DATE, END_DATE,
          DATEDIFF(COALESCE(END_DATE, CURRENT_DATE),
          BEGIN_DATE)
FROM      COMMITTEE_MEMBERS
WHERE     DATEDIFF(COALESCE(END_DATE, CURRENT_DATE),
          BEGIN_DATE)
          > 500
ORDER BY  1
```

Exercise 5.13: Try to calculate the values of the following expressions. (Refer to Appendix B for explanations.)

```
ASCII(SUBSTRING('database',1,1))
LENGTH(RTRIM(SPACE(8)))
LENGTH(CONCAT(CAST(100000 AS CHAR(6)),'000'))
LTRIM(RTRIM('   SQL   '))
REPLACE('database','a','ee')
```

Exercise 5.14: Get the numbers of the penalties that were paid on a Monday.

Exercise 5.15: Get the numbers of the penalties that were paid in 1984.

5.11 Casting of Expressions

Each expression has a data type, regardless of whether this is a simple expression consisting of only one literal or a very complex one consisting of scalar functions and multiplications. If we use an INSERT statement to store a value in a column with a certain data type, it is obvious what the data type of that value is. Unfortunately, it is not always that obvious. We give a few examples here.

If somewhere in an SQL statement the literal 'monkey' is specified, it is obvious what the data type is. Given the possible data types, this expression can have only the data type alphanumeric. The situation is more complex when we specify the literal '1997-01-15'. Does this literal simply have the data type alphanumeric, or is it a date? The answer depends on the context. There are even more choices if simply the number 3 is specified. The data type of this expression can be integer, decimal, or float.

When it is not clear what the data type of an expression is, SQL tries to determine the data type itself. But sometimes we have to specify the data type explicitly. To this end, SQL supports the *cast expression*. Some examples are shown here:

```
Cast expression                 Data type      Value
-----------------------------   -----------    ----------
CAST('123' AS SIGNED INTEGER)   Integer        123
CAST(121314 AS TIME)            Time           12:13:14
CAST('1997-01-15' AS DATE)      Date           1997-01-15
CAST(123 AS CHAR)               Alphanumeric   '123'
```

Explanation: Note the use of the term AS, which is often forgotten. After the word AS, the names of the data types can be specified. The data types allowed are the ones that can be used when defining columns in a CREATE TABLE statement, such as CHAR and DATE. In MySQL, the list of supported data types in the cast expression is different. Permitted are BINARY, CHAR, DATE, DATETIME, SIGNED, SIGNED INTEGER, TIME, UNSIGNED, and UNSIGNED INTEGER. In Chapter 15, we return to the CREATE TABLE statement in detail and explain the characteristics of each data type.

Portability: *In most SQL products, the list of data types that can be specified in the cast expression is equal to the list of data types that can be used in CREATE TABLE statements. MySQL is an exception to the rule. The list of data types supported by MySQL is BINARY, CHAR, DATE, DATETIME, SIGNED, SIGNED INTEGER, TIME, UNSIGNED, and UNSIGNED INTEGER. We use these throughout this book.*

If SQL cannot execute the conversion specified in a cast expression, an error message occurs. By way of illustration, the following two expressions will not be executed:

```
CAST('John' AS SIGNED INTEGER)
CAST('1997' AS DATE)
```

The expression is called cast because in literature specifying a data type or altering the data type of an expression, this is called *casting*. Casting has two forms: *implicit* and *explicit*. When a cast expression or function is used to specify the data type of an expression, it is explicit casting. When a data type is not specified explicitly, SQL tries to derive one. This is called implicit casting.

Example 5.24: Get the payment numbers of the penalties that are higher than $50.

```
SELECT    PAYMENTNO
FROM      PENALTIES
WHERE     AMOUNT > 50
```

Explanation: This SELECT statement contains three expressions: PAYMENTNO, AMOUNT, and 50. The data types of the first two are derived from the data types of the columns. No data type has been specified explicitly for the literal 50. However, because the literal is compared to a column that has the data type decimal, it is assumed that 50 has the same data type. Therefore, we have to conclude that the data type of 50 is integer, and that SQL implicitly executes a casting from integer to decimal.

Obviously, we could have specified a (superfluous) explicit casting as follows:

```
WHERE    AMOUNT > CAST(50 AS DECIMAL(7,2))
```

Casting can be important when expressions with noncomparable data types are compared.

Example 5.25: For each player resident in Inglewood, get the name and the date of birth as one alphanumeric value.

```
SELECT    CONCAT(RTRIM(NAME), CAST(BIRTH_DATE AS CHAR(10)))
FROM      PLAYERS
WHERE     TOWN = 'Inglewood'
```

The result is:

```
CONCAT(...)
-------------------
Newcastle1962-07-08
Baker1963-01-09
```

Explanation: The two columns NAME and BIRTH_DATE do not have the same data types. If we still want to concatenate them, BIRTH_DATE must be cast explicitly to alphanumeric and then the entire expression can be executed.

Portability: *How much implicit casting is done is product-dependent. For example, MySQL does a lot of implicit casting. If MySQL is used for the previous example, no explicit casting is needed.*

With INSERT and UPDATE statements, the data types of the new values are derived from the columns in which they are stored. Implicit casting, therefore, also takes place here.

Exercise 5.16: Transform the value 12 March 2004 into a value with a date data type.

Exercise 5.17: What is the data type of the literal in the SELECT clause of the following statement?

```
SELECT    '2000-12-15'
FROM      PLAYERS
```

Exercise 5.18: Can an alphanumeric literal always be cast explicitly to a date literal, and vice versa?

5.12 The NULL Value as an Expression

In Section 4.7, in Chapter 4, "SQL in a Nutshell," we discussed the NULL value. The specification NULL itself is also a valid scalar expression. It is used, for example, in INSERT statements to enter a NULL value in a new row or to change an existing value of a row in an UPDATE statement to NULL.

Example 5.26: Change the league number of the player with number 2 to the NULL value.

```
UPDATE    PLAYERS
SET       LEAGUENO = NULL
WHERE     PLAYERNO = 2
```

Explanation: In this example, NULL is a singular scalar expression.

   Actually, the scalar expression NULL has no data type. In no way can we derive from those four letters what it is. Is it alphanumeric, numeric, or a date? However, this does not cause problems in the previous UPDATE statement. SQL assumes that the data type of this NULL value is equal to that of the column LEAGUENO. This way, SQL can execute an implicit cast fairly easy, but that does not work all the time. Here is an example.

Example 5.27: For each team, get the number followed by the NULL value.

```
SELECT    TEAMNO, CAST(NULL AS CHAR)
FROM      TEAMS
```

The result is:

```
TEAMNO   CAST(NULL AS CHAR)
------   ------------------
     1   ?
     2   ?
```

Explanation: If we did not execute an implicit casting in this SELECT statement, SQL could not determine the data type. That is why it is always better to execute an explicit casting.

> **Portability:** *Products such as MySQL do not need the NULL value to be explicitly cast, but most SQL products do.*

Exercise 5.19: Does this SELECT statement return all the players without a league number?

```
SELECT    *
FROM      PLAYERS
WHERE     LEAGUENO = NULL
```

Exercise 5.20: What is the result of this SELECT statement: all the rows of the TEAMS table or not even one?

```
SELECT    *
FROM      TEAMS
WHERE     NULL = NULL
```

5.13 The Compound Scalar Expression

The scalar expressions that were shown so far all consist of one component, such as a literal, column specification or system variable. They are all singular scalar expressions. In addition, SQL supports compound scalar expressions; see also Section 5.3. These are expressions that consist of more than one component. The features of a compound expression depend on its data type.

```
<compound scalar expression> ::=
    <compound numeric expression>          |
    <compound alphanumeric expression>  |
    <compound date expression>             |
    <compound time expression>             |
    <compound timestamp expression>        |
    <compound hexadecimal expression>
```

5.13.1 The Compound Numeric Expression

A *compound numeric expression* is a scalar expression that consists of, minimally, a singular scalar numeric expression extended with operators, brackets, and other scalar expressions. The result is a scalar value with a numeric data type.

```
<compound numeric expression> ::=
    [ + | - ] <scalar numeric expression>          |
    ( <scalar numeric expression> )                |
    <scalar numeric expression>
        <mathematical operator> <scalar numeric expression>

<mathematical operator> ::= * | / | + | -
```

Here are some examples:

```
Compound numeric expression  Value
---------------------------  -----
14 * 8                         112
(-16 + 43) / 3                   9
5 * 4 + 2 * 10                  40
18E3 + 10E4                   118E3
12.6 / 6.3                     2.0
```

Table 5.2 lists the mathematical operators that can be used in a compound numeric expression.

Table 5.2	The Mathematical Operators and Their Meaning

MATHEMATICAL OPERATOR	MEANING
*	multiply
/	divide
+	add
−	subtract

Before we give examples, we make the following comments:

- Non-numeric expressions can occur in a compound numeric expression. The only requirement is that the final result of the entire expression returns a numeric value.
- If required, brackets can be used in numeric compound expressions to indicate the order of execution.
- If any component of a numeric compound expression has the value NULL, the value of the entire expression is, by definition, NULL.
- The calculation of the value of a numeric compound expression is performed in keeping with the following priority rules: (1) left to right, (2) brackets, (3) multiplication and division, and (4) addition and subtraction.

Some examples are (we assume that the AMOUNT column has the value 25):

```
Compound numeric expression            Value
--------------------------             --------
6 + 4 * 25                                  106
6 + 4 * AMOUNT                              106
0.6E1 + 4 * AMOUNT                          106
(6 + 4) * 25                                250
(50 / 10) * 5                                25
50 / (10 * 5)                                 1
NULL * 30                                  NULL
```

Incorrect compound numeric expressions are:

```
86 + 'Jim'
((80 + 4)
4/2 (* 3)
```

Example 5.28: Get the match number and the sets won and lost for each match in which the number of sets won is greater than or equal to the number of sets lost multiplied by 2.

```
SELECT    MATCHNO, WON, LOST
FROM      MATCHES
WHERE     WON >= LOST * 2
```

The result is:

```
MATCHNO   WON   LOST
-------   ---   ----
      1    3      1
      3    3      0
      7    3      0
```

Explanation: To answer this query, we need the compound numeric expression LOST * 2.

What are the precision and the scale of the result of a calculation that involves two decimal values? For example, if we multiply a decimal(4,3) by a decimal(8,2), what will be the precision and the scale of that result? Here we show the rules that SQL uses to determine them. We assume that P_1 and S_1, respectively, are the precision and the scale of the first decimal value, and that P_2 and S_2 are those of the second value. In addition, we assume that there exists a function called MAX that enables us to determine the largest of two values.

Multiplication: If we multiply two decimals, the scale of the result is equal to $S_1 + S_2$, and its precision is equal to $P_1 + P_2$. For example, multiplying a decimal(4,3) with a decimal (5,4) returns a decimal(9,7).

Addition: If we add two decimals, the scale of the result is equal to $S_1 + S_2$ and its precision is equal to $MAX(P_1-S_1, P_2-S_2) + MAX(S_1, S_2) + 1$. Adding, for example, a decimal(4,2) to a decimal(7,4) returns a decimal(8,4).

Subtraction: If we subtract a decimal from another, the scale of the result is equal to $S_1 + S_2$, and its precision is equal to $MAX(P_1-S_1, P_2-S_2) + MAX(S_1, S_2) + 1$. In other words, for subtraction and addition, the same rules apply.

SQL products do differ in the rules for division. To illustrate this, we show the rules for two products, namely, for MySQL and DB2.

Division according to MySQL: The scale of the result of a division is equal to $S_1 + 4$, and the precision is equal to $P_1 + 4$. For example, if we divide a decimal(4,3) by a decimal(5,4) the result is a decimal(8,6).

Division according to DB2: The precision of the answer is 31, and the scale is equal to $31 - P_1 + S_1 - S_2$. This means that dividing a decimal(4,3) by a decimal(5,4) leads to a decimal (31,24), and that is different from MySQL.

Exercise 5.21: Determine the values of the following numeric compound expressions:

```
400 - (20 * 10)
(400 - 20) * 10
400 - 20 * 10
400 / 20 * 10
111.11 * 3
222.22 / 2
50.00 * 3.00
```

5.13.2 The Compound Alphanumeric Expression

The value of a *compound alphanumeric expression* has an alphanumeric data type. With a compound expression, the values of alphanumeric expressions are concatenated using the || operator.

If the MySQL database server is started in a standard way, the || operator does not lead to the concatenation of alphanumeric values, but it is regarded as an OR operator to combine predicates. You can change this by changing the value of the system parameter SQL_MODE. Use the following SET statement:

```
SET SQL_MODE= 'PIPES_AS_CONCAT'
```

This specification is needed for the following statements. It applies only to the current session. By specifying the term GLOBAL in front of the system parameter SQL_MODE, it becomes a global specification.

```
<compound alphanumeric expression> ::=
    <scalar alphanumeric expression> "||"
        <scalar alphanumeric expression>
```

Two important rules apply to compound alphanumeric expressions:

- Nonalphanumeric expressions can be used in a compound alphanumeric expression as long as they are first converted into alphanumeric values with, for example, a cast expression.
- If somewhere in a compound alphanumeric expression the value NULL occurs, the value of the whole expression evaluates to NULL.

Examples:

```
Compound alphanumeric expression   Value
--------------------------------   --------
'Jim'                              Jim
'data'||'base'                     database
'da'||'ta'||'ba'||'se'             database
CAST(1234 AS CHAR(4))              1234
'Jim'||CAST(NULL AS CHAR)          NULL
```

Example 5.29: Get the player number and the address of each player who lives in Stratford.

```
SELECT   PLAYERNO, TOWN || ' ' || STREET || ' ' || HOUSENO
FROM     PLAYERS
WHERE    TOWN = 'Stratford'
```

The result is:

```
PLAYERNO  TOWN || ' ' || STREET ...
--------  ---------------------------
       2  Stratford Stoney Road 43
       6  Stratford Haseltine Lane 80
       7  Stratford Edgecombe Way 39
      39  Stratford Eaton Square 78
      57  Stratford Edgecombe Way 16
      83  Stratford Magdalene Road 16a
     100  Stratford Haseltine Lane 80
```

Portability: *In some SQL database servers, the + operator is used instead of the | | operator.*

Exercise 5.22: For each player, get the player number followed by a concatenation of the data elements: the first initial, a full stop, a space, and the full last name.

Exercise 5.23: For each team, get the number and the division of the team followed by the word division.

5.13.3 The Compound Date Expression

It is possible to calculate dates in SQL. For example, a few days, months, or years can be added to a date. The result of such a calculation is always a new date that is later (for addition) or earlier (for subtraction) than the original date expression.

When calculating the new date, the different number of days in the months and the leap years are taken into account. The calculation is done in a *proleptic* way, which means that no adjustment is made because in the Gregorian calendar, the days October 5 to 14 in the year 1582 are missing completely. This also means that we can use a date such as January 1, 1000, even though this date is earlier than the point in time when the Gregorian calendar was introduced. That means that what we call January 1, 1200, according to the Gregorian calendar now, probably was called differently then.

A calculation with dates is specified with a *compound date expression*.

```
<compound date expression> ::=
    <scalar date expression> [ + | - ] <date interval>

<date interval> ::=
    INTERVAL <interval length> <date interval unit>

<interval length> ::= <scalar expression>

<date interval unit> ::=
    DAY | WEEK | MONTH | QUARTER | YEAR
```

A compound date expression starts with a scalar expression (such as a date literal or a column with a date data type) followed by an *interval* that is added to or subtracted from the scalar expression.

An interval does not represent a certain moment in time, but a certain period or length of time. This period is expressed in a number of days, weeks, months, quarters, or years, or a combination of these five. Interval literals can be used to indicate how long, for example, a certain project lasted or how long a match took. Here are a few examples of interval literals:

```
Interval             Value
----------------     --------------------
INTERVAL 10 DAY      period of 10 days
INTERVAL 100 WEEK    period of 100 weeks
INTERVAL 1 MONTH     period of 1 month
INTERVAL 3 YEAR      period of 3 years
```

> **Portability:** *In some SQL products, the keyword* INTERVAL *does not have to be specified or cannot be specified. In MySQL, it is mandatory. And in some products, the plural forms of the interval units can be used. For example, you can also specify* DAYS *or* MONTHS.

An interval is not a complete expression. It must always occur within a compound date expression, and within such an expression, it cannot be specified first.

Example 5.30: Get, for each penalty with a number higher than 5, the payment number, the day on which the penalty was paid and the date 7 days after the payment date.

```
SELECT    PAYMENTNO, PAYMENT_DATE, PAYMENT_DATE + INTERVAL 7 DAY
FROM      PENALTIES
WHERE     PAYMENTNO > 5
```

The result is:

```
PAYMENTNO   PAYMENT_DATE   PAYMENT_DATE + INTERVAL 7 DAY
---------   ------------   ----------------------------
        6   1980-12-08     1980-12-15
        7   1982-12-30     1983-01-06
        8   1984-11-12     1984-11-19
```

Explanation: The SELECT clause contains the expression DATE + INTERVAL 7 DAY. The second part after the plus is the interval. Each interval is preceded by the word INTERVAL. The word DAY is the *interval unit*, and 7 is the *interval length*. In this case, it is an interval of 7 days.

As stated, an interval should always follow an expression with a date data type. The following INSERT statement is, therefore, not allowed:

```
INSERT INTO TABLEX VALUES (INTERVAL 7 DAY)
```

Example 5.31: Get the penalties that were paid between Christmas 1982 (December 25) and New Year's Eve.

```
SELECT    PAYMENTNO, PAYMENT_DATE
FROM      PENALTIES
WHERE     PAYMENT_DATE >= '1982-12-25'
AND       PAYMENT_DATE <= '1982-12-25' + INTERVAL 6 DAY
```

The result is:

```
PAYMENTNO   PAYMENT_DATE
---------   ------------
        7   1982-12-30
```

Explanation: In the second condition of the WHERE clause after the less than or equal to operator, an expression is specified that holds a calculation in which 6 days are added to the date of Christmas 1982.

When a compound date expression contains more than one interval, it is essential that no calculations be made with interval literals only. Interval literals can be added to dates only. The expression DATE + (INTERVAL 1 YEAR + INTERVAL 20 DAY) will be rejected, for example. The reason is that brackets are used, and they force SQL to add the two interval literals to each other first, which is not allowed. The next two formulations cause no problems:

```
DATECOL + INTERVAL 1 YEAR + INTERVAL 20 DAY
(DATECOL + INTERVAL 1 YEAR) + INTERVAL 20 DAY
```

Instead of a literal, complex expressions can be used to specify an interval. In most cases, brackets are required. Here are a few more correct examples:

```
DATECOL + INTERVAL PLAYERNO YEAR + INTERVAL 20*16 DAY
DATECOL + INTERVAL (PLAYERNO*100) YEAR + INTERVAL
LENGTH('SQL') DAY
```

The scalar expression that is used to indicate the interval does not have to be a value with an integer data type; decimals and floats are allowed as well. However, SQL rounds the value first. The part after the decimal point simply is removed, and the value is rounded up or down. So, the following two expressions have the same value.

```
DATECOL + INTERVAL 1.8 YEAR
DATECOL + INTERVAL 2 YEAR
```

> **Portability:** *As indicated, how calculations with dates are specified depends on the SQL product. The examples here show the differences.*

Example 5.32: Add 30 days to a date.

```
DB2           : DATECOL + 30 DAYS
MySQL         : DATECOL + INTERVAL 30 DAY
Oracle        : DATECOL + 30
MS SQL Server : DATEADD(day, 30, DATECOL)
SQL2          : DATECOL + INTERVAL '30' DAY
```

Example 5.33: Move a date 1 month further.

```
DB2           : DATECOL + 1 MONTH
MySQL         : DATECOL + INTERVAL 1 MONTH
Oracle        : ADD_MONTHS(DATECOL, 1)
MS SQL Server : DATEADD(month, 1, DATECOL)
SQL2          : DATECOL + INTERVAL '1' MONTH
```

Exercise 5.24: Determine the result of the following compound date expressions. We assume that the column DATECOL has the value 29 February 2000.

```
DATECOL + INTERVAL 7 DAY
DATECOL - INTERVAL 1 MONTH
(DATECOL - INTERVAL 2 MONTH) + INTERVAL 2 MONTH
CAST('2001-02-28' AS DATE) + INTERVAL 1 DAY
CAST('2001-02-28' AS DATE) + INTERVAL 2 MONTH - INTERVAL 2
   MONTH
```

Exercise 5.25: For each row in the COMMITTEE_MEMBERS table, get the player number, the begin date, and the begin date plus 2 months and 3 days.

5.13.4 The Compound Time Expression

As with dates, it is possible to calculate with times. For example, a number of hours, minutes, or seconds can be added to or subtracted from a specified time. The result after the calculation is always a new time.

Calculations with times are always specified as *compound time expressions*. This type of expression identifies a certain moment of a day to a millionth of a second precisely.

> **Portability:** *MySQL does not support actual compound time expressions yet. However, the scalar function ADDTIME can be used instead. In this book, we use this function as a substitute for the compound time expression.*

```
<compound time expression> ::=
    ADDTIME( <scalar time expression> , <time interval> )

<time interval> ::= <scalar time expression>
```

A compound time expression starts with a scalar expression (such as a time literal or a column with the time data type) followed by an *interval* that is added to or subtracted from that scalar expression.

An interval does not represent a certain moment in time, but a certain period or length of time. This period is expressed in a number of hours, minutes, and seconds or a combination of these three. Time interval literals can be used to indicate how long, for example, a match took. An interval is specified the same way as a time expression:

```
Interval    Value
----------  --------------------
'10:00:00'  period of 10 hours
'00:01:00'  period of 1 minute
'00:00:03'  period of 3 seconds
```

Because times do not occur in the sample database, we create an additional table to show some examples.

Example 5.34: Create a special variant of the MATCHES table that includes the date the match was played, the time it started, and the time it ended.

```
CREATE    TABLE MATCHES_SPECIAL
          (MATCHNO         INTEGER NOT NULL,
          TEAMNO           INTEGER NOT NULL,
          PLAYERNO         INTEGER NOT NULL,
          WON              SMALLINT NOT NULL,
          LOST             SMALLINT NOT NULL,
          START_DATE       DATE NOT NULL,
          START_TIME       TIME NOT NULL,
          END_TIME         TIME NOT NULL,
          PRIMARY KEY      (MATCHNO))

INSERT INTO MATCHES_SPECIAL VALUES
     (1, 1, 6, 3, 1, '2004-10-25', '14:10:12', '16:50:09')

INSERT INTO MATCHES_SPECIAL VALUES
     (2, 1, 44, 3, 2, '2004-10-25', '17:00:00', '17:55:48')
```

Example 5.35: For each match, get the time it starts, plus 8 hours.

```
SELECT    MATCHNO, START_TIME,
          ADDTIME(START_TIME, '08:00:00')
FROM      MATCHES_SPECIAL
```

The result is:

```
MATCHNO   START_TIME   ADDTIME(START_TIME, '08:00:00')
-------   ----------   -------------------------------
      1   14:10:12     22:10:12
      2   17:00:00     25:00:00
```

Example 5.36: Find the matches that ended 6 1/2 hours before midnight.

```
SELECT    MATCHNO , END_TIME
FROM      MATCHES_SPECIAL
WHERE     ADDTIME(END_TIME, '06:30:00') < '24:00:00'
```

The result is:

```
MATCHNO   END_TIME
-------   --------
      2   16:50:09
```

Calculations with times follow predictable rules. When a few seconds are added to a certain time, the sum of the number of seconds in the seconds component of the time and the number of seconds in the interval is calculated. For each 60 seconds that can be removed from the sum without the sum becoming less than 0, 1 is added to the minutes component. A comparable rule applies to the minutes component: For each 60 minutes that can be removed from the sum, 1 is added to the hours component. The hours component, however, can become greater than 24. The expression ADDTIME('10:00:00', '100:00:00') is allowed and returns the value 110:00:00.

Exercise 5.26: Show the expression for adding 10 hours to the point in time 11:34:34.

Exercise 5.27: What is the result of the expression ADDTIME('11:34:34', '24:00:00')?

5.13.5 The Compound Timestamp Expression

The value of a *compound timestamp expression* identifies a certain moment on a day in the Gregorian calendar, such as 4:00 in the afternoon on January 12, 1991.

```
<compound timestamp expression> ::=
    <scalar timestamp expression> [ + | - ]
       <timestamp interval>

<timestamp interval> ::=
    INTERVAL <interval length> <timestamp interval unit>

<interval length> ::= <scalar expression>

<timestamp interval unit> ::=
    MICROSECOND | SECOND | MINUTE | HOUR |
    DAY | WEEK | MONTH | QUARTER | YEAR
```

Just as it is possible to calculate with dates and times, it is possible to calculate with timestamps. For example, a couple months, days, hours, or seconds can be added to or subtracted from a timestamp. The rules for processing are according to those for calculating with dates and times.

If too many hours are added to a time, the surplus is simply thrown away. For a time-stamp expression, this means that the days component increases. So, if 24 hours are added to something, the result would be the same as adding 1 day.

> **Portability:** *In some SQL products, the keyword INTERVAL does not have to be specified or cannot be specified. In MySQL, it is mandatory. And in some products, the plural forms of the interval units can be used. For example, you can also specify HOURS or MINUTES.*

What holds for the timestamp literal also holds for the compound timestamp expression. When the result is stored in a table, SQL cuts off the microseconds part; see the following example.

Example 5.37: Create a table in which timestamps can be stored.

```
CREATE TABLE TSTAMP (COL1 TIMESTAMP)

SET @TIME = TIMESTAMP('1980-12-08 23:59:59.59')

INSERT INTO TSTAMP VALUES (@TIME + INTERVAL 3 MICROSECOND)

SELECT COL1, COL1 + INTERVAL 3 MICROSECOND FROM TSTAMP
```

The result is:

```
COL1                  COL1 + INTERVAL 3 MICROSECOND
-------------------   -----------------------------
1980-12-08 23:59:59   1980-12-08 23:59:59.000003
```

Explanation: It is obvious that the microseconds are missing in the result of the SELECT statement, although they have been entered with an INSERT statement.

Exercise 5.28: Show the expression for adding 1,000 minutes to the timestamp 1995-12-12 11:34:34.

Exercise 5.29: Find for each penalty the payment number and the payment date followed by that same date, plus 3 hours, 50 seconds, and 99 microseconds.

5.14 The Aggregation Function and the Scalar Subquery

For the sake of completeness, we introduce here the last two forms of the scalar expression: the aggregation function and the scalar subquery.

Just like scalar functions, aggregation functions are used to perform calculations. They also have parameters. The big difference between these two types of functions is that a scalar function is always executed on a maximum of one row with values. An aggregation function, on the other hand, is a calculation with a set of rows as input. Table 5.3 shows the different aggregation functions that SQL supports. We discuss aggregation functions extensively in Chapter 9, "SELECT Statement: SELECT Clause and Aggregation Functions."

Table 5.3   *Aggregation Functions in SQL*

AGGREGATION MEANING	FUNCTION
AVG	Determines the weighted average of the values in a column
COUNT	Determines the number of values in a column or the number of rows in a table
MIN	Determines the smallest value in a column
MAX	Determines the largest value in a column
STDDEV	Determines the standard deviation of the values in a column
SUM	Determines the sum of the values in a column
VARIANCE	Determines the variance of the values in a column

The subquery enables us to include SELECT statements within expressions. With this, we can formulate very powerful statement in a compact way. In Section 6.6, in Chapter 6, we return to this subject briefly; in Chapter 8, "SELECT Statement: The WHERE Clause," we discuss the subquery in great detail.

5.15 The Row Expression

Section 5.3 introduced the concept of row expression. The value of a row expression is a row consisting of at least one value. The number of elements in a row expression is called the *degree*. Section 4.8, in Chapter 4, gave examples of rows expressions—namely, in the INSERT statement. There, a row expression is specified after the word VALUES in the INSERT statement.

Example 5.38: Add a new row to the COMMITTEE_MEMBERS table.

```
INSERT    INTO COMMITTEE_MEMBERS
VALUES    (7 + 15, CURRENT_DATE,
          CURRENT_DATE + INTERVAL 17 DAY, 'Member')
```

Explanation: There are four components in this row expression; in other words, the degree of this row expression is 4. First is a compound expression (7 + 15), followed by a system variable and a system variable as part of a compound date expression. The row expression is concluded by a literal.

Row expressions can also be used in SELECT statements, for example, to make a comparison with multiple values simultaneously.

Portability: *MySQL does not support row expressions in the SELECT or the UPDATE statements. So, the next two examples cannot be processed by MySQL.*

Example 5.39: Get the numbers of the players who live on Haseltine Lane in Stratford.

```
SELECT    PLAYERNO
FROM      PLAYERS
WHERE     (TOWN, STREET) = ('Stratford', 'Haseltine Lane')
```

The result is:

```
PLAYERNO
--------
       6
     100
```

Explanation: In the condition of this statement, two row expressions are compared.

Sometimes, it is useful to use a row expression in the UPDATE statement to change multiple columns simultaneously.

Example 5.40: Change the address of player 27 in Haseltine Lane, Stratford.

```
UPDATE    PLAYERS
SET       (TOWN, STREET) = ('Stratford', 'Haseltine Lane')
WHERE     PLAYERNO = 27
```

Explanation: The result of this statement is equal to an UPDATE statement in which the two columns are changed separately.

Each expression has a data type, so that includes a row expression as well. However, a row expression does not have one data type but has a data type for each value from which it is built. So, the previous row expression (TOWN, STREET) has the data type (alphanumeric, alphanumeric).

If row expressions are compared to each other, as in the SET clause of the UPDATE statement previously, the respective degrees should be the same and the data types of the elements with the same order number should be comparable. "Comparable" means that both data types are identical, or that the one can be cast implicitly to the other. Therefore, the following comparisons are syntactically correct:

```
(TOWN, STREET) = (1000, 'USA')
(NAME, BIRTH_DATE, PLAYERNO) = (NULL, '1980-12-12', 1)
```

Exercise 5.30: Get the numbers of the penalties of $25 incurred for player 44 on December 8, 1980.

Exercise 5.31: Get the numbers of the players for whom the last name is equal to the town and the initials equal to the street name, a somewhat peculiar example.

5.16 The Table Expression

Table expressions were discussed briefly in Section 5.3. The value of a table expression is a set of row values. In the INSERT statement, this expression can be used to enter not one, but multiple rows simultaneously.

Example 5.41: Add all eight penalties with just one INSERT statement.

```
INSERT INTO PENALTIES VALUES
    (1,    6, '1980-12-08', 100),
    (2,   44, '1981-05-05',  75),
    (3,   27, '1983-09-10', 100),
    (4,  104, '1984-12-08',  50),
    (5,   44, '1980-12-08',  25),
    (6,    8, '1980-12-08',  25),
    (7,   44, '1982-12-30',  30),
    (8,   27, '1984-11-12',  75)
```

Explanation: The result of this statement is the same as those of eight individual INSERT statements. However, this statement guarantees that either all the eight rows are added or none at all.

Each SELECT statement is also a valid table expression. This is obvious because the result of a SELECT statement is always a set of rows.

Table expressions have data types as well. Just as with the row expression, a table expression is a set of data types. In the earlier INSERT statement, the data type of the table expression is (integer, alphanumeric, alphanumeric, alphanumeric, integer). The rule for all row expressions within one table expression is that they must have the same degree and that they must have comparable data types.

Chapter 6 focuses more attention to the table expression. After all, each SELECT statement is a table expression, and in several places in that same statement, table expressions can be specified.

5.17   Answers

5.1 **1.** Correct; float data type.

   2. Incorrect; there must be quotation marks in front of and after the
          alphanumeric literal.

   3. Correct; alphanumeric data type.

   4. Incorrect; there are characters outside the quotation marks of the
          alphanumeric literal.

   5. Correct; alphanumeric data type.

   6. Correct; integer data type.

   7. Correct; alphanumeric data type.

   8. Correct; alphanumeric data type.

   9. Correct; date data type.

  10. If it is supposed to be an alphanumeric literal, it is correct. If it is supposed
          to be a date literal, it is incorrect because the month component is too high.

  11. Correct; date data type.

  12. Correct; time data type.

  13. If it is supposed to be an alphanumeric literal, it is correct. If it is supposed
          to be a time literal, it is incorrect because if the hours component is equal to
          24, the two other components must be equal to 0.

  14. Correct; timestamp data type.

  15. Incorrect; a hexadecimal data type must consist of an even number of
          characters.

  16. Correct; Boolean data type

5.2 The value of a literal is fixed; that of an expression must be determined by SQL.

5.3 Expressions can be grouped based on their respective data types, the complexity of their values, and their forms. Grouping based on data type refers to the data type of the value of the expression, such as integer, date, or alphanumeric. Grouping based on complexity refers to whether it is a "normal," a row or a table expression. Grouping based on form implies whether it is a singular or compound expression.

5.4
```
SELECT    MATCHNO, WON - LOST AS DIFFERENCE
FROM      MATCHES
```

5.5 Yes, this statement is correct. It is allowed to sort on column headings.

5.6
```
SELECT    PLAYERS.PLAYERNO, PLAYERS.NAME,
          PLAYERS.INITIALS
FROM      PLAYERS
WHERE     PLAYERS.PLAYERNO > 6
ORDER BY  PLAYERS.NAME
```

5.7 This statement is incorrect because of the column specification TEAMS.PLAY-ERNO. The TEAMS table does not occur in the FROM clause; therefore, the SQL statement cannot refer to columns of this table.

5.8
```
SELECT    PRIVILEGE, WITHGRANTOPT
FROM      DATABASE_AUTHS
WHERE     GRANTOR = CURRENT_USER
```

5.9
```
SELECT    PLAYERNO
FROM      COMMITTEE_MEMBERS
WHERE     BEGIN_DATE = CURRENT_DATE
```

5.10
```
SELECT    TEAMNO,
          CASE DIVISION
              WHEN 'first' then 'first division'
              WHEN 'second' THEN 'second division'
              ELSE 'unknown' END AS DIVISION
FROM      TEAMS
```

5.11

```
SELECT    PAYMENTNO, AMOUNT,
          CASE
              WHEN AMOUNT >= 0 AND AMOUNT <= 40
                  THEN 'low'
              WHEN AMOUNT >= 41 AND AMOUNT <= 80
                  THEN 'moderate'
              WHEN AMOUNT >= 81
                  THEN 'high'
              ELSE 'incorrect' END AS CATEGORY
FROM      PENALTIES
```

5.12

```
SELECT    PAYMENTNO, AMOUNT
FROM      PENALTIES
WHERE     CASE
              WHEN AMOUNT >= 0 AND AMOUNT <= 40
                  THEN 'low'
              WHEN AMOUNT > 40 AND AMOUNT <= 80
                  THEN 'moderate'
              WHEN AMOUNT > 80
                  THEN 'high'
              ELSE 'incorrect' END = 'low'
```

5.13 100
     0
     9
     SQL
     deeteebeese

5.14

```
SELECT    PAYMENTNO
FROM      PENALTIES
WHERE     DAYNAME(PAYMENT_DATE) = 'Monday'
```

5.15

```
SELECT    PAYMENTNO
FROM      PENALTIES
WHERE     YEAR(PAYMENT_DATE) = 1984
```

5.16 CAST('2004-03-12' AS DATE)

5.17 Alphanumeric literal

5.18 Not every alphanumeric literal can be converted. It is possible only when the literal satisfies the requirements of a date. Converting a date literal to an alphanumeric literal always works.

5.19 No. When the NULL value is compared to another expression with an equal to operator, the entire condition evaluates to unknown and the corresponding row is not included in the end result.

5.20 Not a single row.

5.21 200
3800
200
200
333,33
111,11
150,0000

5.22
```
SELECT   PLAYERNO, SUBSTR(INITIALS,1,1) || '. ' || NAME
FROM     PLAYERS
```

5.23
```
SELECT   TEAMNO, RTRIM(DIVISION) || ' division'
FROM     TEAMS
```

5.24 2000-03-07
2000-01-29
2000-02-29
2001-03-01
2001-02-28

5.25
```
SELECT   PLAYERNO, BEGIN_DATE,
         BEGIN_DATE + INTERVAL 2 MONTH + INTERVAL 3 DAY
FROM     COMMITTEE_MEMBERS
```

5.26 ADDTIME('11:34:34', '10:00:00')

5.27 35:34:34

5.28 '1995-12-12 11:34:34' + INTERVAL 1000 MINUTE

5.29

```
SELECT    PAYMENTNO, PAYMENT_DATE,
          PAYMENT_DATE + INTERVAL 3 HOUR +
          INTERVAL 50 SECOND + INTERVAL 99 MICROSECOND
FROM      PENALTIES
```

5.30

```
SELECT    PAYMENTNO
FROM      PENALTIES
WHERE     (AMOUNT, PLAYERNO, PAYMENT_DATE) =
          (25, 44, '1980-12-08')
```

5.31

```
SELECT    PLAYERNO
FROM      PLAYERS
WHERE     (NAME, INITIALS) = (TOWN, STREET)
```

SELECT Statements, Table Expressions, and Subqueries

6.1 Introduction

T he SELECT statement and the table expression have already been introduced in this book. These two language constructs are both used for querying data. Within SQL, some other constructs exist, such as the subquery and select block, that are also relevant for querying data. All these constructs have a strong mutual relationship that makes it difficult to keep them apart. However, for someone who is programming SQL, it is important to know the differences. That is why we devote this entire chapter to them. For each construct, we describe what is meant exactly and what the mutual relationships are.

We begin with the SELECT statement. In the preceding chapters, we have already shown several examples of this statement.

6.2 The Definition of the SELECT Statement

Each SELECT statement consists of a *table expression* followed by several specifications. We leave these additional specifications aside for now; they are not included in the following definition.

```
<select statement> ::=
   <table expression>

<table expression> ::=
   <select block head> [ <select block tail> ]
```

(continued)

```
<select block head> ::=
   <select clause>
 [ <from clause>
 [ <where clause> ]
 [ <group by clause>
 [ <having clause> ] ] ]

<select block tail> ::=
 [ <order by clause> ]
```

This chapter is completely devoted to that table expression. The value of a table expression is always a set of (unsorted) rows, in which each row consists of the same number of column values.

As described in Section 5.3, there are two forms of the table expression: the singular and the compound table expression. In this section, we consider only the singular form.

You might wonder what the purpose is of introducing the concept table expression when every SELECT statement exists entirely of a table expression. Aren't the concepts the same? The answer is that every SELECT statement is built from a table expression, but not every table expression is part of a SELECT statement. Table expressions are also used within other SQL statements, such as the CREATE VIEW statement. A certain table expression appears twice in Figure 6.1, the first time as part of a SELECT statement and the next as part of a CREATE VIEW statement.

A table expression consists of one or more *select blocks*. A select block is a set of clauses, such as SELECT, FROM, and ORDER BY. The clauses of a select block are divided into two groups: the *head part* and the *tail part*.

Again, we could wonder why it is useful to make a distinction between table expressions and select blocks. A select block always consists of only one group of clauses—thus, one SELECT clause and one FROM clause—while a table expression, as you will see later, can consist of multiple select blocks—thus, it can also contain multiple SELECT and FROM clauses.

Figure 6.1   *Table expressions as part of various statements*

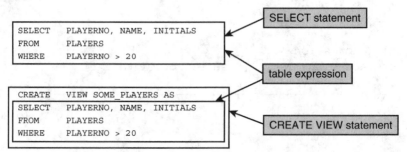

Figure 6.2 shows a graphical representation of the different constructs and their relationships that have been introduced in this section. An arrow indicates which concept has been built from which other concepts. The arrow head points to the concept that forms a part.

Figure 6.2   *The relationships between different language constructs*

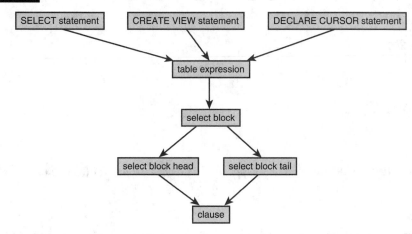

When we use the term select block in this book, we mean the combination of a select block head and a select block tail. The advantage of naming these two parts individually will become clear later in this chapter.

The following rules are important when formulating SELECT statements:

- Each select block (thus, also every table expression and every SELECT statement) consists of at least the SELECT clause. The other clauses, such as WHERE, GROUP BY, and ORDER BY, are optional.

- If a WHERE, GROUP BY, HAVING, or ORDER BY clause is used, SELECT and FROM clauses are required.

- The order of the clauses within a select block is fixed. For example, a GROUP BY clause may never come in front of a WHERE or FROM clause, and the ORDER BY clause (when used) is always the last.

- A HAVING clause can be used within a select block only if there is a GROUP BY clause.

Next, we give a few examples of correct SELECT statements, table expressions, and select blocks. What follows each different clause is, for the sake of convenience, represented as three dots.

```
SELECT    ...
FROM      ...
ORDER BY  ...

SELECT    ...
FROM      ...
GROUP BY  ...
HAVING    ...

SELECT    ...
FROM      ...
WHERE     ...

SELECT    ...
```

> **Portability:** *Not all SQL products support select blocks without a FROM clause. MySQL and SQL Server are examples of products that do.*

Exercise 6.1: Indicate for the following SQL statements whether they are SELECT statements, table expressions, and head parts of select blocks. Multiple answers are possible.

1.

```
SELECT    ...
FROM      ...
WHERE     ...
ORDER BY  ...
```

2.

```
SELECT    ...
FROM      ...
GROUP BY  ...
```

3.

```
CREATE VIEW ...
SELECT   ...
FROM     ...
```

Exercise 6.2: For the following SQL statement, indicate which part is a table expression and which part is the tail part of a select block.

```
SELECT   ...
FROM     ...
WHERE    ...
ORDER BY ...
```

Exercise 6.3: What is the minimum number of clauses that must be present in a SELECT statement?

Exercise 6.4: Can a SELECT statement have an ORDER BY clause but no WHERE clause?

Exercise 6.5: Can a SELECT statement have a HAVING clause but no GROUP BY clause?

Exercise 6.6: Decide what is incorrect in the following SELECT statements:

1.

```
SELECT   ...
WHERE    ...
ORDER BY ...
```

2.

```
SELECT   ...
FROM     ...
HAVING   ...
GROUP BY ...
```

3.

```
SELECT    ...
ORDER BY ...
FROM      ...
GROUP BY ...
```

6.3 Processing the Clauses in a Select Block

Each select block consists of clauses, such as the SELECT, FROM, and ORDER BY clause. In this section, we explain with the use of examples how the different clauses from a select block are processed. In other words, we show the steps SQL performs to come to the desired result. Other examples clearly show what the job of each clause is.

In all these examples, the select block forms the entire table expression and the entire SELECT statement.

Each clause is discussed in detail in separate chapters.

6.3.1 Example 1

Example 6.1: Find the player number for each player who has incurred at least two penalties of more than $25; order the result by player number (the smallest number first).

```
SELECT    PLAYERNO
FROM      PENALTIES
WHERE     AMOUNT > 25
GROUP BY  PLAYERNO
HAVING    COUNT(*) > 1
ORDER BY  PLAYERNO
```

Figure 6.3 shows the order in which SQL processes the different clauses. You will notice immediately that this order differs from the order in which the clauses were entered in the select block (and, therefore, the SELECT statement). Be careful never to confuse these two.

Figure 6.3   *The clauses of the* SELECT *statement*

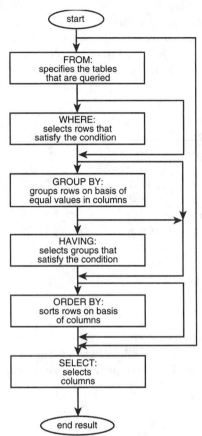

Explanation: Processing each clause results in *one (intermediate result) table* that consists of *zero or more rows* and *one or more columns*. This automatically means that every clause, barring the first, has one table of zero or more rows and one or more columns as its input. The first clause, the FROM clause, retrieves data from the database and has as its input *one or more tables* from the database. Those tables that still have to be processed by a subsequent clause are called *intermediate results*. SQL does not show the user any of the intermediate results; the statement is presented as a single, large process. The only table the end user sees is the final result table.

The developers of every SQL product are allowed to determine themselves how their products will process the SELECT statements internally. They can switch the order of the clauses or combine the processing of clauses. In fact, they can do whatever they want, as long as the final result of the query is equal to the result that we would get if the statement is processed according to the method just described.

Chapter 20, "Using Indexes," examines how statements are actually processed. The method of processing described here, though, is extremely useful if you want to determine the end result of a SELECT statement "by hand."

Let's examine the clauses for the given example one by one.

Only the PENALTIES table is named in the FROM clause. For SQL, this means that it will work with this table. The intermediate result of this clause is an exact copy of the PENALTIES table:

PAYMENTNO	PLAYERNO	PAYMENT_DATE	AMOUNT
1	6	1980-12-08	100.00
2	44	1981-05-05	75.00
3	27	1983-09-10	100.00
4	104	1984-12-08	50.00
5	44	1980-12-08	25.00
6	8	1980-12-08	25.00
7	44	1982-12-30	30.00
8	27	1984-11-12	75.00

The WHERE clause specifies AMOUNT > 25 as a condition. All rows in which the value in the AMOUNT column is greater than 25 satisfy the condition. Therefore, the rows with payment numbers 5 and 6 are discarded, while the remaining rows form the intermediate result table from the WHERE clause:

PAYMENTNO	PLAYERNO	PAYMENT_DATE	AMOUNT
1	6	1980-12-08	100.00
2	44	1981-05-05	75.00
3	27	1983-09-10	100.00
4	104	1984-12-08	50.00
7	44	1982-12-30	30.00
8	27	1984-11-12	75.00

The GROUP BY clause groups the rows in the intermediate result table. The data is divided into groups on the basis of the values in the PLAYERNO column (GROUP BY PLAYERNO). Rows are grouped if, in the relevant column, they contain equal values. The rows with payment numbers 2 and 7, for example, form one group because the PLAYERNO column has the value of 44 in both rows.

This is the intermediate result (the column name PLAYERNO has been shortened to PNO to conserve some space):

PAYMENTNO	PNO	PAYMENT_DATE	AMOUNT
{1}	6	{1980-12-08}	{100.00}
{2, 7}	44	{1981-05-05, 1982-12-30}	{75.00, 30.00}
{3, 8}	27	{1983-09-10, 1984-11-12}	{100.00, 75.00}
{4}	104	{1984-12-08}	{50.00}

Explanation: Thus, for all but the PLAYERNO column, there can be more than one value in one row. The PAYMENTNO column, for example, contains two values in the second and third rows. This is not as strange as it might seem because the data is grouped and each row actually forms a group of rows. Only in the PLAYERNO column is a single value for each row of the intermediate table found because this is the column by which the result is grouped. For the sake of clarity, the groups with values have been enclosed by brackets.

In some ways, you can compare this fourth clause, this HAVING clause, with the WHERE clause. The difference is that the WHERE clause acts on the intermediate table from the FROM clause and the HAVING clause on the grouped intermediate result table from the GROUP BY clause. The effect is the same; in the HAVING clause, rows are also selected with the help of a condition. In this case, the condition is as follows:

```
COUNT(*) > 1
```

This means that all (grouped) rows made up of more than one row must satisfy the condition. Chapter 10, "SELECT Statement: The GROUP BY Clause," looks at this condition in detail.

The intermediate result is:

PAYMENTNO	PNO	PAYMENT_DATE	AMOUNT
{2, 7}	44	{1981-05-05, 1982-12-30}	{75.00, 30.00}
{3, 8}	27	{1983-09-10, 1984-11-12}	{100.00, 75.00}

The SELECT clause specifies which columns must be present in the final result. In other words, the SELECT clause selects columns.

The intermediate result is:

```
PLAYERNO
--------
      44
      27
```

This final clause has no impact on the contents of the intermediate result, but it sorts the final remaining rows. In this example, the result is sorted on PLAYERNO.

This is the end result that is shown to the end user:

```
PLAYERNO
--------
      27
      44
```

6.3.2 Example 2

Example 6.2: Get the player number and the league number of each player resident in Stratford; order the result by league number.

```
SELECT    PLAYERNO, LEAGUENO
FROM      PLAYERS
WHERE     TOWN = 'Stratford'
ORDER BY  LEAGUENO
```

The intermediate result after the FROM clause is:

```
PLAYERNO  NAME        ...   LEAGUENO
--------  ---------   ---   --------
       6  Parmenter   ...   8467
      44  Baker       ...   1124
      83  Hope        ...   1608
       2  Everett     ...   2411
      27  Collins     ...   2513
     104  Moorman     ...   7060
       7  Wise        ...   ?
      57  Brown       ...   6409
      39  Bishop      ...   ?
     112  Bailey      ...   1319
       8  Newcastle   ...   2983
     100  Parmenter   ...   6524
      28  Collins     ...   ?
      95  Miller      ...   ?
```

The intermediate result after the WHERE clause is:

```
PLAYERNO   NAME        ...   LEAGUENO
--------   ---------   ---   --------
       6   Parmenter   ...   8467
      83   Hope        ...   1608
       2   Everett     ...   2411
       7   Wise        ...   ?
      57   Brown       ...   6409
      39   Bishop      ...   ?
     100   Parmenter   ...   6524
```

There is no GROUP BY clause; therefore, the intermediate result remains unchanged. There is also no HAVING clause, so, again, the intermediate result remains unchanged.

In the SELECT clause, the PLAYERNO and LEAGUENO columns are asked for. This gives the following intermediate result:

```
PLAYERNO   LEAGUENO
--------   --------
       6   8467
      83   1608
       2   2411
       7   ?
      57   6409
      39   ?
     100   6524
```

The intermediate result after the ORDER BY clause is:

```
PLAYERNO   LEAGUENO
--------   --------
       7   ?
      39   ?
      83   1608
       2   2411
      57   6409
     100   6524
       6   8467
```

Note that the NULL values are presented first if the result is sorted. This is described in greater depth in Chapter 12, "SELECT Statement: The ORDER BY Clause."

6.3.3 Example 3

The smallest SELECT statement that can be specified consists of one select block with just a SELECT clause.

Example 6.3: How much is 89 times 73?

```
SELECT    89 * 73
```

The result is:

```
89 * 73
-------
   6497
```

The processing of this statement is simple. If no FROM clause is specified, the statement returns a result consisting of one row. This row contains just as many values as there are expressions. In this example, that is also just one.

Exercise 6.7: For the following SELECT statement, determine the intermediate result table after each clause has been processed; give the final result as well.

```
SELECT    PLAYERNO
FROM      PENALTIES
WHERE     PAYMENT_DATE > '1980-12-08'
GROUP BY  PLAYERNO
HAVING    COUNT(*) > 1
ORDER BY  PLAYERNO
```

6.4 Possible Forms of a Table Expression

We already mentioned that the value of each table expression is a set of rows. We also stated that there are two forms: singular and compound. And we indicated that a singular table expression can consist of a select block. This section introduces new forms of the table expression.

```
<table expression> ::=
  { <select block head>           |
    ( <table expression> )        |
    <compound table expression> }
  [ <select block tail> ]

<compound table expression> ::=
    <table expression> <set operator> <table expression>

<set operator> ::= UNION
```

This definition shows that a table expression can have three forms. The first form is the familiar form, in which the head part of a select block is used. With the second form, the table expression is enclosed in brackets. The third form is the compound table expression, which has been mentioned but has not been clarified yet. It is allowed to specify the tail part of a select block after each form.

As usual, in this book, we illustrate the different forms with examples. We skip the first form because it has already been discussed in great detail. In the second form, brackets are used.

Example 6.4: Get the contents of the entire TEAMS table.

```
(SELECT    *
   FROM     TEAMS)
```

Explanation: This statement can also be specified without brackets. The result will be the same. However, the statement can also be formulated as follows:

```
(((((SELECT    *
      FROM     TEAMS)))))
```

Although this is not very useful, it is allowed. Brackets are useful, for example, when multiple select blocks occur within one table expression. We return to this later.

Just as there is a compound version of the scalar expression, there exists a compound version of the table expression. A table expression is built from multiple select blocks that are combined with a so-called *set operator*. SQL supports several set operators. For now, we discuss only one: the UNION operator. Chapter 13, "Combining Table Expressions," explains the others in detail.

Example 6.5: Get the numbers of the players who are captains and the numbers of the players who incurred a penalty.

```
SELECT    PLAYERNO
FROM      TEAMS
UNION
SELECT    PLAYERNO
FROM      PENALTIES
```

The result is:

```
PLAYERNO
--------
       6
       8
      27
      44
     104
```

Explanation: This statement consists of two select blocks. The first selects all the captains, and the second selects all the ticketed players. The intermediate result of the first select block is:

```
PLAYERNO
--------
       6
       8
      27
```

And the intermediate result of the second select block is:

```
PLAYERNO
--------
       6
       8
      27
      27
      44
      44
      44
     104
```

By linking the select blocks with a UNION, SQL places one intermediate result underneath the other:

```
PLAYERNO
--------
       6
       8
      27
       6
       8
      27
      27
      44
      44
      44
     104
```

In the final step, all the duplicate rows are removed automatically from the result. In front of and after a UNION operator, only the head parts of select blocks occur. This means that a select block tail is allowed only after the last select block. Therefore, the following statement is not allowed:

```
SELECT    PLAYERNO
FROM      TEAMS
ORDER BY  PLAYERNO
UNION
SELECT    PLAYERNO
FROM      PENALTIES
```

The tail part of a select block may be used only at the end of the entire table expression, such as here:

```
SELECT    PLAYERNO
FROM      TEAMS
UNION
SELECT    PLAYERNO
FROM      PENALTIES
ORDER BY  PLAYERNO
```

If there is a reason to sort the intermediate result of a select block before it is linked with a UNION operator, brackets must be used. Therefore, the following statement is allowed:

```
(SELECT    PLAYERNO
 FROM      TEAMS
 ORDER BY  1)
UNION
(SELECT    PLAYERNO
 FROM      PENALTIES)
ORDER BY   1
```

If a set operator is used, the degrees of the select blocks must be equal, and the data types of the columns that are placed below one another should be comparable.

Exercise 6.8: For each committee member, get the player number and the begin and end date. However, the dates should not be placed next to each other, but underneath each other.

Exercise 6.9: Following the previous exercise, now every row must express whether it is a begin or end date.

6.5 What Is a SELECT Statement?

To enable SQL to process a table expression, the expression must be wrapped in an SQL statement. A table expression can be used in several statements, including the CREATE VIEW and CREATE TABLE statements. However, the statement that is used most often is the SELECT statement. The first difference between a table expression and a SELECT statement is that the latter can be processed on its own by products such as WinSQL. A table expression, on the other hand, always needs a wrapping statement.

The second difference relates to the clauses of which both can exist. A SELECT statement has an additional clause that cannot be specified within a table expression; see the following definition of the SELECT statement. The use of this extra clause is explained in Chapter 26, "Introduction to Embedded SQL."

```
<select statement> ::=
   <table expression>
 [ <for clause> ]
```

6.6 What Is a Subquery?

Another table expression can be called from within a table expression. The called table expression is called a *subquery*. Alternative names for subquery are *subselect* and *inner-select*. The result of the subquery is passed to the calling table expression that can continue processing.

Grammatically, the difference between a table expression and a subquery is minimal; see the following definition. The difference is mainly in the use.

```
<subquery> ::= ( <table expression> )
```

Example 6.6: Get the numbers of the players with a number less than 10 and who are male.

```
SELECT   PLAYERNO
FROM     (SELECT   PLAYERNO, SEX
          FROM     PLAYERS
          WHERE    PLAYERNO < 10) AS PLAYERS10
WHERE    SEX = 'M'
```

The result is:

```
PLAYERNO
--------
       2
       6
       7
```

Explanation: This statement is special because it contains a table expression in the FROM clause. As is customary, the FROM clause is processed first and with that the sub-query. It is as if the subquery is "called" during the processing of the FROM clause. The table expression in the FROM clause is simple and returns the following intermediate result:

```
PLAYERNO  SEX
--------  ---
       2  M
       6  M
       7  M
       8  V
```

With the specification AS PLAYERS10, this intermediate result receives the name PLAYERS10. This name is called a *pseudonym*; Section 7.5, in Chapter 7, "SELECT State-ment: The FROM Clause," discusses the pseudonym extensively. These types of pseudo-nyms are required when using subqueries within the FROM clause.

The intermediate result is passed on to the WHERE clause where the condition SEX = 'M' is used to select the males. Then, the SELECT clause is used to select only the PLAYERNO column.

Subqueries can also be included within other subqueries. In other words, subqueries can be nested. The following construct is grammatically allowed:

```
SELECT  *
FROM    (SELECT  *
        FROM    (SELECT  *
                FROM    (SELECT  *
                        FROM    PLAYERS) AS S1) AS S2) AS S3
```

Example 6.7: Get the numbers of the players who have a number greater than 10 and less than 100, for whom the year in which they joined the club is greater than 1980, and who are male.

```
SELECT    PLAYERNO
FROM      (SELECT    PLAYERNO, SEX
           FROM      (SELECT    PLAYERNO, SEX, JOINED
                      FROM      (SELECT    PLAYERNO, SEX, JOINED
                                 FROM      PLAYERS
                                 WHERE     PLAYERNO > 10) AS GREATER10
                      WHERE     PLAYERNO < 100) AS LESS100
           WHERE     JOINED > 1980) AS JOINED1980
WHERE     SEX = 'M'
```

The result is:

```
PLAYERNO
--------
      57
      83
```

Explanation: This statement has four levels. The inner subquery is used to search for all the players whose player number is greater than 10:

PLAYERNO	SEX	JOINED
27	F	1983
28	F	1983
39	M	1980
44	M	1980
57	M	1985
83	M	1982
95	M	1972
100	M	1979
104	F	1984
112	F	1984

The next subquery is used to retrieve from the previous intermediate result all the rows in which the player number is less than 100:

```
PLAYERNO   SEX   JOINED
--------   ---   ------
      27   F       1983
      28   F       1983
      39   M       1980
      44   M       1980
      57   M       1985
      83   M       1982
      95   M       1972
```

The third subquery is used to search the intermediate result for all the rows of which the year of joining the club is greater than 1980. Also, the JOINED column is not included in the intermediate result because the table expression on top does not need it. The intermediate result is:

```
PLAYERNO   SEX
--------   ---
      27   V
      28   V
      57   M
      83   M
```

Finally, this intermediate result is searched for the rows in which the SEX column is equal to M.

SQL distinguishes four types of subqueries. The difference among these four is determined by the result of the subquery. The previous subqueries are all *table subqueries*, because the result of each subquery is a set of rows. In addition, we have the *row*, the *column*, and the *scalar subquery*. The result of a row subquery is one row with one or more values. The result of a column subquery is a set of rows in which each row consists of just one value. And the scalar subquery has only one row, consisting of one value as result. This means that each scalar subquery is, by definition, a row subquery and a column subquery as well, but not the other way around; not every row or column subquery is a scalar subquery. It also holds that each row and each column subquery is a table subquery, but not the other way around.

Column subqueries are not discussed until Chapter 8, "SELECT Statement: The WHERE Clause." For now, we just give a few examples of scalar and row subqueries.

Example 6.8: For each player whose number is less than 60, get the number of years between the year in which that player joined the club and that of player 100.

```
SELECT    PLAYERNO, JOINED -
                    (SELECT   JOINED
                     FROM     PLAYERS
                     WHERE    PLAYERNO = 100)
FROM      PLAYERS
WHERE     PLAYERNO < 60
```

The result is:

```
PLAYERNO   JOINED  - (...
--------   --------------
       2              -4
       6              -2
       7               2
       8               1
      27               4
      28               4
      39               1
      44               1
      57               6
```

Explanation: In this statement, the subquery has been placed inside the SELECT clause. The result of this scalar subquery is 1979. After this result has been determined, the following simple SELECT statement is executed:

```
SELECT    PLAYERNO, JOINED - 1979
FROM      PLAYERS
WHERE     PLAYERNO < 60
```

The scalar subquery has to return zero or one row. If the subquery returns more than one row, SQL responds with an error message. Therefore, the next statement will not work because the subquery returns too many rows:

```
SELECT    TEAMNO
FROM      TEAMS
WHERE     PLAYERNO =
          (SELECT    PLAYERNO
           FROM      PLAYERS)
```

Almost everywhere a scalar expression can be specified, a scalar subquery can be used.

Example 6.9: Get the numbers of the players who were born in the same year as player 27.

```
SELECT    PLAYERNO
FROM      PLAYERS
WHERE     YEAR(BIRTH_DATE) = (SELECT    YEAR(BIRTH_DATE)
                              FROM      PLAYERS
                              WHERE     PLAYERNO = 27)
```

The result is:

```
PLAYERNO
--------
       6
      27
```

Explanation: The subquery looks for the year of birth of player 27. The result is one row consisting of one value. In other words, this actually is a scalar subquery. That one value is 1964. Next, the following SELECT statement is executed:

```
SELECT    PLAYERNO
FROM      PLAYERS
WHERE     YEAR(BIRTH_DATE) = 1964
```

Player 27 appears in the end result as well, of course. If that is not the intention, the WHERE clause can be expanded with the condition AND PLAYERNO <> 27.

Portability: *The next examples work only with SQL products that support select blocks without a FROM clause. MySQL and SQL Server are examples of products that do.*

Example 6.10: Get the date of birth of players 27, 44, and 100 as one row (next to each other).

```
SELECT    (SELECT    BIRTH_DATE
           FROM       PLAYERS
           WHERE      PLAYERNO = 27),
          (SELECT    BIRTH_DATE
           FROM       PLAYERS
           WHERE      PLAYERNO = 44),
          (SELECT    BIRTH_DATE
           FROM       PLAYERS
           WHERE      PLAYERNO = 100)
```

The result is:

```
SELECT(...   SELECT(...   SELECT(...
----------   ----------   ----------
1964-12-28   1963-01-09   1963-02-28
```

Explanation: Using the three scalar subqueries on the position of scalar expressions within a SELECT clause produces the desired result.

Example 6.11: Get the numbers of the players who have the same sex as and live in the same town as player 100.

```
SELECT    PLAYERNO
FROM      PLAYERS
WHERE     (SEX, TOWN) = (SELECT    SEX, TOWN
                         FROM       PLAYERS
                         WHERE      PLAYERNO = 100)
```

The result is:

PLAYERNO

       2
       6
       7
      39
      57
      83
     100

Explanation: The result of the subquery is one row with two values: (`'M'`, `'Strat-ford'`). This row value is compared to the row expression: (`SEX`, `TOWN`). See Sections 5.3 and 5.15, in Chapter 5, "`SELECT` Statement: Common Elements," for descriptions of row expressions.

Exercise 6.10: Get the numbers of the committee members who were secretary of the tennis club between January 1, 1990, and December 31, 1994; use subqueries here.

Exercise 6.11: Get the numbers of the teams of which the player with the name Parmenter and initial R is captain; in this example, we assume that there are no two players with the same name and initials.

Exercise 6.12: Get the name of the player who is captain of the team for which match 6 was played.

Exercise 6.13: Get the numbers of the penalties that are higher than the penalties with payment number 4.

Exercise 6.14: Get the numbers of the players who were born on the same day (for example, Monday or Tuesday) as player 2.

Exercise 6.15: Get the numbers of the committee members who took up a position and who resigned that same position on the same day that player 8 took on and resigned his position as treasurer. Player 8 cannot appear in the end result.

Exercise 6.16: Get the divisions of teams 1 and 2, and place them next to each other.

Exercise 6.17: What is the sum of the penalties with payment numbers 1, 2, and 3?

6.7   Answers

6.1   This statement is, in its entirety, a SELECT statement and also a table expression. However, it is not a head part of a select block because an ORDER BY clause belongs to the tail part of a select block.

This statement is, in its entirety, a SELECT statement, a table expression, and the head part of a select block.

This statement is, in its entirety, not a SELECT statement, but a CREATE VIEW statement. From the word SELECT, it actually is a table expression and also the head part of a select block.

6.2   The statement is, in its entirety, a table expression; the ORDER BY clause is the tail part.

6.3   A SELECT statement consists of at least one clause, and that is the SELECT clause.

6.4   Yes.

6.5   No. If a SELECT statement has a HAVING clause, a GROUP BY clause is mandatory.

6.6   There is no FROM clause.

The GROUP BY clause must be specified in front of the HAVING clause.

The ORDER BY clause should be the last clause.

6.7   The FROM clause:

PAYMENTNO	PLAYERNO	PAYMENT_DATE	AMOUNT
1	6	1980-12-08	100.00
2	44	1981-05-05	75.00
3	27	1983-09-10	100.00
4	104	1984-12-08	50.00
5	44	1980-12-08	25.00
6	8	1980-12-08	25.00
7	44	1982-12-30	30.00
8	27	1984-11-12	75.00

The WHERE clause:

PAYMENTNO	PLAYERNO	PAYMENT_DATE	AMOUNT
2	44	1981-05-05	75.00
3	27	1983-09-10	100.00
4	104	1984-12-08	50.00
7	44	1982-12-30	30.00
8	27	1984-11-12	75.00

The GROUP BY clause:

PAYMENTNO	PLAYERNO	PAYMENT_DATE	AMOUNT
{2, 7}	44	{1981-05-05, 1982-12-30}	{75.00, 30.00}
{3, 8}	27	{1983-09-10, 1984-11-12}	{100.00, 75.00}
{4}	104	{1984-12-08}	{50.00}

The HAVING clause:

PAYMENTNO	PLAYERNO	PAYMENT_DATE	AMOUNT
{2, 7}	44	{1981-05-05, 1982-12-30}	{75.00, 30.00}
{3, 8}	27	{1983-09-10, 1984-11-12}	{100.00, 75.00}

The SELECT clause:

PLAYERNO
44
27

The ORDER BY clause:

```
PLAYERNO
--------
      27
      44
```

6.8

```
SELECT    PLAYERNO, BEGIN_DATE
FROM      COMMITTEE_MEMBERS
UNION
SELECT    PLAYERNO, END_DATE
FROM      COMMITTEE_MEMBERS
ORDER BY PLAYERNO
```

6.9

```
SELECT    PLAYERNO, BEGIN_DATE, 'Begin date'
FROM      COMMITTEE_MEMBERS
UNION
SELECT    PLAYERNO, END_DATE, 'End date'
FROM      COMMITTEE_MEMBERS
ORDER BY PLAYERNO
```

6.10

```
SELECT   PLAYERNO
FROM     (SELECT   PLAYERNO
          FROM     (SELECT   PLAYERNO, END_DATE
                    FROM     (SELECT   PLAYERNO, BEGIN_DATE,
                                       END_DATE
                              FROM     COMMITTEE_MEMBERS
                              WHERE    POSITION = 'Secretary')
                              AS SECRETARIES
                    WHERE    BEGIN_DATE >= '1990-01-01')
                    AS AFTER1989
          WHERE    END_DATE <= '1994-12-31') AS BEFORE1995
```

6.11

```
SELECT    TEAMNO
FROM      TEAMS
WHERE     PLAYERNO =
          (SELECT    PLAYERNO
           FROM      PLAYERS
           WHERE     NAME = 'Parmenter'
           AND       INITIALS = 'R')
```

6.12

```
SELECT    TEAMNO
FROM      TEAMS
WHERE     PLAYERNO =
          (SELECT    PLAYERNO
           FROM      PLAYERS
           WHERE     NAME =
                     (SELECT    NAME
                      FROM      PLAYERS
                      WHERE     PLAYERNO = 6)
           AND       PLAYERNO <> 6)

SELECT    NAME
FROM      PLAYERS
WHERE     PLAYERNO =
          (SELECT    PLAYERNO
           FROM      TEAMS
           WHERE     TEAMNO =
                     (SELECT    TEAMNO
                      FROM      MATCHES
                      WHERE     MATCHNO = 6))
```

6.13

```
SELECT    PAYMENTNO
FROM      PENALTIES
WHERE     AMOUNT >
          (SELECT    AMOUNT
           FROM      PENALTIES
           WHERE     PAYMENTNO = 4)
```

6.14

```
SELECT    PLAYERNO
FROM      PLAYERS
WHERE     DAYNAME(BIRTH_DATE) =
          (SELECT    DAYNAME(BIRTH_DATE)
           FROM      PLAYERS
           WHERE     PLAYERNO = 2)
```

6.15

```
SELECT    PLAYERNO
FROM      COMMITTEE_MEMBERS
WHERE     (BEGIN_DATE, END_DATE) =
          (SELECT    BEGIN_DATE, END_DATE
           FROM      COMMITTEE_MEMBERS
           WHERE     PLAYERNO = 8
           AND       POSITION = 'Treasurer')
AND       PLAYERNO <> 8
```

6.16

```
SELECT    (SELECT    DIVISION
           FROM      TEAMS
           WHERE     TEAMNO = 1),
          (SELECT    DIVISION
           FROM      TEAMS
           WHERE     TEAMNO = 2)
```

6.17

```
SELECT    (SELECT    AMOUNT
           FROM      PENALTIES
           WHERE     PAYMENTNO = 1) +
          (SELECT    AMOUNT
           FROM      PENALTIES
           WHERE     PAYMENTNO = 2) +
          (SELECT    AMOUNT
           FROM      PENALTIES
           WHERE     PAYMENTNO = 3)
```

7

SELECT Statement: The FROM Clause

7.1 Introduction

T he processing of a table expression begins at the FROM clause. In fact, this is the starting point of processing a table expression, which is why this clause is discussed in detail first.

In this chapter, we describe the basic features of the FROM clause. In previous chapters, you saw many examples of this clause. The FROM clause is an important clause because each table from which we "use" columns in the other clauses should be specified here. By "using," we mean, for example, that a column appears in a condition or in the SELECT clause. Simply, in the FROM clause, we specify the tables from which the result of a table expression will be retrieved.

The FROM clause has many different forms. We start this chapter with the simplest form.

7.2 Table Specifications in the FROM Clause

The FROM clause is used for specifying which tables are to be queried. This is done by means of *table references*. A table reference consists of a table specification possibly followed by a pseudonym. Table specifications are discussed in this section; pseudonyms are discussed later in this chapter.

```
<from clause> ::=
    FROM <table reference> [ { , <table reference> }... ]

<table reference> ::=
    <table specification> [ [ AS ] <pseudonym> ]

<table specification> ::=
    [ <database name> . | <user name> . ] <table name>

<pseudonym> ::= <name>
```

A table specification normally consists of the name of a table, but you can specify the name of a view. In both cases, we will use the term *table specification*.

Within a table specification another name can be specified in front of a table name. Those two names are separated by a full stop, as in NAME1.PLAYERS. What the extra name refers to depends on the SQL product in use. For one group of products to which MySQL belongs, it has to be the name of an existing database. For other products, it is the name of the owner of the table. In most cases, that is the name of the user who created the table.

MySQL belongs to that second group of products, so let's begin there. Each table is stored in a specific database. It also holds that an application must open a connection to access tables. And a connection always requires one current database. However, sometimes the need arises to stay within the connection and to query a table that is stored outside the current database. We do this by extending table specifications with database names.

Example 7.1: Create a new database called EXTRA with a new table called CITIES.

```
CREATE DATABASE EXTRA

USE EXTRA

CREATE TABLE CITIES
       (CITYNO       INTEGER NOT NULL PRIMARY KEY,
        CITYNAME    CHAR(20) NOT NULL)

INSERT INTO CITIES VALUES
    (1, 'Stratford')

INSERT INTO CITIES VALUES
    (2, 'Inglewood')
```

Explanation: Do not forget to change the current database into EXTRA with the USE statement after the CREATE DATABASE statement.

Example 7.2: Show the entire contents of the CITIES table; assume that a connection has been made to the TENNIS database.

```
SELECT    *
FROM      EXTRA.CITIES
```

Explanation: The compound name EXTRA.CITIES is the table specification. (Note the full stop between the name of the database and the table name; this full stop is mandatory). We say that the table name CITIES is *qualified* with the database name EXTRA.

In fact, a table name can always be qualified, even when a table from the current database is queried.

Example 7.3: Show the contents of the TEAMS table.

```
SELECT    *
FROM      TENNIS.TEAMS
```

Products such as DB2 and Oracle belong to the other group. Here, we can qualify tables with the name of another user. So you can understand this, we first have to explain the concept *owner*.

Every table has an owner. In most cases, the SQL user who enters a CREATE TABLE statement is the owner of the table. Names of tables are unique within a user. In other words, two users can both create a table with the same name, but one user is not allowed to assign the same name to two of his tables. If SQL users want to access tables of others, they have to indicate in some way which table they intend to access. This means that they have to state the owner of the table that they want to access. For this purpose, the definition of the table specification has been extended.

In a FROM clause, if an SQL user wants to refer to a table created by someone else, the name of the owner *must* be specified in front of the table name. This is not required if that user is the *owner* of the table.

Example 7.4: JIM wants to retrieve the entire contents of the PENALTIES table, which has been created by BOB. (Assume that JIM has the authority to query this table.)

```
SELECT    *
FROM      BOB.PENALTIES
```

Explanation: The new compound name BOB.PENALTIES is the table specification. The table name PENALTIES has been qualified by the owner's name BOB.

If user BOB wants to see the contents of the PENALTIES table, he could use the previous statement, but he might also leave out his own name:

```
SELECT    *
FROM      PENALTIES
```

7.3 Again, the Column Specification

In the previous section, we saw that, depending on the SQL product, a table can be qualified with the name of the database or with the name of the owner of the table. When specifying columns (in the SELECT clause, for example), you can also qualify them by specifying the table to which the columns belong. Each column specification consists of three parts; see the definition.

```
<column specification> ::=
    [ <table specification> . ] <column name>

<table specification> ::=
    [ <database name> . | <user name> . ] <table name>
```

The last part is the column name itself, such as PLAYERNO or NAME. This is the only mandatory part. The second part is the table name, such as PLAYERS or TEAMS. The first one is the name of the database or the user. You do not have to specify all these parts, but it is not wrong to do so.

Example 7.5: Find the number of each team. Here are three possible solutions; we assume that the TEAMS table is stored in the TENNIS database and that we use MySQL.

```
SELECT    TEAMNO
FROM      TEAMS
```

and

```
SELECT    TEAMS.TEAMNO
FROM      TEAMS
```

and

```
SELECT    TENNIS.TEAMS.TEAMNO
FROM      TENNIS.TEAMS
```

7.4 Multiple Table Specifications in the FROM Clause

Until now, we have used only one table specification in the FROM clause. If we want to present data from different tables in our result table, we must specify multiple tables in the FROM clause.

Example 7.6: Get the team number and the name of the captain of each team.

The TEAMS table holds information about team numbers and the player numbers of each team. However, the names of the captains are not stored in the TEAMS table but in the PLAYERS table. In other words, we need both tables. Both must be mentioned in the FROM clause.

```
SELECT   TEAMNO, NAME
FROM     TEAMS, PLAYERS
WHERE    TEAMS.PLAYERNO = PLAYERS.PLAYERNO
```

The intermediate result of the FROM clause is:

TEAMNO	PLAYERNO	DIVISION	PLAYERNO	NAME	...
1	6	first	6	Parmenter	...
1	6	first	44	Baker	...
1	6	first	83	Hope	...
1	6	first	2	Everett	...
1	6	first	27	Collins	...
1	6	first	104	Moorman	...
1	6	first	7	Wise	...
1	6	first	57	Brown	...
1	6	first	39	Bishop	...
1	6	first	112	Bailey	...
1	6	first	8	Newcastle	...
1	6	first	100	Parmenter	...
1	6	first	28	Collins	...
1	6	first	95	Miller	...
2	27	second	6	Parmenter	...
2	27	second	44	Baker	...
2	27	second	83	Hope	...

```
         2        27   second         2   Everett     ...
         2        27   second        27   Collins     ...
         2        27   second       104   Moorman     ...
         2        27   second         7   Wise        ...
         2        27   second        57   Brown       ...
         2        27   second        39   Bishop      ...
         2        27   second       112   Bailey      ...
         2        27   second         8   Newcastle   ...
         2        27   second       100   Parmenter   ...
         2        27   second        28   Collins     ...
         2        27   second        95   Miller      ...
```

Explanation: Each row of the PLAYERS table is aligned "beside" each row of the TEAMS table. This results in a table in which the total number of columns equals the number of columns in one table *plus* the number of columns in the other table, and in which the total number of rows equals the number of rows in one table *multiplied* by the number of rows in the other table. We call this result the *Cartesian product* of the tables concerned.

In the WHERE clause, each row where the value in the TEAMS.PLAYERNO column equals the one in the PLAYERS.PLAYERNO column is selected:

```
TEAMNO   PLAYERNO   DIVISION   PLAYERNO   NAME         ...
------   --------   --------   --------   ---------    ---
     1          6   first             6   Parmenter    ...
     2         27   second           27   Collins      ...
```

The end result is:

```
TEAMNO   NAME
------   ---------
     1   Parmenter
     2   Collins
```

In this example, it is essential to specify the table name in front of the PLAYERNO column. Without qualifying the column name, it would be impossible for SQL to determine which column was intended.

Conclusion: If you use a column name that appears in more than one table specified in the FROM clause, it is *mandatory* to include a table specification with the column specification.

Example 7.7: For each penalty, find the payment number, the amount of the penalty, the player number, the name, and the initials of the player who incurred the penalty.

The payment numbers, the amounts, and the player numbers are held in the PENALTIES table, while names and initials are found in the PLAYERS table. Both tables must be included in the FROM clause:

```
SELECT    PAYMENTNO, PENALTIES.PLAYERNO, AMOUNT,
          NAME, INITIALS
FROM      PENALTIES, PLAYERS
WHERE     PENALTIES.PLAYERNO = PLAYERS.PLAYERNO
```

The intermediate result from the FROM clause is (not all the rows have been included):

PAYMENTNO	PLAYERNO	AMOUNT	...	PLAYERNO	NAME	INITIALS	...
1	6	100.00	...	6	Parmenter	R	...
1	6	100.00	...	44	Baker	E	...
1	6	100.00	...	83	Hope	PK	...
1	6	100.00	...	2	Everett	R	..
:	:	:		:	:	:	
2	44	75.00	...	6	Parmenter	R	...
2	44	75.00	...	44	Baker	E	..
2	44	75.00	...	83	Hope	PK	...
2	44	75.00	...	2	Everett	R	...
:	:	:		:	:	:	
3	27	100.00	...	6	Parmenter	R	...
3	27	100.00	...	44	Baker	E	...
3	27	100.00	...	83	Hope	PK	...
3	27	100.00	...	2	Everett	R	...
:	:	:		:	:	:	
:	:	:		:	:	:	

The intermediate result after processing the FROM clause is:

```
PAYMENTNO PLAYERNO AMOUNT ... PLAYERNO NAME      INITIALS  ...
--------- -------- ------ --- -------- --------- --------  ---
        1        6 100.00 ...        6 Parmenter R         ...
        2       44  75.00 ...       44 Baker     E         ...
        3       27 100.00 ...       27 Collins   DD        ...
        4      104  50.00 ...      104 Moorman   D         ...
        5       44  25.00 ...       44 Baker     E         ...
        6        8  25.00 ...        8 Newcastle B         ...
        7       44  30.00 ...       44 Baker     E         ...
        8       27  75.00 ...       27 Collins   DD        ...
```

The end result is:

```
PAYMENTNO  PLAYERNO   AMOUNT  NAME       INITIALS
---------  --------   ------  ---------  --------
        1         6   100.00  Parmenter  R
        2        44    75.00  Baker      E
        3        27   100.00  Collins    DD
        4       104    50.00  Moorman    D
        5        44    25.00  Baker      E
        6         8    25.00  Newcastle  B
        7        44    30.00  Baker      E
        8        27    75.00  Collins    DD
```

To avoid ambiguity, the table name must be specified in front of the PLAYERNO column in the SELECT clause.

The order of the table specifications in a FROM clause does not affect the result of this clause and the end result of the table expression. The SELECT clause is the only clause that determines the order of the columns in the result. The ORDER BY clause is used to determine the order in which the rows will be presented. Thus, the results of the next two statements are equal:

```
SELECT    PLAYERS.PLAYERNO
FROM      PLAYERS, TEAMS
WHERE     PLAYERS.PLAYERNO = TEAMS.PLAYERNO
```

and

```
SELECT    PLAYERS.PLAYERNO
FROM      TEAMS, PLAYERS
WHERE     PLAYERS.PLAYERNO = TEAMS.PLAYERNO
```

Exercise 7.1: Indicate why these SELECT statements are not correctly formulated:

1.

```
SELECT    PLAYERNO
FROM      PLAYERS, TEAMS
```

2.

```
SELECT    PLAYERS.PLAYERNO
FROM      TEAMS
```

Exercise 7.2: For each clause of the following statement, determine the intermediate result and the result. Also, give a description of the question that underlies the statement.

```
SELECT    PLAYERS.NAME
FROM      TEAMS, PLAYERS
WHERE     PLAYERS.PLAYERNO = TEAMS.PLAYERNO
```

Exercise 7.3: For each penalty, find the payment number, the amount, and the number and name of the player who incurred it.

Exercise 7.4: For each penalty incurred by a team captain, find the payment number and the captain's name.

7.5 Pseudonyms for Table Names

When multiple table specifications appear in the FROM clause, it is sometimes easier to use so-called *pseudonyms*. Another name for pseudonym is an *alias*. Pseudonyms are temporary alternative names for table names. In the previous examples, to qualify a column, we specified the full table name. Instead of using table names, we can use pseudonyms.

Example 7.8: For each penalty, get the payment number, the amount of the penalty, the player number, and the name and initials of the player who incurred the penalty. Make use of pseudonyms.

```
SELECT    PAYMENTNO, PEN.PLAYERNO, AMOUNT,
          NAME, INITIALS
FROM      PENALTIES AS PEN, PLAYERS AS P
WHERE     PEN.PLAYERNO = P.PLAYERNO
```

Explanation: In the FROM clause, the pseudonyms are specified or declared after the table names. In other clauses, we must use these pseudonyms instead of the real table names.

Because pseudonyms have been used, it is *not* possible to mention the original table names in the other clauses anymore. The presence of a pseudonym implies that a table name cannot be used in this SQL statement.

The fact that the pseudonym PEN has been used earlier in the statement (in the SELECT clause) than its declaration (in the FROM clause) does not cause any problems. As we have seen, the FROM clause might not be the first clause we specify, but it is the first processed.

The word AS in the definition is optional. So, the previous statement has the same result as the following:

```
SELECT    PAYMENTNO, PEN.PLAYERNO, AMOUNT,
          NAME, INITIALS
FROM      PENALTIES PEN, PLAYERS P
WHERE     PEN.PLAYERNO = P.PLAYERNO
```

In both examples, the use of pseudonyms is not vital. However, later in this book we formulate SELECT statements where table names would have to be repeated many times. Adding pseudonyms makes it easier to formulate and read those statements.

A pseudonym must satisfy the naming rules for table names. More about this subject comes in Section 15.6, in Chapter 15, "Creating Tables." Two pseudonyms in the same statement cannot have the same name.

Exercise 7.5: Get for each team the number and the last name of the captain.

Exercise 7.6: Get for each match the match number, the last name of the player, and the division of the team.

7.6 Various Examples of Joins

This section looks at some examples to illustrate various aspects of the FROM clause. Plus, we introduce several new terms.

Example 7.9: Get the numbers of the captains who have incurred at least one penalty.

```
SELECT    T.PLAYERNO
FROM      TEAMS AS T, PENALTIES AS PEN
WHERE     T.PLAYERNO = PEN.PLAYERNO
```

Explanation: The TEAMS table includes all the players who are captains. By using the player numbers, we can search the PENALTIES table for those captains who have incurred at least one penalty. For that reason, both tables are included in the FROM clause. The intermediate result from the FROM clause becomes:

TEAMNO	PLAYERNO	DIVISION	PAYMENTNO	PLAYERNO	...
1	6	first	1	6	...
1	6	first	2	44	...
1	6	first	3	27	...
1	6	first	4	104	...
1	6	first	5	44	...
1	6	first	6	8	...
1	6	first	7	44	...
1	6	first	8	27	...
2	27	second	1	6	...

```
2        27   second          2         44  ...
2        27   second          3         27  ...
2        27   second          4        104  ...
2        27   second          5         44  ...
2        27   second          6          8  ...
2        27   second          7         44  ...
2        27   second          8         27  ...
```

The intermediate result from the WHERE clause is:

```
TEAMNO   PLAYERNO   DIVISION   PAYMENTNO   PLAYERNO   ...
------   --------   --------   ---------   --------   ---
     1          6   first              1          6   ...
     2         27   second             3         27   ...
     2         27   second             8         27   ...
```

The end result is thus:

```
PLAYERNO
--------
       6
      27
      27
```

When data of different tables is merged into one table, it is called a *join* of tables. The columns on which the join is executed are called the *join columns*. In the previous SELECT statement, these are the columns TEAMS.PLAYERNO and PENALTIES.PLAYERNO. The condition in the WHERE clause, with which we compare the PLAYERNO column of the TEAMS table with the one of the PENALTIES table, is called the *join condition*.

Note that the result of the earlier statement contains duplicate rows. SQL does not automatically remove duplicate rows from the end result. In our example, player 27 appears twice because she incurred two penalties. When you do not want duplicate rows in your result, you should specify the word DISTINCT directly behind the word SELECT. (Chapter 9, "SELECT Statement: SELECT Clause and Aggregation Functions," discusses DISTINCT extensively.)

Example 7.10: Get the numbers of the captains who have incurred at least one penalty. Remove the duplicate numbers.

```
SELECT    DISTINCT T.PLAYERNO
FROM      TEAMS AS T, PENALTIES AS PEN
WHERE     T.PLAYERNO = PEN.PLAYERNO
```

The end result then becomes:

```
PLAYERNO
--------
       6
      27
```

Example 7.11: Get the names and initials of the players who have played at least one match. *Warning:* A competition player does not have to appear in the MATCHES table. (Perhaps he or she has been injured for the whole season.)

```
SELECT    DISTINCT P.NAME, P.INITIALS
FROM      PLAYERS AS P, MATCHES AS M
WHERE     P.PLAYERNO = M.PLAYERNO
```

The result is:

```
NAME        INITIALS
---------   --------
Parmenter   R
Baker       E
Hope        PK
Everett     R
Collins     DD
Moorman     D
Brown       M
Bailey      IP
Newcastle   B
```

Work out for yourself how this SELECT statement could give rise to duplicate values if DISTINCT is not used.

A join is not restricted to two tables. A FROM clause can contain many tables.

Example 7.12: For each match, get the match number, the player number, the team number, the name of the player, and the division in which the team plays.

```
SELECT   M.MATCHNO, M.PLAYERNO, M.TEAMNO, P.NAME, T.DIVISION
FROM     MATCHES AS M, PLAYERS AS P, TEAMS AS T
WHERE    M.PLAYERNO = P.PLAYERNO
AND      M.TEAMNO = T.TEAMNO
```

The result is:

MATCHNO	PLAYERNO	TEAMNO	NAME	DIVISION
1	6	1	Parmenter	first
2	6	1	Parmenter	first
3	6	1	Parmenter	first
4	44	1	Baker	first
5	83	1	Hope	first
6	2	1	Everett	first
7	57	1	Brown	first
8	8	1	Newcastle	first
9	27	2	Collins	second
10	104	2	Moorman	second
11	112	2	Bailey	second
12	112	2	Bailey	second
13	8	2	Newcastle	second

Example 7.13: Get the payment number, the player number, and the date of each penalty incurred in the year in which the player concerned joined the club.

```
SELECT   PEN.PAYMENTNO, PEN.PLAYERNO, PEN.PAYMENT_DATE
FROM     PENALTIES AS PEN, PLAYERS AS P
WHERE    PEN.PLAYERNO = P.PLAYERNO
AND      YEAR(PEN.PAYMENT_DATE) = P.JOINED
```

The result is:

PAYMENTNO	PLAYERNO	PEN.PAYMENT_DATE
3	27	1983-09-10
4	104	1984-12-08
5	44	1980-12-08
6	8	1980-12-08

Explanation: Most join conditions compare key columns with each other. However, that is not a requirement. In this example, the date on which the penalty has been paid is compared to the year in which the player joined the club.

Exercise 7.7: Get the numbers and names of players who have been chairmen.

Exercise 7.8: Get the number of each player who on the same day that he became a committee member also incurred a penalty.

7.7 Mandatory Use of Pseudonyms

In some SELECT statements, there is no choice about whether a pseudonym is to be used. This situation arises when the same table is mentioned more than once in the FROM clause. Consider this example.

Example 7.14: Get the numbers of the players who are older than R. Parmenter; in this example, we assume that the combination of name and initials is unique.

```
SELECT    P.PLAYERNO
FROM      PLAYERS AS P, PLAYERS AS PAR
WHERE     PAR.NAME = 'Parmenter'
AND       PAR.INITIALS = 'R'
AND       P.BIRTH_DATE < PAR.BIRTH_DATE
```

The intermediate result from the WHERE clause is a multiplication of the PLAYERS table by itself. (For simplicity, we have shown only the rows from the PAR.PLAYERS table in which player 6, named R. Parmenter, is found.)

PLAYERNO	...	BIRTH_DATE	...	PLAYERNO	...	BIRTH_DATE	...
6	...	1964-06-25	...	6	...	1964-06-25	...
44	...	1963-01-09	...	6	...	1964-06-25	...
83	...	1956-11-11	...	6	...	1964-06-25	...
2	...	1948-09-01	...	6	...	1964-06-25	...
27	...	1964-12-28	...	6	...	1964-06-25	...
104	...	1970-05-10	...	6	...	1964-06-25	...
7	...	1963-05-11	...	6	...	1964-06-25	...
57	...	1971-08-17	...	6	...	1964-06-25	...
39	...	1956-10-29	...	6	...	1964-06-25	...
112	...	1963-10-01	...	6	...	1964-06-25	...
8	...	1962-07-08	...	6	...	1964-06-25	...
100	...	1963-02-28	...	6	...	1964-06-25	...
28	...	1963-06-22	...	6	...	1964-06-25	...
95	...	1963-05-14	...	6	...	1964-06-25	...
:	:	:	:	:	:	:	:
:	:	:	:	:	:	:	:

The intermediate result of the WHERE clause is:

PLAYERNO	...	BIRTH_DATE	...	PLAYERNO	...	BIRTH_DATE	...
44	...	1963-01-09	...	6	...	1964-06-25	...
83	...	1956-11-11	...	6	...	1964-06-25	...
2	...	1948-09-01	...	6	...	1964-06-25	...
7	...	1963-05-11	...	6	...	1964-06-25	...
39	...	1956-10-29	...	6	...	1964-06-25	...
112	...	1963-10-01	...	6	...	1964-06-25	...
8	...	1962-07-08	...	6	...	1964-06-25	...
100	...	1963-02-28	...	6	...	1964-06-25	...
28	...	1963-06-22	...	6	...	1964-06-25	...
95	...	1963-05-14	...	6	...	1964-06-25	...

The end result is:

```
PLAYERNO
--------
      44
      83
       2
       7
      39
     112
       8
     100
      28
      95
```

In the previous examples, table names were specified in front of column names to identify columns uniquely. That would not help in the previous example because both tables have the same name. In other words, if a FROM clause refers to two tables with the same name, pseudonyms *must* be used.

Note that it would have been sufficient to assign only one of the two tables a pseudonym in the earlier example:

```
SELECT    P.PLAYERNO
FROM      PLAYERS AS P, PLAYERS
WHERE     PLAYERS.NAME = 'Parmenter'
AND       PLAYERS.INITIALS = 'R'
AND       P.BIRTH_DATE < PLAYERS.BIRTH_DATE
```

Exercise 7.9: Get the numbers and names of the players who live in the same town as player 27. Player 27 should not appear in the end result.

Exercise 7.10: Get the number and name of every competition player as well as the number and name of the captain of each team for whom that player has ever competed. The result may *not* contain competition players who are captains of a team. Desired result:

PLAYERNO	NAME (PLAYERS)	PLAYERNO	NAME (CAPTAIN)
44	Baker	6	Parmenter
8	Newcastle	6	Parmenter
8	Newcastle	27	Collins
:	:	:	:
:	:	:	:

Exercise 7.11: Get the numbers of the penalties for which the penalty amount is equal to a penalty amount belonging to player 44. The result should not contain the penalties of player 44.

7.8 Explicit Joins in the FROM Clause

So far, we have talked about the concept of joins, but we have not seen the word JOIN in the table expression yet. The reason is that, until now, we have shown only examples in which the join is "hidden" in the SELECT statement. Sometimes, this join is referred to as an *implicit join*. In this case, a join is then made up of several specifications from the FROM clause (the table specifications), together with one or more conditions from the WHERE clause.

Explicitly adding the join to the SELECT statement started in the SQL2 standard. This new, *explicit join* is entirely specified in the FROM clause, resulting in a considerable increase in features of this clause. The effect is that it is much easier to formulate certain statements. The extended definition of the FROM clause is shown next. Most important in this definition is that a table reference is not restricted to a simple table specification but can form a complete join.

```
<from clause> ::=
    FROM <table reference> [ { , <table reference> }... ]

<table reference> ::=
    { <table specification> |
      <join specification>  }
    [ [ AS ] <pseudonym> ]

<join specification> ::=
    <table reference> <join type> <table reference>
       [ <join condition> ]

<join condition> ::=
     ON <condition> | USING <column list>

<join type> ::=
    [ INNER ] JOIN          |
    LEFT   [ OUTER ] JOIN |
    RIGHT [ OUTER ] JOIN |
    FULL   [ OUTER ] JOIN |
    UNION JOIN              |
    CROSS JOIN

<column list> ::=
    ( <column name> [ { , <column name> }... ] )
```

According to this definition, the following FROM clause is correct:

```
FROM      PLAYERS INNER JOIN PENALTIES
          ON (PLAYERS.PLAYERNO = PENALTIES.PLAYERNO)
```

In this example, PLAYERS and PENALTIES are the tables to be joined, and the join condition is placed between brackets after the word ON. The type of join that must be performed is the *inner join*. We next illustrate with an example the meaning of these specifications.

Example 7.15: For each player born after June 1920, find the player number, the name, and the penalty amounts incurred by him or her.

In the previous chapters, we showed that we can answer this question with the following formulation:

```
SELECT    PLAYERS.PLAYERNO, NAME, AMOUNT
FROM      PLAYERS, PENALTIES
WHERE     PLAYERS.PLAYERNO = PENALTIES.PLAYERNO
AND       BIRTH_DATE > '1920-06-30'
```

which has the result:

```
PLAYERNO  NAME       AMOUNT
--------  ---------  ------
       6  Parmenter  100.00
      44  Baker       75.00
      27  Collins    100.00
     104  Moorman     50.00
      44  Baker       25.00
       8  Newcastle   25.00
      44  Baker       30.00
      27  Collins     75.00
```

There is also a join "hidden" in this statement. The specifications that together form the join are spread out over the FROM and WHERE clauses. With the new definition of the FROM clause, this join can be presented explicitly, and for this, we use the FROM clause we have already given:

```
SELECT    PLAYERS.PLAYERNO, NAME, AMOUNT
FROM      PLAYERS INNER JOIN PENALTIES
          ON (PLAYERS.PLAYERNO = PENALTIES.PLAYERNO)
WHERE     BIRTH_DATE > '1920-06-30'
```

This statement leads to the same result as the previous one; the difference is that now, during the processing of the FROM clause, much more work is done. In the first formulation, the (intermediate) result of the FROM clause is equal to the *Cartesian product* of the two specified tables (see also Section 7.4, in Chapter 7, "SELECT Statement: The FROM Clause"). For the second formulation, the result is the Cartesian product to which the condition already has been applied. For the processing of the WHERE clause, less work has to be done.

Both statements return the same result, but do they satisfy our requirements? The answer is no! These SELECT statements return only the player number and the name of each player who has incurred at least one penalty. That brings us to the specification INNER JOIN. Because SQL is presenting only data about the players appearing in both the tables PLAYERS and PENALTIES, this join is called an *inner* join. Only those players who appear in the intersection of the sets of the two join columns are included in the end result.

Whether an inner join does or does not give what we want depends entirely, on one hand, on our question and, on the other hand, on the relationship between the join columns. In the previous example, we lose players (from the PLAYERS table) because the sets of the two join columns are not equal; one is a subset of the other. Had the question in the example above been 'For each player who incurred at least one penalty, find the player number . . .', the formulation of the statement would have been correct.

There always exists a certain type of relationship between join columns. 'Being a subset of' is just one possibility. There are four types of relationships possible. When a join is specified, it is very important to know what the type of relationship is because it has a serious influence on the result of the SELECT statement in which the join appears.

If C_1 and C_2 are two columns, the four types of relationships between C_1 and C_2 are as follows:

1. The population of C_1 and C_2 are *equal*.
2. The population of C_1 is a *subset* of that of C_2 (or C_2 is a subset of C_1).
3. The populations of C_1 and C_2 are *conjoint*; they have some values in common.
4. The populations of C_1 and C_2 are *disjoint*; they have no values in common.

If C_1 and C_2 are considered to be sets with values, the four relationships can be defined using set theory terminology as follows:

1. $C_1 = C_2$
2. $C_1 \subset C_2$ (or $C_2 \subset C_1$)
3. $C_1 - C_2 \neq \varnothing \wedge C_2 - C_1 \neq \varnothing$
4. $C_1 - C_2 = C_1 \wedge C_2 - C_1 = C_2$

Example 7.16: For each team, find the team number and the name of the captain. With the help of an implicit join:

```
SELECT   TEAMNO, NAME
FROM     TEAMS, PLAYERS
WHERE    TEAMS.PLAYERNO = PLAYERS.PLAYERNO
```

With an explicit join, the previous statement looks as follows:

```
SELECT   TEAMNO, NAME
FROM     TEAMS INNER JOIN PLAYERS
         ON TEAMS.PLAYERNO = PLAYERS.PLAYERNO
```

Explanation: It is obvious, again, that the TEAMS and PLAYERS tables are joined with an inner join. The join condition (after the word ON) is used to compare the PLAYERNO columns in the two tables. The result of these two statements is equal. Because the PLAYERNO column in the TEAMS table is a subset of that of the PLAYERS table, the result contains all those players who appear in the TEAMS table (which is in accordance with the question).

The word INNER in the join specification can be omitted. It has been added only to show which type of join will be executed. Therefore, the previous statement is equal to the next:

```
SELECT   TEAMNO, NAME
FROM     TEAMS JOIN PLAYERS
         ON TEAMS.PLAYERNO = PLAYERS.PLAYERNO
```

Multiple tables can be joined with one FROM clause. Imagine that T_1, T_2, T_3, and T_4 are tables, and C is a join condition to join two tables. Then, the following examples are all allowed:

- T_1 INNER JOIN T_2 ON C
- T_1 INNER JOIN T_2 ON C INNER JOIN T_3 ON C
- (T_1 INNER JOIN T_2 ON C) INNER JOIN T_3 ON C
- T_1 INNER JOIN (T_2 INNER JOIN T_3 ON C) ON C
- (T_1 INNER JOIN T_2 ON C) INNER JOIN (T_3 INNER JOIN T_4 ON C) ON C

Exercise 7.12: For each team, find the number and the name of the captain. In Exercise 7.5, an implicit join was used; use an explicit join now.

Exercise 7.13: Find the numbers and the names of the players who live in the same town as player 27. In Exercise 7.9 an implicit join was used; use an explicit join now.

Exercise 7.14: For each match, get the match number, the name of the player, and the division of the team. In Exercise 7.6, an implicit join was used; use an explicit join now.

7.9 Joins with USING

If the names of the join columns are equal, USING can also be used instead of the condition. Therefore, the following two FROM clauses are equal:

```
FROM      TEAMS INNER JOIN PLAYERS
          ON TEAMS.PLAYERNO = PLAYERS.PLAYERNO
```

and

```
FROM      TEAMS INNER JOIN PLAYERS
          USING (PLAYERNO)
```

The use of USING has no influence on the result and does not create any additional possibilities with respect to the other form. It has only two limited advantages. First, the statement is a little shorter and, therefore, easier to read. Second, when a join of two or more columns must be specified, the formulation becomes much more compact.

Portability: *USING is supported by most SQL products, but not all. For example, DB2 does not support it.*

7.10 Outer Joins

The only join type discussed so far has been the inner join. However, the additional advantages of this type are limited. It is helpful to indicate more explicitly that the statement performs a join, but it is not a huge improvement. For the other join types, such as *left outer join*, however, statements become considerably clearer, more powerful and shorter.

We discuss the left outer, the right outer, and the full outer join, respectively.

7.10.1 The Left Outer Join

We start with an example.

Example 7.17: For *all* the players, find the player number, the name, and the penalties incurred by him or her; order the result by player number.

To answer this question, many of us would use the following SELECT statement:

```
SELECT   PLAYERS.PLAYERNO, NAME, AMOUNT
FROM     PLAYERS, PENALTIES
WHERE    PLAYERS.PLAYERNO = PENALTIES.PLAYERNO
ORDER BY 1
```

The result is:

```
PLAYERNO   NAME        AMOUNT
--------   ---------   ------
       6   Parmenter   100.00
       8   Newcastle    25.00
      27   Collins     100.00
      27   Collins      70.00
      44   Baker        75.00
      44   Baker        25.00
      44   Baker        30.00
     104   Moorman      50.00
```

However, the result is incomplete because all players who have no penalties are missing.

The intention of this question is to get all the players in the result. To get the missing players in the result as well, a so-called *left outer join* must be specified:

```
SELECT   PLAYERS.PLAYERNO, NAME, AMOUNT
FROM     PLAYERS LEFT OUTER JOIN PENALTIES
         ON PLAYERS.PLAYERNO = PENALTIES.PLAYERNO
ORDER BY 1
```

and the result is:

```
PLAYERNO   NAME        AMOUNT
--------   ---------   ------
       2   Everett          ?
       6   Parmenter   100.00
       7   Wise             ?
       8   Newcastle    25.00
      27   Collins     100.00
      27   Collins      75.00
      28   Collins          ?
      39   Bishop           ?
      44   Baker        75.00
      44   Baker        25.00
      44   Baker        30.00
      57   Brown            ?
      83   Hope             ?
      95   Miller           ?
     100   Parmenter        ?
     104   Moorman      50.00
     112   Bailey           ?
```

Explanation: In the FROM clause, the join type is specified between the two tables—in this case, a *left outer join*. In addition, the join condition is specified after the word ON. When the join is specified in this way, SQL knows that *all* rows from the PLAYERS table *must* appear in the intermediate result of the FROM clause. The columns in the SELECT clause that belong to the PENALTIES table are filled automatically with NULL values for all those players for whom no penalty was paid.

Note that with all outer joins, the term OUTER can be omitted without any effect on the end result. Whether outer joins are necessary depends, as mentioned before, on the question and on the relationship between the join columns. Between the populations PLAYERS.PLAYERNO and PENALTIES.PLAYERNO, there is a subset relationship: The population of PENALTIES.PLAYERNO is a subset of the population PLAYERS.PLAYERNO. So, a left outer join is useful. The other way would make no sense; see the following example.

Example 7.18: For *each* penalty, get the payment number and the name of the player.

```
SELECT    PAYMENTNO, NAME
FROM      PENALTIES LEFT OUTER JOIN PLAYERS
          ON PENALTIES.PLAYERNO = PLAYERS.PLAYERNO
ORDER BY 1
```

The result is:

```
PAYMENTNO  NAME
---------  ---------
        1  Parmenter
        2  Baker
        3  Collins
        4  Moorman
        5  Baker
        6  Newcastle
        7  Baker
        8  Collins
```

Explanation: In this statement, PENALTIES is the left table. Because there are no penalties that do not belong to a specific player, no penalties are left out. In other words, a left outer join in this example is superfluous. An inner join would have returned the same result.

Example 7.19: Find, for *each* player, the player number, the name and numbers, and divisions of the teams that he or she captains; order the result by player number.

```
SELECT    P.PLAYERNO, NAME, TEAMNO, DIVISION
FROM      PLAYERS AS P LEFT OUTER JOIN TEAMS AS T
          ON P.PLAYERNO = T.PLAYERNO
ORDER BY P.PLAYERNO
```

The result is:

```
PLAYERNO   NAME       TEAMNO  DIVISION
--------   ---------  ------  --------
       2   Everett       ?    ?
       6   Parmenter     1    first
       7   Wise          ?    ?
       8   Newcastle     ?    ?
      27   Collins       2    second
      28   Collins       ?    ?
      39   Bishop        ?    ?
      44   Baker         ?    ?
      57   Brown         ?    ?
      83   Hope          ?    ?
      95   Miller        ?    ?
     100   Parmenter     ?    ?
     104   Moorman       ?    ?
     112   Bailey        ?    ?
```

Example 7.20: For each player born in Inglewood, find the player number, the name, the list of penalties, and the list of teams for which he or she has played a match.

```
SELECT   PLAYERS.PLAYERNO, NAME, AMOUNT, TEAMNO
FROM     PLAYERS LEFT OUTER JOIN PENALTIES
         ON PLAYERS.PLAYERNO = PENALTIES.PLAYERNO
            LEFT OUTER JOIN MATCHES
            ON PLAYERS.PLAYERNO = MATCHES.PLAYERNO
WHERE    TOWN = 'Inglewood'
```

The result is:

```
PLAYERNO   NAME       AMOUNT  TEAMNO
--------   ---------  ------  ------
       8   Newcastle   25.00     1
       8   Newcastle   25.00     2
      44   Baker       75.00     1
      44   Baker       25.00     1
      44   Baker       30.00     1
```

Explanation: First, the PLAYERS table is joined using a left outer join to the PENAL-TIES table. The result contains 17 rows consisting of two players from Inglewood: players 8 and 44. Player 8 has incurred only one penalty, and player 44 has three penalties. Then, the entire result is joined with the MATCHES table. Because player 8 played for two teams, he appears twice in the result.

Summarizing: A left outer join is useful only if there can exist values in the join column of the left table that do not appear in the join column of the right table.

7.10.2 The Right Outer Join

The right outer join is the mirror image of the left outer join. With the left outer join, it is guaranteed that all rows from the left table appear in the intermediate result of the FROM clause. With the right outer join, this guarantee is given for the right table.

Example 7.21: For *all* players, get the player number, the name, and the numbers of the teams for which they are the captain.

```
SELECT    PLAYERS.PLAYERNO, NAME, TEAMNO
FROM      TEAMS RIGHT OUTER JOIN PLAYERS
          ON TEAMS.PLAYERNO = PLAYERS.PLAYERNO
```

The result is:

PLAYERNO	NAME	TEAMNO
2	Everett	?
6	Parmenter	1
7	Wise	?
8	Newcastle	?
27	Collins	2
28	Collins	?
39	Bishop	?
44	Baker	?
57	Brown	?
83	Hope	?
95	Miller	?
100	Parmenter	?
104	Moorman	?
112	Bailey	?2

Explanation: It is obvious that players such as 2, 7, and 8 have been included in the result even though they are not captains. If a player was captain of two teams, he would appear twice in this result.

7.10.3 The Full Outer Join

What happens when we join two columns that are conjoint regarding their populations? Or in other words, both columns have values that possibly do not appear in the other column. If we want all the values from both columns to appear in the end result, a full outer join is required.

Portability: *MySQL does not support the full outer join. However, because many other products do support full outer joins, we discuss it.*

Example 7.22: Get the result of the full outer join of the MATCHES table with the COMMITTEE_MEMBERS table.

```
SELECT    DISTINCT MATCHES.MATCHNO,
          MATCHES.PLAYERNO AS MATCH_PNO,
          COMMITTEE_MEMBERS.PLAYERNO AS COMMITTEE_PNO
FROM      MATCHES FULL OUTER JOIN COMMITTEE_MEMBERS
          ON MATCHES.PLAYERNO = COMMITTEE_MEMBERS.PLAYERNO
ORDER BY 1, 2, 3
```

The result is:

MATCHNO	MATCH_PNO	COMMITTEE_PNO
1	6	6
2	6	6
3	6	6
4	44	?
5	83	?
6	2	2
7	57	57
8	8	8
9	27	27
10	104	?
11	112	112
12	112	112
13	8	8
?	?	95

Explanation: Rows from both tables appear in the result that, without the full outer join, would not have appeared. The last row in the result has been added because there is a row in the COMMITTEE_MEMBERS table for player 95, and this player does not appear in the MATCHES table. Additionally, the matches with numbers 4, 5, and 10 have been added. The two join columns are really conjoint sets.

You could state that the result of a full outer join (if no duplicate rows appear in the result) is equal to the UNION of the left and right outer joins of the same tables.

Exercise 7.15: Get for all players the player number and the list with penalties incurred by them.

Exercise 7.16: Get for all players the player number and a list with numbers of teams for which they have ever played.

Exercise 7.17: Get for all players the player number, the list with penalties incurred by them, and the list with numbers of team for which they have ever played.

Exercise 7.18: Which of the following FROM clauses would be useful, and which would not?

1.

```
FROM    PENALTIES AS PEN LEFT OUTER JOIN PLAYERS AS P
        ON PEN.PLAYERNO = P.PLAYERNO
```

2.

```
FROM    PENALTIES AS PEN LEFT OUTER JOIN PLAYERS AS P
        ON PEN.PLAYERNO > P.PLAYERNO
```

3.

```
FROM    TEAMS AS T RIGHT OUTER JOIN MATCHES AS M
        ON T.TEAMNO = M.TEAMNO
```

4.

```
FROM    PENALTIES AS PEN FULL OUTER JOIN TEAMS AS T
        ON PEN.PLAYERNO = T.PLAYERNO
```

Exercise 7.19: Determine the results of the following SELECT statements given the tables T1, T2, T3, and T4. Each of these tables has only one column.

```
T1  C          T2  C          T3  C          T4  C
-----          -----          -----          -----
    1              2              ?              ?
    2              3              2              2
    3              4                             3
```

1.

```
SELECT    T1.C, T2.C
FROM      T1 INNER JOIN T2 ON T1.C = T2.C
```

2.

```
SELECT    T1.C, T2.C
FROM      T1 LEFT OUTER JOIN T2 ON T1.C = T2.C
```

3.

```
SELECT    T1.C, T2.C
FROM      T1 RIGHT OUTER JOIN T2 ON T1.C = T2.C
```

4.

```
SELECT    T1.C, T2.C
FROM      T1 RIGHT OUTER JOIN T2 ON T1.C > T2.C
```

5.

```
SELECT    T1.C, T3.C
FROM      T1 RIGHT OUTER JOIN T3 ON T1.C = T3.C
```

6.

```
SELECT    T1.C, T3.C
FROM      T1 LEFT OUTER JOIN T3 ON T1.C = T3.C
```

7.

```
SELECT    T3.C, T4.C
FROM      T3 LEFT OUTER JOIN T4 ON T3.C = T4.C
```

8.

```
SELECT    T3.C, T4.C
FROM      T3 RIGHT OUTER JOIN T4 ON T3.C = T4.C
```

9.

```
SELECT    T1.C, T2.C
FROM      T1 FULL OUTER JOIN T2 ON T1.C = T2.C
```

10.

```
SELECT    T1.C, T2.C, T3.C
FROM      (T1 LEFT OUTER JOIN T3 ON T1.C = T3.C)
          FULL OUTER JOIN T2 ON T3.C = T2.C
```

Exercise 7.20: Which of the following statements are correct? Assume that the column C_1 belongs to the table T_1, and the column C_2 to T_2.

1.   If C_1 is a subset of C_2, the result of $T_1.C_1$ left outer join $T_2.C_2$ is equal to an inner join of the same columns.

2.   If C_2 is a subset of C_1, the result of $T_1.C_1$ left outer join $T_2.C_2$ is equal to an inner join of the same columns.

3.   The result of $T_1.C_1$ left outer join $T_1.C_1$ is equal to an inner join of the same columns.

4.   If the populations of C_1 and C_2 are equal, the result of $T_1.C_1$ full outer join $T_2.C_2$ is equal to an inner join of the same columns.

5.   If the populations of C_1 and C_2 are conjoint, the result of $T_1.C_1$ left outer join $T_2.C_2$ is equal to a full outer join of the same columns.

7.11 Additional Conditions in the Join Condition

The condition in the FROM clause is primarily meant to be used to join tables. Other conditions that do not actually belong to the join are allowed to be included here. However, you should realize that moving a condition from the WHERE clause to the join condition can actually affect the result. The following statement shows that distinction.

Example 7.23: The next SELECT statement contains a left outer join plus an additional condition in the WHERE clause.

```
SELECT    TEAMS.PLAYERNO, TEAMS.TEAMNO, PENALTIES.PAYMENTNO
FROM      TEAMS LEFT OUTER JOIN PENALTIES
          ON TEAMS.PLAYERNO = PENALTIES.PLAYERNO
WHERE     DIVISION = 'second'
```

The result is:

PLAYERNO	TEAMNO	PAYMENTNO
27	2	3
27	2	8

Explanation: The intermediate result of the FROM clause contains all the rows of the TEAMS table of which the captain appears in the PENALTIES table. If teams disappear from this join, they are brought back again because of the left outer join. In other words, that intermediate result looks as follows (on the left are the columns of the TEAMS table, and on the right those of the PENALTIES):

TEAMNO	PLAYERNO	DIVISION	PAYNO	PLAYERNO	PAYMENT_DATE	AMOUNT
1	6	first	1	6	1980-12-08	100.00
2	27	second	3	27	1983-09-10	100.00
2	27	second	8	27	1984-11-12	75.00

Next, the WHERE clause is processed, and that means that only the last two rows are passed on to the SELECT clause.

If we move the condition to the join condition, the following statement arises:

```
SELECT    TEAMS.PLAYERNO, TEAMS.TEAMNO, PENALTIES.PAYMENTNO
FROM      TEAMS LEFT OUTER JOIN PENALTIES
          ON TEAMS.PLAYERNO = PENALTIES.PLAYERNO
          AND DIVISION = 'second'
```

This statement has a result that differs from the previous statement:

PLAYERNO	TEAMNO	PAYMENTNO
6	1	?
27	2	3
27	2	8

Now, team 1 does appear in the result, but how did that happen? SQL processes the explicit join in two steps. During the first step, the join is processed as if no outer join has to be executed, but an inner join does. So, first a Cartesian product is created, and subsequently all conditions are processed, including the condition on the DIVISION column. This leads to the following result:

TEAMNO	PLAYERNO	DIVISION	PAYNO	PLAYERNO	PAYMENT_DATE	AMOUNT
2	27	second	3	27	1983-09-10	100.00
2	27	second	8	27	1984-11-12	75.00

Team 1 does not appear in this intermediate result because it does not play in the second division. During the second step, SQL checks whether rows from the TEAMS table (because that is the table on the left of the left outer join) have disappeared from this intermediate result. Those rows have to be brought back again. As a result, team 1 will be added again:

TEAMNO	PLAYERNO	DIVISION	PAYNO	PLAYERNO	PAYMENT_DATE	AMOUNT
2	27	second	3	27	1983-09-10	100.00
2	27	second	8	27	1984-11-12	75.00
1	6	first	?	?	?	?

Because of the absence of a WHERE clause, all these rows are passed on to the SELECT clause, which means that the end result will differ from that of the first statement.

Example 7.24: The next SELECT statement contains a full outer join plus an additional condition in the WHERE clause.

```
SELECT    TEAMS.PLAYERNO, TEAMS.TEAMNO, PENALTIES.PAYMENTNO
FROM      TEAMS FULL OUTER JOIN PENALTIES
          ON TEAMS.PLAYERNO = PENALTIES.PLAYERNO
          AND TEAMS.PLAYERNO > 1000
```

The result is:

PLAYERNO	TEAMNO	PAYMENTNO
?	?	3
?	?	8
?	?	1
?	?	6

?	?	2
?	?	5
?	?	7
?	?	4
6	1	?
27	2	?

Explanation: After step 1 of the join has been processed, the intermediate result is empty. The reason is that there are no player numbers greater than 1000. Then, during step 2, SQL checks whether there are rows in the tables TEAMS and PENALTIES that do not appear in the result. That involves all the teams and all the penalties, so they are added again and a somewhat strange end result occurs.

Conclusion: If an outer join is used, it absolutely matters where certain conditions are placed: in the join condition or in the WHERE clause. Therefore, consider carefully where you want to place them. This does not apply to the inner join; work out why for yourself.

7.12 The Cross Join

This section discusses the *cross join*. We deal with this topic just briefly because the practical value of this join is restricted and these operators suffer heavily from criticism; see, among others, [DATE97].

With the cross join, we can explicitly ask for a Cartesian product of tables. Usually, we create a Cartesian product as follows:

```
SELECT    TEAMS.*, PENALTIES.*
FROM      TEAMS, PENALTIES
```

This statement couples each row from the TEAMS table with all rows from the PENALTIES table. The following statement, in which we use the cross join, generates the same result:

```
SELECT    *
FROM      TEAMS CROSS JOIN PENALTIES
```

Of course, it is not necessary to include a join condition with the cross join. If we used one, it would not result in a Cartesian product. Therefore, specifying that condition as part of the join is not permitted. However, you can include the condition in a WHERE clause.

Portability: *Not all products support the cross join. MySQL is one that does.*

7.13 The Union Join and the Natural Join

Two join types have been implemented by just a few SQL products: the union and the natural join. However, for the sake of completeness, we discuss them briefly.

Portability: *The union and the natural join are supported by just a few SQL products. MySQL does not support them, either.*

The *union join* is difficult to explain. We try to do this on the basis of an example.

Example 7.25: Get the union join of the TEAMS and the PENALTIES table.

```
SELECT    *
FROM      TEAMS UNION JOIN PENALTIES
```

The result is:

TEAMNO	PLAYERNO	DIVISION	PAYMENTNO	PLAYERNO	PAYMENT_DATE	AMOUNT
1	6	first	?	?	?	?
2	27	second	?	?	?	?
?	?	?	1	6	1980-12-08	100.00
?	?	?	2	44	1981-05-05	75.00
?	?	?	3	27	1983-09-10	100.00
?	?	?	4	104	1984-12-08	50.00
?	?	?	5	44	1980-12-08	25.00
?	?	?	6	8	1980-12-08	25.00
?	?	?	7	44	1982-12-30	30.00
?	?	?	8	27	1984-11-12	75.00

You can see that the TEAMS table is at the top left of the result and the PENALTIES table is at the bottom right. Each row from the TEAMS table occurs only once in the result, which also applies to each row of the PENALTIES table. This result contains all rows that form the difference between a full outer join and an inner join of the same two tables.

In the relational model, the concept of *natural join* has been defined. It has also been included in the SQL2 standard. Here is a statement as an example:

```
SELECT    T.PLAYERNO, T.TEAMNO, T.DIVISION,
          PEN.PAYMENTNO, PEN.PAYMENT_DATE, PEN.AMOUNT
FROM      TEAMS AS T INNER JOIN PENALTIES AS PEN
          ON T.PLAYERNO = PEN.PLAYERNO
WHERE     DIVISION = 'first'
```

The previous statement can have been formulated with a natural join, as follows:

```
SELECT    *
FROM      TEAMS NATURAL INNER JOIN PENALTIES
WHERE     DIVISION = 'first'
```

In this example, we do not have to indicate explicitly which columns must be joined. SQL examines whether the two tables have columns with identical names and assumes that those must be used in the join condition. Also, only one join column is included in the join condition. An ON or USING clause would be superfluous here and, therefore, is not allowed. For each join type (except for the cross join), NATURAL can be specified.

7.14   Equi Joins and Theta Joins

The concepts *equi* and *theta join* are frequently mentioned in the relational model. However, we have not yet seen these concepts applied in SQL; indeed, this is not likely to happen. However, if in the join condition the equal to operator is used, we refer to it as an equi join. So, the following table expressions contain an equi join:

```
SELECT    *
FROM      PLAYERS, TEAMS
WHERE     PLAYERS.PLAYERNO = TEAMS.PLAYERNO
```

and

```
SELECT    *
FROM      PLAYERS LEFT OUTER JOIN TEAMS
          ON PLAYERS.PLAYERNO = TEAMS.PLAYERNO
```

If we simply refer to a join in this book, we imply an equi join. Other joins also exist, such as the *greater than join* (see the example below) and the *less than join*. The term that is used for joins when the join condition does not contain the equal to operator is *non-equi join*.

```
SELECT    *
FROM      PLAYERS, TEAMS
WHERE     PLAYERS.PLAYERNO > TEAMS.PLAYERNO
```

The general join, or *theta join*, takes the following form in SQL; the question mark stands for any comparison operator:

```
SELECT    *
FROM      PLAYERS, TEAMS
WHERE     PLAYERS.PLAYERNO ? TEAMS.PLAYERNO
```

All equi and non-equi joins together form the set of theta joins.

For the sake of clarity, we note the following: The indication equi or non-equi is unrelated to whether a join is an inner, left outer, or full outer join. We can speak of an equi left outer join, an non-equi full outer join, or a greater than inner join.

7.15 The FROM Clause with Table Expressions

In Section 6.6, in Chapter 6, "SELECT Statements, Table Expressions, and Subqueries," we mentioned that the FROM clause itself can contain a table expression. The table expression within the FROM clause is called a table subquery. In this section, we extend the definition of the FROM clause with that table subquery. Next, we present various examples to illustrate the extensive possibilities of table subqueries.

```
<from clause> ::=
    FROM <table reference> [ { , <table reference> }... ]

<table reference> ::=
    { <table specification> |
      <join specification> |
      <table subquery>      }
    [ [ AS ] <pseudonym> ]

<table subquery> ::= ( <table expression> )
```

Example 7.26: Get the numbers of the players resident in Stratford.

```
SELECT    PLAYERNO
FROM      (SELECT    *
          FROM       PLAYERS
          WHERE      TOWN = 'Stratford') AS STRATFORDERS
```

Explanation: A table expression in the form of a table subquery is specified in the FROM clause. This subquery returns all the column values of all players from Stratford. The resulting table is named STRATFORDERS and is passed to the other clauses. The other clauses cannot see that the table, which they receive as input, has been generated with a subquery. This statement could have been formulated in the classical way, but we have used this formulation just to start with a simple example.

Example 7.27: Get the number of each player who is captain of a team playing in the first division.

```
SELECT    SMALL_TEAMS.PLAYERNO
FROM      (SELECT    PLAYERNO, DIVISION
          FROM       TEAMS) AS SMALL_TEAMS
WHERE     SMALL_TEAMS.DIVISION = 'first'
```

The result is:

```
SMALL_TEAMS.PLAYERNO
--------------------
```

6

Explanation: With the table expression in the FROM clause, the following intermediate result is created:

```
PLAYERNO  DIVISION
--------  --------
       6  first
      27  second
```

This intermediate table gets the name SMALL_TEAMS. Next, the condition SMALL_TEAMS.DIVISION = 'first' is executed on this table, after which only the PLAYERNO column is retrieved.

Table expressions can be used, for example, to prevent a repeat of complex scalar expressions.

Example 7.28: Get the match number and the difference between the total number of sets won and the total number of sets lost for each match where that difference is greater than 2.

```
SELECT    MATCHNO, DIFFERENCE
FROM      (SELECT    MATCHNO,
                     ABS(WON - LOST) AS DIFFERENCE
           FROM      MATCHES) AS M
WHERE     DIFFERENCE > 2
```

The result is:

```
MATCHNO  DIFFERENCE
-------  ----------
      3           3
      5           3
      7           3
      8           3
     13           3
```

Explanation: The subquery in the FROM clause returns for each match the match number and the difference between the WON and LOST column. In the main query, a condition is executed on this difference. To refer to that calculation in the main query, a column name has to be introduced in the subquery. For the first time, we have an example in which the specification of a column name is of more use than just to improve the readability of the result.

A special variant of the table expression is the one in which only the SELECT clause is used. This variant can also be used as table subquery.

Example 7.29: Create a virtual table called TOWNS.

```
SELECT   *
FROM     (SELECT 'Stratford' AS TOWN, 4 AS NUMBER
          UNION
          SELECT 'Plymouth', 6
          UNION
          SELECT 'Inglewood', 1
          UNION
          SELECT 'Douglas', 2) AS TOWNS
ORDER BY TOWN
```

The result is:

```
TOWN        NUMBER
---------   ------
Douglas        2
Inglewood      1
Plymouth       6
Stratford      4
```

Explanation: In this FROM clause, a table is created consisting of two columns (the first an alphanumeric one and the second a numeric one) and four rows. This table is named TOWNS. The first column has the name TOWN and contains the name of a town. The second is named NUMBER and contains a relative indication of the number of residents in that city. Note that an end result is created here without so much as querying one of the existing tables.

The table that is created as a result is a normal table to all the other clauses. For example, a WHERE clause does not know whether the intermediate result from the FROM clause is the contents of a "real" table, a subquery, a view, or temporarily created table. So, we can use all the other operations on this temporarily created table.

Example 7.30: Find for each player the number, the name, the town, and the number of residents living in that town.

```
SELECT    PLAYERNO, NAME, PLAYERS.TOWN, NUMBER * 1000
FROM      PLAYERS,
          (SELECT 'Stratford' AS TOWN, 4 AS NUMBER
          UNION
          SELECT 'Plymouth', 6
          UNION
          SELECT 'Inglewood', 1
          UNION
          SELECT 'Douglas', 2) AS TOWNS
WHERE     PLAYERS.TOWN = TOWNS.TOWN
ORDER BY 1
```

The result is:

```
PLAYERNO   NAME        TOWN         NUMBER
--------   ---------   ---------    ------
       2   Everett     Stratford    4000
       6   Parmenter   Stratford    4000
       7   Wise        Stratford    4000
       8   Newcastle   Inglewood    1000
      39   Bishop      Stratford    4000
      44   Baker       Inglewood    1000
      57   Brown       Stratford    4000
      83   Hope        Stratford    4000
      95   Miller      Douglas      2000
     100   Parmenter   Stratford    4000
     112   Bailey      Plymouth     6000
```

Explanation: The PLAYERS table is joined with the TOWNS table. Because an inner join is used, we lose all the players who live in towns that do not appear in the TOWNS table. The next table expression makes sure that we do not lose players from the result:

```
SELECT    PLAYERNO, NAME, PLAYERS.TOWN, NUMBER
FROM      PLAYERS LEFT OUTER JOIN
          (SELECT 'Stratford' AS TOWN, 4 AS NUMBER
          UNION
          SELECT 'Plymouth', 6
          UNION
          SELECT 'Inglewood', 1
          UNION
          SELECT 'Douglas', 2) AS TOWNS
          ON PLAYERS.TOWN = TOWNS.TOWN
ORDER BY 1
```

Example 7.31: Find the numbers of the players who live in a town with a population indicator greater than 2.

```
SELECT    PLAYERNO
FROM      PLAYERS LEFT OUTER JOIN
          (SELECT 'Stratford' AS TOWN, 4 AS NUMBER
          UNION
          SELECT 'Plymouth', 6
          UNION
          SELECT 'Inglewood', 1
          UNION
          SELECT 'Douglas', 2) AS TOWNS
          ON PLAYERS.TOWN = TOWNS.TOWN
WHERE     TOWNS.NUMBER > 2
```

The result is:

```
PLAYERNO
--------
       2
       6
       7
      39
      57
      83
     100
     112
```

Example 7.32: Get all combinations possible of the first names John, Mark, and Arnold, and the last names Berg, Johnson, and Williams.

```
SELECT    *
FROM      (SELECT 'John' AS FIRST_NAME
           UNION
           SELECT 'Mark'
           UNION
           SELECT 'Arnold') AS FIRST_NAMES,
          (SELECT 'Berg' AS LAST_NAME
           UNION
           SELECT 'Johnson'
           UNION
           SELECT 'Williams') AS LAST_NAMES
```

The result is:

FIRST_NAME	LAST_NAME
John	Berg
Mark	Berg
Arnold	Berg
John	Johnson
Mark	Johnson
Arnold	Johnson
John	Williams
Mark	Williams
Arnold	Williams

Example 7.33: For the numbers 10 to 19, find the value to the power of three. However, if the result is greater than 4,000, it should not be included in the result.

```
SELECT    NUMBER, POWER(NUMBER,3)
FROM      (SELECT 10 NUMBER UNION SELECT 11 UNION SELECT 12
           UNION
           SELECT 13 UNION SELECT 14 UNION SELECT 15
           UNION
           SELECT 16 UNION SELECT 17 UNION SELECT 18
           UNION
           SELECT 19) AS NUMBERS
WHERE     POWER(NUMBER,3) <= 4000
```

The result is:

```
NUMBER   POWER (NUMBER)
------   -------------
    10            1000
    11            1331
    12            1728
    13            2197
    14            2744
    15            3375
```

This statement works well if the numbers are limited. When we want to do the same with a hundred or more numbers, the statement would not be as simple. In that case, we could try to avoid the problem by generating a long list of numbers in a more creative way.

Example 7.34: Generate the numbers 0 up to and including 999.

```
SELECT   NUMBER
FROM     (SELECT    CAST(CONCAT(DIGIT1.DIGIT,
                    CONCAT(DIGIT2.DIGIT,
                    DIGIT3.DIGIT)) AS UNSIGNED INTEGER)
                    AS NUMBER
         FROM       (SELECT '0' DIGIT UNION SELECT '1' UNION
                    SELECT '2' UNION SELECT '3' UNION
                    SELECT '4' UNION SELECT '5' UNION
                    SELECT '6' UNION SELECT '7' UNION
                    SELECT '8' UNION SELECT '9') AS DIGIT1,
                    (SELECT '0' DIGIT UNION SELECT '1' UNION
                    SELECT '2' UNION SELECT '3' UNION
                    SELECT '4' UNION SELECT '5' UNION
                    SELECT '6' UNION SELECT '7' UNION
                    SELECT '8' UNION SELECT '9') AS DIGIT2,
                    (SELECT '0' DIGIT UNION SELECT '1' UNION
                    SELECT '2' UNION SELECT '3' UNION
                    SELECT '4' UNION SELECT '5' UNION
                    SELECT '6' UNION SELECT '7' UNION
                    SELECT '8' UNION SELECT '9') AS DIGIT3)
                    AS NUMBERS
ORDER BY 1
```

The result is:

```
NUMBER
------
     0
     1
     2
     :
   998
   999
```

Example 7.35: Find the squares of whole numbers between 0 and 999.

```
SELECT    NUMBER AS SQUARE, ROUND(SQRT(NUMBER)) AS BASIS
FROM      (SELECT   CAST(CONCAT(DIGIT1.DIGIT,
                    CONCAT(DIGIT2.DIGIT,
                    DIGIT3.DIGIT)) AS UNSIGNED INTEGER)
                    AS NUMBER
          FROM      (SELECT '0' DIGIT UNION SELECT '1' UNION
                    SELECT '2' UNION SELECT '3' UNION
                    SELECT '4' UNION SELECT '5' UNION
                    SELECT '6' UNION SELECT '7' UNION
                    SELECT '8' UNION SELECT '9') AS DIGIT1,
                    (SELECT '0' DIGIT UNION SELECT '1' UNION
                    SELECT '2' UNION SELECT '3' UNION
                    SELECT '4' UNION SELECT '5' UNION
                    SELECT '6' UNION SELECT '7' UNION
                    SELECT '8' UNION SELECT '9') AS DIGIT2,
                    (SELECT '0' DIGIT UNION SELECT '1' UNION
                    SELECT '2' UNION SELECT '3' UNION
                    SELECT '4' UNION SELECT '5' UNION
                    SELECT '6' UNION SELECT '7' UNION
                    SELECT '8' UNION SELECT '9') AS DIGIT3)
                    AS NUMBERS
WHERE     SQRT(NUMBER) = ROUND(SQRT(NUMBER))
ORDER BY 1
```

The result is:

```
SQUARE  BASIS
------  -----
     0      0
     1      1
     4      2
     :      :
   900     30
   961     31
```

Exercise 7.21: For each player, get the difference between the year they joined the club and the year in which they were born, but return only those players of which that difference is greater than 20.

Exercise 7.22: Get a list of all combinations of three letters that you can make with the letters a, b, c, and d.

Exercise 7.23: Find 10 random integer numbers between 0 and 1000.

7.16 Answers

7.1   Both tables have a column called PLAYERNO.

The SELECT clause refers to the PLAYERS table even though it is not specified in the FROM clause.

7.2   The question: "Get the name of each player who is captain of a team."

The FROM clause:

```
TEAMNO  PLAYERNO  DIVISION  PLAYERNO  NAME        ...
------  --------  --------  --------  ---------   ---
     1         6  first            6  Parmenter   ...
     1         6  first           44  Baker       ...
     1         6  first           83  Hope        ...
     1         6  first            2  Everett     ...
     1         6  first           27  Collins     ...
     1         6  first          104  Moorman     ...
     1         6  first            7  Wise        ...
```

```
1       6  first        57  Brown       ...
1       6  first        39  Bishop      ...
1       6  first       112  Bailey      ...
1       6  first         8  Newcastle   ...
1       6  first       100  Parmenter   ...
1       6  first        28  Collins     ...
1       6  first        95  Miller      ...
2      27  second        6  Parmenter   ...
2      27  second       44  Baker       ...
2      27  second       83  Hope        ...
2      27  second        2  Everett     ...
2      27  second       27  Collins     ...
2      27  second      104  Moorman     ...
2      27  second        7  Wise        ...
2      27  second       57  Brown       ...
2      27  second       39  Bishop      ...
2      27  second      112  Bailey      ...
2      27  second        8  Newcastle   ...
2      27  second      100  Parmenter   ...
2      27  second       28  Collins     ...
2      27  second       95  Miller      ...
```

The WHERE clause:

TEAMNO	PLAYERNO	DIVISION	PLAYERNO	NAME	...
1	6	first	6	Parmenter	...
2	27	second	27	Collins	...

The SELECT clause and also the end result:

```
NAME
---------
Parmenter
Collins
```

7.3

```
SELECT    PAYMENTNO, AMOUNT, PLAYERS.PLAYERNO, NAME
FROM      PENALTIES, PLAYERS
WHERE     PENALTIES.PLAYERNO = PLAYERS.PLAYERNO
```

7.4

```
SELECT    PAYMENTNO, NAME
FROM      PENALTIES, PLAYERS, TEAMS
WHERE     PENALTIES.PLAYERNO = TEAMS.PLAYERNO
AND       TEAMS.PLAYERNO = PLAYERS.PLAYERNO
```

7.5

```
SELECT    T.TEAMNO, P.NAME
FROM      TEAMS AS T, PLAYERS AS P
WHERE     T.PLAYERNO = P.PLAYERNO
```

7.6

```
SELECT    M.MATCHNO, P.NAME, T.DIVISION
FROM      MATCHES AS M, PLAYERS AS P, TEAMS AS T
WHERE     M.PLAYERNO = P.PLAYERNO
AND       M.TEAMNO = T.TEAMNO
```

7.7

```
SELECT    P.PLAYERNO, P.NAME
FROM      PLAYERS AS P, COMMITTEE_MEMBERS AS C
WHERE     P.PLAYERNO = C.PLAYERNO
AND       B.POSITION = 'Chairman'
```

7.8

```
SELECT    DISTINCT CM.PLAYERNO
FROM      COMMITTEE_MEMBERS AS CM, PENALTIES AS PEN
WHERE     CM.PLAYERNO = PEN.PLAYERNO
AND       CM.BEGIN_DATE = PEN.PAYMENT_DATE
```

7.9

```
SELECT    P.PLAYERNO, P.NAME
FROM      PLAYERS AS P, PLAYERS AS P27
WHERE     P.TOWN = P27.TOWN
AND       P27.PLAYERNO = 27
AND       P.PLAYERNO <> 27
```

7.10

```
SELECT    DISTINCT P.PLAYERNO AS PLAYER_PLAYERNO,
          P.NAME AS PLAYER_NAME,
          CAP.PLAYERNO AS CAPTAIN_PLAYERNO,
          CAP.NAME AS CAPTAIN_NAME
FROM      PLAYERS AS P, PLAYERS AS CAP,
          MATCHES AS M, TEAMS AS T
WHERE     M.PLAYERNO = P.PLAYERNO
AND       T.TEAMNO = M.TEAMNO
AND       M.PLAYERNO <> T.PLAYERNO
AND       CAP.PLAYERNO = T.PLAYERNO
```

7.11

```
SELECT    PEN1.PAYMENTNO, PEN1.PLAYERNO
FROM      PENALTIES AS PEN1, PENALTIES AS PEN2
WHERE     PEN1.AMOUNT = PEN2.AMOUNT
AND       PEN2.PLAYERNO = 44
AND       PEN1.PLAYERNO <> 44
```

7.12

```
SELECT    T.TEAMNO, P.NAME
FROM      TEAMS AS T INNER JOIN PLAYERS AS P
          ON T.PLAYERNO = P.PLAYERNO
```

7.13

```
SELECT    P.PLAYERNO, P.NAME
FROM      PLAYERS AS P INNER JOIN PLAYERS AS P27
          ON P.TOWN = P27.TOWN
AND       P27.PLAYERNO = 27
AND       P.PLAYERNO <> 27
```

7.14

```
SELECT    M.MATCHNO, P.NAME, T.DIVISION
FROM      (MATCHES AS M INNER JOIN PLAYERS AS P
          ON M.PLAYERNO = P.PLAYERNO)
          INNER JOIN TEAMS AS T
          ON M.TEAMNO = T.TEAMNO
```

7.15

```
SELECT    PLAYERS.PLAYERNO, PENALTIES.AMOUNT
FROM      PLAYERS LEFT OUTER JOIN PENALTIES
          ON PLAYERS.PLAYERNO = PENALTIES.PLAYERNO
```

7.16

```
SELECT    P.PLAYERNO, M.TEAMNO
FROM      PLAYERS AS P LEFT OUTER JOIN MATCHES AS M
          ON P.PLAYERNO = M.PLAYERNO
```

7.17

```
SELECT    P.PLAYERNO, M.TEAMNO
FROM      (PLAYERS AS P LEFT OUTER JOIN MATCHES AS M
          ON P.PLAYERNO = M.PLAYERNO)
          LEFT OUTER JOIN PENALTIES AS PEN
          ON P.PLAYERNO = PEN.PLAYERNO
```

7.18   **1.** The left outer join indicates that all rows that possibly disappear from the left table (the PENALTIES table) still have to be included in the end result. But there are no rows in the PENALTIES table of which the player number does not appear in the PLAYERS table. So, the outer join in this FROM clause has no use; an inner join would return the same result.

2. The left outer join indicates that all rows that possibly disappear from the left table (the PENALTIES table) still have to be included in the end result. In this example, rows could disappear because a greater than operator is used in the join condition. Therefore, this FROM clause serves a purpose.

3. The right outer join indicates that all rows that possibly disappear from the right table (the MATCHES table) still have to be included in the end result. But there are no rows in the MATCHES table of which the team number does not appear in the TEAMS table. So, this FROM clause has no use; an inner join would give a similar result.

4. The full outer join indicates that all rows that possibly disappear from the left table (the PENALTIES table) and the right table (the TEAM table) still have to be included in the end result. In this situation, it is indeed possible. So, this FROM clause is useful.

7.19

1.

```
T1.C   T2.C
----   ----
   2      3
   2      3
```

2.

```
T1.C   T2.C
----   ----
   1      ?
   2      2
   3      3
```

3.

T1.C	T2.C
2	2
3	3
?	4

4.

T1.C	T2.C
3	2
?	3
?	4

5.

T1.C	T3.C
2	2
?	?

6.

T1.C	T3.C
1	?
2	2
3	?

7.

T3.C	T4.C
?	?
2	2

8.

```
T3.C  T4.C
----  ----
  ?     ?
  2     2
  ?     3
```

9.

```
T1.C  T2.C
----  ----
  1     ?
  2     2
  3     3
  ?     4
```

10.

```
T1.C  T2.C  T3.C
----  ----  ----
  1     ?     ?
  2     2     2
  3     ?     ?
  ?     3     ?
  ?     4     ?
```

7.20 Correct.

Incorrect.

Correct.

Correct.

Incorrect.

7.21

```
SELECT    PLAYERNO, DIFFERENCE
FROM      (SELECT    PLAYERNO,
                     JOINED - YEAR(BIRTH_DATE) AS DIFFERENCE
           FROM      PLAYERS) AS DIFFERENCES
WHERE     DIFFERENCE > 20
```

7.22

```
SELECT    LETTER1 || LETTER2 || LETTER3
FROM      (SELECT 'a' AS LETTER1 UNION SELECT 'b'
           UNION SELECT 'c' UNION SELECT 'd') AS LETTERS2,
          (SELECT 'a' AS LETTER3 UNION SELECT 'b'
           UNION SELECT 'c' UNION SELECT 'd') AS LETTERS3
```

7.23

```
SELECT    ROUND(RAND() * 1000)
FROM      (SELECT 0 NUMBER UNION SELECT 1 UNION SELECT 2
           UNION
           SELECT 3 UNION SELECT 4 UNION SELECT 5
           UNION
           SELECT 6 UNION SELECT 7 UNION SELECT 8
           UNION
           SELECT 9) AS NUMBERS
```

8

SELECT Statement:
The WHERE Clause

8.1 Introduction

In the WHERE clause, a condition is used to select rows from the intermediate result of the FROM clause. These selected rows form the intermediate result of the WHERE clause. The WHERE clause acts as a kind of filter. In this chapter, we describe the different conditions permitted in this clause.

How is a WHERE clause processed? One by one, each row that appears in the intermediate result table of a FROM clause is evaluated, and the value of the condition is determined. That value can be true, false, or unknown. A row is included in the (intermediate) result of the WHERE clause only if the condition is true. If the condition is false or unknown, the row is kept out of the result. This process can be formally described in the following way:

```
WHERE-RESULT := [];
FOR EACH R IN FROM-RESULT DO
    IF CONDITION = TRUE THEN
        WHERE-RESULT :+ R;
ENDFOR;
```

Explanation: The WHERE-RESULT and FROM-RESULT represent two sets in which rows of data can be temporarily stored. R represents a row from a set. The symbol [] represents the empty set. A row is added to the set with the operator :+. This pseudo programming language is used later in the book.

The definition of the term *condition* is shown next. In this book, we consider the terms *condition* and *predicate* as equivalents and use them interchangeably.

```
<condition> ::=
    <predicate>                          |
    <predicate> OR <predicate>           |
    <predicate> AND <predicate>          |
    ( <condition> )                      |
    NOT <condition>

<predicate> ::=
    <predicate with comparison>  |
    <predicate with in>          |
    <predicate with between>     |
    <predicate with like>        |
    <predicate with null>        |
    <predicate with exists>      |
    <predicate with any all>
```

In the previous chapters, we gave some examples of possible conditions in the WHERE clause. In this chapter, the following forms are described:

- The comparison operators
- The comparison operators with subquery
- Conditions coupled with AND, OR, and NOT
- The IN operator with expression list
- The IN operator with subquery
- The BETWEEN operator
- The LIKE operator
- The NULL operator
- The EXISTS operator
- The ANY and ALL operators

All the conditions described in this chapter consist of one or more expressions. In Chapter 5, "SELECT Statement: Common Elements," you saw that an aggregation function can be a valid expression. However, aggregation functions are not permitted in the condition of a WHERE clause.

8.2 Conditions Using Comparison Operators

The best-known condition is the one in which the values of two expressions are compared. The condition is formed by an expression (for example, 83 or 15 * 100), a *comparison operator* or *relation operator* (for example, < or =), and another expression. The value on the left of the operator is compared with the expression on the right. The condition is true, false, or unknown, depending on the operator. SQL supports the comparison operators shown in Table 8.1.

Table 8.1   *Overview of Comparison Operators*

COMPARISON OPERATOR	MEANING
=	Equal to
<	Less than
>	Greater than
<=	Less than or equal to
>=	Greater than or equal to
<>	Not equal to

The definition of this condition form is as follows:

```
<predicate with comparison> ::=
    <scalar expression> <comparison operator>
      <scalar expression> |
    <row expression> <comparison operator> <row expression>

<comparison operator> ::=
    = | < | > | <= | >= | <>
```

The definition shows that there are two forms of this predicate. The best known is the one in which the values of scalar expressions are compared. In the other form, row expressions are used. We start with the first form.

Example 8.1: Get the numbers of the players resident in Stratford.

```
SELECT    PLAYERNO
FROM      PLAYERS
WHERE     TOWN = 'Stratford'
```

The result is:

```
PLAYERNO
--------
       2
       6
       7
      39
      57
      83
     100
```

Explanation: Only for rows in which the value of the TOWN column is equal to Strat-ford is the PLAYERNO printed because then the condition TOWN = 'Stratford' is true.

Example 8.2: Get the number, the date of birth, and the year of joining the club for each player who joined 17 years after the year in which he or she was born.

```
SELECT    PLAYERNO, BIRTH_DATE, JOINED
FROM      PLAYERS
WHERE     YEAR(BIRTH_DATE) + 17 = JOINED
```

The result is:

```
PLAYERNO  BIRTH_DATE    JOINED
--------  ----------    ------
      44  1963-01-09      1980
```

The condition in this statement could also be expressed in other ways:

```
WHERE  YEAR(BIRTH_DATE) = JOINED - 17
WHERE  YEAR(BIRTH_DATE) - JOINED + 17 = 0
```

In the first section, we mentioned that if the condition for a row is unknown, it is excluded from the result. Here is an example.

Example 8.3: Get the player numbers for players who have league number 7060.

```
SELECT    PLAYERNO
FROM      PLAYERS
WHERE     LEAGUENO = '7060'
```

The result is:

```
PLAYERNO
--------
     104
```

Explanation: The PLAYERNO is displayed only for rows in which the LEAGUENO is 7060 because only then is the condition true. The rows in which the LEAGUENO column has the NULL value (players 7, 28, 39, and 95) are not displayed because the value of such a condition is unknown.

If one of the scalar expressions in a condition has the NULL value, regardless of the data type of the expression (numeric, alphanumeric, or date), the condition evaluates to unknown. The following table shows what the result of a certain condition can be, depending on whether one or two of the scalar expressions concerned are equal to the NULL value. Here, the question mark represents any comparison operator:

```
Condition                            Result
---------------------------------    ------------
non-NULL value ? non-NULL value      true or false
non-NULL value ? NULL value          unknown
NULL value ? NULL value              unknown
```

For some statements, the NULL value can lead to unexpected results. Here is an example in which the condition at first looks a little peculiar.

Example 8.4: Get the numbers and league numbers of players who actually have a league number.

```
SELECT    PLAYERNO, LEAGUENO
FROM      PLAYERS
WHERE     LEAGUENO = LEAGUENO
```

The result is:

```
PLAYERNO  LEAGUENO
--------  --------
       2  2411
       6  8467
       8  2983
      27  2513
      44  1124
      57  6409
      83  1608
     100  6524
     104  7060
     112  1319
```

Explanation: Each row in which the LEAGUENO column is filled will be printed because here LEAGUENO is equal to LEAGUENO. If the LEAGUENO column is not filled, the condition evaluates to unknown. Section 8.10 describes a "cleaner" way to formulate the previous query.

For that matter, the condition LEAGUENO <> LEAGUENO does not return one single row. If the value of the LEAGUENO column is not equal to NULL, the condition evaluates to false, and if the value equals NULL, the condition evaluates to unknown.

The comparison operators <, <=, >, and >= are used to check which value is greater. For numeric values, the answer is always obvious: 1 is less than 2, and 99.99 is greater than 88.3. But how does that work with alphanumeric values, dates, and times? For alphanumeric values, the answer is simple: An alphanumeric value is less than another if it comes first when those values are sorted. Some examples:

```
Condition             Result
------------------    ------
'Jim' < 'Pete'        true
'Truth' >= 'Truck'    true
'Jim' = 'JIM'         false
```

> **Portability:** *In MySQL, comparisons with alphanumeric values are not case-sensitive—in other words, uppercase letters and lowercase letters are considered to be equal. In the previous example, the condition* `'Jim' = 'JIM'` *evaluates to true in MySQL. In almost all other products, these comparisons are case-sensitive.*

But what do we do with special symbols such as the β and æ? And let us not forget é, â, and ç? Should é come before or after è? And when a rule applies here, does it hold for every language? In other words, what exactly is the order of all kinds of alphanumeric characters? How letters and digits are sorted depends on so-called *character set* and *collating sequences*. These topics are discussed in detail in Chapter 17, "Character Sets and Collating Sequences."

One date, time, or timestamp is less than another if it comes earlier in time. Some examples are:

```
Condition                       Result
---------------------------     ------
'1985-12-08' < '1995-12-09'     true
'1980-05-02' > '1979-12-31'     true
'12:00:00'   < '14:00:00'       true
```

Row expressions were already described in Section 5.3. With comparisons between row expressions, the values with identical positions are compared.

Example 8.5: Find the numbers of the matches in which the number of sets won is equal to 2 and the number of sets lost is equal to 3.

```
SELECT    MATCHNO
FROM      MATCHES
WHERE     (WON, LOST) = (2, 3)
```

The result is:

```
MATCHNO
-------
      2
     11
```

Explanation: SQL rewrites the condition internally as (WON = 2) AND (LOST = 3).

Instead of the equal to operator, other comparison operators can be used. However, attention must then be paid to how a certain comparison is processed. For example, the condition

```
(2, 4) > (1, 3)
```

is not equal to

```
(2 = 4) AND (1 = 3)
```

but to

```
(2 > 1) OR (2 = 1 AND 4 > 3)
```

So first, the first values of both row expressions are compared. If this comparison returns the value true, the entire condition is true straight away. If this first comparison is not true, a check is done to see whether the first two values are equal and whether the second value of the first row expression is greater than the second value of the second row expression. This also means that if the second value of the second row expression is equal to NULL, the entire condition still can be true.

For the different comparison operators in the following table, we have indicated how the condition is converted to scalar expressions. The question mark represents one of the operators <, >, <=, and >=, and E_1, E_2, E_3, and E_4 represent random scalar expressions.

Predicate	Converted to scalar expressions
$(E_1, E_2) = (E_3, E_4)$	$(E_1 = E_3)$ AND $(E_2 = E_4)$
$(E_1, E_2) <> (E_3, E_4)$	$(E_1 <> E_3)$ OR $(E_2 <> E_4)$
$(E_1, E_2) \; ? \; (E_3, E_4)$	$(E_1 \; ? \; E_3)$ OR $(E_1 = E_3$ AND $E_2 \; ? \; E_4)$
$(E_1, E_2, E_3) \; ? \; (E_4, E_5, E_6)$	$(E_1 \; ? \; E_4)$ OR $(E_1 = E_4$ AND $E_2 \; ? \; E_5)$ OR $(E_1 = E_4$ AND $E_2 = E_5$ AND $E_3 \; ? \; E_6)$

The next table contains several examples of comparisons between row expressions and the corresponding results. In particular, pay attention to the examples with NULL values. If a NULL value appears in the condition, it does not automatically evaluate to unknown; see the last example.

```
Predicate                     Result
--------------------          ------
(2, 1) > (1, 2)               true
(2, 2) > (1, 1)               true
(1, 2) > (1, 1)               true
(1, 2) > (1, 2)               false
(1, 2) > (1, 3)               false
(2, NULL) > (1, NULL)         true
(NULL, 2) > (1, 1)            unknown
(NULL, 2) > (NULL, 1)         unknown
(2, 1) <> (2, 1)              false
(2, 2) <> (2, 1)              true
(3, 2) <> (2, 1)              true
(3, NULL) <> (2, 1)           true
```

Portability: *In some SQL products, the comparison operator <> is sometimes represented as ∧=, ! =, ¬=, or #. Not all products support conditions based on row expressions.*

Exercise 8.1: Get the payment number of each penalty greater than $60. (Give at least two formulations.)

Exercise 8.2: Get the number of each team for which the captain is not player 27.

Exercise 8.3: What is the result of the following SELECT statement?

```
SELECT    PLAYERNO, NAME
FROM      PLAYERS
WHERE     LEAGUENO > LEAGUENO
```

Exercise 8.4: Get the number of each player who won at least one match.

Exercise 8.5: Get the number of each player who played at least one match of five sets.

8.3 Comparison Operators with Subqueries

In Chapter 5, we mentioned that a scalar expression can also be a subquery. But if it is, it must be a scalar subquery.

Example 8.6: Get the number and name of the player who captains team 1.

```
SELECT    PLAYERNO, NAME
FROM      PLAYERS
WHERE     PLAYERNO =
          (SELECT   PLAYERNO
           FROM     TEAMS
           WHERE    TEAMNO = 1)
```

Explanation: It is obvious in this example that in the condition of the WHERE clause, the value of a "normal" scalar expression, consisting of the column name PLAYERNO, is compared with the value of a subquery. The intermediate result of the subquery is player number 6. This value can now replace the subquery. Next, the following SELECT statement occurs:

```
SELECT    PLAYERNO, NAME
FROM      PLAYERS
WHERE     PLAYERNO = 6
```

The result is:

```
PLAYERNO  NAME
--------  ---------
       6  Parmenter
```

Note that subqueries can be used as expressions only if the subquery returns precisely one value at all times. In other words, it has to be a *scalar subquery*. A scalar subquery has one row as result, consisting of one value. Therefore, the following statement is incorrect and is not processed by SQL:

```
SELECT    *
FROM      PLAYERS
WHERE     BIRTH_DATE <
          (SELECT   BIRTH_DATE
           FROM     PLAYERS)
```

Example 8.7: Find the number, the name, and initials of each player who is older than the player with league number 8467.

```
SELECT    PLAYERNO, NAME, INITIALS
FROM      PLAYERS
WHERE     BIRTH_DATE <
          (SELECT   BIRTH_DATE
           FROM     PLAYERS
           WHERE    LEAGUENO = '8467')
```

This subquery always returns at maximum one value because, as indicated in Section 2.4, in Chapter 2, "The Tennis Club Sample Database," the LEAGUENO column is an alternate key. The intermediate result of that subquery is the date June 25, 1964. The result that the user sees is:

```
PLAYERNO   NAME        INITIALS
--------   ---------   --------
       2   Everett     R
       7   Wise        GWS
       8   Newcastle   B
      28   Collins     C
      39   Bishop      D
      44   Baker       E
      83   Hope        PK
      95   Miller      P
     100   Parmenter   P
     112   Bailey      IP
```

But what if the subquery does not return a result? In this case, the result of the subquery is equal to the NULL value.

The next, somewhat strange statement returns all the rows because there is no player with league number 9999.

```
SELECT    PLAYERNO, NAME, INITIALS
FROM      PLAYERS
WHERE     (SELECT    BIRTH_DATE
           FROM      PLAYERS
           WHERE     LEAGUENO = '9999') IS NULL
```

Example 8.8: Get the numbers of the matches played for the team that is captained by player 27.

```
SELECT    MATCHNO
FROM      MATCHES
WHERE     TEAMNO =
           (SELECT    TEAMNO
            FROM      TEAMS
            WHERE     PLAYERNO = 27)
```

The result is:

```
MATCHNO
-------
      9
     10
     11
     12
     13
```

Explanation: The subquery is used to determine the number of the team that is captained by player 27. Next, that result is used in the condition of the main query.

Example 8.9: Find the number, the town, and the sex of each player living in the same town as player 7 and having the same sex as player 2.

```
SELECT    PLAYERNO, TOWN, SEX
FROM      PLAYERS
WHERE     (TOWN, SEX) =
          ((SELECT   TOWN
            FROM      PLAYERS
            WHERE     PLAYERNO = 7),
           (SELECT   SEX
            FROM      PLAYERS
            WHERE     PLAYERNO = 2))
```

The result is:

```
PLAYERNO  TOWN        SEX
--------  ---------   ---
       2  Stratford   M
       6  Stratford   M
       7  Stratford   M
      39  Stratford   M
      57  Stratford   M
      83  Stratford   M
     100  Stratford   M
```

Explanation: The two scalar subqueries are processed separately. One returns Stratford as the answer and the other returns M. After that, the condition (TOWN, SEX) = ('Stratford ', 'M ') is checked for each player separately in the WHERE clause. So, the two scalar subqueries form one row expression.

If comparisons with row expressions are made, row subqueries can be included.

Portability: *Not all SQL products allow conditions in which row expressions are compared with row subqueries.*

Example 8.10: Player 6 became secretary of the tennis club on January 1, 1990. Find the numbers of the players who took up a committee position on that same date and also resigned on the same date as player 6.

```
SELECT    DISTINCT PLAYERNO
FROM      COMMITTEE_MEMBERS
WHERE     (BEGIN_DATE, END_DATE) =
          (SELECT    BEGIN_DATE, END_DATE
           FROM      COMMITTEE_MEMBERS
           WHERE     PLAYERNO = 6
           AND       POSITION = 'Secretary'
           AND       BEGIN_DATE = '1990-01-01')
```

The result is:

```
PLAYERNO
--------
       6
       8
      27
```

Explanation: The subquery is a typical row subquery. The result consists of one row with two values at the most because each player can hold only one position on a certain date. The combination PLAYERNO and BEGIN_DATE is the primary key of the COMMITTEE_MEMBERS table. After the subquery has been processed, those two values are compared with the row expression (BEGIN_DATE, END_DATE). Here the same processing rules apply as described in the previous section.

Example 8.11: Get the numbers, names, and initials of all players whose combination of name and initials comes before player 6 in alphabetical order.

```
SELECT    PLAYERNO, NAME, INITIALS
FROM      PLAYERS
WHERE     (NAME, INITIALS) <
          (SELECT    NAME, INITIALS
           FROM      PLAYERS
           WHERE     PLAYERNO = 6)
ORDER BY NAME, INITIALS
```

The result is:

```
PLAYERNO  NAME       INITIALS
--------  ---------  --------
     112  Bailey     IP
      44  Baker      E
      39  Bishop     D
      57  Brown      M
      28  Collins    C
      27  Collins    DD
       2  Everett    R
      83  Hope       PK
      95  Miller     P
     104  Moorman    D
       8  Newcastle  B
     100  Parmenter  P
```

In the next example, we use the MATCHES_SPECIAL table that was used in Example 5.34.

Example 8.12: Get the numbers of the matches that started after match 1.

```
SELECT    MATCHNO
FROM      MATCHES_SPECIAL
WHERE     (START_DATE, START_TIME) >
          (SELECT    START_DATE, START_TIME
           FROM      MATCHES_SPECIAL
           WHERE     MATCHNO = 1)
```

Explanation: Even though two matches start on the same day, if they start at different times, they can be included in the end result. Without using row expressions, it would become a complex statement. Try to write this statement without making use of row expressions.

Exercise 8.6: Find the player number, the name, and the initials of the player who belongs to penalty 4.

Exercise 8.7: Find the player number, the name, and the initials of the player who captains the team belonging to match 2.

Exercise 8.8: Find the player number and name of each player who has the same age as R. Parmenter whose name and number may not appear in the result.

Exercise 8.9: Find the numbers of all matches played by team 2 in which the number of sets won is equal to the number of sets won in the match with number 6. Exclude match 6 from the result.

Exercise 8.10: Find the number of every match that has the same number of sets won as match 2 and the same number of sets lost as match 8.

Exercise 8.11: Find the numbers, names, and initials of all players whose combination of town, street, and house number comes alphabetically before player 100.

8.4 Comparison Operators with Correlated Subqueries

The previous section contains examples of scalar subqueries, and the previous chapter contains examples of table subqueries. Processing these subqueries is simple for SQL: Before the main query is processed, the subquery is processed first, and this intermediate result is passed to the main query. However, scalar subqueries can also refer to columns of the main query. We call this *correlated subqueries*.

Example 8.13: Get the numbers of the matches played by players living in Inglewood.

```
SELECT    MATCHNO
FROM      MATCHES
WHERE     'Inglewood' =
          (SELECT    TOWN
           FROM      PLAYERS
           WHERE     PLAYERS.PLAYERNO = MATCHES.PLAYERNO)
```

The result is:

```
MATCHNO
-------
      4
      8
     13
```

Explanation: The subquery of this table expression refers to a column belonging to the table specified in the main query: MATCHES.PLAYERNO. For this reason, we call such a subquery a *correlated subquery*. By using the qualified column specification, we establish a relationship or correlation between the subquery and the main query.

The effect of a correlated subquery is that SQL cannot determine the result of the subquery first, but for each row in the main query (every match), the result of the subquery must be determined separately. Because the player belonging to the first match is equal to 6, the following subquery is executed for this player:

```
SELECT    TOWN
FROM      PLAYERS
WHERE     PLAYERS.PLAYERNO = 6
```

This player does not live in Inglewood, so the first match does not appear in the end result. The next subquery is executed for match 4 with player 44, and he lives in Inglewood. Therefore, match 4 will appear in the end result.

```
SELECT    TOWN
FROM      PLAYERS
WHERE     PLAYERS.PLAYERNO = 44
```

The processing of this statement could also be presented as follows with the pseudo programming language:

```
END-RESULT := [];
FOR EACH M IN MATCHES DO
   FOR EACH P IN PLAYERS DO
      COUNTER := 0;
      IF M.PLAYERNO = P.PLAYERNO THEN
         IF 'Inglewood' = P.TOWN THEN
            COUNTER := COUNTER + 1;
         ENDIF;
      ENDIF;
   ENDFOR;
   IF COUNTER > 0 THEN
      END-RESULT :+ W;
   ENDIF;
ENDFOR;
```

Example 8.14: Get the match numbers, the player numbers, and the team numbers of all the matches played by a player who also captains that team.

```
SELECT    MATCHNO, PLAYERNO, TEAMNO
FROM      MATCHES
WHERE     PLAYERNO =
          (SELECT    PLAYERNO
           FROM      TEAMS
           WHERE     TEAMS.PLAYERNO = MATCHES.PLAYERNO)
```

The result is:

MATCHNO	PLAYERNO	TEAMNO
1	6	1
2	6	1
3	6	1
9	27	2

Explanation: The correlated subquery is processed for each match separately. For each match, SQL determines whether there are teams on which the captain is equal to the player who played the match. If so, that match is included in the end result.

Example 8.15: Get the numbers of the matches played by players whose third letter of his name is equal to the third letter of the division in which the team plays.

```
SELECT    MATCHNO
FROM      MATCHES
WHERE     SUBSTR((SELECT    DIVISION
                  FROM      TEAMS
                  WHERE     TEAMS.TEAMNO =
                            MATCHES.TEAMNO),3,1)
          =
          SUBSTR((SELECT    NAME
                  FROM      PLAYERS
                  WHERE     PLAYERS.PLAYERNO =
                            MATCHES.PLAYERNO),3,1)
```

The result is:

MATCHNO

      1
      2
      3

Exercise 8.12: Get the numbers of the penalties incurred by players who were born after 1965.

Exercise 8.13: Get the payment numbers and the player numbers of all penalties of which the player is also captain of a team.

8.5 Conditions Coupled with AND, OR, and NOT

A WHERE clause can contain multiple conditions if the *logical operators* AND, OR, and NOT are used. Table 8.2 contains the truth table for two conditions C_1 and C_2, and all possible values for the conditions C_1 AND C_2, C_1 OR C_2, and NOT C_1.

Table 8.2   *Truth Table for the Logical Operators*

C_1	C_2	C_1 AND C_2	C_1 OR C_2	NOT C_1
True	True	True	True	False
True	False	False	True	False
True	Unknown	Unknown	True	False
False	True	False	True	True
False	False	False	False	True
False	Unknown	False	Unknown	True
Unknown	True	Unknown	True	Unknown
Unknown	False	False	Unknown	Unknown
Unknown	Unknown	Unknown	Unknown	Unknown

Example 8.16: Get the number, name, sex, and birth date of each male player born after 1970.

```
SELECT   PLAYERNO, NAME, SEX, BIRTH_DATE
FROM     PLAYERS
WHERE    SEX = 'M'
AND      BIRTH_DATE > '1970-12-31'
```

The result is:

```
PLAYERNO  NAME   SEX  BIRTH_DATE
--------  -----  ---  ----------
      57  Brown  M    1971-08-17
```

Explanation: For every row in the PLAYERS table in which the value in the SEX column equals M and the value in the BIRTH_DATE column is greater than 31 December 1970, four columns are displayed.

Example 8.17: Get the numbers, the names, and the towns of all players who live in Plymouth or Eltham.

```
SELECT   PLAYERNO, NAME, TOWN
FROM     PLAYERS
WHERE    TOWN = 'Plymouth'
OR       TOWN = 'Eltham'
```

The result is:

```
PLAYERNO  NAME     TOWN
--------  -------  --------
      27  Collins  Eltham
     104  Moorman  Eltham
     112  Bailey   Plymouth
```

Note that this SELECT statement would produce *no* result if the logical operator OR were replaced by AND. Work this out for yourself why.

If a WHERE clause contains AND plus OR operators, the AND operators are processed first. So, in the following WHERE clause (assume C_1 to C_3 represent conditions)

```
WHERE  C₁  OR  C₂  AND  C₃
```

C_2 AND C_3 is evaluated first. Imagine that the result is A_1, and after this C_1 OR A_1 is evaluated. This is the final result. This process can also be represented as follows:

```
C₂  AND  C₃  ->  A₁
C₁  OR  A₁   ->  result
```

By using brackets, you can influence the order in which the conditions are evaluated. Consider the following WHERE clause:

```
WHERE  (C₁  OR  C₂)  AND  C₃
```

The processing sequence now becomes:

```
C₁  OR  C₂   ->  A₁
A₁  AND  C₃  ->  result
```

With any given value for C_1, C_2, and C_3, the result of the first example can be different from the result of the second. Imagine, for example, that C_1 and C_2 are true and that C_3 is false. Then, the result of the first example without brackets is true and that of the second with brackets is false.

The NOT operator can be specified in front of each condition. The NOT operator changes the value of a condition to false if it is true and true if it is false; if the condition is unknown, it remains unknown.

Example 8.18: Get the numbers, names, and towns of players who do *not* live in Stratford.

```
SELECT    PLAYERNO, NAME, TOWN
FROM      PLAYERS
WHERE     TOWN <> 'Stratford'
```

The result is

```
PLAYERNO   NAME        TOWN
--------   ---------   ---------
       8   Newcastle   Inglewood
      27   Collins     Eltham
      28   Collins     Midhurst
      44   Baker       Inglewood
      95   Miller      Douglas
     104   Moorman     Eltham
     112   Bailey      Plymouth
```

This example can also be formulated as follows:

```
SELECT    PLAYERNO, NAME, TOWN
FROM      PLAYERS
WHERE     NOT (TOWN = 'Stratford')
```

Explanation: Each row in which the condition TOWN = 'Stratford' is true or unknown is not printed because the NOT operator switches the value true to false, and NOT (unknown) remains unknown.

Example 8.19: Get the number, town, and date of birth of each player who lives in Stratford or was born in 1963, but do not include those who live in Stratford and were born in 1963.

```
SELECT    PLAYERNO, TOWN, BIRTH_DATE
FROM      PLAYERS
WHERE     (TOWN = 'Stratford' OR  YEAR(BIRTH_DATE) = 1963)
AND NOT   (TOWN = 'Stratford' AND YEAR(BIRTH_DATE) = 1963)
```

The result is:

```
PLAYERNO   TOWN        BIRTH_DATE
--------   ---------   ----------
       2   Stratford   1948-09-01
       6   Stratford   1964-06-25
```

```
 28  Midhurst   1963-06-22
 39  Stratford  1956-10-29
 44  Inglewood  1963-01-09
 57  Stratford  1971-08-17
 83  Stratford  1956-11-11
 95  Douglas    1963-05-14
112  Plymouth   1963-10-01
```

Exercise 8.14: Get the number, name, and town of each female player who is *not* a resident of Stratford.

Exercise 8.15: Find the player numbers of those who joined the club between 1970 and 1980.

Exercise 8.16: Find the numbers, names, and dates of birth of players born in a leap year. If you need a reminder, a leap year is one in which the year figure is divisible by 4, except centuries, in which the year figure must be divisible by 400. Therefore, 1900 is not a leap year, but 2000 is.

Exercise 8.17: For each competition player born after 1965 who has won at least one match, get the match number, the name and initials, and the division of the teams in which the player has ever played.

8.6 The IN Operator with Expression List

The condition with the IN operator has two forms. This section describes the form in which a series of values is listed; Section 8.7 explains the form in which subqueries are used.

```
<predicate with in> ::=
   <scalar expression> [ NOT ] IN <scalar expression list> |
   <row expression> [ NOT ] IN <row expression list>

<row expression list> ::=
   ( <scalar expression list>
     [ { , <scalar expression list> }... ] )

<scalar expression list> ::=
   ( <scalar expression> [ { , <scalar expression> }... ] )
```

Conditions can become lengthy if we have to check whether a specific value appears within a long list of given values. Let's use an example to illustrate this.

Example 8.20: Find the number, name, and town of each player who lives in Inglewood, Plymouth, Midhurst, or Douglas.

```
SELECT    PLAYERNO, NAME, TOWN
FROM      PLAYERS
WHERE     TOWN = 'Inglewood'
OR        TOWN = 'Plymouth'
OR        TOWN = 'Midhurst'
OR        TOWN = 'Douglas'
```

The result is:

```
PLAYERNO  NAME       TOWN
--------  ---------  ---------
       8  Newcastle  Inglewood
      28  Collins    Midhurst
      44  Baker      Inglewood
      95  Miller     Douglas
     112  Bailey     Plymouth
```

The statement and the result are correct, but the statement is rather long winded. The IN operator can be used to simplify the statement:

```
SELECT    PLAYERNO, NAME, TOWN
FROM      PLAYERS
WHERE     TOWN IN ('Inglewood', 'Plymouth', 'Midhurst',
                   'Douglas')
```

This condition is to be read as follows: Each row whose TOWN value occurs in the set of four town names satisfies the condition. In this example, the four town names form the *expression list*.

Example 8.21: Get the numbers and years of birth of the players born in 1962, 1963, or 1970.

```
SELECT     PLAYERNO, YEAR(BIRTH_DATE)
FROM       PLAYERS
WHERE      YEAR(BIRTH_DATE) IN (1962, 1963, 1970)
```

The result is:

```
PLAYERNO   YEAR(BIRTH_DATE)
--------   ----------------
       7               1963
       8               1962
      28               1963
      44               1963
      95               1963
     100               1963
     104               1970
     112               1963
```

The previous examples use only literals within the expression list. All forms of scalar expressions can be specified here, including column specifications and scalar subqueries.

Example 8.22: Get the match numbers and the number of sets won and lost for all matches that have two sets won or two sets lost.

```
SELECT     MATCHNO, WON, LOST
FROM       MATCHES
WHERE      2 IN (WON, LOST)
```

The result is:

```
MATCHNO   WON   LOST
-------   ---   ----
      2     2      3
      4     3      2
      9     3      2
     10     3      2
     11     2      3
```

Example 8.23: Find the numbers of the player whose number is equal to 100, equal to the player number of the penalty with number 1, or equal to the number of the captain of team 2.

```
SELECT    PLAYERNO
FROM      PLAYERS
WHERE     PLAYERNO IN
          (100,
          (SELECT    PLAYERNO
           FROM      PENALTIES
           WHERE     PAYMENTNO = 1),
          (SELECT    PLAYERNO
           FROM      TEAMS
           WHERE     TEAMNO = 2))
```

The result is:

```
PLAYERNO
--------
       6
      27
     100
```

Explanation: The expression list consists of three scalar expressions, of which one is a literal and the other two are scalar subqueries. Make sure that each of the subqueries is really scalar and that they do not return more than one row consisting of one value.

Example 8.24: Get the match numbers and the number of sets won and lost of all matches in which the number of sets won is equal to the match number divided by 2, or equal to the number of sets lost or equal to the number of sets lost belonging to match 1.

```
SELECT    MATCHNO, WON, LOST
FROM      MATCHES
WHERE     WON IN
          (TRUNCATE(MATCHNO / 2,0), LOST,
          (SELECT    LOST
           FROM      MATCHES
           WHERE     MATCHNO = 1))
```

The result is:

```
MATCHNO  WON  LOST
-------  ---  ----
      6    1     3
      7    3     0
     12    1     3
```

Example 8.25: Get the numbers of the matches played by players whose names begin with the capital letter *B*, *C*, or *E*.

```
SELECT    MATCHNO
FROM      MATCHES
WHERE     (SELECT    SUBSTR(NAME,1,1)
           FROM      PLAYERS
           WHERE     PLAYERS.PLAYERNO = MATCHES.PLAYERNO)
          IN ('B','C','E')
```

The result is:

```
MATCHNO
-------
      4
      6
      7
      9
     11
     12
```

The following rules apply to the scalar expressions used with the IN operator: The data types must be comparable and not every expression form can be used.

How exactly is a condition with IN processed? Imagine that E_1, E_2, E_3, and E_4 are scalar expressions. Then, the condition:

```
E₁ IN (E₂, E₃, E₄)
```

is equivalent to the condition:

```
(E₁ = E₂) OR (E₁ = E₃) OR (E₁ = E₄)
```

This means that if one of the expressions between brackets is equal to NULL, the value of the entire condition can still be true. It also means that if E_1 itself is equal to NULL, the entire condition evaluates to unknown.

Simultaneously, it follows that the condition:

```
E_1 NOT IN (E_2, E_3, E_4)
```

is equivalent to the condition:

```
NOT (E_1 IN (E_2, E_3, E_4))
```

and equivalent to:

```
(E_1 <> E_2) AND (E_1 <> E_3) AND (E_1 <> E_4)
```

The definition shows that the IN operator can also deal with row expressions.

Example 8.26: Find the match numbers and the number of sets won and lost of all matches that were won with 3-1 or 3-2.

```
SELECT    MATCHNO, WON, LOST
FROM      MATCHES
WHERE     (WON, LOST) IN ((3,1),(3,2))
```

The result is:

```
MATCHNO   WON   LOST
-------   ---   ----
      1     3      1
      4     3      2
      9     3      2
     10     3      2
```

Explanation: Because a row expression consisting of two expressions occurs to the left of the IN operator, the expression list should also be a list consisting of row expressions.

Example 8.27: Get the numbers, names, and initials of all players whose name and initials are equal to that of player 6 or of 27.

```
SELECT    PLAYERNO, NAME, INITIALS
FROM      PLAYERS
WHERE     (NAME, INITIALS) IN
          ((SELECT    NAME, INITIALS
            FROM      PLAYERS
            WHERE     PLAYERNO = 6),
           (SELECT    NAME, INITIALS
            FROM      PLAYERS
            WHERE     PLAYERNO = 27))
```

The result is:

```
PLAYERNO  NAME       INITIALS
--------  ---------  --------
       6  Parmenter  R
      27  Collins    DD
```

Portability: *Which expression forms can and cannot be used inside the list of expressions depends strongly on the product you are using. Some SQL products allow only literals and system variables.*

Exercise 8.18: Get the payment numbers of every penalty of $50, $75, or $100.

Exercise 8.19: Get the numbers of the players who do not live in Stratford and not in Douglas.

Exercise 8.20: Get the numbers of the penalties of which the amount is equal to 100, equal to five times the payment number, or equal to the amount belonging to penalty 2.

Exercise 8.21: Get the numbers of the players who live in the town Stratford and the street Haseltine Lane, or in the town Stratford and the street Edgecombe Way.

8.7 The IN Operator with Subquery

Section 8.6 discussed the first form of the IN operator. A row from a table satisfies a condition with the IN operator if the value of a particular column occurs in a *fixed* set of expressions. The number of elements in the set has been defined by the user. The IN operator can also take another form in which the set of expressions is not listed but is *variable*. The set is determined by SQL at the point that the statement is processed. This process is the subject of this section.

In Section 8.6, we gave a definition of the condition with the IN operator. The definition is extended as follows:

```
<predicate with in> ::=
    <scalar expression> [ NOT ] IN <scalar expression list> |
    <scalar expression> [ NOT ] IN <column subquery>       |
    <row expression> [ NOT ] IN <row expression list>      |
    <row expression> [ NOT ] IN <table subquery>

<row expression list> ::=
    ( <scalar expression list>
        [ { , <scalar expression list> }... ] )

<scalar expression list> ::=
    ( <scalar expression> [ { , <scalar expression> }... ] )

<column subquery> ;
<table subquery> ::= ( <table expression> )
```

Example 8.28: Get the player number, name, and initials of each player who has played at least one match.

The question in this example actually consists of two parts. First, you need to work out which players have played at least one match. Then you need to look for the numbers, the names, and the initials of these players. The MATCHES table contains the numbers of the players who have played at least one match, so with the following simple SELECT statement, you can find out these numbers:

```
SELECT    PLAYERNO
FROM      MATCHES
```

The result is:

```
PLAYERNO
--------
       6
       6
```

```
      6
     44
     83
      2
     57
      8
     27
    104
    112
    112
      8
```

But how do we use those numbers to look up the relevant names and initials of the players from the PLAYERS table? If we use the IN operator, we have to remember the numbers of the previous statement somehow and then type in the following statement:

```
SELECT    PLAYERNO, NAME, INITIALS
FROM      PLAYERS
WHERE     PLAYERNO IN (6, 44, 83, 2, 57, 8, 27, 104, 112)
```

The result is:

```
PLAYERNO  NAME       INITIALS
--------  ---------  --------
       2  Everett    R
       6  Parmenter  R
       8  Newcastle  B
      27  Collins    DD
      44  Baker      E
      57  Brown      M
      83  Hope       PK
     104  Moorman    D
     112  Bailey     IP
```

This method works, but it is very clumsy and would be impractical if the MATCHES table contains a large set of different player numbers. Because this type of query is common, SQL offers the possibility of specifying column subqueries together with the IN operator. (Note that it is also allowed to use subqueries with the previous form of the IN operator, but those are scalar subqueries.) The SELECT statement for the previous example now looks like this:

```
SELECT   PLAYERNO, NAME, INITIALS
FROM     PLAYERS
WHERE    PLAYERNO IN
         (SELECT   PLAYERNO
          FROM     MATCHES)
```

We have no longer specified an expression list after the IN operator as we did in the examples in Section 8.6; we have specified a column subquery. A column subquery has as a result multiple rows, with each row consisting of one value. In the example, the result would look like the following (remember that this is an intermediate result that is not seen by the users):

```
(6, 44, 83, 2, 57, 8, 27, 104, 112)
```

When SQL processes the table expression, it replaces the subquery with the (intermediate) result of the subquery (this is done behind the scenes):

```
SELECT   PLAYERNO, NAME, INITIALS
FROM     PLAYERS
WHERE    PLAYERNO IN (6, 44, 83, 2, 57, 8, 27, 104, 112)
```

This is now a familiar statement. The result of this statement is the same as the end result that we have already shown.

The most important difference between the IN operator with a set of scalar expressions and a column subquery is that, in the first instance, the set of values is fixed in advance by the user, whereas in the second instance, the values are variable and are determined by SQL during the processing.

Example 8.29: Get the player number and the name of each player who has played at least one match for the first team.

```
SELECT   PLAYERNO, NAME
FROM     PLAYERS
WHERE    PLAYERNO IN
         (SELECT   PLAYERNO
          FROM     MATCHES
          WHERE    TEAMNO = 1)
```

The intermediate result of the subquery is:

```
(2, 6, 6, 44, 57, 83)
```

The result of the entire statement is:

```
PLAYERNO  NAME
--------  ---------
       2  Everett
       6  Parmenter
       8  Newcastle
      44  Baker
      57  Brown
      83  Hope
```

As you can see, a subquery can also contain conditions; even other subqueries are allowed.

Example 8.30: Get the number and name of each player who has played at least one match for the team that is *not* captained by player 6.

```
SELECT    PLAYERNO, NAME
FROM      PLAYERS
WHERE     PLAYERNO IN
          (SELECT    PLAYERNO
           FROM      MATCHES
           WHERE     TEAMNO NOT IN
                     (SELECT    TEAMNO
                      FROM      TEAMS
                      WHERE     PLAYERNO = 6))
```

The intermediate result of the *sub-subquery* is:

```
(1)
```

The subquery searches all players who do *not* appear in the set of teams captained by player 6. The intermediate result is:

```
(8, 27, 104, 112)
```

The result of the statement is:

```
PLAYERNO  NAME
--------  ---------
       8  Newcastle
      27  Collins
     104  Moorman
     112  Bailey
```

Again, users do not see any of the intermediate results.

When is a condition with an IN operator and a subquery true, when is it false, and when is it unknown? Imagine that C is the name of a column and that v_1, v_1, . . . , and v_n are values from which the intermediate result of subquery S is formed. It follows that:

```
C IN (S)
```

is equivalent to:

```
(C = C) AND ((C = v₁) OR (C = v₂) OR ... OR (C = vₙ) OR false)
```

The following should be noted concerning certain specific situations:

- If C is equal to the NULL value, the entire condition evaluates to unknown because the condition C = C is equal to unknown; this rule holds independently of the numbers of values in the result of the subquery.
- If C is not equal to the NULL value and if the subquery returns no result, the condition evaluates to false because the last "term" of this "longhand" condition is false.
- If C is not equal to the NULL value, and if one of the v values is equal to the NULL value and one of the other v values is not equal to NULL, the condition can be true or unknown.
- If C is not equal to the NULL value, and if all v values are equal to the NULL value, the condition evaluates to unknown.

Note that not all SQL products interpret the IN operator this way. For some products, such as DB2, it holds that

```
C IN (S)
```

is equivalent to:

```
(C = v₁) OR (C = v₂) OR ... OR (C = vₙ) OR false
```

The following should be noted concerning certain specific situations:

- Regardless of the value of C, if the subquery returns no result, the entire condition evaluates to false because the last "term" of this "longhand" condition is false.
- If C is equal to the NULL value, and if the subquery returns a result of one or more values, the entire condition evaluates to unknown because every condition $C = v_i$ is equal to unknown.
- If one of the v values is equal to the NULL value and one of the other v values is not equal to NULL, the condition can be true or unknown.

We can apply the same reasoning to NOT IN. The following condition:

```
C NOT IN (S)
```

is equivalent to:

```
(C = C) AND (C <> v₁) AND (C <> v₂) AND ... AND (C <> vₙ) AND
true
```

The following should be noted concerning certain specific situations:

- If C is equal to the NULL value, the entire condition evaluates to unknown because the condition C = C is equal to unknown; this rule holds independently of the numbers of values in the result of the subquery.
- If C is not equal to the NULL value, and if the subquery returns no result, the condition evaluates to true because the last "term" of this "longhand" condition is true.
- If C is not equal to the NULL value, and if one of the v values is equal to the NULL value and one of the other v values is not equal to NULL, the condition can be true or unknown.
- If C is not equal to the NULL value, and if all v values are equal to the NULL value, the condition evaluates to unknown.

Again, not all SQL products interpret the NOT IN operator this way. For some products, such as DB2, it holds that

```
C NOT IN (S)
```

is equivalent to:

```
(C <> v₁) AND (C <> v₂) AND ... AND (C <> vₙ) AND true
```

Here, the following should be noted concerning certain specific situations:

■   Regardless of the value of C, if the subquery returns no result, the entire condition evaluates to true because the last "term" of this "longhand" condition is true.

■   If C is equal to the NULL value, and if the subquery returns a result, the entire condition evaluates to unknown because every condition $C = v_i$ is equal to unknown. This rule holds independently of the numbers of rows in the result of the subquery.

■   If one of the v values is equal to the NULL value and one of the other v values is not equal to NULL, the condition is unknown or false.

Imagine that the year of birth of player 27 is unknown. Will player 27 appear in the end result of the following SELECT statement?

```
SELECT    *
FROM      PLAYERS
WHERE     BIRTH_DATE NOT IN
          (SELECT    BIRTH_DATE
           FROM      PLAYERS
           WHERE     Town = 'London')
```

The answer is no. Only players whose date of birth is known will be included in the end result, so player 27 will not appear.

This IN operator with subquery can be extended with row expressions. In this case, after the IN operator, we have to specify a table expression. The number of expressions in the row expression and the number of expressions in the SELECT clause of the table expressions must be equal. The data types must also be comparable.

Example 8.31: Get all the details of all the rows in the COMMITTEE MEMBERS table that have the same begin and end date as one of those rows for which the position is equal to secretary.

```
SELECT    *
FROM      COMMITTEE_MEMBERS
WHERE     (BEGIN_DATE, END_DATE) IN
          (SELECT    BEGIN_DATE, END_DATE
           FROM      COMMITTEE_MEMBERS
           WHERE     POSITION = 'Secretary')
```

The result is:

```
PLAYERNO   BEGIN_DATE   END_DATE     POSITION
--------   ----------   ----------   ---------
       6   1990-01-01   1990-12-31   Secretary
       8   1990-01-01   1990-12-31   Treasurer
       8   1991-01-01   1991-12-31   Secretary
      27   1990-01-01   1990-12-31   Member
      27   1991-01-01   1991-12-31   Treasurer
      57   1992-01-01   1992-12-31   Secretary
     112   1992-01-01   1992-12-31   Member
```

Almost all the tables of the standard example in this book have simple primary keys consisting of one column. Imagine that the situation is different and that the primary key of the PLAYERS table is formed by the columns NAME and INITIALS. Foreign keys referring to this primary key will all be compound. In that case, formulating queries is simple if row expressions are used. We illustrate this with a few examples in which we use slightly adapted versions of the familiar tables PLAYERS and PENALTIES. We assume that the primary key in the PLAYERS_NI table is indeed formed by the combination NAME with INITIALS. In the PENALTIES_NI table, the column PAYMENTNO is still the primary key, but it has been extended with the columns NAME and INITIALS.

Example 8.32: Create the two tables and insert several rows.

```
CREATE TABLE PLAYERS_NI
      (NAME          CHAR(10) NOT NULL,
       INITIALS      CHAR(3) NOT NULL,
       TOWN          VARCHAR(30) NOT NULL,
       PRIMARY KEY (NAME, INITIALS))

INSERT INTO PLAYERS_NI VALUES ('Parmenter', 'R', 'Stratford')
INSERT INTO PLAYERS_NI VALUES ('Parmenter', 'P', 'Stratford')
INSERT INTO PLAYERS_NI VALUES ('Miller', 'P', 'Douglas')

CREATE TABLE PENALTIES_NI
      (PAYMENTNO     INTEGER NOT NULL,
       NAME          CHAR(10) NOT NULL,
       INITIALS      CHAR(3) NOT NULL,
       AMOUNT        DECIMAL(7,2) NOT NULL,
```

```
        PRIMARY KEY (PAYMENTNO),
        FOREIGN KEY (NAME, INITIALS)
           REFERENCES PLAYERS_NI (NAME, INITIALS))

INSERT INTO PENALTIES_NI VALUES (1, 'Parmenter', 'R', 100.00)
INSERT INTO PENALTIES_NI VALUES (2, 'Miller', 'P', 200.00)
```

The remaining examples in this section relate to the earlier two tables.

Example 8.33: Get the name, initials, and town of each player who has incurred at least one penalty.

The following SELECT statement, in which no row expressions are used, does not give the correct answer to this question, even though it looks like it will:

```
SELECT    NAME, INITIALS, TOWN
FROM      PLAYERS_NI
WHERE     NAME IN
          (SELECT    NAME
           FROM      PENALTIES_NI)
AND       INITIALS IN
          (SELECT    INITIALS
           FROM      PENALTIES_NI)
```

The result is:

```
NAME            INITIALS   TOWN
---------       --------   ---------
Parmenter       R          Stratford
Parmenter       P          Stratford
Miller          P          Douglas
```

This result is the correct answer with respect to the SELECT statement, but it is *not* the answer to the original question. The fact is, player P. Parmenter has *not* incurred a penalty according to the PENALTIES_NI table. A correct formulation of this question is:

```
SELECT    NAME, INITIALS, TOWN
FROM      PLAYERS_NI
WHERE     (NAME, INITIALS) IN
          (SELECT   NAME, INITIALS
           FROM     PENALTIES_NI)
```

The result is:

```
NAME        INITIALS  TOWN
---------   --------  ---------
Parmenter   R         Stratford
Miller      P         Douglas
```

Another correct solution for this example is given next. This solution does not make use of row expressions, which makes it more difficult to fathom.

```
SELECT    NAME, INITIALS, TOWN
FROM      PLAYERS_NI
WHERE     NAME IN
          (SELECT   NAME
           FROM     PENALTIES_NI
           WHERE    PLAYERS_NI.INITIALS =
                    PENALTIES_NI.INITIALS)
```

Explanation: For every row in the main query (thus, in the PLAYERS_NI table), the subquery looks for rows in the PENALTIES_NI table with identical initials. Next, a verification is carried out to see whether the NAME of the player also appears in those rows (WHERE NAME IN ...).

Example 8.34: Get the name, initials, and town of each player who has *not* incurred a penalty.

```
SELECT    NAME, INITIALS, TOWN
FROM      PLAYERS_NI
WHERE     (NAME, INITIALS) NOT IN
          (SELECT   NAME, INITIALS
           FROM     PENALTIES_NI)
```

The result is:

```
NAME          INITIALS   TOWN
---------     --------   ---------
Parmenter     P          Stratford
```

Explanation: The details of a player in the PLAYERS_NI table are included in the result only if there is not one row in the PENALTIES_NI table with the same combination of NAME and INITIALS as the player in the PLAYERS_NI table.

Section 8.13 deals more extensively with the features and limitations of subqueries.

Exercise 8.22: Get the player number and the name of each player who has incurred at least one penalty.

Exercise 8.23: Get the player number and the name of each player who has incurred at least one penalty of more than $50.

Exercise 8.24: Find the team numbers and player numbers of the team captains from the first division who live in Stratford.

Exercise 8.25: Get the player number and the name of each player for whom at least one penalty has been paid and who is not a captain of any team playing in the first division.

Exercise 8.26: What is the result of the following *SELECT* statement?

```
SELECT    *
FROM      PLAYERS
WHERE     LEAGUENO NOT IN
          (SELECT    LEAGUENO
          FROM      PLAYERS
          WHERE     PLAYERNO IN (28, 95))
```

Exercise 8.27: Get the match number and player number of each match in which the number of sets won and the number of sets lost is equal to at least one of the set scores of a match played by a team from the second division.

Exercise 8.28: Get the numbers and names of those players who live at the same address as at least one other player. "Address" is defined as the combination of town, street, house number, and postcode.

8.8 The BETWEEN Operator

SQL supports a special operator that enables you to determine whether a value occurs within a given range of values.

```
<predicate with between> ::=
    <scalar expression> [ NOT ] BETWEEN <scalar expression>
        AND <scalar expression>
```

Example 8.35: Find the number and date of birth of each player born between 1962 and 1964.

```
SELECT    PLAYERNO, BIRTH_DATE
FROM      PLAYERS
WHERE     BIRTH_DATE >= '1962-01-01'
AND       BIRTH_DATE <= '1964-12-31'
```

The result is:

```
PLAYERNO  BIRTH_DATE
--------  ----------
       6  1964-06-25
       7  1963-05-11
       8  1962-07-08
      27  1964-12-28
      28  1963-06-22
      44  1963-01-09
      95  1963-10-01
     100  1963-02-28
     112  1963-10-01
```

This statement can also be written using the BETWEEN operator (the result remains the same):

```
SELECT    PLAYERNO, BIRTH_DATE
FROM      PLAYERS
WHERE     BIRTH_DATE BETWEEN '1962-01-01' AND '1964-12-31'
```

If E_1, E_2, and E_3 are expressions, the condition:

```
E1 BETWEEN E2 AND E3
```

is equivalent to the condition:

```
(E1 >= E2) AND (E1 <= E3)
```

From this, we can derive that if one of the three expressions is equal to the NULL value, the entire condition is unknown or false. Additionally, it follows that:

```
E1 NOT BETWEEN E2 AND E3
```

is equivalent to:

```
NOT (E1 BETWEEN E2 AND E3)
```

and equivalent to:

```
(E1 < E2) OR (E1 > E3)
```

If, in this case, E_1 has the NULL value; then the condition evaluates to unknown. The condition is true, for example, if E_1 is not NULL, E_2 is NULL, and E_1 is greater than E_3.

Example 8.36: Get the numbers of the matches in which the sum of the number of sets won and lost is equal to 2, 3, or 4.

```
SELECT    MATCHNO, WON + LOST
FROM      MATCHES
WHERE     WON + LOST BETWEEN 2 AND 4
```

The result is:

MATCHNO	WON + LOST
1	4
3	3
5	3
6	4
7	3
8	3
12	4
13	3

Example 8.37: Get the player number, the date of birth, and the name and initials of each player whose birth date is between that of B. Newcastle and P. Miller.

```
SELECT    PLAYERNO, BIRTH_DATE, NAME, INITIALS
FROM      PLAYERS
WHERE     BIRTH_DATE BETWEEN
          (SELECT   BIRTH_DATE
           FROM     PLAYERS
           WHERE    NAME = 'Newcastle'
           AND      INITIALS = 'B')
          AND
          (SELECT   BIRTH_DATE
           FROM     PLAYERS
           WHERE    NAME = 'Miller'
           AND      INITIALS = 'P')
```

The result is:

```
PLAYERNO  BIRTH_DATE  NAME       INITIALS
--------  ----------  ---------  --------
       7  1963-05-11  Wise       GWS
       8  1962-07-08  Newcastle  B
      44  1963-01-09  Baker      E
      95  1963-05-14  Miller     P
     100  1963-02-28  Parmenter  P
```

Exercise 8.29: Get the payment number of each penalty between $50 and $100.

Exercise 8.30: Get the payment number of each penalty that is *not* between $50 and $100.

Exercise 8.31: Get the numbers of the players who joined the club after the age of 16 and before reaching their 40s. (Remember that players can join the club only on the first of January of each year.)

8.9 The LIKE Operator

The LIKE operator is used to select alphanumeric values with a particular pattern or mask.

```
<predicate with like> ::=
    <scalar expression> [ NOT ] LIKE <like pattern>
        [ ESCAPE <character> ]

<like pattern> ::= <scalar alphanumeric expression>
```

Example 8.38: Find the name and number of each player whose name begins with an uppercase *B*.

```
SELECT    NAME, PLAYERNO
FROM      PLAYERS
WHERE     NAME LIKE 'B%'
```

The result is:

```
NAME      PLAYERNO
------    --------
Bishop         39
Baker          44
Brown          57
Bailey        112
```

Explanation: After the LIKE operator, you find an alphanumeric literal: 'B%'. Because this literal comes after a LIKE operator and not after a comparison operator, two characters, the percentage sign and the underscore, have a special meaning. Such a literal is called a *pattern* or a *mask*. In a pattern, the percentage sign stands for zero, one, or more characters. The underscore stands for exactly one random character.

In the earlier SELECT statement, we, therefore, asked for the players whose names begin with uppercase *B* followed by zero, one, or more characters.

Example 8.39: Get the name and number of each player whose name ends with a lowercase *r*.

```
SELECT   NAME, PLAYERNO
FROM     PLAYERS
WHERE    NAME LIKE '%r'
```

The result is:

```
NAME        PLAYERNO
---------   --------
Parmenter          6
Baker             44
Miller            95
Parmenter        100
```

Example 8.40: Get the name and number of each player whose name has the lower-case letter *e* as the penultimate letter.

```
SELECT   NAME, PLAYERNO
FROM     PLAYERS
WHERE    NAME LIKE '%e_'
```

The result is:

```
NAME        PLAYERNO
---------   --------
Parmenter          6
Baker             44
Miller            95
Bailey           112
Parmenter        100
```

The pattern does not have to be a simple alphanumeric literal. Each alphanumeric expression is permitted.

Example 8.41: Get the name, town, and number of each player whose name ends with a letter that is equal to the third letter of his or her town.

```
SELECT    NAME, TOWN, PLAYERNO
FROM      PLAYERS
WHERE     NAME LIKE CONCAT('%', SUBSTR(TOWN,3,1))
```

The result is:

```
NAME         TOWN        PLAYERNO
---------    ---------   --------
Parmenter    Stratford          6
Parmenter    Stratford        100
Bailey       Plymouth         112
```

In a pattern, if both the percentage sign and the underscore are absent, the equal to operator can be used. In that case, the condition

```
NAME LIKE 'Baker'
```

is equivalent to:

```
NAME = 'Baker'
```

Imagine that A is an alphanumeric column and P a pattern, then:

```
A NOT LIKE P
```

is equivalent to:

```
NOT (A LIKE P)
```

If you want to search for one or both of the two special symbols (_ and %), you have to use an *escape symbol*.

Example 8.42: Find the name and number of each player whose name contains an underscore.

```
SELECT    NAME, PLAYERNO
FROM      PLAYERS
WHERE     NAME LIKE '%#_%' ESCAPE '#'
```

Explanation: Because no player satisfies this condition, there will be no result. Every character can be specified as an escape symbol. We chose # for this, but symbols such as @, $, and ~ are also allowed. The symbol that follows the escape symbol in a pattern then loses its special meaning. If we had not used the escape symbol in this example, SQL would have looked for players whose names contain at least one character.

Exercise 8.32: Find the number and name of each player whose name contains the string of letters *is*.

Exercise 8.33: Find the number and name of each player whose name is six characters long.

Exercise 8.34: Find the number and name of each player whose name is at least six characters long.

Exercise 8.35: Find the number and name of each player whose name has an *r* as the third and penultimate letters.

Exercise 8.36: Get the number and name of each player whose town name has the percentage sign on the second and penultimate position.

8.10 The IS NULL Operator

Use the IS NULL operator to select rows that have no value in a particular column.

```
<predicate with null> ::=
    <scalar expression> IS [ NOT ] NULL
```

In Example 8.4, we showed how all players with a league number can be found. This statement can also be formulated in another way, one that corresponds more to the original question.

Example 8.43: Get the player number and the league number of each player who has a league number.

```
SELECT    PLAYERNO, LEAGUENO
FROM      PLAYERS
WHERE     LEAGUENO IS NOT NULL
```

Explanation: Note that the word IS may *not* be replaced by the equals sign.
    If NOT is left out, we get all the players who have *no* league number.

Example 8.44: Get the name, the number, and the league number of each player whose league number is *not* equal to 8467.

```
SELECT    NAME, PLAYERNO, LEAGUENO
FROM      PLAYERS
WHERE     LEAGUENO <> '8467'
OR        LEAGUENO IS NULL
```

The result is:

NAME	PLAYERNO	LEAGUENO
Everett	2	2411
Wise	7	?
Newcastle	8	2983
Collins	27	2513
Collins	28	?
Bishop	39	?
Baker	44	1124
Brown	57	6409
Hope	83	1608
Miller	95	?
Parmenter	100	6524
Moorman	104	7060
Bailey	112	1319

If the condition LEAGUENO IS NULL were left out, the result would contain only rows in which the LEAGUENO column is not equal to NULL and not equal to 8467 (see result table below). This is because the value of the condition LEAGUENO <> '8467' is unknown if the LEAGUENO column has the value NULL. The result table is:

NAME	PLAYERNO	LEAGUENO
Everett	2	2411
Newcastle	8	2983
Collins	27	2513
Baker	44	1124
Brown	57	6409
Hope	83	1608
Parmenter	100	6524
Moorman	104	7060
Bailey	112	1319

Imagine that E_1 is an expression, then:

```
E₁ IS NOT NULL
```

is equivalent to:

```
NOT (E₁ IS NULL)
```

Note: *A condition with* IS NULL *or* IS NOT NULL *can never have the value unknown; work this out by yourself.*

Exercise 8.37: Get the number of each player who has *no* league number.

Exercise 8.38: Why is the condition in the following SELECT statement not useful?

```
SELECT   *
FROM     PLAYERS
WHERE    NAME IS NULL
```

8.11 The EXISTS Operator

In this section, we discuss another operator with which subqueries can be used in conjunction with main queries: the EXISTS operator:

```
<predicate with exists> ::= EXISTS <table subquery>

<table subquery> ::= ( <table expression> )
```

Example 8.45: Find the names and initials of players for whom at least one penalty has been paid.

The question in this example can be answered using an IN operator:

```
SELECT    NAME, INITIALS
FROM      PLAYERS
WHERE     PLAYERNO IN
          (SELECT    PLAYERNO
           FROM      PENALTIES)
```

The result is:

```
NAME        INITIALS
--------    --------
Parmenter   R
Baker       E
Collins     DD
Moorman     D
Newcastle   B
```

The question can also be answered using the EXISTS operator:

```
SELECT    NAME, INITIALS
FROM      PLAYERS
WHERE     EXISTS
          (SELECT    *
          FROM      PENALTIES
          WHERE     PLAYERNO = PLAYERS.PLAYERNO)
```

But what does this statement mean exactly? For every player in the PLAYERS table, SQL determines whether the subquery returns a row. In other words, it checks to see whether there is a nonempty result (EXISTS). If the PENALTIES table contains at least one row with a player number that is equal to that of the player concerned, that row satisfies the condition. We give an example next. For the first row in the PLAYERS table, player 6, the following subquery is executed (behind the scenes):

```
SELECT    *
FROM      PENALTIES
WHERE     PLAYERNO = 6
```

The (intermediate) result consists of one row, so in the end result, we see the name and initials of the player whose number is 6.

The previous subquery will be executed for the second, third, and subsequent rows of the PLAYERS table. The only thing that changes each time is the value for PLAYERS.PLAYERNO in the condition of the WHERE clause. The subquery can, therefore, have a different intermediate result for each player in the PLAYERS table.

The difference between how these two different solutions work can best be explained by examples written in the pseudo language that we introduced in Section 8.1. The formulation with the IN operator is as follows:

```
SUBQUERY-RESULT := [];
FOR EACH PEN IN PENALTIES DO
   SUBQUERY-RESULT :+ PEN;
ENDFOR;
END-RESULT := [];
FOR EACH P IN PLAYERS DO
   IF P.PLAYERNO IN SUBQUERY-RESULT THEN
      END-RESULT :+ P;
   ENDIF;
ENDFOR;
```

The formulation with the EXISTS operator is:

```
END-RESULT := [];
FOR EACH P IN PLAYERS DO
   FOR EACH PEN IN PENALTIES DO
      COUNTER := 0;
      IF P.PLAYERNO = PEN.PLAYERNO THEN
         COUNTER := COUNTER + 1;
      ENDIF;
   ENDFOR;
   IF COUNTER > 0 THEN
      END-RESULT :+ P;
   ENDIF;
ENDFOR;
```

Example 8.46: Get the names and initials of the players who are not team captains.

```
SELECT    NAME, INITIALS
FROM      PLAYERS
WHERE     NOT EXISTS
          (SELECT    *
           FROM      TEAMS
           WHERE     PLAYERNO = PLAYERS.PLAYERNO)
```

The result is:

```
NAME        INITIALS
---------   --------
Everett     R
Wise        GWS
Newcastle   B
Collins     C
Bishop      D
Baker       E
Brown       M
Hope        PK
Miller      P
Parmenter   P
Moorman     D
Bailey      IP
```

A condition that contains only an EXISTS operator always has the value `true` or `false` and is never unknown. In Section 8.13, we return to the EXISTS operator and correlated subqueries.

As mentioned before, during the evaluation of a condition with the EXISTS operator, SQL looks to see if the result of the subquery returns rows but does not look at the contents of the rows. This makes what you specify in the SELECT clause completely irrelevant. You can even specify a literal. Therefore, the previous statement is equivalent to the following statement:

```
SELECT    NAME, INITIALS
FROM      PLAYERS
WHERE     NOT EXISTS
          (SELECT    'nothing'
           FROM      TEAMS
           WHERE     PLAYERNO = PLAYERS.PLAYERNO)
```

Exercise 8.39: Get the name and initials of each player who is captain of at least one team.

Exercise 8.40: Get the name and initials of each player who is not a captain of any team in which player 112 has ever played.

8.12 The ALL and ANY Operators

Another way of using a subquery is with the ALL and ANY operators. These operators resemble the IN operator with subquery. The SOME operator has the same meaning as the ANY operator; ANY and SOME are just synonyms of each other.

As the following definition shows, in the ANY and ALL operators, only scalar expressions can be used, not row expressions.

```
<predicate with any all> ::=
    <scalar expression> <any all operator> <column subquery>

<column subquery> ::= ( <table expression> )

<any all operator> ::=
    <comparison operator> { ALL | ANY | SOME }
```

Example 8.47: Get the player numbers, names, and dates of birth of the oldest players. The oldest players are those whose date of birth is less than or equal to that of every other player.

```
SELECT    PLAYERNO, NAME, BIRTH_DATE
FROM      PLAYERS
WHERE     BIRTH_DATE <= ALL
          (SELECT    BIRTH_DATE
           FROM      PLAYERS)
```

The result is:

```
PLAYERNO  NAME     BIRTH_DATE
--------  -------  ----------
       2  Everett  1948-09-01
```

Explanation: The intermediate result of the subquery consists of the dates of birth of all players. Next, SQL evaluates each player in the main query and checks whether the date of birth of that player is less than or equal to each date of birth that is in the intermediate result of the subquery.

Example 8.48: Get the player numbers and dates of birth of the players who are older than all the players who have ever played for team 2.

```
SELECT    PLAYERNO, BIRTH_DATE
FROM      PLAYERS
WHERE     BIRTH_DATE < ALL
          (SELECT    BIRTH_DATE
           FROM      PLAYERS AS P INNER JOIN MATCHES AS M
                     ON P.PLAYERNO = M.PLAYERNO
           WHERE     M.TEAMNO = 2)
```

The result is:

```
PLAYERNO  BIRTH_DATE
--------  ----------
       2  1948-09-01
      39  1956-10-29
      83  1956-11-11
```

Explanation: The subquery is used to retrieve the dates of birth of all the players who have ever played a match for team 2. These are in chronological order 1962-07-08, 1964-12-28, 1970-05-10, 1963-10-01, and 1963-10-01. Next, the main query is used to determine for each player whether his or her date of birth is less than all these five dates. If we would have used <= in the condition, player 8 would also have appeared in the result. However, that would not have been right because player 8 has played for team 2, and he is not older than all players because he cannot be older than himself.

Example 8.49: For each team, find the team number and the number of the player with the lowest number of sets won.

```
SELECT    DISTINCT TEAMNO, PLAYERNO
FROM      MATCHES AS M1
WHERE     WON <= ALL
          (SELECT   WON
           FROM     MATCHES AS M2
           WHERE    M1.TEAMNO = M2.TEAMNO)
```

The result is:

```
TEAMNO  PLAYERNO
------  --------
     1        83
     1         8
     2         8
```

Explanation: Again, the SELECT statement contains a correlated subquery. The result is that, for each match (that is found in the main query), a set of matches is retrieved with the subquery. For example, for match 1 (played by team 1), the (intermediate) result of the subquery will consist of the matches 1, 2, 3, 4, 5, 6, 7, and 8. These are all matches played with a team number that is equal to the team number belonging to match 1. The final result of the subquery for this first match consists of the won values of those matches—respectively, 3, 2, 3, 3, 0, 1, 3, and 0. Next, SQL checks whether the won value is smaller than or equal to each of these values. For any match where this is so, the number of the team and player is printed.

For the IN operator, we have shown precisely when such a condition is true, false, or unknown. We can do the same for the ALL operator. Imagine that C is the name of the column and that $w_1, w_1, \ldots,$ and w_n are values that form the intermediate result of subquery (S). It follows that:

```
C <= ALL (S)
```

is equivalent to:

```
(C = C) AND (C <= v₁) AND (C = v₂) AND ... AND (C = vₙ)
    AND true
```

The following should be noted concerning certain specific situations:

■ If C is equal to the NULL value, the entire condition evaluates to unknown because the condition C = C is equal to unknown; this rule holds independently of the numbers of values in the result of the subquery.

■ If C is not equal to the NULL value, and if the subquery returns no result, the condition evaluates to true because at the end of this "longhand" condition, true is specified.

■ If C is not equal to the NULL value, and if one of the v values is equal to the NULL value and one of the other v values is not equal to NULL, the condition can be unknown or false.

■ If C is not equal to the NULL value, and if all v values are equal to the NULL value, the condition evaluates to unknown.

Note that not all SQL products interpret the ALL operator this way. For some products, such as DB2, it holds that

```
C <= ALL (S)
```

is equivalent to:

```
(C <= v₁) AND (C <= v₂) AND ... AND (C <= vₙ) AND true
```

The following should be noted concerning certain specific situations:

■ Regardless of the value of C, if the subquery returns no result, the entire condition evaluates to true because at the end of this "longhand" condition true is specified.

■ If C is equal to the NULL value, and if the subquery returns a result of one or more values, the entire condition evaluates to unknown because then every condition C <= v_i is equal to unknown.

■   If one of the v values is equal to the NULL value and one of the other v values is
not equal to the NULL value, the condition is unknown or false.

The following examples illustrate some of these rules.

Example 8.50: Get the highest league number and the corresponding player number.

```
SELECT    LEAGUENO, PLAYERNO
FROM      PLAYERS
WHERE     LEAGUENO >= ALL
          (SELECT    LEAGUENO
           FROM      PLAYERS)
```

Because the LEAGUENO column contains NULL values, the intermediate result of the
subquery will also have NULL values. Therefore, the following condition will be evaluated for each row:

```
(LEAGUENO >= 2411) AND
(LEAGUENO >= 8467) AND
(LEAGUENO >= NULL) AND ... AND true
```

This condition can be true only if all conditions are true, and that does not hold for,
among other things, the third condition. So, this statement will return an empty result.
We must add a condition to the subquery to eliminate the NULL value.

```
SELECT    LEAGUENO, PLAYERNO
FROM      PLAYERS
WHERE     LEAGUENO >= ALL
          (SELECT    LEAGUENO
           FROM      PLAYERS
           WHERE     LEAGUENO IS NOT NULL)
```

The result is:

```
LEAGUENO   PLAYERNO
--------   --------
8467              6
```

This result also shows that when a player does not have a league number, he or she will not appear in the final result.

Example 8.51: Find the player number, the town, and the league number for each player who has the lowest league number of all players resident in his or her town.

The statement that many people will execute will look as follows:

```
SELECT    PLAYERNO, TOWN, LEAGUENO
FROM      PLAYERS AS P1
WHERE     LEAGUENO <= ALL
          (SELECT   P2.LEAGUENO
           FROM     PLAYERS AS P2
           WHERE    P1.TOWN = P2.TOWN)
```

The result is:

PLAYERNO	TOWN	LEAGUENO
27	Eltham	2513
44	Inglewood	1124
112	Plymouth	1319

Explanation: The result of this statement is unexpected. Where is Stratford? Where is player 83? Don't forget, he is the one with the lowest league number in Stratford. This statement looks correct, but it is not. We explain the problem step by step.

For player 6 who lives in Stratford, for example, the (intermediate) result of the subquery consists of the league numbers 8467, 1608, 2411, 6409, and 6524, and two NULL values. These are the league numbers of all players resident in Stratford. Because the result of the subquery contains a NULL value, the entire condition evaluates to unknown, and player 6 is not included in the result.

You might think that you can correct this omission by extending the condition in the subquery, as follows:

```
SELECT    PLAYERNO, TOWN, LEAGUENO
FROM      PLAYERS AS P1
WHERE     LEAGUENO <= ALL
          (SELECT   P2.LEAGUENO
           FROM     PLAYERS AS P2
           WHERE    P1.TOWN = P2.TOWN
           AND      LEAGUENO IS NOT NULL)
```

The result that MySQL presents is now correct:

```
PLAYERNO  TOWN       LEAGUENO
--------  ---------  --------
      27  Eltham     2513
      44  Inglewood  1124
      83  Stratford  1608
     112  Plymouth   1319
```

Player 83 from Stratford has correctly been added to the result. But products such as DB2 present a different result:

```
PLAYERNO  TOWN       LEAGUENO
--------  ---------  --------
      27  Eltham     2513
      28  Midhurst   ?
      44  Inglewood  1124
      83  Stratford  1608
      95  Douglas    ?
     112  Plymouth   1319
```

Player 83 from Stratford has also been included in the result, but players from Midhurst and Douglas have been added, even though there are no players in those two cities with league numbers. The rule in the first bullet point now applies: If the subquery returns no result, the condition evaluates, by definition, to true. For DB2, the statement should be:

```
SELECT    PLAYERNO, TOWN, LEAGUENO
FROM      PLAYERS AS P1
WHERE     LEAGUENO <= ALL
          (SELECT  P2.LEAGUENO
          FROM     PLAYERS AS P2
          WHERE    P1.TOWN = P2.TOWN
          AND      LEAGUENO IS NOT NULL)
AND       TOWN IN
          (SELECT  TOWN
          FROM     PLAYERS
          WHERE    LEAGUENO IS NOT NULL)
```

Explanation: The second subquery determines whether the player lives in a town in which players who have a league number live.

The ANY operator is the counterpart of ALL. We illustrate this with an example.

Example 8.52: Get the player numbers, names, and dates of birth of all players except the oldest.

```
SELECT    PLAYERNO, NAME, BIRTH_DATE
FROM      PLAYERS
WHERE     BIRTH_DATE > ANY
          (SELECT   BIRTH_DATE
           FROM     PLAYERS)
```

The result is:

```
PLAYERNO  NAME        BIRTH_DATE
--------  ---------   ----------
       6  Parmenter   1964-06-25
       7  Wise        1963-05-11
       8  Newcastle   1962-07-08
      27  Collins     1964-12-28
      28  Collins     1963-06-22
      39  Bishop      1956-10-29
      44  Baker       1963-01-09
      57  Brown       1971-08-17
      83  Hope        1956-11-11
      95  Miller      1963-05-14
     100  Parmenter   1963-02-28
     104  Moorman     1970-05-10
     112  Bailey      1963-10-01
```

Explanation: Again, the intermediate result of the subquery contains all the dates of birth. However, this time we are searching for all the players whose date of birth is greater than at least one date of birth of one other player. When such a date of birth is found, the player is not the oldest. The result of this statement consists of all players except the oldest one, and that is Everett; see the answer in the previous example.

Imagine that C is the name of a column and that $v_1, v_1, \ldots,$ and v_n are values that form the intermediate result of subquery (S). It follows that:

```
C > ANY (S)
```

is equivalent to:

```
(C = C) AND ((C > v₁) OR (C > v₂) OR ... OR (C > vₙ) OR false)
```

The following should be noted concerning certain specific situations:

- If C is equal to the NULL value, the entire condition evaluates to unknown because the condition C = C is equal to unknown; this rule holds independently of the numbers of values in the result of the subquery.
- If C is not equal to the NULL value and if the subquery returns no result, the condition evaluates to false because at the end of this "longhand" condition, false is specified.
- If C is not equal to the NULL value, and if one of the v values is equal to the NULL value and one of the other v values is not equal to NULL, the condition can be unknown or true.
- If C is not equal to the NULL value, and if all v values are equal to the NULL value, the condition evaluates to unknown.

Note that not all SQL products interpret the ANY operator this way. For some products, such as DB2, it holds that

```
C > ANY (S)
```

is equivalent to:

```
(C > v₁) OR (C > v₂) OR ... OR (C > vₙ) OR false
```

The following should be noted concerning certain specific situations:

- Regardless of the value of C, if the subquery returns no result, the entire condition evaluates to false because at the end of this "longhand" condition, false is specified.
- If C is equal to the NULL value, and the subquery returns a result, the entire condition evaluates to unknown because then every condition $C > v_i$ is equal to unknown; this rule holds independently of the number of rows in the result of the subquery.
- If C is not equal to the NULL value, and if all v values are equal to the NULL values, the condition is unknown.

Instead of the greater than (>) and the less than or equal to (<=) operators that we used in this section in our two examples, any of the other comparison operators may be used.

Example 8.53: Get the numbers of the players who have incurred at least one penalty that is higher than a penalty paid for player 27; this player may not appear in the result.

```
SELECT    DISTINCT PLAYERNO
FROM      PENALTIES
WHERE     PLAYERNO <> 27
AND       AMOUNT > ANY
          (SELECT    AMOUNT
           FROM      PENALTIES
           WHERE     PLAYERNO = 27)
```

The result is:

```
PLAYERNO
--------
       6
```

Explanation: The main query contains the additional condition PLAYERNO <> 27 because otherwise this player might also appear in the final result.

Example 8.54: Get the player number, the date of birth, and the town of each player who is younger than at least one other player from the same town.

```
SELECT    PLAYERNO, BIRTH_DATE, TOWN
FROM      PLAYERS AS P1
WHERE     BIRTH_DATE > ANY
          (SELECT    BIRTH_DATE
           FROM      PLAYERS AS P2
           WHERE     P1.TOWN = P2.TOWN)
```

The result is:

```
PLAYERNO  BIRTH_DATE  TOWN
--------  ----------  ---------
       6  1964-06-25  Stratford
       7  1963-05-11  Stratford
```

39	1956-10-29	Stratford
44	1963-01-09	Inglewood
57	1971-08-17	Stratford
83	1956-11-11	Stratford
100	1963-02-28	Stratford
104	1970-05-10	Eltham

Explanation: Because the subquery is correlated, for each player, the subquery returns another result. The subquery gives the list with dates of birth of all players who live in the same town.

Finally, try to deduce for yourself that the condition C = ANY (S) is equivalent to C IN (S). Also try to prove that the condition C <> ALL (S) is equivalent to C NOT IN (S) and equivalent to NOT (C IN (S)).

The condition C = ALL (S) is, by definition, false if the subquery returns multiple, distinct values because the value in a column can never be equal to two or more different values simultaneously. We can illustrate this proposition with a simple example. Imagine that v_1 and v_2 are two different values from the intermediate result of subquery S; it follows that C = ALL (S) is equal to (C = v1) AND (C = v2). By definition, this is false.

The opposite applies for the condition C <> ANY (S). If the subquery returns multiple values, the condition is, by definition, true. This is because, again, if the intermediate result of subquery S consists of the values v_1 and v_2, it follows that C <> ANY (S) is equivalent to (C <> v1) OR (C <> v2). This, by definition, is true.

Exercise 8.41: Find the player number of the oldest players from Stratford.

Exercise 8.42: Find the player number and name of each player who has incurred at least one penalty. (Do not use the IN operator.)

Exercise 8.43: Get the payment number, the penalty amount, and the payment date for each penalty that is the highest of all penalties incurred in the same year.

Exercise 8.44: Get the lowest and the highest player number in the PLAYER table, and present these two values as one row.

8.13 Scope of Columns in Subqueries

In this chapter, we have shown many SQL statements with subqueries. In this section, we linger over an important aspect of the subquery: the *scope* of columns. To explain this concept well, we again use *select blocks*. The following table expression, for example, is constructed from five select blocks: S_1, S_2, S_3, S_4, and S_5.

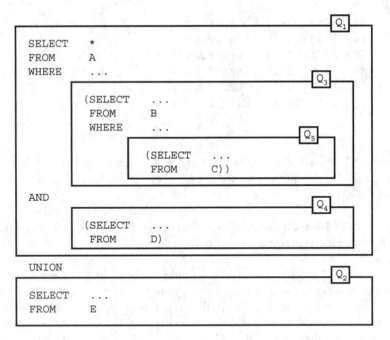

A SELECT clause marks the beginning of a select block. A subquery belongs to the select block formed by the table expression of which it is a subquery. The columns of a table can be used anywhere in the select block in which the table is specified. Therefore, in the example, columns from table A can be used in select blocks S_1, S_3, S_4, and S_5, but not in S_2. We can say, then, that S_1, S_3, S_4, and S_5 together form the scope of the columns from table A. Columns from table B can be used only in select blocks S_3 and S_5, making S_3 and S_5 the scope of the table B columns.

Example 8.55: Get the number and name of each player who has incurred at least one penalty.

The columns from the PLAYERS table can be used in select blocks S_1 and S_2, but columns from the PENALTIES table can be used only in select block S_2.

In this example the PLAYERNO column from the PLAYERS table is used in S_2. What would happen if, instead of PLAYERS.PLAYERNO, only PLAYERNO were specified? In that case, SQL would interpret the column as being PLAYERNO from the PENALTIES table. This would give another result: The NAME of *each* player would be printed because PLAYERNO = PLAYERNO is valid for every row in the PENALTIES table.

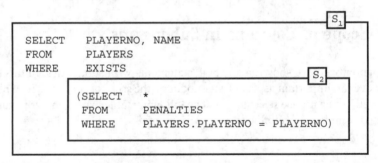

Select block S$_2$ is a *correlated subquery*, because it contains a column that belongs to a table specified in another select block.

If no table name is specified in front of a column name in a subquery, SQL first checks whether that column belongs to one of the tables in the FROM clause of the subquery. If so, SQL assumes that the column belongs to that table. If not, SQL checks whether the column belongs to one of the tables in the FROM clause in the select block of which the subquery is part. However, a statement is much easier to read when the table name is explicitly specified in front of the column name.

How does SQL process the previous statement? Again, we illustrate this by using the intermediate results from the various clauses. The intermediate result of the FROM clause in select block S$_1$ is a copy of the PLAYERS table:

```
PLAYERNO   NAME        ...
--------   ---------   ---
       6   Parmenter   ...
      44   Baker       ...
      83   Hope        ...
       2   Everett     ...
      27   Collins     ...
       :   :             :
       :   :             :
```

When processing the WHERE clause, the subquery is executed for each row in the intermediate result. The intermediate result of the subquery for the first row, in which the player number is equal to 6, looks as follows:

```
PAYMENTNO   PLAYERNO   DATE         AMOUNT
---------   --------   ----------   ------
        1          6   1980-12-08   100.00
```

There is only one row in the PENALTIES table in which the player number equals the player number from the row in the PLAYERS table. The condition of select block S$_1$ is true because the intermediate result of the select block consists of at least one row.

The intermediate result of the subquery for the second row from select block S$_1$ consists of three rows:

```
PAYMENTNO   PLAYERNO   DATE         AMOUNT
---------   --------   ----------   ------
        2         44   1981-05-05    75.00
        5         44   1980-12-08    25.00
        7         44   1982-12-30    30.00
```

We see, then, that player 44 will appear in the end result. The next player, number 83, will not be included in the end result because no row in the PENALTIES table records a player number of 83.

The final result of the statement is:

```
PLAYERNO   NAME
--------   ---------
       6   Parmenter
      44   Baker
      27   Collins
     104   Moorman
       8   Newcastle
```

In processing a correlated subquery, a column from the outer or enveloping select block is considered to be a constant for the subquery.

As mentioned in Chapter 5, in reality, SQL tries to find a more efficient method. However, regardless of the method, the result is always the same.

The following are a couple of alternatives for the previous example.

```
SELECT    PLAYERNO, NAME
FROM      PLAYERS
WHERE     EXISTS
          (SELECT    *
           FROM      PENALTIES
           WHERE     PLAYERS.PLAYERNO = PLAYERS.PLAYERNO)
```

The subquery is executed separately for each player. The WHERE clause in the subquery contains a condition that is always true, so the subquery always returns rows. The conclusion is, therefore, that this statement returns the names of all players.

The result would be different if the PLAYERNO column in the PLAYERS table did (could) contain NULL values (work out why for yourself).

This next statement has the same effect as the first example in this section:

```
SELECT    PLAYERNO, NAME
FROM      PLAYERS AS P
WHERE     EXISTS
          (SELECT    *
           FROM      PENALTIES AS PEN
           WHERE     P.PLAYERNO = PEN.PLAYERNO)
```

Note that the pseudonym for the PENALTIES table can be omitted without affecting the result.

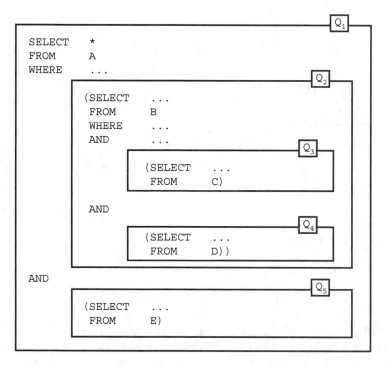

Exercise 8.45: Indicate, for each of the following columns, in which select blocks of the SELECT statement they can be used.

A. C_1
B. C_1
C. C_1
D. C_1
E. C_1

Exercise 8.46: Get the name and initials of each player who has played for a first division team, who has won at least one match, and who has not incurred a single penalty.

Exercise 8.47: Get the number and name of each player who has played for both the first and second teams.

8.14 More Examples with Correlated Subqueries

A correlated subquery is defined as a subquery in which a column is used that belongs to a table specified in another select block. This section presents more examples of this form of the subquery because it shows that, in practice, the use of correlated subquery causes problems.

Example 8.56: Get the team number and division of each team in which player 44 has played.

```
SELECT    TEAMNO, DIVISION
FROM      TEAMS
WHERE     EXISTS
          (SELECT    *
          FROM      MATCHES
          WHERE     PLAYERNO = 44
          AND       TEAMNO = TEAMS.TEAMNO)
```

The result is:

```
TEAMNO  DIVISION
------  --------
     1  first
```

Explanation: Look in the MATCHES table to check whether, for each team, there is at least one row in which the TEAMNO value equals the team number of the team concerned and the player number is 44. We now rewrite this statement in the pseudo language already used in other parts of this book.

```
RESULT := [];
FOR EACH T IN TEAMS DO
   RESULT-SUB := [];
   FOR EACH M IN MATCHES DO
      IF (M.PLAYERNO = 44)
      AND (T.TEAMNO = M.TEAMNO) THEN
         RESULT-SUB :+ M;
   ENDFOR;
   IF RESULT-SUB <> [] THEN
      RESULT :+ T;
ENDFOR;
```

Example 8.57: Get the player number of each player who has incurred more than one penalty.

```
SELECT    DISTINCT PLAYERNO
FROM      PENALTIES AS PEN
WHERE     PLAYERNO IN
          (SELECT    PLAYERNO
           FROM      PENALTIES
           WHERE     PAYMENTNO <> PEN.PAYMENTNO)
```

The result is:

```
PLAYERNO
--------
      27
      44
```

Explanation: For each row in the PENALTIES table, SQL checks whether there is another row in this table with the same player number, but with a different payment number. If so, these players have incurred at least two penalties.

Example 8.58: Get the number and the name of each player who has *not* played matches for team 1.

```
SELECT    PLAYERNO, NAME
FROM      PLAYERS
WHERE     1 <> ALL
          (SELECT    TEAMNO
           FROM      MATCHES
           WHERE     PLAYERNO = PLAYERS.PLAYERNO)
```

The result is:

```
PLAYERNO   NAME
--------   ---------
       7   Wise
      27   Collins
      28   Collins
      39   Bishop
      95   Miller
     100   Parmenter
     104   Moorman
     112   Bailey
```

Explanation: The subquery produces a list of team numbers for which a given player has played. The main query presents the names of those players for whom team number 1 does not appear on the list.

Example 8.59: Get the team number of each team in which player 57 has *not* played.

```
SELECT   TEAMNO
FROM     TEAMS
WHERE    NOT EXISTS
         (SELECT    *
          FROM      MATCHES
          WHERE     PLAYERNO = 57
          AND       TEAMNO = TEAMS.TEAMNO)
```

The result is:

```
TEAMNO
------
     2
```

Explanation: Get the numbers of the teams for which, in the MATCHES table, no row appears with the same team number and player number 57.

Example 8.60: Which players have played for all teams named in the TEAMS table?

```
SELECT    PLAYERNO
FROM      PLAYERS AS P
WHERE     NOT EXISTS
          (SELECT    *
           FROM      TEAMS AS T
           WHERE     NOT EXISTS
                     (SELECT    *
                      FROM      MATCHES AS M
                      WHERE     T.TEAMNO = M.TEAMNO
                      AND       P.PLAYERNO = M.PLAYERNO))
```

The result is:

```
PLAYERNO
--------
       8
```

Explanation: We can formulate the original question in another way: Find each player for whom no team exists for which the player concerned has never played. The two sub-queries together produce a list of teams for which a specific player has not played. The main query presents those players for whom the result table of the subquery is empty. SQL determines for each player, separately, whether the subquery yields *no* result. Consider player 27 as an example. SQL checks whether the following statement has a result for this player:

```
SELECT    *
FROM      TEAMS T
WHERE     NOT EXISTS
          (SELECT    *
           FROM      MATCHES M
           WHERE     T.TEAMNO = M.TEAMNO
           AND       M.PLAYERNO = 27)
```

This statement has a result if there is a team for which player 27 has never played. Player 27 has not played for team 1 but has for team 2. We conclude that the result of this statement consists of the data from team 1. This means that player 27 does not appear in the end result because the WHERE clause specifies players for whom the result of the subquery is empty (NOT EXISTS).

We can do the same with player number 8. The result of the subquery, in this case, is empty because she has played for team 1 as well as for team 2. This means that the condition in the main query is true, and player 8 is included in the end result.

Example 8.61: Get the player number of each player who has played for at least all the teams for which player 57 has ever played.

```
SELECT    PLAYERNO
FROM      PLAYERS
WHERE     NOT EXISTS
          (SELECT   *
          FROM      MATCHES AS M1
          WHERE     PLAYERNO = 57
          AND       NOT EXISTS
                    (SELECT   *
                    FROM      MATCHES AS M2
                    WHERE     M1.TEAMNO = M2.TEAMNO
                    AND       PLAYERS.PLAYERNO = M2.PLAYERNO))
```

The result is:

```
PLAYERNO
--------
       2
       6
       8
      44
      57
      83
```

Explanation: This statement is very similar to the previous one. However, the question asks not for players who have played for *all* teams, but for teams for which player 57 has also played. This difference is apparent in the first subquery. Here, SQL does not check all the teams (in contrast to the subquery in the previous example), but only teams for which player 57 has played.

Example 8.62: Get the player number of each player who has played for the same teams as player 57.

We can formulate this question differently: Get the numbers of the players who, first of all, have played for all the teams for which player 57 has played and, second, have not played for teams for which player 57 has not played. The first part of the question is like the previous one. The second part of the question can be answered with the following SELECT statement. This statement retrieves all players who have competed in teams for which player 57 has not competed:

```
SELECT    PLAYERNO
FROM      MATCHES
WHERE     TEAMNO IN
          (SELECT   TEAMNO
           FROM     TEAMS
           WHERE    TEAMNO NOT IN
                    (SELECT   TEAMNO
                     FROM     MATCHES
                     WHERE    PLAYERNO = 57))
```

Combining this statement with that of the previous question supplies us with our answer:

```
SELECT    PLAYERNO
FROM      PLAYERS AS P
WHERE     NOT EXISTS
          (SELECT   *
           FROM     MATCHES AS M1
           WHERE    PLAYERNO = 57
           AND      NOT EXISTS
                    (SELECT   *
                     FROM     MATCHES AS M2
                     WHERE    M1.TEAMNO = M2.TEAMNO
                     AND      P.PLAYERNO = M2.PLAYERNO))
AND       PLAYERNO NOT IN
          (SELECT   PLAYERNO
           FROM     MATCHES
           WHERE    TEAMNO IN
                    (SELECT   TEAMNO
                     FROM     TEAMS
                     WHERE    TEAMNO NOT IN
                              (SELECT   TEAMNO
                               FROM     MATCHES
                               WHERE    PLAYERNO = 57)))
```

The result is:

```
PLAYERNO
--------
       2
       6
      44
      57
      83
```

Explanation: Player 57 also appears in the result, of course, but can be removed with a simple condition. Player 8 does not appear in the result because she has played for team 1 as well as for team 2, and player 57 played only for team 1. Try to fill in a few other player numbers for yourself to check whether the statement is correct.

Exercise 8.48: Find the player number and name of each player who has incurred at least one penalty; use a correlated subquery.

Exercise 8.49: Find the player number and name of each player who has won at least two matches.

Exercise 8.50: Find the player number and name of each player who has won in total more sets than lost.

Exercise 8.51: Get the name and initials of each player who incurred no penalties between January 1, 1980, and December 31, 1980.

Exercise 8.52: Get the player number of each player who has incurred at least one penalty that is equal to an amount that has occurred at least twice.

8.15 Conditions with Negation

In this section, we discuss an error that programmers often make. This error refers to *conditions with negation*. A condition in which we search for the rows that do not contain a specific value in a column is (informally) called a condition with negation. A negative condition can be made by placing a NOT in front of a positive condition. Here are two examples to demonstrate the problem.

Example 8.63: Get the player numbers of each player who lives in Stratford.

```
SELECT    PLAYERNO
FROM      PLAYERS
WHERE     TOWN = 'Stratford'
```

The result is:

```
PLAYERNO
--------
       2
       6
       7
      39
      57
      83
     100
```

By placing the NOT operator in front of the condition, we get a SELECT statement with a negative condition:

```
SELECT    PLAYERNO
FROM      PLAYERS
WHERE     NOT (TOWN = 'Stratford')
```

The result is:

```
PLAYERNO
--------
       8
      27
      28
      44
      95
     104
     112
```

In this example, we can also specify a negative condition using the comparison operator <> (not equal to):

```
SELECT    PLAYERNO
FROM      PLAYERS
WHERE     TOWN <> 'Stratford'
```

In the last example, we found the players who do *not* live in Stratford by simply adding NOT to the condition. All went well because the SELECT clause contains one of the candidate keys of the PLAYERS table completely, and that is the primary key PLAYERNO. There are problems, however, if the SELECT clause contains only a part of a candidate key or no candidate key. This is illustrated in the next example.

Example 8.64: Get the number of each player who has incurred a penalty of $25.

This example and the corresponding SELECT statement appear similar to those of the previous example:

```
SELECT    PLAYERNO
FROM      PENALTIES
WHERE     AMOUNT = 25
```

Now, find the players who have not incurred a penalty of $25. If we do it in the same way as in the last example, the statement looks like this:

```
SELECT    PLAYERNO
FROM      PENALTIES
WHERE     AMOUNT <> 25
```

The result of this is:

```
PLAYERNO
--------
       6
      44
      27
     104
      44
      27
```

If you examine the PENALTIES table, you will see that player 44 incurred a penalty of $25. In other words, the SELECT statement does not return the correct result to our original question. The reason for this is that the SELECT clause of this statement contains none of the candidate keys of the PENALTIES table. (This table has only one candidate key: PAYMENTNO.) The correct answer is obtained by formulating an entirely different statement. We use a subquery coupled with the NOT operator:

```
SELECT    PLAYERNO
FROM      PLAYERS
WHERE     PLAYERNO NOT IN
          (SELECT   PLAYERNO
           FROM     PENALTIES
           WHERE    AMOUNT = 25)
```

The subquery determines which players have incurred a penalty of $25. In the main query, SQL looks to see which players do *not* appear in the result of the subquery. However, pay attention to the fact that the main query searches not the PENALTIES table, but the PLAYERS table. If the PENALTIES table had been used in the FROM clause in this statement, we would have received a list of all players who had incurred *at least one* penalty that was not equal to $25, and this was not the original question.

Now that we have a negative statement defined using NOT IN, it is possible to create the positive SELECT statement with a comparable structure:

```
SELECT    PLAYERNO
FROM      PLAYERS
WHERE     PLAYERNO IN
          (SELECT   PLAYERNO
           FROM     PENALTIES
           WHERE    AMOUNT = 25)
```

The result is:

```
PLAYERNO
--------
       8
      44
```

Conclusion: If a SELECT clause does not contain a complete candidate key of the table in the FROM clause, and if the WHERE clause has a negative condition, be very careful!

Exercise 8.53: Get the player number of each player who has not won a single match by winning three sets.

Exercise 8.54: Get the team number and the division of each team for which player 6 has not competed.

Exercise 8.55: Get the player number for each player who has played only on teams for which player 57 has never competed.

8.16 Future Conditions

To finish this chapter, we discuss several conditions that have been added to the SQL2 standard but have not been implemented in most SQL products. This section gives a general description of the features of these conditions, but because you cannot yet use them anywhere, we do not give you elaborate or exact definitions. After reading this section, you should have a general understanding of these conditions.

The first new condition is the one with the UNIQUE operator. This operator can be used to determine whether the result of a subquery contains duplicate rows.

Example 8.65: Get the player numbers of the players who have incurred precisely one penalty.

```
SELECT    P.PLAYERNO
FROM      PENALTIES AS P
WHERE     UNIQUE
          (SELECT    PEN.PLAYERNO
           FROM      PENALTIES AS PEN
           WHERE     PEN.PLAYERNO = P.PLAYERNO)
```

The result is:

```
PLAYERNO
--------
       6
       8
     104
```

Example 8.66: Get the player numbers of the players who have incurred at least two penalties.

```
SELECT    P.PLAYERNO
FROM      PENALTIES AS P
WHERE     NOT UNIQUE
          (SELECT   PEN.PLAYERNO
           FROM     PENALTIES AS PEN
           WHERE    PEN.PLAYERNO = P.PLAYERNO)
```

The result is:

```
PLAYERNO
--------
      27
      44
```

Another new operator that was introduced in SQL2 is OVERLAPS. If the begin and end dates of activities, such as sport events, projects, work contracts, and marriages, are stored, often questions are asked concerning whether two activities have some overlap in time. By "overlap," we mean that one event begins before the other finishes. It is difficult to specify this with classical SQL conditions, but with the OVERLAPS operator, it is straightforward.

```
<predicate with overlaps> ::=
    <period specification> OVERLAPS <period specification>

<period specification> ::=
    ( <date expression> , <date expression> )          |
    ( <date expression> , <interval expression> )      |
    ( <time expression> , <time expression> )          |
    ( <time expression> , <interval expression> )      |
    ( <timestamp expression> , <timestamp expression> ) |
    ( <timestamp expression> , <interval expression> )
```

To illustrate this operator, we use the COMMITTEE_MEMBERS table.

Example 8.67: Get the numbers and positions of the players who were on the board during the entire time player 8 was treasurer.

```
SELECT    OTHERS.PLAYERNO, OTHERS.POSITION
FROM      COMMITTEE_MEMBERS AS OTHERS, COMMITTEE_MEMBERS AS P8
WHERE     P8.PLAYERNO = 8
AND       P8.POSITION = 'Treasurer'
AND       OTHERS.PLAYERNO <> 8
AND       OTHERS.BEGIN_DATE <= P8.BEGIN_DATE
AND       OTHERS.END_DATE >= P8.END_DATE
```

The result is:

```
PLAYERNO  POSITION
--------  ---------
       2  Chairman
       6  Secretary
      27  Member
```

Explanation: This result looks correct at first sight. We are looking for players for whom the begin date is equal to or smaller than that of player 8, and for whom the end date is equal to or greater than that of player 8. However, there is a problem when the end dates of the other players are not known because they are still active on the board. We can solve this in two ways. Replace the last condition with the following:

```
AND       COALESCE(OTHERS.END_DATE, '9999-12-31')
          >= P8.END_DATE
```

or replace the entire WHERE clause with the following:

```
WHERE     P8.PLAYERNO = 8
AND       P8.POSITION = 'Treasurer'
AND       OTHERS.PLAYERNO <> 8
AND       OTHERS.BEGIN_DATE <= P8.BEGIN_DATE
AND       (OTHERS.END_DATE >= P8.END_DATE
           OR OTHERS.END_DATE IS NULL)
```

Example 8.68: Get the numbers and positions of the players who were on the board from January 1, 1991, up to and including December 31, 1993.

```
SELECT    PLAYERNO, POSITION
FROM      COMMITTEE_MEMBERS
WHERE     BEGIN_DATE >= '1991-01-01'
AND       END_DATE <= '1993-12-31'
```

However, the NULL values have not been taken in account. What happens when a committee member is still active? Although this problem can be solved by using the COALESCE function for the END_DATE, as we did in the last example, a much more elegant solution uses the OVERLAPS operator.

```
SELECT    PLAYERNO, POSITION
FROM      COMMITTEE_MEMBERS
WHERE     (BEGIN_DATE, END_DATE) OVERLAPS
          ('1991-01-01', '1993-12-31')
```

Explanation: On the left and the right of the OVERLAPS operator, two periods are specified. A period consists of a begin moment and an end moment. A begin moment can be represented by a date, time, or timestamp expression. The end moment can also be a date, time, or timestamp expression, but it can also be an interval.

8.17 Answers

8.1

```
SELECT    PAYMENTNO
FROM      PENALTIES
WHERE     AMOUNT > 60
```

or

```
SELECT    PAYMENTNO
FROM      PENALTIES
WHERE     60 < AMOUNT
```

or

```
SELECT    PAYMENTNO
FROM      PENALTIES
WHERE     AMOUNT - 60 > 0
```

8.2

```
SELECT    TEAMNO
FROM      TEAMS
WHERE     PLAYERNO <> 27
```

8.3   No row in the PLAYERS table satisfies the condition. No row in which the
LEAGUENO column has a value satisfies the condition because the condition is
false. In addition, each row in which the LEAGUENO column has no value (and
thus contains the NULL value) is not returned.

8.4

```
SELECT    DISTINCT PLAYERNO
FROM      MATCHES
WHERE     WON > LOST
```

8.5

```
SELECT    DISTINCT PLAYERNO
FROM      MATCHES
WHERE     WON + LOST = 5
```

8.6

```
SELECT    PLAYERNO, NAME, INITIALS
FROM      PLAYERS
WHERE     PLAYERNO =
          (SELECT    PLAYERNO
           FROM      PENALTIES
           WHERE     PAYMENTNO = 4)
```

8.7

```
SELECT    PLAYERNO, NAME, INITIALS
FROM      PLAYERS
WHERE     PLAYERNO =
          (SELECT   PLAYERNO
           FROM     TEAMS
           WHERE    TEAMNO =
                    (SELECT   TEAMNO
                     FROM     MATCHES
                     WHERE    MATCHNO = 2))
```

8.8

```
SELECT    PLAYERNO, NAME
FROM      PLAYERS
WHERE     BIRTH_DATE =
          (SELECT   BIRTH_DATE
           FROM     PLAYERS
           WHERE    NAME = 'Parmenter'
           AND      INITIALS = 'R')
AND       NOT (NAME = 'Parmenter'
              AND INITIALS = 'R')
```

8.9

```
SELECT    MATCHNO
FROM      MATCHES
WHERE     WON =
          (SELECT   WON
           FROM     MATCHES
           WHERE    MATCHNO = 6)
AND       MATCHNO <> 6
AND       TEAMNO = 2
```

8.10

```
SELECT    MATCHNO
FROM      MATCHES
WHERE     (WON, LOST) =
          ((SELECT   WON
            FROM      MATCHES
            WHERE     MATCHNO = 2),
           (SELECT   LOST
            FROM      MATCHES
            WHERE     MATCHNO = 8))
```

8.11

```
SELECT    PLAYERNO, TOWN, STREET, HOUSENO
FROM      PLAYERS
WHERE     (TOWN, STREET, HOUSENO) <
          (SELECT    TOWN, STREET, HOUSENO
           FROM       PLAYERS
           WHERE      PLAYERNO = 100)
ORDER BY TOWN, STREET, HOUSENO
```

8.12

```
SELECT    PAYMENTNO
FROM      PENALTIES
WHERE     1965 <
          (SELECT    YEAR(BIRTH_DATE)
           FROM       PLAYERS
           WHERE      PLAYERS.PLAYERNO = PENALTIES.PLAYERNO)
```

8.13

```
SELECT    PAYMENTNO, PLAYERNO
FROM      PENALTIES
WHERE     PLAYERNO =
          (SELECT    PLAYERNO
           FROM       TEAMS
           WHERE      TEAMS.PLAYERNO = PENALTIES.PLAYERNO)
```

8.14

```
SELECT    PLAYERNO, NAME, TOWN
FROM      PLAYERS
WHERE     SEX = 'F'
AND       TOWN <> 'Stratford'
```

or

```
SELECT    PLAYERNO, NAME, TOWN
FROM      PLAYERS
WHERE     SEX = 'F'
AND       NOT (TOWN = 'Stratford')
```

8.15

```
SELECT    PLAYERNO
FROM      PLAYERS
WHERE     JOINED >= 1970
AND       JOINED <= 1980
```

or

```
SELECT    PLAYERNO
FROM      PLAYERS
WHERE     NOT (JOINED < 1970 OR JOINED > 1980)
```

8.16

```
SELECT    PLAYERNO, NAME, BIRTH_DATE
FROM      PLAYERS
WHERE     MOD(YEAR(BIRTH_DATE), 400) = 0
OR        (MOD(YEAR(BIRTH_DATE), 4) = 0
          AND NOT(MOD(YEAR(BIRTH_DATE), 100) = 0))
```

8.17

```
SELECT    MATCHNO, NAME, INITIALS, DIVISION
FROM      MATCHES AS M, PLAYERS AS P, TEAMS AS T
WHERE     M.PLAYERNO = P.PLAYERNO
AND       M.TEAMNO = T.TEAMNO
AND       YEAR(BIRTH_DATE) > 1965
AND       WON > LOST
```

8.18

```
SELECT    PAYMENTNO
FROM      PENALTIES
WHERE     AMOUNT IN (50, 75, 100)
```

8.19

```
SELECT    PLAYERNO
FROM      PLAYERS
WHERE     TOWN NOT IN ('Stratford', 'Douglas')
```

or

```
SELECT    PLAYERNO
FROM      PLAYERS
WHERE     NOT (TOWN IN ('Stratford', 'Douglas'))
```

or

```
SELECT    PLAYERNO
FROM      PLAYERS
WHERE     TOWN <> 'Stratford'
AND       TOWN <> 'Douglas'
```

8.20

```
SELECT    PAYMENTNO
FROM      PENALTIES
WHERE     AMOUNT IN
          (100, PAYMENTNO * 5,
          (SELECT    AMOUNT
           FROM      PENALTIES
           WHERE     PAYMENTNO = 2))
```

8.21

```
SELECT    PLAYERNO, TOWN, STREET
FROM      PLAYERS
WHERE     (TOWN, STREET) IN
          (('Stratford','Haseltine Lane'),
           ('Stratford',' Edgecombe Way'))
```

8.22

```
SELECT    PLAYERNO, NAME
FROM      PLAYERS
WHERE     PLAYERNO IN
          (SELECT    PLAYERNO
           FROM      PENALTIES)
```

8.23

```
SELECT    PLAYERNO, NAME
FROM      PLAYERS
WHERE     PLAYERNO IN
          (SELECT    PLAYERNO
           FROM      PENALTIES
           WHERE     AMOUNT > 50)
```

8.24

```
SELECT    TEAMNO, PLAYERNO
FROM      TEAMS
WHERE     DIVISION = 'first'
AND       PLAYERNO IN
          (SELECT    PLAYERNO
           FROM      PLAYERS
           WHERE     TOWN = 'Stratford')
```

8.25

```
SELECT    PLAYERNO, NAME
FROM      PLAYERS
WHERE     PLAYERNO IN
          (SELECT    PLAYERNO
           FROM      PENALTIES)
AND       PLAYERNO NOT IN
          (SELECT    PLAYERNO
           FROM      TEAMS
           WHERE     DIVISION = 'first')
```

or

```
SELECT    PLAYERNO, NAME
FROM      PLAYERS
WHERE     PLAYERNO IN
          (SELECT    PLAYERNO
           FROM      PENALTIES
           WHERE     PLAYERNO NOT IN
                     (SELECT    PLAYERNO
                      FROM      TEAMS
                      WHERE     DIVISION = 'first'))
```

8.26 The result is empty.

8.27

```
SELECT    MATCHNO, PLAYERNO
FROM      MATCHES
WHERE     (WON, LOST) IN
          (SELECT    WON, LOST
           FROM      MATCHES
           WHERE     TEAMNO IN
                     (SELECT    TEAMNO
                      FROM      TEAMS
                      WHERE     DIVISION = 'second'))
```

8.28

```
SELECT    PLAYERNO, NAME
FROM      PLAYERS AS P1
WHERE     (TOWN, STREET, HOUSENO, POSTCODE) IN
          (SELECT    TOWN, STREET, HOUSENO, POSTCODE
           FROM      PLAYERS AS P2
           WHERE     P1.PLAYERNO <> P2.PLAYERNO)
```

8.29

```
SELECT    PAYMENTNO
FROM      PENALTIES
WHERE     AMOUNT BETWEEN 50 AND 100
```

8.30

```
SELECT    PAYMENTNO
FROM      PENALTIES
WHERE     NOT (AMOUNT BETWEEN 50 AND 100)
```

or

```
SELECT     PAYMENTNO
FROM       PENALTIES
WHERE      AMOUNT NOT BETWEEN 50 AND 100
```

or

```
SELECT     PAYMENTNO
FROM       PENALTIES
WHERE      AMOUNT < 50
OR         AMOUNT > 100
```

8.31

```
SELECT     PLAYERNO
FROM       PLAYERS
WHERE      JOINED BETWEEN
           YEAR(BIRTH_DATE + INTERVAL 16 YEAR + INTERVAL 1 DAY)
           AND YEAR(BIRTH_DATE + INTERVAL 40 YEAR -
                    INTERVAL 1 DAY)
```

8.32

```
SELECT     PLAYERNO, NAME
FROM       PLAYERS
WHERE      NAME LIKE '%is%'
```

8.33

```
SELECT     PLAYERNO, NAME
FROM       PLAYERS
WHERE      NAME LIKE '_____'
```

8.34

```
SELECT     PLAYERNO, NAME
FROM       PLAYERS
WHERE      NAME LIKE '_____%'
```

or

```
SELECT    PLAYERNO, NAME
FROM      PLAYERS
WHERE     NAME LIKE '%_____'
```

or

```
SELECT    PLAYERNO, NAME
FROM      PLAYERS
WHERE     NAME LIKE '%_____%'
```

or

```
SELECT    PLAYERNO, NAME
FROM      PLAYERS
WHERE     LENGTH(RTRIM(NAME)) > 6
```

8.35

```
SELECT    PLAYERNO, NAME
FROM      PLAYERS
WHERE     NAME LIKE '_r%r_'
```

8.36

```
SELECT    PLAYERNO, NAME
FROM      PLAYERS
WHERE     TOWN LIKE '_@%%@%_' ESCAPE '@'
```

8.37

```
SELECT    PLAYERNO
FROM      PLAYERS
WHERE     LEAGUENO IS NULL
```

8.38 The NAME column has been defined as NOT NULL. Therefore, the column will never contain a NULL value, which is why the condition is false for each row.

8.39

```
SELECT    NAME, INITIALS
FROM      PLAYERS
WHERE     EXISTS
          (SELECT    *
          FROM      TEAMS
          WHERE     PLAYERNO = PLAYERS.PLAYERNO)
```

8.40

```
SELECT    NAME, INITIALS
FROM      PLAYERS AS P
WHERE     NOT EXISTS
          (SELECT    *
          FROM      TEAMS AS T
          WHERE     T.PLAYERNO = P.PLAYERNO
          AND       EXISTS
                    (SELECT    *
                    FROM      MATCHES AS M
                    WHERE     M.TEAMNO = T.TEAMNO
                    AND       M.PLAYERNO = 112))
```

8.41

```
SELECT    PLAYERNO
FROM      PLAYERS
WHERE     BIRTH_DATE <= ALL
          (SELECT    BIRTH_DATE
          FROM      PLAYERS
          WHERE     TOWN = 'Stratford')
AND       TOWN = 'Stratford'
```

8.42

```
SELECT    PLAYERNO, NAME
FROM      PLAYERS
WHERE     PLAYERNO = ANY
          (SELECT    PLAYERNO
           FROM      PENALTIES)
```

8.43

```
SELECT    PAYMENTNO, AMOUNT, PAYMENT_DATE
FROM      PENALTIES AS PEN1
WHERE     AMOUNT >= ALL
          (SELECT    AMOUNT
           FROM      PENALTIES AS PEN2
           WHERE     YEAR(PEN1.PAYMENT_DATE) =
                     YEAR(PEN2.PAYMENT_DATE))
```

8.44

```
SELECT    (SELECT    PLAYERNO
           FROM      PLAYERS
           WHERE     PLAYERNO <= ALL
                     (SELECT    PLAYERNO
                      FROM      PLAYERS)),
          (SELECT    PLAYERNO
           FROM      PLAYERS
           WHERE     PLAYERNO >= ALL
                     (SELECT    PLAYERNO
                      FROM      PLAYERS))
```

8.45 A. C1: S_1, S_2, S_3, S_4, S_5

B. C1: S_2, S_3, S_4

C. C1: S_3

D. C1: S_4

E. C1: S_5

8.46

```
SELECT    NAME, INITIALS
FROM      PLAYERS
WHERE     PLAYERNO IN
          (SELECT   PLAYERNO
           FROM     MATCHES
           WHERE    TEAMNO IN
                    (SELECT   TEAMNO
                     FROM     TEAMS
                     WHERE    DIVISION = 'first'))
AND       PLAYERNO IN
          (SELECT   PLAYERNO
           FROM     MATCHES
           WHERE    WON > LOST)
AND       PLAYERNO NOT IN
          (SELECT   PLAYERNO
           FROM     PENALTIES)
```

8.47

```
SELECT    PLAYERNO, NAME
FROM      PLAYERS
WHERE     PLAYERNO IN
          (SELECT   PLAYERNO
           FROM     MATCHES
           WHERE    TEAMNO = 1)
AND       PLAYERNO IN
          (SELECT   PLAYERNO
           FROM     MATCHES
           WHERE    TEAMNO = 2)
```

8.48

```
SELECT    PLAYERNO, NAME
FROM      PLAYERS
WHERE     EXISTS
          (SELECT   *
           FROM     PENALTIES
           WHERE    PLAYERNO = PLAYERS.PLAYERNO)
```

8.49

```
SELECT    PLAYERNO, NAME
FROM      PLAYERS
WHERE     PLAYERNO IN
          (SELECT  PLAYERNO
           FROM    MATCHES AS M1
           WHERE   WON > LOST
           AND     EXISTS
                   (SELECT  *
                    FROM    MATCHES AS M2
                    WHERE   M1.PLAYERNO = M2.PLAYERNO
                    AND     WON > LOST
                    AND     M1.MATCHNO <> M2.MATCHNO))
```

or

```
SELECT    PLAYERNO, NAME
FROM      PLAYERS
WHERE     1 < (SELECT  COUNT(*)
              FROM     MATCHES
              WHERE    WON > LOST
              AND      PLAYERS.PLAYERNO = PLAYERNO)
```

8.50

```
SELECT    P.PLAYERNO, P.NAME
FROM      PLAYERS AS P, MATCHES AS M1
WHERE     P.PLAYERNO = M1.PLAYERNO
GROUP BY  P.PLAYERNO, P.NAME
HAVING    SUM(WON) >
          (SELECT   SUM(LOST)
           FROM     MATCHES AS M2
           WHERE    M2.PLAYERNO = P.PLAYERNO
           GROUP BY M2.PLAYERNO)
```

8.51

```
SELECT    NAME, INITIALS
FROM      PLAYERS
WHERE     NOT EXISTS
          (SELECT   *
          FROM      PENALTIES
          WHERE     PLAYERS.PLAYERNO = PLAYERNO
          AND       PAYMENT_DATE BETWEEN '1980-01-01'
                    AND '1980-12-31')
```

8.52

```
SELECT    DISTINCT PLAYERNO
FROM      PENALTIES AS PEN1
WHERE     EXISTS
          (SELECT   *
          FROM      PENALTIES AS PEN2
          WHERE     PEN1.AMOUNT = PEN2.AMOUNT
          AND       PEN1.PAYMENTNO <> PEN2.PAYMENTNO)
```

8.53

```
SELECT    PLAYERNO
FROM      PLAYERS
WHERE     PLAYERNO NOT IN
          (SELECT   PLAYERNO
          FROM      MATCHES WHERE WON = 3)
```

8.54

```
SELECT    TEAMNO, DIVISION
FROM      TEAMS
WHERE     TEAMNO NOT IN
          (SELECT   TEAMNO
          FROM      MATCHES
          WHERE     PLAYERNO = 6)
```

8.55

```
SELECT    DISTINCT PLAYERNO
FROM      MATCHES
WHERE     PLAYERNO NOT IN
          (SELECT   PLAYERNO
           FROM     MATCHES
           WHERE    TEAMNO IN
                    (SELECT   TEAMNO
                     FROM     MATCHES
                     WHERE    PLAYERNO = 57))
```

SELECT Statement: SELECT Clause and Aggregation Functions

9.1 Introduction

The WHERE clause described in the previous chapter selects rows. The intermediate result from this clause forms a *horizontal subset* of a table. In contrast, the SELECT clause selects only columns and not rows; the result forms a *vertical subset* of a table.

The features, limitations, and use of the SELECT clause depend on the presence or absence of a GROUP BY clause. This chapter discusses table expressions *without* a GROUP BY clause. In Chapter 10, "SELECT Statement: The GROUP BY Clause," which concentrates on the GROUP BY clause, we discuss the features of the SELECT clause when the table expression *does* contain a GROUP BY clause.

A large part of this chapter is devoted to so-called *aggregation functions*. In Chapter 5, "SELECT Statement: Common Elements," we referred to these functions but did not explore them in any depth.

```
<select clause> ::=
    SELECT [ DISTINCT | ALL ] <select element list>

<select element list> ::=
    <select element> [ { , <select element> }... ] |
    *

<select element> ::=
    <scalar expression> [[ AS ] <column name> ] |
    <table specification>.*                       |
    <pseudonym>.*

<column name> ::= <name>
```

9.2   Selecting All Columns (*)

The shortest SELECT clause is the one in which only an asterisk (*) is specified. This asterisk is a shorthand notation for all columns in each table mentioned in the FROM clause. Two equivalent SELECT statements are in the following example:

Example 9.1: Get the entire PENALTIES table.

```
SELECT    *
FROM      PENALTIES
```

and

```
SELECT    PAYMENTNO, PLAYERNO, PAYMENT_DATE, AMOUNT
FROM      PENALTIES
```

Explanation: The * symbol, then, does not mean multiplication in this context.

When a FROM clause contains two or more tables, it is sometimes necessary to use a table specification in front of the * symbol to clarify which columns should be presented.

Example 9.2: Get all the information on all the penalties incurred by players who are also captains.

The following three statements are equivalent:

```
SELECT    PENALTIES.*
FROM      PENALTIES INNER JOIN TEAMS
          ON PENALTIES.PLAYERNO = TEAMS.PLAYERNO

SELECT    PENALTIES.PAYMENTNO, PENALTIES.PLAYERNO,
          PENALTIES.PAYMENT_DATE, PENALTIES.AMOUNT
FROM      PENALTIES INNER JOIN TEAMS
          ON PENALTIES.PLAYERNO = TEAMS.PLAYERNO

SELECT    PEN.*
FROM      PENALTIES AS PEN INNER JOIN TEAMS
          ON PEN.PLAYERNO = TEAMS.PLAYERNO
```

The result is:

PAYMENTNO	PLAYERNO	PAYMENT_DATE	AMOUNT
1	6	1980-12-08	100.00
3	27	1983-09-10	100.00
8	27	1984-11-12	75.00

9.3 Expressions in the SELECT Clause

In processing the SELECT clause, the intermediate result is evaluated row by row. Each expression gives rise to a value in each result row. Most of the examples of the SELECT clause described so far contain only column names, but an expression can also take the form of a literal, a calculation, or a scalar function.

Example 9.3: For each match, get the match number, the word Tally, the difference between the columns WON and LOST and the value of the WON column multiplied by 10.

```
SELECT    MATCHNO, 'Tally', WON - LOST,
          WON * 10
FROM      MATCHES
```

The result is:

MATCHNO	TALLY	WON - LOST	WON * 10
1	Tally	2	30
2	Tally	-1	20
3	Tally	3	30
4	Tally	1	30
5	Tally	-3	0
6	Tally	-2	10
7	Tally	3	30
8	Tally	-3	0
9	Tally	1	30
10	Tally	1	30
11	Tally	-1	20
12	Tally	-2	10
13	Tally	-3	0

9.4 Removing Duplicate Rows with DISTINCT

A SELECT clause can consist of a number of expressions preceded by the word DIS-
TINCT. (See the definition at the beginning of this chapter.) When DISTINCT is specified, SQL removes duplicate rows from the intermediate result.

Example 9.4: Find all the different town names from the PLAYERS table.

```
SELECT   TOWN
FROM     PLAYERS
```

The result is:

```
TOWN
---------
Stratford
Stratford
Stratford
Inglewood
Eltham
Midhurst
Stratford
Inglewood
Stratford
Stratford
Douglas
Stratford
Eltham
Plymouth
```

In this result table, the towns Stratford, Inglewood, and Eltham appear seven, two,
and two times, respectively. If the statement is expanded to include DISTINCT:

```
SELECT   DISTINCT TOWN
FROM     PLAYERS
```

it produces the following result, in which all duplicate rows are removed:

```
TOWN
---------
Stratford
Midhurst
Inglewood
Plymouth
Douglas
Eltham
```

Example 9.5: Get every existing combination of street and town names.

```
SELECT    STREET, TOWN
FROM      PLAYERS
```

The result is:

```
STREET            TOWN
--------------    ---------
Stoney Road       Stratford
Haseltine Lane    Stratford
Edgecombe Way     Stratford
Station Road      Inglewood
Long Drive        Eltham
Old Main Road     Midhurst
Eaton Square      Stratford
Lewis Street      Inglewood
Edgecombe Way     Stratford
Magdalene Road    Stratford
High Street       Douglas
Haseltine Lane    Stratford
Stout Street      Eltham
Vixen Road        Plymouth
```

This result also contains duplicate rows; for example, Edgecombe Way and Haseltine Lane in Stratford are each mentioned twice. When DISTINCT is added:

```
SELECT    DISTINCT STREET, TOWN
FROM      PLAYERS
```

the result is:

```
STREET            TOWN
--------------    ---------
Edgecombe Way     Stratford
Eaton Square      Stratford
Haseltine Lane    Stratford
High Street       Douglas
Lewis Street      Inglewood
Long Drive        Eltham
Magdalena Road    Stratford
Old Main Road     Midhurst
Station Road      Inglewood
Stoney Road       Stratford
Stout Street      Eltham
Vixen Road        Plymouth
```

DISTINCT, then, is concerned with the *whole row*, and not only with the expression that directly follows the word DISTINCT in the statement. In these two constructs, the use of DISTINCT is superfluous (but not forbidden):

■ When the SELECT clause includes at least one candidate key for each table specified in the FROM clause, DISTINCT is superfluous. The most important property of a candidate key is that the set of columns that forms the candidate key never allows duplicate values, so a table that has a candidate key never has duplicate rows. The inclusion of a candidate key in the SELECT clause offers a guarantee that no duplicate rows will appear in the end result.

■ When the table expression results in none or only one row with values, DISTINCT is superfluous. For equal rows, at least two rows are necessary. For example, if you are looking for players with a certain player number (WHERE PLAYERNO = 45), the statement results in one row if that player number exists, and otherwise no rows.

The user is allowed to specify the word ALL in the same position in the statement as where DISTINCT appears. Note that ALL actually has the opposite effect to DISTINCT and does not alter the result of a "normal" table expression. In other words, the results of the following two statements are equivalent:

```
SELECT    TOWN
FROM      PLAYERS
```

and

```
SELECT    ALL TOWN
FROM      PLAYERS
```

Exercise 9.1: In which of the following statements is DISTINCT superfluous?

1.

```
SELECT    DISTINCT PLAYERNO
FROM      TEAMS
```

2.

```
SELECT    DISTINCT PLAYERNO
FROM      MATCHES
WHERE     TEAMNO = 2
```

3.

```
SELECT    DISTINCT *
FROM      PLAYERS
WHERE     PLAYERNO = 100
```

4.

```
SELECT    DISTINCT M.PLAYERNO
FROM      MATCHES AS M, PENALTIES AS PEN
WHERE     M.PLAYERNO = PEN.PLAYERNO
```

5.

```
SELECT    DISTINCT PEN.PAYMENTNO
FROM      MATCHES AS M, PENALTIES AS PEN
WHERE     M.PLAYERNO = PEN.PLAYERNO
```

6.

```
SELECT    DISTINCT PEN.PAYMENTNO, M.TEAMNO,
          PEN.PLAYERNO
FROM      MATCHES AS M, PENALTIES AS PEN
WHERE     M.PLAYERNO = PEN.PLAYERNO
```

9.5 When Are Two Rows Equal?

When are two rows identical or equal? At first sight, this seems a trivial question, but are two rows still equal when one of the values is equal to the NULL value? We answer these two questions somewhat formally.

Imagine that two rows, R_1 and R_2, both consist of n values w_i ($1 <= i <= n$). These two rows R_1 and R_2 are equal under the following conditions:

- The number of values in the rows is equal.
- For each i ($1 <= i <= n$), it holds that R_1w_i is equal to R_2w_i or that R_1w_i and R_2w_i are both equal to the NULL value.

This means that if, for example, the value R_1w_3 is equal to the NULL value and R_2w_3 is not, the rows R_1 and R_2 cannot be equal (regardless of the other values). However, if both R_1w_3 and R_2w_3 are equal to the NULL value, they could be equal.

Example 9.6: Get all the different league numbers.

```
SELECT    DISTINCT LEAGUENO
FROM      PLAYERS
```

The result is:

```
LEAGUENO
--------
1124
1319
1608
2411
2513
2983
6409
6524
7060
8467
?
```

Explanation: The NULL value appears only once in the result because rows that consist of only a NULL value are equal to each other.

This rule does not seem to be in line with the rules described in Section 8.2, in Chapter 8, "SELECT Statement: The WHERE Clause." There, we stated that two NULL values are not equal to each other. Also, when comparing row expressions, two NULL values are not considered to be equal or unequal. For example, the next two conditions both evaluate to unknown.

```
NULL = 4
(1, NULL) = (1, NULL)
```

Informally, we could say that SQL executes a *horizontal comparison* with conditions. The values that must be compared are, besides each other, or to the left or right of the comparison operator. And that is the difference with DISTINCT. We could state that DISTINCT rows "underneath" each other in the intermediate result are compared, instead of rows that are "next to" each other. In other words, with DISTINCT, a *vertical comparison* takes place. In that case, NULL values are equal to each other. Imagine the intermediate result of a certain table expression that looks as follows:

```
(1, NULL)
(1, NULL)
```

Two rows are compared vertically when processing DISTINCT. In the end result, only one of the two rows is left. This rule might look somewhat strange, but it is in accordance with the rules of the original relational model.

Example 9.7: Determine which rows will be deleted by DISTINCT.

```
SELECT    DISTINCT *
FROM      (SELECT   1 AS A, 'Hello' AS B, 4 AS C UNION
           SELECT   1, 'Hello', NULL UNION
           SELECT   1, 'Hello', NULL UNION
           SELECT   1, NULL, NULL) AS X
```

The result is:

```
A   B       C
-   -----   -
1   Hello   4
1   Hello   ?
1   ?       ?
```

Exercise 9.2: Determine the results of these SELECT statements for the following T table:

```
T:  C1  C2  C3
--  --  --  --
    c1  c2  c3
    c2  c2  c3
    c3  c2  ?
    c4  c2  ?
    c5  ?   ?
    c6  ?   ?
```

1.

```
SELECT    DISTINCT C2
FROM      T
```

2.

```
SELECT    DISTINCT C2, C3
FROM      T
```

9.6 An Introduction to Aggregation Functions

Expressions in the SELECT clause can contain so-called *aggregation functions* (also called *statistical, group, set,* or *column functions*). If the table expression has *no* GROUP BY clause, an aggregation function in a SELECT clause operates on all rows. If a SELECT clause does contain an aggregation function, the entire table expression yields only one row as an end result. (Remember, we are still assuming here that the table expression has *no* GROUP BY clause.) In fact, the values of a group rows are aggregated to one value. For example, all penalty amounts in the PENALTIES table are added up to one value with the SUM function.

```
<aggregation function> ::=
    COUNT    ( [ DISTINCT | ALL ] { * | <expression> } ) |
    MIN      ( [ DISTINCT | ALL ] <expression> )         |
    MAX      ( [ DISTINCT | ALL ] <expression> )         |
    SUM      ( [ DISTINCT | ALL ] <expression> )         |
    AVG      ( [ DISTINCT | ALL ] <expression> )         |
    STDDEV   ( [ DISTINCT | ALL ] <expression> )         |
    VARIANCE ( [ DISTINCT | ALL ] <expression> )
```

Example 9.8: How many players are registered in the PLAYERS table?

```
SELECT    COUNT(*)
FROM      PLAYERS
```

The result is:

```
COUNT(*)
--------
      14
```

Explanation: The function COUNT(*) counts the number of rows that remain after processing the FROM clause. In this case, the number equals the number of rows in the PLAYERS table.

Example 9.9: How many players live in Stratford?

```
SELECT    COUNT(*)
FROM      PLAYERS
WHERE     TOWN = 'Stratford'
```

The result is:

```
COUNT(*)
--------
       7
```

Explanation: Because the SELECT clause is processed *after* the WHERE clause, the number of rows in which the TOWN column has the value Stratford is counted.

We look at various aggregation functions in more detail in the following sections.

Several general rules apply to the use of aggregation functions. These rules apply when the concerning table expression contains no GROUP BY clause.

- A table expression with an aggregation function yields only one row as a result. This can be a row consisting of only NULL values, but there is always one row. The result can never consist of zero rows or more than one row.
- It is not allowed to nest aggregation functions. Several expression forms can be used as parameters for an aggregation function but not an aggregation function itself. Therefore, this expression is not allowed: COUNT(MAX(...)).
- If the SELECT clause contains one or more aggregation functions, a column specification in the SELECT clause can occur only within an aggregation function.

The last rule requires some explanation. According to this rule, the following statement is not correct because the SELECT clause contains an aggregation function as an expression, while the column name PLAYERNO occurs outside an aggregation function.

```
SELECT    COUNT(*), PLAYERNO
FROM      PLAYERS
```

The reason for this limitation is that the result of an aggregation function always consists of one value, while the result of a column specification consists of a set of values. SQL considers this to be incompatible results.

Note, however, that this rule applies only to column specifications and not to, for example, literals and system variables. Therefore, the following statement is correct:

```
SELECT    'The number of players', COUNT(*)
FROM      PLAYERS
```

The result is:

```
'The number of players is'  COUNT(*)
--------------------------  --------
The number of players is         14
```

In Chapter 10, we extend these rules for the SELECT clause for table expressions that *do* contain a GROUP BY clause.

Exercise 9.3: Is the following SELECT statement correct?

```
SELECT    TEAMNO, COUNT(*)
FROM      MATCHES
```

Exercise 9.4: Find the number of penalties and the highest penalty amount.

9.7 The COUNT Function

With the COUNT function, an asterisk (*) or an expression can be specified between brackets. The first case in which an asterisk is used was discussed in the previous section. In this section, we discuss the other possibilities.

Example 9.10: How many league numbers are there?

```
SELECT    COUNT(LEAGUENO)
FROM      PLAYERS
```

The result is:

```
COUNT(LEAGUENO)
----------------
            10
```

Explanation: The function COUNT(LEAGUENO) is used to count the number of *non-NULL values* in the LEAGUENO column instead of the number of rows in the intermediate result. So, the result is 10 and not 14 (the number of non-NULL and all values in the column, respectively).

Specifying does not change the result of the query. This applies to all the aggregation functions. Therefore, the previous statement could have been written as follows:

```
SELECT    COUNT(ALL LEAGUENO)
FROM      PLAYERS
```

The COUNT function can also be used to calculate the number of *different* values in a column.

Example 9.11: How many different town names are there in the TOWN column?

```
SELECT    COUNT(DISTINCT TOWN)
FROM      PLAYERS
```

The result is:

```
COUNT(DISTINCT TOWN)
--------------------
              6
```

Explanation: When DISTINCT is specified in front of the column name, all the duplicate values are removed first and then the addition is carried out.

Example 9.12: Get the number of different characters that start the names of the players.

```
SELECT    COUNT(DISTINCT SUBSTR(NAME, 1, 1))
FROM      PLAYERS
```

The result is:

```
COUNT(DISTINCT SUBSTR(NAME, 1, 1))
-----------------------------------
                                  8
```

Explanation: This example shows clearly that all kinds of expression forms can be used within aggregation functions, including scalar functions (see Appendix B, "Scalar Functions," for a description of the SUBSTR function).

Example 9.13: Get the number of different years that appear in the PENALTIES table.

```
SELECT    COUNT(DISTINCT YEAR(PAYMENT_DATE))
FROM      PENALTIES
```

The result is:

```
COUNT(DISTINCT YEAR(PAYMENT_DATE))
-----------------------------------
                                  5
```

Example 9.14: Get the number of different town names and the number of sexes represented.

```
SELECT    COUNT(DISTINCT TOWN), COUNT(DISTINCT SEX)
FROM      PLAYERS
```

The result is:

```
COUNT(DISTINCT TOWN)   COUNT(DISTINCT SEX)
--------------------   -------------------
                   6                     2
```

Explanation: More than one aggregation function can be specified in a SELECT clause.

Example 9.15: Get the numbers and names of players who incurred more penalties than they played matches.

```
SELECT    PLAYERNO, NAME
FROM      PLAYERS AS P
WHERE     (SELECT    COUNT(*)
          FROM       PENALTIES AS PEN
          WHERE      P.PLAYERNO = PEN.PLAYERNO)
          >
          (SELECT    COUNT(*)
          FROM       MATCHES AS M
          WHERE      P.PLAYERNO = M.PLAYERNO)
```

The result is:

```
PLAYERNO  NAME
--------  -------
      27  Collins
      44  Baker
```

Explanation: Aggregation functions can appear in the SELECT clause of each table expression, including subqueries.

Example 9.16: For each player, find the player number, the name, and the number of penalties incurred by him or her, but only for players who have at least two penalties.

```
SELECT    PLAYERNO, NAME,
          (SELECT   COUNT(*)
          FROM      PENALTIES
          WHERE     PENALTIES.PLAYERNO = PLAYERS.PLAYERNO)
          AS NUMBER
FROM      PLAYERS
WHERE     (SELECT   COUNT(*)
          FROM      PENALTIES
          WHERE     PENALTIES.PLAYERNO = PLAYERS.PLAYERNO) >= 2
```

The result is:

```
PLAYERNO   NAME      NUMBER
--------   -------   ------
      27   Collins        2
      44   Baker          3
```

Explanation: The correlated subquery in the SELECT clause calculates the number of penalties for each player. That same subquery checks whether that number is greater than 1.

This statement can also be formulated in a more compact way by placing the subquery within the FROM clause:

```
SELECT    PLAYERNO, NAME, NUMBER
FROM      (SELECT   PLAYERNO, NAME,
                    (SELECT   COUNT(*)
                    FROM      PENALTIES
                    WHERE     PENALTIES.PLAYERNO =
                              PLAYERS.PLAYERNO)
                    AS NUMBER
          FROM      PLAYERS) AS PN
WHERE     NUMBER >= 2
```

Explanation: The subquery in the FROM clause determines the number, the name, and the number of penalties for each player. Next, this number becomes a column in the intermediate result. After that, a condition can be specified (NUMBER >= 2); finally, the value of that column in the SELECT clause is retrieved.

Example 9.17: Get the total number of penalties followed by the total number of matches.

```
SELECT (SELECT    COUNT(*)
        FROM      PENALTIES),
       (SELECT    COUNT(*)
        FROM      MATCHES)
```

The result is:

```
SELECT ...   SELECT ...
----------   ----------
         8           13
```

Exercise 9.5: Get the number of different committee positions.

Exercise 9.6: Get the number of league numbers of players resident in Inglewood.

Exercise 9.7: Find for each team the number, the division, and the number of matches played for that team.

Exercise 9.8: For each player, get the number, the name, and the number of matches won.

Exercise 9.9: Create a SELECT statement that results in the following table:

```
TABLES               NUMBERS
------------------   -------
Number of players        14
Number of teams           2
Number of matches        13
```

9.8 The MAX and MIN Functions

With the MAX and MIN functions, you can determine the largest and smallest values, respectively, in a column.

Example 9.18: What is the highest penalty?

```
SELECT    MAX(AMOUNT)
FROM      PENALTIES
```

The result is:

```
MAX(AMOUNT)
-----------
     100.00
```

Example 9.19: What is the lowest penalty incurred by a player resident in Stratford?

```
SELECT    MIN(AMOUNT)
FROM      PENALTIES
WHERE     PLAYERNO IN
          (SELECT    PLAYERNO
           FROM      PLAYERS
           WHERE     TOWN = 'Stratford')
```

The result is:

```
MIN(AMOUNT)
-----------
     100.00
```

Example 9.20: How many penalties are equal to the lowest one?

```
SELECT    COUNT(*)
FROM      PENALTIES
WHERE     AMOUNT =
          (SELECT    MIN(AMOUNT)
           FROM      PENALTIES)
```

The result is:

```
COUNT(AMOUNT)
-------------
            2
```

Explanation: The subquery calculates the lowest penalty, which is $25. The SELECT statement calculates the number of penalties equal to the amount of this lowest penalty.

Example 9.21: For each team, find the team number followed by the player number of the player who has won the most matches for that team.

```
SELECT    DISTINCT TEAMNO, PLAYERNO
FROM      MATCHES AS M1
WHERE     WON =
          (SELECT    MAX(WON)
          FROM      MATCHES AS M2
          WHERE     M1.TEAMNO = M2.TEAMNO)
```

The result is:

```
TEAMNO   PLAYERNO
------   --------
     1          6
     1         44
     1         57
     2         27
     2        104
```

Explanation: In the result, more than one player appears for each team because several players won a match in three sets.

Aggregation functions can occur in calculations. Here are two examples.

Example 9.22: What is the difference between the highest and lowest penalty in cents?

```
SELECT    (MAX(AMOUNT) - MIN(AMOUNT)) * 100
FROM      PENALTIES
```

The result is:

```
(MAX(AMOUNT) - MIN(AMOUNT)) * 100
---------------------------------
                          7500.00
```

Example 9.23: Get the first letter of the last name of all players, alphabetically.

```
SELECT    SUBSTR(MAX(NAME), 1, 1)
FROM      PLAYERS
```

The result is:

```
SUBSTR(MAX(NAME), 1, 1)
-----------------------
W
```

Explanation: First, the MAX function finds the last name in alphabetical order, and then the scalar function SUBSTR picks out the first letter from this name. See Appendix B for a description of this and other functions.

In principle, DISTINCT can be used with the MAX and MIN functions, but this, of course, does not change the end result (work out why for yourself).

When MAX and MIN functions are processed, two special situations must be taken into consideration:

■ If a column in a given row contains only NULL values, the values of the MIN and MAX functions are also NULL.

■   If the MIN and MAX functions are executed on an empty intermediate result, the
value of these functions is also NULL.

Here is an example of each.

Example 9.24: What is the highest league number of all players from Midhurst?

```
SELECT    MAX(LEAGUENO)
FROM      PLAYERS
WHERE     TOWN = 'Midhurst'
```

The result is:

```
MAX(LEAGUENO)
-------------
?
```

Explanation: The PLAYERS table contains only one player from Midhurst, and she has
no league number. That is why the answer of this statement has only one row consisting of the NULL value.

Example 9.25: What is the lowest league number of all players from Amsterdam? If a
player does not exist, print the text Unknown.

```
SELECT    CASE WHEN MIN(LEAGUENO) IS NULL
               THEN 'Unknown'
               ELSE MIN(LEAGUENO)
          END
FROM      PLAYERS
WHERE     TOWN = 'Amsterdam'
```

The result is:

```
CASE WHEN ...
-------------
Unknown
```

Example 9.26: For each player who incurred at least one penalty, find the player number, the highest penalty, and the date on which that penalty was paid.

```
SELECT    PLAYERNO, AMOUNT, PAYMENT_DATE
FROM      PENALTIES AS PEN1
WHERE     AMOUNT =
          (SELECT   MAX(AMOUNT)
           FROM     PENALTIES AS PEN2
           WHERE    PEN2.PLAYERNO = PEN1.PLAYERNO)
```

The result is:

```
PLAYERNO   AMOUNT   PAYMENT_DATE
--------   ------   ------------
       6   100.00    1980-12-08
       8    25.00    1980-12-08
      27   100.00    1983-09-10
      44    75.00    1981-05-05
     104    50.00    1984-12-08
```

Example 9.27: For each player, get the player number, the highest penalty amount that was paid for him or her, and the highest number of sets won in a match.

```
SELECT    PLAYERNO,
          (SELECT   MAX(AMOUNT)
           FROM     PENALTIES
           WHERE    PENALTIES.PLAYERNO = PLAYERS.PLAYERNO)
          AS HIGHESTPENALTY,
          (SELECT   MAX(WON)
           FROM     MATCHES
           WHERE    MATCHES.PLAYERNO = PLAYERS.PLAYERNO)
          AS NUMBEROFSETS
FROM      PLAYERS
```

The result is:

.

.

PLAYERNO	HIGHESTPENALTY	NUMBEROFSETS
2	?	1
6	100.00	3
7	?	?
8	25.00	0
27	100.00	3
28	?	?
39	?	?
44	75.00	3
57	?	3
83	?	0
95	?	?
100	?	?
104	50.00	3
112	?	2

Explanation: The two correlated subqueries are processed for each player separately. When no rows are found, the subquery returns a NULL value.

Example 9.28: Get the number of each player whose lowest penalty amount is equal to his or her highest penalty amount.

```
SELECT    PLAYERNO
FROM      PLAYERS
WHERE     (SELECT    MIN(AMOUNT)
           FROM      PENALTIES
           WHERE     PENALTIES.PLAYERNO = PLAYERS.PLAYERNO) =
          (SELECT    MAX(AMOUNT)
           FROM      PENALTIES
           WHERE     PENALTIES.PLAYERNO = PLAYERS.PLAYERNO)
```

The result is:

```
PLAYERNO
--------
       6
       8
     104
```

Exercise 9.10: Get the lowest number of sets by which a match has been won.

Exercise 9.11: For each player, get the number and the difference between his or her lowest and highest penalty amounts.

Exercise 9.12: Get the number and the date of birth of each player born in the same year as the youngest player who played for the first team.

9.9 The SUM and AVG Functions

The SUM function calculates the sum of all values in a particular column. The AVG function calculates the *arithmetic average* of the values in a particular column. Both functions are, of course, applicable only to columns with a numeric data type.

Example 9.29: What is the total amount of penalties incurred by players from Inglewood?

```
SELECT    SUM(AMOUNT)
FROM      PENALTIES
WHERE     PLAYERNO IN
          (SELECT    PLAYERNO
           FROM      PLAYERS
           WHERE     TOWN = 'Inglewood')
```

The result is:

```
SUM(AMOUNT)
-----------
     155.00
```

You can specify the word ALL in front of the column name without affecting the result. By adding ALL, you explicitly demand that *all* values are considered. In contrast, the use of DISTINCT within the SUM function can alter the end result. If you extend the SUM function in the previous SELECT statement with DISTINCT, you get the following result:

```
SELECT    SUM(DISTINCT AMOUNT)
FROM      PENALTIES
WHERE     PLAYERNO IN
          (SELECT   PLAYERNO
           FROM     PLAYERS
           WHERE    TOWN = 'Inglewood')
```

The result is:

```
SUM(AMOUNT)
-----------
     130.00
```

Note that, unlike the COUNT, MIN, and MAX functions, the SUM function is applicable only to columns with a numeric data type. The former three functions can also be applied to columns with alphanumeric and temporal data types.

Example 9.30: Get the average amount of penalties incurred by player 44.

```
SELECT    AVG(AMOUNT)
FROM      PENALTIES
WHERE     PLAYERNO = 44
```

The result is:

```
AVG(AMOUNT)
-----------
      43.33
```

Explanation: The amount $43.33 is the average of the amounts $75, $25, and $30.

Example 9.31: Which players have ever incurred a penalty greater than the average penalty?

```
SELECT    DISTINCT PLAYERNO
FROM      PENALTIES
WHERE     AMOUNT >
          (SELECT    AVG(AMOUNT)
           FROM      PENALTIES)
```

The result is:

```
PLAYERNO
--------
       6
      27
      44
```

Explanation: The average penalty is $60.

Adding the word ALL does not affect the result because it simply reinforces the idea that *all* values are included in the calculation. On the other hand, adding DISTINCT within the AVG function does influence the result.

Example 9.32: What is the *unweighted* arithmetic mean of the penalty amounts? (By "unweighted," we mean that each value is considered only once in the calculation, even when it occurs more than once.)

```
SELECT    AVG(DISTINCT AMOUNT)
FROM      PENALTIES
```

The result is:

```
AVG(DISTINCT AMOUNT)
--------------------
               56.00
```

Explanation: The amount $56 is equal to $100 + $75 + $50 + $30 + $25 divided by 5.

Example 9.33: What is the average length (in number of characters) of the names of the players, and how long is the longest name?

```
SELECT    AVG(LENGTH(RTRIM(NAME))), MAX(LENGTH(RTRIM(NAME)))
FROM      PLAYERS
```

The result is:

```
AVG(LENGTH(RTRIM(NAME)))   MAX(LENGTH(RTRIM(NAME)))
------------------------   ------------------------
                6.5000                            9
```

Example 9.34: For each penalty, get the payment number, the amount, and the difference between the amount and the average penalty amount.

```
SELECT    PAYMENTNO, AMOUNT,
          ABS(AMOUNT - (SELECT AVG(AMOUNT)
                        FROM   PENALTIES)) AS DIFFERENCE
FROM      PENALTIES AS P
```

The result is:

PAYMENTNO	AMOUNT	DIFFERENCE
1	100.00	40.00
2	75.00	15.00
3	100.00	40.00
4	50.00	10.00
5	25.00	35.00
6	25.00	35.00
7	30.00	30.00
8	75.00	15.00

Explanation: In this example, the subquery is part of a compound expression. The result of the subquery is subtracted from the AMOUNT column, and next the absolute value of this result is calculated with the scalar function ABS.

For the SUM and AVG functions, the same rules apply as for MIN and MAX:

- If a column in a given row contains only NULL values, the value of the function is equal to NULL.
- If some of the values in a column are NULL, the value of the function is equal to the sum of the average of all *non*-NULL values divided by the number of *non*-NULL values (and, therefore, not divided by the total number of values).
- If the intermediate result for which SUM or AVG must be calculated is empty, the result of the function is equal to the NULL value.

Exercise 9.13: Determine the value of these functions for the following set of values in the NUMBER column: { 1, 2, 3, 4, 1, 4, 4, NULL, 5 }.

```
COUNT(*)
COUNT(NUMBER)
MIN(NUMBER)
MAX(NUMBER)
SUM(NUMBER)
AVG(NUMBER)
COUNT(DISTINCT NUMBER)
MIN(DISTINCT NUMBER)
MAX(DISTINCT NUMBER)
SUM(DISTINCT NUMBER)
AVG(DISTINCT NUMBER)
```

Exercise 9.14: What is the average penalty for players who have ever competed for team 1?

Exercise 9.15: Get the numbers and names of the players for whom the total amount of penalties is higher than 100.

Exercise 9.16: Get the names and initials of the players who have won more sets in at least one of their matches than player 27 has won in total.

Exercise 9.17: Get the numbers and names of the players for whom the sum of all sets won is equal to 8.

Exercise 9.18: Get the numbers and names of the players for whom the length of their name is greater than the average length.

Exercise 9.19: Get for each player (also those without penalties) the player number and the difference between his or her maximum and the average penalty.

Exercise 9.20: Get for each player the average penalty amount in the form of a simple, horizontal histogram. Make use of the scalar function REPEAT.

9.10 The VARIANCE and STDDEV Functions

The VARIANCE and STDDEV functions calculate, respectively, the *variance* and the *standard deviation* of the values in a particular column. These functions are, of course, applicable only to columns with a numeric data type.

> **Portability:** *Not every SQL product supports the functions VARIANCE and STDDEV. That is why we also illustrate in this section how these values can be calculated with standard SQL.*

The VARIANCE function, or the VAR function, for short, calculates the variance. Variance is a measurement that indicates how close all values are to the average. In other words, it refers to the *distribution* of all values. The closer each value is to the average, the lower the variance is.

Example 9.35: Get the variance of all penalties incurred by player 44.

```
SELECT    VARIANCE(AMOUNT)
FROM      PENALTIES
WHERE     PLAYERNO = 44
```

The result is:

```
VARIANCE(AMOUNT)
----------------
         505.555
```

Explanation: The variance is calculated on the basis of the following steps:

- Calculate the average of the column concerned.
- Determine for each value in the column how much the absolute value differs from the average.

- Calculate the sum of the squares of the differences.
- Divide the sum by the number of values (in the column).

If you execute these steps for the previous statement, the first step returns the answer: 43.33333, the average of the three values 75, 25, and 30. Next, for each of the three values, the difference with the average is calculated. You can determine this with the following SELECT statement:

```
SELECT   AMOUNT -
         (SELECT    AVG(AMOUNT)
          FROM      PENALTIES
          WHERE     PLAYERNO = 44)
FROM     PENALTIES
WHERE    PLAYERNO = 44
```

This gives the result: 31.666667, −18.33333, and −13.33333. You can use the following SELECT statement to calculate this intermediate result:

```
SELECT   SUM(P)
FROM     (SELECT    POWER(AMOUNT -
                    (SELECT    AVG(AMOUNT)
                     FROM      PENALTIES
                     WHERE     PLAYERNO = 44),2) AS P
          FROM      PENALTIES
          WHERE     PLAYERNO = 44) AS POWERS
```

The result is 1516.6666666667. In the final step, this amount is divided by the number of values, which gives an end result of 505.5555. To calculate all these steps without the VARIANCE function, the following statement can be used:

```
SELECT   SUM(P) /
         (SELECT COUNT(*) FROM PENALTIES WHERE PLAYERNO = 44)
FROM     (SELECT    POWER(AMOUNT -
                    (SELECT    AVG(AMOUNT)
                     FROM      PENALTIES
                     WHERE     PLAYERNO = 44),2) AS P
          FROM      PENALTIES
          WHERE     PLAYERNO = 44) AS POWERS
```

The STDDEV function calculates the *standard deviation* of a set of values. Standard deviation is another measure of distribution for determining how close the values are to the average. By definition, the standard deviation is equal to the square root of the variance. In other words, the following two expressions are equal: STDDEV (...) and SQRT (VARIANCE (...)).

Example 9.36: Get the standard deviation for all penalties incurred by player 44.

```
SELECT    STDDEV (AMOUNT)
FROM      PENALTIES
WHERE     PLAYERNO = 44
```

The result is:

```
STDDEV (AMOUNT)
--------------
      22.484563
```

Exercise 9.21: Get the standard deviation of all penalties of player 44 *without* using the STDDEV function.

9.11 Answers

9.1 Not superfluous.
Not superfluous.
Superfluous because a condition appears on the primary key.
Not superfluous.
Not superfluous.
Not superfluous.

9.2

1.

```
C2
—
c2
?
```

2.

```
C2   C3
—    —
c2   c3
c2   ?
?    ?
```

9.3 This statement is not correct. An aggregation function is used in the SELECT clause; therefore, all other column names must appear within an aggregation function.

9.4

```
SELECT    COUNT(*), MAX(AMOUNT)
FROM      PENALTIES
```

9.5

```
SELECT    COUNT(DISTINCT POSITION)
FROM      COMMITTEE_MEMBERS
```

9.6

```
SELECT    COUNT(LEAGUENO)
FROM      PLAYERS
WHERE     TOWN = 'Inglewood'
```

9.7

```
SELECT    TEAMNO, DIVISION,
          (SELECT    COUNT(*)
           FROM      MATCHES
           WHERE     TEAMS.TEAMNO = MATCHES.TEAMNO)
FROM      TEAMS
```

9.8

```
SELECT    PLAYERNO, NAME,
          (SELECT    COUNT(*)
          FROM       MATCHES
          WHERE      MATCHES.PLAYERNO = PLAYERS.PLAYERNO
          AND        WON > LOST)
FROM      PLAYERS
```

9.9

```
SELECT 'Number of players' ,
        (SELECT COUNT(*) FROM PLAYERS) UNION
SELECT 'Number of teams',
        (SELECT COUNT(*) FROM TEAMS) UNION
SELECT 'Number of matches',
        (SELECT COUNT(*) FROM MATCHES)
```

9.10

```
SELECT    MIN(WON)
FROM      MATCHES
WHERE     WON > LOST
```

9.11

```
SELECT    PLAYERNO,
          ABS((SELECT    MIN(AMOUNT)
               FROM       PENALTIES
               WHERE      PENALTIES.PLAYERNO =
                          PLAYERS.PLAYERNO) -
              (SELECT    MAX(AMOUNT)
               FROM       PENALTIES
               WHERE      PENALTIES.PLAYERNO =
                          PLAYERS.PLAYERNO))
FROM      PLAYERS
```

9.12

```
SELECT    PLAYERNO, BIRTH_DATE
FROM      PLAYERS
WHERE     YEAR(BIRTH_DATE) =
          (SELECT    MAX(YEAR(BIRTH_DATE))
           FROM      PLAYERS
           WHERE     PLAYERNO IN
                     (SELECT    PLAYERNO
                      FROM      MATCHES
                      WHERE     TEAMNO = 1))
```

9.13 9
    8
    1
    5
    24
    3
    5
    1
    5
    15
    15 / 5 = 3

9.14

```
SELECT    AVG(AMOUNT)
FROM      PENALTIES
WHERE     PLAYERNO IN
          (SELECT    PLAYERNO
           FROM      MATCHES
           WHERE     TEAMNO = 1)
```

9.15

```
SELECT    PLAYERNO, NAME
FROM      PLAYERS
WHERE     (SELECT    SUM(AMOUNT)
           FROM      PENALTIES
           WHERE     PENALTIES.PLAYERNO = PLAYERS.PLAYERNO)
          > 100
```

9.16

```
SELECT    NAME, INITIALS
FROM      PLAYERS
WHERE     PLAYERNO IN
          (SELECT    PLAYERNO
           FROM      MATCHES
           WHERE     WON >
                     (SELECT    SUM(WON)
                      FROM      MATCHES
                      WHERE     PLAYERNO = 27))
```

9.17

```
SELECT    PLAYERNO, NAME
FROM      PLAYERS
WHERE     (SELECT    SUM(WON)
           FROM      MATCHES
           WHERE     MATCHES.PLAYERNO =
                     PLAYERS.PLAYERNO) = 8
```

9.18

```
SELECT    PLAYERNO, NAME
FROM      PLAYERS
WHERE     LENGTH(RTRIM(NAME)) >
          (SELECT    AVG(LENGTH(RTRIM(NAME)))
           FROM      PLAYERS)
```

9.19

```
SELECT    PLAYERNO,
          ABS((SELECT    AVG(AMOUNT)
               FROM      PENALTIES
               WHERE     PENALTIES.PLAYERNO =
                         PLAYERS.PLAYERNO) -
              (SELECT    MAX(AMOUNT)
               FROM      PENALTIES
               WHERE     PENALTIES.PLAYERNO =
                         PLAYERS.PLAYERNO))
FROM      PLAYERS
```

9.20

```
SELECT    PLAYERNO,
          REPEAT('*',
             CAST((SELECT    AVG(AMOUNT)
                   FROM      PENALTIES
                   WHERE     PENALTIES.PLAYERNO =
                             PLAYERS.PLAYERNO)/10
                  AS SIGNED INTEGER))
FROM      PLAYERS
```

9.21

```
SELECT    SQRT(SUM(P) /
          (SELECT COUNT(*) FROM PENALTIES WHERE
                      PLAYERNO = 44))
FROM      (SELECT    POWER(AMOUNT -
                      (SELECT    AVG(AMOUNT)
                       FROM      PENALTIES
                       WHERE     PLAYERNO = 44),2) AS P
           FROM      PENALTIES
           WHERE     PLAYERNO = 44) AS POWERS
```

10

SELECT Statement:
The GROUP BY Clause

10.1 Introduction

T he GROUP BY clause groups rows on the basis of similarities between them. You could, for example, group all the rows in the PLAYERS table on the basis of the place of residence; the result would be one group of players per town. From there you could query how many players there are in each group. The question that is actually answered is then: How many players live in each town? Other examples follow: How many matches have been played per team, and how much has been incurred in penalties per player? In short, the GROUP BY clause is frequently used to formulate questions based on the word per.

By adding aggregation functions, such as COUNT and SUM, to a select block with the use of a GROUP BY clause, data can be *aggregated*. These functions owe their name to this. Aggregation means that you ask not for the individual values, but for summations, averages, frequencies, and subtotals.

```
<group by clause> ::=
    GROUP BY <group by specification list>
            [ WITH { ROLLUP | CUBE } ]

<group by specification list> ::=
    <group by specification> [ { , <group by specification> }... ]

<group by specification> ::=
    <group by expression>          |
    <grouping sets specification> |
    <rollup specification>

<grouping sets specification> ::=
    GROUPING SETS ( <grouping sets specification list> )
```

(continued)

```
<grouping sets specification list> ::=
    <grouping sets specification>
    [ { , <grouping sets specification> }... ]

<grouping sets specification> ::=
    <group by expression>                    |
    <rollup specification>                   |
    ( <grouping sets specification list> )

<rollup specification> ::=
    ROLLUP ( <group by expression list> ) |
    CUBE ( <group by expression list> )   |
    ( )

<group by expression> ::= <scalar expression>
```

10.2 Grouping on One Column

The simplest form of the GROUP BY clause is the one in which only one column is grouped. In the previous chapters, we gave several examples of statements with such a GROUP BY clause. For the sake of clarity, we specify several other examples in this section.

Example 10.1: Get all the different town names from the PLAYERS table.

```
SELECT   TOWN
FROM     PLAYERS
GROUP BY TOWN
```

The intermediate result from the GROUP BY clause could look like this:

```
TOWN        PLAYERNO                        NAME
---------   ---------------------------     ---------------------
Stratford   {6, 83, 2, 7, 57, 39, 100}      {Parmenter, Hope, ...}
Midhurst    {28}                            {Collins}
Inglewood   {44, 8}                         {Baker, Newcastle}
Plymouth    {112}                           {Bailey}
Douglas     {95}                            {Miller}
Eltham      {27, 104}                       {Collins, Moorman}
```

Explanation: All rows with the same TOWN form one group. Each row in the interme-diate result has one value in the TOWN column, whereas all other columns can contain multiple values. To indicate that these columns are special, the values are placed between brackets. We show those columns in this way for illustrative purposes only; you should realize that SQL probably would solve this internally in a different way. Fur-thermore, these two columns *cannot* be presented like this. In fact, a column that is not grouped is completely omitted from the end result, but we return to this later in the chapter.

The end result of the statement is:

```
TOWN
---------
Stratford
Midhurst
Inglewood
Plymouth
Douglas
Eltham
```

A frequently used term in this particular context is *grouping*. The GROUP BY clause in the previous statement has one grouping, which consists of only one column: the TOWN column. In this chapter, we sometimes represent this as follows: The result is grouped by [TOWN]. Later in this chapter, we give examples of groupings with multi-ple columns and GROUP BY clauses consisting of multiple groupings.

We could have solved the earlier question more easily by leaving out the GROUP BY clause and adding DISTINCT to the SELECT clause (work this out for yourself). Using the GROUP BY clause becomes interesting when we extend the SELECT clause with aggregation functions.

Example 10.2: For each town, find the number of players.

```
SELECT    TOWN, COUNT(*)
FROM      PLAYERS
GROUP BY  TOWN
```

The result is:

TOWN	COUNT(*)
Stratford	7
Midhurst	1
Inglewood	2
Plymouth	1
Douglas	1
Eltham	2

Explanation: In this statement, the result is grouped by [TOWN]. The COUNT(*) function is now executed against each grouped row instead of against all rows. In other words, the function COUNT(*) is calculated for each grouped row (for each town).

In this result, it is obvious that the data is aggregated. The individual data of players cannot be displayed anymore, and the data is aggregated by TOWN. Or the aggregation level of this result is TOWN.

Example 10.3: For each team, get the team number, the number of matches that has been played for that team, and the total number of sets won.

```
SELECT    TEAMNO, COUNT(*), SUM(WON)
FROM      MATCHES
GROUP BY  TEAMNO
```

The result is:

TEAMNO	COUNT(*)	SUM(WON)
1	8	15
2	5	9

Explanation: This statement contains one grouping consisting of the TEAMNO column.

Example 10.4: For each team that is captained by a player resident in Eltham, get the team number and the number of matches that has been played for that team.

```
SELECT    TEAMNO, COUNT(*)
FROM      MATCHES
WHERE     TEAMNO IN
          (SELECT  TEAMNO
           FROM     TEAMS INNER JOIN PLAYERS
                    ON TEAMS.PLAYERNO = PLAYERS.PLAYERNO
           WHERE    TOWN = 'Eltham')
GROUP BY TEAMNO
```

The result is:

```
TEAMNO   COUNT(*)
------   --------
    2        5
```

The column on which the result has been grouped might also appear in the SELECT clause as a parameter within an aggregation function. This does not happen often, but it is allowed.

Example 10.5: Get each different penalty amount, followed by the number of times that the amount occurs, in the PENALTIES table, and also show the result of that amount multiplied by the number.

```
SELECT    AMOUNT, COUNT(*), SUM(AMOUNT)
FROM      PENALTIES
GROUP BY AMOUNT
```

The PENALTIES table is grouped on the AMOUNT column first. The intermediate result could be presented as follows:

PAYMENTNO	PLAYERNO	PAYMENT_DATE	AMOUNT
{5, 6}	{44, 8}	{1980-12-08, 1980-12-08}	25.00
{7}	{44}	{1982-12-30}	30.00
{4}	{104}	{1984-12-08}	50.00
{2, 8}	{44, 27}	{1981-05-05, 1984-11-12}	75.00
{1, 3}	{6, 27}	{1980-12-08, 1983-09-10}	100.00

Again, the values of the columns that are not grouped are placed between brackets, and the AMOUNT column shows only one value. However, that is not entirely correct. Behind the scenes, SQL also creates a group for this column. So, the intermediate result should, in fact, be presented as follows:

PAYMENTNO	PLAYERNO	PAYMENT_DATE	AMOUNT
{5, 6}	{44, 8}	{1980-12-08, 1980-12-08}	{25.00, 25.00}
{7}	{44}	{1982-12-30}	{30.00}
{4}	{104}	{1984-12-08}	{50.00}
{2, 8}	{44, 27}	{1981-05-05, 1984-11-12}	{75.00, 75.00}
{1, 3}	{6, 27}	{1980-12-08, 1983-09-10}	{100.00, 100.00}

The values in the AMOUNT column are also represented as a group now. Of course, only equal values appear in each group. And because it is a group, aggregation functions can be used.

The result is:

AMOUNT	COUNT(*)	SUM(AMOUNT)
25.00	2	50.00
30.00	1	30.00
50.00	1	50.00
75.00	2	150.00
100.00	2	200.00

However, in this book, we do not present the values of the grouped columns between brackets.

Exercise 10.1: Show the different years in which players joined the club; use the PLAYERS table.

Exercise 10.2: For each year, show the number of players who joined the club.

Exercise 10.3: For each player who has incurred at least one penalty, give the player number, the average penalty amount, and the number of penalties.

Exercise 10.4: For each team that has played in the first division, give the team number, the number of matches, and the total number of sets won.

10.3 Grouping on Two or More Columns

A GROUP BY clause can contain two or more columns—or, in other words, a grouping can consist of two or more columns. We illustrate this with two examples.

Example 10.6: For the MATCHES table, get all the different combinations of team numbers and player numbers.

```
SELECT     TEAMNO, PLAYERNO
FROM       MATCHES
GROUP BY   TEAMNO, PLAYERNO
```

   The result is grouped not on one column, but on two. All rows with the same team number and the same player number form a group.
   The intermediate result from the GROUP BY clause is:

TEAMNO	PLAYERNO	MATCHNO	WON	LOST
1	2	{6}	{1}	{3}
1	6	{1, 2, 3}	{3, 2, 3}	{1, 3, 0}
1	8	{8}	{0}	{3}
1	44	{4}	{3}	{2}
1	57	{7}	{3}	{0}
1	83	{5}	{0}	{3}
2	8	{13}	{0}	{3}
2	27	{9}	{3}	{2}
2	104	{10}	{3}	{2}
2	112	{11, 12}	{2, 1}	{3, 3}

The end result is:

```
TEAMNO   PLAYERNO
------   --------
    1           2
    1           6
    1           8
    1          44
    1          57
    1          83
    2           8
    2          27
    2         104
    2         112
```

The sequence of the columns in the GROUP BY clause has no effect on the end result of a statement. The following statement, therefore, is equivalent to the previous one:

```
SELECT    TEAMNO, PLAYERNO
FROM      MATCHES
GROUP BY PLAYERNO, TEAMNO
```

As an example, let us add some aggregation functions to the previous SELECT statement:

```
SELECT    TEAMNO, PLAYERNO, SUM(WON),
          COUNT(*), MIN(LOST)
FROM      MATCHES
GROUP BY TEAMNO, PLAYERNO
```

The result is:

TEAMNO	PLAYERNO	SUM(WON)	COUNT(*)	MIN(LOST)
1	2	1	1	3
1	6	8	3	0
1	8	0	1	3
1	44	3	1	2
1	57	3	1	0
1	83	0	1	3
2	8	0	1	3
2	27	3	1	2
2	104	3	1	2
2	112	3	2	3

In this example, the grouping is equal to [TEAMNO, PLAYERNO] and the aggregation level of the result is the combination of team number with player number. This aggregation level is lower than that of a statement in which the grouping is equal to [TEAMNO] or [TOWN].

Example 10.7: For each player who has ever incurred at least one penalty, get the player number, the name, and the total amount in penalties incurred.

```
SELECT    P.PLAYERNO, NAME, SUM(AMOUNT)
FROM      PLAYERS AS P INNER JOIN PENALTIES AS PEN
          ON P.PLAYERNO = PEN.PLAYERNO
GROUP BY P.PLAYERNO, NAME
```

The result is:

P.PLAYERNO	NAME	SUM(AMOUNT)
6	Parmenter	100.00
8	Newcastle	25.00
27	Collins	175.00
44	Baker	130.00
104	Moorman	50.00

Explanation: This example also has a grouping consisting of two columns. The statement would have given the same result if the PEN.PLAYERNO column had been included in the grouping. Work this out for yourself.

Exercise 10.5: For each combination of won–lost sets, get the number of matches won.

Exercise 10.6: For each combination of year–month, get the number of committee members who started in that year and that month.

Exercise 10.7: Group the matches on town of player and division of team, and get the sum of the sets won for each combination of town[nd]division.

Exercise 10.8: For each player who lives in Inglewood, get the name, initials, and number of penalties incurred by him or her.

Exercise 10.9: For each team, get the team number, the division, and the total number of sets won.

10.4 Grouping on Expressions

Up to now, we have shown only examples in which the result was grouped on one or more columns, but what happens when we group on expressions? Again, here are two examples.

Example 10.8: For each year present in the PENALTIES table, get the number of penalties paid.

```
SELECT    YEAR(PAYMENT_DATE), COUNT(*)
FROM      PENALTIES
GROUP BY  YEAR(PAYMENT_DATE)
```

The intermediate result from the GROUP BY clause is:

YEAR(PAYMENT_DATE)	PAYMENTNO	PLAYERNO	PAYMENT_DATE	AMOUNT
1980	{1, 5, 6}	{6, 44, 8}	{1980-12-08, 1980-12-08, 1980-12-08}	{100.00, 25,00, 25,00}
1981	{2}	{44}	{1981-05-05}	{75,00}
1982	{7}	{44}	{1982-12-30}	{30,00}
1983	{3}	{27}	{1983-09-10}	{100,00}
1984	{4, 8}	{104, 27}	{1984-12-08, 1984-11-12}	{50,00, 75,00}

The result is:

```
YEAR(PAYMENT_DATE)   COUNT(*)
------------------   --------
1980                        3
1981                        1
1982                        1
1983                        1
1984                        2
```

Explanation: The result is now grouped on the values of the scalar expression YEAR(PAYMENT_DATE). Rows for which the value of the expression YEAR(PAYMENT_DATE) is equal form a group.

Example 10.9: Group the players on the basis of their player numbers. Group 1 should contain the players with number 1 up to and including 24. Group 2 should contain the players with numbers 25 up to and including 49, and so on. For each group, get the number of players and the highest player number.

```
SELECT     TRUNCATE(PLAYERNO/25,0), COUNT(*), MAX(PLAYERNO)
FROM       PLAYERS
GROUP BY   TRUNCATE(PLAYERNO/25,0)
```

The result is:

```
TRUNCATE(PLAYERNO/25,0)   COUNT(*)   MAX(PLAYERNO)
-----------------------   --------   -------------
                      0          4               8
                      1          4              44
                      2          1              57
                      3          2              95
                      4          3             112
```

The scalar expression on which is grouped can be rather complex. This can consist of system variables, functions and calculations. Even certain scalar subqueries are allowed. Section 10.7 gives a few examples.

Portability: *Several SQL products do not allow you to group on compound expressions, but require on column specifications only. However, a comparable result can be obtained by using views; see Chapter 21, "Views."*

Exercise 10.10: Group the players on the length of their names and get the number of players for each length.

Exercise 10.11: For each match, determine the difference between the number of sets won and lost, and group the matches on that difference.

10.5   Grouping of NULL Values

If grouping is required on a column that contains NULL values, all these NULL values form one group. When rows are grouped, NULL values are also considered to be equal. The reason is that, with a GROUP BY, a vertical comparison is applied. This is in accordance with the rules described in Section 9.5, in Chapter 9, "SELECT Statement: SELECT Clause and Aggregation Functions."

Example 10.10: Find the different league numbers.

```
SELECT    LEAGUENO
FROM      PLAYERS
GROUP BY  LEAGUENO
```

The result is:

```
LEAGUENO
--------
1124
1319
1608
2411
2513
2983
6409
6524
7060
8467
?
```

Explanation: Players 7, 28, 39, and 95 do not have a league number and, therefore, form one group (the last row) in the end result.

10.6   General Rules for the GROUP BY Clause

This section describes a number of important rules that relate to select blocks with a GROUP BY clause.

Rule 1: In Section 9.6, in Chapter 9, we gave several rules for the use of aggregation functions in the SELECT clause. We now add the following rule: If a select block does have a GROUP BY clause, any column specification specified in the SELECT clause must exclusively occur as a parameter of an aggregated function or in the list of columns given in the GROUP BY clause, or in both.

Therefore, the following statement is incorrect because the TOWN column appears in the SELECT clause, yet it is *not* the parameter of an aggregation function and does not occur in the list of columns by which the result is grouped.

```
SELECT    TOWN, COUNT(*)
FROM      PLAYERS
GROUP BY  PLAYERNO
```

The reason for this restriction is as follows. The result of an aggregation function always consists of one value for each group. The result of a column specification on which grouping is performed also always consists of one value per group. These results are compatible. In contrast, the result of a column specification on which *no* grouping is performed consists of a set of values. This would not be compatible with the results of the other expressions in the SELECT clause.

Rule 2: In most examples, the expressions that are used to form groups also occur in the SELECT clause. However, that is not necessary. An expression that occurs in the GROUP BY clause *can* appear in the SELECT clause.

Rule 3: An expression that is used to form groups can also occur in the SELECT clause within a compound expression. We give an example next.

Example 10.11: Get the list with the different penalty amounts in cents.

```
SELECT    CAST(AMOUNT * 100 AS SIGNED INTEGER)
          AS AMOUNT_IN_CENTS
FROM      PENALTIES
GROUP BY  AMOUNT
```

The result is:

```
AMOUNT_IN_CENTS
---------------
           2500
           3000
           5000
           7500
          10000
```

Explanation: A grouping is performed on a simple expression consisting of a column name: AMOUNT. In the SELECT clause, that same AMOUNT column occurs within a compound expression. This is allowed.

This rule is followed by the fact that no matter how complex a compound expression is, if it occurs in a GROUP BY clause, it can be included in its entirety only in the SELECT clause. For example, if the compound expression PLAYERNO * 2 occurs in a GROUP BY clause, the expressions PLAYERNO * 2, (PLAYERNO * 2) - 100, and MOD(PLAYERNO * 2, 3) - 100 can occur in the SELECT clause. On the other hand, the expressions PLAYERNO, 2 * PLAYERNO, PLAYERNO * 100, and 8 * PLAYERNO * 2 are not allowed.

Rule 4: If an expression occurs twice or more in a GROUP BY clause, double expressions are simply removed. The GROUP BY clause GROUP BY TOWN, TOWN is converted to GROUP BY TOWN. Also, GROUP BY SUBSTR(TOWN,1,1), SEX, SUBSTR(TOWN,1,1) is converted to GROUP BY SUBSTR(TOWN,1,1), SEX. Therefore, it has no use for double expressions.

Rule 5: In Section 9.4, in Chapter 9, we described the cases in which the use of DISTINCT in the SELECT clause is superfluous. The rules given in that section apply to SELECT statements without a GROUP BY clause. We add a rule for SELECT statements with a GROUP BY clause: DISTINCT (if used outside an aggregation function) that is superfluous when the SELECT clause includes all the columns specified in the GROUP BY clause. The GROUP BY clause groups the rows in such a way that the columns on which they are grouped no longer contain duplicate values.

Exercise 10.12: Describe why the following statements are incorrect:

1.

```
SELECT   PLAYERNO, DIVISION
FROM     TEAMS
GROUP BY PLAYERNO
```

2.

```
SELECT    SUBSTR(TOWN,1,1), NAME
FROM      PLAYERS
GROUP BY  TOWN, SUBSTR(NAME,1,1)
```

3.

```
SELECT    PLAYERNO * (AMOUNT + 100)
FROM      PENAL TIES
GROUP BY  AMOUNT + 100
```

Exercise 10.13: In which of the following statements is DISTINCT superfluous?

1.

```
SELECT    DISTINCT PLAYERNO
FROM      TEAMS
GROUP BY  PLAYERNO
```

2.

```
SELECT    DISTINCT COUNT(*)
FROM      MATCHES
GROUP BY  TEAMNO
```

3.

```
SELECT    DISTINCT COUNT(*)
FROM      MATCHES
WHERE     TEAMNO = 2
GROUP BY  TEAMNO
```

10.7   Complex Examples with GROUP BY

Here are several other examples to illustrate the extensive possibilities of the GROUP BY clause.

Example 10.12: What is the average total amount of penalties for players who live in Stratford and Inglewood?

```
SELECT    AVG(TOTAL)
FROM      (SELECT   PLAYERNO, SUM(AMOUNT) AS TOTAL
           FROM     PENALTIES
           GROUP BY PLAYERNO) AS TOTALS
WHERE     PLAYERNO IN
          (SELECT   PLAYERNO
           FROM     PLAYERS
           WHERE    TOWN = 'Stratford' OR TOWN = 'Inglewood')
```

The result is:

```
AVG(TOTAL)
----------
        85
```

Explanation: The intermediate result of the subquery in the FROM clause is a table consisting of two columns, called PLAYERNO and TOTAL, and contains five rows (players 6, 8, 27, 44, and 104). This table is passed on to the WHERE clause, where a subquery selects players from Stratford and Inglewood (players 6, 8, and 44). Finally, the average is calculated in the SELECT clause of the column TOTAL.

Example 10.13: For each player who incurred penalties and is captain, get the player number, the name, the number of penalties that he or she incurred, and the number of teams that he or she captains.

```
SELECT    PLAYERS.PLAYERNO, NAME, NUMBER_OF_PENALTIES,
          NUMBER_OF_TEAMS
FROM      PLAYERS,
          (SELECT   PLAYERNO, COUNT(*) AS NUMBER_OF_PENALTIES
           FROM     PENALTIES
           GROUP BY PLAYERNO) AS NUMBER_PENALTIES,
          (SELECT   PLAYERNO, COUNT(*) AS NUMBER_OF_TEAMS
           FROM     TEAMS
           GROUP BY PLAYERNO) AS NUMBER_TEAMS
WHERE     PLAYERS.PLAYERNO = NUMBER_PENALTIES.PLAYERNO
AND       PLAYERS.PLAYERNO = NUMBER_TEAMS.PLAYERNO
```

The result is:

```
PLAYERNO   NAME        NUMBER_OF_PENALTIES   NUMBER_OF_TEAMS
--------   ---------   -------------------   ---------------
       6   Parmenter                     1                 1
      27   Collins                       2                 1
```

Explanation: The FROM clause contains two subqueries that both have a GROUP BY clause.

The previous statement could have been formulated more easily by including subqueries in the SELECT clause, which makes GROUP BY clauses no longer required; see the next example. Now, the only difference is that all players appear in the result.

```
SELECT    PLAYERS.PLAYERNO, NAME,
          (SELECT   COUNT(*)
           FROM     PENALTIES
           WHERE    PLAYERS.PLAYERNO =
                    PENALTIES.PLAYERNO) AS NUMBER_OF_PENALTIES,
          (SELECT   COUNT(*)
           FROM     TEAMS
           WHERE    PLAYERS.PLAYERNO =
                    TEAMS.PLAYERNO) AS NUMBER_OF_TEAMS
FROM      PLAYERS
```

Example 10.14: Get the player number and the total number of penalties for each player who played a match.

```
SELECT    DISTINCT M.PLAYERNO, NUMBERP
FROM      MATCHES AS M LEFT OUTER JOIN
             (SELECT    PLAYERNO, COUNT(*) AS NUMBERP
              FROM      PENALTIES
              GROUP BY PLAYERNO) AS NP
          ON M.PLAYERNO = NP.PLAYERNO
```

Explanation: In this statement, the subquery creates the following intermediate result (this is the NP table):

PLAYERNO	NUMBERP
6	1
8	1
27	2
44	3
104	1

Next, this table is joined with the MATCHES table. We execute a left outer join, so no players disappear from this table. The final result is:

PLAYERNO	NUMBERP
2	?
6	1
8	1
27	2
44	3
57	?
83	?
104	1
112	?

Example 10.15: Group the penalties on the basis of payment date. Group 1 should contain all penalties between January 1, 1980, and June 30, 1982; group 2 should contain all penalties between July 1, 1981, and December 31, 1982; and group 3 should contain all penalties between January 1, 1983, and December 31, 1984. Get for each group the sum of all penalties.

```
SELECT    GROUPS.PGROUP, SUM(P.AMOUNT)
FROM      PENALTIES AS P,
          (SELECT 1 AS PGROUP, '1980-01-01' AS START,
                  '1981-06-30' AS END
          UNION
          SELECT 2, '1981-07-01', '1982-12-31'
          UNION
          SELECT 3, '1983-01-01', '1984-12-31') AS GROUPS
WHERE     P.PAYMENT_DATE BETWEEN START AND END
GROUP BY  GROUPS.PGROUP
ORDER BY  1
```

The result is:

```
GROUP   SUM(P.AMOUNT)
-----   -------------
    1          225.00
    2           30.00
    3          225.00
```

Explanation: In the FROM clause, a new (virtual) table is created in which the three groups have been defined. This GROUPS table is joined with the PENALTIES table. A BETWEEN operator is used to join the two tables. If there are penalties that fall outside these groups with respect to payment date, they will not be included in the result.

Example 10.16: For each penalty, get the penalty amount plus the sum of that amount and the amounts of all penalties with a lower payment number (cumulative value).

```
SELECT    P1.PAYMENTNO, P1.AMOUNT, SUM(P2.AMOUNT)
FROM      PENALTIES AS P1, PENALTIES AS P2
WHERE     P1.PAYMENTNO >= P2. PAYMENTNO
GROUP BY  P1. PAYMENTNO, P1.AMOUNT
ORDER BY  P1. PAYMENTNO
```

For convenience, we assume that the PENALTIES table consists of the following three rows only (you can create this, too, by temporarily removing all penalties with a number greater than 3):

PAYMENTNO	PLAYERNO	PAYMENT_DATE	AMOUNT
1	6	1980-12-08	100
2	44	1981-05-05	75
3	27	1983-09-10	100

The desired result is:

PAYMENTNO	AMOUNT	SUM
1	100	100
2	75	175
3	100	275

The intermediate result of the FROM clause (we show only the columns PAYMENTNO and AMOUNT):

P1.PAYNO	P1.AMOUNT	P2.PAYNO	P2.AMOUNT
1	100	1	100
1	100	2	75
1	100	3	100
2	75	1	100
2	75	2	75
2	75	3	100
3	100	1	100
3	100	2	75
3	100	3	100

The intermediate result of the WHERE clause:

P1.PAYNO	P1.AMOUNT	P2.PAYNO	P2.AMOUNT
1	100	1	100
2	75	1	100
2	75	2	75
3	100	1	100
3	100	2	75
3	100	3	100

The intermediate result of the GROUP BY clause:

P1.PAYNO	P1.AMOUNT	P2.PAYNO	P2.AMOUNT
1	100	{1}	{100}
2	75	{1, 2}	{100, 75}
3	100	{1, 2, 3}	{100, 75, 100}

The intermediate result of the SELECT clause:

P1.PAYNO	P1.AMOUNT	SUM(P2.AMOUNT)
1	100	100
2	75	175
3	100	275

This final result is equal to the desired table.

Most joins in this book and in reality are equi joins. Non-equi joins are rare. The previous statement is an example that shows that non-equi joins can be useful and that powerful statements can be formulated with them.

Example 10.17: For each penalty, get the payment number, the penalty amount, and the percentage that the amount forms of the sum of all amounts (again, we use the same PENALTIES table as in the previous example).

```
SELECT    P1.PAYMENTNO, P1.AMOUNT,
          (P1.AMOUNT * 100) / SUM(P2.AMOUNT)
FROM      PENALTIES AS P1, PENALTIES AS P2
GROUP BY  P1.PAYMENTNO, P1.AMOUNT
ORDER BY  P1.PAYMENTNO
```

The intermediate result of the FROM clause is equal to that of the previous example. However, the intermediate result of the GROUP BY clause differs:

P1.PAYNO	P1.AMOUNT	P2.PAYNO	P2.AMOUNT
1	100	{1, 2, 3}	{100, 75, 100}
2	75	{1, 2, 3}	{100, 75, 100}
3	100	{1, 2, 3}	{100, 75, 100}

The intermediate result of the SELECT clause:

P1.PAYNO	P1.AMOUNT	(P1.AMOUNT * 100) / SUM(P2.AMOUNT)
1	100	36.36
2	75	27.27
3	100	36.36

Find out whether this is the final result as well.

Exercise 10.14: How many players live in a town, on average?

Exercise 10.15: For each team, get the team number, the division, and the number of players that played matches for that team.

Exercise 10.16: For each player, get the player number, the name, the sum of all penalties that he or she incurred, and the number of teams from the first division that he or she captains.

Exercise 10.17: For each team captained by a player who lives in Stratford, get the team number and the number of players who have won at least one match for that team.

Exercise 10.18: For each player, get the player number, the name, and the difference between the year in which he or she joined the club and the average year of joining the club.

Exercise 10.19: For each player, get the player number, the name, and the difference between the year in which he or she joined the club and the average year in which players who live in the same town joined the club.

10.8 Grouping with WITH ROLLUP

The GROUP BY clause has many features to group data and to calculate aggregated data, such as the total number of penalties or the sum of all penalties. However, so far all statements return results in which all data is on the same level of aggregation. But what if we want to see data belonging to different aggregation levels within one statement? Imagine that we want to see in one statement the total penalty amount for each player and also the total penalty amount for all players. This is not possible with the forms of the GROUP BY clauses that we have discussed so far. For this purpose, more than two groupings within one GROUP BY clause are required. By adding the specification WITH ROLLUP to the GROUP BY clause, it becomes possible.

Portability: *Not all SQL products support* WITH ROLLUP. *However, because many products, including MySQL, offer this feature, we discuss it here.*

Example 10.18: For each player, find the sum of all his or her penalties, plus the sum of all penalties.

A way to combine these two groupings in one statement is to use the UNION operator.

```
SELECT    PLAYERNO, SUM(AMOUNT)
FROM      PENALTIES
GROUP BY  PLAYERNO
UNION
SELECT    CAST(NULL AS SIGNED INTEGER), SUM(AMOUNT)
FROM      PENALTIES
```

The result is:

```
PLAYERNO   SUM(AMOUNT)
--------   -----------
       6        100.00
       8         25.00
      27        175.00
      44        130.00
     104         50.00
       ?        480.00
```

Explanation: The rows in this intermediate result in which the PLAYERNO column is filled form the result of the first select block. The rows in which PLAYERNO is equal to NULL make up the result of the second select block. The first five rows contain data on the aggregation level of the player numbers, and the last row contains data on the aggregation level of all rows.

The specification WITH ROLLUP has been introduced to simplify this kind of statement. WITH ROLLUP can be used to ask for multiple groupings with one GROUP BY clause. The previous statement will then be:

```
SELECT    PLAYERNO, SUM(AMOUNT)
FROM      PENALTIES
GROUP BY PLAYERNO WITH ROLLUP
```

Explanation: The result of this statement is the same as the previous one. The specification WITH ROLLUP indicates that after the result has been grouped with [PLAYERNO], another grouping is needed—in this case, on all rows.

We give a formal description here. Imagine that in a GROUP BY clause, the expressions E_1, E_2, E_3, and E_4 are specified. The grouping that is performed then is [E_1, E_2, E_3, E_4]. When we add the specification WITH ROLLUP to this GROUP BY, an entire set of groupings will be performed: [E_1, E_2, E_3, E_4], [E_1, E_2, E_3], [E_1, E_2], [E_1], and finally []. The specification [] means that all rows are grouped into one group. The specified grouping is seen as the highest aggregation level that is asked, and also indicates that all higher aggregation levels must be calculated again. To aggregate upward is called *rollup* in literature. So, the result of this statement contains data on five different levels of aggregation.

If in the SELECT clause an expression occurs in which the result of a certain grouping is not grouped, the NULL value is placed in the result.

Example 10.19: For each combination of sex–town, get the number of players, and get the total number of players per sex and the total number of players in the entire table as well.

```
SELECT    SEX, TOWN, COUNT(*)
FROM      PLAYERS
GROUP BY SEX, TOWN WITH ROLLUP
```

The result is:

```
SEX  TOWN        COUNT(*)
---  ---------   --------
M    Stratford          7
M    Inglewood          1
M    Douglas            1
M    ?                  9
V    Midhurst           1
V    Inglewood          1
V    Plymouth           1
V    Eltham             2
V    ?                  5
?    ?                 14
```

Explanation: This result has three levels of aggregation. Rows 1, 2, 3, 5, 6, 7, and 8 form the lowest level and have been added because of the grouping [SEX, TOWN]; rows 4 and 9 have been added because of the grouping [SEX]; and the last row forms the highest level of aggregation and has been added because of the grouping []. It contains the total number of players.

Exercise 10.20: For each team, get the number of matches played and also the total number of matches.

Exercise 10.21: Group the matches by the name of the player and the division of the team, and execute a ROLLUP.

10.9 Grouping with WITH CUBE

Another way to get multiple groupings within one GROUP BY clause is to use the WITH CUBE specification.

Portability: *Not all SQL products support* WITH CUBE. *However, because many products, including MySQL, offer this feature, we discuss it here.*

Again, we use a formal way to explain this new specification. Imagine that the specification WITH CUBE is added to a GROUP BY clause consisting of the expressions E_1, E_2, and E_3. As a result, many groupings are performed: $[E_1, E_2, E_3]$, $[E_1, E_2]$, $[E_1, E_3]$, $[E_2, E_3]$, $[E_1]$, $[E_2]$, $[E_3]$, and finally []. The list begins with a grouping on all three expressions, followed by three groupings with each two expressions (one grouping for each possible combination of two expressions), and followed by a grouping for each expression separately; it closes with a grouping of all rows.

Example 10.20: Group the PLAYERS table on the columns SEX with TOWN and add a WITH CUBE specification.

```
SELECT    ROW_NUMBER() OVER () AS SEQNO,
          SEX, TOWN, COUNT(*)
FROM      PLAYERS
GROUP BY SEX, TOWN WITH CUBE
ORDER BY SEX, TOWN
```

The result is:

SEQNO	SEX	TOWN	COUNT(*)
1	M	Stratford	7
2	M	Inglewood	1
3	M	Douglas	1
4	M	?	9
5	F	Midhurst	1
6	F	Inglewood	1
7	F	Plymouth	1
8	F	Eltham	2
9	F	?	5
10	?	Stratford	7
11	?	Midhurst	1
12	?	Inglewood	2
13	?	Plymouth	1
14	?	Douglas	1
15	?	Eltham	2
16	?	?	14

Explanation: Rows 1, 2, 3, 5, 6, 7, and 8 have been added because of the grouping [SEX, TOWN]. Rows 4 and 9 have been added because of the grouping [SEX]. Rows 10 through 15 have been added because of the grouping on [TOWN], and row 16 has been included because of the grouping of all rows.

Exercise 10.22: Describe what the difference is between a WITH ROLLUP and a WITH CUBE specification.

Exercise 10.23: Group the MATCHES table on the columns TEAMNO, PLAYERNO, and WON, and add a WITH CUBE specification.

10.10 Grouping Sets

The GROUP BY clauses that have been described so far use the short notation for the specification of groupings. SQL also has a more extensive notation. So-called *grouping sets specifications* indicate on which expressions groupings must be performed.

Portability: *Not all SQL products support grouping sets. However, because many products, including MySQL, offer this feature, we discuss it here.*

Example 10.21: For each town, get the most recent date of birth.
With the shortest notation form, this statement looks as follows:

```
SELECT    TOWN, MIN(BIRTH_DATE)
FROM      PLAYERS
GROUP BY  TOWN
```

When the extensive notation form is used, this similar formulation occurs:

```
SELECT    TOWN, MIN(BIRTH_DATE)
FROM      PLAYERS
GROUP BY  GROUPING SETS ((TOWN))
```

The result of both statements is:

```
TOWN        MIN(BIRTH_DATE)
---------   ---------------
Stratford   1948-09-01
Midhurst    1963-06-22
Inglewood   1962-07-08
Plymouth    1963-10-01
Douglas     1963-05-14
Eltham      1964-12-28
```

Explanation: Behind the term GROUPING SETS, the grouping sets specifications can be found. Within such a specification, several groupings can be specified. Each grouping is placed between brackets and the whole should also be placed between brackets—hence, the double brackets.

The advantage of the extensive notation form is that it offers more ways to group data. Several groupings can be specified, among other things, and combinations of ROLLUP and CUBE can be used.

Example 10.22: For each town, get the number of players, and for each sex, get the number of players as well.

Because a grouping is needed on two different columns, this question cannot be formulated with one GROUP BY clause (in which the short notation form is used). A way to combine these two groupings in one statement is to use an UNION operator.

```
SELECT    CAST(NULL AS CHAR), TOWN, COUNT(*)
FROM      PLAYERS
GROUP BY  TOWN
UNION
SELECT    SEX, CAST(NULL AS CHAR), COUNT(*)
FROM      PLAYERS
GROUP BY  SEX
ORDER BY  2, 1
```

The result is:

SEX	TOWN	COUNT(*)
?	Stratford	7
?	Midhurst	1
?	Inglewood	2
?	Plymouth	1
?	Douglas	1
?	Eltham	2
M	?	9
F	?	5

Explanation: The rows in this intermediate result in which the TOWN column has been filled came from the first select block. The rows in which TOWN is equal to NULL form the intermediate result of the second select block. In fact, these two rows form subtotals for each sex.

To simplify this type of statement, the grouping sets specification has been added to SQL. With this, one GROUP BY clause can be used to specify several groupings. The previous statement becomes:

```
SELECT    SEX, TOWN, COUNT(*)
FROM      PLAYERS
GROUP BY GROUPING SETS ((TOWN), (SEX))
ORDER BY 2, 1
```

Explanation: Behind the words GROUPING SETS, two groupings are now specified: (TOWN) and (SEX).

If one grouping consists of one expression, the brackets can be removed. So, GROUP BY GROUPING SETS ((TOWN), (SEX)) is equivalent to GROUP BY GROUPING SETS (TOWN, SEX).

Again, the GROUP BY clause, as we discussed in the previous chapters, is, in fact, a shortened notation for the one with grouping sets. Table 10.1 contains several examples of original formulations without grouping sets and their equivalents with grouping sets.

Table 10.1   *Original GROUP BY Clauses and Their Equivalent Grouping Sets Specifications*

ORIGINAL SPECIFICATION	SPECIFICATION WITH GROUPING SETS
GROUP BY A	GROUP BY GROUPING SETS ((A)) or GROUP BY GROUPING SETS (A)
GROUP BY A, B	GROUP BY GROUPING SETS ((A, B))
GROUP BY YEAR(A), SUBSTR(B)	GROUP BY GROUPING SETS ((YEAR(A), SUBSTR(B)))

A special grouping is (). There is no expression between the brackets. In this case, all rows are placed in one group. We can calculate a grand total with that, for example.

Example 10.23: Find for each combination of sex–town the number of players, get for each sex the number of players, and get the total number of players in the entire table.

```
SELECT    SEX, TOWN, COUNT(*)
FROM      PLAYERS
GROUP BY GROUPING SETS ((SEX, TOWN), (SEX), ())
ORDER BY 1, 2
```

The result is:

```
SEX  TOWN        COUNT(*)
---  ---------   --------
M    Stratford       7
M    Inglewood       1
M    Douglas         1
M    ?               9
F    Midhurst        1
F    Inglewood       1
F    Plymouth        1
F    Eltham          2
F    ?               5
?    ?              14
```

Explanation: The last row contains the total number of players and is added because of the grouping ().

Example 10.24: Get for each team and for each player individually the number of matches played.

```
SELECT    TEAMNO, PLAYERNO, COUNT(*)
FROM      MATCHES
GROUP BY GROUPING SETS (TEAMNO, PLAYERNO)
ORDER BY 1, 2
```

The result is:

```
TEAMNO  PLAYERNO  COUNT(*)
------  --------  --------
     1         ?         8
     2         ?         5
     ?         2         1
     ?         6         3
     ?         8         2
     ?        27         1
     ?        44         1
     ?        57         1
     ?        83         1
     ?       104         1
     ?       112         2
```

Explanation: The first two rows in the result have been included because of the grouping on the TEAMNO column and the other rows because of the grouping on the PLAYERNO column.

This example clearly shows that brackets are important. The specification GROUPING SETS (TEAMNO, PLAYERNO) returns a different result than GROUPING SETS ((TEAMNO, PLAYERNO)). The second grouping sets specification results in one grouping on the combination of the two columns specified and the second grouping sets specification leads to two groupings.

Finally, here are a few abstract examples of certain GROUP BY clauses, including the groupings that are executed. E1, E2, and E3 stand for random expressions, and the symbol ∪ represents the union operator.

Table 10.2   *The Relationship Between Grouping Sets Specifications and Groupings*

GROUP BY CLAUSE	GROUPINGS
GROUP BY E1, E2, E3	[E1, E2, E3]
GROUP BY GROUPING SETS (())	[]
GROUP BY GROUPING SETS ((E1, E2, E3))	[E1, E2, E3]
GROUP BY GROUPING SETS (E1, E2, E3)	[E1] ∪ [E2] ∪ [E3]
GROUP BY GROUPING SETS ((E1), (E2), (E3))	[E1] ∪ [E2] ∪ [E3]
GROUP BY GROUPING SETS ((E1, E2), (E3))	[E1, E2] ∪ [E3]
GROUP BY GROUPING SETS ((E1, E2), E3)	[E1, E2] ∪ [E3]
GROUP BY GROUPING SETS ((E1, E2), (E3, E4))	[E1, E2] ∪ [E3, E4]
GROUP BY GROUPING SETS ((E1, (E2, E3)))	Not allowed

Exercise 10.24: Get the total number of penalties by using a grouping sets specification.

Exercise 10.25: Get for each combination of team number and player number the number of matches, give the number of matches for each team number, and find the total number of matches as well.

Exercise 10.26: Indicate which groupings must be specified for the following GROUP BY clauses:

1. GROUP BY GROUPING SETS ((), (), (E1), (E2))
2. GROUP BY GROUPING SETS (E1, (E2, E3),(E3, E4, E5))
3. GROUP BY GROUPING SETS ((E1, E2), (), E3, (E2, E1))

10.11   Grouping with ROLLUP and CUBE

Section 10.8 describes the WITH ROLLUP specification. This specification cannot be used if the GROUP BY clause contains grouping sets specifications. In that case, an alternative specification must be used.

> **Portability:** *Many SQL products, including MySQL, do not support grouping with ROLLUP and CUBE. But because several other products offer this feature, it is discussed here.*

It often happens that data has to be aggregated on different levels. Example 10.23 is a clear example. For such a situation, a short notation form has been added, the ROLLUP. Imagine that E1 and E2 are two expressions. In that case, the specification GROUP BY ROLLUP (E1, E2) is equal to the specification GROUP BY GROUPING SETS ((E1, E2), ((E1), ())). So, ROLLUP does not offer extra functionality; it makes only the formulation of some GROUP BY clauses easier. This means that the SELECT statement in Example 10.23 can be simplified by using ROLLUP.

Example 10.25: Get for each combination of sex–town the number of players, get for each sex the number of players, and get the total number of players in the entire table.

```
SELECT    SEX, TOWN, COUNT(*)
FROM      PLAYERS
GROUP BY ROLLUP (SEX, TOWN)
ORDER BY 1, 2
```

The result is (of course, equal to that of Example 10.23):

SEX	TOWN	COUNT(*)
M	Stratford	7
M	Inglewood	1
M	Douglas	1
M	?	9
F	Midhurst	1
F	Inglewood	1
F	Plymouth	1
F	Eltham	2
F	?	5
?	?	14

Explanation: The term ROLLUP comes from the OLAP world. It is an operator that is supported by many OLAP tools. It indicates that data must be aggregated on different levels, beginning at the lowest level. That lowest level is, of course, specified at ROLLUP. In this example, it is formed by the combination of the SEX and TOWN columns. After that, the data is aggregated by sex and then the total.

Example 10.26: For each combination of sex–town–year of birth, get the number of players; for each combination of sex–town, get the number of players; for each sex, get the number of players; and, finally, get the total number of players.

```
SELECT    ROW_NUMBER() OVER () AS SEQNO,
          SEX, TOWN, YEAR(BIRTH_DATE), COUNT(*)
FROM      PLAYERS
GROUP BY ROLLUP (SEX, TOWN, YEAR(BIRTH_DATE))
ORDER BY 2, 3, 4
```

The result is:

SEQNO	SEX	TOWN	YEAR(BIRTH_DATE)	COUNT(*)
1	M	Stratford	1948	1
2	M	Stratford	1956	2
3	M	Stratford	1963	2
4	M	Stratford	1964	1
5	M	Stratford	1971	1
6	M	Stratford		7
7	M	Inglewood	1963	1
8	M	Inglewood		1
9	M	Douglas	1963	1
10	M	Douglas		1
11	M			9
12	F	Midhurst	1963	1
13	F	Midhurst		1
14	F	Inglewood	1962	1
15	F	Inglewood		1
16	F	Plymouth	1963	1
17	F	Plymouth		1
18	F	Eltham	1964	1
19	F	Eltham	1970	1
20	F	Eltham		2
21	F			5
22				14

Explanation: The grouping [SEX, TOWN, YEAR(BIRTH_DATE)] returns the rows 1, 2, 3, 4, 5, 7, 9, 12, 14, 16, 18, and 19. The grouping [SEX, TOWN] results in the rows 6, 8, 10, 13, 15, 17, and 20. The grouping [SEX] leads up to the rows 11 and 21, and, finally, the grouping [] returns the last row.

By adding more brackets, certain aggregation levels can be skipped.

Example 10.27: For each combination of sex–town–year of birth, get the number of players; for each sex, get the number of players; and, finally, get the total number of players.

```
SELECT    ROW_NUMBER() OVER () AS SEQNO,
          SEX, TOWN, YEAR(BIRTH_DATE), COUNT(*)
FROM      PLAYERS
GROUP BY ROLLUP (SEX, (TOWN, YEAR(BIRTH_DATE)))
ORDER BY 2, 3, 4
```

The result is:

SEQNO	SEX	TOWN	YEAR(BIRTH_DATE)	COUNT(*)
1	M	Stratford	1948	1
2	M	Stratford	1956	2
3	M	Stratford	1963	2
4	M	Stratford	1964	1
5	M	Stratford	1971	1
6	M	Inglewood	1963	1
7	M	Douglas	1963	1
8	M			9
9	F	Midhurst	1963	1
10	F	Inglewood	1962	1
11	F	Plymouth	1963	1
12	F	Eltham	1964	1
13	F	Eltham	1970	1
14	F			5
15				14

Explanation: Because the TOWN column is placed between brackets together with the expression YEAR(BIRTH_DATE), it is considered to be a group. The groupings that are performed because of this are, successively, [SEX, TOWN, YEAR(BIRTH_DATE)], [SEX], and []. The grouping [SEX, TOWN] is skipped.

By way of illustration, the specification ROLLUP ((SEX, TOWN), YEAR(BIRTH_DATE)) would lead to the groupings [SEX, TOWN, YEAR(BIRTH_DATE)], [SEX, TOWN], and []. Only the grouping on the SEX column is absent here. Another example: The specification ROLLUP ((SEX, TOWN), (YEAR(BIRTH_DATE), MONTH(BIRTH_DATE))) results in the following groupings: [SEX, TOWN, YEAR(BIRTH_DATE), MONTH(BIRTH_DATE)], [SEX, TOWN], and [].

Besides ROLLUP, SQL has a second specification to simplify long GROUP BY clauses: the CUBE. If E_1 and E_2 are two expressions, the specification GROUP BY CUBE (E_1, E_2, E_3) is equal to the specification GROUP BY GROUPING SETS ((E_1, E_2, E_3), (E_1, E_2), (E_1, E_3), (E_2, E_3), (E_1), (E_2), (E_3), ()).

Example 10.28: Get the number of players for each combination of sex–town, for each sex and for each town, and also get the total number of players in the entire table.

```
SELECT   ROW_NUMBER() OVER () AS SEQNO,
         SEX, TOWN, COUNT(*)
FROM     PLAYERS
GROUP BY CUBE (SEX, TOWN)
ORDER BY 2, 3
```

The result is:

SEQNO	SEX	TOWN	COUNT(*)
1	M	Stratford	7
2	M	Inglewood	1
3	M	Douglas	1
4	M		9
5	F	Midhurst	1
6	F	Inglewood	1
7	F	Plymouth	1
8	F	Eltham	2
9	F		5
10		Stratford	7
11		Midhurst	1
12		Inglewood	2
13		Plymouth	1
14		Douglas	1
15		Eltham	2
16			14

Explanation: Rows 1, 2, 3, 5, 6, 7, and 8 have been included because of the grouping [SEX, TOWN]. Rows 4 and 9 have been included because of the grouping [SEX]. Rows 10 up to and including 15 form the result of the grouping [TOWN]. Finally, row 16 forms the result of a total grouping.

The GROUPING function can also be used in combination with ROLLUP and CUBE.

As in Section 10.10, we show several other abstract examples of certain GROUP BY clauses in which ROLLUP and CUBE appear, including the groupings that are executed. Again, E_1, E_2, E_3 and E_4 represent random expressions, and the symbol ∪ represents the union operator.

Table 10.3   *The Relationship Between Grouping Sets Specifications and Groupings*

GROUP BY CLAUSE	GROUPINGS
GROUP BY ROLLUP (())	[]
GROUP BY ROLLUP (E1)	[E1] ∪ []
GROUP BY ROLLUP (E1, E2)	[E1, E2] ∪ [E1] ∪ []
GROUP BY ROLLUP (E1, (E2, E3))	[E1, E2, E3] ∪ [E1] ∪ []
GROUP BY ROLLUP ((E1, E2), E3)	[E1, E2, E3] ∪ [E1, E2] ∪ []
GROUP BY ROLLUP ((E1, E2), (E3, E4))	[E1, E2, E3, E4] ∪ [E1, E2] ∪ []
GROUP BY CUBE (())	[]
GROUP BY CUBE (E1)	[E1] ∪ []
GROUP BY CUBE (E1, E2)	[E1, E2] ∪ [E1] ∪ [E2] ∪ []
GROUP BY CUBE (E1, E2, E3)	[E1, E2, E3] ∪ [E1, E2] ∪ [E1, E3] ∪ [E2, E3] ∪ [E1] ∪ [E2] ∪ [E3] ∪ []
GROUP BY CUBE (E1, E2, E3, E4)	[E1, E2, E3, E4] ∪ [E1, E2, E3] [E1, E2, E4] ∪ [E1, E3, E4] ∪ [E2, E3, E4] ∪ [E1, E2] ∪ [E1, E3] ∪ [E1, E4] ∪ [E2, E3] ∪ [E2, E4] ∪ [E3, E4] ∪ [E1] ∪ [E2] ∪ [E3] ∪ [E4] ∪ []
GROUP BY CUBE (E1, (E2, E3))	[E1, E2, E3] ∪ [E1] ∪ [E2, E3] ∪ []
GROUP BY CUBE ((E1, E2), (E3, E4))	[E1, E2, E3, E4] ∪ [E1, E2] ∪ [E3, E4] ∪ []
GROUP BY CUBE (E1, ())	[E1] ∪ []

Exercise 10.27: For each combination of team number–player number, get the number of matches, and also get the number of matches for each team and the total number of matches. In this result, include only those matches that have been won in this result.

Exercise 10.28: Execute a CUBE on the column town, sex, and team number after the two tables PLAYERS and TEAMS have been joined.

10.12 Combining Grouping Sets

Multiple groupings can be included in one select block. Simple group by expressions may be combined with grouping sets specifications, multiple grouping sets specifications may be specified and even two rollups may be specified. However, the effect of this combining needs some explanation.

If a grouping sets specification is combined with one or more simple group by expressions, the latter simply is added to the grouping sets specification. For example, the specification GROUPING SETS ((E$_1$)), E$_2$, E$_3$ is equal to GROUPING SETS ((E$_1$, E$_2$, E$_3$)). If the grouping sets specification contains two groupings, the simple expressions are added to both groupings. The specification GROUPING SETS ((E$_1$), (E$_2$)), E$_3$ is, for example, equal to GROUPING SETS ((E$_1$,E$_3$),(E$_2$,E$_3$)).

If two grouping sets specifications are included in one GROUP BY clause, some kind of multiplication of the specifications takes place. For example, the specification GROUPING SETS ((E$_1$), (E$_2$)), GROUPING SETS ((E$_3$)) contains two grouping sets specifications, in which the first consists of two groupings and the second of one grouping. SQL turns it into GROUPING SETS ((E$_1$, E$_3$), (E$_2$, E$_3$)). Now the expression E$_3$ has been added to both groupings of the first grouping sets specification. The specification GROUPING SETS ((E$_1$), (E$_2$)), GROUPING SETS ((E$_3$), (E$_4$)) is turned into GROUPING SETS ((E$_1$, E$_3$), (E$_1$, E$_4$), (E$_2$, E$_3$), (E$_2$, E$_4$)). It is obvious that E$_1$ is linked to both groupings of the other grouping sets specifications. The same applies to E$_2$.

Finally, the specification GROUPING SETS ((E$_1$), (E$_2$)), GROUPING SETS ((E$_3$), (E$_4$)), E$_5$ is turned into GROUPING SETS ((E$_1$, E$_3$, E$_5$)), (E$_1$, E$_4$, E$_5$), (E$_2$, E$_3$, E$_5$), (E$_2$, E$_4$, E$_5$)).

Table 10.4 gives a few abstract examples of certain GROUP BY clauses in which several grouping sets specifications appear, including the groupings that are executed. Again, E$_1$, E$_2$, E$_3$, and E$_4$ stand for random expressions, and the symbol ∪ represents the union operator.

Table 10.4   *Combining Grouping Sets Specifications*

GROUP BY CLAUSE	GROUPINGS
GROUP BY GROUPING SETS (E1, E2), E3	[E1, E3] ∪ [E2, E3]
GROUP BY E1, GROUPING SETS (E2, E3)	[E1, E2] ∪ [E1, E3]
GROUP BY GROUPING SETS ((E1, E2)), E3	[E1, E2, E3]
GROUP BY GROUPING SETS ((E1, E2), (E3, E4)), E5	[E1, E2, E5] ∪ [E3, E4, E5]
GROUP BY ROLLUP (E1, E2)), E3	[E1, E2, E3] ∪ [E1, E2] ∪ [E1] ∪ []
GROUP BY GROUPING SETS (E1, E2), GROUPING SETS (E3, E4)	[E1, E3] ∪ [E1, E4] ∪ [E2, E3] ∪ [E2, E4] ∪
GROUP BY GROUPING SETS (E1, ROLLUP (E2, E3))	[E1] ∪ [E2, E3] ∪ [E2] ∪ []
GROUP BY GROUPING SETS ((E1, ROLLUP (E2)))	[E1, E2] ∪ [E1] ∪ []
GROUP BY ROLLUP (E1, E2), ROLLUP (E3, E4)	[E1, E2, E3, E4] ∪ [E1, E3, E4] ∪ [E3, E4] ∪ [E1, E2, E3] ∪ [E1, E3] ∪ [E3] ∪ [E1, E2] ∪ [E1] ∪ []

10.13   Answers

10.1

```
SELECT    JOINED
FROM      PLAYERS
GROUP BY JOINED
```

10.2

```
SELECT    JOINED, COUNT(*)
FROM      PLAYERS
GROUP BY JOINED
```

10.3

```
SELECT    PLAYERNO, AVG(AMOUNT), COUNT(*)
FROM      PENALTIES
GROUP BY PLAYERNO
```

10.4

```
SELECT    TEAMNO, COUNT(*), SUM(WON)
FROM      MATCHES
WHERE     TEAMNO IN
          (SELECT   TEAMNO
           FROM     TEAMS
           WHERE    DIVISION = 'first')
GROUP BY TEAMNO
```

10.5

```
SELECT    WON, LOST, COUNT(*)
FROM      MATCHES
WHERE     WON > LOST
GROUP BY WON, LOST
ORDER BY 1, 2
```

10.6

```
SELECT    YEAR(BEGIN_DATE), MONTH(BEGIN_DATE), COUNT(*)
FROM      COMMITTEE_MEMBERS
GROUP BY YEAR(BEGIN_DATE), MONTH(BEGIN_DATE)
ORDER BY 1, 2
```

10.7

```
SELECT    P.NAME, T.DIVISION, SUM(WON)
FROM      (MATCHES AS M INNER JOIN PLAYERS AS P
           ON M.PLAYERNO = P.PLAYERNO)
           INNER JOIN TEAMS AS T
           ON M.TEAMNO = T.TEAMNO
GROUP BY P.NAME, T.DIVISION
ORDER BY 1
```

10.8

```
SELECT    NAME, INITIALS, COUNT(*)
FROM      PLAYERS AS P INNER JOIN PENALTIES AS PEN
           ON P.PLAYERNO = PEN.PLAYERNO
WHERE     P.TOWN = 'Inglewood'
GROUP BY P.PLAYERNO, NAME, INITIALS
```

10.9

```
SELECT    T.TEAMNO, DIVISION, SUM(WON)
FROM      TEAMS AS T, MATCHES AS M
WHERE     T.TEAMNO = M.TEAMNO
GROUP BY T.TEAMNO, DIVISION
```

10.10

```
SELECT    LENGTH(RTRIM(NAME)), COUNT(*)
FROM      PLAYERS
GROUP BY LENGTH(RTRIM(NAME))
```

10.11

```
SELECT    ABS(WON - LOST), COUNT(*)
FROM      MATCHES
GROUP BY ABS(WON - LOST)
```

10.12 **1.** The result of the `DIVISION` column has not been grouped, while this column appears in the `SELECT` clause.

2. The `NAME` column cannot appear like this in the `SELECT` clause because the result has not been grouped on the full `NAME` column.

3. The `PLAYERNO` column appears in the `SELECT` clause, while the result has not been grouped; furthermore, the column does not appear as parameter of an aggregation function.

10.13 Superfluous.
Not superfluous.
Superfluous.

10.14

```
SELECT    AVG(NUMBERS)
FROM      (SELECT    COUNT(*) AS NUMBERS
          FROM       PLAYERS
          GROUP BY TOWN) AS TOWNS
```

10.15

```
SELECT    TEAMS.TEAMNO, DIVISION, NUMBER_PLAYERS
FROM      TEAMS LEFT OUTER JOIN
          (SELECT    TEAMNO, COUNT(*) AS NUMBER_PLAYERS
          FROM       MATCHES
          GROUP BY TEAMNO) AS M
          ON (TEAMS.TEAMNO = M.TEAMNO)
```

10.16

```
SELECT    PLAYERS.PLAYERNO, NAME, SUM_AMOUNT,
          NUMBER_TEAMS
FROM      (PLAYERS LEFT OUTER JOIN
          (SELECT    PLAYERNO, SUM(AMOUNT) AS SUM_AMOUNT
          FROM       PENALTIES
          GROUP BY PLAYERNO) AS TOTALS
```

```
        ON (PLAYERS.PLAYERNO = TOTALS.PLAYERNO))
           LEFT OUTER JOIN
           (SELECT   PLAYERNO, COUNT(*) AS NUMBER_TEAMS
            FROM      TEAMS
            WHERE     DIVISION = 'first'
            GROUP BY PLAYERNO) AS NUMBERS
            ON (PLAYERS.PLAYERNO = NUMBERS.PLAYERNO)
```

10.17

```
SELECT    TEAMNO, COUNT(DISTINCT PLAYERNO)
FROM      MATCHES
WHERE     TEAMNO IN
          (SELECT   TEAMNO
           FROM     PLAYERS AS P INNER JOIN TEAMS AS T
                    ON P.PLAYERNO = T.PLAYERNO
           AND      TOWN = 'Stratford')
AND       WON > LOST
GROUP BY TEAMNO
```

10.18

```
SELECT    PLAYERNO, NAME, JOINED - AVERAGE
FROM      PLAYERS,
          (SELECT   AVG(JOINED) AS AVERAGE
           FROM     PLAYERS) AS T
```

10.19

```
SELECT    PLAYERNO, NAME, JOINED - AVERAGE
FROM      PLAYERS,
          (SELECT   TOWN, AVG(JOINED) AS AVERAGE
           FROM     PLAYERS
           GROUP BY TOWN) AS TOWNS
WHERE     PLAYERS.TOWN = TOWNS.TOWN
```

10.20

```
SELECT    TEAMNO, COUNT(*)
FROM      MATCHES
GROUP BY TEAMNO WITH ROLLUP
```

10.21

```
SELECT    P.NAME, T.DIVISION, SUM(WON)
FROM      (MATCHES AS M INNER JOIN PLAYERS AS P
          ON M.PLAYERNO = P.PLAYERNO)
          INNER JOIN TEAMS AS T
          ON M.TEAMNO = T.TEAMNO
GROUP BY P.NAME, T.DIVISION WITH ROLLUP
```

10.22 The WITH ROLLUP specification calculates all levels of aggregation; at the bottom is a grouping based upon the expressions specified. The WITH CUBE specification returns much more data. For every possible combination of expressions specified, groupings are performed.

10.23

```
SELECT    ROW_NUMBER() OVER () AS SEQNO,
          TEAMNO, PLAYERNO, WON, COUNT(*)
FROM      MATCHES
GROUP BY TEAMNO, PLAYERNO, WON WITH CUBE
ORDER BY 2, 3
```

10.24

```
SELECT    COUNT(*)
FROM      MATCHES
GROUP BY GROUPING SETS (())
```

10.25

```
SELECT    TEAMNO, PLAYERNO, COUNT(*)
FROM      MATCHES
GROUP BY GROUPING SETS ((TEAMNO, PLAYERNO), (TEAMNO), ())
ORDER BY 1, 2
```

10.26 1. [] ∪ [E1] ∪ [E2]

2. [E1] ∪ [E2, E3] ∪ [E3, E4, E5]

3. [E1, E2] ∪ [] ∪ [E3]

10.27

```
SELECT    TEAMNO, PLAYERNO, COUNT(*)
FROM      MATCHES
WHERE     WON > LOST
GROUP BY ROLLUP (TEAMNO, PLAYERNO)
ORDER BY 1, 2
```

10.28

```
SELECT    P.TOWN, P.SEX, M.TEAMNO, COUNT(*)
FROM      MATCHES AS M INNER JOIN PLAYERS AS P
          ON M.PLAYERNO = P.PLAYERNO
GROUP BY CUBE (P.TOWN, P.SEX, M.TEAMNO)
ORDER BY 1, 2, 3
```

SELECT Statement: The HAVING Clause

11.1 Introduction

The purpose of the HAVING clause of a select block is comparable to that of the WHERE clause. The difference is that the WHERE clause selects rows after the FROM clause has been processed, whereas the HAVING clause selects rows after a GROUP BY clause has been executed. You can use a HAVING clause only in combination with a GROUP BY clause.

```
<having clause> ::=
    HAVING <condition>
```

In the previous chapter, you saw that the GROUP BY clause groups the rows of the result from the FROM clause. The HAVING clause enables you to select groups (with rows) based upon their particular group properties. The condition in the HAVING clause looks a lot like a "normal" condition in the WHERE clause. Nevertheless, there is one difference: Expressions in the condition of a HAVING clause can contain aggregation functions, whereas this is not possible for expressions in the condition of a WHERE clause (unless they appear within a subquery).

Example 11.1: Get the number of each player who has incurred more than one penalty.

```
SELECT    PLAYERNO
FROM      PENALTIES
GROUP BY  PLAYERNO
HAVING    COUNT(*) > 1
```

The intermediate result of the GROUP BY clause looks like this:

PAYMENTNO	PLAYERNO	PAYMENT_DATE	AMOUNT
{1}	6	{1980-12-08}	{100.00}
{6}	8	{1980-12-08}	{25.00}
{3, 8}	27	{1983-09-10, 1984-11-12}	{100.00, 75.00}
{2, 5, 7}	44	{1981-05-05, 1980-12-08, 1982-12-30}	{75.00, 25.00, 30.00}
{4}	104	{1984-12-08}	{50.00}

In the HAVING condition, we specified the selection of groups in which the number of rows exceeds 1. The intermediate result of the HAVING clause is:

PAYMENTNO	PLAYERNO	PAYMENT_DATE	AMOUNT
{3, 8}	27	{1983-09-10, 1984-11-12}	{100.00, 75.00}
{2, 5, 7}	44	{1981-05-05, 1980-12-08, 1982-12-30}	{75.00, 25.00, 30.00}

Finally, the end result is:

PLAYERNO
27
44

Explanation: Just as with the SELECT clause, the value of an aggregation function in a HAVING clause is calculated for each group separately. In the previous example, the number of rows for each group in the intermediate result of the GROUP BY is counted.

11.2   Examples of the HAVING Clause

This section contains examples of applications of aggregation functions in the HAVING clause.

Example 11.2: Get the player number of each player whose last penalty was incurred in 1984.

```
SELECT    PLAYERNO
FROM      PENALTIES
GROUP BY  PLAYERNO
HAVING    MAX(YEAR(PAYMENT_DATE)) = 1984
```

The result is:

```
PLAYERNO
--------
      27
     104
```

Explanation: The intermediate result of the GROUP BY clause is equal to the one in Example 11.1. The scalar function YEAR pulls out the year figure from each date during the processing of the HAVING clause. So, SQL searches in the PAYMENT_DATE column for the highest year figures for each row. They are, respectively, 1980–12–08, 1980–12–08, 1984–11–12, 1982–12–30, and 1984–12–08.

Example 11.3: For each player who has incurred more than $150 worth of penalties in total, find the player number and the total amount of penalties.

```
SELECT    PLAYERNO, SUM(AMOUNT)
FROM      PENALTIES
GROUP BY  PLAYERNO
HAVING    SUM(AMOUNT) > 150
```

The result is:

```
PLAYERNO   SUM(AMOUNT)
--------   -----------
      27        175.00
```

Example 11.4: For each player who is a captain and who has incurred more than $80 worth of penalties in total, find the player number and the total amount of penalties.

```
SELECT    PLAYERNO, SUM(AMOUNT)
FROM      PENALTIES
WHERE     PLAYERNO IN
          (SELECT    PLAYERNO
          FROM       TEAMS)
GROUP BY  PLAYERNO
HAVING    SUM(AMOUNT) > 80
```

The result is:

```
PLAYERNO    SUM(AMOUNT)
--------    -----------
       6        100.00
      27        175.00
```

Example 11.5: Get the player number and the total amount of penalties for the player with the highest penalty total.

```
SELECT    PLAYERNO, SUM(AMOUNT)
FROM      PENALTIES
GROUP BY  PLAYERNO
HAVING    SUM(AMOUNT) >= ALL
          (SELECT    SUM(AMOUNT)
          FROM       PENALTIES
          GROUP BY   PLAYERNO)
```

The intermediate result of the GROUP BY clause is equal to the one in Example 11.1. The result from the subquery is:

```
AMOUNT
------
100.00
 25.00
175.00
130.00
 50.00
```

For each group (read: player), SQL determines whether the result of the function SUM(AMOUNT) is greater than or equal to all values in the result of the subquery. The final result is:

```
PLAYERNO   SUM(AMOUNT)
--------   -----------
      27        175.00
```

11.3 General Rule for the HAVING Clause

In Section 10.6, we outlined rules for the use of columns and aggregation functions in the SELECT clause. The HAVING clause requires a similar type of rule, as follows: Each column specification specified in the HAVING clause must occur within an aggregation function or in the list of columns named in the GROUP BY clause. Therefore, the following statement is incorrect because the BIRTH_DATE column appears in the HAVING clause but does *not* appear within an aggregation function or in the list of columns by which grouping is performed.

```
SELECT    TOWN, COUNT(*)
FROM      PLAYERS
GROUP BY  TOWN
HAVING    BIRTH_DATE > '1970-01-01'
```

The reason for this limitation is the same as that for the SELECT clause rule. The result of an aggregation function always consists of one value for each group. The result of the column specification on which the result is grouped always consists of only one value for each group as well. On other hand, the result of a column specification, where it has *not* been grouped, consists of a set of values. We are then dealing with incompatible results.

Exercise 11.1: In which town do more than four players live?

Exercise 11.2: Get the player number of each player who has incurred more than $150 in penalties.

Exercise 11.3: Get the name, initials, and number of penalties of each player who has incurred more than one penalty.

Exercise 11.4: Get the number of the team for which most players have played, and give the number of players who have played for this team.

Exercise 11.5: Get the team number and the division of each team for which more than four players have competed.

Exercise 11.6: Get the name and initials of each player who has incurred two or more penalties of more than $40.

Exercise 11.7: Get the name and initials of each player whose total amount of penalties is the highest.

Exercise 11.8: Get the number of each player who has incurred twice as many penalties as player 104.

Exercise 11.9: Get the numbers of the players who have incurred as many penalties as player 6.

11.4 Answers

11.1

```
SELECT    TOWN
FROM      PLAYERS
GROUP BY  TOWN
HAVING    COUNT(*) > 4
```

11.2

```
SELECT    PLAYERNO
FROM      PENALTIES
GROUP BY  PLAYERNO
HAVING    SUM(AMOUNT) > 150
```

11.3

```
SELECT     NAME, INITIALS, COUNT(*)
FROM       PLAYERS INNER JOIN PENALTIES
           ON PLAYERS.PLAYERNO = PENALTIES.PLAYERNO
GROUP BY   PLAYERS.PLAYERNO, NAME, INITIALS
HAVING     COUNT(*) > 1
```

11.4

```
SELECT     TEAMNO, COUNT(*)
FROM       MATCHES
GROUP BY   TEAMNO
HAVING     COUNT(*) >= ALL
           (SELECT    COUNT(*)
            FROM      MATCHES
            GROUP BY  TEAMNO)
```

11.5

```
SELECT     TEAMNO, DIVISION
FROM       TEAMS
WHERE      TEAMNO IN
           (SELECT    TEAMNO
            FROM      MATCHES
            GROUP BY  TEAMNO
            HAVING    COUNT(DISTINCT PLAYERNO) > 4)
```

11.6

```
SELECT     NAME, INITIALS
FROM       PLAYERS
WHERE      PLAYERNO IN
           (SELECT    PLAYERNO
            FROM      PENALTIES
            WHERE     AMOUNT > 40
            GROUP BY  PLAYERNO
            HAVING    COUNT(*) >= 2)
```

11.7

```
SELECT    NAME, INITIALS
FROM      PLAYERS
WHERE     PLAYERNO IN
          (SELECT    PLAYERNO
           FROM      PENALTIES
           GROUP BY PLAYERNO
           HAVING    SUM(AMOUNT) >= ALL
                     (SELECT    SUM(AMOUNT)
                      FROM      PENALTIES
                      GROUP BY PLAYERNO))
```

11.8

```
SELECT    PLAYERNO
FROM      PENALTIES
WHERE     PLAYERNO <> 104
GROUP BY PLAYERNO
HAVING    SUM(AMOUNT)  =
          (SELECT    SUM(AMOUNT) * 2
           FROM      PENALTIES
           WHERE     PLAYERNO = 104)
```

11.9

```
SELECT    PLAYERNO
FROM      PENALTIES
WHERE     PLAYERNO <> 6
GROUP BY PLAYERNO
HAVING    COUNT(*) =
          (SELECT    COUNT(*)
           FROM      PENALTIES
           WHERE     PLAYERNO = 6)
```

12

SELECT Statement: The ORDER BY Clause

12.1 Introduction

What is actually the sequence in which the rows in the result of a SELECT statement are presented? If the SELECT statement has no ORDER BY clause, the sequence is unpredictable. When working through the examples or exercises, you might have found once or twice that the sequence of the rows in your result is different from the one in the book. The addition of an ORDER BY clause at the end of a SELECT statement is the only guarantee that the rows in the end result will be sorted in a certain way.

```
<order by clause> ::=
    ORDER BY <sorting> [ { , <sorting> }... ]

<sorting> ::=
    <scalar expression> [ <sort direction> ] |
    <sequence number> [<sort direction> ]    |
    <column heading> [ <sort direction> ]

<sort direction> ::= ASC | DESC
```

12.2 Sorting on Column Names

Sorting on one column is the simplest method. In this case, the *sorting* consists of one column specification. You are allowed to sort on each column specified in the SELECT clause.

Example 12.1: Find the payment number and the player number of each penalty incurred; sort the result by player number.

```
SELECT    PAYMENTNO, PLAYERNO
FROM      PENALTIES
ORDER BY  PLAYERNO
```

The result is:

```
PAYMENTNO   PLAYERNO
---------   --------
        1          6
        6          8
        3         27
        8         27
        5         44
        2         44
        7         44
        4        104
```

Explanation: The rows are sorted based upon the values in the PLAYERNO column, with the lowest value first and the highest value last.

You are allowed to sort on more than one column. This could be relevant if the first column consists of duplicate values. For example, the PLAYERNO column in the PENAL-TIES table contains duplicate values. If you sort on one column only, SQL is allowed to determine itself how the rows with duplicate player numbers are sorted. When you add another column for sorting, you explicitly indicate how the duplicate values must be sorted.

Example 12.2: Find all player numbers and penalty amounts; sort the result on both columns.

```
SELECT    PLAYERNO, AMOUNT
FROM      PENALTIES
ORDER BY  PLAYERNO, AMOUNT
```

The result is:

```
PLAYERNO   AMOUNT
--------   ------
       6   100.00
       8    25.00
      27    75.00
      27   100.00
      44    25.00
      44    30.00
      44    75.00
     104    50.00
```

Explanation: The result shows that if the player numbers are equal, the penalty amount is used to sort. Two sort keys are needed to get the rows in the desired sequence.

In most cases, a sorting is specified on columns and expressions that also appear in the SELECT clause. However, this is not a necessity. The ORDER BY clause can contain expressions that do not appear in the SELECT clause.

Example 12.3: Get all penalty amounts, and sort the result on player number and penalty amount.

```
SELECT     AMOUNT
FROM       PENALTIES
ORDER BY   PLAYERNO, AMOUNT
```

The result is:

```
AMOUNT
------
100.00
 25.00
 75.00
100.00
 25.00
 30.00
 75.00
 50.00
```

Explanation: When the previous result is compared to the result of Example 12.2, we can see that the rows are indeed sorted on player number, even though this column does not appear in the SELECT clause.

12.3 Sorting on Expressions

Besides sorting on column names, a sorting can consist of scalar expressions.

Example 12.4: Get for all players the last name, the initials, and the player number, and sort the result on the first letter of the last name.

```
SELECT    NAME, INITIALS, PLAYERNO
FROM      PLAYERS
ORDER BY  SUBSTR(NAME, 1, 1)
```

The result is:

NAME	INITIALS	PLAYERNO
Bishop	D	39
Baker	E	44
Brown	M	57
Bailey	IP	112
Collins	DD	27
Collins	C	28
Everett	R	2
Hope	PK	83
Miller	P	95
Moorman	D	104
Newcastle	B	8
Parmenter	R	6
Parmenter	P	100
Wise	GWS	7

Explanation: Because several names begin with the same letter, SQL can decide for itself the sequence in which the rows with equal letters are presented.

The expressions in the ORDER BY clause can even contain subqueries.

Example 12.5: Get the player number and the amount of all penalties, and sort the result on the difference between the amount and the average penalty amount.

```
SELECT    PLAYERNO, AMOUNT
FROM      PENALTIES
ORDER BY ABS(AMOUNT - (SELECT AVG(AMOUNT) FROM PENALTIES))
```

The result is:

```
PLAYERNO  AMOUNT
--------  ------
     104   50.00
      44   75.00
      27   75.00
      44   30.00
      44   25.00
       8   25.00
       6  100.00
      27  100.00
```

Explanation: The value of the subquery is calculated first. Next, the value of the scalar expression is calculated for each row individually, and the result is sorted on that.

Subqueries that are used in the ORDER BY clause can even be correlated.

Example 12.6: Get the player number and the amount of all penalties, and sort the result on the average penalty amount of each player.

```
SELECT    PLAYERNO, AMOUNT
FROM      PENALTIES AS P1
ORDER BY (SELECT    AVG(AMOUNT)
          FROM      PENALTIES AS P2
          WHERE     P1.PLAYERNO = P2.PLAYERNO)
```

The result is:

```
PLAYERNO   AMOUNT
--------   ------
       8    25.00
      44    75.00
      44    25.00
      44    30.00
     104    50.00
      27   100.00
      27    75.00
       6   100.00
```

Explanation: The average penalty amount of player 8 is $25, so this amount comes first, followed by the penalties of player 44 because his average penalty amount is $43.33. The average of player 104 is $50, that of player 27 is $87.50 and, finally, the average penalty amount of player 6 is $100.

Portability: *Not all SQL products allow correlated subqueries in the ORDER BY clause.*

12.4   Sorting with Sequence Numbers and Column Headings

In the ORDER BY clause, we can replace a sorting consisting of column names or expressions with *sequence numbers*. A sequence number assigns a number to the expression in the SELECT clause on which sorting is performed. This next two statements are, therefore, equivalent:

```
SELECT    PAYMENTNO, PLAYERNO
FROM      PENALTIES
ORDER BY  PLAYERNO
```

and

```
SELECT    PAYMENTNO, PLAYERNO
FROM      PENALTIES
ORDER BY 2
```

The sequence number 2 stands for the second expression in the SELECT clause. It is not essential to use sequence numbers, but this can simplify the formulation of a statement.

Example 12.7: For each player who has incurred at least one penalty, get the total penalty amount; sort the result on this total.

```
SELECT    PLAYERNO, SUM(AMOUNT)
FROM      PENALTIES
GROUP BY PLAYERNO
ORDER BY 2
```

The result is:

```
PLAYERNO   SUM(AMOUNT)
--------   -----------
       8         25.00
     104         50.00
       6        100.00
      44        130.00
      27        175.00
```

Example 12.8: For each player, get the player number, the last name, and the sum of his penalties; sort the result on this sum.

```
SELECT    PLAYERNO, NAME,                     •
          (SELECT    SUM(AMOUNT)
           FROM      PENALTIES AS PEN
           WHERE     PEN.PLAYERNO=P.PLAYERNO)
FROM      PLAYERS AS P
ORDER BY 3
```

The result is:

```
PLAYERNO   NAME         SELECT SUM
--------   ---------    ----------
       2   Everett              ?
     100   Parmenter            ?
      95   Miller               ?
      83   Hope                 ?
      57   Brown                ?
     112   Bailey               ?
      39   Bishop               ?
      28   Collins              ?
       7   Wise                 ?
       8   Newcastle        25.00
     104   Moorman          50.00
       6   Parmenter       100.00
      44   Baker           130.00
      27   Collins         175.00
```

Your question might be: Isn't a sequence number a form of an expression as well? The answer is, no! In the ORDER BY clause, the sequence number is not considered to be an expression consisting of one literal. A sequence number is regarded an exception here.

The previous problem can also be solved by using column headings. The specification of column headings was introduced in Section 5.4. Column headings can also be used to sort rows. The next statement is equivalent, then, to the previous one:

```
SELECT    PLAYERNO, NAME,
          (SELECT   SUM(AMOUNT)
          FROM      PENALTIES AS PEN
          WHERE     PEN.PLAYERNO=P.PLAYERNO) AS TOTAL
FROM      PLAYERS AS P
ORDER BY  TOTAL
```

12.5   Sorting in Ascending and Descending Order

If you do not specify anything after a sorting, SQL sorts the result in *ascending* order. The same result can be achieved by explicitly specifying ASC (*ascending*) after the sorting. If you specify DESC (*descending*), the rows in the result are presented in *descending* order. Sorting values in a descending order always returns the reverse presentation of sorting in an ascending order, regardless of the data type of the values.

Example 12.9: For each penalty, get the player number and the penalty amount; sort the result in descending order on player number and in ascending order on penalty amount.

```
SELECT    PLAYERNO, AMOUNT
FROM      PENALTIES
ORDER BY  PLAYERNO DESC, AMOUNT ASC
```

The result is:

```
PLAYERNO  AMOUNT
--------  ------
     104   50.00
      44   25.00
      44   30.00
      44   75.00
      27   75.00
      27  100.00
       8   25.00
       6  100.00
```

Sorting numeric values in ascending order is obvious. It means that the lowest value is presented first and the highest is presented last. Sorting on dates, times, and time-stamps is also obvious. An ascending sort of dates means that dates are presented in chronological order. The same applies to time and timestamp values.

Sorting alphanumeric values in ascending order is the same as alphabetical sorting of words (such as in a dictionary). First come the words beginning with the letter *A*, then those with the letter *B*, and so on. Sorting alphanumeric values is, nevertheless, not as simple as it seems. For example, does the lowercase letter *a* come before or after the uppercase *A*, and do digits come before or after letters? And what do we do with symbols such as ё, é, and è? And let us not forget ç, œ, β, and æ? How letters and digits are sorted depends on the *character set* with which you work. In a character set, an internal value is defined for each character. Well-known character sets are *ASCII* (American Standard Code for Information Interchange), *EBCDIC* (Extended Binary Coded Decimal Interchange Code), and *Unicode*. A given operating system usually works with a specific character set. Modern versions of Windows, for example, use the Unicode character set, while the classic IBM mainframes support the EBCDIC character set. The sequence also depends on the so-called *collating sequences*. In Chapter 17, "Character Sets and Collating Sequences," we discuss character sets and collating sequences in detail.

In this book, we assume that you work with the Unicode character set. Under Windows, it is simple to examine the Unicode character set with the program Character Map, which is one of the accessories of Windows; see Figure 12.1. This figure shows that all uppercase letters come before the lowercase letters, and that digits come before uppercase letters.

Figure 12.1   *The program Character Map that shows the Unicode character set*

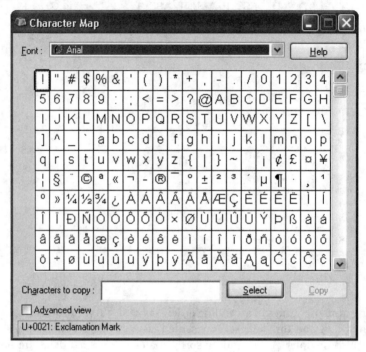

Example 12.10: Create the following PEOPLE table, add the six rows, and see how the different values are sorted.

```
CREATE TABLE CODES
       (CODE    CHAR(4) NOT NULL)

INSERT INTO CODES VALUES ('abc')
INSERT INTO CODES VALUES ('ABC')
INSERT INTO CODES VALUES ('-abc')
INSERT INTO CODES VALUES ('a bc')
INSERT INTO CODES VALUES ('ab')
INSERT INTO CODES VALUES ('9abc')
```

The SELECT statement:

```
SELECT     *
FROM       CODES
ORDER BY   CODE
```

The result is:

```
CODE
----
-abc
9abc
a bc
ab
abc
ABC
```

Explanation: This result clearly shows that digits come before letters, that the hyphen comes before the digits, and that short values are placed before long values. We can also see that uppercase letters come after lowercase letters.

12.6 Sorting of NULL Values

NULL values introduce a problem with sorting, and the various SQL products handle the ordering of NULL values in different ways. You should consult the relevant SQL manuals for more details. Four options exist:

- NULL values are always presented first, regardless of whether the ordering is ascending or descending.
- NULL values are always presented last, regardless of whether the ordering is ascending or descending.
- NULL values are seen as the lowest values.
- NULL values are seen as the highest values.

MySQL treats NULL values as the lowest values in a column. Therefore, they are always placed at the bottom of the result if the order is descending and at the top if the order is ascending; see the following example and the accompanying result.

Example 12.11: Get the different league numbers, and sort the result in descending order.

```
SELECT    DISTINCT LEAGUENO
FROM      PLAYERS
ORDER BY  1 DESC
```

The result is:

```
LEAGUENO
--------
8467
7060
6524
6409
2983
2513
2411
1608
1319
1124
?
```

Exercise 12.1: Show at least three different ORDER BY clauses that would sort the PLAYERS table in ascending order by player number.

Exercise 12.2: Indicate which of the following SELECT statements are incorrect:

1.

```
SELECT    *
FROM      PLAYERS
ORDER BY  2
```

2.

```
SELECT    *
FROM      PLAYERS
ORDER BY  20 DESC
```

3.

```
SELECT    PLAYERNO, NAME, INITIALS
FROM      PLAYERS
ORDER BY 2, INITIALS DESC, 3 ASC
```

4.

```
SELECT    *
FROM      PLAYERS
ORDER BY 1, PLAYERNO DESC
```

Exercise 12.3: For each match, get the player number, the team number, and the difference between the number of sets won and the number of sets lost; order the result in ascending order on this difference.

12.7 Answers

12.1
  1. ORDER BY 1
  2. ORDER BY PLAYERNO
  3. ORDER BY 1 ASC
  4. ORDER BY PLAYERNO ASC

12.2
  1. Correct.
  2. Incorrect because there is no twentieth column in the PLAYERS table.
  3. Incorrect because sorting is specified twice on the INITIALS column.
  4. Incorrect because a column in an ORDER BY clause cannot be specified twice.

12.3

```
SELECT    PLAYERNO, TEAMNO, WON - LOST
FROM      MATCHES
ORDER BY 3 ASC
```

13

Combining Table Expressions

13.1 Introduction

In Section 6.4, in Chapter 6, "SELECT Statements, Table Expressions, and Subqueries," we introduce the term *compound table expression*. With the help of *set operators,* the results of individual table expressions can be combined. In that section and several other chapters, examples are given of the set operator called UNION. With this operator, results of table expressions are placed underneath each other. SQL supports other set operators besides the UNION operator. Here is the complete list:

- UNION
- INTERSECT
- EXCEPT

- UNION ALL
- INTERSECT ALL
- EXCEPT ALL

Chapter 6 defines the table expression and the compound table expression. However, only the UNION operator is mentioned there. Now, we extend that definition with the complete set of set operators.

```
<table expression> ::=
  { <select block head>       |
    ( <table expression> )    |
    <compound table expression> }
[ <select block tail> ]

<compound table expression> ::=
    <table expression> <set operator> <table expression>

<set operator> ::=
    UNION | INTERSECT | EXCEPT |
    UNION ALL | INTERSECT ALL | EXCEPT ALL
```

13.2 Combining with UNION

If two table expressions are combined with the UNION operator, the end result consists of every row that appears in the result of one of the two table expressions or in both. UNION is the equivalent of the operator *union* from set theory.

Example 13.1: Get the player number and the town of each player from Inglewood and Plymouth.

```
SELECT     PLAYERNO, TOWN
FROM       PLAYERS
WHERE      TOWN = 'Inglewood'
UNION
SELECT     PLAYERNO, TOWN
FROM       PLAYERS
WHERE      TOWN = 'Plymouth'
```

The result is:

```
PLAYERNO  TOWN
--------  ---------
       8  Inglewood
      44  Inglewood
     112  Plymouth
```

Explanation: Each of the two table expressions returns a table consisting of two columns and zero or more rows. As mentioned, the UNION operator puts the two tables underneath each other. The end result of the entire statement is one table.

Note: *The previous statement could, of course, also have been formulated using an OR operator:*

```
SELECT     PLAYERNO, TOWN
FROM       PLAYERS
WHERE      TOWN = 'Inglewood'
OR         TOWN = 'Plymouth'
```

However, it is not always possible to replace the UNION operator with an OR operator. Here is an example.

Example 13.2: Get a list of all the dates that appear in the PLAYERS and the PENALTIES table.

```
SELECT    BIRTH_DATE AS DATES
FROM      PLAYERS
UNION
SELECT    PAYMENT_DATE
FROM      PENALTIES
```

The result is:

```
DATES
----------
1948-09-01
1956-10-29
1956-11-11
1962-07-08
1963-01-09
1963-02-28
1963-05-11
1963-05-14
1963-06-22
1963-10-01
1964-06-25
1964-12-28
1970-05-10
1971-08-17
1980-12-08
1981-05-05
1982-12-30
1983-09-10
1984-11-12
1984-12-08
```

This statement cannot be formulated with OR because rows from different tables are combined and are not, as in the previous example, from the same table.

A special property of the UNION operator is that all duplicate (or equal) rows are removed automatically from the end result. Section 9.5, in Chapter 9, "SELECT

Statement: SELECT Clause and Aggregation Functions," describes the rule for the equality of two rows with regard to DISTINCT in the SELECT clause. The same rule also applies, of course, to the UNION operator.

Example 13.3: Get the number of each player who has incurred at least one penalty, or who is a captain, or for whom both conditions apply.

```
SELECT      PLAYERNO
FROM        PENALTIES
UNION
SELECT      PLAYERNO
FROM        TEAMS
```

   The result is:

```
PLAYERNO
--------
       6
       8
      27
      44
     104
```

Explanation: The result obviously shows that all the duplicate rows have been deleted.

   You can combine more than two table expressions into one table expression. The following is an example.

Example 13.4: Get the player number of each player who has incurred at least one penalty, who is a captain, who lives in Stratford, or for whom two or three of these conditions apply.

```
SELECT      PLAYERNO
FROM        PENALTIES
UNION
SELECT      PLAYERNO
FROM        TEAMS
UNION
SELECT      PLAYERNO
FROM        PLAYERS
WHERE       TOWN = 'Stratford'
```

The result is:


```
PLAYERNO
--------
       2
       6
       7
       8
      27
      39
      44
      57
      83
     100
     104
```

Exercise 13.1: Get a list of numbers of the players who have ever been committee members, plus the numbers of the players who have incurred at least two penalties.

Exercise 13.2: Determine what the most recent date is: the most recent date of birth or the most recent date on which a penalty has been paid.

13.3 Rules for Using UNION

The following rules for using the UNION operator must be observed:

- The SELECT clauses of all relevant table expressions must have the same number of expressions, and the expressions that will be placed under one another must have comparable data types. If this applies, the table expressions are *union compatible*. Note that two data types are comparable if they are the same or if the expressions can be transformed into the same data type by an implicit case.
- An ORDER BY clause can be specified only after the last table expression. The sorting is performed on the entire end result, after all intermediate results have been combined.
- The SELECT clauses should not contain DISTINCT because SQL automatically removes duplicate rows when using UNION; thus, an additional DISTINCT is superfluous but allowed.

The following SELECT statements have not been not written according to these rules (work through them for yourself):

```
SELECT    *
FROM      PLAYERS
UNION
SELECT    *
FROM      PENALTIES
```

```
SELECT    PLAYERNO
FROM      PLAYERS
WHERE     TOWN = 'Stratford'
ORDER BY 1
UNION
SELECT    PLAYERNO
FROM      TEAMS
ORDER BY 1
```

The UNION operator in combination with the GROUP BY clause offers the possibility of calculating subtotals and totals. Yet the use of WITH ROLLUP results in simpler statements.

Example 13.5: For each combination of team number and player number, give the sum of all sets won and sets lost, and find for each team a subtotal and final total.

```
SELECT    CAST(TEAMNO AS CHAR(4)) AS TEAMNO,
          CAST(PLAYERNO AS CHAR(4)) AS PLAYERNO,
          SUM(WON + LOST) AS TOTAL
FROM      MATCHES
GROUP BY TEAMNO, PLAYERNO
UNION
SELECT    CAST(TEAMNO AS CHAR(4)),
          'subtotal',
          SUM(WON + LOST)
FROM      MATCHES
GROUP BY TEAMNO
UNION
SELECT    'total', 'total', SUM(WON + LOST)
FROM      MATCHES
ORDER BY 1, 2
```

The result is:

TEAMNO	PLAYERNO	TOTAL
1	2	4
1	44	5
1	57	3
1	6	2
1	8	3
1	83	3
1	subtotal	30
2	104	5
2	112	9
2	27	5
2	8	3
2	subtotal	22
total	total	52

Explanation: The statement consists of three table expressions. The first calculates the sum of all sets played for each combination of team number and player number. The second table expression calculates the sum of sets won and lost for each team. In the column PLAYERNO, the word *subtotal* is represented. To make the two table expressions union compatible, the player number in the first table expression of the SELECT clause is converted to an alphanumeric value. The third table expression calculates the total of all sets in the two columns. The ORDER BY clause ensures that the rows in the final result are in the correct sequence.

Exercise 13.3: Indicate which of the following (parts of the) SELECT statements are correct and which are incorrect, and state why:

1.

```
SELECT    ...
FROM      ...
GROUP BY ...
HAVING    ...
UNION
SELECT    ...
FROM      ...
ORDER BY ...
```

2.

```
SELECT    PLAYERNO, NAME
FROM      PLAYERS
UNION
SELECT    PLAYERNO, POSTCODE
FROM      PLAYERS
```

3.

```
SELECT    TEAMNO
FROM      TEAMS
UNION
SELECT    PLAYERNO
FROM      PLAYERS
ORDER BY 1
```

4.

```
SELECT    DISTINCT PLAYERNO
FROM      PLAYERS
UNION
SELECT    PLAYERNO
FROM      PENALTIES
ORDER BY 1
```

5.

```
SELECT    ...
FROM      ...
GROUP BY ...
ORDER BY ...
UNION
SELECT    ...
FROM      ...
```

Exercise 13.4: If we assume the original contents of the sample tables, how many rows appear in the end result of each of the following statements?

1.

```
SELECT    TOWN
FROM      PLAYERS
UNION
SELECT    TOWN
FROM      PLAYERS
```

2.

```
SELECT    PLAYERNO
FROM      PENALTIES
UNION
SELECT    PLAYERNO
FROM      PLAYERS
```

3.

```
SELECT    YEAR(BIRTH_DATE)
FROM      PLAYERS
UNION
SELECT    YEAR(PAYMENT_DATE)
FROM      PENALTIES
```

13.4 Combining with INTERSECT

This section describes another set operator, the INTERSECT. If two table expressions are combined with the INTERSECT operator, the end result consists of those rows that appear in the results of both table expressions. INTERSECT is the equivalent of the *intersection* operator from set theory. Just as with the UNION operator, duplicate rows are automatically removed from the result.

> **Portability:** *Several SQL products, including MySQL, do not support the INTERSECT operator.*

Example 13.6: Get the player number and the date of birth of each player who is living in Stratford and who was born after 1960.

```
SELECT    PLAYERNO, BIRTH_DATE
FROM      PLAYERS
WHERE     TOWN = 'Stratford'
INTERSECT
SELECT    PLAYERNO, BIRTH_DATE
FROM      PLAYERS
WHERE     BIRTH_DATE > '1960-12-31'
ORDER BY 1
```

The result is:

```
PLAYERNO  BIRTH_DATE
--------  ----------
       6  1964-06-25
       7  1963-05-11
      57  1971-08-17
     100  1963-02-28
```

Explanation: Both table expressions produce a table with two columns and zero or more rows. The INTERSECT operator looks for the rows that appear in the results of both table expressions. The end result of the entire statement is one table.

For the use of the INTERSECT operator, the same rules hold as for the UNION operator; see Section 13.3. The SELECT clauses have to be union compatible, an ORDER BY can be specified only behind the last table expression, and DISTINCT is superfluous.

The previous statement could, of course, have been formulated with the AND operator:

```
SELECT    PLAYERNO, BIRTH_DATE
FROM      PLAYERS
WHERE     TOWN = 'Stratford'
AND       BIRTH_DATE > '1960-12-31'
ORDER BY 1
```

However, it is not always possible to substitute the INTERSECT operator for the AND operator; see the following example.

Example 13.7: Get the player number of each player who is a captain and who has incurred at least one penalty.

```
SELECT    PLAYERNO
FROM      TEAMS
INTERSECT
SELECT    PLAYERNO
FROM      PENALTIES
```

The result is:

```
PLAYERNO
--------
       6
      27
```

All set operators, including the INTERSECT operator, can be used within subqueries.

Example 13.8: Get the player number and name of each player who is a captain and who incurred at least one penalty.

```
SELECT    PLAYERNO, NAME
FROM      PLAYERS
WHERE     PLAYERNO IN
          (SELECT    PLAYERNO
           FROM      TEAMS
           INTERSECT
           SELECT    PLAYERNO
           FROM      PENALTIES)
```

The result is:

```
PLAYERNO  NAME
--------  ---------
       6  Parmenter
      27  Collins
```

Example 13.9: Get the numbers less than 5000 that represent an integer to the power of two and three.

```
SELECT    POWER(NUMBER,2) AS POWERS
FROM      (SELECT    CAST(DIGIT1. DIGIT || DIGIT2. DIGIT
                     AS UNSIGNED INTEGER) AS NUMBER
           FROM      (SELECT '0' DIGIT UNION SELECT '1' UNION
                      SELECT '2' UNION SELECT '3' UNION
                      SELECT '4' UNION SELECT '5' UNION
                      SELECT '6' UNION SELECT '7' UNION
                      SELECT '8' UNION SELECT '9') AS DIGIT1,
                     (SELECT '0' DIGIT UNION SELECT '1' UNION
                      SELECT '2' UNION SELECT '3' UNION
                      SELECT '4' UNION SELECT '5' UNION
                      SELECT '6' UNION SELECT '7' UNION
                      SELECT '8' UNION SELECT '9') AS DIGIT2)
                     AS NUMBERS
WHERE     POWER(NUMBER,2) < 5000
INTERSECT
SELECT    POWER(NUMBER,3) AS POWERS
FROM      (SELECT    CAST(DIGIT1.DIGIT || DIGIT2.DIGIT
                     AS UNSIGNED INTEGER) AS NUMBER
           FROM      (SELECT '0' DIGIT UNION SELECT '1' UNION
                      SELECT '2' UNION SELECT '3' UNION
                      SELECT '4' UNION SELECT '5' UNION
                      SELECT '6' UNION SELECT '7' UNION
                      SELECT '8' UNION SELECT '9') AS DIGIT1,
                     (SELECT '0' DIGIT UNION SELECT '1' UNION
                      SELECT '2' UNION SELECT '3' UNION
                      SELECT '4' UNION SELECT '5' UNION
                      SELECT '6' UNION SELECT '7' UNION
                      SELECT '8' UNION SELECT '9') AS DIGIT2)
                     AS NUMBERS
WHERE     POWER(NUMBER,3) < 5000
```

The result is:

```
POWERS
------
     0
     1
    64
   729
  4096
```

Explanation: This result is based upon the SELECT statement in Example 7.34, in Chapter 7, "SELECT Statement: The FROM Clause."

Exercise 13.5: Get the numbers of the players who have once been committee members and who have incurred at least two penalties.

Exercise 13.6: Get the number of players who have ever been committee members and for whom at least two penalties have been incurred.

13.5 Combining with EXCEPT

The third set operator is the EXCEPT operator. If two table expressions are combined with the EXCEPT operator, the end result consists of only the rows that appear in the result of the first table expression but do not appear in the result of the second. EXCEPT is the equivalent of the *difference* operator from set theory. Just as with the UNION operator, duplicate rows are automatically removed from the result.

> **Portability:** *Several SQL products, including MySQL, do not support the EXCEPT operator.*

Example 13.10: Get the player number and the date of birth of each player who lives in Stratford but was *not* born after 1960.

```
SELECT    PLAYERNO, BIRTH_DATE
FROM      PLAYERS
WHERE     TOWN = 'Stratford'
EXCEPT
SELECT    PLAYERNO, BIRTH_DATE
FROM      PLAYERS
WHERE     BIRTH_DATE > '1960-12-31'
ORDER BY 1
```

The result is:


```
PLAYERNO  BIRTH_DATE
--------  ----------
       2  1948-09-01
      39  1956-10-29
      83  1956-11-11
```


Explanation: Each of the two table expressions returns a table with two columns and zero or more rows. The EXCEPT operator looks first for all rows appearing in the first table expression. These are the following players:


```
PLAYERNO  BIRTH_DATE
--------  ----------
       6  1964-06-25
      83  1956-11-11
       2  1948-09-01
       7  1963-05-11
      57  1971-08-17
      39  1956-10-29
     100  1963-02-28
```


Next, the operator looks for all the rows appearing in the second table expression:


```
PLAYERNO  BIRTH_DATE
--------  ----------
     112  1963-10-01
       8  1962-07-08
     100  1963-02-28
      28  1963-06-22
       6  1964-06-25
      44  1963-01-09
      27  1964-12-28
     104  1970-05-10
       7  1963-05-11
      57  1971-08-17
```

Finally, all rows appearing in the first intermediate result but not in the second are recorded in the end result. The end result of the entire statement is, of course, one table again.

The previous statement could also have been formulated as follows:

```
SELECT    PLAYERNO, BIRTH_DATE
FROM      PLAYERS
WHERE     TOWN = 'Stratford'
AND       NOT(BIRTH_DATE > '1960-12-31')
ORDER BY 1
```

Just as with the UNION and INTERSECT operators, the same rules that were described in Section 13.3 apply when using the EXCEPT operator.

However, it is not always possible to replace the EXCEPT operator the way we did earlier. If the rows come from different tables, the trick does not work.

Example 13.11: Get the player number and name of each player who has incurred at least one penalty and is *not* a captain.

```
SELECT    PLAYERNO, NAME
FROM      PLAYERS
WHERE     PLAYERNO IN
          (SELECT    PLAYERNO
           FROM      PENALTIES
           EXCEPT
           SELECT    PLAYERNO
           FROM      TEAMS)
```

The result is:

```
PLAYERNO  NAME
--------  ---------
       8  Newcastle
      44  Baker
     104  Moorman
```

Theoretically, the existence of the EXCEPT operator makes the INTERSECT operator superfluous. Work out for yourself that the following two statements produce the same result under all circumstances.

```
SELECT     PLAYERNO
FROM       TEAMS
INTERSECT
SELECT     PLAYERNO
FROM       PENALTIES
```

```
SELECT     PLAYERNO
FROM       TEAMS
EXCEPT    (SELECT     PLAYERNO
           FROM       TEAMS
           EXCEPT
           SELECT     PLAYERNO
           FROM       PENALTIES)
```

Example 13.12: Get the numbers of the players from the PENALTIES tables minus numbers 6, 27, and 58.

```
SELECT     PLAYERNO
FROM       PENALTIES
EXCEPT
SELECT     6 UNION SELECT 27 UNION SELECT 58
```

The result is:

```
PLAYERNO
--------
       8
      44
     104
```

Portability: *Some SQL products use the term MINUS instead of EXCEPT.*

Exercise 13.7: Get the numbers of the players who have ever been committee members and for whom no penalties have been incurred.

Exercise 13.8: Which payment numbers between 1 and 20 are not currently in use?

13.6 Keeping Duplicate Rows

All previous examples made it clear that duplicate rows are automatically removed from the end result if one of the set operators UNION, INTERSECT, or EXCEPT is used. Removing duplicate rows can be suppressed by using the ALL version of these operators. We illustrate this with the UNION ALL operator.

If two table expressions are combined with the UNION ALL operator, the end result consists of the resulting rows from both of the table expressions. The only difference between UNION and UNION ALL is that when you use UNION, the duplicate rows are automatically removed, and when you use UNION ALL, they are kept.

The result of the following statement shows that duplicate rows are not removed.

Example 13.13: Combine the set of player numbers from the PENALTIES table with the one from the TEAMS table. Do not remove duplicate rows.

```
SELECT    PLAYERNO
FROM      PENALTIES
UNION ALL
SELECT    PLAYERNO
FROM      TEAMS
```

The result is:

```
PLAYERNO
--------
       6
      44
      27
     104
      44
       8
      44
      27
       6
      27
```

ALL can also be added to the operators INTERSECT and EXCEPT. The effect is comparable to that of the UNION operator: Duplicate rows are not removed.

Example 13.14: Subtract the set of player numbers of the TEAMS table from the set of player numbers of PENALTIES table. Keep the duplicate rows.

```
SELECT     PLAYERNO
FROM       PENALTIES
EXCEPT ALL
SELECT     PLAYERNO
FROM       TEAMS
```

Explanation: The result of the first table expression holds the values 6, 8, 27, 27, 44, 44, 44, and 104. The result of the second table expression holds the values 6 and 27. The final result will be:

```
PLAYERNO
--------
       8
      27
      44
      44
      44
     104
```

Notice that 27 does appear in the final result. The reason for this is that 27 appears twice in the intermediate result of the first table expression, so only one 27 value is removed.

Exercise 13.9: Get the numbers of players and add the number of teams.

Exercise 13.10: Get the squares for the numbers 0 up to and including 9, and carry the numbers to the third power. Do not remove duplicate numbers.

13.7 Set Operators and the NULL Value

SQL automatically removes duplicate rows from the result if the set operators UNION, INTERSECT, and EXCEPT are specified. That is why the following (somewhat peculiar) SELECT statement produces only one row, even if both individual table expressions have one row as their intermediate result:

```
SELECT    PLAYERNO, LEAGUENO
FROM      PLAYERS
WHERE     PLAYERNO = 27
UNION
SELECT    PLAYERNO, LEAGUENO
FROM      PLAYERS
WHERE     PLAYERNO = 27
```

But what will happen to NULL values? What is the result of the previous statement if we substitute player number 7 for 27? Player 7 has no league number. Maybe you think that the statement will produce two rows now because the two NULL values are not considered equivalent. However, this is not true. SQL will produce only one row in this situation. SQL considers NULL values to be equivalent when set operators are processed. In other words, the rule used here to determine whether two rows are equal is the same as the one for DISTINCT; see Section 9.5, in Chapter 9. This is in accordance with the theory of the original relational model as defined by E. F. Codd (see [CODD90]).

13.8 Combining Multiple Set Operators

We have already seen a few examples in which multiple set operators are used within a single SELECT statement. Here is another example.

Example 13.15: Get the numbers of each player who incurred at least one penalty and who is not a captain; add the numbers of the players who live in Eltham.

```
SELECT    PLAYERNO
FROM      PENALTIES
EXCEPT
SELECT    PLAYERNO
FROM      TEAMS
UNION
SELECT    PLAYERNO
FROM      PLAYERS
WHERE     TOWN = 'Eltham'
```

The result is:

```
PLAYERNO
--------
       8
      27
      44
     104
```

Explanation: The method of processing is as follows. First, the result of the second table expression is subtracted from that of the first; only then is the intermediate result combined with the result of the third table expression.

We can place brackets around table expressions to affect the sequence of processing. Next, we give the earlier SELECT statement, but now we have placed brackets around the last two table expressions. The result shows that the SELECT statement has been processed differently.

```
SELECT    PLAYERNO
FROM      PENALTIES
EXCEPT
( SELECT    PLAYERNO
  FROM      TEAMS
  UNION
  SELECT    PLAYERNO
  FROM      PLAYERS
  WHERE     TOWN = 'Eltham' )
```

The result is:

```
PLAYERNO
--------
       8
      44
```

13.9 Set Operators and the Theory

We conclude this chapter with a rather theoretical discussion of set operators. We give a number of rules for working with multiple different set operators within one SELECT statement. All the rules are based on general rules (laws) that apply to mathematical operators and set theory. We define and explain each of these rules, and we use the following symbols and definitions:

- The symbol T_i represents the result of a random table expression (i is 1, 2, or 3).
- For each T_i, it holds that the SELECT clauses are union compatible.
- The symbol $T\varnothing$ represents the empty result of a table expression.
- The symbol $\cup$ represents the UNION operator.
- The symbol $\cap$ represents the INTERSECT operator.
- The symbol $-$ represents the EXCEPT operator.
- The symbol $\cup^A$ represents the UNION ALL operator.
- The symbol $\cap^A$ represents the INTERSECT ALL operator.
- The symbol $-^A$ represents the EXCEPT ALL operator.
- The symbol $=$ means "is equal to."
- The symbol $\neq$ means "is not always equal to."
- The symbol θ represents a random set operator.
- The symbol $\varnothing$ represents an empty result.

Therefore, the results of two table expressions are equivalent if the number of rows of the two is equivalent and if, after the results have been sorted, the rows with identical reference numbers are equivalent.

General rules:

$T_1 \cup T_2 = T_2 \cup T_1$

In mathematics, this law is called the *commutative law* for the UNION operator. A set operator is commutative if the order of the table expressions can be changed without affecting the final result. In other words, a set operator θ is commutative if $T_1 \theta T_2$ is equivalent to $T_2 \theta T_1$ for each pair (T_1, T_2). Notice that $T_1 - T_2 \neq T_2 - T_1$ because $T_1 \neq T_2$. Thus, the EXCEPT operator (and also the EXCEPT ALL operator) is an example of a noncommutative operator.

$T_1 \cup^A T_2 = T_2 \cup^A T_1$

For the UNION ALL operator, the commutative law also holds.

$T_1 \cap T_2 = T_2 \cap T_1$

For the INTERSECT operator, the commutative law also holds.

$T_1 \cap^A T_2 = T_2 \cap^A T_1$

For the INTERSECT ALL operator, the commutative law also holds.

$T_1 \cup T\emptyset \neq T_1$

Adding an empty result to a non-empty result T_1 with the UNION operator does not always lead to the result T_1. The comparison is correct only if T_1 does not have duplicate rows.

$T_1 \cup^A T\emptyset = T_1$

Adding an empty result to a non-empty result with the UNION ALL operator has no effect.

$T_1 \cap T\emptyset = \emptyset$ and $T_1 \cap^A T\emptyset = \emptyset$

The intersection of a result with an empty result leads to an empty end result, regardless of whether T_1 contains duplicate rows.

$T_1 - T\emptyset = T_1$ and $T_1 -^A T\emptyset = T_1$

The result of subtracting an empty result from a non-empty result T_1 with the EXCEPT operator does not always lead to the result T_1 itself. The comparison is correct only if T_1 contains no duplicate rows.

$T_1 \cup (T_2 \cup T_3) = (T_1 \cup T_2) \cup T_3$ and
$T_1 \cup^A (T_2 \cup^A T_3) = (T_1 \cup^A T_2) \cup^A T_3$

This law is called the *associative law* for the UNION operator. A set operator θ is associative if $(T_1 \, \theta \, T_2) \, \theta \, T_3$ is equivalent to $T_1 \, \theta \, (T_2 \, \theta \, T_3)$ for each combination of (T_1, T_2, T_3). For the UNION ALL operator, the associative law also holds. Brackets can be omitted for associative set operators, so $T_1 \cup (T_2 \cup T_3)$ is equivalent to $T_1 \cup T_2 \cup T_3$.

$T_1 \cap (T_2 \cap T_3) = (T_1 \cap T_2) \cap T_3$

The rules of the associative law also apply to the INTERSECT operator.

$T_1 \cup (T_2 \cap T_3) = (T_1 \cup T_2) \cap (T_1 \cup T_3)$
and
$T_1 \cap (T_2 \cup T_3) = (T_1 \cap T_2) \cup (T_1 \cap T_3)$

These laws are called the *distributive laws*. The analogy between the properties of union and intersection, and the properties of adding and multiplying numbers is worth noting.

$T_1 \cup T_1 \neq T_1$

The union of a result with itself leads to the same result only if T_1 contains no duplicate rows.

$T_1 \cup^A T_1 \neq T_1$

In mathematics, this law is called the *idempotent law*. The rule is true only if T_1 is empty.

$T_1 \cap T_1 \neq T_1$

The intersection of a result with itself leads to the same result only if T_1 contains no duplicate rows.

$T_1 - T_1 = T\emptyset$

Subtracting a result from itself always leads to an empty result, regardless of whether T_1 contains duplicate rows.

$T_1 -^A T_1 = T\emptyset$

See the previous rule.

$T_1 \cup (T_1 \cap T_2) = T_1$ and
$T_1 \cap (T_1 \cup T_2) = T_1$

This applies only if T_1 and T_2 contain no duplicate rows.

$(T_1 \cup^A T_2) \cup T_3 = T_1 \cup (T_2 \cup^A T_3)$

If the UNION operator is the last operator to be executed, all UNION ALL operators can be replaced by UNION operators and the result remains the same. The following rule is therefore also correct: $(T_1 \cup T_2) \cup^A T_3 \neq T_1 \cup (T_2 \cup^A T_3)$.

$T_1 - (T_1 - T_2) = T_1 \cap T_2$ and
$T_2 - (T_2 - T_1) = T_1 \cap T_2$

These rules apply only if neither T_1 nor T_2 contains duplicate rows.

$(T_1 \cup T_2) \cap T_1 = T_1 - T_2$

This rule always applies, even if T_1 and T_2 do contain duplicate rows.

$T_1 \cup T_2 = (T_1 - T_2) \cup (T_1 \cap T_2)$
$\cup (T_2 - T_1)$

This rule is called *inner identity* in [CODD90].

13.10 Answers

13.1

```
SELECT    PLAYERNO
FROM      COMMITTEE_MEMBERS
UNION
SELECT    PLAYERNO
FROM      PENALTIES
GROUP BY  PLAYERNO
HAVING    COUNT(*) >= 2
```

13.2

```
SELECT    MAX(ADATE)
FROM      (SELECT    MAX(BIRTH_DATE) AS ADATE
           FROM      PLAYERS
           UNION
           SELECT    MAX(PAYMENT_DATE) AS ADATE
           FROM      PENALTIES) AS TWODATES
```

13.3   Correct.

Correct, even though the lengths of the columns NAME and POSTCODE are not equal.

Correct.

Correct, even though in a SELECT clause, DISTINCT is superfluous with an UNION operator.

Incorrect because when a UNION operator is used, only the last SELECT statement can include an ORDER BY clause.

13.4   6

14

12

13.5

```
SELECT    PLAYERNO
FROM      COMMITTEE_MEMBERS
INTERSECT
SELECT    PLAYERNO
FROM      PENALTIES
GROUP BY PLAYERNO
HAVING    COUNT(*) >= 2
```

13.6

```
SELECT    COUNT(*)
FROM      (SELECT    PLAYERNO
           FROM      COMMITTEE_MEMBERS
           INTERSECT
           SELECT    PLAYERNO
           FROM      PENALTIES
           GROUP BY PLAYERNO
           HAVING    COUNT(*) >= 2) AS PLAYERS
```

13.7

```
SELECT    PLAYERNO
FROM      COMMITTEE_MEMBERS
EXCEPT
SELECT    PLAYERNO
FROM      PENALTIES
```

13.8

```
VALUES   (1),(2),(3),(4),(5),(6),(7),(8),(9),(10),
         (11),(12),(13),(14),(15),(16),(17),(18),(19),(20)
EXCEPT
SELECT   PAYMENTNO
FROM     PENALTIES
```

13.9

```
SELECT   SUM(NUMBER)
FROM     (SELECT   COUNT(*) AS NUMBER
          FROM     PLAYERS
          UNION ALL
          SELECT   COUNT(*) AS NUMBER
          FROM     TEAMS) AS NUMBERS
```

13.10

```
SELECT   POWER(DIGIT,2)
FROM     (SELECT '0' DIGIT UNION SELECT '1' UNION
          SELECT '2' UNION SELECT '3' UNION
          SELECT '4' UNION SELECT '5' UNION
          SELECT '6' UNION SELECT '7' UNION
          SELECT '8' UNION SELECT '9') AS DIGITS1
UNION ALL
SELECT   POWER(DIGIT,3)
FROM     (SELECT '0' DIGIT UNION SELECT '1' UNION
          SELECT '2' UNION SELECT '3' UNION
          SELECT '4' UNION SELECT '5' UNION
          SELECT '6' UNION SELECT '7' UNION
          SELECT '8' UNION SELECT '9') AS DIGITS2
ORDER BY 1
```

14

Updating Tables

14.1 Introduction

S QL offers various statements for updating the contents (the column values in the rows) of tables—statements for inserting new rows, for changing column values, and for deleting rows. This chapter describes the extensive features of these statements.

> **Note:** *In most examples of this book, we assume that the tables contain their original contents. If you execute the statements discussed in this chapter, you change the contents of the tables. Consequently, the results of your statements in the next examples can differ from those in the book. On the Web site of the book, www.r20.nl, you can read how to restore the original contents of the tables after an update.*

14.2 Inserting New Rows

In SQL, you can use the INSERT statement to add rows to an existing table. With this statement, you can add new rows and populate a table with rows taken from another table.

```
<insert statement> ::=
    INSERT INTO <table specification> <insert specification>

<insert specification> ::=
    [ <column list> ] <values clause>      |
    [ <column list> ] <table expression>
```

(continued)

```
<column list> ::=
    ( <column name> [ { , <column name> }... ] )

<values clause> ::=
    VALUES <row expression> [ { , <row expression> } ... ]

<row expression> ::=
    ( <scalar expression> [ { , <scalar expression> }... ]
```

Section 4.8, in Chapter 4, "SQL in a Nutshell," among others, contains several examples of INSERT statements. In this section, we show other simple examples to illustrate the possibilities of the INSERT statement.

Example 14.1: The tennis club has a new team. This third team will be captained by player 100 and will compete in the third division.

```
INSERT INTO TEAMS (TEAMNO, PLAYERNO, DIVISION)
VALUES (3, 100, 'third')
```

Explanation: Behind the term INSERT INTO, the name of the table is specified for which rows must be added. Following that are the names of the columns of that table; finally, a VALUES clause is used to specify the values of the new row. The structure of a VALUES clause is simple and consists of one or more row expressions, with each row expression consisting of one or more scalar expressions.

The word INTO can be left out, but with all other SQL products, it is required; therefore, we recommend including the word always.

You do not have to specify column names if a value is specified for all columns of the table concerned. The TEAMS table contains three columns, and three values have been specified, which means that we could have omitted the column names:

```
INSERT INTO TEAMS
VALUES (3, 100, 'third')
```

If column names are omitted, SQL assumes that the order in which the values are entered is the same as the default sequence of the columns (see COLUMN_NO in the COLUMNS table).

You are not required to specify columns in the default sequence. Therefore, the next statement is equivalent to the previous two:

```
INSERT INTO TEAMS (PLAYERNO, DIVISION, TEAMNO)
VALUES (100, 'third', 3)
```

If the column names had *not* been specified in this statement, the result would have been entirely different. SQL would have considered the value 100 to be a TEAMNO, the value third a PLAYERNO, and the value 3 a DIVISION. Of course, the insert would not have been performed at all because the value third is an alphanumeric literal and the PLAYERNO column has a numeric data type.

For all columns in the CREATE TABLE statement that have been defined as NOT NULL, a value *must* be specified (work out for yourself why). The following statement is, therefore, not correct because the PLAYERNO column has been defined as NOT NULL and does not have a value in the INSERT statement:

```
INSERT INTO TEAMS
        (TEAMNO, DIVISION)
VALUES (3, 'third')
```

However, the next example is correct.

Example 14.2: Add a new player.

```
INSERT INTO PLAYERS
        (PLAYERNO, NAME, INITIALS, SEX,
        JOINED, STREET, TOWN)
VALUES (611, 'Jones', 'GG', 'M', 1977, 'Green Way',
        'Stratford')
```

In all columns that have not been specified in the INSERT statement, NULL values will be entered.

Instead of a literal, a NULL value can be specified. Then, the concerning row will be filled, in that row, with the NULL value. In the following statement, the LEAGUENO column, among other things, will be filled with NULL:

```
INSERT INTO PLAYERS
        (PLAYERNO, NAME, INITIALS, BIRTH_DATE,
        SEX, JOINED, STREET, HOUSENO, POSTCODE,
        TOWN, PHONENO, LEAGUENO)
VALUES (611, 'Jones', 'GG', NULL, 'M', 1977,
        'Green Way', NULL, NULL, 'Stratford', NULL, NULL)
```

Because it is possible to specify more than one row expression in a VALUES clause, you can add multiple new rows with one INSERT statement.

Example 14.3: Add four new teams.

```
INSERT INTO TEAMS (TEAMNO, PLAYERNO, DIVISION)
VALUES (6, 100, 'third'),
        (7,  27, 'fourth'),
        (8,  39, 'fourth'),
        (9, 112, 'sixth')
```

Explanation: The new rows are separated by apostrophes within the VALUES clause.
  Instead of literals, you can also include expressions within the VALUES clause, and these expressions can be compound. Therefore, calculations, scalar functions, and even scalar subqueries are allowed.

Example 14.4: Create a new table in which the number of players and the sum of all penalties will be stored.

```
CREATE TABLE TOTALS
        (NUMBERPLAYERS   INTEGER NOT NULL,
        SUMPENALTIES    DECIMAL(9,2) NOT NULL)

INSERT INTO TOTALS (NUMBERPLAYERS, SUMPENALTIES)
VALUES ((SELECT COUNT(*) FROM PLAYERS),
        (SELECT SUM(AMOUNT) FROM PENALTIES))
```

Explanation: Remember that each subquery must be placed between brackets in this construct.

14.3 Populating a Table with Rows from Another Table

In the previous section, we showed only examples of INSERT statements in which new rows are added. With the INSERT statement, we can fill a table with rows from another table (or other tables). You could say that data is *copied* from one table to another. Instead of the VALUES clause, we use a table expression in the INSERT statement.

Example 14.5: Create a separate table in which the number, name, town, and telephone number of each noncompetition player is recorded.

We start with creating a new table:

```
CREATE TABLE RECR_PLAYERS
      (PLAYERNO    SMALLINT NOT NULL,
       NAME        CHAR(15) NOT NULL,
       TOWN        CHAR(10) NOT NULL,
       PHONENO     CHAR(13),
       PRIMARY KEY (PLAYERNO))
```

The following INSERT statement populates the RECR_PLAYERS table with data about recreational players registered in the PLAYERS table:

```
INSERT    INTO RECR_PLAYERS
          (PLAYERNO, NAME, TOWN, PHONENO)
SELECT    PLAYERNO, NAME, TOWN, PHONENO
FROM      PLAYERS
WHERE     LEAGUENO IS NULL
```

After this INSERT statement, the contents of the new table look like this:

```
PLAYERNO  NAME     TOWN       PHONENO
--------  -------  ---------  ----------
       7  Wise     Stratford  070-347689
      28  Collins  Midhurst   071-659599
      39  Bishop   Stratford  070-393435
      95  Miller   Douglas    070-867564
```

Explanation: The first part of the INSERT statement is a normal INSERT statement. The second part is based not on a VALUES clause, but on a table expression. The result of a table expression is a number of rows with values. However, these rows are not displayed on the screen, but are stored directly in the RECR_PLAYERS table.

The rules that apply to the first form of the INSERT statement also apply here. The next two statements, then, have an equivalent result to the previous INSERT statement:

```
INSERT    INTO RECR_PLAYERS
SELECT    PLAYERNO, NAME, TOWN, PHONENO
FROM      PLAYERS
WHERE     LEAGUENO IS NULL

INSERT    INTO RECR_PLAYERS
          (TOWN, PHONENO, NAME, PLAYERNO)
SELECT    TOWN, PHONENO, NAME, PLAYERNO
FROM      PLAYERS
WHERE     LEAGUENO IS NULL
```

Several other rules apply:

- The table to which rows are added can be the same as the one from which they are copied.
- The table expression is a fully fledged table expression and, therefore, can include subqueries, joins, set operators, GROUP BY and ORDER BY clauses, functions, and so on.
- The number of columns in the INSERT INTO clause must be equal to the number of expressions in the SELECT clause of the table expression.
- The data types of the columns in the INSERT INTO clause must conform to the data types of the expressions in the SELECT clause.

We use two examples to illustrate the first rule.

Example 14.6: Duplicate the number of rows in the RECR_PLAYERS table.

```
INSERT    INTO RECR_PLAYERS
          (PLAYERNO, NAME, TOWN, PHONENO)
SELECT    PLAYERNO + 1000, NAME, TOWN, PHONENO
FROM      RECR_PLAYERS
```

Explanation: One thousand is added to the value of the PLAYERNO column to make sure that no problems occur with the primary key.

Example 14.7: Add all penalties to the PENALTIES table for which the amount is greater than the average amount.

```
INSERT    INTO PENALTIES
SELECT    PAYMENTNO + 100, PLAYERNO, PAYMENT_DATE, AMOUNT
FROM      PENALTIES
WHERE     AMOUNT >
          (SELECT    AVG(AMOUNT)
           FROM      PENALTIES)
```

Exercise 14.1: Add a new row to the PENALTIES table; the payment number is 15, this concerns player 27, the payment date was 1985-11-08, and the penalty amount is $75.

Exercise 14.2: Add all the penalties to the PENALTIES table for which the amount is smaller than the average amount, plus all penalties of player 27. Make sure that the penalty numbers remain unique.

14.4 Updating Values in Rows

With the UPDATE statement, you can change values in a table. Use a table reference to indicate which table needs to be updated. The WHERE clause of an UPDATE statement specifies which rows must be changed; the SET clause assigns new values to one or more columns.

```
<update statement> ::=
   UPDATE <table reference>
   SET    <column assignment> [ { , <column assignment> }... ]
   [ WHERE  <condition> ]

<table reference> ::=
   <table specification> [ [ AS ] <pseudonym> ]

<pseudonym> ::= <name>

<column assignment> ::=
   <column name> = <scalar expression>
```

Example 14.8: Update the league number for player 95 to 2000.

```
UPDATE    PLAYERS
SET       LEAGUENO = '2000'
WHERE     PLAYERNO = 95
```

Explanation: For *every* row in the PLAYERS table (UPDATE PLAYERS) in which the player number equals 95 (WHERE PLAYERNO = 95), you must change the LEAGUENO to 2000 (SET LEAGUENO = '2000'). The last specification is called a column assignment.

In most examples, it is not necessary, but you can specify a pseudonym behind a table name, just as in a SELECT statement. The earlier UPDATE statement has the same result as the following:

```
UPDATE    PLAYERS AS P
SET       P.LEAGUENO = '2000'
WHERE     P.PLAYERNO = 95
```

A literal is specified in the column assignment of this first example. Because of this, the LEAGUENO column gets a complete new value, one that replaces the existing value completely. A column assignment can also contain complex expressions that can even refer to the column that will be updated.

Example 14.9: Increase all penalties by 5%.

```
UPDATE    PENALTIES
SET       AMOUNT = AMOUNT * 1.05
```

Explanation: Because the WHERE clause has been omitted, as in the previous example, the update is performed on all rows in the table concerned. In this example, the amount in each row of the PENALTIES table is increased by 5%.

Example 14.10: Set the number of sets won to 0 for all competitors resident in Stratford.

```
UPDATE     MATCHES
SET        WON = 0
WHERE      PLAYERNO IN
           (SELECT   PLAYERNO
           FROM      PLAYERS
           WHERE     TOWN = 'Stratford')
```

The earlier examples show SET clauses with only one column assignment. You can update multiple columns with one statement simultaneously.

Example 14.11: The Parmenter family has moved to 83 Palmer Street in Inglewood; the postcode has become 1234UU, and the telephone number is unknown.

```
UPDATE     PLAYERS
SET        STREET    = 'Palmer Street',
           HOUSENO   = '83',
           TOWN      = 'Inglewood',
           POSTCODE  = '1234UU',
           PHONENO   = NULL
WHERE      NAME      = 'Parmenter'
```

Explanation: In this case, the PHONENO column has been filled with the NULL value. Remember the comma between each item. With this statement, both players named Parmenter are moved to the same address.

We must be careful when the column that will be updated is used in the expressions of column assignments. The following statement could give the impression that the values of the STREET and TOWN columns for player 44 are exchanged:

```
UPDATE     PLAYERS
SET        STREET    = TOWN,
           TOWN      = STREET
WHERE      PLAYERNO  = 44
```

Explanation: The original contents of the PLAYERS table are:

```
PLAYERNO   STREET        TOWN
--------   ------------  ---------
44         Lewis Street  Inglewood
```

The result of the UPDATE statement is:

```
PLAYERNO   STREET        TOWN
--------   ------------  ---------
44         Inglewood     Lewis Street
```

So, the values of the columns have not been processed, but now the question is, why not? This is caused by the processing method of the UPDATE statement. For each row, SQL checks whether the condition in the WHERE clause is true. If so, the value of the expression of the first column assignment is determined first, and this value is assigned to the column concerned. The value of the second expression is determined next, and that value also is assigned to the column concerned. In this example, it means that first the value of the TOWN column is assigned to the STREET column. After that, the value of the STREET column in the second column assignment is calculated, which already is the TOWN column. It looks as if SQL has processed the following statements in succession:

```
UPDATE    PLAYERS
SET       STREET    = TOWN
WHERE     PLAYERNO = 44

UPDATE    PLAYERS
SET       TOWN     = STREET
WHERE     PLAYERNO = 44
```

When exchanging values, the values of one of the columns must be entered in a temporary table.

Portability: *Not all SQL products would process the previous example as described. For example, products such as DB2 would switch the values of the two columns TOWN and STREET.*

Expressions consisting of scalar subqueries can also be used in the SET clause.

Example 14.12: Create a new table to store for each player the player number, the number of matches she played, and the sum of all penalties incurred by her.

```
CREATE TABLE PLAYERS_DATA
        (PLAYERNO          INTEGER NOT NULL PRIMARY KEY,
        NUMBER_MAT         INTEGER,
        SUM_PENALTIES      DECIMAL(7,2))

INSERT INTO PLAYERS_DATA (PLAYERNO)
SELECT PLAYERNO FROM PLAYERS

UPDATE     PLAYERS_DATA AS PD
SET        NUMBER_MAT =      (SELECT    COUNT(*)
                             FROM       MATCHES AS M
                             WHERE      M.PLAYERNO = PD.PLAYERNO),
           SUM_PENALTIES = (SELECT      SUM(AMOUNT)
                             FROM        PENALTIES AS PEN
                             WHERE       PEN.PLAYERNO = PD.PLAYERNO)
```

Explanation: In the UPDATE clause of the UPDATE statement, a pseudonym (PD) is used for reference in the subqueries to this table.

In a subquery that is used in a SET clause, you can specify the table that will be updated.

Example 14.13: Subtract the average penalty amount from each penalty amount.

```
UPDATE     PENALTIES
SET        AMOUNT = AMOUNT - (SELECT    AVG(AMOUNT)
                              FROM       PENALTIES)
```

Explanation: SQL calculates the value of the scalar subquery before the actual UPDATE statement is processed.

Portability: *Not all SQL products allow the use of subqueries in the SET clause.*

Exercise 14.3: Change the value F in the SEX column of the PLAYERS table to W (woman).

Exercise 14.4: Update the SEX column in the PLAYERS table as follows: Where M is recorded, change it to F, and where F exists, change it to M.

Exercise 14.5: Increase all penalties higher than the average penalty by 20%.

14.5 Deleting Rows from a Table

The DELETE statement removes rows from a table. The definition of the DELETE statement reads:

```
<delete statement> ::=
    DELETE
    FROM    <table reference>
    [ <where clause> ]

<table reference> ::=
    <table specification> [ [ AS ] <pseudonym> ]

<pseudonym> ::= <name>
```

Example 14.14: Delete all penalties incurred by player 44.

```
DELETE
FROM      PENALTIES
WHERE     PLAYERNO = 44
```

or

```
DELETE
FROM      PENALTIES AS PEN
WHERE     PEN.PLAYERNO = 44
```

If the WHERE clause is omitted, all the rows of the specified table are deleted. This is not the same as dropping a table with the DROP statement. DELETE removes only the contents, whereas the DROP statement deletes not only the contents of the table, but also the definition of the table from the catalog. After the DELETE statement, the table remains intact.

Example 14.15: Delete all players for whom the year in which they joined the club is greater than the average year that all players from Stratford joined the club.

```
DELETE
FROM     PLAYERS
WHERE    JOINED >
         (SELECT   AVG(JOINED)
          FROM     PLAYERS
          WHERE    TOWN = 'Stratford')
```

Explanation: Just as with the UPDATE statement, some SQL products do not allow subqueries in the WHERE clause of a DELETE statement to refer to the table from which rows are deleted. Again, this restriction does not apply to SQL.

Exercise 14.6: Delete all penalties incurred by player 44 in 1980.

Exercise 14.7: Delete all penalties incurred by players who have ever played for a team in the second division.

Exercise 14.8: Delete all players who live in the same town as player 44, but keep the data about player 44.

14.6 Answers

14.1

```
INSERT INTO PENALTIES
VALUES (15, 27, '1985-11-08', 75)
```

14.2

```
INSERT    INTO PENALTIES
SELECT    PAYMENTNO + 1000, PLAYERNO, PAYMENT_DATE, AMOUNT
FROM      PENALTIES
WHERE     AMOUNT >
          (SELECT   AVG(AMOUNT)
          FROM      PENALTIES)
UNION
SELECT    PAYMENTNO + 2000, PLAYERNO, PAYMENT_DATE, AMOUNT
FROM      PENALTIES
WHERE     PLAYERNO = 27
```

14.3

```
UPDATE    PLAYERS
SET       SEX = 'W'
WHERE     SEX = 'F'
```

14.4

```
UPDATE    PLAYERS
SET       SEX = 'X'
WHERE     SEX = 'F'

UPDATE    PLAYERS
SET       SEX = 'F'
WHERE     SEX = 'M'

UPDATE    PLAYERS
SET       SEX = 'M'
WHERE     SEX = 'X'
```

or

```
UPDATE    PLAYERS
SET       SEX = CASE SEX
                   WHEN 'F' THEN 'M'
                   ELSE 'F' END
```

14.5

```
UPDATE    PENALTIES
SET       AMOUNT = AMOUNT * 1.2
WHERE     AMOUNT >
          (SELECT    AVG(AMOUNT)
          FROM       PENALTIES)
```

14.6

```
DELETE
FROM      PENALTIES
WHERE     PLAYERNO = 44
AND       YEAR(PAYMENT_DATE) = 1980
```

14.7

```
DELETE
FROM      PENALTIES
WHERE     PLAYERNO IN
          (SELECT    PLAYERNO
          FROM       MATCHES
          WHERE      TEAMNO IN
                     (SELECT    TEAMNO
                     FROM       TEAMS
                     WHERE      DIVISION = 'second'))
```

14.8

```
DELETE
FROM      PLAYERS
WHERE     TOWN =
          (SELECT    TOWN
          FROM       PLAYERS
          WHERE PLAYERNO = 44)
AND       PLAYERNO <> 44
```

III | Creating Database Objects

This third part describes how *database objects* are created. *Database object* is the generic term for, among other things, tables, keys, views, and indexes. These are the objects we have to create and that together form a database.

Chapter 15, "Creating Tables," describes all the statements for creating and changing tables. We discuss in detail the properties of the different data types.

When tables are created, it is possible to specify integrity constraints. These constraints are explained separately in Chapter 16, "Specifying Integrity Constraints." This chapter also reviews primary keys, alternate keys, foreign keys, and check integrity constraints, along with some other topics.

In Chapter 17, "Character Sets and Collating Sequences," we explain what the terms *character set* and *collating sequence* mean and illustrate how SQL supports them. In this chapter, we have chosen an explanation that applies to MySQL because support for these two concepts is implemented very differently among various products.

Chapter 18, "Changing and Dropping Tables," concentrates entirely on the SQL statements and the features for changing and deleting existing tables. Examples of changes are adding new columns, updating data types, and deleting columns.

Chapter 19, "Designing Tables," discusses several simple guidelines for designing tables.

Chapter 20, "Using Indexes," describes how, with the help of indexes, the required processing time of certain SQL statements can be reduced. This chapter gives an overview of how indexes work internally and discusses the different types of indexes, such as virtual column indexes and bitmap indexes. We also give guidelines on which columns to index.

Chapter 21, "Views," deals with views, or virtual tables. With views, we define a "layer" on top of the tables so that the users can see the tables in a form that is most suitable for them.

Chapter 22, "Creating Databases," discusses creating, updating, and deleting entire databases.

Chapter 23, "Users and Data Security," handles data security. We explain which SQL statements to use to create new users (with passwords), and how these users can be authorized to perform certain statements against certain data.

Chapter 24, "Creating Sequences," deals with sequences. SQL can use this database object to generate numbers that we can use, for example, to add new values to primary keys.

Schemas offer an opportunity to group tables logically. This short topic is explained in Chapter 25, "Creating Schemas."

15

Creating Tables

15.1 Introduction

T his chapter describes the statements for creating, updating, and deleting tables. We take the view that the user knows what data must be stored and what the structure of the data is—that is, what tables are to be created and what the appropriate columns are. In other words, the user has a ready-to-use database design at his or her disposal. The topic of database design is covered in Chapter 19, "Designing Tables."

15.2 Creating New Tables

The CREATE TABLE statement is used to construct new tables, in which rows of data can be stored. The definition of this statement is complex and extensive. For that reason, we explain the statement's features step by step and build up the definition slowly. The concepts of column definition, table integrity constraint, column integrity constraint, data type, and index definition are explained in the following sections and chapters. First, we focus on the core of the CREATE TABLE statement.

```
<create table statement> ::=
   CREATE [ TEMPORARY ] TABLE <table specification>
      <table schema>

<table schema> ::=
   ( <table element> [ { ,<table element> }... ] )

<table element> ::=
   <column definition>          |
   <table integrity constraint>
```

(continued)

```
<column definition> ::=
   <column name> <data type> [ <null specification> ]
   [ <column integrity constraint> ]

<null specification> ::= NOT NULL

<column integrity constraint> ::=
   PRIMARY KEY                        |
   UNIQUE                             |
   <check integrity constraint>

<table integrity constraint> ::=
   <primary key>                      |
   <alternate key>                    |
   <foreign key>                      |
   <check integrity constraint>
```

We begin with a simple example.

Example 15.1: Show the statement to create the PLAYERS table in the tennis club database.

```
CREATE    TABLE PLAYERS
          (PLAYERNO      INTEGER NOT NULL PRIMARY KEY,
          NAME          CHAR(15) NOT NULL,
          INITIALS      CHAR(3) NOT NULL,
          BIRTH_DATE    DATE,
          SEX           CHAR(1) NOT NULL,
          JOINED        SMALLINT NOT NULL,
          STREET        VARCHAR(30) NOT NULL,
          HOUSENO       CHAR(4),
          POSTCODE      CHAR(6),
          TOWN          VARCHAR(30) NOT NULL,
          PHONENO       CHAR(13),
          LEAGUENO      CHAR(4) UNIQUE)
```

We explain this statement step by step. The name of this table is PLAYERS. The user who enters a CREATE TABLE statement automatically becomes the owner. Two tables belonging to the same database cannot have the same name.

The *table schema* of a table consists of one or more *table elements*. These elements determine how the table looks and what data we can store in it. Examples of table elements are column definitions and integrity constraints, such as primary and foreign keys. We discuss these concepts in Chapter 16, "Specifying Integrity Constraints." In this chapter, we concentrate primarily on column definitions and primary keys.

A *column definition* contains a column name, a data type, possibly a null specification, and possibly a column integrity constraint. It is not allowed to have duplicate column names in one table. However, two different tables may have similar column names, such as the columns with the name PLAYERNO that appear in all tables.

Specifying a data type for a column is mandatory. By means of the data type, we indicate what kind of values can be entered in a column. In other words, the data type of a column restricts the type of values that can be entered. Therefore, it is important to choose a suitable data type. Section 5.2, in Chapter 5, "SELECT Statement: Common Elements," described the data types of literals in detail. In the next section, we discuss all data types and their respective qualities as they appear in a CREATE TABLE statement.

For every column, a *null specification* can be specified; see Section 4.7, in Chapter 4, "SQL in a Nutshell." Once again, we emphasize that SQL supports the NULL value as a possible value for a column in a row. The NULL value can be compared to "value unknown" or "value not present," and should not be confused with the number zero or a set of spaces. In a CREATE TABLE statement, you can specify NOT NULL after the data type of a column. This indicates which columns *cannot* contain NULL values. In other words, every NOT NULL column must contain a value in every row. Not including a null specification implies that NULL values are allowed.

A column definition may end with a column integrity constraint. This could be a primary key, for example. By specifying the term PRIMARY KEY after a column, this column becomes the primary key of the table. In the previous example, PLAYERNO is the primary key. This specification can appear only within one column definition of a table. After this, SQL guarantees that the column concerned does not contain duplicate values. If PRIMARY KEY is specified, the column can no longer contain NULL values. It is as if the null specification NOT NULL has been included implicitly.

Another column integrity constraint is UNIQUE, with which we define an alternate key. After this specification, SQL again makes sure that this column does not contain duplicate values. For multiple column definitions belonging to the same table, UNIQUE can be specified. The same rule that applied to PRIMARY KEY applies to UNIQUE columns: NOT NULL must be specified.

The check integrity constraint is discussed in Section 16.6, in Chapter 16.

A new table is built in the current database. If we want to create a table in another database, we must specify a database name in front of the table name.

Example 15.2: Create the PENALTIES table in the database called TEST.

```
CREATE    TABLE TEST.PENALTIES
          (PAYMENTNO        INTEGER NOT NULL PRIMARY KEY,
          PLAYERNO         INTEGER NOT NULL,
          PAYMENT_DATE     DATE NOT NULL,
          AMOUNT           DECIMAL(7,2) NOT NULL)
```

Explanation: However, the TEST database should exist. (See Section 4.4, in Chapter 4, to create databases.) After this statement, the TEST database is not automatically the current database; the current database remains unchanged.

Portability: *This feature works only for SQL products in which table names in table specifications can be qualified by database names.*

Exercise 15.1: Do you have to specify a data type for each column?

Exercise 15.2: What should be defined first in a column definition: the null specification or the data type?

15.3 Data Types of Columns

Chapter 5 extensively discussed the concept of data type. We showed how literals and expressions can have different data types. In this section, we explain how these data types within CREATE TABLE statements have to be defined. We also discuss the properties and limitations of each data type. The definition of *data type* is given next.

```
<data type> ::=
    <numeric data type>      |
    <alphanumeric data type> |
    <temporal data type>     |
    <boolean data type>      |
    <blob data type>
```

(continued)

```
<numeric data type> ::=
   <integer data type> |
   <decimal data type> |
   <float data type>

<integer data type> ::=
   SMALLINT |
   INTEGER  |
   INT      |
   BIGINT

<decimal data type> ::=
   DECIMAL [ ( <precision> [ ,<scale> ] ) ] |
   DEC     [ ( <precision> [ ,<scale> ] ) ] |
   NUMERIC [ ( <precision> [ ,<scale> ] ) ] |
   NUM     [ ( <precision> [ ,<scale> ] ) ]

<float data type> ::=
   FLOAT [ ( <length> ) ] |
   REAL                   |
   DOUBLE [ PRECISION ]

<alphanumeric data type> ::=
   CHAR [ ( <length> ) ]             |
   CHARACTER [ ( <length> ) ]        |
   VARCHAR ( <length> )              |
   CHAR VARYING ( <length> )         |
   CHARACTER VARYING ( <length> )    |
   LONG VARCHAR

<temporal data type> ::=
   DATE      |
   TIME      |
   TIMESTAMP

<boolean data type> ::= BOOLEAN

<blob data type> ::= BLOB

<precision> ;
<scale>     ;
<length>    ::= <whole number>
```

15.3.1 The Integer Data Types

Columns with an integer data type can be used to store whole numbers or integers. For example, all primary keys in the tables of the sample database are integers and, for that reason, have an integer data type.

SQL supports various integer data types. The differences between the data types stem from their respective sizes—that is, they differ in range. Table 15.5 shows which integer data types are supported and what their respective range is. For example, in columns with the data type INTEGER, we can store values that are less than or equal to 2.147.483.647. After that, the column is "full."

Table 15.1 *Ranges of Different Integer Data Types*

INTEGER LITERAL	RANGE
SMALLINT	-2^{15} up to and including $+2^{15} - 1$ or $-32{,}768$ up to and including $32{,}767$
INTEGER	-2^{31} up to and including $+2^{31} - 1$ or $-2{,}147{,}483{,}648$ up to and including $-2{,}147{,}483{,}647$
BIGINT	-2^{63} up to and including $+2^{63}-1$ or $-9{,}223{,}372{,}036{,}854{,}775{,}808$ up to and including $9{,}223{,}372{,}036{,}854{,}775{,}807$

The data type INTEGER may be abbreviated to INT.

Portability: *If possible, try to use the data types SMALLINT and INTEGER as much as possible. These are the only two that are supported by almost every SQL product.*

15.3.2 The Decimal Data Types

For the storage of nonwhole numbers, SQL has several decimal data types. This data type can be used to store, for example, amounts and measurement data. For this data type, you can specify how many digits you can have in front of and after the decimal point. For example, in DECIMAL(12,4), the first number (12) represents the *precision*, and the second number (4) the *scale*. This means that columns with this data type can have a maximum of eight digits in front of the decimal point (scale minus precision) and four after it (the precision), or the range of this data type is $-99{,}999{,}999.9999$, up to and including $99{,}999{,}999.9999$. The scale of a decimal data type must always be equal to or smaller than the precision.

If the precision is specified and the scale is not, the scale is equal to 0. If neither is specified, the precision is equal to 10 and the scale is equal to 0. The precision is at least equal to 1 but never more than 30. Note that when the specified precision is equal to 0, SQL thinks that no precision has been specified, and, therefore, it becomes equal to 10.

The name DECIMAL may be abbreviated to DEC. The name NUMERIC can be used as a synonym for DECIMAL. And NUMERIC itself can be abbreviated to NUM.

15.3.3 The Float Data Types

The float data type is used to store very big or very small numbers. This could be numbers consisting of, for example, 30, 100, or even more digits in front of the decimal point. Or it could be numbers with many, many digits after the decimal point. Consider numbers in which the number of digits after the decimal point is infinite, such as the well-known number pi and the fraction [1/3]. However, because a restricted amount of storage space is available for a float value, the real numbers are not stored. If a number is very big or very small, a rough estimate, or approximation, of that number is stored. That is why they are sometimes called *estimated* values.

In columns with a decimal data type, the decimal point has the same position in every value. This does not apply to the float data type; in every value, the decimal point can be somewhere else. In other words, the decimal point "floats around." That is why we call it a floating decimal point.

SQL has two float data types: *single precision* and *double precision*. They differ in the amount of storage space that is reserved for a value. Because of this, they differ in range. The range of the single-precision float data type is between $-3.402823466E38$ and $-1.175494351E-38$, and between $1,175494351E-38$ and $3.402823466E38$. The range of the double precision is bigger: from $-1.7976931348623157E308$ to $-2,2250738585072014E-308$ and from $2.2250738585072014E-308$ to $1.7976931348623157E308$.

The length that can be specified in a float data type determines the type of the float data type. It is a single precision if the length is between 0 and 24, and a double-precision data type if the length is between 25 and 53.

Example 15.3: Create a new table consisting of two columns; one has a single precision data type. Store several float values in it and show the contents of this table next.

```
CREATE TABLE MEASUREMENTS
       (NR INTEGER, MEASUREMENT_VALUE FLOAT(1))

INSERT INTO MEASUREMENTS VALUES
    (1, 99.99),
    (2, 99999.99),
    (3, 99999999.99),
    (4, 99999999999.99),
    (5, 99999999999999.99),
    (6, 0.999999),
    (7, 0.9999999),
    (8, 99999999.9999),
    (9, (1.0/3))

SELECT * FROM MEASUREMENTS
```

The result is:

```
NO   MEASUREMENT_VALUE
--   -----------------
 1               99.99
 2              100000
 3               1e+008
 4               1e+011
 5               1e+014
 6            0.999999
 7                   1
 8               1e+008
 9            0.333333
```

Explanation: In the first row, the value is still such that the actual value can be stored; therefore, an estimate is not necessary. However, that is not the case in rows 2, 3, 4, and 5. The number of digits in front of the decimal point is too big. For that reason, the value is rounded in these four rows and SQL can just store the simple value 1.0E+xx. Row 6 is stored accurately. The number of digits after the decimal point is high, but not in front of the decimal point. In row 7, the number of digits after the decimal point is indeed too big, and the value is rounded to 1. For the value in row 8, an estimate is stored as well. The result of the division 1.0 / 3 is rounded after six digits after the decimal point.

If we do the same, but now with FLOAT(30) instead of FLOAT(1), the following result arises:

```
NO   MEASUREMENT_VALUE
--   -----------------
 1               99.99
 2            99999.99
 3         99999999.99
 4      99999999999.99
 5     100000000000000
 6            0.999999
 7           0.9999999
 8       99999999.9999
 9         0.333333333
```

Explanation: There is more storage space available, so the need to store an estimate has been reduced. Rows 1, 2, 3, 4, 6, 7, and 8 all contain actual numbers and not estimates. In row 4, an estimate is stored, and in row 9, the number is rounded after 9 digits after the decimal point.

> **Portability:** *Although most SQL products support the FLOAT data type, differences do exist in how they are being handled—calculations with floats can lead to differences.*

15.3.4 The Alphanumeric Data Types

SQL supports the following alphanumeric data types (*string data types*) to store alphanumeric values: CHAR, VARCHAR, and LONG VARCHAR. Each alphanumeric data type is suitable for storing words, names, text, and codes.

Each column with an alphanumeric data type has an assigned character set and collating sequence; see Chapter 17, "Character Sets and Collating Sequences." SQL has to be sure that if we store letters and special symbols, such as é, %, and ā in the database and retrieve them later, they still look the same. This could mean that SQL has to perform several translations. Imagine that the data is stored in a database that has been installed on a UNIX machine. However, the data is displayed on a Windows machine. It could very well be that the different machines present a certain letter or symbol internally in a different way. By using an alphanumeric data type, we indicate that all internal translations must be done automatically and transparently. SQL is responsible for this.

An alphanumeric column has a *maximum length*. This length indicates how many characters can be stored in the column concerned. However, do not confuse the number of characters with the number of bytes that those values will occupy on disk. This depends on the chosen character set. If the ASCII character set is used, each character uses 1 byte; in other character sets, this could go up to 4 bytes per character (which means that an alphanumeric value of, for example, ten characters could occupy 40 bytes on disk); again, see Chapter 17.

The alphanumeric data types can be divided into two groups: those with a fixed length (CHAR) and those with a variable length (VARCHAR and LONG VARCHAR). Fixed or variable has to do with the way in which the values will be stored on the hard disk. For example, if CHARACTER(20) is used in a CREATE TABLE statement, we have to assume that each value that we store in that column indeed occupies 20 characters on disk. If we store a value consisting of only 4 characters, 16 spaces are added to fill the 20 characters. The variable alphanumeric data types store only relevant characters. That is how the data types VARCHAR and LONG VARCHAR derived their names; VARCHAR stands for "varying character," which means "alphanumeric value with variable length." In many SQL statements, the difference between CHAR and VARCHAR has, in itself, no effect. It mainly has to do with performance and storage space.

Table 15.2 shows the maximum length for the different alphanumeric data types.

Table 15.2   *Maximum Length of Alphanumeric Data Types*

ALPHANUMERIC DATA TYPE	MAXIMUM LENGTH
CHAR	254
VARCHAR	32,672 characters
LONG VARCHAR	32,700 characters

For the CHAR data type, a value between 0 and 255 *may* be specified, and at VAR-CHAR, a value between 0 and 255 *must* be specified. If the length is equal to 0, only the NULL value or an empty numeric value (' ') can be stored.

A number of these data types have synonyms. A synonym for the CHAR data type is CHARACTER. VARCHAR has two synonyms: CHAR VARYING and CHARACTER VARYING. We recommend that you use the names given in Table 15.2 as much as possible, to simplify a possible port to other SQL products.

Section 19.4, in Chapter 19, describes when to use which alphanumeric data type. In this section, several recommendation are given.

Using the data type LONG VARCHAR has certain specific restrictions. Many SQL products do not allow, for example, indexing of this type of column, and other products are not capable of concatenating such a value with another alphanumeric value. If you use this data type, be sure you know which restrictions apply to your own SQL product.

15.3.5 The Temporal Data Types

SQL supports three temporal data types: DATE, TIME, and TIMESTAMP. The DATE data type is used to record dates in a column. The TIME data type represents a time of the day. The TIMESTAMP data type is a combination of a date and a time. Chapter 5 extensively describes these data types and their features.

15.3.6 The Boolean Data Type

The value of a column with the Boolean data type can hold only two values: TRUE or FALSE, or, in other words, 1 or 0. This can be used for columns such as MARRIED and INSURED. For both, the two permitted values are yes and no, or TRUE and FALSE.

Example 15.4: Get the internal value of the Boolean value TRUE.

```
SELECT TRUE
```

The result is:

```
TRUE
----
   1
```

> **Portability:** *Most SQL products do not support the Boolean data type yet. MySQL does. However, in MySQL, this data type has been implemented internally as a* TINYINT *data type. This means that any integer value between* −128 *and* 127 *can be stored in such a column. And if the value is equal to 0, it is treated as* FALSE; *any other value is treated as* TRUE.

15.3.7 The Blob Data Types

Section 15.3.4 illustrated that when alphanumeric columns are used, SQL must make sure that an *a* remains an *a* and a *b* a *b*. Sometimes, we want to store strings of bytes that SQL does not use at all. The bytes must be stored and retrieved again without any form of translation. This is necessary for the storage of, for example, digital photographs, video, and scanned documents. For the storage of these data, SQL supports the *blob data type*. *Blob* stands for "basic large object"—in other words, it is an object that consists of many bytes.

Blob data types have several features in common with the alphanumeric data types. First, both have two versions: those with a fixed length and those with a variable length. Second, blob data types have a maximum length.

The maximum length of the blob data type is 2,147,483,647 characters.

Exercise 15.3: Describe in your own words the differences among the numeric data types integer, decimal, and float.

Exercise 15.4: When would you prefer an alphanumeric data type with a variable length above one with a fixed length?

Exercise 15.5: Determine acceptable data types for the following columns:

- Phone number at which a player can be reached
- Age of a player in whole months
- Name of the company where the player works
- Number of children a player has
- Date of a player's first match for the club

Exercise 15.6: Write a CREATE TABLE statement for a table with the name DEPART-MENT and with the columns: DEPNO (unique code consisting of always five characters), BUDGET (maximum amount of 999,999), and LOCATION (name of maximum 30 characters). The DEPNO column always has a value.

15.4 Creating Temporary Tables

In most cases, the tables that we create will be granted a long life. For months or even years, applications will make use of them. The tables that are created with a CREATE TABLE statement are, therefore, sometimes called *permanent tables*. Usually, permanent tables are used by multiple SQL users and several applications.

However, sometimes there is a need for *temporary tables*. Unlike permanent tables, temporary tables have a short life and are also visible only for the SQL user who is responsible for creating the table. The temporary table is essentially owned by one SQL user for a limited time span. Temporary tables are useful, for example, for temporarily storing the results of complex SELECT statements. Afterward, those tables can be accessed repeatedly by other statements.

SQL supports temporary tables. After they have been created, they act as permanent tables. Every SELECT, UPDATE, INSERT, and DELETE statement can be executed on these tables. They can be removed with a DROP TABLE statement, but if that does not happen, SQL removes them automatically when the application ends.

Temporary table are created with the CREATE TABLE statement. Only the word TEMPORARY has to be added.

Example 15.5: Create the temporary table SUMPENALTIES and store in it the sum of all penalties.

```
CREATE TEMPORARY TABLE SUMPENALTIES
       (TOTAL DECIMAL(10,2))

INSERT INTO SUMPENALTIES
SELECT SUM(AMOUNT)
FROM   PENALTIES
```

Explanation: From now on, this new table can be accessed only by the SQL user who started the application in which this table was created.

The name of a temporary table can be equal to the name of an existing permanent table. In that case, the permanent table will not be removed, but the temporary table of the current SQL user will hide the permanent one. See the following example.

Example 15.6: Create a permanent table and a temporary table with similar names.

```
CREATE TABLE TESTTABLE (C1 INTEGER)

INSERT INTO TESTTABLE VALUES (1)

CREATE TEMPORARY TABLE TESTTABLE (C1 INTEGER, C2 INTEGER)

INSERT INTO TESTTABLE VALUES (2, 3)

SELECT * FROM TESTTABLE
```

The result is:

```
C1   C2
--   --
 2    3
```

Explanation: The result of the SELECT statement clearly shows that the contents of the temporary table are presented, and not those of the permanent table. This example also shows that, in this situation, it is not necessary for the two tables involved to have the same table schema.

If a DROP TABLE statement is executed on the TESTTABLE after the SELECT statement, and subsequently a SELECT statement is executed again, the original permanent table appears again and the following result is presented:

```
C1
--
 1
```

Portability: *More SQL products support the concept of temporary tables. Those that do have not implemented this special table type in the way it is described here. For example, in DB2 for Windows and UNIX, a special SQL statement called DECLARE GLOBAL TEMPORARY TABLE is introduced for this.*

15.5 Copying Tables

All CREATE TABLE statements shown in this chapter and the previous chapters assume that the table is created from scratch. However, it is also possible to create a new table that is based on an existing table. The specifications and the contents of the existing tables are used to create the new table and possibly fill it as well.

```
<create table statement> ::=
   CREATE [ TEMPORARY ] TABLE
      <table specification> <table structure>

<table structure> ::=
   LIKE <table specification>              |
   ( LIKE <table specification> )          |
   <table contents>                        |
   <table schema> [ <table contents> ]

<table contents> ::= [ AS ] <table expression>

<table schema> ::=
   ( <table element> [ { , <table element> }... ] )
```

Example 15.7: Create a copy of the TEAMS table called TEAMS_COPY1.

```
CREATE TABLE TEAMS_COPY1 LIKE TEAMS
```

Explanation: A new table has been created with the same structure as the TEAMS table. Column names, data types, null specifications, and indexes have all been copied, but not the contents of the table. Therefore, this table is still empty after this statement. The foreign keys and the specialized privileges that might be present have not been copied, either.

The specification LIKE TEAMS also can be placed between brackets, but this does not affect the result.

Another way of copying, one that includes copying the data, is the one in which a table expression is used.

Example 15.8: Create a copy of the TEAMS table called TEAM_COPY2, and copy the contents as well.

```
CREATE TABLE TEAMS_COPY2 AS
(SELECT    *
 FROM      TEAMS)
```

Explanation: The first thing that is done during the processing of the statement is to determine the structure of the result of the SELECT statement. This involves determining how many columns the result contains (three, in this example) and what the data types of these columns are (INTEGER for TEAMNO, INTEGER for PLAYERNO, and CHAR(6) for DIVISION, respectively). SQL also determines what the null specification is: Each column is checked to see whether NULL values are allowed. Next, a CREATE TABLE statement is executed behind the scenes. The table that is created has the same table schema as the original TEAMS table. Finally, the result of the SELECT statement is added to the new table. In fact, the TEAMS table is copied in its entirety in this example.

The word AS and the brackets around the table expression can be left out. However, we recommend using them as much as possible because many other SQL products require them.

When you create a copy like this, indexes and integrity constraints are not copied along. SQL cannot derive from a SELECT statement what the indexes and integrity constraints should be.

In this example, a simple table expression is used. However, any table expression can be used, including the complex forms. The table expression can contain subqueries, set operators, and GROUP BY clauses.

If we want the column names of the new table to be different from those in the original table, we must specify those new names in the table expression.

Example 15.9: Create a copy of the TEAMS table and assign the columns TEAMNO and PLAYERNO different names—respectively, TNO and PNO. Show the contents of this new table next.

```
CREATE TABLE TEAMS_COPY3 AS
(SELECT    TEAMNO AS TNO, PLAYERNO AS PNO, DIVISION
 FROM      TEAMS)

SELECT    *
FROM      TEAMS_COPY3
```

The result is:

```
TNO  PNO  DIVISION
---  ---  --------
  1    6  first
  2   27  second
```

Example 15.10: Create a copy of the TEAMS table, but without the DIVISION column and only with the teams of player 27.

```
CREATE TABLE TEAMS_COPY4 AS
(SELECT    TEAMNO, PLAYERNO
 FROM      TEAMS
 WHERE     PLAYERNO = 27)
```

Example 15.11: Create a *temporary* copy of the TEAMS table and assign this table the same name.

```
CREATE TEMPORARY TABLE TEAMS AS
 (SELECT    *
  FROM      TEAMS
```

Explanation: Chapter 14, "Updating Tables," contains several INSERT, UPDATE, and DELETE statements that change the contents of the permanent TEAMS table. If you want to get the original contents of the tables back, you must remove the available rows and add the common rows again. This process can be simplified by using temporary tables. After the earlier CREATE TABLE statement has been processed, you can process transactions on the TEAMS table to your heart's content. If the application is stopped or started again, or after the temporary table has been removed, the original TEAMS table, including the original contents, appears again.

If you want to change certain properties of a column, such as the data type or the null specification, during the copying, you have to add a table schema to the CREATE TABLE statement.

Example 15.12: Create a copy of the TEAMS table in which NULL values are allowed in the PLAYERNO column and in which the data type of the DIVISION column is extended from 6 to 10 characters.

```
CREATE TABLE TEAMS_COPY5
        (TEAMNO      INTEGER NOT NULL PRIMARY KEY,
        PLAYERNO     INTEGER NULL,
        DIVISION     CHAR(10) NOT NULL) AS
(SELECT    *
 FROM      TEAMS)
```

Explanation: Columns in which the properties do not change can be omitted from the table schema. The following statement would have given the same result:

```
CREATE TABLE TEAMS_COPY5
        (PLAYERNO     INTEGER NULL,
        DIVISION      CHAR(10) NOT NULL) AS
(SELECT    *
 FROM      TEAMS)
```

Be sure that all column names that appear in the table schema are equal to the names of the original columns. SQL considers columns with unfamiliar names as new columns.

Example 15.13: Create a copy of the TEAMS table, but the PLAYERNO column should now allow NULL values. Plus, a new column called COMMENT must be added. Show the contents of this table next.

```
CREATE TABLE TEAMS_COPY6
        (PLAYERNO     INTEGER NULL,
        COMMENT       VARCHAR(100)) AS
(SELECT    *
 FROM      TEAMS)

SELECT * FROM TEAMS_COPY6
```

The result is:

COMMENT	TEAMNO	PLAYERNO	DIVISION
?	1	6	first
?	2	27	second

Explanation: The result shows that the TEAMS_COPY6 table has an additional column compared to the TEAMS table. This new column is filled with NULL values, of course. There is another way to add columns to existing tables, but that is explained in Chapter 18, "Changing and Dropping Tables."

Exercise 15.7: Create a table called P_COPY with the same table schema as the PLAYERS table.

Exercise 15.8: Create a table called P2_COPY with the same table schema and contents as the PLAYERS table.

Exercise 15.9: Create a table called NUMBERS that contains only the player numbers of players resident in Stratford.

15.6 Naming Tables and Columns

Users can select names for columns and tables. SQL has only the following restrictions:

- Two tables belonging to the same database may not have the same name.
- Two columns in a table may not have the same name.
- The length of the name of a table or column is restricted. The maximum length differs from product to product. Sometimes, it is 18 characters, and sometimes, names of 128 characters are allowed.
- A name may consist of only letters, digits, and the special symbols _ and $.
- The name must begin with a letter.
- Table and column names may not be reserved words; Appendix A, "Syntax of SQL," includes a list of all reserved words.

The restrictions imposed by the last two rules can be avoided by placing double quotes in front of and after the table name. The table names SELECT and FAMOUS PLAYERS are incorrect, but "SELECT" and "FAMOUS PLAYERS" are correct. However, this means that everywhere these table names are used, the double quotes must be included.

> **Portability:** *By default, MySQL does not use double quotes around names. To set this to the double quotes, the* `SQL_MODE` *system parameter must be set to* `ANSI_QUOTES`:
>
> ```
> SET SQL_MODE='ANSI_QUOTES'
> ```

Defining sensible names for tables and columns is extremely important. Column and table names are used in almost every statement. Awkward names, especially during interactive use of SQL, can lead to irritating mistakes, so observe the following naming conventions:

- Keep the table and column names short but not cryptic (so PLAYERS instead of PLYRS).
- Use the plural form for table names (so PLAYERS instead of PLAYER) so that statements "flow" better.
- Do not use *information-bearing names* (so PLAYERS instead of PLAYERS_2, where the digit 2 represents the number of indexes on the table); if this information were to change, it would be necessary to change the table name together with all the statements that use the table.
- Be consistent (PLAYERNO and TEAMNO instead of PLAYERNO and TEAMNUM).
- Avoid names that are too long (so STREET instead of STREETNAME).
- As much as possible, give columns with comparable populations the same name (so PLAYERNO in PLAYERS, PLAYERNO in TEAMS, and PLAYERNO in PENALTIES).

To prevent potential problems, avoid words that have a special meaning within the operating system, such as CON and LPT.

15.7 Column Options: Default and Comment

A table schema consists of column definitions, among other things. In Section 15.2, we mentioned that a column definition consists of a column name, a data type, possibly a null specification, and some column integrity constraints. To each column definition, several column options can be added as well. Column options are the subject of this section.

```
<column definition> ::=
    <column name> <data type> [ <null specification> ]
    [ <column integrity constraint> ] [ <column option>... ]

<column option> ::=
    DEFAULT <literal>                    |
    COMMENT <alphanumeric literal>
```

The first column option is the *default value*. A default value is used when a new row is added to a table and no value has been specified for that column.

Example 15.14: Create the PENALTIES table in which the default value of the AMOUNT column is equal to 50 and the default value for the PAYMENT_DATE is 1 January 1990.

```
CREATE TABLE PENALTIES
        (PAYMENTNO      INTEGER NOT NULL PRIMARY KEY,
         PLAYERNO       INTEGER NOT NULL,
         PAYMENT_DATE   DATE NOT NULL DEFAULT '1990-01-01',
         AMOUNT         DECIMAL(7,2) NOT NULL DEFAULT 50.00)
```

Next, we add a new row with an INSERT statement in which we do not specify a value for the columns PAYMENT_DATE and AMOUNT.

```
INSERT    INTO PENALTIES
          (PAYMENTNO, PLAYERNO)
VALUES    (15, 27)
```

After this statement, the new PENALTIES table contains the following contents:

PAYMENTNO	PLAYERNO	PAYMENT_DATE	AMOUNT
15	27	1990-01-01	50.00

Instead of specifying no value in the INSERT statement, the specification DEFAULT can be included. The previous INSERT statement would look as follows:

```
INSERT    INTO PENALTIES
          (PAYMENTNO, PLAYERNO, PAYMENT_DATE, AMOUNT)
VALUES    (15, 27, DEFAULT, DEFAULT)
```

DEFAULT can also be used in the UPDATE statement to replace an existing value by the default value of the column.

Example 15.15: Replace the amount of all penalties by the default value.

```
UPDATE    PENALTIES
SET       AMOUNT = DEFAULT
```

Note that DEFAULT is not a system variable and can, therefore, not appear within compound expressions. The scalar function DEFAULT can be used to retrieve the default value of a column. This function can, of course, be included within expressions.

Example 15.16: Replace the amount of all penalties by the year of the default value of the PAYMENT_DATE column and multiply this by 10.

```
UPDATE    PENALTIES
SET       AMOUNT = YEAR(DEFAULT(PAYMENT_DATE))*10
```

Default values cannot be specified for columns with the data types BLOB or TEXT, or one of the geometric data types.

The second column option is COMMENT, with which a comment can be added to each column. This documentation about the columns is stored in the catalog and is available to every SQL user. The comment can be 255 characters long at the most.

Example 15.17: Create the PENALTIES table and add a comment to each column. Show the comment as it is stored in the catalog tables next.

```
CREATE TABLE PENALTIES
        (PAYMENTNO   INTEGER  NOT NULL PRIMARY KEY
            COMMENT     'Primary key of the table',
         PLAYERNO      INTEGER  NOT NULL
            COMMENT     'Player who has incurred the penalty',
         PAYMENT_DATE DATE      NOT NULL
            COMMENT     'Date on which the penalty has been paid',
         AMOUNT        DECIMAL(7,2) NOT NULL
            COMMENT     'Amount of the penalty in dollars')

SELECT    COLUMN_NAME, COLUMN_COMMENT
FROM      INFORMATION_SCHEMA.COLUMNS
WHERE     TABLE_NAME = 'PENALTIES'
```

The result is:

```
COLUMN_NAME    COLUMN_COMMENT
-----------    ----------------------------------------
PAYMENTNO      Primary key of the table
PLAYERNO       Player who has incurred the penalty
PAYMENT_DATE   Date on which the penalty has been paid
AMOUNT         Amount of the penalty in dollars
```

15.8 Derived Columns

Normally, the columns of a table contain data. Every time that we insert a new row into a table, a value is stored for each column. Some products (but not MySQL) allow the creation of columns that do not really contain values and, therefore, do not take up disk space. These columns are called *computed columns* or *virtual columns*. The values of those columns are derived (computed) from other columns.

Example 15.18: Create a new version of the MATCHES table that contains an extra column called BALANCE, which holds the difference between the columns WON and LOST.

```
CREATE TABLE MATCHES
    (MATCHNO     INTEGER NOT NULL PRIMARY KEY,
     TEAMNO      INTEGER NOT NULL,
     PLAYERNO    INTEGER NOT NULL,
     WON         SMALLINT NOT NULL,
     LOST        SMALLINT NOT NULL,
     BALANCE     AS ABS(WON - LOST))
```

Explanation: We define an expression instead of a data type for the column called BAL-ANCE. This expression represents the values of the BALANCE column. The data type of the column is derived from that of the expression.

The use of computed columns becomes clear when we start to query the data.

Example 15.19: For each match with a balance greater than 1, get the match number and that balance.

```
SELECT    MATCHNO, BALANCE
FROM      MATCHES
WHERE     BALANCE > 1
```

The result is:

```
MATCHNO  BALANCE
-------  -------
      1        2
      3        3
      7        3
```

In this example, the expression is quite simple, but more complex compound expressions are allowed and can be useful. For example, it is possible to create computed columns that return the age of a player or the length in days that a player was a member of the committee. However, not all expressions can be used to define computed columns, and some restrictions apply. For example, no aggregation functions or subqueries are allowed.

Portability: *Computed columns are supported by, for example, Microsoft SQL Server and Apache Derby.*

15.9   Tables and the Catalog

In Section 4.17, in Chapter 4, we mentioned that descriptions of tables are stored in the catalog. Two of these catalog tables record tables and columns: TABLES and COLUMNS. The descriptions of these tables are given next. Some of the columns are explained in other chapters.

The TABLE_CREATOR and TABLE_NAME columns form the primary key of the table, as shown in Table 15.3.

The three columns TABLE_CREATOR, TABLE_NAME, and COLUMN_NAME form the primary key of the COLUMNS table, as shown in Table 15.4.

Table 15.3   *Columns of the TABLES Catalog Table*

COLUMN NAME	DATA TYPE	DESCRIPTION
TABLE_CREATOR	CHAR	Name of the database (not the owner) in which the table was created. MySQL does not recognize an owner of a table, as other SQL products do, which is why the database name has been chosen.
TABLE_NAME	CHAR	Name of the table.
CREATE_TIMESTAMP	TIMESTAMP	Date and time when the table was created.
COMMENT	CHAR	Comments that have been entered using the COMMENT statement.

Table 15.4   *Columns of the COLUMNS Catalog Table*

COLUMN NAME	DATA TYPE	DESCRIPTION
TABLE_CREATOR	CHAR	Name of the database in which the table was created; see the TABLES table.
TABLE_NAME	CHAR	Name of the table in which the column is a part.
COLUMN_NAME	CHAR	Name of the column.
COLUMN_NO	NUMERIC	Sequence number of the column within the table. This sequence reflects the order in which columns appear in the CREATE TABLE statement.
DATA_TYPE	CHAR	Data type of the column.
CHAR_LENGTH	NUMERIC	If the DATA_TYPE is equal to alphanumeric, the length is indicated here.
PRECISION	NUMERIC	If the value of DATA_TYPE is equal to N(umeric), the number of digits in front of the decimal point is indicated; for all other data types, the value is equal to zero.

COLUMN NAME	DATA TYPE	DESCRIPTION
SCALE	NUMERIC	If the value of DATA_TYPE is equal to N(umeric), the number of digits after the decimal point is indicated; for all other data types, the value is equal to zero.
NULLABLE	CHAR	If the column has been defined as NOT NULL, the value is equal to NO; otherwise, it is equal to YES.
COMMENT	CHAR	Comments that have been entered using the COMMENT statement.

Example 15.20: For each column in the PLAYERS table (that has been created in the TENNIS database), get the name, the data type, and the length, and indicate whether it is a NULL column.

```
SELECT    COLUMN_NAME, DATA_TYPE, CHAR_LENGTH, NULLABLE
FROM      COLUMNS
WHERE     TABLE_NAME = 'PLAYERS'
AND       TABLE_CREATOR = 'TENNIS'
ORDER BY COLUMN_NO
```

The result is:

```
COLUMN_NAME  DATA_TYPE  CHAR_LENGTH  NULLABLE
-----------  ---------  -----------  --------
PLAYERNO     INT                  ?  NO
NAME         CHAR                15  NO
INITIALS     CHAR                 3  NO
BIRTH_DATE   DATE                 ?  YES
SEX          CHAR                 1  NO
JOINED       SMALLINT             ?  NO
STREET       VARCHAR             30  NO
HOUSENO      CHAR                 4  YES
POSTCODE     CHAR                 6  YES
TOWN         VARCHAR             30  NO
PHONENO      CHAR                13  YES
LEAGUENO     CHAR                 4  YES
```

Example 15.21: For each of the tables of the tennis club, get the number of rows, the number of columns, and the number of rows and columns of the tables together.

```
SELECT    'PLAYERS' AS TABLE_NAME, COUNT(*) AS NUMBER_ROWS,
          (SELECT   COUNT(*)
           FROM     COLUMNS
           WHERE    TABLE_NAME = 'PLAYERS'
           AND      TABLE_CREATOR = 'TENNIS') AS P
FROM      PLAYERS
UNION
SELECT    'TEAMS', COUNT(*),
          (SELECT   COUNT(*)
           FROM     COLUMNS
           WHERE    TABLE_NAME = 'TEAMS'
           AND      TABLE_CREATOR = 'TENNIS') AS T
FROM      TEAMS
UNION
SELECT    'PENALTIES', COUNT(*),
          (SELECT   COUNT(*)
           FROM     COLUMNS
           WHERE    TABLE_NAME = 'PENALTIES'
           AND      TABLE_CREATOR = 'TENNIS') AS PEN
FROM      PENALTIES
UNION
SELECT    'MATCHES', COUNT(*),
          (SELECT   COUNT(*)
           FROM     COLUMNS
           WHERE    TABLE_NAME = 'MATCHES'
           AND      TABLE_CREATOR = 'TENNIS') AS M
FROM      MATCHES
UNION
SELECT    'COMMITTEE_MEMBERS', COUNT(*),
          (SELECT   COUNT(*)
           FROM     COLUMNS
           WHERE    TABLE_NAME = 'COMMITTEE_MEMBERS'
           AND      TABLE_CREATOR = 'TENNIS') AS CM
FROM      COMMITTEE_MEMBERS
ORDER BY 1
```

The result is:

```
TABLE_NAME            NUMBER_ROWS   NUMBER_COLUMNS
-----------------     -----------   --------------
COMMITTEE_MEMBERS          17            4
PENALTIES                   8            4
PLAYERS                    14           13
TEAMS                       2            3
MATCHES                    13            5
```

Exercise 15.10: Show how the TABLES and COLUMNS tables are filled after the execution of the CREATE TABLE statement in Exercise 15.6.

15.10 Answers

15.1 Yes, a data type is mandatory.

15.2 First the data type.

15.3 Own words.

15.4 Variable length is useful when the difference between the longest value possible for a column and the average length is considerable. If both are equal, a fixed length for a column is preferable.

15.5 CHARACTER(13); no phone number in the world is longer than 13 digits.

SMALLINT or DECIMAL(3,0)

VARCHAR(50); company names can be very long.

SMALLINT

DATE

15.6

```
CREATE TABLE DEPARTMENT
      ( DEPNO      CHAR(5) NOT NULL PRIMARY KEY,
        BUDGET     DECIMAL(8,2),
        LOCATION   VARCHAR(30))
```

15.7

```
CREATE TABLE P_COPY
   LIKE PLAYERS
```

15.8

```
CREATE TABLE P2_COPY AS
  (SELECT * FROM PLAYERS)
```

15.9

```
CREATE TABLE NUMBERS AS
(SELECT    PLAYERNO
 FROM      PLAYERS
 WHERE     TOWN = 'Stratford')
```

15.10

The TABLES table:

CREATOR	TABLE_NAME	CREATE_TIMESTAMP	COMMENT
TENNIS	DEPARTMENT	2005-08-29 11:43:48	InnoDB free: 10240 kB

The COLUMNS table:

TABLE_CREATOR	TABLE_NAME	COLUMN_NAME	COLUMN_NO
TENNIS	DEPARTMENT	DEPNO	1
TENNIS	DEPARTMENT	BUDGET	2
TENNIS	DEPARTMENT	LOCATION	3

DATA_TYPE	CHAR_LENGTH	PRECISION	SCALE	NULLABLE	COMMENT
CHAR	5	?	?	NO	?
DECIMAL	?	8	2	YES	?
VARCHAR	30	?	?	YES	?

16

Specifying Integrity Constraints

16.1 Introduction

C hapter 1, "Introduction to SQL," discusses enforcement of data *integrity* in the data-base as one of the most important responsibilities of a database server. By *data integrity*, we mean *consistency* and *correctness* of the data. Data is consistent if individual items do not contradict one another. Data is correct if it satisfies all relevant rules, which can be company rules but may also be tax rules, laws of nature, and so on. For example, if in the example database the total number of sets in a match is greater than five, this data item is incorrect.

SQL can handle data integrity if so-called *integrity constraints* (or constraints) are defined. After each update, SQL tests whether the new database contents still comply with the relevant integrity constraints. In other words, it checks whether the state of the database is still *valid*. A valid update transforms the valid state of a database to a new valid state. Therefore, the specification of integrity constraints places restrictions on the possible values of a table.

> Integrity constraints are the rules with which the contents of a database must comply at all times, and they describe which updates to the database are permitted.

Several integrity constraints can be defined within a CREATE TABLE statement. For each column, NOT NULL can be specified, for example. This means that the NULL value is not permitted, or, in other words, that it is mandatory to populate the column. Section 15.2 discusses integrity constraints. Primary and foreign keys are other examples of integrity constraints.

```
<create table statement> ::=
    CREATE TABLE <table name> <table schema>

<table schema> ::=
    ( <table element> [ { ,<table element> }... ] )

<table element> ::=
    <column definition> | <table integrity constraint>

<column definition> ::=
    <column name> <data type> [ <null specification> ]
    [ <column integrity constraint> ]

<null specification> ::= NOT NULL

<column integrity constraint> ::=
    PRIMARY KEY                     |
    UNIQUE                          |
    <check integrity constraint>

<table integrity constraint> ::=
    [ CONSTRAINT <constraint name> ]
    { <primary key>                 |
      <alternate key>              |
      <foreign key>                |
      <check integrity constraint> }

<primary key> ::= PRIMARY KEY <column list>

<alternate key> ::= UNIQUE <column list>

<foreign key> ::=
    FOREIGN KEY <column list> <referencing specification>

<referencing specification> ::=
    REFERENCES <table specification> [ <column list> ]
    [ <referencing action>... ]

<referencing action> ::=
    ON UPDATE { CASCADE | RESTRICT | SET NULL } |
    ON DELETE { CASCADE | RESTRICT | SET NULL }

<column list> ::=
    ( <column name> [ { , <column name> }... ] )

<check integrity constraint> ::= CHECK ( <condition> )
```

16.2 Primary Keys

A *primary key* is (informally) known as a column or group of columns of a table of which the values are always unique. NULL values are not permitted in columns that form part of a primary key. In the example in Section 15.2, in Chapter 15, the column PLAY-ERNO is defined as the primary key of the PLAYERS table.

Primary keys can be defined in two ways: as column or table integrity constraints. In the first case, the term PRIMARY KEY is simply added to the column definition.

Example 16.1: Create the PLAYERS table, including the primary key.

```
CREATE TABLE PLAYERS (
        PLAYERNO        INTEGER NOT NULL PRIMARY KEY,
        :               :
        LEAGUENO        CHAR(4))
```

Explanation: The primary key is defined after the null specification. The null specification may be specified behind the primary key.

In this example, we can also define the primary key as a table integrity constraint:

```
CREATE TABLE PLAYERS (
        PLAYERNO        INTEGER NOT NULL,
        :               :
        LEAGUENO        CHAR(4),
        PRIMARY KEY     (PLAYERNO))
```

You can define primary keys over multiple columns in a table. These are called *composite* primary keys. The COMMITTEE_MEMBERS table contains such a composite primary key. A composite primary key can be defined as only a table integrity constraint. All relevant columns are placed between brackets.

Example 16.2: Create a DIPLOMAS table to record, among other things, which course members followed which course on which date; the STUDENT, COURSE, and DDATE columns will form a composite primary key.

```
CREATE    TABLE DIPLOMAS
          (STUDENT      INTEGER NOT NULL,
          COURSE        INTEGER NOT NULL,
          DDATE         DATE NOT NULL,
          SUCCESSFUL    CHAR(1),
          LOCATION      VARCHAR(5),
          PRIMARY KEY (STUDENT, COURSE, DDATE))
```

Explanation: By defining the primary key on the three columns, you can ensure that a student can obtain only one diploma for only one course on a specific date.

If a column that is part of a primary key has not been defined as NOT NULL, SQL defines the column as NOT NULL. The specification NOT NULL in the PLAYERNO column in the previous examples can be left out; however, we do not recommend that. For the sake of clarity, it is better to include this null specification.

Portability: *Some SQL products handle the NULL differently if a column is part of a primary key. In those products, if a primary key column has not been defined as NOT NULL, they do not endorse the CREATE TABLE statement. In this case, each primary key column must explicitly be defined as NOT NULL.*

Any column or group of columns can, in principle, function as a primary key. Nevertheless, primary key columns must follow a number of rules. Some of these rules stem from the theory of the relational model; others are enforced by SQL. We advise you to follow these rules when you define primary keys:

- Only one primary key can be defined for each table. This rule comes from the relational model and applies to SQL as well.
- The theory (the relational model) requires that one primary key should be defined for each table. SQL, however, does not enforce this; you can create tables without a primary key. However, we strongly recommend that you specify a primary key for each base table. The main reason is that, without a primary key, it is possible (accidentally or deliberately) to store two identical rows in a table; as a result, the two rows no longer would be distinguishable from one another. In query processes, they will satisfy the same conditions, and in updating, they will always be updated together, so there is a high probability that eventually the database will become corrupted.
- Two different rows in a table may never have the same value for the primary key. In the literature, this is called the *uniqueness rule*. As an example, the TOWN column in the PLAYERS table should not be specified as a primary key because many players live in the same town.

- A primary key is not correct if it is possible to delete a column from the primary key and have this "smaller" primary key still satisfy the uniqueness rule. This rule is called the *minimality rule*. In short, this means that a primary key should not consist of an unnecessarily high number of columns. Imagine that we would define PLAYERNO with NAME as the primary key for the PLAYERS table. We already know that player numbers are unique, so, in this case, the primary key contains more columns than necessary and, therefore, does not satisfy the minimality rule.

- A column name may occur only once in the column list of a primary key.

- The populations of the columns belonging to a primary key may not contain NULL values. This rule is known either as the *first integrity constraint* or as the *entity integrity constraint*. What would happen if we allowed NULL values in a primary key? It would be possible to insert two rows with NULL values as the primary key values and other columns with identical data. These two rows would not be uniquely identifiable and would always satisfy the same conditions for selection or updating. You cannot infringe this rule because SQL requires that the columns concerned be defined as NOT NULL.

Exercise 16.1: Do you have to specify a NOT NULL integrity constraint for a column defined as the primary key?

Exercise 16.2: What is the minimum and maximum number of primary keys that can be defined for each table?

Exercise 16.3: Define the primary key for the MATCHES table.

16.3 Alternate Keys

In the relational model, an alternate key is, like a primary key, a column or group of columns of a table, of which the values are unique at all times. Chapter 1 indicates that an alternate key is a candidate key that is not chosen to be the primary key. There are two important distinctions between primary and alternate keys. First, a table may have many alternate keys but only one primary key. Second, according to the theory of the relational model, primary keys cannot contain NULL values, whereas alternate keys can (unless it is explicitly forbidden with a NOT NULL integrity rule). However, SQL also follows the rule that alternate keys can never contain NULL values.

Example 16.3: Define the PLAYERNO column in the TEAMS table as an alternate key. (We assume in this example that a player may captain only one team.)

```
CREATE    TABLE TEAMS
             (TEAMNO      INTEGER NOT NULL,
              PLAYERNO    INTEGER NOT NULL UNIQUE,
              DIVISION    CHAR(6) NOT NULL,
              PRIMARY KEY (TEAMNO))
```

Explanation: The word UNIQUE indicates that PLAYERNO is an alternate key and that the values must remain unique.

The previous statement could also have been defined as follows. The alternate key is defined as table integrity constraint:

```
CREATE    TABLE TEAMS
          (TEAMNO      INTEGER NOT NULL,
           PLAYERNO    INTEGER NOT NULL,
           DIVISION    CHAR(6) NOT NULL,
           PRIMARY KEY (TEAMNO),
           UNIQUE (PLAYERNO))
```

Each table can have several alternate keys, and they may even overlap. We can define one alternate key on the columns C_1 and C_2, and another on C_2 with C_3. There is overlap on the C_2 column, then, which SQL allows. Alternative keys may also overlap with the primary key. However, it makes no sense to define a set of columns as an alternate key when that set is a superset of the columns of another key. If a primary key has been defined, for example, on the column C_1, the definition of an alternate key on the columns C_1 and C_2 is unnecessary. The uniqueness of the combination C_1, C_2 is already guaranteed by the primary key. However, SQL allows this construct, so be careful that you do not make mistakes.

Exercise 16.4: Indicate what is incorrect in the following CREATE TABLE statements.

1.

```
CREATE TABLE T1
       (C1   INTEGER NOT NULL,
        C2   INTEGER NOT NULL UNIQUE,
        C3   INTEGER NOT NULL,
        PRIMARY KEY (C1, C4))
```

2.

```
CREATE TABLE T1
       (C1   INTEGER NOT NULL PRIMARY KEY,
        C2   INTEGER NOT NULL,
        C3   INTEGER UNIQUE,
        PRIMARY KEY (C1))
```

3.

```
CREATE TABLE T1
       (C1  INTEGER NOT NULL PRIMARY KEY,
        C2  INTEGER NOT NULL,
        C3  INTEGER UNIQUE,
        UNIQUE (C2, C3))
```

16.4 Foreign Keys

In the sample database, a number of rules are associated with the relationships between the tables; see Chapter 2, "The Tennis Club Sample Database." For example, all player numbers stored in the TEAMS table must occur in the PLAYERNO column of the PLAYERS table. Also, all team numbers in the MATCHES table must appear in the TEAMNO column of the TEAMS table. This type of relationship is called a *referential integrity constraint*. Referential integrity constraints are a special type of integrity constraint that can be implemented as a foreign key with the CREATE TABLE statements. We give a number of examples.

Example 16.4: Create the TEAMS table such that all player numbers (captains) must appear in the PLAYERS table. Assume that the PLAYERS table has already been created with the PLAYERNO column as the primary key.

```
CREATE   TABLE TEAMS
         (TEAMNO      INTEGER NOT NULL,
          PLAYERNO    INTEGER NOT NULL,
          DIVISION    CHAR(6) NOT NULL,
          PRIMARY KEY (TEAMNO),
          FOREIGN KEY (PLAYERNO)
             REFERENCES PLAYERS (PLAYERNO))
```

Explanation: The foreign key specification has been added to the CREATE TABLE statement. Each foreign key specification consists of three parts. The first part indicates which column (or combination of columns) is the foreign key. This is the specification FOREIGN KEY (PLAYERNO). In the second part, we indicate the table and column(s) the foreign key refers to (REFERENCES PLAYERS (PLAYERNO)). The third part is the referencing action. The referencing action does not appear in this example and is discussed in the next section.

> **Portability:** *In most SQL products, foreign keys can refer to only primary keys. A foreign key cannot refer to an alternate key or any other set of columns; it must be an outright primary key. MySQL is an exception because it does allow a reference to alternate keys.*

Before we give an explanation of this example in detail, we introduce two new terms. The table in which a foreign key is defined is called a *referencing table*. A table to which a foreign key points is called a *referenced table*. Thus, in the previous example, TEAMS is the referencing table and PLAYERS is the referenced table.

What is the actual effect of defining a foreign key? After the statement has been executed, SQL guarantees that each non-NULL value inserted in the foreign key already occurs in the primary key of the referenced table. In the previous example, this means that for each new player number in the TEAMS table, a check is carried out as to whether that number already occurs in the PLAYERNO column (primary key) of the PLAYERS table. If this is not the case, the user or application receives an error message and the update is rejected. This also applies to updating the PLAYERNO column in the TEAMS table with the UPDATE statement. We could also say that SQL guarantees that the population of the PLAYERNO column in the TEAMS table is always a subset of the PLAYERNO column in the PLAYERS table. This means, for example, that the following SELECT statement never returns any rows:

```
SELECT    *
FROM      TEAMS
WHERE     PLAYERNO NOT IN
          (SELECT    PLAYERNO
           FROM      PLAYERS)
```

Naturally, the definition of a foreign key has a huge influence on the updating of the tables involved. We illustrate this with a number of examples. We assume here that the PLAYERS and TEAM tables have the same data as the tables described in Chapter 2.

1. Deleting a player from the PLAYERS table is now permitted only if that player is not a captain.
2. Updating a player number of a player in the PLAYERS table is possible only if that player is not a captain.
3. For inserting new players into the PLAYERS table, no restrictions are enforced by the foreign key.
4. For deleting existing teams from the TEAMS table, no restrictions are enforced by the foreign key.
5. Updating a player number of a captain in the TEAMS table is permitted only if the new player number already occurs in the PLAYERS table.

6. Inserting new teams into the TEAMS table is permitted only if the player number of the captain already occurs in the PLAYERS table.

For clarity as far as the terminology is concerned, we refer to the PLAYERNO column in the TEAMS table as the foreign key; the referential integrity constraint is the check that says that each player number added to the TEAMS table must occur in the PLAYERS table.

The following rules apply when a foreign key is specified:

- The referenced table must already have been created by a CREATE TABLE statement, or must be the table that is currently being created. In the latter case, the referencing table is the same as the referenced table.
- A primary key *must* be defined for the referenced table.
- A column name (or combination of column names) must be specified behind the referenced table name. If this is done, this column (combination) must be the primary key of this table. When no column name is specified, the referenced table must have a primary key, and the column name of the foreign key must be the same as that of the primary key.
- A NULL value is permitted in a foreign key, although a primary key can never contain NULL values. This means that the contents of a foreign key are correct if each non-NULL value occurs in a specific primary key.
- The number of columns in the foreign key must be the same as the number of columns in the primary key of the referenced table.
- The data types of the columns in the foreign key must match those of the corresponding columns in the primary key of the referenced table.

Next, we give the definitions of three tables from the sample database, including all primary and foreign keys.

Example 16.5: Create the TEAMS table, including all relevant primary and foreign keys.

```
CREATE    TABLE TEAMS
          (TEAMNO      INTEGER NOT NULL,
          PLAYERNO    INTEGER NOT NULL,
          DIVISION    CHAR(6) NOT NULL,
          PRIMARY KEY (TEAMNO),
          FOREIGN KEY (PLAYERNO) REFERENCES PLAYERS (PLAYERNO))
```

Explanation: Team captains must be players who occur in the PLAYERS table. Players who are captains cannot be deleted.

Example 16.6: Create the MATCHES table, including all relevant primary and foreign keys.

```
CREATE    TABLE MATCHES
          (MATCHNO     INTEGER NOT NULL,
          TEAMNO       INTEGER NOT NULL,
          PLAYERNO     INTEGER NOT NULL,
          WON          INTEGER NOT NULL,
          LOST         INTEGER NOT NULL,
          PRIMARY KEY (MATCHNO),
          FOREIGN KEY (TEAMNO) REFERENCES TEAMS (TEAMNO),
          FOREIGN KEY (PLAYERNO) REFERENCES PLAYERS (PLAYERNO))
```

Explanation: A match may be played only by someone who appears in the PLAYERS table and may be played only for a team that appears in the TEAMS table. Players and teams may be deleted only if their numbers do not occur in the MATCHES table.

Example 16.7: Create the PENALTIES table, including all relevant primary and foreign keys.

```
CREATE    TABLE PENALTIES
          (PAYMENTNO     INTEGER NOT NULL,
          PLAYERNO       INTEGER NOT NULL,
          PAYMENT_DATE   DATE NOT NULL,
          AMOUNT         DECIMAL(7,2) NOT NULL,
          PRIMARY KEY (PAYMENTNO),
          FOREIGN KEY (PLAYERNO) REFERENCES PLAYERS (PLAYERNO))
```

Explanation: A penalty can be inserted only for a player who appears in the PLAYERS table. If a player is deleted from the PLAYERS table, his penalties will be removed automatically.

For the sake of clarity, the following constructs *are* permitted:

- A foreign key may consist of one or more columns. This means that if a foreign key consists of, for example, two columns, the primary key of the referenced table must also consist of two columns.
- A column may be part of several different foreign keys.

- A subset of columns in a primary key, or the entire set of columns in a primary key, may form a foreign key.
- The referenced and referencing table associated with a foreign key may be the same. Such a table is called a *self-referencing table*, and the construct is *self-referential integrity*. Example:

```
CREATE    TABLE EMPLOYEES
        (EMPLOYEE_NO  CHAR(10) NOT NULL,
        MANAGER_NO    CHAR(10),
        PRIMARY KEY   (EMPLOYEE_NO),
        FOREIGN KEY   (MANAGER_NO)
            REFERENCES EMPLOYEES (EMPLOYEE_NO))
```

Exercise 16.5: Describe the reason for defining foreign keys.

Exercise 16.6: Tell which updates are no longer allowed after the following definition.

```
CREATE    TABLE MATCHES
        (MATCHNO      INTEGER NOT NULL,
        TEAMNO        INTEGER NOT NULL,
        PLAYERNO      INTEGER NOT NULL,
        WON           INTEGER NOT NULL,
        LOST          INTEGER NOT NULL,
        PRIMARY KEY   (MATCHNO),
        FOREIGN KEY   (TEAMNO)
            REFERENCES TEAMS (TEAMNO),
        FOREIGN KEY   (PLAYERNO)
            REFERENCES PLAYERS (PLAYERNO))
```

Exercise 16.7: Describe the concept of self-referential integrity.

Exercise 16.8: Can a self-referencing table be created with one CREATE TABLE statement?

16.5   The Referencing Action

In the previous section, we deferred the discussion of one part of the foreign key: the *referencing action*. In that section, we assumed that a player can be deleted only if he or she had not played a match. By defining a referencing action, we can change this "behavior."

Referencing actions can be defined for each foreign key. A referencing action consists of two parts: In the first part, we indicate the statement to which the referencing action applies. Two statements are relevant here: the UPDATE and DELETE statements. In the second part, we specify which action will be taken. There are three possible actions: CAS-CADE, RESTRICT, and SET NULL. We explain what these different actions mean next.

If you do not specify referencing actions, by default, the following two referencing actions are used:

```
ON UPDATE RESTRICT

ON DELETE RESTRICT
```

Example 16.8: Create the PENALTIES table with two referencing actions.

```
CREATE    TABLE PENALTIES
          (PAYMENTNO      INTEGER NOT NULL,
          PLAYERNO       INTEGER NOT NULL,
          PAYMENT_DATE   DATE NOT NULL,
          AMOUNT         DECIMAL(7,2) NOT NULL,
          PRIMARY KEY    (PAYMENTNO),
          FOREIGN KEY    (PLAYERNO) REFERENCES PLAYERS (PLAYERNO)
              ON UPDATE    RESTRICT
              ON DELETE    RESTRICT)
```

Explanation: The first referencing action specifies explicitly that the update must be rejected (RESTRICT) if the number of a player for whom penalties occur in the PENAL-TIES table is updated (UPDATE). The same applies to the second referencing action: If a player for whom penalties occur in the PENALTIES table is removed (DELETE), the delete must be rejected (RESTRICT).

When CASCADE is used instead of RESTRICT, the behavior changes.

Example 16.9: Create the PENALTIES table with a CASCADE referencing action for the DELETE statement.

```
CREATE    TABLE PENALTIES
          (PAYMENTNO      INTEGER NOT NULL,
          PLAYERNO       INTEGER NOT NULL,
          PAYMENT_DATE   DATE NOT NULL,
          AMOUNT         DECIMAL(7,2) NOT NULL,
          PRIMARY KEY (PAYMENTNO),
          FOREIGN KEY (PLAYERNO) REFERENCES PLAYERS (PLAYERNO)
              ON DELETE CASCADE)
```

Explanation: If a player is deleted, all his or her penalties are automatically removed as well. Imagine that the following DELETE statement is executed:

```
DELETE
FROM      PLAYERS
WHERE     PLAYERNO = 127
```

SQL automatically executes the following DELETE statement (behind the scenes):

```
DELETE
FROM      PENALTIES
WHERE     PLAYERNO = 127
```

If you had specified ON UPDATE CASCADE, the same would have applied to changing the player numbers. If a player number in the PLAYERS table is updated, all player number in the PENALTIES table are updated accordingly.

If you replace the word CASCADE with SET NULL, which is the third possibility, you have another result again:

Example 16.10: Create the PENALTIES table with a SET NULL referencing action for the DELETE statement.

```
CREATE    TABLE PENALTIES
          (PAYMENTNO      INTEGER NOT NULL,
           PLAYERNO       INTEGER NOT NULL,
           PAYMENT_DATE   DATE NOT NULL,
           AMOUNT         DECIMAL(7,2) NOT NULL,
           PRIMARY KEY   (PAYMENTNO),
           FOREIGN KEY   (PLAYERNO) REFERENCES PLAYERS (PLAYERNO)
              ON DELETE SET NULL)
```

If you delete a player, the player number is replaced by the NULL value in all rows of the PENALTIES table in which that player number appears.

Note: *The previous statement is not actually correct. This is because the PLAYERNO column in the PENALTIES table has been defined as NOT NULL, which means that no NULL values can be entered. Therefore, SQL will not accept the previous CREATE TABLE statement.*

A foreign key may use different actions for the two statements. For example, you can define a foreign key with the referencing actions ON UPDATE RESTRICT and ON DELETE CASCADE.

Portability: *Not every SQL product supports referencing actions.*

Exercise 16.9: Not specifying referencing actions is equal to specifying which referencing actions?

Exercise 16.10: Which update restrictions are imposed by the following definition?

```
CREATE   TABLE MATCHES
         (MATCHNO       SMALLINT NOT NULL,
          TEAMNO        SMALLINT NOT NULL,
          PLAYERNO      SMALLINT NOT NULL,
          WON           SMALLINT NOT NULL,
          LOST          SMALLINT NOT NULL,
          PRIMARY KEY   (MATCHNO),
          FOREIGN KEY   (TEAMNO)
             REFERENCES TEAMS
             ON UPDATE CASCADE
             ON DELETE RESTRICT,
          FOREIGN KEY   (PLAYERNO)
             REFERENCES PLAYERS
             ON UPDATE RESTRICT
             ON DELETE CASCADE )
```

16.6 Check Integrity Constraints

Primary, alternate, and foreign keys are examples of integrity constraints that occur frequently in practice. In addition, each database has a number of special integrity constraints. For example, the SEX column in the PLAYERS table can contain only two types of values: M or F, or the value of the AMOUNT column must be greater than 0. You can specify such rules with *check integrity constraints*.

Portability: *In MySQL, check integrity constraints can be included in the CREATE TABLE statements. Unfortunately, they are not enforced yet. However, this will change in one of the future versions.*

Example 16.11: Create a special version of the PLAYERS table with only the columns PLAYERNO and SEX, and take into account that the SEX column may contain only the values M or F.

```
CREATE    TABLE PLAYERS_X
          (PLAYERNO  INTEGER NOT NULL,
           SEX     CHAR(1) NOT NULL
                   CHECK(SEX IN ('M', 'F')))
```

Explanation: The check integrity constraint specifies which values are permitted. Because CHECK is included within the definition of the column itself, only the column SEX may occur in the condition. That is why this form is called a *column integrity constraint*.

Example 16.12: Create another version of the PLAYERS table containing only the columns PLAYERNO and BIRTH_DATE, and take into account that all values in the BIRTH_DATE column must be greater than 1 January 1920.

```
CREATE    TABLE PLAYERS_Y
          (PLAYERNO    INTEGER NOT NULL,
           BIRTH_DATE  DATE
                       CHECK(BIRTH_DATE > '1920-01-01'))
```

If an integrity constraint is specified in which two or more columns of a table are compared to each other, the column integrity constraint must be defined as a *table integrity constraint*.

Example 16.13: Create another version of the PLAYERS table containing only the columns PLAYERNO, BIRTH_DATE, and JOINED, and take into account that all the values in the BIRTH_DATE column must be smaller than the values in the JOINED column. In other words, a player can join the tennis club only after he or she has been born.

```
CREATE    TABLE PLAYERS_Z
          (PLAYERNO    SMALLINT NOT NULL,
           BIRTH_DATE  DATE,
           JOINED      SMALLINT NOT NULL,
           CHECK(YEAR(BIRTH_DATE) < JOINED))
```

The specification NOT NULL is, in fact, a special variant of the check integrity constraint. Instead of NOT NULL, you can specify the following column integrity constraint for all columns concerned: CHECK(COLUMN IS NOT NULL). However, we advise you to use the null specification because SQL checks this in a more efficient way.

Be sure that a combination of check integrity constraints does not mean that a table (or column) can no longer be filled. SQL does not check this. For example, after the following statement, it is no longer possible to enter rows in the PLAYERS_W table:

```
CREATE    TABLE PLAYERS_W
          (PLAYERNO     SMALLINT,
          BIRTH_DATE    DATE      NOT NULL,
          JOINED        SMALLINT NOT NULL,
          CHECK(YEAR(BIRTH_DATE) < JOINED),
          CHECK(BIRTH_DATE > '1920-01-01'),
          CHECK(JOINED   < 1880))
```

The scalar expressions we used in the check integrity constraints in the earlier examples are all simple. SQL products differ in what they allow as scalar expression here. Many products would not support the following construct.

Example 16.14: Create another version of the PLAYERS table containing only the columns PLAYERNO and SEX, and be sure that all values in the SEX column appear in the SEX column of the original PLAYERS table.

```
CREATE    TABLE PLAYERS_V
          (PLAYERNO    SMALLINT NOT NULL,
          SEX          CHAR(1) NOT NULL
                       CHECK(SEX IN
                          (SELECT SEX FROM PLAYERS)))
```

Exercise 16.11: Define a check integrity constraint that guarantees that each penalty amount in the PENALTIES table is greater than zero.

Exercise 16.12: Define a check integrity constraint that guarantees that in the MATCHES table the total number of sets won is always greater than the number of sets lost, and be sure that the total is less than 6.

Exercise 16.13: Define a check integrity constraint that guarantees that in the COMMITTEE_MEMBERS table the begin date is always less than the end date, and that the begin date must be after 31 December 1989.

16.7 Naming Integrity Constraints

If an integrity constraint is violated with an INSERT, UPDATE, or DELETE statement, SQL returns an error message and rejects the update. One update can result in the violation of more than one integrity constraints. In that case, the application will receive several error messages. To indicate exactly which integrity constrains have been violated, a name can be assigned to each integrity constraint. This name is included in the error message to make the message more meaningful to the application.

If no names have been specified, SQL comes up with a name itself. You can look up what that is in the catalog tables; see Section 16.9.

Example 16.15: Create the same DIPLOMAS table as in Example 16.2; however, the primary key should get a name this time.

```
CREATE    TABLE DIPLOMAS
          (STUDENT      INTEGER NOT NULL,
           COURSE       INTEGER NOT NULL,
           DDATE        DATE NOT NULL,
           SUCCESSFUL   CHAR(1),
           LOCATION     VARCHAR(50),
           CONSTRAINT   PRIMARY_KEY_DIPLOMAS
              PRIMARY KEY (STUDENT, COURSE, DDATE))
```

Assigning the name is done by specifying the name behind the word CONSTRAINT in front of the integrity constraint (in this case, the primary key).

Example 16.16: Create the PLAYERS table and assign names to the primary key and to the check integrity constraint of the SEX column.

```
CREATE    TABLE PLAYERS
          (PLAYERNO INTEGER NOT NULL
              CONSTRAINT PRIMARY_KEY_PLAYERS
              PRIMARY KEY,
           :
           SEX CHAR(1) NOT NULL
              CONSTRAINT ALLOWED_VALUES_SEX
              CHECK(SEX IN ('M', 'F')),
           :
```

We recommend assigning names as often as possible when defining integrity constraints. This makes it easier to refer to them when deleting integrity constraints, for example. This implies that we prefer the table integrity constraint to the column integrity constraint because it is not possible to assign a name to the latter.

16.8 Deleting Integrity Constraints

If a table is deleted with a DROP TABLE statement, all integrity constraints are, of course, automatically deleted. All foreign keys for which the table is the referenced table are also deleted. With the ALTER TABLE statement, integrity constraints can be dropped independently without dropping the table itself. This feature is described in detail in Chapter 18, "Changing and Dropping Tables."

16.9 Integrity Constraints and the Catalog

SQL uses several catalog tables for recording data on integrity constraints. Various products have chosen their own different solutions for this. Because the solutions are completely different, we do not discuss them any further. We advise you to study the solution that your product uses.

16.10 Answers

16.1 A primary key cannot and may not contain NULL values. SQL requires that, for each column belonging to a primary key, NOT NULL must be defined.

16.2 For each table, only one primary key can be defined, but it is not mandatory.

16.3

```
CREATE   TABLE MATCHES
        (MATCHNO        INTEGER NOT NULL,
         TEAMNO         INTEGER NOT NULL,
         PLAYERNO       INTEGER NOT NULL,
         WON            INTEGER NOT NULL,
         LOST           INTEGER NOT NULL,
         PRIMARY KEY    (MATCHNO))
```

or

```
CREATE    TABLE MATCHES
          (MATCHNO      INTEGER NOT NULL PRIMARY KEY,
          TEAMNO        INTEGER NOT NULL,
          PLAYERNO      INTEGER NOT NULL,
          WON           INTEGER NOT NULL,
          LOST          INTEGER NOT NULL)
```

16.4 Column C4 in the definition of the primary key does not exist.

Column C1 is defined as the primary key twice; this is not permitted.

The first alternate key on the column C3 is a subset of the second on the columns C2 and C3.

16.5 Foreign keys are defined to force SQL to check that no incorrect data can be entered in the tables.

16.6 The following updates are no longer permitted:

Deleting a player from the PLAYERS table is now permitted only if that player has played no matches.

Updating a player number in the PLAYERS table is possible only if that player has played no matches.

Deleting a team from the TEAMS table is now permitted only if no matches have been played by that team.

Updating a team number in the TEAMS table is possible only if no matches have been played by that team.

No restrictions are imposed by the foreign keys on inserting new players into the PLAYERS table.

No restrictions are imposed by the foreign keys on inserting new teams into the TEAMS table.

No restrictions are imposed by the foreign keys on deleting matches from the MATCHES table.

Updating a player number in the MATCHES table is permitted only if the new player number already occurs in the PLAYERS table.

Updating a team number in the MATCHES table is permitted only if the new team number already occurs in the TEAMS table.

Inserting new matches in the MATCHES table is permitted only if the new player number already occurs in the PLAYERS table and the new team number already occurs in the TEAMS table.

16.7   If the referencing table and the referenced table are the same for the same foreign key, we call this self-referential integrity.

16.8   Yes.

16.9   This is the same as the specification of ON UPDATE RESTRICT and ON DELETE RESTRICT.

16.10   The following updates are no longer permitted:

Deleting a player from the PLAYERS table is now permitted only if that player has played no matches: ON UPDATE RESTRICT.

Updating a player number in the PLAYERS table is allowed: ON DELETE CASCADE.

Deleting a team from the TEAMS table is not permitted: ON DELETE RESTRICT.

Updating a team number in the TEAMS table is allowed: ON UPDATE CASCADE.

No restrictions are imposed by the foreign keys on inserting new players into the PLAYERS table.

No restrictions are imposed by the foreign keys on inserting new teams into the TEAMS table.

No restrictions are imposed by the foreign keys on deleting matches from the MATCHES table.

Updating a player number in the MATCHES table is permitted only if the new player number already occurs in the PLAYERS table.

Updating a team number in the MATCHES table is permitted only if the new team number already occurs in the TEAMS table.

Inserting new matches in the MATCHES table is permitted only if the new player number already occurs in the PLAYERS table and the new team number already occurs in the TEAMS table.

16.11   CHECK(AMOUNT > 0)

16.12   CHECK(WON > LOST AND WON + LOST < 6)

16.13   CHECK(BEGIN_DATE BETWEEN '1990-01-01' AND
          COALESCE(END_DATE, '9999-01-01')

Character Sets and Collating Sequences

17.1 Introduction

I n this book, the concepts *character sets* and *collating sequence* have been mentioned a few times. What these concepts exactly mean and how SQL handles them is the topic of this chapter.

Portability: *In the various SQL products, support for character sets and collating sequences has been implemented very differently. For that reason, we describe the form implemented in MySQL.*

To store alphanumeric values, characters such as *A*, *b*, and *ĕ*, but also special symbols such as {, &, and =, they must be converted into numeric codes. Something like a translation table must be built that contains a unique numeric code for each relevant character. Each character, therefore, gets a position in that translation table. Such a translation table is called a character set in the SQL world. In the literature, the terms *code character set* and *character encoding* are sometimes used as well.

For a character set, an *encoding scheme* must be invented. The character set indicates only that, for example, the uppercase letter *A* has the position or the code 41 and that the lowercase letter *h* has the position 68. But how will we store that in bytes? For each translation table, several encoding schemes can be invented; the more creative you are, the more schemes you can create. At first, you always think of a fixed number of bits and bytes for each character. So, for the storage of a character set consisting of a maximum of 256 characters, you can decide to reserve 8 bits for each character. But you could also decide to use flexible storage. For characters that occur frequently, you reserve, for example, 4 bits; for the others, you reserve 8 or 12.

Flexible lengths are also used in Morse code. In Morse, letters are represented by dots and dashes. However, not every letter has the same number of dots or dashes. The letter *e*, for example, is only one dash, whereas the *c* is built up from a dash, a dot, a dash and finally a dot—four symbols for one letter. You can also use such a solution as an encoding scheme for a character set.

So, the encoding scheme contains information about how positions such as 1, 100, and 1,000 are stored on hard disk or in internal memory.

In SQL the concepts of character sets and encoding scheme are seen as synonyms. A character set is a combination of a translation table with an encoding scheme.

Through the years, many character sets have been invented. The first standardized character set was ASCII (American Standard Code for Information Interchange), and its first version was defined in 1960 by ANSI. Another well-known character set is EBCDIC (Extended Binary Coded Decimal Interchange Code), invented by IBM. It has been the standard on the IBM mainframes for a long time.

With ASCII, the number of characters was limited to a maximum of 256 (2^8) characters. That used to be enough, but nowadays applications and their users require much more. Applications must be capable of handling special letters, such as β, Ð, Œ, and æ. Also, letters with all sorts of accents, such as ş, ū, ų, and š must be processed. And then we have not even mentioned the languages in which other letters are used. Think about languages from the Middle East and the Far East. In short, 256 positions are no longer sufficient. It was time to come up with character sets that could be used to code thousands of different characters. *Unicode* (short for Universal Code) is one of the most used new character sets, but there are more that can hold large sets of characters.

Unicode has different encoding schemes, including *UTF-8*, *UTF-16*, and *UTF-32*. UTF stands for Unicode Transformation Format. These encoding schemes vary in the number of different characters they can handle and in the number of bytes they reserve for certain characters.

The concept of *collating sequence* deals with the sort order or the grouping of the characters. If numeric values are sorted or compared, it is always obvious how that must be done. The number 10 is smaller than the number 100, so 10 comes before 100 when sorted. Sorting and comparing alphanumeric values is not always that simple. If you have to place the words *Monkey* and *monkey* in alphabetical order, which one comes first, the spelling with the uppercase letter or the one with the lowercase letter? If you sort on the positions of the characters, the spelling with the uppercase letters will come first with character sets such as ASCII and Unicode. But is that what you want? And if that is what you want, does that mean that a user living in Georgia wants that as well? It becomes even more difficult when you want to sort the Dutch words *scène*, *schaaf*, and *scepter*. It is only on the third letter that these words are different. When you look at the ASCII codes for these three letters, *scepter* comes first, then *schaaf*, and finally *scène* sorted last. However, most users would like to see *scepter* and *scène* behind each other. But then the question is, which of these two comes first? To throw some light on this, the collating sequence has been added. For example, if a character set is assigned to a column, a collating sequence can be specified. For one character set, several collating sequences can be relevant. A collating sequence always belongs to only one character set.

17.2 Available Character Sets and Collating Sequences

During the installation of SQL, a number of character sets are introduced. This list can be retrieved by using a special SHOW statement or by querying a catalog table.

Example 17.1: Show the available character sets.

```
SHOW CHARACTER SET
```

or

```
SELECT    CHARACTER_SET_NAME, DESCRIPTION,
          DEFAULT_COLLATE_NAME, MAXLEN
FROM      INFORMATION_SCHEMA.CHARACTER_SETS
```

The result is:

```
CHARSET   DESCRIPTION                     DEFAULT COLLATION   MAXLEN
-------   -----------------------------   -----------------   ------
big5      Big5 Traditional Chinese        big5_chinese_ci        2
dec8      DEC West European               dec8_swedish_ci        1
cp850     DOS West European               cp850_general_ci       1
hp8       HP West European                hp8_english_ci         1
koi8r     KOI8-R Relcom Russian           koi8r_general_ci       1
latin1    ISO 8859-1 West European        latin1_swedish_ci      1
latin2    ISO 8859-2 Central European     latin2_general_ci      1
swe7      7bit Swedish                    swe7_swedish_ci        1
ascii     US ASCII                        ascii_general_ci       1
  :
utf8      UTF-8 Unicode                   utf8_general_ci        3
ucs2      UCS-2 Unicode                   ucs2_general_ci        2
  :
cp932     SJIS for Windows Japanese       cp932_japanese_ci      2
eucjpms   UJIS for Windows Japanese       eucjpms_japanese_ci    3
```

Explanation: The column on the right contains the name of the character set. This is the name that we use in other statements to indicate which character set must be applied. The second column contains a short description of each character set. The third column contains the default collating sequence of each character set. And on the complete right side you can find the maximum number of bytes that is reserved for a character. Note that this is 3 bytes for the last one.

In the SELECT statement, the column names, not a *, have been specified to make sure that the SELECT statement presents the columns in the same order as the SHOW statement.

All available collating sequences can be retrieved as well.

Example 17.2: Show the available collating sequences for the character set utf8.

```
SHOW COLLATION LIKE 'utf8%'
```

or

```
SELECT    *
FROM      INFORMATION_SCHEMA.COLLATIONS
WHERE     COLLATION_NAME LIKE 'utf8%'
```

The result is:

```
COLLATION            CHARSET   ID   DEFAULT   COMPILED   SORTLEN
-------------------  -------   ---  -------   --------   -------
utf8_general_ci      utf8       33  Yes       Yes              1
utf8_bin             utf8       83            Yes              1
utf8_unicode_ci      utf8      192            Yes              8
utf8_icelandic_ci    utf8      193            Yes              8
utf8_latvian_ci      utf8      194            Yes              8
utf8_romanian_ci     utf8      195            Yes              8
utf8_slovenian_ci    utf8      196            Yes              8
utf8_polish_ci       utf8      197            Yes              8
utf8_estonian_ci     utf8      198            Yes              8
utf8_spanish_ci      utf8      199            Yes              8
utf8_swedish_ci      utf8      200            Yes              8
utf8_turkish_ci      utf8      201            Yes              8
utf8_czech_ci        utf8      202            Yes              8
utf8_danish_ci       utf8      203            Yes              8
utf8_lithuanian_ci   utf8      204            Yes              8
utf8_slovak_ci       utf8      205            Yes              8
utf8_spanish2_ci     utf8      206            Yes              8
utf8_roman_ci        utf8      207            Yes              8
utf8_persian_ci      utf8      208            Yes              8
```

Explanation: The column on the left contains the names of the collating sequences that we can use in SQL statements. The second column contains the name of the character set to which the collating sequence belongs. ID contains a unique number of the sequence. The DEFAULT column indicates whether the collating sequence is the default for this character set. The last two columns contain technical information.

17.3   Assigning Character Sets to Columns

Each alphanumeric column has a character set. When a table is created, a character set can explicitly be assigned to each column. For this, a data type option is used.

Example 17.3: Create a new table with two alphanumeric columns, and assign the character set ucs2 to both.

```
CREATE TABLE TABUCS2
      (C1   CHAR(10)     CHARACTER SET ucs2 NOT NULL PRIMARY KEY,
       C2   VARCHAR(10)  CHARACTER SET ucs2)
```

Explanation: The character set is included as data type option and is, therefore, placed after the data type and in front of the null specification and primary key. The name of the character set may be entered in uppercase or lowercase letters. The name may also be specified as an alphanumeric literal. CHARACTER SET may be abbreviated to CHAR SET or CHARSET.

   Columns belonging to the same table can have different character sets. This can be useful for the registration of, for example, a company name in different languages.

   If a character set has not explicitly been defined for a column, the default character set is used.

Example 17.4: Create a new table with two alphanumeric columns, do not assign a character set, and look in the catalog tables next to see what the default character set is.

```
CREATE TABLE TABDEFKARSET
      (C1   CHAR(10) NOT NULL,
       C2   VARCHAR(10))

SELECT    COLUMN_NAME, CHARACTER_SET_NAME
FROM      INFORMATION_SCHEMA.COLUMNS
WHERE     TABLE_NAME = 'TABDEFKARSET'
```

The result is:

```
COLUMN_NAME  CHARACTER_SET_NAME
-----------  ------------------
C1           latin1
C2           latin1
```

The default character set is latin1 for both columns. But where exactly has that default been defined? A default character set can be defined on two levels, on the table and on the database level. With a so-called *table option*, a default character set can be defined for a table.

Example 17.5: Create a new table with two alphanumeric columns, and define utf8 as the default character set.

```
CREATE TABLE TABUTF8
       (C1   CHAR(10) NOT NULL,
        C2   VARCHAR(10))
    DEFAULT CHARACTER SET utf8

SELECT    COLUMN_NAME, CHARACTER_SET_NAME
FROM      INFORMATION_SCHEMA.COLUMNS
WHERE     TABLE_NAME = 'TABUTF8'
```

The result is:

```
COLUMN_NAME   CHARACTER_SET_NAME
-----------   ------------------
C1            utf8
C2            utf8
```

If no default character set has been defined for a table, SQL checks whether one has been defined on the database level.

Each created database has a default character set, which is latin1 if nothing has been specified. In Chapter 22, "Creating Databases," we show how this default character set can be specified and changed.

Character sets that have been assigned once explicitly do not change when you change the default of the table or database later.

Exercise 17.1: Are the internal byte codes of two characters, belonging to the same character set but with different collating sequences, equal?

Exercise 17.2: Show the SELECT statement with which the number of collating sequences for each character set can be determined.

17.4 Assigning Collating Sequences to Columns

Each column should also have a collating sequence. If it has not been specified, SQL uses the default collating sequence that belongs to the character set. The next example shows how such a default collating sequence of a character set can be retrieved.

Example 17.6: Get the collating sequences of the columns of the tables that were created in Examples 17.3 and 17.4.

```
SELECT    TABLE_NAME, COLUMN_NAME, COLLATION_NAME
FROM      INFORMATION_SCHEMA.COLUMNS
WHERE     TABLE_NAME IN ('TABUCS2', 'TABDEFKARSET')
```

The result is:

```
TABLE_NAME      COLUMN_NAME  COLLATION_NAME
------------    -----------  ------------------
tabdefkarset    C1           latin1_swedish_ci
tabdefkarset    C2           latin1_swedish_ci
tabucs2         C1           ucs2_general_ci
tabucs2         C2           ucs2_general_ci
```

Of course, it is possible to specify explicitly a collating sequence with the data type option COLLATE.

Example 17.7: Create a new table with two alphanumeric columns, define utf8 as the character set, and use two different collating sequences.

```
CREATE TABLE TABCOLLATE
      (C1   CHAR(10)
            CHARACTER SET utf8
            COLLATE utf8_romanian_ci NOT NULL,
       C2   VARCHAR(10)
            CHARACTER SET utf8
            COLLATE utf8_spanish_ci)

SELECT    COLUMN_NAME, CHARACTER_SET_NAME, COLLATION_NAME
FROM      INFORMATION_SCHEMA.COLUMNS
WHERE     TABLE_NAME = 'TABCOLLATE'
```

The result is:

```
COLUMN_NAME   CHARACTER_SET_NAME   COLLATION_NAME
-----------   ------------------   ----------------
C1            utf8                 utf8_romanian_ci
C2            utf8                 utf8_spanish_ci
```

Explanation: The name of the collating sequence may also be written in uppercase let-ters and may be placed between brackets. If a character set and a collating sequence are specified, the character set should go first.

If all alphanumeric columns of a table need to have the same collating sequence, a default collating sequence can be defined for the entire table. Even though the charac-ter sets have their own collating sequences, that of the table still has priority.

Example 17.8: Create a new table with two alphanumeric columns, and define utf8 as character set and utf8_romanian_ci as the collating sequence.

```
CREATE TABLE TABDEFCOL
      (C1   CHAR(10) NOT NULL,
       C2   VARCHAR(10))
   CHARACTER SET = utf8
   COLLATE =  utf8_romanian_ci

SELECT   COLUMN_NAME, CHARACTER_SET_NAME, COLLATION_NAME
FROM     INFORMATION_SCHEMA.COLUMNS
WHERE    TABLE_NAME = 'TABDEFCOL'
```

The result is:

```
COLUMN_NAME   CHARACTER_SET_NAME   COLLATION_NAME
-----------   ------------------   ----------------
C1            utf8                 utf8_romanian_ci
C2            utf8                 utf8_romanian_ci
```

It is also possible to specify a default collating sequence on the database level; see Chapter 22.

17.5 Expressions with Character Sets and Collating Sequences

The character set and the collating sequence play a big part in the processing of alphanumeric expressions. Especially when making comparisons and sorting data, SQL must include the character sets and collating sequence of the expressions concerned. It is not allowed to compare two alphanumeric values belonging to two different collating sequences. We can conclude that two expressions with two different character sets cannot be compared, either, because, by definition, they have different collating sequences.

Example 17.9: Create a new table with two columns based upon different character sets.

```
CREATE TABLE TWOCHARSETS
       (C1   CHAR(10) CHARACTER SET 'latin1' NOT NULL,
        C2   VARCHAR(10) CHARACTER SET 'utf8')

INSERT INTO TWOCHARSETS VALUES ('A', 'A')

SELECT    *
FROM      TWOCHARSETS
WHERE     C1 = C2
```

SQL returns an error message when processing this SELECT.

Example 17.10: Create a new table with two columns based upon the same character set, but with different collating sequences.

```
CREATE TABLE TWOCOLL
       (C1   CHAR(10) COLLATE   'latin1_general_ci' NOT NULL,
        C2   VARCHAR(10) COLLATE 'latin1_danish_ci')

INSERT INTO TWOCOLL VALUES ('A', 'A')

SELECT    *
FROM      TWOCOLL
WHERE     C1 = C2
```

Explanation: Both the columns C1 and C2 have the character set latin1 (the default of the database), but their collating sequences differ; as a result, comparisons, such as in the earlier SELECT statement, will lead to error messages.

To compare two values with different collating sequences, you could change the collating sequence of one. Specify the term COLLATE behind the column concerned then, followed by the name of the sequence:

```
SELECT    *
FROM      TWOCOLL
WHERE     C1 COLLATE latin1_danish_ci = C2
```

Because of this, the definition of the alphanumeric expression is extended somewhat:

```
<alphanumeric expression> ::=
   <alphanumeric scalar expression> |
   <alphanumeric row expression>    |
   <alphanumeric table expression>

<alphanumeric scalar expression> ::=
   <singular alphanumeric scalar expression> COLLATE <name> |
   <compound alphanumeric scalar expression>

<alphanumeric singular scalar expression> ::=
   _<collating sequence name> <alphanumeric literal> |
   <alphanumeric column specification>               |
   <alphanumeric user variable>                      |
   <alphanumeric system variable>                    |
   <alphanumeric cast expression>                    |
   <alphanumeric case expression>                    |
   NULL                                              |
   ( <alphanumeric scalar expression> )              |
   <alphanumeric scalar function>                    |
   <alphanumeric aggregation function>               |
   <alphanumeric scalar subquery>
```

It is obvious that you can specify only a collating sequence that belongs to the character set of the column or expression. The following statement also returns an error message because utf8_general_ci is not a collating sequence that belongs to latin1:

```
SELECT    *
FROM      TWOCOLL
WHERE     C1 COLLATE utf8_general_ci = C2
```

What exactly is the character set of an alphanumeric literal? If nothing is specified, that is the default character set of the database. If you want to assign a literal another character set, you should place the name of the character set in front of the literal. And in front of that name, the underscore symbol must be placed.

Example 17.11: Present the word *database* in the utf8 character set.

```
SELECT    _utf8'database'
```

To retrieve the collating sequence of a certain expression, the COLLATE function has been added.

Example 17.12: Get the collating sequence of the expressions _utf8'database', _utf8'database' COLLATE utf8_bin, and of the NAME column of the PLAYERS table.

```
SELECT    COLLATION(_utf8'database'),
          COLLATION(_utf8'database' COLLATE utf8_bin),
          COLLATION((SELECT MAX(NAME) FROM PLAYERS))
```

The result is:

```
COLLATION(_utf8'database')   COLLATION(...)   COLLATION(...)
--------------------------   --------------   --------------
utf8_general_ci              utf8_bin
latin1_swedish_ci
```

With the CHARSET function, you retrieve the character set.

Example 17.13: Get the character sets of the expression _utf8'database' and of the NAME column of the PLAYERS table.

```
SELECT    CHARSET(_utf8'database'),
          CHARSET((SELECT MAX(NAME) FROM PLAYERS))
```

The result is:

```
CHARSET(_utf8'database')   CHARSET((...))
------------------------   --------------
utf8                       latin1
```

Exercise 17.3: How does a comparison look in which two alphanumeric expressions with different collating sequences are compared on the basis of a third collating sequence?

17.6 Sorting and Grouping with Collating Sequences

COLLATE may also be used in ORDER BY clauses to specify a sorting on another collating sequence.

Example 17.14: Sort the two names Muller and Müller with two different collating sequences: latin1_swedish_ci and latin1_german2_ci.

```
SELECT _latin1'Muller' AS NAME
UNION
SELECT CONCAT('M', _latin1 x'FC', 'ller')
ORDER BY NAME COLLATE latin1_swedish_ci
```

The result is:

```
NAME
------
Muller
Müller
```

Explanation: The first select block returns the name Muller with the character set latin1; the second select block returns the name Müller. When you change the collating sequence into latin1_german2_ci in this statement, the two rows are turned around in sequence, as the following result shows:

```
NAME
------
Müller
Muller
```

For the grouping of data, a check is done to see whether values in a column are equal. If that is the case, they are joined in one group. If the column contains alphanumeric values, the collating sequence plays a big part. In one collating sequence, two different characters can be seen as equal, while in another sequence they are considered to be unequal.

Example 17.15: Create a table in which the characters *e*, *é*, and *ë* are stored.

```
CREATE TABLE LETTERS
    (SEQNO    INTEGER NOT NULL PRIMARY KEY,
     LETTER   CHAR(1) CHARACTER SET UTF8 NOT NULL)

INSERT INTO LETTERS VALUES (1, 'e'), (2, x'E9'),(3, x'EB')

SELECT    LETTER
FROM      (SELECT    LETTER COLLATE utf8_general_ci AS LETTER
           FROM      LETTERS) AS L
GROUP BY LETTER
```

The result is:

```
LETTER
------

e
```

Explanation: The hexadecimal code of *é* is E9 and *ë* becomes EB. In the subquery, all letters are converted into the utf8_general_ci collating sequence. The result shows that *é* and *ë* are considered to be equal, while a separate group is formed for the character *e*. If you change the collating sequence, you get another result:

```
SELECT    LETTER
FROM      (SELECT    LETTER COLLATE utf8_swedish_ci AS L
           FROM      LETTERS) AS LETTER
GROUP BY LETTER
```

The result is:

```
LETTER
------
e
```

Now all three characters form one group and can be joined together. So be careful when you group and sort alphanumeric values when collating sequences are involved.

Exercise 17.4: Determine what the character set and collating sequence is of the TOWN column in the PLAYERS table.

Exercise 17.5: Sort the players on the basis of the TOWN column, but use another collating sequence than the one in the previous exercise.

17.7 The Coercibility of Expressions

For many expressions and statements, SQL can decide for itself which collating sequence must be used. For example, if you sort the values of a column or you compare a column with itself, the collating sequence of the relevant column will be used; see the following example.

Example 17.16: Use the LETTERS table from Example 17.15 and sort this table on the LETTER column.

```
SELECT    LETTER
FROM      LETTERS
ORDER BY LETTER
```

Which collating sequence will be used if you compare values that are of the same character set but that have different collating sequences? SQL solves this problem by means of the *coercibility*. Each expression has a coercibility value between 0 and 5. If two expressions are compared with different coercibility values, the collating sequence of the expression with the lowest coercibility value is selected. The rules for coercibility follow:

- If an explicit collating sequence is assigned to an expression, the coercibility is equal to 0.
- The concatenation of two alphanumeric expressions with different collating sequences gives a coercibility that is equal to 1.
- The coercibility of a column specification is 2.
- The value of functions such as USER() and VERSION() has a coercibility of 3.
- The coercibility of an alphanumeric literal is 4.
- The NULL value of an expression that has NULL as result has 5 as coercibility.

For the comparison COLUMN1 = 'e', the column specification COLUMN1 has a coercibility of 2 and that the literal has a coercibility of 4. This implies that SQL will use the collating sequence of the column specification.

You can retrieve the coercibility of an expression with the COERCIBILITY function.

Example 17.17: Get the coercibility value of several expressions.

```
SELECT    COERCIBILITY('Rick' COLLATE latin1_general_ci) AS C0,
          COERCIBILITY(TEAMNO) AS C2,
          COERCIBILITY(USER()) AS C3,
          COERCIBILITY('Rick') AS C4,
          COERCIBILITY(NULL) AS C5
FROM      TEAMS
WHERE     TEAMNO = 1
```

The result is:

C0	C2	C3	C4	C5
0	2	3	4	5

17.8   Related System Variables

Various system variables have a relationship with character sets and collating sequences. Table 17.1 contains their names and the corresponding explanations.

Table 17.1   *System Variables for Character Sets and Collating Sequences*

SYSTEM VARIABLE	EXPLANATION
CHARACTER_SET_CLIENT	The character set of the statements that are sent from the client to the server.
CHARACTER_SET_CONNECTION	The character set of the client/server connection.
CHARACTER_SET_DATABASE	The default character set of the current database. The value of this variable can change every time the USE statement is used to "jump" to another database. If no current database exists, this variable has the value of the CHARACTER_SET_SERVER variable.
CHARACTER_SET_RESULTS	The character set of the end results of SELECT statements that are sent from the server to the client.
CHARACTER_SET_SERVER	The default character set of the server.
CHARACTER_SET_SYSTEM	The character set of the system. This character set is used for the names of database objects, such as tables and columns, but also for the names of functions that are stored in the catalog tables. The value of this variable is always equal to utf8.
CHARACTER_SET_DIR	The name of the directory in which the files with all the character sets are registered.
COLLATION_CONNECTION	The character set of the present connection.
COLLATION_DATABASE	The default collating sequence of the current database. The value of this variable can change every time the USE statement is used to "jump" to another database. If no current database exists, this variable has the value of the COLLATION_SERVER variable.
COLLATION_SERVER	The default collating sequence of the server.

Besides CHARACTER_SET_DIR, the value of each of these system variables can be retrieved with the help of "at" symbols within SQL statements.

Example 17.18: Give the value of the default collating sequence of the current database.

```
SELECT @@COLLATION_DATABASE
```

The result is:

```
@@COLLATION_DATABASE
--------------------
latin1_swedish_ci
```

Example 17.19: Give the values of the system variables whose name begins with CHARACTER_SET.

```
SHOW VARIABLES LIKE 'CHARACTER_SET%'
```

The result is:

```
VARIABLE_NAME              VALUE
-------------             ---------------
character_set_client       latin1
character_set_connection   latin1
character_set_database     latin1
character_set_results      latin1
character_set_server       latin1
character_set_system       utf8
character_sets_dir         C:\Program Files\MySQL\MySQL Server
                           5.0\share\charsets/
```

17.9 Answers

17.1   The internal byte codes are not equal then.

17.2

```
SELECT    COLLATION_NAME, COUNT(*)
FROM      INFORMATION_SCHEMA.COLLATIONS
GROUP BY COLLATION_NAME
```

17.3

```
EXPRESSION1 COLLATE utf8 = EXPRESSION2 COLLATE ut8
```

17.4

```
SELECT CHARSET((SELECT MAX(TOWN) FROM PLAYERS)),
       COLLATION((SELECT MAX(TOWN) FROM PLAYERS))
```

17.5

```
SELECT    TOWN
FROM      PLAYERS
ORDER BY TOWN COLLATE latin1_danish_ci
```

18

Changing and Dropping Tables

18.1 Introduction

The UPDATE, INSERT, and DELETE statements update the contents of a table. With SQL, we can also change the *structure* of a table, even when that table contains millions of rows. We can add columns, change the data type of an existing column, add integrity constraints, and can even delete entire tables. This chapter describes all the features to drop tables (with the DROP TABLE statement), to rename them (the RENAME statement), and to change them (the ALTER TABLE statement).

> **Note:** *In most examples in this book, we assume that each table contains its original contents. If you execute the statements in this chapter with SQL, you change the structure and the contents, of course. Because of this, the results of your statements in the following examples could differ from those in the book. On the Web site of the book, www.r20.nl, you can find information on how the tables can be restored to their original state.*

18.2 Deleting Entire Tables

The DROP TABLE statement deletes a table. SQL also removes the descriptions of the table from all relevant catalog tables, along with all integrity constraints, indexes, and privileges that are "linked" to that table. In fact, SQL removes each database object that has no right to exist after the table has been deleted.

```
<drop table statement> ::=
   DROP TABLE <table specification>
```

Example 18.1: Delete the PLAYERS table.

```
DROP TABLE PLAYERS
```

Explanation: After this statement has been processed, the table no longer exists. Furthermore, all linked database objects, such as indexes, views, and privileges, have been removed as well.

A table can be removed only if there are no foreign keys pointing to the table—or, in other words, the table cannot be a referenced table. In that case, either the relevant foreign key or the entire referencing table must be removed first.

> **Portability:** *Following the SQL2 standard, several SQL products have added an option called CASCADE to the DROP TABLE statement. If this option is used, all tables that are "linked" to this table via foreign keys are removed. Thus, the following statement removes the PLAYERS table, but also, among other things, removes the PENALTIES and TEAMS tables:*
>
> DROP TABLE PLAYERS CASCADE

18.3 Renaming Tables

The RENAME TABLE statement gives an existing table a new name.

```
Rename table statement> ::=
    RENAME TABLE <table name change>

<table name change> ::= <table name> TO <table name>
```

Example 18.2: Change the name of the PLAYERS table to TENNIS_PLAYERS.

```
RENAME TABLE PLAYERS TO TENNIS_PLAYERS
```

All other database objects that refer to this table are changed accordingly. Assigned privileges do not disappear, foreign keys remain, and views that use this renamed table keep on working.

> **Portability:** *Most SQL products support the RENAME TABLE statement, but still not all.*

18.4   Changing the Table Structure

You can change many aspects of the table structure. SQL supports the ALTER TABLE statement for this. Because this statement offers so many possibilities, we describe its features in several sections. This section describes the possibilities for altering the table itself. The following section discusses the ways to change the specifications of columns. Section 18.6 covers the possibilities of changing integrity constraints. How we should change existing indexes is described in Section 20.5, in Chapter 20, "Using Indexes," (after we explain how indexes are created).

Portability: *Most SQL products support the* ALTER TABLE *statement, but they differ in what can be done with this statement. For example, some products do not allow data types of existing columns to be changed, others do not allow columns to be deleted, and with others you cannot change the name of a table.*

```
<alter table statement> ::=
    ALTER TABLE <table specification> <table structure change>

<table structure change> ::=
    <table change>               |
    <column change>              |
    <integrity constraint change> |
    <index change>

<table change> ::=
    RENAME [ TO | AS ] <table name>                              |
    CONVERT TO CHARACTER SET { <character set name> | DEFAULT }
       [ COLLATE <collating sequence name> ]

<table name>                ;
<column name>               ;
<character set name>        ;
<collating sequence name> ::= <name>
```

Example 18.3: Change the name of the PLAYERS table to TENNIS_PLAYERS.

```
ALTER TABLE PLAYERS TO TENNIS_PLAYERS
```

Explanation: The result of this statement is, of course, equal to that of the RENAME TABLE statement; see Section 18.3. The word TO can be replaced by AS.

If you want to change the character set of existing columns, use the CONVERT feature of the ALTER TABLE statement.

Example 18.4: For all alphanumeric columns in the PLAYERS table, change the character set to utf8 and set the collating sequence to utf8_general_ci.

```
ALTER TABLE PLAYERS
    CONVERT TO CHARACTER SET utf8 COLLATE utf8_general_ci
```

18.5 Changing Columns

Many properties of columns can be changed with the ALTER TABLE statement.

```
<alter table statement> ::=
    ALTER TABLE <table specification>
    <table structure change>

<table structure change> ::=
    <table change>               |
    <column change>              |
    <integrity constraint change> |
    <index change>

<column change> ::=
    ADD [ COLUMN ] <column definition>
      [ FIRST | AFTER <column name> ]                            |
    ADD [ COLUMN ] <table schema>                                |
    DROP [ COLUMN ] <column name> [ RESTRICT | CASCADE ]         |
    CHANGE [ COLUMN ] <column name> <column definition>
      [ FIRST | AFTER <column name> ]                            |
    MODIFY [ COLUMN ] <column definition>
      [ FIRST | AFTER <column name> ]                            |
    ALTER [ COLUMN ] { SET DEFAULT <expression> | DROP DEFAULT }

<column definition> ::=
    <column name> <data type> [ <null specification> ]
    [ <column integrity constraint> ] [ <column option>... ]
```

(continued)

```
<column list> ::= <column name> [ { , <column name> }... ]

<table name>                ;
<column name>               ;
<index name>               ;
<constraint name>          ;
<character set name>       ;
<collating sequence name> ::= <name>
```

Example 18.5: Add a new column called TYPE to the TEAMS table. This column shows whether it is a ladies' or a men's team.

```
ALTER    TABLE TEAMS
ADD      TYPE CHAR(1)
```

The TEAMS table now looks like this:

```
TEAMNO   PLAYERNO   DIVISION   TYPE
------   --------   --------   ----
     1          6   first      ?
     2         27   second     ?
```

Explanation: In all rows, the TYPE column is filled with the NULL value. This is the only possible value that SQL can use to fill the column. (How would SQL know whether, for example, team 1 is a men's team?)

Because you may specify a full column definition, you may also enter a null specification, integrity constraints, and column options.

The word COLUMN may be added but does not change the result. The new column automatically becomes the last column unless the "position" is specified.

Example 18.6: Add a new column called TYPE to the TEAMS table. This column shows whether it is a ladies' or a men's team. The column must be placed right behind the TEAMNO column.

```
ALTER    TABLE TEAMS
ADD      TYPE CHAR(1) AFTER TEAMNO
```

This TEAMS table now looks like this:

```
TEAMNO   TYPE   PLAYERNO   DIVISION
------   ----   --------   --------
     1   ?             6   first
     2   ?            27   second
```

Explanation: By replacing AFTER TEAMNO with FIRST, the new column will be positioned at the beginning.

  With a somewhat different formulation, you can add two or more new columns at one time.

Example 18.7: Add two new columns to the TEAMS table.

```
ALTER    TABLE TEAMS
ADD      (CATEGORY   VARCHAR(20) NOT NULL,
         IMAGO       INTEGER DEFAULT 10)
```

Explanation: The CATEGORY column has been defined as NOT NULL. This means that SQL cannot assign a NULL value to each row for this column. Depending on the data type, SQL fills in an actual value: the value 0 for numeric columns, the empty string for alphanumeric columns, the date 0000-00-00 for date data types, and the time 00:00:00 for time data types.

Example 18.8: Delete the TYPE column from the TEAMS table.

```
ALTER    TABLE TEAMS
DROP     TYPE
```

Explanation: All other database objects that depend on this column, such as privileges, indexes, and views, will also be deleted.

Example 18.9: In the TEAMS table, change the column name BIRTH_DATE to DATE_OF_BIRTH.

```
ALTER    TABLE PLAYERS
CHANGE   BIRTH_DATE DATE_OF_BIRTH DATE
```

Explanation: Behind the column name, a new column definition is specified. Because we want to change only the column name, we'll leave the other specifications the way they are, so they remain equal to those of the original column. But we are allowed to change those as well.

Example 18.10: Increase the length of the TOWN column from 30 to 40.

```
ALTER    TABLE PLAYERS
CHANGE   TOWN TOWN VARCHAR(40) NOT NULL
```

The length of a data type may be increased or reduced. In the case of the latter, the existing values are shortened.

Example 18.11: Shorten the length of the TOWN column to five characters.

```
ALTER    TABLE PLAYERS
CHANGE   TOWN TOWN VARCHAR(5) NOT NULL
```

Example 18.12: Change the data type of the PLAYERNO column in the PLAYERS table from INTEGER to TINYINT.

```
ALTER    TABLE PLAYERS
CHANGE   PLAYERNO PLAYERNO TINYINT
```

When data types are changed, the usual rule is that it must be possible to transform the values in the column into the new data type. So, the previous example will be executed correctly because the current player numbers fit into the TINYINT data type.

Example 18.13: Move the TOWN column to the second position.

```
ALTER    TABLE PLAYERS
CHANGE   TOWN TOWN VARCHAR(5) NOT NULL AFTER PLAYERNO
```

Specifications that are not mentioned, such as the comment and the character set, remain unchanged.

ALTER TABLE MODIFY can also be used to change properties of columns. The only thing is that the column name does not have to be mentioned first. That also means that, when using MODIFY, the column name itself cannot be changed.

Example 18.14: Rewrite Example 18.13 with MODIFY.

```
ALTER    TABLE PLAYERS
MODIFY   TOWN VARCHAR(5) NOT NULL AFTER PLAYERNO
```

Example 18.15: Assign the default value Member to the POSITION column of the COM-MITTEE_MEMBERS table.

```
ALTER    TABLE COMMITTEE_MEMBERS
ALTER    POSITION SET DEFAULT 'Member'
```

Example 18.16: Delete the default value of the POSITION column in the COMMIT-TEE_MEMBERS table.

```
ALTER    TABLE COMMITTEE_MEMBERS
ALTER    POSITION DROP DEFAULT
```

Exercise 18.1: Change the column name POSITION in the COMMITTEE_MEMBERS table to COMMITTEE_POSITION.

Exercise 18.2: Next, increase the length of the COMMITTEE_POSITION column from 20 to 30.

Exercise 18.3: Assign the default value Stratford to the TOWN column in the PLAY-ERS table.

18.6 Changing Integrity Constraints

In Chapter 16, "Specifying Integrity Constraints," we extensively discussed all different kinds of integrity constraints that can be added to a table. With the ALTER TABLE statement, constraints can be added or deleted afterward.

```
<alter table statement> ::=
   ALTER TABLE <table specification>
   <table structure change>

<table structure change> ::=
   <table change>               |
   <column change>              |
   <integrity constraint change> |
   <index change>

<integrity constraint change> ::=
   ADD <table integrity constraint>  |
   DROP PRIMARY KEY                  |
   DROP CONSTRAINT <constraint name>

<table integrity constraint> ::=
   [ CONSTRAINT [ <constraint name> ] ]
   { <primary key>              |
     <alternate key>            |
     <foreign key>              |
     <check integrity constraint> }

<primary key> ::= PRIMARY KEY <column list>

<alternate key> ::= UNIQUE <column list>

<foreign key> ::=
   FOREIGN KEY <column list> <referencing specification>

<check integrity constraint> ::= CHECK ( <condition> )

<column list> ::= ( <column name> [ { , <column name> }... ] )

<table name>        ;
<column name>       ;
<constraint name> ::= <name>
```

The syntax that is needed to add integrity constraints with an ALTER TABLE statement is identical to the syntax for table integrity constraints in the CREATE TABLE statement. We refer to Chapter 16 for this.

There is a special situation that we would like to discuss here. Imagine that there are two tables: T_1 and T_2. And imagine that both have a foreign key referring to the other table. This is called *cross-referential integrity*. Cross-referential integrity can cause problems. If T_1 is defined and T_2 does not yet exist, the foreign key cannot be defined. This problem can be solved by adding one of the two foreign keys later with an ALTER TABLE statement.

Example 18.17: Create the two tables T_1 and T_2.

```
CREATE TABLE T1
       (A INTEGER NOT NULL PRIMARY KEY,
        B INTEGER NOT NULL)

CREATE TABLE T2
       (A INTEGER NOT NULL PRIMARY KEY,
        B INTEGER NOT NULL CONSTRAINT C1 CHECK (B > 0),
        CONSTRAINT FK1 FOREIGN KEY (A) REFERENCES T1 (A))

ALTER TABLE T1
   ADD CONSTRAINT FK2 FOREIGN KEY (A) REFERENCES T2 (A)
```

Explanation: After these three statements, the cross-referential integrity is defined.

To remove integrity constraints, you can use the DROP version of the ALTER TABLE statement. Here are some examples:

Example 18.18: Delete the primary key from the PLAYERS table.

```
ALTER TABLE PLAYERS DROP PRIMARY KEY
```

Example 18.19: Delete the foreign key called FK$_2$ that refers from the T_1 to the T_2 table; see the previous example.

```
ALTER TABLE T1 DROP CONSTRAINT FK2
```

With DROP CONSTRAINT, you can remove all kinds of integrity constraints, including primary and alternate keys and check integrity constraints as well.

Example 18.20: Delete the check integrity constraint called C_1 that is defined on the B column of the T_2 table.

```
ALTER TABLE T2 DROP CONSTRAINT C1
```

It is easier to delete an integrity constraint later if a name has explicitly been specified because then it is not necessary to find out which name SQL has assigned to it.

18.7 Answers

18.1

```
ALTER TABLE COMMITTEE_MEMBERS
    CHANGE POSITION COMMITTEE_POSITION CHAR(20)
```

18.2

```
ALTER TABLE COMMITTEE_MEMBERS
    MODIFY COMMITTEE_POSITION CHAR(30)
```

18.3

```
ALTER TABLE PLAYERS
    ALTER TOWN SET DEFAULT 'Stratford'
```

19

Designing Tables

19.1 Introduction

I n Chapters 15, "Creating Tables," and 16, "Specifying Integrity Constraints," we
have shown which statements we can use to create tables with their integrity constraints. This chapter looks more closely at the process of *designing a database structure.*
Before you can create a database, you must have designed a structure for it. During this
design process, you decide which tables should be defined and which columns should
be included in each table. The process of designing databases, then, is comparable to the
work of an architect, while creating tables resembles the construction job.

For any given application, there are generally several possible table structures. This
choice can be subject to different factors:

■ Storage space available
■ Maximum acceptable processing time for updates
■ Maximum acceptable processing time for SELECT statements
■ Security

Before starting the actual design, the designer must decide which factors are most
relevant to the situation. Is it essential to save as much storage space as possible? Should
SELECT statements take, at most, 3 seconds of processing time? Or should we take into
consideration several different factors simultaneously?

Having to consider a combination of factors nearly always leads to conflicts. A sav-
ings in storage space, for example, means that SELECT statements will take longer to
process. Looking at this another way, if every SELECT statement must be processed
quickly, much of the data must be stored repeatedly, and this, of course, requires more
storage space. Additionally, data redundancy leads to slower processing of updates
because each logical update requires an update to more than one table.

Many different techniques exist for designing a table structure. We do not describe
these techniques here because they fall outside the context of this book. However, in the
following sections, we present ten basic guidelines for designing a database structure. For
each guideline, we try to indicate its influence on the first four factors listed previously.

19.2   Which Tables and Columns?

Determining the tables and columns in a database design is the most important aspect of the design process. Much has already been written about the subject. We concentrate only on the most important guidelines. You can find more comprehensive coverage of the database design process in [DATE95] and [SIMS04].

Guideline 1: Define a Primary Key for Each Table

If a table has several candidate keys, you must make a choice. Always choose the one that consists of the smallest number of columns as the primary key. This simplifies the process of joining tables for, among other things, SELECT statements.

If this criterion does not lead to a good solution for some reason, choose the column that contains "internal" values. By "internal," we mean values for which your own organization is the owner. For example, do not choose passport number as a key because the government is the owner of this number.

If this criterion does not work, choose the primary key that uses the least amount of storage space—for example, a CHAR(5) column instead of a VARCHAR(30) column.

Guideline 2: Each Determinant in a Table
Must Be a Candidate Key of That Table

This guideline is often referred to in the literature as the Boyce-Codd normal form; see, among others, [DATE95].

This is the first time we have used the term *determinant*, so it needs to be explained. Column A is a determinant of column B if, for each different value in A there is, at most, one associated value in B. The PLAYERNO column in the PLAYERS table, for example, is a determinant of all other columns in the table. A determinant can consist of more than one column.

Imagine that the column DETER in table T is a determinant of column C. The following SELECT statement will *never* return a result (work it out for yourself):

```
SELECT    DETER
FROM      T
GROUP BY  DETER
HAVING    COUNT(DISTINCT C) > 1
```

Here is an example of a table design that does not follow the second guideline:

```
PLAYERNO  NAME       TEAMNO  DIVISION
--------  ---------  ------  --------
       6  Parmenter  1       first
      44  Baker      1       first
      27  Collins    2       second
     104  Moorman    2       second
```

The PLAYERNO column is the primary key. Thus, the table follows the first guideline. The determinant of the NAME column is PLAYERNO. This is also true for TEAMNO and DIVISION; every PLAYERNO belongs to, at most, one TEAMNO and one DIVISION. However, TEAMNO is also a determinant of DIVISION because every TEAMNO has, at most, one associated DIVISION. TEAMNO, then, is a determinant but not a candidate key. The conclusion is that the table does not follow the second guideline.

The most significant disadvantage of a table that does not comply with the second guideline is that certain "facts" are recorded several times. In the previous example, the fact that team 1 plays in the first division is recorded more than once. This situation leads to more complex updating requirements and inefficient use of storage space and, finally, to inconsistent data.

Guideline 3: Do Not Use Repeating Groups in a Table

Columns that contain the same type of data, have the same meaning, and are placed in the same table form what is known a *repeating group*. Imagine that each player must register the first name of his or her children (to participate in a club Christmas party). A possible table structure for the CHILDREN table is:

```
PLAYERNO  CNAME1   CNAME2  CNAME3
--------  -------  ------  ------
       6  Milly    Diana   Judy
      44  ?        ?       ?
      83  William  Jimmy   ?
```

The columns CNAME1, CNAME2, and CNAME3 form a repeating group. They contain the same type of data—that is, the name of a child. They also have the same significance; they are children belonging to one player. Up to three children may be registered for each player. What are the consequences of such a design, for example, for SELECT and UPDATE statements? An example of each follows.

Example 19.1: Find, for each player, the number of registered children.

```
SELECT    PLAYERNO, 0
FROM      CHILDREN
WHERE     CNAME1 IS NULL
AND       CNAME2 IS NULL
AND       CNAME3 IS NULL
UNION
SELECT    PLAYERNO, 1
FROM      CHILDREN
WHERE     CNAME1 IS NOT NULL
AND       CNAME2 IS NULL
AND       CNAME3 IS NULL
UNION
SELECT    PLAYERNO, 2
FROM      CHILDREN
WHERE     CNAME1 IS NOT NULL
AND       CNAME2 IS NOT NULL
AND       CNAME3 IS NULL
UNION
SELECT    PLAYERNO, 3
FROM      CHILDREN
WHERE     CNAME1 IS NOT NULL
AND       CNAME2 IS NOT NULL
AND       CNAME3 IS NOT NULL
UNION
SELECT    PLAYERNO, 0
FROM      PLAYERS
WHERE     PLAYERNO NOT IN
          (SELECT    PLAYERNO
           FROM      CHILDREN)
```

And the result is:

```
PLAYERNO
------------------
        6         3
       44         0
       83         2
        2         0
       27         0
        :         :
```

Example 19.2: The name Diana (one of the children belonging to player 6) must be changed to Diane.

First, we look for the column in which Diana is recorded:

```
SELECT    *
FROM      CHILDREN
WHERE     PLAYERNO = 6
```

From the result, we see that the column CNAME2 must be updated. The UPDATE statement looks like this:

```
UPDATE    CHILDREN
SET       CNAME2 = 'Diane'
WHERE     PLAYERNO = 6
```

Allowing repeating groups makes many statements rather complex. The CHILDREN table can also be designed without a repeating group:

The CHILDREN table:

```
PLAYERNO   CNAME
--------   -------
       6   Milly
       6   Diana
       6   Judy
      83   William
      83   Jimmy
```

The primary key of this CHILDREN table is formed by the columns PLAYERNO and CNAME. The formulation of the two previous statements looks as follows:

The first statement is:

```
SELECT    PLAYERNO, COUNT(*)
FROM      PLAYERS LEFT OUTER JOIN CHILDREN
          ON PLAYERS.PLAYERNO = CHILDREN.PLAYERNO
GROUP BY PLAYERNO
```

The second statement is:

```
UPDATE    CHILDREN
SET       CNAME = 'Diane'
WHERE     PLAYERNO = 6
AND       CNAME = 'Diana'
```

It seems that repeating groups often give rise to more complex statements and, therefore, should be avoided as much as possible. Moreover, the number of columns in a repeating group must be adapted to the maximum number of values possible. In the previous example, this might be as many as ten children! This applies to every row, of course, and puts excessive pressure on storage space.

Guideline 4: Do Not Concatenate Columns

The PLAYERS table consists of 13 columns. Some of these could be joined to make a single column. For example, the columns STREET, HOUSENO, and TOWN could be merged into one column called ADDRESS. This can make some SELECT statements easier to formulate.

Example 19.3: Get the address of player 44.

```
SELECT    ADDRESS
FROM      PLAYERS
WHERE     PLAYERNO = 44
```

The result is:

```
ADDRESS
--------------------------
23 Lewis Street, Inglewood
```

On the other hand, other questions are very difficult to formulate:

■ To retrieve the TOWN of a player, we have to use a complex expression in which some scalar functions are combined. We assume that the town name is preceded by a comma and a space:

```
SUBSTR(ADDRESS, LOCATE(',', ADDRESS) + 2, LENGTH(ADDRESS))
```

Note that not all SQL products support these functions. For those that do not, it is not possible to retrieve just a part of a column value with only one statement.

- When you select rows on the basis of town name, the previous expression must be used. You can be sure that this statement will take a long time to process.

- Selecting rows on the basis of the street name is not possible because the LIKE operator must be used.

- Selecting rows by house number will be impossible. Where does the house number begin? After a space? No, because some street names consist of several words. Does the house number begin at the first number? No, because some house numbers consist of letters. To answer this question, we have to include a special symbol between the street name and the house number.

- Imagine that Edgecombe Way is renamed Park Way and that this change must be reflected throughout the table. SQL must look at each row separately and possibly perform the update.

These disadvantages are specific to this example but provide a clear basis for generalization.

Exercise 19.1: Which column in the PLAYERS table does not obey the fourth guideline?

Exercise 19.2: Create an alternative design for the PLAYERS table so that it follows the second and fourth guidelines. Here, we assume that for each town there exists only one area code.

19.3 Adding Redundant Data

A design that satisfies the guidelines given in the previous section simplifies the formulation of SELECT and UPDATE statements. Processing update statements is fast because each "fact" is registered only once. Processing SELECT statements is another story. Precisely because each fact is recorded only once, many joins must be executed. Processing joins and other SELECT statements can be very time-consuming. One way to tackle this problem is to include *redundant data* in a table. Here is an example of a join and another SELECT statement, both of which can be executed faster when redundant data has been added.

Example 19.4: Get the name of each player who incurred at least one penalty.

```
SELECT   NAME, AMOUNT
FROM     PENALTIES AS PEN, PLAYERS AS P
WHERE    PEN.PLAYERNO = P.PLAYERNO
```

SQL must perform a join to process this statement. The join can be avoided by storing the NAME column as redundant data in the PENALTIES table.

The new PENALTIES table is:

PAYMENTNO	PLAYERNO	NAME	PAYMENT_DATE	AMOUNT
1	6	Parmenter	1980-12-08	100.00
2	44	Baker	1981-05-05	75.00
3	27	Collins	1983-09-10	100.00
4	104	Moorman	1984-12-08	50.00
5	44	Baker	1980-12-08	25.00
6	8	Newcastle	1980-12-08	25.00
7	44	Baker	1980-12-30	30.00
8	27	Collins	1984-11-12	75.00

The statement then becomes:

```
SELECT    NAME, AMOUNT
FROM      PENALTIES
```

This SELECT statement will definitely be executed faster than the previous one.

This method of adding redundant data is sometimes called *denormalization*. A disadvantage of denormalization is the need to store some facts more than once. The names of players, for example, are now recorded in the PLAYERS table and in the PENALTIES table. Updating the name of a player requires two separate update statements. Another disadvantage of denormalization is that recording the same fact in more than one place uses twice as much storage space. With denormalization, you must weigh the relative importance of faster execution time of SELECT statements against slower execution time of updates and the storage space needed. In practice, this means that denormalization is used more often for data warehouses than for transaction databases.

Example 19.5: Get, for each player, the total amount of penalties incurred by him or her.

```
SELECT    PLAYERNO, SUM(AMOUNT) AS TOTAL
FROM      PLAYERNO LEFT OUTER JOIN PENALTIES
          ON PLAYERS.PLAYERNO = PENALTIES.PLAYERNO
GROUP BY PLAYERNO
ORDER BY 1
```

The result is:

```
PLAYERNO    TOTAL
--------   ------
       2     0.00
       6   100.00
       7     0.00
       8    25.00
      27   175.00
      28     0.00
      39     0.00
      44   130.00
      57     0.00
      83     0.00
      95     0.00
     100     0.00
     104    50.00
     112     0.00
```

This statement could be greatly simplified if the total amount of penalties were registered in the PLAYERS table. The statement then would become:

```
SELECT    PLAYERNO, TOT_AMOUNT
FROM      PLAYERS
```

In this way, the processing time would be greatly reduced, but here also the same disadvantages as for denormalization are found: more updates and duplication of data. We have to conclude, however, that the performance of OLAP and other business intelligence tools improves considerably as a result of denormalization.

In both examples, redundancy took the form of adding one extra column. Creating an entirely new redundant table is sometimes an attractive alternative. (Invent an example for yourself.) Guideline 5 can be derived from this story now.

Guideline 5: Add Redundant Data When the Processing Time of SELECT Statements Is Not Acceptable

Exercise 19.3: Create a design for the MATCHES table so that the following query would no longer need a join. Additionally, give the changed formulation of the SELECT statement.

```
SELECT    M.MATCHNO, M.TEAMNO, T.DIVISION
FROM      MATCHES AS M INNER JOIN TEAMS AS T
          ON M.TEAMNO = T.TEAMNO
```

Exercise 19.4: Give an alternative design for the PLAYERS table so that the following query can be answered without joins and subqueries: Find the number and name of each player who has, for a given team, won more sets than the average number of sets won for any team.

19.4   Choosing a Data Type for a Column

The design of a database includes the task of choosing a data type for each column. This section presents a number of guidelines that can assist you in this choice.

Guideline 6: Use the Same Data Types for Columns That Will Be Compared with One Another

In SELECT and UPDATE statements, columns are compared with one another. The columns WON and LOST are compared in the following statement:

```
SELECT    MATCHNO
FROM      MATCHES
WHERE     WON - 2 > LOST
```

In contrast to this example, the following statement compares two columns that come from different tables:

```
SELECT    NAME
FROM      PLAYERS INNER JOIN PENALTIES
          ON PLAYERS.PLAYERNO = PENALTIES.PLAYERNO
```

Two data types are the same if the data type (CHAR, SMALLINT, and so on) and the defined length are the same.

Portability: *Some SQL products process statements that compare columns of different data types extremely slowly.*

Guideline 7: Assign a Column a Numeric Data Type Only if It Will Be Used in Calculations

If you perform calculations on values in a column, the column must be defined with a numeric data type. Otherwise, the calculations might be impossible. Sometimes, you might be inclined to give a numeric data type to a column that records specific codes (with no intrinsic significance) that consist entirely of digits (for example, the league number). The advantage of a numeric column is that it requires little storage space. Coding systems, on the other hand, change frequently. During the design, all the codes might be numeric, but the question is whether that will always be the case. Conversions from numeric to alphanumeric values, should the need arise, are not simple. Therefore, define a column as numeric only if this is necessary for calculations.

Guideline 8: Do Not Skimp on the Length of Columns

Independent of the data type, a column must have a length defined that allows its longest value to be accommodated. Work out how long the longest value is for each column. Do not assume that the largest value is one of your existing values; think also about possible future values.

Guideline 9: Do Not Use the Data Type VARCHAR for All Alphanumeric Columns

For columns with an alphanumeric data type, there is a choice between values with a variable length and values with a fixed length. Variable length has been designed to save storage space. In the first instance, it often appears to be the best choice, but be careful: It is not always as good as it seems. Columns with a variable length have two disadvantages. First, for each value in such a column, the length of the particular value is recorded (this is not visible for users). This, of course, uses extra storage space. Second, in SELECT and UPDATE statements, columns with a variable length perform more slowly than columns with a fixed length. The general guideline is to use alphanumeric data types with a variable length only if, on average, there would be at least 15 unused positions for most values.

19.5 When Should You Use NOT NULL?

When must you specify NOT NULL behind a column in a CREATE TABLE statement?

Guideline 10: Use NOT NULL When a Column Must Contain a Value for Every Row

Never use the NULL value in an artificial manner. Never use it to represent something other than an unknown value because working with NULL values in calculations can be tricky, especially in conjunction with aggregation functions (see Chapter 9, "SELECT Statement: SELECT Clause and Aggregation Functions").

> **Portability:** *Additionally, it must be stated that, for some products, such as DB2, for each value in a column that has not been defined NOT NULL, an extra (invisible) byte is stored. This byte is used by the product to indicate whether the value is NULL. In other words, a NOT NULL column uses less storage space than an identical column with the same data type, but without NOT NULL.*

Closing remark: Many more factors and guidelines can influence the design of a database structure than we have mentioned here. Nevertheless, we have discussed the most important ones in this chapter.

Exercise 19.5: Design a database for recording data about one-man shows. For each show, the name of the show and the name of the artist should be recorded. The location and date of each performance should also be recorded, as well as the names of participating musicians and their instruments—at most, two instruments for each musician. The musical setting (that is, musicians and instruments) will be the same for each performance of a particular show. Of course, each musician may take part in several shows.

Write the necessary CREATE TABLE statements, including primary and foreign keys. (Determine suitable data types for the columns yourself.)

19.6 Answers

19.1   The PHONENO column contains the area code and the subscription number. It is better, therefore, to replace it with two columns.

19.2   A determinant of the AREACODE column is the TOWN column. (For each town, there is a maximum of one area code.) A separate table must be created with the columns TOWN (primary key) and AREACODE. The AREACODE column then disappears from the PLAYERS table. The columns that remain are PLAYERNO, NAME, INITIALS, BIRTH_DATE, SEX, JOINED, STREET, HOUSENO, TOWN, SUBSCRIPNO, and LEAGUENO.

19.3 The MATCHES table must be extended with a column called DIVISION, in which the division in which the match has been played is recorded. The SELECT statement would then look like this:

```
SELECT   MATCHNO, TEAMNO, DIVISION
FROM     MATCHES
```

19.4 The PLAYERS table must have two columns added: WON and AVERAGE. The first column contains the total number of matches won by the player; the second column presents the average number of matches won. The statement would take the following form:

```
SELECT   PLAYERNO, NAME
FROM     PLAYERS
WHERE    WON > AVERAGE
```

19.5

```
CREATE TABLE PERFORMANCE
       (NAME_SHOW    CHAR(20) NOT NULL,
        LOCATION     CHAR(20) NOT NULL,
        PERF_DATE    DATE NOT NULL,
        PRIMARY KEY  (NAME_SHOW, LOCATION, PERF_DATE))

CREATE TABLE SHOWS
       (NAME_SHOW    CHAR(20) NOT NULL,
        ARTIST       CHAR(20) NOT NULL,
        PRIMARY KEY  (NAME_SHOW))

CREATE TABLE SETTING
       (NAME_SHOW    CHAR(20) NOT NULL,
        MUSICIAN     CHAR(20) NOT NULL,
        INSTRUMENT   CHAR(20) NOT NULL,
        PRIMARY KEY  (NAME_SHOW, MUSICIAN, INSTRUMENT))
```

20

Using Indexes

20.1 Introduction

Some SQL statements have a reasonably constant execution time. Examples include the CREATE TABLE and GRANT statements. It does not matter under which circumstances such statements are executed; they always need a certain execution time. There is no way to reduce their execution time. However, this is not the case for all statements. The time required to process SELECT, UPDATE, and DELETE statements varies from one statement to the next. One SELECT statement might be processed in 2 seconds, while another could take minutes. The required execution time of this type of statements can indeed be influenced.

Many techniques are available for reducing the execution time of SELECT, UPDATE, and DELETE statements. These techniques range from reformulating statements to purchasing faster computers. In this book, we discuss three of them. In Chapter 19, "Designing Tables," we looked at adding redundant data, as a result of which the execution time of certain statements can be improved. This chapter describes indexes and how their presence or absence can strongly influence execution times. In Chapter 29, "Optimization of Statements," we deal with reformulating statements. Improving execution times is also known as *optimization*.

Note in advance: The first sections that follow do not so much cover SQL statements as provide useful background information on how SQL uses indexes.

> **Portability:** *The syntax for creating and dropping indexes is reasonably the same in most SQL products. However, there are differences in how indexes work internally and how SQL products use them. Therefore, in this chapter, we keep the explanations general so that they apply to most SQL products.*

20.2   Rows, Tables, and Files

In this book, we assume that if we add rows, they are stored in tables. However, a table is a concept that SQL understands but the operating system does not. This section provides some insight into how rows are actually stored on hard disk. This information is important to understand before we concentrate on the workings of an index.

Rows are stored in *files*. In some SQL products, a file is created separately for each table. In other products, tables can also share a file, and sometimes the rows of one table can be spread over multiple files (and also over multiple hard disks).

Each file is divided into *data pages*, or *pages*, for short. Figure 20.1 is a graphical representation of a file that contains the data of the PLAYERS table. The file consists of five pages (the horizontal, gray strips form the boundaries between the pages). In other words, the data of the PLAYERS table is spread over five pages of this file.

In this example, it is clear that each page has enough space for four rows and that each page is not completely filled. How do these "gaps" arise? When new rows are added, SQL automatically stores these after the last row of the final page. If that page is full, an empty page is added to the file. So, a gap is created not during the process of adding rows, but when rows are deleted. SQL does not fill the gaps automatically. If it did, SQL would have to find an empty space when a row is added, and for large tables, this would take too much time. Imagine that the table contains one million rows and that all pages are full except for the penultimate page. If a new row had to be stored in a gap, first all other rows would have to be accessed to locate a gap. Again, this would delay the process too much; that is why rows are inserted at the end.

Figure 20.1   *The rows of a table are stored in pages*

6	Parmenter	...
44	Baker	...
83	Hope	...
		...
2	Everett	...
27	Collins	...
		...
104	Moorman	...
7	Wise	...
57	Brown	...
		...
		...
39	Bishop	...
112	Bailey	...
8	Newcastle	...
		...
100	Parmenter	...
28	Collins	...
		...
95	Miller	...

page

In this example, we have also assumed that a page consists of a maximum of four rows. How many rows really fit in a page is determined by two factors: the size of the page and the length of the rows. The size of a page depends on the operating system and the SQL product itself. Sizes such as 2K, 4K, 8K, and 32K are very common. The length of a row from the PLAYERS table is about 90 bytes. This means that approximately 45 rows would fit into a page of size 4K.

It is important to realize that pages always form the unit of I/O. If an operating system retrieves data from a hard disk, this is done page by page. Systems such as UNIX or Windows do not retrieve 2 bytes from disk. Instead, they collect the page in which these 2 bytes are stored. A database server, therefore, can ask an operating system to retrieve one page from the file, but not just one row.

Two steps are required to retrieve a row from a table. First, the page in which the row is recorded is collected from disk. Second, we have to find the row in the page. Some products handle this problem very simply: They just browse through the entire page until they find the relevant row. Because this process takes place entirely within internal memory, it is carried out relatively fast. Other products use a more direct method; each page contains a simple list with numbered entities in which the locations of all rows that occur on that page can be found. This list has a maximum number of entities and can record a certain number of locations; let us assume that this number is 256. In addition, each row has a unique identification. This *row identification* consists of two parts: a page identification and a number that indicates a row in the list. Now, we can find a row by first selecting the correct page and then retrieving the actual location of the row within the page. We return to this subject in the next section.

20.3 How Does an Index Work?

SQL has several methods of accessing rows in a table. The two best known are the *sequential access method* (also called *scanning* or *browsing*) and the *indexed access method*.

The sequential access method is best described as "browsing through a table row by row." Each row in a table is read. If only one row has to be found in a table with many rows, this method is, of course, very time-consuming and inefficient. It is comparable to going through a telephone book page by page. If you are looking for the number of someone whose name begins with an *L*, you certainly do not want to start looking under the letter *A*.

When SQL uses the indexed access method, it reads only the rows that exhibit the required characteristics. To do this, however, an *index* is necessary. An index is a type of alternative access to a table and can be compared with the index in a book.

An index in SQL is built like a *tree* consisting of a number of *nodes*. Figure 20.2 is a pictorial representation of an index. Notice that this is a simplification of what an index tree really looks like. Nevertheless, the example is detailed enough to understand how SQL handles indexes. At the top of the figure (in the light gray area) is the index itself, and at the bottom are two columns of the PLAYERS table: PLAYERNO and NAME. The nodes of the index are represented by the long rectangles. The node at the top forms the starting point of the index and is known as the *root*. Each node contains up to three values from the PLAYERNO column. Each value in a node points to another node or to a row in the PLAYERS table, and each row in the table is referenced through at least one node. A node that points to a row is called a *leaf page*. The values in a node have been ordered. For each node, apart from the root, the values in that node are always less than or equal to the value that points to that node. Leaf pages are themselves linked to one another. A leaf page has a pointer to the leaf page with the next set of values. In Figure 20.2, we represent these pointers with open arrows.

Figure 20.2   *Example of an index tree*

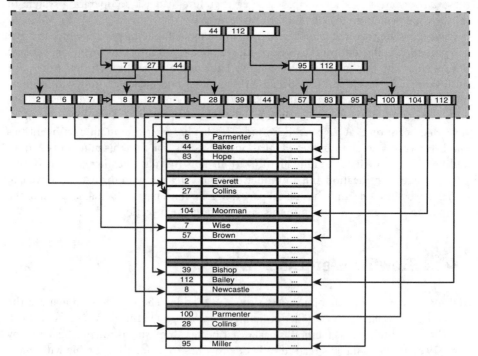

What does a pointer really look like? A pointer is nothing more than a row identification. We introduced this concept in the previous section. Because a row identification consists of two parts, the same also applies to an index pointer: the page in which the row occurs and the entity of the list that indicates the location of the row within the page.

Broadly speaking, SQL supports three algorithms for using indexes. The first algorithm is for searching rows in which a particular value occurs. The second algorithm is for browsing through an entire table or a part of a table via an ordered column. Finally, the third algorithm is used if several values of a column must be retrieved. We illustrate these algorithms with three examples. The first example is of how SQL uses the index to select particular rows.

Example 20.1: Imagine that all rows with player number 44 must be found.

Step 1.   Look for the root of the index. This root becomes the active node.

Step 2.   Is the active node a leaf page? If so, continue with step 4. If not, continue with step 3.

Step 3.   Does the active node contain the value 44? If so, the node to which this value points becomes the active node; go back to step 2. If not, choose the lowest value that is greater than 44 in the active node. The node to which this value points becomes the active node; go back to step 2.

Step 4.   Look for the value 44 in the active node. Now this value points to all pages in which rows of the PLAYERS table appear where the value of the PLAY-ERNO column is 44. Retrieve all these pages from the database for further processing.

Step 5.   Find for each page the row where the value PLAYERNO column is equal to 44.

Without browsing through all the rows, SQL has found the desired row(s). In most cases, the time spent answering this type of question can be reduced considerably if SQL can use an index.

In the next example, SQL uses the index to retrieve ordered rows from a table.

Example 20.2: Get all players ordered by player number.

Step 1.   Look for the leaf page with the lowest value. This leaf page becomes the active node.

Step 2.   Retrieve all pages to which the values in the active node are pointing for further processing.

Step 3.   If there is a subsequent leaf page, make this the active node and continue with step 2.

The disadvantage of this method is that if players are retrieved from disk, there is a good chance that a page must be fetched several times. For example, the second page in Figure 20.2 must be fetched first to retrieve player 2. Next, the first page is needed for player 6, then the third page for player 7, and finally the fourth page for player 8. So far, there is no problem. However, if player 27 is to be retrieved next, the second page must be retrieved from disk again. Meanwhile, many other pages have been fetched, and because of that, the odds are that the second page is no longer in internal memory and, therefore, cannot be read again. The conclusion is that because the rows were not ordered in the file, many pages must be fetched several times, and that does not exactly improve the processing time.

To speed up this process, most products support *clustered* indexes. Figure 20.3 contains an example. With a clustered index, the sequence of the rows in the file is determined by the index, and this can improve the execution time for the sorting process considerably. If we now retrieve the players from the file in an ordered way, each page will be fetched only once. SQL understands that when player 6 is retrieved, the correct page is already in the internal memory; the retrieval of player 2 caused this. The same applies to player 7.

Figure 20.3   *Example of a clustered index*

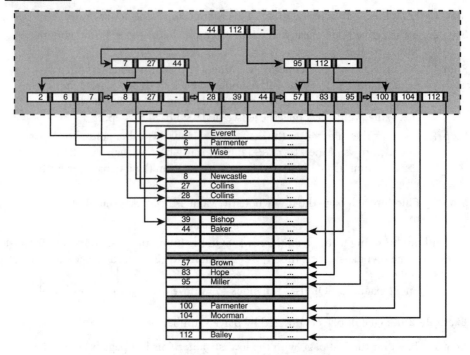

Clustered indexes offer no additional advantages for direct access (the first algorithm) to rows. Working with this index form is recommended when you want to retrieve ordered rows often.

The third algorithm is a combination of the first two.

Example 20.3: Get all players with number 39 up to and including 95.

Step 1.   Look for the root of the index. This root becomes the active node.

Step 2.   Is the active node a leaf page? If so, continue with step 4. If not, continue with step 3.

Step 3.   Does the active node contain the value 39? If so, the node to which this value points becomes the active node; go back to step 2. If not, choose the lowest value that is greater than 39 in the active node. The node to which this value points becomes the active node; go back to step 2.

Step 4.   Look for the value 39 in the active node.

Step 5.   In the active node, retrieve all rows that belong to the values between 39 and 95. If 95 appears in this node, you are ready. Otherwise, continue with the following step.

Step 6.   If there is a subsequent leaf page, make this the active node and continue with step 5.

This algorithm can be useful when a SELECT statement contains conditions in which, for example, BETWEEN, a greater than operator, or certain LIKE operators occur.

Here are some remarks concerning indexes:

- If values in a table are updated, or if rows are added or deleted, SQL automatically updates the index. So, the index tree is always consistent with the contents of the table.

- In the previous table, an index was defined on the PLAYERNO column of the PLAYERS table. This is the primary key of this table and contains no duplicate values. An index can also be defined on a nonunique column, such as the NAME column. The result of this is that one value in a leaf page points to multiple rows—one pointer for each row in which the value occurs.

- It is possible to define many indexes on a table, but because a clustered index affects the way in which rows are stored, each table may contain only one clustered index.

- Indexes can also be defined on combinations of values. Those are called *composite indexes*. Each value in a node is then a concatenation of the individual values. The leaf pages point to rows in which that combination of values appears.

Several other important observations can be made about the use of indexes. The two most important are these:

- Nodes of an index are just like rows in a table, stored in files. Therefore, an index takes up physical storage space (just like an index in a book).

- Updates to tables can lead to updates to indexes. When an index must be updated, SQL tries, where it can, to fill the gaps in the nodes to complete the process as quickly as possible; however, an index can become so "full" that new nodes must be added. This can necessitate a total *reorganization* of the index which can be very time-consuming.

Several types of indexes exist. In this section, we discussed what is called the *B-tree* index. The letter *B* stands for "balanced." A characteristic feature of a B-tree index is that all the branches of the tree have roughly the same length. Later in this chapter, we describe other types of index.

As we already mentioned, this section presents a very simplified picture of the workings of an index. In practice, for example, a node in an index tree can accommodate not just three, but many values. For a more detailed description of indexes, see [DATE95].

20.4 Processing a SELECT Statement: The Steps

Chapter 5, "SELECT Statement: Common Elements," described which clauses are executed successively during the processing of a SELECT statement. These clauses form a *basic strategy* for processing a statement. In a basic strategy, we assume sequential access to the data. This section discusses how the use of an index can change the basic strategy to an *optimized strategy*.

SQL tries to choose the most efficient strategy for processing each statement. This analysis is performed by a module within SQL, called the *optimizer*. (The analysis of statements is also referred to as *query optimization*.) The optimizer defines a number of alternative strategies for each statement. It estimates which strategy is likely to be the most efficient, based upon factors such as the expected execution time, the number of rows, and the presence of indexes. (In the absence of indexes, this can be the basic strategy.) SQL then executes the statement according to its chosen strategy.

Following are some examples to show what optimized processing strategies can look like.

Example 20.4: Get all information about player 44. (We assume that there is an index defined on the PLAYERNO column.)

```
SELECT    *
FROM      PLAYERS
WHERE     PLAYERNO = 44
```

The **FROM** clause: Usually, all rows would be retrieved from the PLAYERS table. Speeding up the processing by using an index means that only the rows in which the value in the PLAYERNO column is 44 are fetched.

The intermediate result is:

```
PLAYERNO   NAME    ...
--------   -----   ---
      44   Baker   ...
```

The **WHERE** clause: In this example, this clause was processed simultaneously with the FROM clause.

The **SELECT** clause: All columns are presented.

The difference between the basic strategy and this "optimized" strategy can be represented in another way.

The basic strategy is:

```
RESULT := [];
FOR EACH P IN PLAYERS DO
    IF P.PLAYERNO = 44 THEN
        RESULT :+ P;
ENDFOR;
```

The optimized strategy is:

```
RESULT := [];
FOR EACH P IN PLAYERS WHERE PLAYERNO = 44 DO
    RESULT :+ P;
ENDFOR;
```

With the first strategy, all rows are fetched by the FOR EACH statement. The second strategy works much more selectively. When an index is used, only those rows in which the player number is 44 are retrieved.

Example 20.5: Get the player number and town of each player whose number is less than 10 and who lives in Stratford; order the result by player number.

```
SELECT    PLAYERNO, TOWN
FROM      PLAYERS
WHERE     PLAYERNO < 10
AND       TOWN = 'Stratford'
ORDER BY  PLAYERNO
```

The **FROM** clause: Fetch all rows where the player number is less than 10. Again, use the index on the PLAYERNO column. Fetch the rows in ascending order, thus accounting for the ORDER BY clause. This is simple because the values in an index are always ordered.

The intermediate result is:

```
PLAYERNO   ...   TOWN         ...
--------   ---   ---------    ---
       2   ...   Stratford    ...
       6   ...   Stratford    ...
       7   ...   Stratford    ...
       8   ...   Inglewood    ...
```

The **WHERE** clause: The WHERE clause specifies two conditions. Each row in the intermediate result satisfies the first condition, which has already been evaluated in the FROM clause. Now, only the second condition must be evaluated.

The intermediate result is:

```
PLAYERNO   ...   TOWN        ...
--------   ---   ---------   ---
       2   ...   Stratford   ...
       6   ...   Stratford   ...
       7   ...   Stratford   ...
```

The **SELECT** clause: Two columns are selected.
The intermediate result is:

```
PLAYERNO   TOWN
--------   ---------
       2   Stratford
       6   Stratford
       7   Stratford
```

The **ORDER BY** clause: Because of the use of an index during the processing of the FROM clause, no extra sorting needs to be done. The end result, then, is the same as the last intermediate result shown.

Next, we show the basic strategy and the optimized strategy for this example.

The basic strategy is:

```
RESULT := [];
FOR EACH P IN PLAYERS DO
   IF (P.PLAYERNO < 10)
   AND (P.TOWN = 'Stratford') THEN
      RESULT :+ P;
ENDFOR;
```

The optimized strategy is:

```
RESULT := [];
FOR EACH P IN PLAYERS WHERE PLAYERNO < 10 DO
   IF P.TOWN = 'Stratford' THEN
      RESULT :+ P;
ENDFOR;
```

Example 20.6: Get the name and initials of each player who lives in the same town as player 44.

```
SELECT    NAME, INITIALS
FROM      PLAYERS
WHERE     TOWN =
          (SELECT    TOWN
           FROM      PLAYERS
           WHERE     PLAYERNO = 44)
```

Here are both strategies.
The basic strategy is:

```
RESULT := [];
FOR EACH P IN PLAYERS DO
   HELP := FALSE;
   FOR EACH P44 IN PLAYERS DO
      IF (P44.TOWN = P.TOWN)
      AND (P44.PLAYERNO = 44) THEN
         HELP := TRUE;
   ENDFOR;
   IF HELP = TRUE THEN
      RESULT :+ P;
ENDFOR;
```

The optimized strategy is:

```
RESULT := [];
FIND P44 IN PLAYERS WHERE PLAYERNO = 44;
FOR EACH P IN PLAYERS WHERE TOWN = P44.TOWN DO
   RESULT :+ P;
ENDFOR;
```

These were three relatively simple examples. As the statements become more complex, it also becomes more difficult for SQL to determine the optimal strategy. This, of course, also adds to the processing time. There is a noticeable quality difference among the optimizers of the various SQL products. Some SQL products have reasonably good optimizers, but others seldom find an optimal strategy and choose the basic strategy.

If you want to know more about the optimization of SELECT statements, see [KIM85]. However, you do not actually need this knowledge to understand SQL statements, which is why we have given only a summary of the topic.

Exercise 20.1: For the following two statements, write the basic strategy and an optimized strategy; assume that there is an index defined on each column.

1.

```
SELECT    *
FROM      TEAMS
WHERE     TEAMNO > 1
AND       DIVISION = 'second'
```

2.

```
SELECT    P.PLAYERNO
FROM      PLAYERS AS P, MATCHES AS M
WHERE     P.PLAYERNO = M.PLAYERNO
AND       BIRTH_DATE > '1963-01-01'
```

20.5 Creating Indexes

The definition of the CREATE INDEX statement is as follows:

```
<create index statement> ::=
    CREATE <index type> INDEX <index name>
    ON <table specification>
    ( <column in index> [ { , <column in index> }... ] )

<index type> ::= UNIQUE | CLUSTERED

<column in index> ::= <column name> [ ASC | DESC ]
```

Example 20.7: Create an index on the POSTCODE column of the PLAYERS table.

```
CREATE    INDEX PLAY_PC
ON        PLAYERS (POSTCODE ASC)
```

Explanation: In this example, a nonunique index is created (correctly). The inclusion of ASC or DESC indicates whether the index should be built in ascending (ASC) or descending (DESC) order. If neither is specified, SQL takes ASC as its default. If a certain column in a SELECT statement is sorted in descending order, processing is quicker if a descending-order index is defined on that column.

Example 20.8: Create a compound index on the columns WON and LOST of the MATCHES table.

```
CREATE    INDEX MAT_WL
ON        MATCHES (WON, LOST)
```

Explanation: Multiple columns may be included in the definition of index, as long as they all belong to the same table.

Example 20.9: Create a unique index on the columns NAME and INITIALS of the PLAYERS table.

```
CREATE    UNIQUE INDEX NAMEINIT
ON        PLAYERS (NAME, INITIALS)
```

Explanation: After this statement has been entered, SQL prevents two equal combinations of name and initials from being inserted into the PLAYERS table. The same could have been achieved by defining the column combination as alternate key.

Portability: *For some SQL products, a column on which a unique index has been defined can contain one NULL value at the most, whereas a column with a nonunique index can contain multiple NULL values.*

Example 20.10: Create a clustered and unique index on the PLAYERNO column of the PLAYERS table:

```
CREATE    UNIQUE CLUSTERED INDEX PLAYERS_CLUSTERED
ON        PLAYERS (PLAYERNO)
```

Explanation: After this statement has been entered, the index makes sure that rows are recorded on hard disk in an ordered way; see the explanation of Example 20.1.

It should be noted that MySQL does not support clustered indexes.

Indexes can be created at any time. You do not have to create all the indexes for a table right after the CREATE TABLE statement. You can also create indexes on tables that already have data in them. Obviously, creating a unique index on a table in which the column concerned already contains duplicate values is not possible. SQL notes this and does not create the index. The user has to remove the duplicate values first. The following SELECT statement helps locate the duplicate C values (C is the column on which the index must be defined):

```
SELECT    C
FROM      T
GROUP BY  C
HAVING    COUNT(*) > 1
```

Indexes can also be entered with an ALTER TABLE statement; see the following definition.

```
<alter table statement> ::=
    ALTER TABLE <table specification> <table structure change>

<table structure change> ::=
    <table change>                 |
    <column change>                |
    <integrity constraint change>  |
    <index change>
```

(continued)

```
<index change> ::=
   ADD <index type> INDEX <index name>
   ( <column in index> [ { , <column in index> }... ] )

<index type> ::= UNIQUE | CLUSTERED

<column in index> ::= <column name> [ ASC | DESC ]
```

Example 20.11: Create a nonunique index on the DIVISION column of the TEAMS table.

```
ALTER TABLE TEAMS
ADD    INDEX TEAMS_DIVISION USING BTREE (DIVISION)
```

20.6 Dropping Indexes

The DROP INDEX statement is used to remove indexes.

```
<drop index statement> ::=
   DROP INDEX <index name>
```

Example 20.12: Remove the three indexes that have been defined in the previous examples.

```
DROP INDEX PLAY_PC

DROP INDEX MAT_WL

DROP INDEX NAMEINIT
```

Explanation: When you drop an index, the index type is not mentioned. In other words, you cannot specify the words UNIQUE and CLUSTERED.

20.7 Indexes and Primary Keys

Many SQL products (including MySQL) create a unique index automatically if a primary or alternate key is included within a CREATE TABLE statement. The name of the index is determined by the SQL product itself.

Example 20.13: Create the T1 table with one primary key and three alternate keys.

```
CREATE TABLE T1
        (COL1    INTEGER NOT NULL,
         COL2    DATE NOT NULL UNIQUE,
         COL3    INTEGER NOT NULL,
         COL4    INTEGER NOT NULL,
         PRIMARY KEY (COL1, COL4),
         UNIQUE (COL3, COL4),
         UNIQUE (COL3, COL1) )
```

After the table has been created, SQL executes the following CREATE INDEX statements behind the scenes:

```
CREATE UNIQUE INDEX "PRIMARY" USING BTREE
ON      T1 (COL1, COL4)

CREATE UNIQUE INDEX COL2 USING BTREE
ON      T1 (COL2)

CREATE UNIQUE INDEX COL3 USING BTREE
ON      T1 (COL3, COL4)

CREATE UNIQUE INDEX COL3_2 USING BTREE
ON      T1 (COL3, COL1)
```

Be sure that the name PRIMARY is placed between double quotes because it is a reserved word.

20.8   The Big PLAYERS_XXL Table

In the next sections, as well as in other chapters, we use a special version of the PLAYERS table. This new table contains the same columns as the original PLAYERS table. The difference, however, is that that table might hold thousands of rows and not just 14. That is why the table is called PLAYERS_XXL.

The original PLAYERS table contains normal values, such as Inglewood and Parmenter. The PLAYERS_XXL table contains artificially created data. The POSTCODE column, for example, contains values such as p4 and p25, and the STREET column contains values as street164 and street83. The following sections show how this big table can be created and filled.

Example 20.14: Create the PLAYERS_XXL table.

```
CREATE TABLE PLAYERS_XXL
        (PLAYERNO        INTEGER NOT NULL PRIMARY KEY,
         NAME            CHAR(15) NOT NULL,
         INITIALS        CHAR(3) NOT NULL,
         BIRTH_DATE      DATE,
         SEX             CHAR(1) NOT NULL,
         JOINED          SMALLINT NOT NULL,
         STREET          VARCHAR(30) NOT NULL,
         HOUSENO         CHAR(4),
         POSTCODE        CHAR(6),
         TOWN            VARCHAR(30) NOT NULL,
         PHONENO         CHAR(13),
         LEAGUENO        CHAR(4))
```

Example 20.15: Create the stored procedure FILL_PLAYERS_XXL next.

```
CREATE PROCEDURE FILL_PLAYERS_XXL
    (IN NUMBER_PLAYERS INTEGER)
BEGIN
    DECLARE COUNTER INTEGER;
    TRUNCATE TABLE PLAYERS_XXL;
    COMMIT WORK;
    SET COUNTER = 1;
    WHILE COUNTER <= NUMBER_PLAYERS DO
      INSERT INTO PLAYERS_XXL VALUES(
```

```
      COUNTER,
      CONCAT('name',CAST(COUNTER AS CHAR(10))),
      CASE MOD(COUNTER,2) WHEN 0 THEN 'vl1' ELSE 'vl2' END,
      DATE('1960-01-01') + INTERVAL (MOD(COUNTER,300)) MONTH,
      CASE MOD(COUNTER,20) WHEN 0 THEN 'F' ELSE 'M' END,
      1980 + MOD(COUNTER,20),
      CONCAT('street',CAST(COUNTER /10 AS UNSIGNED INTEGER)),
      CAST(CAST(COUNTER /10 AS UNSIGNED INTEGER)+1 AS CHAR(4)),
      CONCAT('p',MOD(COUNTER,50)),
      CONCAT('town',MOD(COUNTER,10)),
      '070-6868689',
      CASE MOD(COUNTER,3) WHEN 0 THEN '0' ELSE COUNTER END);
    IF MOD(COUNTER,1000) = 0 THEN
      COMMIT WORK;
    END IF;
    SET COUNTER = COUNTER + 1;
  END WHILE;
  COMMIT WORK;
  UPDATE PLAYERS_XXL SET LEAGUENO = NULL WHERE LEAGUENO = '0';
  COMMIT WORK;
END
```

Explanation: After this stored procedure has been created, the table is not yet filled.

Example 20.16: Fill the PLAYERS_XXL table.

```
CALL FILL_PLAYERS_XXL(100000)
```

Explanation: With this statement, the PLAYERS_XXL table is filled with 100,000 rows. The stored procedure begins with emptying the table completely. After that, as many rows as specified in the CALL statement will be added.

Example 20.17: Create the following indexes on the PLAYERS_XXL table.

```
CREATE INDEX PLAYERS_XXL_INITIALS
   ON PLAYERS_XXL(INITIALS)

CREATE INDEX PLAYERS_XXL_POSTCODE
   ON PLAYERS_XXL(POSTCODE)

CREATE INDEX PLAYERS_XXL_STREET
   ON PLAYERS_XXL(STREET)
```

20.9 Choosing Columns for Indexes

To be absolutely sure that inefficient processing of SELECT statements is not due to the absence of an index, you could create an index on every column and combination of columns. If you intend to enter only SELECT statements against the data, this could well be a good approach. However, such a solution raises a number of problems; not least is the cost of index storage space. Another important disadvantage is that each update (INSERT, UPDATE, or DELETE statement) requires a corresponding index update and reduces the processing speed. So, a choice has to be made. We discuss some guidelines next.

20.9.1 A Unique Index on Candidate Keys

In CREATE TABLE statements, we can specify primary and alternate keys. The result is that the relevant column(s) will never contain duplicate values. It is recommended that an index be defined on each candidate key so that the uniqueness of new values can be checked quickly. In fact, as mentioned in Section 20.7, SQL automatically creates a unique index for each candidate key.

20.9.2 An Index on Foreign Keys

Joins can take a long time to execute if there are no indexes defined on the join columns. For a large percentage of joins, the join columns are also keys of the tables concerned. They can be primary and alternate keys, but they may also be foreign keys. According to the first rule of thumb, you should define an index on the primary and alternate key columns. What remains now are indexes on foreign keys.

20.9.3 An Index on Columns Included in Selection Criteria

In some cases, SELECT, UPDATE, and DELETE statements can be executed faster if an index has been defined on the columns named in the WHERE clause.
    Example:

```
SELECT    *
FROM      PLAYERS
WHERE     TOWN = 'Stratford'
```

    Rows are selected on the basis of the value in the TOWN column, and processing this statement could be more efficient if there were an index on this column. This was discussed extensively in the earlier sections of this chapter.

An index is worthwhile not just when the = operator is used, but also for <, <=, >, and >=. (Note that the <> operator does not appear in this list.) However, this gains time only when the number of rows selected is a small percentage of the number of rows in the table.

This section started with "In some cases." So, when is it necessary to define an index, and when is it not? This depends on several factors, of which the most important are the number of rows in the table (or the cardinality of the table), the number of different values in the column concerned (or the cardinality of the column), and the distribution of values within the column. We explain these rules and illustrate them with some figures resulting from a test performed with SQL.

This test uses the PLAYERS_XXL table; see the previous section. The results of the tests are represented in three diagrams; see Figure 20.4. Diagrams (a), (b), and (c) contain the processing times of the following SELECT statements, respectively:

```
SELECT    COUNT(*)
FROM      PLAYERS_XXL
WHERE     INITIALS = 'in1'

SELECT    COUNT(*)
FROM      PLAYERS_XXL
WHERE     POSTCODE = 'p25'

SELECT    COUNT(*)
FROM      PLAYERS_XXL
WHERE     STREET = 'street164'
```

Each SELECT statement has been executed on the PLAYERS_XXL table with three different sizes: small (100,000 rows), medium (500,000 rows), and large (1,000,000 rows). Each statement has also been executed with (light gray bars) and without (dark gray bars) an index. Each of the three statements was run in six different environments. To give reliable figures, each statement was run several times in each environment, and the average processing speed is shown in seconds in the diagrams.

It is important to know that the INITIALS column contains only two different values, in1 and in2; the POSTCODE column contains 50 different values; and, finally, in the STREET column, every value occurs ten times at the most. All this means that the first SELECT statement contains a condition on a column with a low cardinality, the third statement has a condition on a column with a high cardinality, and the second statement has a condition on a column with an average cardinality.

The following rules can be derived from the results. First, all three diagrams show that the larger the table is, the bigger the impact of the index is. Of course, we can define an index on a table consisting of 20 rows, but the effect will be minimal. Whether a table is large enough for it to be worth defining an index depends entirely on the system on which the application runs. You have to try for yourself.

Figure 20.4   *The impact of the cardinality of a column on the processing speed*

(a)

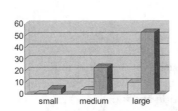

(b)

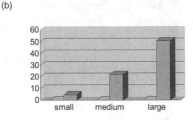

(c)

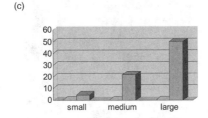

Second, the diagrams show that the effect of an index on a column with a low car-dinality (so few different values) is minimal; see diagram (a) in Figure 20.4. As the table becomes larger, the processing speed starts to improve somewhat, but it remains mini-mal. For the third statement with a condition on the STREET column, the opposite applies. Here, the presence of an index has a major impact on the processing speed. Moreover, as the database gets larger, that difference becomes more apparent. Diagram (b) in Figure 20.4 confirms the results for a table with an average cardinality.

The third factor that is significant in deciding whether you will define an index is the distribution of the values within a column. In the previous statements, each column concerned had an equal distribution of values. Each value occurred just as many times within the column. What if that is not the case? Figure 20.5 shows the results of the following two statements:

```
SELECT    COUNT (*)
FROM      PLAYERS_XXL
WHERE     SEX = 'M'
```

```
SELECT    COUNT(*)
FROM      PLAYERS_XXL
WHERE     SEX = 'F'
```

For these tests, the division of the values in the SEX column were as follows: The M value was present in 95% of the rows, and the F value in 5%. This is an extreme example of a nonequal distribution and indicates the difference clearly. In diagram (a) in Figure 20.5, we can see that the impact of the index is minimal, while the impact in diagram (b) in that figure is large. If an index is defined, counting all women in the large PLAYERS table is carried out approximately 180 times faster.

Figure 20.5   *The impact on the processing speed of the distribution of values within a column*

(a)

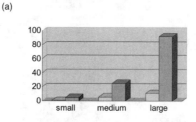

(b)

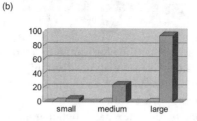

20.9.4 An Index on a Combination of Columns

If a WHERE clause contains an AND operator, an index is usually defined on the combination of columns to ensure a more efficient processing.

Example:

```
SELECT    *
FROM      PLAYERS
WHERE     NAME = 'Collins'
AND       INITIALS = 'DD'
```

The associated index is:

```
CREATE     INDEX NAMEINIT
ON         PLAYERS (NAME, INITIALS)
```

In some cases, when you are executing such a SELECT statement, it can suffice to have an index on only one of the columns. Imagine that duplicate names seldom occur in the NAME column and that this is the only column with an index. Usually, SQL will find all the rows that satisfy the condition NAME = 'Collins' by using this index. Only infrequently will it retrieve a few too many rows. In this case, an index on the combination of columns will take up more storage space than necessary and will not significantly improve the processing of the SELECT statement.

Indexes defined on combinations of columns are also used for selections in which only the first column (or columns) of the index are specified. Therefore, SQL uses the previous NAMEINIT index to process the condition NAME = 'Collins' but not for INITIALS = 'DD' because the INITIALS column is not the first one in the NAMEINIT index.

20.9.5 An Index on Columns Used for Sorting

If SQL needs to sort the result of a SELECT statement by a column that has no index, a separate (time-consuming) sort process must be performed. This extra sorting can be avoided if you define a clustered index on the relevant column. When the rows are fetched from the database (with the FROM clause), this index can be used. The intermediate result from the FROM clause is already ordered by the correct column. After that, no extra sorting is necessary. This rule is valid only if the column concerned does not contain many NULL values (because NULL values are not stored in an index), and if the SELECT statement does not have a WHERE clause with a condition that can be optimized.

When exactly does SQL perform a sort? If you add an ORDER BY clause to a SELECT statement, there is a good chance that SQL performs a sort. In addition, when columns are to be grouped (with the GROUP BY clause), all the rows must be sorted first. SQL can process a GROUP BY clause more quickly when the rows are already ordered. If you use DISTINCT in the SELECT clause, all rows must be ordered (behind the scenes) to determine whether they are equal. Therefore, the order rule is again applicable: SQL can process DISTINCT more quickly when the rows are already ordered.

Finally, note that it naturally makes little sense to define two indexes on the same column or combination of columns. Therefore, consult the COLUMNS_IN_INDEX table to check whether an index has already been defined on a column or on a combination of columns.

20.10 Special Index Forms

For a long time, SQL products supported only the B-tree index form, as described in previous sections. Other index forms have now been added, mainly because of the increasing popularity of data warehousing (see Section 1.8, in Chapter 1, "Introduction to SQL"). In this section, we discuss five types: the multitable index, the virtual column index, the selective index, the hash index, and the bitmap index.

> **Portability:** *Not all SQL products support these new index forms. MySQL, for example, does not; therefore, it is not possible to try them with this product. The products that do support them have all implemented different syntaxes. That is why we use an imaginary syntax in the examples.*

20.10.1 The Multitable Index

In the previous sections, an index could be defined only on columns of the same table. For *multitable indexes* (also called *join* indexes), this restriction does not apply. This type of index enables you to define an index on columns of two or more tables.

Example 20.18: Create a multitable index on the PLAYERNO columns of the PLAYERS and MATCHES table.

```
CREATE  INDEX PLAY_MAT
ON      PLAYERS(PLAYERNO),  MATCHES(PLAYERNO)
```

The advantage of this multitable index is that if the two tables are linked with a join to PLAYERNO, this join can be processed very quickly. This is the main reason why this type of index has been added. Try to imagine that the pointers point from a player number (in the index) to multiple rows in different tables.

The index tree that is built for a multitable index is still a B-tree. The only difference is what is stored in the leaf pages.

20.10.2 The Virtual Column Index

The second type that we discuss here is the *virtual column index*. This type of index defines an index not on an entire column, but on an expression.

Example 20.19: Create a virtual column index on the result of the expression (WON − LOST)/2 in the MATCHES table.

```
CREATE  INDEX MAT_HALFBALANCE
ON      MATCHES((WON - LOST)/2)
```

Explanation: Instead of storing the values of the columns in the index tree, first the expression is calculated for each row of the table, and the results are recorded in the index tree. The values in the index tree point to the rows in which the result of the expression is equal to that value. Certain restrictions apply to the expression that may be used in the index definition. For example, aggregation functions and subqueries are not permitted.

The main advantage of this index is the improvement of the processing speed of statements in which the relevant expression in the WHERE clause is used. The index MAT_HALFBALANCE increases the performance of this SELECT statement.

```
SELECT  *
FROM    MATCHES
WHERE   (WON - LOST)/2 > 1
```

The index tree of a virtual column index also has the structure of a B-tree. The main difference is that none of the values stored in the index tree is a value that occurs in the table itself.

20.10.3 The Selective Index

For a *selective index*, only some of the rows are indexed, in contrast to a "normal" B-tree index. Imagine that the MATCHES table contains one million rows and that most users are mainly interested in the data of the last two years, which makes up only 200,000 rows. All their questions contain the condition in which the date is not older than two years. However, other users need the other 800,000 rows. For indexes, the more rows there are, the larger the index tree becomes and the slower it is. So, for a large group of users, the index is unnecessarily large and slow. Selective indexes can be used to prevent this.

Example 20.20: Create a selective index on the PAYMENT_DATE column of the PENAL-TIES table.

```
CREATE  INDEX PEN_PAYMENT_DATE
ON      PENALTIES
WHERE   PAYMENT_DATE > '1996-12-31'
```

Explanation: A WHERE clause is used to indicate which rows in the PENALTIES table need to be indexed. In this case, the optimizer must be smart enough not only to use the index for statements in which information is requested concerning penalties that were paid after 1996; it also has to access the table directly for those rows that have not been indexed.

20.10.4 The Hash Index

The last three types of indexes discussed are all variations on the B-tree index. The *hash index*, however, has a completely different structure. This index is not based on the B-tree. However, the hash index has something in common with the B-tree index: the possibility of accessing the rows in a table directly. The main difference is that no index tree is created. Nevertheless, the term *hash index* is used often in the literature, and we also use this term in this book.

How does the hash index work? An important difference between the previous types of index and the hash index is that the latter must be created before the table is filled. Therefore, the table must exist but may not contain any rows. When a hash index is created, a certain amount of disk space is reserved automatically. Initially, this hash space is completely empty and will be used to store rows. The size of it is deduced from the size of the hash and is specified when the hash index is created.

Example 20.21: Create a direct-access mechanism for the PLAYERNO column in the PLAYERS table through hashing.

```
CREATE HASH INDEX PLAYERNO_HASH
ON      PLAYERS (PLAYERNO)
WITH    PAGES=100
```

Explanation: This statement puts aside a hash space of 100 pages for the PLAYERS table. In addition, it indicates that direct access to these rows will go through the PLAYERNO column.

However, the most important aspect is that, when a hash index is created, this leads to the development of a hash function. This hash function converts a player number to an address in the hash space. Here, the address is just the page number. In the previous example, the hash function converts a player number to a page number between 1 and 100. SQL does not show how this function exactly works. For most products, the core of the function is formed by a modulo function (with the number of pages as basis). This would mean that player 27 ends up in page 27, and player 12 and 112 both end up in page 12.

But how and when is this hash function used? In the first place, the function can be used to add new rows. If we add a new row with an INSERT statement, the address is calculated behind the scenes, and the row is stored in the relevant page, although we do not see or notice anything. The process becomes more interesting when we want to fetch rows. If we want to retrieve a player with a SELECT statement, the hash function will also be used. With this, the location of the appropriate row is determined (in which page). SQL immediately jumps to that page and looks for the row in the page. If the row is not present in that page, it does not occur at all in the table. This shows the power of the hash index. A hash index can be even faster than a B-tree index. A B-tree index browses through the entire index tree before the actual rows are found. The hash index allows us to jump to the row almost directly.

Although the hash index provides the fastest access for retrieving several rows from a table, it also has some disadvantages:

- If the values in the hash column are distributed equally, the pages in the hash space are also filled equally. For the PLAYERNO column, we could assume that the number of a new player is always equal to that of the player who was entered last plus 1, in which case the rows are distributed equally. But what if that is not the case? Imagine that player numbers 30 to 50 are absent. Then, certain pages remain much emptier than others, and that shows a disadvantage of the hash index: If the hash function cannot distribute the rows equally over the hash space, certain pages will be very empty and others will be overcrowded. As a result, the execution time of the statements will differ considerably.

- The second disadvantage is, in fact, another aspect of the first one. If the pages have not been distributed equally, certain pages will not be filled correctly, which means that we are wasting storage space.

- A third disadvantage is related to how the pages are filled. A page always takes maximum space, and, because of this, it can be full. What happens when the hash function returns this (full) page for another new row? Then, so-called *chained pages* have to be created with a pointer from the first page. The chained page can be compared to the trailer of a truck: The more chained pages there are, the slower it becomes. If we ask for a certain row, the system goes to the first page to see whether the row occurs there; if not, it looks at the chained page and maybe another chained page. If we take the comparison with the truck further, this would mean that if we were looking for a parcel, we would always look into the truck first, then in the first trailer, then the second, and so on.

- What happens when the hash space is full? In that case, a new hash space must be created, and for this, all products have specific SQL statements or special programs that are easy to use. However, although these programs are easy for the user, for SQL, the enlargement of the hash space involves a lot of work; all rows must be fetched from the table, a new space must be made ready, a new hash function must be created (because there are more pages), and, finally, all rows must be placed in the hash space again. If a table contains only ten rows, this process can be performed quickly, but if there are thousands of rows, you can imagine how much time this will take. Thus, the fourth disadvantage of the hash index is that it makes the environment rather static because reorganizing the hash space is something we prefer not to do.

20.10.5 The Bitmap Index

All the types of indexes that we have discussed so far lead to an improvement of the processing speed if the number of different values of the indexed column is not too small. The more duplicate values a column contains, the less advantages an index has. An index on the SEX column of the sample database would not add much to the processing speed of SELECT statements. For many products, the rule of thumb holds that if we are looking for 15% or more of all rows in a table, a serial browsing of the table is faster than direct access through an index. For example, if we are looking for all male players, we are looking for more than 50% of all players. In such a case, an index on the SEX column is pointless. However, browsing through an entire table could take a very long time. Therefore, several vendors have added the *bitmap index* to their SQL product to improve the performance.

Creating a bitmap index is very much like creating one of the previous indexes.

Example 20.22: Create a bitmap index on the SEX column of the PLAYERS table.

```
CREATE  BITMAP  INDEX  PLAYERS_SEX
ON      PLAYERS(SEX)
```

The internal structure of a bitmap index cannot be compared with that of a B-tree or hash index. It falls outside the context of this book to explain this in detail. However, it is important to remember that these indexes can improve considerably the speed of SELECT statements with conditions on columns containing duplicate values. The more duplicate values a column contains, the slower the B-tree index gets and the faster the bitmap index is. A bitmap index is no use when you are looking for a few rows (or using direct access).

The bitmap index has the same disadvantages as the B-tree index: It slows the updating of data and it takes up storage space. Because the first disadvantage is the more important, bitmap indexes are seldom or never used in a transaction environment, although they are in data warehouses.

20.11 Indexes and the Catalog

Just as with tables and columns, indexes are recorded in catalog tables. These are the INDEXES table and the COLUMNS_IN_INDEX table. The descriptions of the columns of the first table are given in Table 20.1. The columns INDEX_CREATOR and INDEX_NAME are the primary key of the INDEXES table.

Table 20.1   *Columns of the INDEXES Catalog Table*

COLUMN NAME	DATA TYPE	DESCRIPTION
INDEX_CREATOR	CHAR	Name of the user who created the index (in MySQL, this is the name of the database in which the index is created)
INDEX_NAME	CHAR	Name of the index
CREATE_TIMESTAMP	DATETIME	Date and time when the index is created
TABLE_CREATOR	NUMERIC	Owner of the table on which the index is defined
TABLE_NAME	CHAR	Name of the table on which the index is defined
UNIQUE_ID	CHAR	Whether the index is unique (YES) or not (NO)
INDEX_TYPE	CHAR	Form of the index: BTREE, HASH, or BITMAP

The columns on which an index is defined are recorded in a separate table, the COLUMNS_IN_INDEX table. The primary key of this table is formed by the columns INDEX_CREATOR, INDEX_NAME, and COLUMN_NAME, described in Table 20.2.

Table 20.2   *Columns of the COLUMNS_IN_INDEX Catalog Table*

COLUMN NAME	DATA TYPE	DESCRIPTION
INDEX_CREATOR	CHAR	Name of the user who created the index (in MySQL, this is the name of the database in which the index is created)
INDEX_NAME	CHAR	Name of the index
TABLE_CREATOR	NUMERIC	Owner of the table on which the index is defined
TABLE_NAME	CHAR	Name of the table on which the index is defined
COLUMN_NAME	CHAR	Name of the column on which the index is defined
COLUMN_SEQ	NUMERIC	Sequence number of the column in the index
ORDERING	CHAR	Has the value ASC if the index has been built in ascending order; otherwise, has the value DESC

The sample indexes from this section are recorded in the INDEXES and the COLUMNS_IN_INDEX tables, as follows (we assume that all the tables and indexes are created in the TENNIS database):

INDEX_CREATOR	INDEX_NAME	TABLE_NAME	UNIQUE_ID	INDEX_TYPE
TENNIS	PLAY_PC	PLAYERS	NO	BTREE
TENNIS	MAT_WL	MATCHES	NO	BTREE
TENNIS	NAMEINIT	PLAYERS	YES	BTREE

INDEX_NAME	TABLE_NAME	COLUMN_NAME	COLUMN_SEQ	ORDERING
PLAY_PC	PLAYERS	POSTCODE	1	ASC
MAT_WL	MATCHES	WON	1	ASC
MAT_WL	MATCHES	LOST	2	ASC
NAMEINIT	PLAYERS	NAME	1	ASC
NAMEINIT	PLAYERS	INITIALS	2	ASC

Example 20.23: Which base table has more than one index?

```
SELECT    TABLE_CREATOR, TABLE_NAME, COUNT(*)
FROM      INDEXES
GROUP BY  TABLE_CREATOR, TABLE_NAME
HAVING    COUNT(*) > 1
```

Explanation: If a particular index appears more than once in the INDEXES table, it is based upon more than one base table.

Example 20.24: Which base table does not have any unique index?

```
SELECT    TABLE_CREATOR, TABLE_NAME
FROM      TABLES AS TAB
WHERE     NOT EXISTS
          (SELECT    *
          FROM      INDEXES AS IDX
          WHERE     TAB.TABLE_CREATOR = IDX.TABLE_CREATOR
          AND       TAB.TABLE_NAME = TAB.TABLE_NAME
          AND       IDX.UNIQUE_ID = 'YES')
```

20.12 Answers

20.1

1. Basic strategy:

```
RESULT := [];
FOR EACH T IN TEAMS DO
   IF (T.TEAMNO > 1)
   AND (T.DIVISION = 'second') THEN
      RESULT :+ T;
ENDFOR;
```

Optimized strategy:

```
RESULT := [];
FOR EACH T IN TEAMS
WHERE DIVISION = 'second' DO
   IF T.TEAMNO > 1 THEN
      RESULT :+ T;
ENDFOR;
```

2. Basic strategy:

```
RESULT := [];
FOR EACH P IN PLAYERS DO
   FOR EACH M IN MATCHES DO
      IF P.PLAYERNO = M.PLAYERNO AND
         P.BIRTH_DATE > '1963-01-01' THEN
         RESULT :+ P;
   ENDFOR;
ENDFOR;
```

Optimized strategy:

```
RESULT := [];
FOR EACH P IN PLAYERS
WHERE P.BIRTH_DATE > '1963-01-01' DO
    FOR EACH M IN MATCHES DO
        IF P.PLAYERNO = M.PLAYERNO THEN
            RESULT :+ P;
    ENDFOR;
ENDFOR;
```

Views

21.1 Introduction

S QL supports two types of tables: real tables, generally known as base tables, and derived tables, also called *views*. Base tables are created with CREATE TABLE statements and are the only ones in which data can be stored. Examples are the PLAYERS and TEAMS tables from the tennis club database.

A derived table, or view, stores *no* rows itself. Instead, it exists, and can be seen, as a prescription or formula for combining certain data from base tables to make a "virtual" table. The word *virtual* is used because the contents of a view exist only when it is used in a statement. At that moment, SQL executes the prescription that makes up the *view formula* and presents the user with what seems to be a real table.

This chapter describes how views are created and how they can be used. Some useful applications include the simplification of routine statements and the reorganization of tables. Two sections look at restrictions on querying and updating views.

21.2 Creating Views

Views are created with the CREATE VIEW statement.

```
<create view statement> ::=
    CREATE [ OR REPLACE ] VIEW <view name>
        [ <column list> ] AS
        <table expression>
        [ WITH [ CASCADED | LOCAL ] CHECK OPTION ]
```

Example 21.1: Create a view that holds all town names from the PLAYERS table, and show the virtual contents of this new view.

```
CREATE    VIEW TOWNS AS
SELECT    DISTINCT TOWN
FROM      PLAYERS

SELECT    *
FROM      TOWNS
```

The result is:

```
TOWN
---------
Stratford
Inglewood
Eltham
Midhurst
Douglas
Plymouth
```

Example 21.2: Create a view that holds the player numbers and league numbers of all players who have a league number, and show the virtual contents of this view.

```
CREATE    VIEW CPLAYERS AS
SELECT    PLAYERNO, LEAGUENO
FROM      PLAYERS
WHERE     LEAGUENO IS NOT NULL

SELECT    *
FROM      CPLAYERS
```

The result is:

```
PLAYERNO   LEAGUENO
--------   --------
      44   1124
     112   1319
      83   1608
       2   2411
      27   2513
       8   2983
      57   6409
     100   6524
     104   7060
       6   8467
```

These two CREATE VIEW statements create two views: TOWNS and CPLAYERS. The contents of each view are defined by a table expression. Such a table expression forms the view formula of the view. These two views can be queried just like base tables, and the CPLAYERS view can even be updated.

Example 21.3: Get the player and league numbers for competition players whose numbers run from 6 to 44 inclusive.

```
SELECT    *
FROM      CPLAYERS
WHERE     PLAYERNO BETWEEN 6 AND 44
```

The result is:

```
PLAYERNO   LEAGUENO
--------   --------
       6   8467
      44   1124
      27   2513
       8   2983
```

If we did not use the CPLAYERS view for the same question, but accessed the PLAY-ERS table directly, we would need a more complex SELECT statement to retrieve the same information:

```
SELECT    PLAYERNO, LEAGUENO
FROM      PLAYERS
WHERE     LEAGUENO IS NOT NULL
AND       PLAYERNO BETWEEN 6 AND 44
```

Example 21.4: Remove the competition player whose league number is 7060.

```
DELETE
FROM      CPLAYERS
WHERE     LEAGUENO = '7060'
```

When this statement is executed, the row in the base table, the PLAYERS table, in which the LEAGUENO column equals 7060, is deleted.

The contents of a view are not stored but are derived when the view is referenced. This means that the contents, by definition, are always in line with the contents of the base tables. Every update made to the data in a base table is immediately visible in a view. Users never need to be concerned about the integrity of the contents of the view, as long as the integrity of the base tables is maintained. In Section 21.8, we return to the subject of updating views.

Another view may be specified in a view formula. In other words, we may nest views.

Example 21.5: Create a view that holds all competition players whose player numbers run from 6 to 27 inclusive, and show the virtual contents of this view.

```
CREATE    VIEW SEVERAL AS
SELECT    *
FROM      CPLAYERS
WHERE     PLAYERNO BETWEEN 6 AND 27

SELECT    *
FROM      SEVERAL
```

The result is:

```
PLAYERNO   LEAGUENO
--------   --------
       6   8467
       8   2983
      27   2513
```

Note that not every form of the table expression may be used as a view formula. These rules are vendor-dependent, however.

In most cases, table expressions retrieve data from base tables or views, but not necessarily. Table expressions can give a result without accessing so much as one table; for example, see Example 7.34, in Chapter 7, "SELECT Statement: The FROM Clause." Therefore, views do not have to be defined on base tables. Here is an example:

Example 21.6: Create a view in which the number 0 up to and including 9 appear, and show the contents of this view next.

```
CREATE VIEW DIGITS AS
SELECT '0' DIGIT UNION SELECT '1' UNION
SELECT '2' UNION SELECT '3' UNION
SELECT '4' UNION SELECT '5' UNION
SELECT '6' UNION SELECT '7' UNION
SELECT '8' UNION SELECT '9'

SELECT * FROM DIGITS
```

The result is:

```
DIGIT
-----
    0
    1
    2
    3
    4
    5
    6
    7
    8
    9
```

Behind the word CREATE, we can specify OR REPLACE. If the name of the view already exists, the old view formula is overwritten by the new one.

21.3 The Column Names of Views

By default, the column names in a view are the same as the column names in the SELECT clause. For example, the two columns in the SEVERAL view are called PLAYERNO and LEAGUENO. A view, therefore, inherits the column names. You can also explicitly define the column names of views.

Example 21.7: Create a view that holds the player number, name, initials, and date of birth of each player who lives in Stratford.

```
CREATE    VIEW STRATFORDERS (PLAYERNO, NAME, INIT, BORN) AS
SELECT    PLAYERNO, NAME, INITIALS, BIRTH_DATE
FROM      PLAYERS
WHERE     TOWN = 'Stratford'

SELECT    *
FROM      STRATFORDERS
WHERE     PLAYERNO > 90
```

The result is (note the column names):

```
PLAYERNO  NAME       INITIALS  BORN
--------  --------   --------  ----------
     100  Parmenter  P         1963-02-08
```

These new column names are permanent. You can no longer refer to the columns PLAYERNO or BIRTH_DATE in the STRATFORDERS view.

If an expression in the SELECT clause of a view formula does *not* consist of a column specification, but is a function or calculation, it is mandatory to provide names for the columns of the view.

Example 21.8: For each town, create a view that holds the place–name and the number of players who live in that town.

```
CREATE    VIEW RESIDENTS (TOWN, NUMBER) AS
SELECT    TOWN, COUNT(*)
FROM      PLAYERS
GROUP BY TOWN
```

Explanation: In this view, you may not leave out the column names TOWN and NUM-BER_OF.

Exercise 21.1: Create a view called NUMBERPLS that contains all the team numbers and the total number of players who have played for that team. (Assume that at least one player has competed for each team.)

Exercise 21.2: Create a view called WINNERS that contains the number and name of each player who, for at least one team, has won one match.

Exercise 21.3: Create a view called TOTALS that records the total amount of penalties for each player who has incurred at least one penalty.

21.4 Updating Views: WITH CHECK OPTION

We have already shown a number of examples of views being updated. In fact, the underlying tables are being updated. Nevertheless, updating views can have unexpected results. Let us illustrate this with the following example:

Example 21.9: Create a view that holds all players born before 1960.

```
CREATE    VIEW VETERANS AS
SELECT    *
FROM      PLAYERS
WHERE     BIRTH_DATE < '1960-01-01'
```

Now we would like to change the date of birth of the veteran whose player number is 2 from 1 September 1948 to 1 September 1970. The update statement reads:

```
UPDATE    VETERANS
SET       BIRTH_DATE = '1970-09-01'
WHERE     PLAYERNO = 2
```

This is a correct update. The date of birth of player number 2 in the PLAYERS table is changed. The unexpected effect of this update, though, is that if we look at the *view* using a SELECT statement, player 2 no longer appears. This is because when the update occurred, the player ceased to satisfy the condition specified in the view formula.

If you extend the view definition using the so-called WITH CHECK OPTION, SQL ensures that such an unexpected effect does not arise.

The view definition then becomes:

```
CREATE    VIEW VETERANS AS
SELECT    *
FROM      PLAYERS
WHERE     BIRTH_DATE < '1960-01-01'
WITH      CHECK OPTION
```

If a view includes the WITH CHECK OPTION clause, all changes with UPDATE, INSERT, and DELETE statements are checked for validity:

- An UPDATE statement is correct if the rows that are updated still belong to the (virtual) contents of the view after the update.
- An INSERT statement is correct if the new rows belong to the (virtual) contents of the view.
- A DELETE statement is correct if the rows that are deleted belong to the (virtual) contents of the view.

As said, a view can be stacked on top of another view. The question that comes to mind then is to what extent the check of the WITH CHECK OPTION can be carried out. If we specify WITH CASCADED CHECK OPTION, all views are checked. When WITH LOCAL CHECK OPTION is used, only those checks are carried out that relate to conditions that appear in the view that will be updated. CASCADED is the default.

Example 21.10: Create a view of all players born before 1960 and living in Inglewood.

```
CREATE    VIEW INGLEWOOD_VETERANS AS
SELECT    *
FROM      VETERANS
WHERE     TOWN = 'Inglewood'
WITH      CASCADED CHECK OPTION
```

Explanation: If we use an INSERT statement to add a player to this view, he or she must live in Inglewood and must be born before January 1, 1960. When we leave out CAS-CADED, every player who we add to the INGLEWOOD_VETERANS table must live in Inglewood. SQL no longer carries out the check.

The WITH CHECK OPTION can be used only in conjunction with views that can be updated according to the rules mentioned in Section 21.8.

21.5 Deleting Views

The DROP VIEW statement deletes a view. Every other view that references this dropped view is also dropped automatically. Of course, this can lead to the removal of other views. When a base table is dropped, all views that have been defined directly or indirectly on that table are also dropped.

```
<drop view statement> ::=
    DROP VIEW <table specification>
```

Example 21.11: Drop the CPLAYERS view.

```
DROP VIEW CPLAYERS
```

21.6 Views and the Catalog

Information about views is recorded in various tables. In the VIEWS table, a row is stored for each view. The primary key of this catalog table is formed by the column VIEW_ID. The columns VIEW_NAME and CREATOR form an alternate key.

Table 21.1   *Columns of the VIEWS Catalog Table*

COLUMN NAME	DATA TYPE	DESCRIPTION
VIEW_CREATOR	CHAR	Name of the owner (or creator) of the view (in MySQL, this is the name of the database to which the view belongs)
VIEW_NAME	CHAR	Name of the view
CREATE_TIMESTAMP	TIMESTAMP	Date on which the view was created
WITHCHECKOPT	CHAR	Has the value YES (if the view is defined with the WITH CHECK OPTION), CASCADED, LOCAL; otherwise, it has the value NO

(continued)

Table 21.1   *Columns of the VIEWS Catalog Table (continued)*

COLUMN NAME	DATA TYPE	DESCRIPTION
IS_UPDATABLE	CHAR	Has the value YES if the view can be updated; otherwise, it has the value NO
COMMENT	CHAR	Comment that is entered with the COMMENT statement
VIEWFORMULA	CHAR	The view formula (table expression)

The columns of the view inherit the data type of the column expressions from the SELECT clause of the view formula.

Example 21.12: Can a table called STOCK be created in the TENNIS DATABASE, or does that name already exist?

```
SELECT    TABLE_NAME
FROM      TABLES
WHERE     TABLE_NAME = 'STOCK'
AND       TABLE_CREATOR = 'TENNIS'
UNION
SELECT    VIEW_NAME
FROM      VIEWS
WHERE     VIEW_NAME = 'STOCK'
AND       VIEW_CREATOR = 'TENNIS'
```

Explanation: The SELECT statement checks whether a table or view was created with the name STOCK in the TENNIS database. If the statement has a result, this table name cannot be used again.

21.7 Restrictions on Querying Views

The SELECT, INSERT, UPDATE, and DELETE statements may be executed on views. However, a number of restrictions exist. For example, some views may not be queried in certain ways, and the rows of some views may not be deleted.

Portability: *The restrictions that apply to querying views can be different per SQL product. The following restrictions do not apply to MySQL.*

Restriction 1: When a column in a view is based on an aggregation function in the SELECT clause of the view formula, this column may be used only in the SELECT or ORDER BY clauses of the SELECT statement that queries the view—not, for example, in the WHERE clause.

Example:

```
CREATE    VIEW TOTALS
          (PLAYERNO, TOT_AMOUNT) AS
SELECT    PLAYERNO, SUM(AMOUNT)
FROM      PENALTIES
GROUP BY  PLAYERNO
```

The following SELECT statement is, therefore, *not* allowed because the TOT_AMOUNT column is based on a function in the view formula. It cannot be used in the WHERE clause.

```
SELECT    *
FROM      TOTALS
WHERE     TOT_AMOUNT > 100
```

Restriction 2: If a column of a view is based on an aggregation function in a view formula, this column may *not* be used in a function in the SELECT clause of the statement that uses the view.

Consider the TOTALS view again. The following statement is not permitted because the MAX function is specified for the TOT_AMOUNT column from the TOTALS view. TOT_AMOUNT itself is based on a function (SUM(AMOUNT)).

```
SELECT    MAX(TOT_AMOUNT)
FROM      TOTALS
```

Restriction 3: If a view formula contains a GROUP BY clause, the view may not be joined with another view or table.

As an illustration, we use the TOTALS view again. This view contains a GROUP BY clause, and that makes the following join invalid:

```
SELECT    NAME, TOT_AMOUNT
FROM      PLAYERS, TOTALS
WHERE     PLAYERS.PLAYERNO = TOTALS.PLAYERNO
```

21.8   Restrictions on Updating Views

As mentioned, there are also restrictions on updating views. (MySQL has some restrictions as well.) A view can be updated only if the view formula satisfies the following conditions. The first eight conditions apply to all update statements.

- The view definition must be based, directly or indirectly, on one or more base tables.
- The SELECT clause may *not* contain DISTINCT.
- The SELECT clause may *not* contain aggregation functions.
- The FROM clause may not contain more than *one* table.
- The SELECT statement may *not* contain a GROUP BY clause (and, therefore, also no HAVING clause).
- The SELECT statement may *not* contain an ORDER BY clause.
- The SELECT statement may *not* contain set operators.
- For the UPDATE statement, a virtual column may *not* be updated.
- The BEGIN_AGE column in the following view may not be updated (though the PLAYERNO column may be updated):

```
CREATE    VIEW AGE (PLAYERNO, BEGIN_AGE) AS
SELECT    PLAYERNO, JOINED - YEAR(BIRTH_DATE)
FROM      PLAYERS
```

- For the INSERT statement, the SELECT clause must contain, from the table that is specified in the FROM clause, all columns in which the NOT NULL value is allowed or for which a default value is specified.

That is why INSERT statements may not be performed against the following view. The view does not contain all NOT NULL columns, such as SEX and TOWN:

```
CREATE    VIEW PLAYERS_NAMES AS
SELECT    PLAYERNO, NAME, INITIALS
FROM      PLAYERS
```

Exercise 21.4: This chapter has shown many examples of views. For each of the following views, say whether an UPDATE, INSERT, or DELETE statement may be performed:

TOWNS

CPLAYERS

SEVERAL

STRATFORDERS

RESIDENTS

VETERANS

TOTALS

AGE

21.9 Processing View Statements

How will statements that access views be processed? The processing steps (see Chapter 5, "SELECT Statement: Common Elements") cannot be executed one by one, as happens for base tables. SQL reaches the FROM clause and attempts to fetch rows from the database; it has a problem because a view contains no stored rows. So which rows must be retrieved from the database when a statement refers to a view? SQL knows that it is dealing with a view (thanks to a routine look in the catalog). To process the steps, SQL can choose between two methods, called *substitution* and *materialization*.

With the first method, the view formula is merged into the SELECT statement. This method is called substitution because the view name in the SELECT statement is replaced (substituted) by the view formula. Next, the obtained SELECT statement is processed. We show how this works with an example.

Example 21.13: Create a view of all data of the players who incurred a penalty. Next, give the number of each player from the COST_RAISERS view who has incurred at least one penalty and lives in Stratford.

```
CREATE    VIEW COST_RAISERS AS
SELECT    *
FROM      PLAYERS
WHERE     PLAYERNO IN
          (SELECT   PLAYERNO
           FROM     PENALTIES)

SELECT    PLAYERNO
FROM      COST_RAISERS
WHERE     TOWN = 'Stratford'
```

The first processing step comprises the merging of the view formula into the SELECT statement. This step produces the following statement:

```
SELECT    PLAYERNO
FROM      (SELECT    *
          FROM       PLAYERS
          WHERE      PLAYERNO IN
                     (SELECT    PLAYERNO
                      FROM       PENALTIES)) AS VIEWFORMULA
WHERE     TOWN = 'Stratford'
```

Now, this statement can be processed by moving through the steps. In short, an additional step emerges that SQL performs before the other steps.

The final result is:

```
PLAYERNO
--------
       6
```

Here is another example, using the STRATFORDERS view from Section 21.3.

Example 21.14: Delete all Stratford people born after 1965.

```
DELETE
FROM      STRATFORDERS
WHERE     BORN > '1965-12-31'
```

After the name has been substituted by the view formula, the statement reads:

```
DELETE
FROM      PLAYERS
WHERE     BIRTH_DATE > '1965-12-31'
AND       TOWN = 'Stratford'
```

Another method of processing is called materialization. Here, the table expression of the view formula is processed first, which gives an intermediate result. Next, the actual

SELECT statement is executed on that intermediate result. If we would process Example 21.13 through materialization, the following statement would be executed first:

```
SELECT   *
FROM     PLAYERS
WHERE    PLAYERNO IN
         (SELECT   PLAYERNO
          FROM     PENALTIES)
```

This gives the following intermediate result (for the sake of convenience, only the columns PLAYERNO and TOWN have been displayed):

```
PLAYERNO  TOWN
--------  ---------
       6  Stratford
       8  Inglewood
      27  Eltham
      44  Inglewood
     104  Eltham
```

SQL keeps this intermediate result in internal memory. After that, the following statement is executed:

```
SELECT   PLAYERNO
FROM     <intermediate result>
WHERE    TOWN = 'Stratford'
```

Both methods have their advantages and disadvantages. SQL determines which method can be used best in which situation.

Exercise 21.5: What will the following statements look like after the view formula has been included through the method substitution?

1.

```
SELECT   YEAR(BORN) - 1900, COUNT(*)
FROM     STRATFORDERS
GROUP BY 1
```

2.

```
SELECT    PLAYERNO
FROM      COST_RAISERS, STRATFORDERS
WHERE     COST_RAISERS.PLAYERNO = STRATFORDERS.PLAYERNO
```

3.

```
UPDATE    STRATFORDERS
SET       BORN = 1950
WHERE     PLAYERNO = 7
```

21.10 Application Areas for Views

You can use views in a great variety of applications. In this section, we look at some of them. There is no special significance to the order in which they are discussed.

21.10.1 Simplification of Routine Statements

Statements that are used frequently, or are structurally similar, can be simplified through the use of views.

Example 21.15: Imagine that these two statements are frequently entered.

```
SELECT    *
FROM      PLAYERS
WHERE     PLAYERNO IN
          (SELECT   PLAYERNO
           FROM     PENALTIES)
AND       TOWN = 'Stratford'
```

and

```
SELECT    TOWN, COUNT(*)
FROM      PLAYERS
WHERE     PLAYERNO IN
          (SELECT   PLAYERNO
           FROM     PENALTIES)
GROUP BY TOWN
```

Both statements are concerned with the players who have incurred at least one penalty, so this subset of players can be defined by a view:

```
CREATE    VIEW PPLAYERS AS
SELECT    *
FROM      PLAYERS
WHERE     PLAYERNO IN
          (SELECT   PLAYERNO
           FROM     PENALTIES)
```

Now, the two previous SELECT statements can be greatly simplified by using the PPLAYERS view:

```
SELECT    *
FROM      PPLAYERS
WHERE     TOWN = 'Stratford'
```

and

```
SELECT    TOWN, COUNT(*)
FROM      PPLAYERS
GROUP BY TOWN
```

Example 21.16: Imagine that the PLAYERS table is often joined with the MATCHES table.

```
SELECT    ...
FROM      PLAYERS, MATCHES
WHERE     PLAYERS.PLAYERNO = MATCHES.PLAYERNO
AND       ...
```

In this case, the SELECT statement becomes simpler if the join is defined as a view:

```
CREATE    VIEW PLAY_MAT AS
SELECT    ...
FROM      PLAYERS, MATCHES
WHERE     PLAYERS.PLAYERNO = MATCHES.PLAYERNO
```

The join now takes this simplified form:

```
SELECT    ...
FROM      PLAY_MAT
WHERE     ...
```

21.10.2 Reorganizing Tables

The structure of tables is designed and implemented on the basis of a particular situation. This situation can change from time to time, which means that the structure also changes. For example, a new column is added to a table, or two tables are joined to make a single table. In most cases, the reorganization of a table structure requires altering already developed and operational statements. Such changes can be time-consuming and expensive. Appropriate use of views can keep this time and cost to a minimum. Let us see how.

Example 21.17: Get the name and initials of each competition player, and give also the divisions in which he or she has ever played.

```
SELECT    DISTINCT NAME, INITIALS, DIVISION
FROM      PLAYERS AS P, MATCHES AS M, TEAMS AS T
WHERE     P.PLAYERNO = M.PLAYERNO
AND       M.TEAMNO = T.TEAMNO
```

The result is:

```
NAME          INITIALS  DIVISION
---------     --------  --------
Parmenter     R         first
Baker         E         first
Hope          PK        first
Everett       R         first
Collins       DD        second
Moorman       D         second
Brown         M         first
Bailey        IP        second
Newcastle     B         first
Newcastle     B         second
```

For some presently unknown reasons, the TEAMS and MATCHES tables have to be reorganized; they are combined to form one table, the RESULT table, shown here:

MATCH_NO	TEAMNO	PLAYERNO	WON	LOST	CAPTAIN	DIVISION
1	1	6	3	1	6	first
2	1	6	2	3	6	first
3	1	6	3	0	6	first
4	1	44	3	2	6	first
5	1	83	0	3	6	first
6	1	2	1	3	6	first
7	1	57	3	0	6	first
8	1	8	0	3	6	first
9	2	27	3	2	27	second
10	2	104	3	2	27	second
11	2	112	2	3	27	second
12	2	112	1	3	27	second
13	2	8	0	3	27	second

The CAPTAIN column in the RESULT table is the former PLAYERNO column from the TEAMS table. This column has been given another name; otherwise, there would have been two columns called PLAYERNO. All statements that refer to the two tables now have to be rewritten, including the previous SELECT statement. A solution, which

renders a total rewrite unnecessary, is to define two views that represent the former
TEAMS and MATCHES tables, respectively:

```
CREATE    VIEW TEAMS (TEAMNO, PLAYERNO, DIVISION) AS
SELECT    DISTINCT TEAMNO, CAPTAIN, DIVISION
FROM      RESULT

CREATE    VIEW MATCHES AS
SELECT    MATCHNO, TEAMNO, PLAYERNO,
          WON, LOST
FROM      RESULT
```

The virtual contents of each of these two views are the same as the contents of the
two original tables. Not one statement has to be rewritten, including the SELECT statement from the beginning of this section.

Of course, you cannot manage every reorganization of a table with views. It might be
decided, for example, to store data about male and female players in separate tables.
Both tables acquire the same columns as the PLAYERS table but omit the SEX column.
It is no longer possible to reconstruct the original PLAYERS table with a view because
the UNION operator would be required, and inserts on this view are not allowed.

21.10.3 Stepwise Development of SELECT Statements

Imagine that you have to complete the following task: Get the name and initials of each
player from Stratford who has incurred a penalty that is greater than the average penalty
for players from the second team and who played for at least one first-division team. You
could write a huge SELECT statement to answer this, but you could also develop a query
in a stepwise fashion.

First, we create a view of all the players who have incurred at least one penalty that
is greater than the average penalty for players from the second team:

```
CREATE    VIEW GREATER AS
SELECT    DISTINCT PLAYERNO
FROM      PENALTIES
WHERE     AMOUNT >
          (SELECT   AVG(AMOUNT)
           FROM     PENALTIES
           WHERE    PLAYERNO IN
                    (SELECT   PLAYERNO
                     FROM     MATCHES
                     WHERE    TEAMNO = 2))
```

Then we create a view of all players who have competed for a team in the first division:

```
CREATE   VIEW FIRST AS
SELECT   DISTINCT PLAYERNO
FROM     MATCHES
WHERE    TEAMNO IN
         (SELECT   TEAMNO
          FROM     TEAMS
          WHERE    DIVISION = 'first')
```

Using these two views, answering the original question is quite simple:

```
SELECT   NAME, INITIALS
FROM     PLAYERS
WHERE    TOWN = 'Stratford'
AND      PLAYERNO IN
         (SELECT   PLAYERNO
          FROM     GREATER)
AND      PLAYERNO IN
         (SELECT   PLAYERNO
          FROM     FIRST)
```

We can split the problem into "mini problems" and execute this in steps. In this way, you can create one long SELECT statement.

21.10.4 Specifying Integrity Constraints

By using the WITH CHECK OPTION clause, you can implement rules that restrict the possible set of values that may be entered into columns.

Example 21.18: The SEX column in the PLAYERS table may contain either the value M or the value F. You can use the WITH CHECK OPTION clause to provide an automatic control for this. The following view should be defined:

```
CREATE   VIEW PLAYERSS AS
SELECT   *
FROM     PLAYERS
WHERE    SEX IN ('M', 'F')
WITH     CHECK OPTION
```

To follow this up, we give nobody the privilege of accessing the PLAYERS table directly; instead they have to do so via the PLAYERSS view. The WITH CHECK OPTION clause tests every update (that is, every UPDATE and INSERT statement) to see whether the value in the SEX column falls into the permitted range.

Note: *If the desired check can be defined with a check integrity constraint, we recommend that you use it in this application.*

21.10.5 Data Security

Views can also be used to protect parts of tables. Chapter 23, "Users and Data Security," deals with this topic in detail.

Exercise 21.6: Decide whether the following reorganizations of the database structure are possible through the use of views.

- The NAME column is added to the PENALTIES table but also remains in the PLAYERS table.
- The TOWN column is removed from the PLAYERS table and placed together with the PLAYERNO column in a separate table.

21.11 Answers

21.1

```
CREATE    VIEW NUMBERPLS (TEAMNO, NUMBER) AS
SELECT    TEAMNO, COUNT(*)
FROM      MATCHES
GROUP BY  TEAMNO
```

21.2

```
CREATE    VIEW WINNERS AS
SELECT    PLAYERNO, NAME
FROM      PLAYERS
WHERE     PLAYERNO IN
          (SELECT    PLAYERNO
           FROM      MATCHES
           WHERE     WON > LOST)
```

21.3

```
CREATE    VIEW TOTALS (PLAYERNO, SUM_PENALTIES) AS
SELECT    PLAYERNO, SUM(AMOUNT)
FROM      PENALTIES
GROUP BY PLAYERNO
```

21.4

VIEW	UPDATE	INSERT	DELETE
TOWNS	No	No	No
CPLAYERS	Yes	No	Yes
SEVERAL	Yes	No	Yes
STRATFORDERS	Yes	No	Yes
RESIDENTS	No	No	No
VETERANS	Yes	Yes	Yes
TOTALS	No	No	No
AGE	Yes	No	Yes

21.5

1.

```
SELECT    YEAR(BORN) - 1900, COUNT(*)
FROM      (SELECT    PLAYERNO, NAME,
                     INITIALS, BIRTH_DATE AS BORN
          FROM       PLAYERS
          WHERE      TOWN = 'Stratford') AS STRATFORDERS
GROUP BY BORN
```

2.

```
SELECT    EXPENSIVE.PLAYERNO
FROM      (SELECT    *
          FROM       PLAYERS
          WHERE      PLAYERNO IN
                     (SELECT    PLAYERNO
                      FROM      PENALTIES)) AS EXPENSIVE,
```

```
          (SELECT    PLAYERNO, NAME,
                     INITIALS, BIRTH_DATE AS BORN
           FROM      PLAYERS
           WHERE     TOWN = 'Stratford') AS STRATFORDERS
WHERE     EXPENSIVE.PLAYERNO = STRATFORDERS.PLAYERNO
```

3.

```
UPDATE    PLAYERS
SET       BIRTH_DATE = '1950-04-04'
WHERE     PLAYERNO = 7
```

21.6 Yes, but the view can be only queried, not updated, because the view formula
contains a join.

22

Creating Databases

22.1 Introduction

E ach table that is created is stored in a database. During the installation of MySQL, two databases are created automatically and used to store the catalog tables. We do not recommend adding your own tables to these databases. It is better to create new databases for this by using the CREATE DATABASE statement. Section 4.4 contains an example of this statement. In this relatively short chapter, we deal with this statement at great length.

> **Portability:** *Creating and dropping databases is an area in which huge differences between the SQL products exist. Because MySQL is supplied on the CD-ROM, we explain how this product treats this topic.*

22.2 Databases and the Catalog

In MySQL, databases are stored in the catalog table called INFORMATION_SCHEMA.

Example 22.1: Show the names of all databases.

```
SELECT    SCHEMA_NAME
FROM      INFORMATION_SCHEMA.SCHEMATA
```

The result is:

```
SCHEMA_NAME
-----------------
information_schema
mysql
tennis
test
```

Explanation: A catalog table called DATABASES does not exist. Instead, this table is called SCHEMATA. This is somewhat confusing. MySQL is one of the few products that uses the terms and schema interchangeably.

The previous result contains four databases. The first two were created by MySQL during the installation: INFORMATION_SCHEMA and MYSQL. If you remove these databases, MySQL no longer can function. The last two databases were created separately.

The tables of a database can be retrieved by querying the catalog table TABLES and specifying the database name or schema name in the condition.

Example 22.2: Show the names of the tables belonging to the TENNIS database.

```
SELECT    TABLE_NAME
FROM      INFORMATION_SCHEMA.TABLES
WHERE     TABLE_SCHEMA = 'TENNIS'
ORDER BY 1
```

The result is:

```
TABLE_NAME
-----------------
COMMITTEE_MEMBERS
PENALTIES
PLAYERS
TEAMS
MATCHES
```

22.3 Creating Databases

With the CREATE DATABASE statement, you can create new databases. During that process, you can specify a default character set and a default collating sequence.

```
<create database statement> ::=
    CREATE DATABASE [ IF NOT EXISTS ] <database name>
        [ <database option>... ]

<database option> ::=
    [ DEFAULT ] CHARACTER SET <character set name> |
    [ DEFAULT ] COLLATE <collating sequence name>

<database name>              ;
<character set name>         ;
<collating sequence name> ::= <name>
```

Example 22.3: Create a new database called TENNIS2.

```
CREATE DATABASE TENNIS2
    DEFAULT CHARACTER SET utf8
    DEFAULT COLLATE utf8_general_ci
```

Explanation: This creates a new database without tables. If you want to use this database, do not forget to make it the current database using the USE statement.

Example 22.4: For each database, get the name and the default character set and collating sequence.

```
SELECT    SCHEMA_NAME, DEFAULT_CHARACTER_SET_NAME,
          DEFAULT_COLLATION_NAME
FROM      INFORMATION_SCHEMA.SCHEMATA
```

The result is:

```
SCHEMA_NAME            DEFAULT_CHARACTER_SET_NAME   DEFAULT_COLLATION_NAME
------------------     --------------------------   ----------------------
information_schema     utf8                         utf8_general_ci
mysql                  latin1                       latin1_swedish_ci
tennis                 latin1                       latin1_swedish_ci
tennis2                utf8                         utf8_general_ci
test                   latin1                       latin1_swedish_ci
```

22.4 Updating Databases

You can change the existing default character set and collating sequence with an ALTER
DATABASE statement. These new defaults apply only to the tables and columns that will
be created after the update.

```
<alter database statement> ::=
    ALTER DATABASE [ <database name> ]
        [ <database option>... ]

<database option> ::=
    [ DEFAULT ] CHARACTER SET <character set name> |
    [ DEFAULT ] COLLATE <collating sequence name>

<database name>              ;
<character set name>         ;
<collating sequence name> ::= <name>
```

Example 22.5: Change the character set and collating sequence of the TENNIS2
database.

```
ALTER DATABASE TENNIS2
    DEFAULT CHARACTER SET sjis
    DEFAULT COLLATE sjis_japanese_ci
```

Explanation: The TENNIS2 database does not have to be current for this statement.

Example 22.6: Define hp8 as the default character set for the TENNIS database; then create a new table with two alphanumeric columns. Do not assign a character set. Look in the catalog tables to see the default collating sequence.

```
ALTER DATABASE TENNIS CHARACTER SET hp8

CREATE TABLE CHARSETHP8
       (C1   CHAR(10) NOT NULL,
        C2   VARCHAR(10))

SELECT    COLUMN_NAME, CHARACTER_SET_NAME, COLLATION_NAME
FROM      INFORMATION_SCHEMA.COLUMNS
WHERE     TABLE_NAME = 'CHARSETHP8'
```

The result is:

```
COLUMN_NAME    CHARACTER_SET_NAME    COLLATION_NAME
-----------    ------------------    --------------
K1             hp8                   hp8_english_ci
K2             hp8                   hp8_english_ci
```

The default of the database is, of course, the default collating sequence (latin1_swedish_ci) of the default character set (latin1). With an ALTER DATA-BASE, this default can be changed.

Example 22.7: Change the default collating sequence of the TENNIS database to hp8_bin.

```
ALTER DATABASE TENNIS COLLATE hp8_bin
```

22.5 Dropping Databases

One of the most drastic SQL statements is the DROP DATABASE statement. This statement removes the entire database at once. All tables of that database disappear permanently, so be very careful!

```
<drop database statement> ::=
    DROP DATABASE <database name>

<database name> ::= <name>
```

Example 22.8: Drop the TENNIS2 database.

```
DROP DATABASE TENNIS2
```

23

Users and Data Security

23.1 Introduction

In this chapter, we describe the features that SQL offers for protecting data in the tables against deliberate or accidental unauthorized use. For the security of data, SQL users, passwords, and privileges are required.

SQL users must be known to SQL before they can access the database data. In Chapter 3, "Installing the Software," we showed you how one user is created automatically during SQL installation. In Chapter 4, "SQL in a Nutshell," we showed how a new SQL user called BOOKSQL was introduced. Logging on to SQL without an existing user name is just not possible.

To each SQL user, a password can be assigned. When a password is required, accessing the database data becomes even more difficult because the name of an SQL user is no longer sufficient. After following the procedure to install the sample database as described in this book, the user BOOKSQL has the password BOOKSQLPW. You have probably entered this password many times, and you already have discovered what happens if you make a typing error: no access!

New SQL users are not allowed to access tables belonging to other SQL users, even with the SELECT statement. Nor can they create their own tables. New SQL users must explicitly be granted privileges. We can indicate, for example, that an SQL user is allowed to query a certain table or change specific columns of a table. Another SQL user might be allowed to create tables, and the third to create and remove complete databases.

The privileges that can be granted are divided into four groups:

- *Column privileges* relate to one specific column of a table—for example, the privilege to update the values in the AMOUNT column of the PENALTIES table with UPDATE statements.
- *Table privileges* relate to all data of one specific table—for example, the privilege to query all the data of the PLAYERS table with SELECT statements.

- *Database privileges* relate to all tables of one specific database—for example, the privilege to create new tables in the existing TENNIS database.
- *User privileges* relate to all databases that are known to SQL—for example, the privilege to remove existing databases or to create new ones.

In this chapter, we explain how new SQL users can be entered and how privileges can be assigned with the GRANT statement. All privileges are stored in the catalog, of course. We also describe how privileges can be recalled with the REVOKE statement and how SQL users can be removed from the catalog.

Note: *In the following sections of this chapter, we use the term* user *instead of the somewhat longer* SQL user, *for convenience; see Section 4.3, in Chapter 4, to find out the difference between the two.*

23.2 Adding and Removing Users

Besides BOOKSQL, we can add other users. In Section 4.13, in Chapter 4, we used an example to show how a new user can be added. In this section, we explain it in more detail.

To add new users in the catalog, SQL uses the simple CREATE USER statement.

```
<create user statement> ::=
    CREATE USER <user name> IDENTIFIED BY <password>

<user name> ;
<password>  ::= <name>
```

In a CREATE USER statement, a *username* and a *password* are entered. In most SQL products, the username is just a name consisting of letters and numbers. The password is a simple name as well.

Example 23.1: Introduce two new users: CHRIS with the password CHRISSEC, and PAUL with the password LUAP.

```
CREATE USER CHRIS IDENTIFIED BY CHRISSEC

CREATE USER PAUL IDENTIFIED BY LUAP
```

Products such as DB2 and Oracle can process both statements without any problem. On the other hand, they do not work with MySQL because the definitions of the concepts username and password differ; see the following definition:

```
    <name> | '<name>' | '<name>'@'<host name>'

<password> ::= <alphanumeric literal>
```

The first difference is that, in MySQL, the password must be placed between quotation marks. The second difference is that if the username is specified as a name, for example as CHRIS, this name is changed to the specification 'CHRIS'@'%'. The first statement in the previous code could have been written in full as follows:

```
CREATE USER 'CHRIS'@'%' IDENTIFIED BY 'CHRISSEC'
```

The specification behind the @ sign represents the name of the host. Users log on from a certain machine. The machine on which the database server runs is called localhost. We used this specification in Chapter 4 for the user BOOKSQL. After the following CREATE USER statement, for example, user SAM can log on only from the machine called TEST. From the previous statement, CHRIS is allowed to log on from any machine.

```
CREATE USER 'SAM'@'TEST' IDENTIFIED BY 'CHRISSEC'
```

Users who have just been introduced do not have many privileges yet. They can log on to SQL and perform all operations for which no privileges are required. For example, they can use the HELP function or execute a COMMIT statement. However, whether they can access tables remains to be seen.

Each user has the right to use the ALTER USER statement to change his or her password.

```
<alter user statement> ::=
    ALTER USER <user name> IDENTIFIED BY <password>
```

Example 23.2: Change the password of JIM to JIM1.

```
ALTER USER JIM IDENTIFIED BY JIM1
```

The DROP USER statement is used to remove users from the system in a simple way. All their privileges are also removed automatically.

```
<drop user statement> ::=
    DROP USER <user name>
```

Example 23.3: Drop the user JIM.

```
DROP USER JIM
```

Portability: *If the removed user has created tables and indexes, what happens next depends on the product. SQL removes only users who are not the owner of any database object. Therefore, these objects have to be removed first. Many other SQL products work like this. Other products drop the user but keep all tables and indexes of this user. Finally, some products remove the user together with all his or her database objects.*

Exercise 23.1: Create a user with the name RONALDO and password NIKE.

Exercise 23.2: Remove user RONALDO.

23.3 Granting Table and Column Privileges

SQL supports the following table privileges.

- SELECT—This privilege gives a user the right to access the specified table with the SELECT statement. He or she can also include the table in a view formula. However, a user must have the SELECT privilege for every table (or view) specified in a view formula.
- INSERT—This privilege gives a user the right to add rows to the specified table with the INSERT statement.
- DELETE—This privilege gives a user the right to remove rows from the specified table with the DELETE statement.
- UPDATE—This privilege gives a user the right to change values in the specified table with the UPDATE statement.
- REFERENCES—This privilege gives a user the right to create foreign keys that refer to the specified table.
- ALTER—This privilege gives a user the right to change the table with the ALTER TABLE statement.

- INDEX—This privilege gives a user the right to define indexes on the table.
- ALL or ALL PRIVILEGES—This privilege is a shortened form for all the privileges just named.

A table privilege may be granted only by users who have enough privileges themselves.

```
<grant statement> ::=
   <grant table privilege statement>

<grant table privilege statement> ::=
   GRANT  <table privileges>
   ON     <table specification>
   TO     <grantees>
   [ WITH GRANT OPTION ]

<table privileges> ::=
   ALL [ PRIVILEGES ] |
   <table privilege> [ { , <table privilege> }... ]

<table privilege> ::=
   SELECT                       |
   INSERT                       |
   DELETE                       |
   UPDATE [ <column list> ]     |
   REFERENCES [ <column list> ] |
   ALTER                        |
   INDEX

<column list> ::=
   ( <column name> [ { , <column name> }... ] )

<grantees> ::=
   PUBLIC |
   <user name> [ { , <user name> }... ]
```

Here are a few examples of how table privileges must be granted. We assume, unless otherwise mentioned, that the user called BOOKSQL enters the statements.

Example 23.4: Give JAMIE the SELECT privilege on the PLAYERS table.

```
GRANT   SELECT
ON      PLAYERS
TO      JAMIE
```

Explanation: After this GRANT statement has been processed, JAMIE may use any SELECT statement to query the PLAYERS table, regardless of who has created the table.

Multiple table privileges can be granted to multiple users simultaneously.

Example 23.5: Give JAMIE and PETE the INSERT and UPDATE privilege for all columns of the TEAMS table.

```
GRANT     INSERT, UPDATE
ON        TEAMS
TO        JAMIE, PIET
```

A certain table privilege does not automatically lead to another. If we grant an INSERT privilege to a user, he or she does not automatically receive the SELECT privilege; it has to be granted separately.

A privilege can be granted to one user, to a number of users, or to PUBLIC (MySQL does not support this feature). If a privilege is granted to PUBLIC, each user who has been introduced gets that privilege. This also applies to all users introduced after the granting of the privilege, so after a user is entered into the system, he or she automatically receives all the privileges granted to PUBLIC.

Example 23.6: Give all users the SELECT and INSERT privileges on the PENALTIES table.

```
GRANT     SELECT, INSERT
ON        PENALTIES
TO        PUBLIC
```

With several privileges, including UPDATE and REFERENCES, you can indicate the columns to which the privilege applies. In that case, we call it *column privileges*. When you do not specify a column, as in the previous examples, it means that the privilege applies to *all* columns of the table.

Example 23.7: Give PETE the UPDATE privilege for the columns PLAYERNO and DIVISION of the TEAMS table.

```
GRANT     UPDATE (PLAYERNO, DIVISION)
ON        TEAMS
TO        PETE
```

Exercise 23.3: Give RONALDO the SELECT and INSERT privileges on the PLAYERS table.

Exercise 23.4: Give everyone all privileges on the COMMITTEE_MEMBERS table.

Exercise 23.5: Give RONALDO the UPDATE privilege for the columns STREET, HOUSENO, POSTCODE, and TOWN of the PLAYERS table.

23.4 Granting Database Privileges

Table privileges are effective for a certain table. SQL also supports privileges for an entire database, such as the privilege to create tables or views in a certain database.

Portability: *Granting privileges on the database level is not supported by all SQL products.*

SQL supports the following database privileges:

- SELECT—This privilege gives the user the right to access all tables of the specified database with the SELECT statement.
- INSERT—This privilege gives the user the right to add rows to all tables of the specified database with the INSERT statement.
- DELETE—This privilege gives the user the right to remove rows from all tables of the specified database with the DELETE statement.
- UPDATE—This privilege gives the user the right to update values in all tables of the specified database with the UPDATE statement.
- REFERENCES—This privilege gives the user the right to create foreign keys that point to tables of the specified database.
- CREATE—This privilege gives the user the right to create new tables in the specified database with the CREATE TABLE statement.
- ALTER—This privilege gives the user the right to alter all tables of the specified database with the ALTER TABLE statement.
- DROP—This privilege gives the user the right to remove all tables of the specified database.
- INDEX—This privilege gives the user the right to define and remove indexes on all tables of the specified database.
- CREATE TEMPORARY TABLES—This privilege gives the user the right to create temporary tables in the specified database.
- CREATE VIEW—This privilege gives the user the right to create new views in the specified database with the CREATE VIEW statement.
- CREATE ROUTINE—This privilege gives the user the right to create new stored procedures and functions for the specified database; see Chapters 30, "Stored Procedures" and 31, "Stored Functions."

- ALTER ROUTINE—This privilege gives the user the right to update and remove existing stored procedures and functions of the specified database.

- EXECUTE ROUTINE—This privilege gives the user the right to invoke existing stored procedures and functions of the specified database.

- LOCK TABLES—This privilege gives the user the right to block existing tables of the specified database; see Section 27.10, in Chapter 27, "Transactions and Multi-user Usage."

- ALL or ALL PRIVILEGES—This privilege is a shortened form for all the privileges just named.

The definition of this GRANT statement resembles the one for granting table privileges. However, there are two important differences. First, the list with privileges is longer and the ON clause looks different.

```
<grant statement> ::=
   <grant database privilege statement>

<grant database privilege statement> ::=
   GRANT <database privileges>
   ON    [ <database name> . ] *
   TO    <grantees>
   [ WITH GRANT OPTION ]

<database privileges> ::=
   ALL [ PRIVILEGES ] |
   <database privilege> [ { , <database privilege> }... ]

<database privilege> ::=
   SELECT                    |
   INSERT                    |
   DELETE                    |
   UPDATE                    |
   REFERENCES                |
   CREATE                    |
   ALTER                     |
   DROP                      |
   INDEX                     |
   CREATE TEMPORARY TABLES   |
   CREATE VIEW               |
   CREATE ROUTINE            |
   ALTER ROUTINE             |
   EXECUTE ROUTINE           |
   LOCK TABLES
```

Example 23.8: Give PETE the SELECT privilege for all tables in the TENNIS database.

```
GRANT    SELECT
ON       TENNIS.*
TO       PETE
```

Explanation: So, this privilege is effective for all existing tables and also the tables that will be added to the TENNIS database later.

Example 23.9: Give JIM the privilege to create, update, and remove new tables and views in the TENNIS database.

```
GRANT    CREATE, ALTER, DROP, CREATE VIEW
ON       TENNIS.*
TO       JIM
```

Note that one database privilege does not imply the other here as well. JIM is allowed to create new tables and views now, but he may not access them yet. For that, he needs to be granted a separate SELECT privilege or more privileges.

Example 23.10: Give PETE the SELECT privilege to query all catalog tables in the INFORMATION_SCHEMA database.

```
GRANT    SELECT
ON       INFORMATION_SCHEMA.*
TO       PETE
```

Example 23.11: Give ALYSSA the SELECT and INSERT privileges for all tables in the current database.

```
GRANT    SELECT, INSERT
ON       *
TO       ALYSSA
```

Explanation: The asterisk represents the current database here.

Exercise 23.6: Give JACO and DIANE the INSERT privilege on all tables of the TEN-NIS database.

23.5 Granting User Privileges

The most effective privileges are the user privileges. For all statements for which database privileges need to be granted, user privileges can be defined as well. For example, by granting someone the privilege CREATE on the user level, this user can create tables in all databases (instead of in one specific database). In addition, SQL supports the following additional user privileges:

■ CREATE USER—This privilege gives a user the right to create and remove new users.

```
<grant statement> ::=
    <grant user privilege statement>

<grant user privilege statement> ::=
    GRANT <user privileges>
    ON    *.*
    TO    <grantees>
    [ WITH GRANT OPTION ]

<user privileges> ::=
    ALL [ PRIVILEGES ] |
    <user privilege> [ { , <user privilege> }... ]

<user privilege> ::=
    SELECT                     |
    INSERT                     |
    DELETE                     |
    UPDATE                     |
    REFERENCES                 |
    CREATE                     |
    ALTER                      |
    DROP                       |
    INDEX                      |
    CREATE TEMPORARY TABLES    |
    CREATE VIEW                |
    CREATE ROUTINE             |
    ALTER ROUTINE              |
    EXECUTE ROUTINE            |
    LOCK TABLES                |
    CREATE USER
```

Example 23.12: Give MAX the CREATE, ALTER, and DROP privileges for all tables of all databases.

```
GRANT    CREATE, ALTER, DROP
ON       *.*
TO       MAX
```

Explanation: So, these privileges apply to all existing databases and also to all future databases.

Example 23.13: Give ALYSSA the privilege to create new users.

```
GRANT    CREATE USER
ON       *.*
TO       ALYSSA
```

The user called *root* gets the following privilege during the installation of MySQL:

```
GRANT    ALL PRIVILEGES
ON       *.*
TO       ROOT
```

By way of conclusion, Table 23.1 lists the levels at which privileges for certain SQL statements can be granted.

Table 23.1   *Overview of Privileges*

STATEMENT	USER PRIVILEGE	DATABASE PRIVILEGE	TABLE PRIVILEGE	COLUMN PRIVILEGE
SELECT	Yes	Yes	Yes	No
INSERT	Yes	Yes	Yes	No
DELETE	Yes	Yes	Yes	Yes
UPDATE	Yes	Yes	Yes	Yes

(continued)

Table 23.1   *Overview of Privileges (continued)*

STATEMENT	USER PRIVILEGE	DATABASE PRIVILEGE	TABLE PRIVILEGE	COLUMN PRIVILEGE
REFERENCES	Yes	Yes	Yes	Yes
CREATE	Yes	Yes	Yes	No
ALTER	Yes	Yes	Yes	No
DROP	Yes	Yes	Yes	No
INDEX	Yes	Yes	Yes	Yes
CREATE TEMPORARY TABLES	Yes	Yes	No	No
CREATE VIEW	Yes	Yes	No	No
CREATE ROUTINE	Yes	Yes	No	No
ALTER ROUTINE	Yes	Yes	No	No
EXECUTE ROUTINE	Yes	Yes	No	No
LOCK TABLES	Yes	Yes	No	No
CREATE USER	Yes	No	No	No

23.6 Passing on Privileges: WITH GRANT OPTION

A GRANT statement can be concluded with the WITH GRANT OPTION. This means that all users specified in the TO clause can *themselves* pass on the privilege (or part of the privilege) to other users. In other words, if a user is given a table privilege via the WITH GRANT OPTION, he or she can grant that privilege on the table without being the owner of it.

Example 23.14: Give JIM the REFERENCES privilege on the TEAMS table and allow him to pass it on to other users:

```
GRANT    REFERENCES
ON       TEAMS
TO       JOHN
WITH     GRANT OPTION
```

Because of the WITH GRANT OPTION clause, JIM can pass on this privilege to PETE, for example:

```
GRANT     REFERENCES
ON        TEAMS
TO        PETE
```

JIM can himself extend the statement with WITH GRANT OPTION so that PETE, in turn, can pass on the privilege.

23.7 Working with Roles

Granting privileges to individual users is acceptable if there are not that many. But imagine that the database consists of 300 tables and has 500 users. If everyone is to be given privileges, at least 500 GRANT statements are required. However, it is likely that many more statements are necessary, and this is very difficult to manage. That is why the concept of role has been added to SQL.

Portability: *MySQL supports no roles.*

A *role* is a defined set of privileges (the same privileges we have already described) that is granted to users. If the privileges of one role are altered (a table privilege is added, for example), the privileges of all users belonging to that role are changed automatically. It is easier to manage the privileges this way. A user may have several roles.

With the CREATE ROLE statement, new roles can be created.

```
<create role statement> ::=
    CREATE ROLE <role name>
```

To assign privileges to roles, the definition of the concept grantees has been extended so that all kinds of privileges can be assigned to roles.

```
<grantees> ::=
    PUBLIC                                          |
    <user name> [ { , <user name> }... ] |
    <role name> [ { , <role name> }... ]
```

A special version of the GRANT statement has also been created to assign roles to users.

```
<grant statement> ::=
   <grant role statement>

<grant role statement> ::=
   GRANT <role name> [ { , <role name> }... ]
   TO <grantees>
```

Example 23.15: Create the role SALES and give this role the SELECT and INSERT privileges on the PENALTIES table. Next, grant the SALES role to users ILENE, KELLY, JIM, and MARC.

```
CREATE ROLE SALES

GRANT    SELECT, INSERT
ON       PENALTIES
TO       SALES

GRANT SALES TO ILENE, KELLY, JIM, MARC
```

Explanation: The first statement creates the new role. With the GRANT statement, table privileges are granted. The structure of this statement is the same as the one used for granting privileges to users. Next, with a special version of the GRANT statement, we give the role to the four users. It is now possible to extend the privileges of the SALES role with one statement instead of using an entire set of GRANT statements.

Roles can be removed with the DROP ROLE statement. And, of course, all privileges belonging to that role also are removed; in turn, the users lose their privileges.

Example 23.16: Remove the role SALES.

```
DROP ROLE SALES
```

Exercise 23.7: Create the users JOE, JACO, and CHRIS with the password JAZZ. Then, create the role ADMIN and give this role all privileges on the COMMITTEE_MEMBERS table. Grant this new role to the users just created.

23.8 Recording Privileges in the Catalog

Several catalog tables are used to record users, roles, and privileges:

- Users are recorded in the USERS table.
- Roles are stored in the ROLES table.
- The USER_ROLES table is used to record which user has which role.
- The COLUMN_AUTHS table contains information about the privileges granted on specific columns.
- The TABLE_AUTHS table contains information about privileges on specific tables.

Contrary to many other SQL products, SQL does *not* remember who granted a privilege. When SQL has approved and processed a granted privilege, it does not record who granted the privilege. In the various catalog views, the column GRANTOR (the grantor of the privilege) has been included but has the value UNKNOWN everywhere. The GRANTEE (the person who receives the privilege), however, has been filled everywhere.

The USERS table contains only one column, the name of the user. This column also forms the primary key of this table.

Table 23.2 *Columns of the USERS Catalog Table*

COLUMN NAME	DATA TYPE	DESCRIPTION
USER_NAME	CHAR	Name of the user.

The ROLES table also consists of only one column, the name of the role.

Table 23.3 *Columns of the ROLES Catalog Table*

COLUMN NAME	DATA TYPE	DESCRIPTION
ROLE_NAME	CHAR	Name of the role.

The USER_ROLES table has the following structure. (The columns USER_NAME and ROLE_NAME form the primary key of this table.)

Table 23.4 *Columns of the USER_ROLES Catalog Table*

COLUMN NAME	DATA TYPE	DESCRIPTION
USER_NAME	CHAR	Name of the user.
ROLE_NAME	CHAR	Name of the role.

The column privileges are recorded in a separate catalog table, the COLUMN_AUTHS table. The primary key of this table is formed by the columns GRANTOR, TABLE_NAME, GRANTEE, and COLUMN_NAME. The table has the following structure:

Table 23.5   *Columns of the COLUMN_AUTHS Catalog Table*

COLUMN NAME	DATA TYPE	DESCRIPTION
GRANTOR	CHAR	User who granted the privilege.
GRANTEE	CHAR	User who received the privilege.
TABLE_CREATOR	CHAR	Name of the owner of the table on which the privilege is granted. (In MySQL, this is the name of the database to which the table belongs.)
TABLE_NAME	CHAR	Table or view on which the privilege is granted.
COLUMN_NAME	CHAR	Column name on which the UPDATE privilege is granted.
PRIVILEGE	CHAR	Indication of what kind of privilege it is.
WITHGRANTOPT	LOGICAL	If this column is filled with the value YES, the user can pass on the privilege to other users; otherwise, the value of this column is equal to NO.

The TABLE_AUTHS table has the following structure. The primary key of this table is formed by the columns GRANTOR, GRANTEE, TABLE_CREATOR, TABLE_NAME, and PRIVILEGE. You can see that the column privileges are *not* recorded in this table.

Table 23.6   *Columns of the TABLE_AUTHS Catalog Table*

COLUMN NAME	DATA TYPE	DESCRIPTION
GRANTOR	CHAR	User who granted the privilege.
GRANTEE	CHAR	User who received the privilege.
TABLE_CREATOR	CHAR	Name of the owner of the table on which the privilege is granted. (In MySQL, this is the name of the database to which the table belongs.)
TABLE_NAME	CHAR	Table or view on which the privilege is granted.
PRIVILEGE	CHAR	Indication of what kind of privilege it is.
WITHGRANTOPT	CHAR	If this column is filled with the value YES, the user can pass on the privilege to other users; otherwise, the value of this column is equal to NO.

The DATABASE_AUTHS table has the following structure. The primary key of this table is formed by the columns GRANTOR, GRANTEE, DATABASE_NAME, and PRIVILEGE.

Table 23.7   *Columns of the DATABASE_AUTHS Catalog Table*

COLUMN NAME	DATA TYPE	DESCRIPTION
GRANTOR	CHAR	User who granted the privilege.
GRANTEE	CHAR	User who received the privilege.
DATABASE_NAME	CHAR	Database on which the privilege is granted.
PRIVILEGE	CHAR	Indication of what kind of privilege it is.
WITHGRANTOPT	CHAR	If this column is filled with the value YES, the user can pass on the privilege to other users; otherwise, the value of this column is equal to NO.

The USER_AUTHS table has the following structure. The primary key of this table is formed by the columns GRANTOR, GRANTEE, and PRIVILEGE.

Table 23.8   *Columns of the USER_AUTHS Catalog Table*

COLUMN NAME	DATA TYPE	DESCRIPTION
GRANTOR	CHAR	User who granted the privilege.
GRANTEE	CHAR	User who received the privilege.
PRIVILEGE	CHAR	Indication of what kind of privilege it is; if this column is filled with the value USAGE, this user does not have any user privilege.
WITHGRANTOPT	CHAR	If this column is filled with the value YES, the user can pass on the privilege to other users; otherwise, the value of this column is equal to NO.

Example 23.17: Which users are allowed to query the PLAYERS table in the TENNIS database?

```
SELECT    GRANTEE
FROM      USER_AUTHS
WHERE     PRIVILEGE = 'SELECT'
UNION
SELECT    GRANTEE
FROM      DATABASE_AUTHS
WHERE     DATABASENAME = 'TENNIS'
AND       PRIVILEGE = 'SELECT'
UNION
SELECT    GRANTEE
FROM      TABLE_AUTHS
WHERE     TABLE_CREATOR = 'TENNIS'
AND       PRIVILEGE = 'SELECT'
```

Explanation: This example requires a search in three tables because SELECT privileges can be defined on three levels.

Exercise 23.8: What does the TABLE_AUTHS table look like after the following GRANT statements?
     The first two statements have been entered by BOOKSQL:

```
GRANT    SELECT
ON       PLAYERS
TO       PUBLIC

GRANT    INSERT
ON       PLAYERS
TO       RUDY
WITH     GRANT OPTION
```

     RUDY enters these statements:

```
GRANT    INSERT
ON       PLAYERS
TO       REGINA

GRANT    INSERT
ON       PLAYERS
TO       SUSAN
WITH     GRANT OPTION
```

     SUSAN enters the following statement:

```
GRANT    INSERT
ON       PLAYERS
TO       REGINA
```

23.9 Revoking Privileges

The REVOKE statement withdraws privileges from a user without deleting that user from the USERS table. This statement has the opposite effect of the GRANT statement.

```
<revoke statement> ::=
   <revoke table privilege statement>    |
   <revoke database privilege statement> |
   <revoke user privilege statement>     |
   <revoke role statement>

<revoke table privilege statement> ::=
   REVOKE   <table privileges>
   ON       <table specification>
   FROM     <grantees>

<table privileges> ::=
   ALL [ PRIVILEGES ] |
   <table privilege> [ { , <table privilege> }... ]

<table privilege> ::=
   SELECT                         |
   INSERT                         |
   DELETE                         |
   UPDATE [ <column list> ]       |
   REFERENCES [ <column list> ]   |
   ALTER                          |
   INDEX

<revoke database privilege statement> ::=
   REVOKE   <database privileges>
   ON       [ <database name> . ] *
   FROM     <user name> [ { , <user name> }... ]

<database privileges> ::=
   ALL [ PRIVILEGES ] |
   <database privilege> [ { , <database privilege> }... ]

<database privilege> ::=
   SELECT                         |
   INSERT                         |
   DELETE                         |
   UPDATE                         |
   REFERENCES                     |
   CREATE                         |
   ALTER                          |
   DROP                           |
   INDEX                          |
```

(continued)

```
      CREATE TEMPORARY TABLES  |
      CREATE VIEW              |
      CREATE ROUTINE           |
      ALTER ROUTINE            |
      EXECUTE ROUTINE          |
      LOCK TABLES

<revoke user privilege statement> ::=
      REVOKE  <user privileges>
      ON      *.*
      FROM    <user name> [ { , <user name> }... ]

<user privileges> ::=
      ALL [ PRIVILEGES ] |
      <user privilege> [ { , <user privilege> }... ]

<user privilege> ::=
      SELECT                   |
      INSERT                   |
      DELETE                   |
      UPDATE                   |
      REFERENCES               |
      CREATE                   |
      ALTER                    |
      DROP                     |
      INDEX                    |
      CREATE TEMPORARY TABLES  |
      CREATE VIEW              |
      CREATE ROUTINE           |
      ALTER ROUTINE            |
      EXECUTE ROUTINE          |
      LOCK TABLES              |
      CREATE USER

<column list> ::=
      ( <column name> [ { , <column name> }... ]

<revoke role statement> ::=
      REVOKE <role name> [ { , <role name> }... ]
      FROM   <grantees>

<grantees> ::=
      PUBLIC |
      <user name> [ { , <user name> }... ]
```

Example 23.18: The SELECT privilege of JIM on the PLAYERS table is to be withdrawn. (We assume that the situation is as it was at the end of Section 23.8.)

```
REVOKE    SELECT
ON        PLAYERS
FROM      JIM
```

The relevant privilege is now deleted from the catalog.

Example 23.19: Withdraw the REFERENCES privilege on the TEAMS table from JIM.

```
REVOKE    REFERENCES
ON        TEAMS
FROM      JIM
```

This privilege is withdrawn, together with all the privileges that are directly or indirectly dependent on it. In the example, PETE also loses his REFERENCES privilege on the TEAMS table.

With the REVOKE statement, a role of a user can also be deleted and privileges of roles can be withdrawn. Examples of both features follow.

Example 23.20: Withdraw the SALES role of ILENE.

```
REVOKE SALES FROM ILENE
```

Example 23.21: Withdraw the SELECT privilege on the PENALTIES table of the role called SALES.

```
REVOKE    SELECT
ON        PENALTIES
FROM      SALES
```

It could be that a user has been granted overlapping privileges. He received, for example, the table privilege UPDATE on the PLAYERS table and also the user privilege UPDATE for all tables in all databases. If one of the two is withdrawn, the other privilege remains.

23.10 Security of and Through Views

A GRANT statement can refer not only to tables, but also to views. (See the definition of the GRANT statement in Section 23.3.) Let's look at this more closely.

Because privileges can also be granted for views, you can provide users with access to only a part of a table or only to information derived or summarized from tables. The following are examples of both features.

Example 23.22: Give DIANE the privilege to read only the names and addresses of non-competitive players.

First, DIANE must be entered with a CREATE USER statement.

```
CREATE USER DIANE IDENTIFIED BY 'SECRET'
```

Second, a view is created specifying which data she may see:

```
CREATE     VIEW NAME_ADDRESS AS
SELECT     NAME, INITIALS, STREET, HOUSENO,
           TOWN
FROM       PLAYERS
WHERE      LEAGUENO IS NULL
```

The last step is to grant DIANE the SELECT privilege on the NAME_ADDRESS view:

```
GRANT    SELECT
ON       NAME_ADDRESS
TO       DIANE
```

With this statement, DIANE has access to only that part of the PLAYERS table defined in the view formula of NAME_ADDRESS.

Example 23.23: Make sure that user GERARD can look at only the number of players in each town.

First, we introduce GERARD.

```
CREATE USER GERARD IDENTIFIED BY 'XYZ1234'
```

The view that we use looks like this:

```
CREATE    VIEW RESIDENTS (TOWN, NUMBER_OF) AS
SELECT    TOWN, COUNT(*)
FROM      PLAYERS
GROUP BY TOWN
```

Now we give GERARD the privilege for the previous view:

```
GRANT    SELECT
ON       RESIDENTS
TO       GERARD
```

All types of table privilege can be granted on views.

23.11 Answers

23.1 CREATE   USER RONALDO IDENTIFIED BY 'NIKE'

23.2 DROP   USER RONALDO

23.3

```
GRANT    SELECT, INSERT
ON       PLAYERS
TO       RONALDO
```

23.4

```
GRANT    ALL
ON       COMMITTEE_MEMBERS
TO       PUBLIC
```

23.5

```
GRANT     UPDATE(STREET, HOUSENO, POSTCODE, TOWN)
ON        PLAYERS
TO        RONALDO
```

23.6

```
GRANT     INSERT
ON        TENNIS.*
TO        JACO, DIANE
```

23.7

```
CREATE    USER JOE    IDENTIFIED BY 'JAZZ'
CREATE    USER JACO   IDENTIFIED BY 'JAZZ'
CREATE    USER CHRIS  IDENTIFIED BY 'JAZZ'

CREATE    ROLE ADMIN

GRANT     ALL
ON        COMMITTEE_MEMBERS
TO        ADMIN
```

23.8

GRANTOR	GRANTEE	TABLE_NAME	S	I	D	U	R	WITHGRANTOPT
BOOKSQL	PUBLIC	PLAYERS	Y	N	N	N	N	NO
BOOKSQL	RUDY	PLAYERS	N	Y	N	N	N	YES
RUDY	REGINE	PLAYERS	N	Y	N	N	N	NO
RUDY	SUSANNE	PLAYERS	N	Y	N	N	N	YES
SUSANNE	REGINE	PLAYERS	N	Y	N	N	N	NO

24

Creating Sequences

24.1 Introduction

Many tables that are created have a column with unique numbers. These numbers identify the rows. Usually, they also form the primary keys of the tables. We have given several examples in this book of those primary keys. All tables of the sample database contain a column with unique numbers. For example, the player numbers in the PLAYERS table and the team numbers in the TEAMS table are unique. The numbers of the database objects in the catalog tables of the SQL products are often unique as well.

Generating numbers is rather difficult, which is why SQL supports a database object with which it can generate a series of numbers in a simple way. This database object is called the *sequence*. With sequences, we can generate ascending or descending, unique or nonunique, cyclic or noncyclic series of numbers.

> **Portability:** *Not every SQL product supports the sequence; MySQL is one of them. Those that do support it do not implement the sequence in exactly the same way. For that reason, in this book we describe the syntax as it is described in the SQL standard.*

24.2 Why Do We Need Sequences?

Do we actually need a sequence to generate numbers? Can't the applications create numbers themselves? Of course they can, but it is much more complex than you would think. Imagine that we want to enter a new team in the TEAMS table. But before the new team can be added to the TEAMS table with an INSERT statement, the next team number must be determined. We could do that with the following SELECT statement:

```
SELECT    CASE
               WHEN MAX(TEAMNO) IS NULL THEN 0
               ELSE MAX(TEAMNO) + 1
          END
FROM      TEAMS
```

Of course, this works if two users never try to determine a next number like this simultaneously. Those numbers would certainly not be unique.

In other applications, the problem of generating unique numbers is solved by creating a special table. In this table, records are kept on the last number issued for each relevant table. This value is fetched, increased, and used, and a new value is stored in the special table. This solution can work properly but causes much traffic on that special table. In addition, several SQL statements must be executed, which slows the total processing speed.

SQL supports the sequence to generate a series of numbers in a much more elegant way. A sequence can be seen as a number generator and can be used in INSERT, UPDATE, and SELECT statements. With a CREATE SEQUENCE statement, a sequence can be created.

Example 24.1: Create a new table called COUNTRIES and create a sequence to generate unique numbers for the country numbers in this table.

```
CREATE TABLE COUNTRIES
        (COUNTRYNO     INTEGER NOT NULL PRIMARY KEY,
         COUNTRYNAME   VARCHAR(30) NOT NULL)

CREATE SEQUENCE COUNTRYNUMBERS
```

Next, a simple INSERT statement can be used to enter a country:

```
INSERT    INTO COUNTRIES
          (COUNTRYNO, COUNTRYNAME)
VALUES    (NEXT VALUE FOR COUNTRYNUMBERS, 'China')
```

Explanation: The specification NEXT VALUE FOR COUNTRYNUMBERS is a special scalar expressions and returns the next number belonging to the sequence called COUNTRYNUMBERS. This is the first time the next number for COUNTRYNUMBERS is retrieved; therefore, the number 1 is generated. So, a new country with number 1 is added to the table. From now on, every time you use NEXT VALUE FOR COUNTRYNUMBERS, this expression returns a higher number. So, the series of numbers ascends.

```
<scalar expression> ::=
   NEXT VALUE FOR <sequence name>
```

If you enter the following UPDATE statement immediately after the previous INSERT statement:

```
UPDATE    COUNTRIES
SET       COUNTRYNO = NEXT VALUE FOR COUNTRYNUMBERS
WHERE     COUNTRYNO = 1
```

you change the value of the COUNTRYNO column to 2. The column is set to 2 because it is the second time you invoke NEXT VALUE for the COUNTRYNUMBERS sequence.

What you have done for country numbers can also be done for player numbers, payment numbers, and match numbers.

If you ask for the next value of a sequence in a SELECT statement, and the statement concerned gives multiple rows as result, for each row in the result, a new number is generated.

Example 24.2: For each player, get the player number, and use the COUNTRYNUMBERS sequence to generate unique numbers.

```
SELECT    PLAYERNO, NEXT VALUE FOR COUNTRYNUMBERS
FROM      PLAYERS
```

The result is:

```
PLAYERNO  NEXT VALUE FOR COUNTRYNUMBERS
--------  -----------------------------
       2                              1
       6                              2
       7                              3
       8                              4
      27                              5
      28                              6
      39                              7
```

44	8
57	9
83	10
95	11
100	12
104	13
112	14

Whether you actually get the next number also depends on whether other concurrent applications request new numbers using the same sequence. If that happens, both applications discover gaps in their series of numbers.

If the database server stops and restarts, the sequences will not show their first number. This is because XPRODUCTS remembers for every sequence what the last generated number is.

Portability: *In a few SQL products that support the sequence, the specification* SEQUENCE1.NEXTVAL *is used instead of the expression* NEXT VALUE FOR SEQUENCE1. *The result is the same.*

24.3 Options of the Sequences

In the first example of the previous section, the country numbers form a series of numbers beginning at 1 and incremented by 1. In some situations, we would like to deviate from that. When creating a sequence, several options can be specified to indicate how the series of numbers must be generated.

```
<create sequence statement> ::=
    CREATE SEQUENCE [ <user name>. ] <sequence name>
       [ <sequence option>... ]

<sequence option> ::=
    START WITH <integer literal>                          |
    INCREMENT BY <integer literal>                        |
    { MAXVALUE <integer literal> | NOMAXVALUE }           |
    { MINVALUE <integer literal> | NOMINVALUE }           |
    { CYCLE | NOCYCLE }                                   |
    { ORDER | NOORDER }                                   |
    { CACHE <integer literal> | NOCACHE }
```

The option START WITH can be used to indicate what the first number of the series must be. If this option is omitted, the value of the first number depends on whether the series is generated in ascending or descending order. In case of an ascending order, the value of the MINVALUE option is the first one. If this is not specified either, 1 is the first one. In case of a descending order, the value of the MAXVALUE option is generated first. If this is not specified, −1 is generated.

Example 24.3: Create a series of numbers beginning with 100.

```
CREATE  SEQUENCE  HUNDRED  START  WITH  100

SELECT    NEXT  VALUE  FOR  HUNDRED  AS  NUMBERS
FROM      MATCHES
WHERE     MATCHES  <=  5
```

The result is:

```
NUMBERS
-------
    100
    101
    102
    103
    104
```

With the option INCREMENT BY, we indicate what the next number in the series should be—or, in other words, by how much the number should be increased. If this option is omitted, the number is increased by 1. If the number is positive, an ascending series of numbers is generated. The number that is specified can be negative. In that case, the numbers are generated in descending order.

Example 24.4: Create a series of numbers that begins at 1 and increments by 100.

```
CREATE  SEQUENCE  BIG_STEPS
    INCREMENT  BY  100

SELECT    NEXT  VALUE  FOR  BIG_STEPS  AS  NUMBERS
FROM      MATCHES
WHERE     MATCHNO  <=  5
```

The result is:

```
NUMBERS
-------
      1
    101
    201
    301
    401
```

Example 24.5: Create a series of numbers that begins with −1 and *decrements* by 10.

```
CREATE  SEQUENCE  BACKWARDS
    INCREMENT  BY  -10

SELECT    NEXT  VALUE  FOR  BACKWARDS  AS  NUMBERS
FROM      MATCHES
WHERE     MATCHNO <= 5
```

The result is:

```
NUMBERS
-------
     -1
    -11
    -21
    -31
    -41
```

Explanation: Again, because the numbers are generated in descending order, the series does not start with 1, but −1.

Example 24.6: Create a series of numbers that begins with 1 and increments by 100.

```
CREATE SEQUENCE BIG_STEPS
    INCREMENT BY 100

SELECT    NEXT VALUE FOR BIG_STEPS AS NUMBERS
FROM      MATCHES
WHERE     MATCHNO <= 5
```

The result is:

```
NUMBERS
-------
      1
    101
    201
    301
    401
```

The MINVALUE option for sequences indicates what the lowest number should be that is generated in a descending series of numbers. Omitting this option is equivalent to specifying NOMINVALUE.

Example 24.7: Create a series of numbers that begins with 100 and descends by 1; the smallest value may be 98.

```
CREATE SEQUENCE MIN98
    START WITH 100
    INCREMENT BY -1
    MINVALUE 98

SELECT    NEXT VALUE FOR MIN98 AS NUMBERS
FROM      MATCHES
WHERE     MATCHNO <= 5
```

The result is:

```
NUMBERS
-------
    100
     99
     98
```

Explanation: Five rows should appear in this result. However, after the third, SQL returns an error message because the series has to stop at 98.

MAXVALUE indicates what the highest number can be that is generated in an ascending series of numbers. Omitting this option is equal to specifying NOMAXVALUE.

> **Portability:** *The lowest (MINVALUE) and highest (MAXVALUE) numbers that can be generated (and, therefore, can be specified), depend on the SQL product that you use. For example, with DB2, those are, respectively, $2^{31} - 1$ (2.147.483.647) and $-2^{31}+1$ ($-$2.147.483.647), and, with Oracle 10^{28} and -10^{28}.*

When the maximum number has been reached, the option CYCLE can indicate that the numbering should start all over again. In other words, a cyclic series of numbers is generated. Omitting this option is equal to specifying NOCYCLE, which means that if the highest number has been reached, when another number is requested, SQL will return an error message and *not* generate a new number. If CYCLE is not specified but START WITH is, the MINVALUE option can be left out.

Example 24.8: Create a series of number that begins with 1 and increases by 1, with the highest number of 3.

```
CREATE SEQUENCE CYCLE3
    START WITH 1
    INCREMENT BY 1
    MAXVALUE 3
    CYCLE

SELECT    NEXT VALUE FOR CYCLE3 AS NUMBERS
FROM      MATCHES
```

The result is:

```
NUMBERS
-------
      1
      2
      3
      1
      2
      3
      1
      2
      3
      1
      2
      3
      1
```

Explanation: If we use CYCLE, it is obvious that unique numbers are no longer generated.

ORDER indicates that the numbers are indeed generated in the right order. This is a standard implementation (note, however, that gaps in the numbering can occur). If NOORDER is specified, there is no guarantee that the numbers are generated in the right order.

The CACHE option does not relate so much to the numbers that are generated but to the speed with which that happens. The speed of applications can be increased by raising the CACHE size. In many products, the default value of the CACHE option is 20. SQL determines 20 numbers in advance and stores these number somewhere in internal memory. However, there is a chance that if the system fails, the already generated but so far unused numbers have disappeared.

Portability: *In several SQL products that support the sequence, some options have different names. For example, in DB2, NOMAXVALUE, NOMINVALUE, NOCYCLE, NOCACHE, and NOORDER are called, respectively, NO MAXVALUE, NO MINVALUE, NO CYCLE, NO CACHE, and NO ORDER.*

Example 24.9: Create a sequence called STANDARD that has the standard value (in accordance with DB2) for each option.

```
CREATE SEQUENCE STANDARD
    MINVALUE 1
    MAXVALUE 2147483647
    START WITH 1
    INCREMENT BY 1
    NOCYCLE
    CACHE 20
    ORDER
```

The use of the expression NEXT VALUE FOR is restricted to a number of rules. The expression can be specified only at the following places:

- In the SELECT clause of the main query SELECT statement (so not in that of a subquery)

  The SELECT statement in itself has to fulfill the following conditions:

  - It cannot be a part of a view.
  - It cannot contain DISTINCT.
  - It cannot contain an ORDER BY clause.
  - It cannot contain a GROUP BY clause.
  - It cannot contain set operators such as UNION.
- In the VALUES clause of an INSERT statement
- In the SET clause of an UPDATE statement

Exercise 24.1: Create sequences that generate the following series of numbers:

1. 2, 4, 6, 8, 10, . . .
2. 80, 70, 60, . . ., 10, 0, −10, −20, . . .
3. 1, 2, 3, 4, 1, 2, 3, 4, 1, 2, . . .
4. 0, 1, 0, 1, 0, 1, 0, . . .

24.4 Retrieving the Last Generated Number

Sometimes, you must retrieve the value of the number that was created last, without having to create a new number again. This number can be retrieved with the expression PREVIOUS VALUE FOR.

Example 24.10: Create a sequence for the team numbers, enter a team next, and change the team number of match 10 to this new team number.

```
CREATE SEQUENCE TEAMNUMBERS

INSERT    INTO TEAMS
          (TEAMNO, PLAYERNO, DIVISION)
VALUES    (NEXT VALUE FOR TEAMNUMBERS, 6, 'first')
```

Next, the change:

```
UPDATE    MATCHES
SET       TEAMNO = PREVIOUS VALUE FOR TEAMNUMBERS
WHERE     MATCHNO = 10
```

Explanation: The expression PREVIOUS VALUE FOR returns for a certain sequence—in this case, TEAMNUMBERS—the last generated number.

The last generated number can be retrieved only if the application concerned has asked for a NEXT VALUE. So, even when another application has made sure that the number is on 100, an application that has just logged on can retrieve that number 100 only after it has asked to generate a value itself.

> **Portability:** *In some SQL products that support the sequence, the specification* SEQUENCE1.CURRVAL *is used instead of the expression* PREVIOUS VALUE FOR SEQUENCE1. *The result is the same.*

24.5   Altering and Deleting Sequences

The options of a sequence can be altered with the ALTER SEQUENCE statement.

```
<alter sequence statement> ::=
    ALTER SEQUENCE [ <user name>. ] <sequence name>
        [ <sequence option>... ]

<sequence option> ::=
    RESTART [ WITH <integer literal> ]            |
    INCREMENT BY <integer literal>                |
    { MAXVALUE < integer literal> | NOMAXVALUE }  |
    { MINVALUE < integer literal> | NOMINVALUE }  |
    { CYCLE  | NOCYCLE }                           |
    { ORDER  | NOORDER }                           |
    { CACHE < integer literal> | NOCACHE }
```

Example 24.11: Make sure that the COUNTRYNUMBERS sequence starts all over again.

```
ALTER SEQUENCE COUNTRYNUMBERS
    RESTART
```

Example 24.12: Make sure that the COUNTRYNUMBERS sequence starts all over, but now at 100.

```
ALTER SEQUENCE COUNTRYNUMBERS
    RESTART WITH 100
```

Example 24.13: Change the FIVES sequence in such a way that it stops when the number 800 is reached.

```
ALTER SEQUENCE FIVES
        MAXVALUE 800
```

When we want sequences to start all over, it could happen that certain numbers are generated that have already been used. Those numbers are no longer unique. Make sure that the applications are aware of this fact.

Portability: *Not all SQL products allow sequences to be started over again.*

A sequence can be removed with the DROP SEQUENCE statement.

```
<drop sequence statement> ::=
   DROP SEQUENCE [ <user name>. ] <sequence name>
```

Example 24.14: Remove the DECREASE sequence.

```
DROP SEQUENCE DECREASE
```

24.6 Privileges for Sequences

Before users and applications may use a sequence, they must be granted the right privileges. With the ALTER privilege, users can adjust the options of a sequence; with USAGE, they are allowed to use the privilege.

```
<grant statement> ::=
   <grant sequence privilege statement>

<grant sequence privilege statement> ::=
   GRANT <sequence privileges>
   ON    SEQUENCE <sequence name>
   TO    <grantees>
   [ WITH GRANT OPTION ]

<sequence privileges> ::=
   <sequence privilege> [ { , <sequence privilege> }... ]

<sequence privilege> ::=
   ALTER | USAGE

<grantees> ::=
   PUBLIC |
   <user name> [ { , <user name> }... ]
```

Example 24.15: Give BEN the privilege to use and adjust the COUNTRYNUMBERS sequence.

```
GRANT    ALTER, USAGE
ON       SEQUENCE COUNTRYNUMBERS
TO       BEN
```

And, of course, there is a comparable REVOKE statement to withdraw these privileges.

24.7 Answers

24.1   1.

```
CREATE SEQUENCE EVEN_NUMBERS
    START WITH 2
    INCREMENT BY 2
```

2.

```
CREATE SEQUENCE TENS
    START WITH 80
    INCREMENT BY -10
```

3.

```
CREATE SEQUENCE FROM_1_TO_4
    START WITH 1
    INCREMENT BY 1
    MINVALUE 1
    MAXVALUE 4
    NOCACHE
    CYCLE
```

4.

```
CREATE SEQUENCE BIT
    START WITH 0
    MINVALUE 0
    MAXVALUE 1
    NOCACHE
    CYCLE
```

25

Creating Schemas

25.1 What Is a Schema?

T he term *database* was explained in Chapter 22, "Creating Databases." A database is an object to group tables physically, like a storage rack groups a set of boxes. A *schema*, on the other hand, is a method to group database objects, such as tables and views. With a schema, objects are grouped logically, like boxes can be grouped logically be giving them special labels. For example, all boxes labeled *purchase* might contain documents belonging to the purchasing department.

To explain the term *schema* correctly, we have to throw light on the difference between *owner* and *creator*. Every table and index is created by a user. Usually, we call this user the owner. However, we should call this user the creator. The reason is that some products distinguish between the owner and the creator of the table. (In most cases, they are the same user.) If user U_1 creates a table for another user U_2, U_1 is the creator and U_2 is the owner.

Example 25.1: Create the TEST table with BRADLEY as owner, and assume that this statement is entered by MICHAEL.

```
CREATE TABLE BRADLEY.TEST
      (COLUMN1   INTEGER)
```

Explanation: In front of the table name, the name of the owner BRADLEY is specified (separated by a full stop). If this name is not specified, the table is owned by the user who enters the statement. He is then the owner and creator. In this example, BRADLEY is the owner and MICHAEL is the creator.

What exactly is a schema? In fact, the terms *owner* and *schema* are equivalent. All database objects with the same owner belong to the same schema. The name of the schema is equal to the name of the owner. This means that with the previous CREATE TABLE statement, a table is created that is assigned to the schema BRADLEY.

Not only tables can belong to a schema. Indexes, for example, can also belong to a schema.

Example 25.2: Create an index on the COLUMN1 column of the TEST table with BRADLEY as owner.

```
CREATE INDEX BRADLEY.INDEXA ON TEST (COLUMN1)
```

For the sake of clarity, tables belonging to the same schema belong to the same owner. Also note that tables belonging to different schemas can still belong to the same database.

Portability: *Not all SQL products support schemas; MySQL is one of them.*

25.2 Creating a Schema

In the first example in the previous section, a schema was created implicitly. To create a new schema explicitly, use the CREATE SCHEMA statement.

```
<create schema statement> ::=
   CREATE SCHEMA <schema name>
      <schema statement>...

<schema statement> ::=
   <create table statement> |
   <create view statement>  |
   <create index statement> |
   <grant statement>
```

Example 25.3: Create a schema called TENNIS_SCHEMA.

```
CREATE SCHEMA TENNIS_SCHEMA
```

Explanation: After processing this statement, a schema exists with the name TEN-NIS_SCHEMA. Of course, this schema does not contain any database objects yet.

Example 25.4: Add a view to TENNIS_SCHEMA.

```
CREATE VIEW TENNIS_SCHEMA.SEVERAL_MATCHES AS
SELECT    *
FROM      MATCHES
WHERE     MATCHENO < 5
```

With a CREATE SCHEMA statement, we can also create several objects simultaneously that all belong to the new schema. In this case, it is not necessary to repeatedly specify the schema name explicitly in, for example, the CREATE TABLE statement.

Example 25.5: Create a schema consisting of two tables and one index.

```
CREATE SCHEMA TWO_TABLES
     CREATE TABLE TABLE1 (COLUMN1 INTEGER)
     CREATE TABLE TABLE2 (COLUMN1 INTEGER)
     CREATE INDEX INDEX1 ON TABLE1(COLUMN1)
```

Explanation: Note that this is one SQL statement in which an entire schema, two tables, and one index are created at once. The last three all have TWO_TABLES as owner and belong to the same schema.

The advantage of combining a set of CREATE statements within a CREATE SCHEMA statement is that they are all processed together or not at all. Therefore, when a problem arises with one of the CREATE statements and a few database objects have already been created, they will all be removed. It is truly all or nothing.

Portability: *The types of database objects that can belong to a schema depend on the SQL product.*

25.3 Removing a Schema

With the DROP SCHEMA statement, an existing schema can be removed.

```
<drop schema statement> ::=
   DROP SCHEMA <schema name> [ RESTRICT ]
```

If a schema is removed that still contains database objects, those objects are removed as well. If the DROP statement is extended with RESTRICT, the statement is rejected if there are still objects left in the schema.

Portability: *Because schemas are the same as owners, some SQL products use the DROP USER statement to remove schemas.*

25.4 Schema Versus SQL User

If the concept of a schema is similar to the concept of an owner, and if each owner is an SQL user, you probably wonder why this concept of schema has been introduced. Does it actually add something? Sufficient differences exist between a schema and an SQL user to justify their respective existences:

■ A schema does not have a password, but for every SQL user (and this include all the owners), a password can be defined.

■ It is not possible to log on with a schema name.

■ It is not possible to assign privileges to schemas with the GRANT statement, but it is for owners.

■ A schema cannot be a builder, but an SQL user can.

■ With one CREATE SCHEMA statement, a set of database objects can be created, but not with a CREATE USER statement.

This means that a schema and an SQL user have overlapping functionalities, but each also has unique features.

IV Programming with SQL

SQL can be used in two ways: *interactively* and *pre-programmed*. Preprogrammed SQL is used primarily in programs developed for end users who do not have to learn SQL statements but who work with easy-to-use menus and screens instead.

Previous chapters have assumed interactive use of the language. Interactive means that statements are processed as soon as they are entered, whereas, with preprogrammed SQL, statements are included in a program that has been written in another programming language. Most products support, among others, the languages C, C++, Java, Visual Basic, PHP, Perl, and COBOL. These languages are known as *host languages*. When using preprogrammed SQL, the results of the SQL statements are not immediately visible to the user but are processed by the *enveloping* program. You can use most of the SQL statements discussed in the earlier chapters in preprogrammed SQL. Apart from a few minor additions, preprogrammed SQL is the same as interactive SQL.

Several forms of preprogrammed SQL exist. The oldest is embedded SQL. With the arrival of client/server technology, the use of preprogrammed SQL through so-called Call Level Interfaces (CLIs) became very popular. The first standardized CLI was Open DataBase Connectivity (ODBC), from Microsoft. The advent of the Internet and the World Wide Web led to the development of other CLIs, among them Java DataBase Connectivity (JDBC) and Microsoft's OLE DB. JDBC has a resemblance to ODBC but has been designed specifically for applications developed in Java. Additionally, special CLIs have been developed for languages such as PHP and Perl to access SQL database servers.

When programmers include SQL statements in a host language for the first time, they all have the same questions initially. What does the statement to log on look like? How do we include parameters within SQL statements? How does a program process the result of a SELECT statement? How do we know that an SQL statement has been processed correctly? The answers to these questions depend on the host language and the form of preprogrammed SQL. Still, they are not completely different. Clearly, commonalities do exist. Whatever language and CLI are selected, several general principles apply. That is why it is recommended to study those principles before you get bogged down in those details. For that reason, we decided to describe embedded SQL first. This form is rather detail-free, which makes it possible to focus on those general principles.

Note: *MySQL does not support embedded SQL, so you cannot use this form later. The first chapter of this part is purely added for educational reasons.*

Introduction to Embedded SQL

26.1 Introduction

T he primary concern of this chapter is to introduce the principles of embedded SQL. As the title states, it is an introduction rather than a complete description of the features of embedded SQL. We strongly advise those who want to develop programs with embedded SQL to carefully study the SQL manuals supplied with products.

The host language used in this chapter is not an existing programming language, but a so-called *pseudo programming language*. Again, we selected a pseudo programming language to avoid getting bogged down in all sorts of details that are concerned with the link between a host language and embedded SQL.

In Chapter 30, "Stored Procedures," we describe stored procedures. For a better understanding of that chapter, we also advise you to read this chapter about embedded SQL because many of the principles that apply to embedded SQL hold true for stored procedures.

Portability: *Not every SQL product supports embedded SQL, including MySQL. Some only offer CLIs.*

26.2 The Pseudo Programming Language

Before we start to look at the examples of embedded SQL, we need to outline a few points about the pseudo programming language that we will use.

■ In many programming languages, each SQL statement in embedded SQL usually starts with the words EXEC SQL. We omit this in our examples.

■ In many programming languages, each SQL statement has to end with END-SQL (in COBOL, for example) or a semicolon (in C, C++, PL/I, and Pascal, for example). We use the semicolon in our examples.

■ Every non-SQL statement also ends with a semicolon.

- Everything on a line that follows the symbol # is considered to be a comment.
- All the host variables (variables belonging to the host language) used must be declared at the beginning of a program, and a data type must be assigned to the variable. For this, we use the SQL data types (see Chapter 15, "Creating Tables")

26.3 DDL and DCL Statements and Embedded SQL

Including DDL and DCL statements, such as CREATE TABLE and GRANT, in a program is simple. No difference exists between the functions and the syntax of these two types of statement for interactive or embedded use.

Example 26.1: Develop a program that creates or drops an index on the PLAYERS table, depending on the choice the end user makes.

```
PROGRAM PLAYERS_INDEX;
DECLARATIONS
    choice : CHAR(1);
BEGIN
    WRITE 'Do you want to create (C) or drop
          (D) the PLAY index?';
    READ choice;
    # Dependent on choice, create or drop the index
    IF choice = 'C' THEN
       CREATE UNIQUE INDEX PLAY ON PLAYERS (PLAYERNO);
       WRITE 'Index PLAY is created!';
    ELSE IF choice = 'D' THEN
       DROP INDEX PLAY;
       WRITE 'Index PLAY is dropped!';
    ELSE
       WRITE 'Unknown choice!';
    ENDIF;
END
```

The result is:

```
Do you want to create (C) or drop (D) the PLAY index? C
Index PLAY is created!
```

Explanation: You can see in this program that an embedded SQL statement is the same as its interactive counterpart. A semicolon follows each SQL statement in this program, which has not been included in any of the previous chapters. This is because we were focused on the SQL statements themselves, not how they should be entered.

SQL supports several statements for changing the data in tables, such as DELETE, INSERT, and UPDATE. These statements are included in a program in the same way as DDL and DCL statements.

Example 26.2: Develop a program that deletes all rows from the PENALTIES table.

```
PROGRAM DELETE_PENALTIES;
DECLARATIONS
    choice : CHAR(1);
BEGIN
    WRITE 'Do you want to delete all rows';
    WRITE 'from the PENALTIES table (Y/N)?';
    READ choice;
    # Determine what the answer is.
    IF choice = 'Y' THEN
        DELETE FROM PENALTIES;
        WRITE 'The rows are deleted!';
    ELSE
        WRITE 'The rows are not deleted!';
    ENDIF;
END
```

26.4 Processing Programs

In the previous section, we gave a number of examples of programs with embedded SQL, but how can we run these programs? Programs written in a language such as C, Java, COBOL, or Pascal must be processed by a *compiler* and a *link/editor* before they can be executed. The compiler generates an *object module* that will be converted to a *load module* by the link/editor. A load module is a program that is ready to be loaded into the internal memory of the computer for processing. Compilers and link/editors are not part of a database server but are separate programs or utilities.

To make things easy and clear, we assume in the rest of this section that we are working with C as the host language. For other host languages, the same comments and rules usually apply.

In the previous section, we gave a few examples of programs with embedded SQL. Perhaps you have already asked yourself, what does the C compiler do with embedded SQL? The answer is clear: It gives error messages because SQL statements are not a part of the C language. We have to do something with the program before the compiler can process it. We need to *precompile* the program.

The precompiler translates a program written with C and SQL statements into a program that contains only pure C statements but still guarantees that the desired SQL statements are processed in some way. Most vendors of SQL products supply a number of *precompilers* (also called *preprocessors*) to precompile programs. A precompiler is a stand-alone program (a utility program) that is supplied with the database server. A separate precompiler is generally available for each host language. Figure 26.1 illustrates the process of precompiling, compiling, and link/editing.

Figure 26.1   *Preparation of programs with embedded SQL statements*

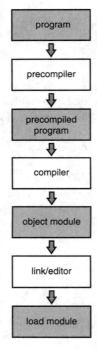

What is the job of a precompiler? We give a general outline of a precompiler's tasks by listing the steps executed before a SQL statement, included in a program, can be processed. These are the steps:

1. Identify the SQL statements in the program.
2. Translate the SQL statements into C statements.
3. Check the syntactical correctness of the SQL statements.
4. Check that tables and columns mentioned in the statements actually exist.
5. Check that the privileges (granted with GRANT statements) required to execute the SQL statements are available.
6. Determine the processing strategy.
7. Execute the SQL statements.

The steps that a precompiler executes depend on the product. Each precompiler executes steps 1 and 2. Identifying SQL statements has been made easier by demanding that each SQL statement be preceded by the words EXEC SQL. The differences between the products begin at step 2. The C code generated by the DB2 precompiler is different from that generated by the Oracle precompiler. Is this important? No. The code that is generated is not intended to be modified by human hand, just as code generated by a compiler should not be modified.

As an illustration, we show you the C code that the Oracle precompiler (Version 1.2.14) generates for the statement: DELETE FROM PENALTIES.

```
/* SQL stmt #4
   EXEC SQL DELETE FROM PENALTIES;
*/
{      /* beginning of SQL code gen stmt */
sqlsca(&sqlca);
if ( !sqlusi[0] )
   {  /* OPEN SCOPE */
sq001.sq001T[0] = (unsigned short)10;
SQLTM[0] = (int)4;
sqlbs2(&sq001.sq001N, sq001.sq001V,
   sq001.sq001L, sq001.sq001T, sq001.sq001I,
   &SQLTM[0], &sqlusi[0]);
   }  /* CLOSE SCOPE */
sqlsch(&sqlusi[0]);
sqlscc(&sqlcun[0]);
sqltfl(&SQLTM[0], &SQLBT0);
if ( !SQLTM[0] )
   {  /* OPEN SCOPE */
SQLTM[0] = (int)16384;
sqlopn(&SQLTM[0], &SQLBT3, &sqlvsn);
SQLTM[0] = (int)19;
sqlosq(sq002, &SQLTM[0]);
   }  /* CLOSE SCOPE */
SQLTM[0] = (int)1;
sqlexe(&SQLTM[0]);
sqlwnr();
}   /* ending of SQL code gen stmt */
```

Not all precompilers check the syntactical correctness of SQL statements (step 3). Some just assume that what follows EXEC SQL is correct SQL. This means that you can have an error message during the execution of the program in step 7.

In explaining step 4 onward, we should make a distinction between the products that compile the SQL statements and those that interpret the statements at *run time* (that is, during the execution of the program). Examples of the first group are DB2 and Ingres. Examples of interpreters are Oracle and Informix.

In an interpreter environment, steps 4, 5, and 6 are not executed by the precompiler. Those steps are executed at runtime during step 7. At runtime, SQL determines whether the tables that are used actually exist. This also means that the precompiler can run without the database server being started.

The SQL statements in a compiler environment are placed in a separate file by the precompiler. In some products, this file is called the *Database Request Module* (DBRM). In other words, the precompiler has two output files: the adapted C program from which the SQL statements have been removed and the DBRM that contains the SQL statements. The adapted program can be compiled, but the program is not yet ready to be executed. First, the DBRM must be processed by a specific utility program, called the *binder*.

The binder is a program that is supplied by the vendor of the SQL product and can run only when the database server has been started. In fact, the binder executes steps 4, 5, and 6 for each statement in the DBRM. It checks whether the tables and columns actually exist, checks the privileges, and determines the processing strategy to be used for the SQL statement. (In Chapter 20, "Using Indexes," we discussed how to determine the processing strategy.) The result is a set of compiled SQL statements that can be processed. The binder stores them in a special catalog table. To summarize, the following activities are executed in a compiler environment before a program can run: precompiling, binding, compiling, and link/editing.

Step 7, executing an SQL statement, takes place when the program is run. In a compiler environment, this means that when an SQL statement is to be processed, the compiled SQL statement is retrieved from the catalog so that it can be executed. In an interpreter environment, SQL must first check whether the tables and columns exist, and whether the correct privileges exist. And it must also determine the processing strategy.

26.5 Using Host Variables in SQL Statements

In the next example, we show that in those SQL statements where expressions may be used, such as SELECT and UPDATE, *host variables* can also be specified (see Chapter 5, "SELECT Statement: Common Elements").

Example 26.3: Develop a program that increases the number of sets won by one for a given match.

```
PROGRAM RAISE_WON;
DECLARATIONS
   mno : SMALLINT;
BEGIN
   WRITE 'Enter the match number: ';
```

```
        READ mno;
        # Increase the number of sets won
        UPDATE    MATCHES
        SET       WON = WON + 1
        WHERE     MATCHNO = :mno;
        WRITE 'Ready!';
    END
```

Explanation: In the WHERE clause, we use the host variable MNO at a place where we otherwise would use an expression. This is allowed in embedded SQL. To differentiate host variables from columns, functions, and so on, you must specify a colon in front of them.

A host variable that is used within SQL statements must be specified according to precise rules. These rules depend on the column with which the host variable is compared, and each host language has its own rules. For example, the MNO variable must have a data type that is compatible with the data type of the MATCHNO column because that is the column with which it is being compared. Again, we refer to the manuals of the various products for these rules. We will use the SQL data types.

Example 26.4: Develop a program for entering data about a penalty.

```
PROGRAM ENTER_PENALTIES;
DECLARATIONS
    pno       : SMALLINT;
    payno     : SMALLINT;
    pay_date  : DATE;
    amount    : DECIMAL(7,2);
BEGIN
    WRITE 'Enter the payment number of the penalty: ';
    READ payno;
    WRITE 'Enter the player number of the penalty: ';
    READ pno;
    WRITE 'Enter the date on which the penalty is paid: ';
    READ pay_date;
    WRITE 'Enter the penalty amount: ';
    READ amount;
    # Add the new data to the PENALTIES table
    INSERT  INTO PENALTIES
            (PAYMENTNO, PLAYERNO, PAYMENT_DATE, AMOUNT)
    VALUES (:payno, :pno, :payment_date, :amount);
    WRITE 'Ready!';
END
```

Explanation: After the values have been entered, new data is inserted with an INSERT statement.

When working with a real programming language, you are required to place the following statements around the declarations of the host variables used within SQL statements:

```
BEGIN DECLARE SECTION
```

and

```
END DECLARE SECTION
```

An example of this is given in Section 26.18.

26.6 The SQLCODE Host Variable

The RAISE_WON program from the previous section used an UPDATE statement to increase the value in the WON column by one. But how do we know whether this increase has actually taken place? Perhaps there was no row in the MATCHES table corresponding to the match number entered. We can test this by checking the value in the SQLCODE host variable. SQLCODE is a host variable that is assigned a specific value by SQL after any SQL statement has been executed, not just after DML statements. If the value of SQLCODE is equal to zero, the SQL statement has executed correctly. If its value is negative, something has gone wrong. A positive value of SQLCODE indicates a warning. The value 100, for example, means that no rows have been found.

Example 26.5: Extend the RAISE_WON program to include a test on SQLCODE.

```
PROGRAM RAISE_WON_2;
DECLARATIONS
   mno : SMALLINT;
BEGIN
   WRITE ' Enter the match number: ';
   READ mno;
   # Increase the number of sets won
   UPDATE    MATCHES
   SET       WON = WON + 1
   WHERE     MATCHNO = :mno;
   # Determine if it has executed successfully
   IF sqlcode > 0 THEN
      WRITE ' Update has occurred';
   ELSE
      WRITE ' The match entered does not exist';
   ENDIF;
END
```

Perhaps you noticed that we did not declare the SQLCODE host variable in this program. We do not declare this host variable in the usual way, but instead we use a special statement, the INCLUDE statement. This makes the beginning of the previous program look as follows:

```
PROGRAM RAISE_WON_2;
DECLARATIONS
    mno : SMALLINT;
    INCLUDE SQLCA;
BEGIN
    WRITE 'Enter the match number: ';
    :
```

Explanation: The effect of this INCLUDE statement is that a file called SQLCA is imported. In that file, SQLCODE has been declared in the correct way. This prevents errors. The most important reason for declaring SQLCODE in this way is that SQL also supports other special host variables. By using this statement, they are all declared simultaneously.

In almost all the example programs, we test the value of the SQLCODE host variable after an SQL statement has been processed. We conclude this section with two remarks on this host variable.

■ Despite that all the possible SQLCODE values that can be generated by SQL are documented in the manuals of the SQL products, we recommend that you never test on these specific codes. These codes can change in new versions, and it is always difficult to determine all the possible codes that might be returned.

■ Try to develop a procedure, function, or routine that hides and encapsulates the SQLCODE completely. Besides that this is a "cleaner" way of programming, SQL-CODE is described in ISO's SQL2 standard as a *deprecated feature*, which means that it will disappear from the standard in a subsequent version.

26.7 Executable Versus Nonexecutable SQL Statements

So far, we have discussed three new statements that we are not allowed to use and, indeed, cannot use interactively: BEGIN DECLARE, END DECLARE, and INCLUDE. These are not "real" SQL statements but statements processed by the precompiler instead of by SQL. The first two statements tell the precompiler which host variables can occur within SQL statements and what the data types are. The precompiler reads in the file that is specified in the INCLUDE statements.

In the literature, statements that SQL processes are called *executable* statements. Statements that the precompiler processes are called *nonexecutable* statements. We describe a few more in this chapter.

Nonexecutable SQL statements are used only in embedded SQL. It is not possible to state the opposite, however—that all executable statements may be used interactively. Later in this chapter, we discuss other executable SQL statements that may be used only with embedded SQL.

26.8 The WHENEVER Statement

In Section 26.6, we stated that a value is assigned to SQLCODE after processing each SQL statement. However, this applies only to executable SQL statements, not to the nonexecutable statements. The possible values of SQLCODE can be divided into three groups:

- The statement has been processed correctly.
- During the statement, something went wrong. (The statement was probably not executed.)
- During the statement, a warning appeared. (The statement was executed.)

Ideally, the value of the SQLCODE host variable should be checked after each SQL statement, for example, with an IF-THEN-ELSE statement. However, a large program can consist of hundreds of statements, and this would lead to many IF-THEN-ELSE statements. To avoid this, SQL supports the WHENEVER statement. With the WHENEVER statement, you specify where the program should proceed according to the value of the SQLCODE host variable.

```
<whenever statement> ::=
    WHENEVER <whenever condition> <whenever action>

<whenever condition> ::=
    SQLWARNING | SQLERROR | NOT FOUND

<whenever action> ::=
    CONTINUE | GOTO <label>
```

To show how this statement can be used, what it means, and how it actually works, we rewrite the PLAYERS_INDEX example from Section 26.3.

Example 26.6: Develop a program that creates or drops the index on the PLAYERS table, depending on the user's choice.

In the original program, the SQLCODE host variable was not checked. Let us first change this example without using the WHENEVER statement.

```
PROGRAM PLAYERS_INDEX_2;
DECLARATIONS
    choice : CHAR(1);
BEGIN
    WRITE 'Do you want to create (C) or delete
           (D) the PLAY index ?';
    READ choice;
    # Depending on the choice, create or delete the index
    IF choice = 'C' THEN
        CREATE INDEX PLAY ON PLAYERS (PLAYERNO);
        IF sqlcode >= 0 THEN
            WRITE 'Index PLAY is created!';
        ELSE
            WRITE 'SQL statement is not processed';
            WRITE 'Reason is ', sqlcode;
        ENDIF;
    ELSE IF choice = 'D' THEN
        DROP INDEX PLAY;
        IF sqlcode => 0 THEN
            WRITE 'Index PLAY is deleted!';
        ELSE IF
            WRITE 'SQL statement is not processed';
            WRITE 'Reason is ', sqlcode;
        ENDIF;
    ELSE
        WRITE 'Unknown choice!';
    ENDIF;
END
```

The program has grown considerably. We now add a WHENEVER statement:

```
PROGRAM PLAYERS_INDEX_3;
DECLARATIONS
    choice : CHAR(1);
BEGIN
    WHENEVER SQLERROR GOTO STOP;
    WHENEVER SQLWARNING CONTINUE;
    WRITE 'Do you want to create (C) or delete
           (D) the PLAY index?';
    READ choice;
```

```
# Depending on the choice, create or delete the index
IF choice = 'C' THEN
   CREATE INDEX PLAY ON PLAYERS (PLAYERNO);
   WRITE 'Index PLAY is created!';
ELSE IF choice = 'D' THEN
   DROP INDEX PLAY;
   WRITE 'Index PLAY is deleted!';
ELSE
   WRITE 'Unknown choice!';
ENDIF;

STOP:
  WRITE 'SQL statement is not processed';
  WRITE 'Reason is ', sqlcode;
END
```

Explanation: The effect of the first WHENEVER statement is that when an error occurs during the processing of an SQL statement, the program automatically "jumps" to the label called STOP. This statement replaces the two IF-THEN-ELSE statements in the program PLAYERS_INDEX_2. The effect of the second WHENEVER statement is nil; with this statement, you specify that if the value of the SQLCODE host variable is greater than zero (SQLWARNING), the program should continue.

The WHENEVER statement is a nonexecutable statement, which means that the statement is processed by the precompiler. In other words, the precompiler converts this statement to statements of the host language. The precompiler generates an IF-THEN-ELSE statement for each SQL statement. For example, the precompiler generates the following IF-THEN-ELSE statement for the first WHENEVER statement:

```
IF sqlcode < 0 GOTO STOP
```

This IF-THEN-ELSE statement is placed directly behind each SQL statement. No IF-THEN-ELSE statements are generated for the other WHENEVER statement. This is not needed because CONTINUE has been specified.

If a program contains the following three WHENEVER statements:

```
WHENEVER SQLWARNING GOTO HELP
WHENEVER SQLERROR   GOTO STOP
WHENEVER NOT FOUND  GOTO AGAIN
```

the following statements are generated and placed behind each SQL statement:

```
IF sqlcode = 100 GOTO AGAIN
IF sqlcode > 0    GOTO HELP
IF sqlcode < 0    GOTO STOP
```

WHENEVER statements may be specified in more than one place in a program. A WHENEVER statement is applicable to all SQL statements that follow it, until the end of the program or the next WHENEVER statement.

In practice, some developers make the error of thinking that the precompiler follows the "flow" of the program. This is certainly not true. The precompilers consider a program to be a series of lines. If the line contains an SQL statement, something will be done with it. The precompiler cannot see the difference between, for example, an IF-THEN-ELSE and a WHILE-DO statement. In the following example, we show the kind of logical error that can be made:

```
BEGIN
    WHENEVER SQLERROR GOTO STOP1;
    :
    WHILE ... DO
       :
       WHENEVER SQLERROR GOTO STOP2;
       UPDATE PENALTIES SET AMOUNT = AMOUNT * 1.05;
       :
    ENDWHILE;
    :
    DELETE FROM TEAMS WHERE TEAMNO = 1;
    :
    STOP1:
    :
    STOP2:
    :
END;
```

An important question we should ask ourselves is, to which label will the program jump if the DELETE statement fails and the program has not executed the statements within the WHILE-DO statement? You might think that it will jump to label STOP1 because that is the only WHENEVER statement that has been processed. This is not true, however. A precompiler considers a program to be a series of statements without meaning. It is

interested only in the SQL statements. The precompiler replaces each WHENEVER statement with IF-THEN-ELSE statements, resulting in the following program:

```
BEGIN
   :
   WHILE ... DO
      :
      UPDATE PENALTIES SET AMOUNT = AMOUNT * 1.05;
      IF sqlcode < 0 GOTO STOP2;
      :
   ENDWHILE;
   :
   DELETE FROM TEAMS WHERE TEAMNO = 1;
   IF sqlcode < 0 GOTO STOP2;
   :
END;
```

In other words, if the DELETE statement fails, the program jumps to the STOP2 label,
even though the statements within the WHILE-DO statement have not been processed.

26.9   Logging On to SQL

Just as a username and password must be given for interactive SQL to let SQL know who
you are, this should happen with embedded SQL. We use the CONNECT statement to do
this.

Example 26.7: Develop a program that logs on to SQL and reports whether this has
succeeded.

```
PROGRAM LOGIN;
DECLARATIONS
   user     : CHAR(30);
   password : CHAR(30);
BEGIN
   WRITE 'What is your name?';
   READ user;
   WRITE 'What is your password?';
```

```
      READ password;
      CONNECT TO :user IDENTIFIED BY :password;
      IF sqlcode = 0 THEN
         WRITE 'Logging on has succeeded';
      ELSE
         WRITE 'Logging on has not succeeded';
         WRITE 'Reason: ', sqlcode;
      ENDIF;
   END
```

Explanation: If SQL rejects the CONNECT statement, SQLCODE has a negative value.

The first SQL statement processed in a program should always be a CONNECT statement. The reason is that SQL rejects all the SQL statements if the application has not logged on properly. So, all the previous examples are incorrect because they do not contain a CONNECT statement. However, we continue this practice of omitting the CONNECT statement from all the examples to avoid making the programs too large and too complex.

The opposite of the CONNECT statement is, of course, the DISCONNECT statement. The use of this statement is simple. After the execution of DISCONNECT, the tables are no longer accessible.

Portability: *Not every product supports the CONNECT statement. Furthermore, the features of this statement vary considerably among the products that do support it.*

26.10   SELECT Statements Returning One Row

In many cases, you will want to capture the result of a SELECT statement in a program. This can be done by saving the result in host variables. Here, you need to distinguish between SELECT statements that always return one row and those in which the result consists of an indeterminate number of rows. The former type is described in this section, and the latter is discussed in Section 26.12.

Embedded SQL supports a version of the SELECT statement intended for those statements for which the result table consists of one row. A new clause is added to this SELECT statement: the INTO clause. In the INTO clause of this statement, we specify one host variable for each expression in the SELECT clause. These types of statements are known as SELECT INTO statements. The reason for differentiating them from "normal" SELECT statements is that, first, they contain the INTO clause and, second, they produce only one row.

```
<select into statement> ::=
   <select clause>
   <into clause>
 [ <from clause>
 [ <where clause> ]
 [ <group by clause>
 [ <having clause> ] ] ]

<into clause> ::=
   INTO <host variable> [ { , <host variable> }... ]

<host variable> ::=
   ":" <host variable name>
```

Example 26.8: Develop a program that prints a player's address line by line after a particular player number is entered.

```
PROGRAM ADDRESS;
DECLARATIONS
    pno      : SMALLINT;
    name     : CHAR(15);
    init     : CHAR(3);
    street   : CHAR(15);
    houseno  : CHAR(4);
    town     : CHAR(10);
    postcode : CHAR(6);
BEGIN
    WRITE 'Enter the player number: ';
    READ pno;
    # Search for address data
    SELECT   NAME, INITIALS, STREET,
             HOUSENO, TOWN, POSTCODE
    INTO     :name, :init, :street,
             :houseno, :town, :postcode
    FROM     PLAYERS
    WHERE    PLAYERNO = :pno;
    IF sqlcode >= 0 THEN
        # Present address data
```

```
        WRITE 'Playerno       :', pno;
        WRITE 'Surname        :', name;
        WRITE 'Initials       :', init;
        WRITE 'Street         :', street, ' ', houseno;
        WRITE 'Town           :', town;
        WRITE 'Postcode       :', postcode;
     ELSE
        WRITE 'There is no player with number ', pno;
     ENDIF;
END
```

The result is:

```
Enter the player number:27

Player number :27
Surname       :Collins
Initials      :DD
Street        :Long Drive 804
Town          :Eltham
Postcode      :8457DK

Enter the player number :112

Player number :112
Surname       :Bailey
Initials      :IP
Street        :Vixen Road 8
Town          :Plymouth
Postcode      :6392LK
```

Explanation: The SELECT INTO statement retrieves data about the player whose number has been entered. The values of the expressions from the SELECT clause are assigned to the host variables that have been specified in the INTO clause. This SELECT INTO statement can return, at most, one row because the PLAYERNO column is the primary key of the PLAYERS table. By using the SQLCODE host variable, we can check whether the player whose number has been entered actually appears in the table.

Example 26.9: Develop a program that prints the number of players who live in a given town after a given town is entered.

```
PROGRAM NUMBER_PLAYERS;
DECLARATIONS
   number  : INTEGER;
   town    : CHAR(10);
BEGIN
   WRITE 'Enter the town: ';
   READ town;
   # Determine the number of players
   SELECT    COUNT(*)
   INTO      :number
   FROM      PLAYERS
   WHERE     TOWN = :town;
   IF sqlcode <> 0 THEN
      number := 0;
   ENDIF;
   WRITE 'There are ', number, ' players in ', town;
END
```

Example 26.10: With the ENTER_PENALTIES program from Section 26.3, the users have to enter a payment number themselves.

Of course, you can let the program itself decide on the next payment number by using a SELECT INTO statement.

```
PROGRAM ENTER_PENALTIES _2;
DECLARATIONS
   pno       : SMALLINT;
   payno     : SMALLINT;
   pay_date  : DATE;
   amount    : DECIMAL(7,2);
BEGIN
   # Have the user enter the data
   READ pno;
   READ pay_date;
   READ amount;
   # Determine the highest payment number already entered
   SELECT    COALESCE(MAX(PAYMENTNO),0) + 1
   INTO      :payno
```

```
FROM       PENALTIES;
# Add the new data to the PENALTIES table
INSERT   INTO PENALTIES
         (PAYMENTNO, PLAYERNO, PAYMENT_DATE, AMOUNT)
VALUES (:payno, :pno, :pay_date, :amount);
WRITE 'Ready!';
END
```

Explanation: The SELECT INTO statement finds the highest payment number in the table and adds 1 to it. This becomes the new payment number.

Beware of using SELECT * with embedded SQL! Such a SELECT clause returns all columns from a given table. It is still the case that a host variable has to be specified for every column in the INTO clause of the same statement. The number of columns in a table can increase, though, with the ALTER TABLE statement. If this happens, the SELECT statement will no longer work because there will not be enough host variables available in the INTO clause. Therefore, avoid the use of * in SELECT clauses in the embedded SQL environment.

26.11 NULL Values and the NULL Indicator

The result of a SELECT INTO statement may contain a NULL value. If this is possible, that NULL value must be intercepted. You can accomplish this by including so-called NULL indicators.

Example 26.11: Get the league number of player 27.

```
PROGRAM GET_LEAGUENO;
DECLARATIONS
    leagueno      : CHAR(4);
    null_leagueno : INTEGER;
BEGIN
    SELECT   LEAGUENO
    INTO     :leagueno:null_leagueno
    FROM     PLAYERS
    WHERE    PLAYERNO = 27;
    IF sqlcode = 0 THEN
        IF null_leagueno = 0 THEN
            WRITE 'The league number is ', leagueno;
```

```
        ELSE
           WRITE 'Player 27 has no league number';
        ENDIF;
     ELSE
        WRITE 'Player 27 does not exist';
     ENDIF;
  END
```

Explanation: The INTO clause in this SELECT INTO statement contains something that we have not seen so far. Right behind the LEAGUENO host variable, another variable is specified: NULL_LEAGUENO. If the result of the SELECT INTO statement equals the NULL value, no value is assigned to the LEAGUENO host variable, and a negative value is assigned to NULL_LEAGUENO. The NULL_LEAGUENO variable is called a NULL indicator. If an expression in a SELECT clause can return a NULL value, the use of such a NULL indicator is mandatory. If you do not do this in the previous program and an expression returns NULL, a negative value is assigned to SQLCODE. The program will then state (incorrectly) that player 27 does not exist.

The use of NULL indicators is not restricted to the SELECT statement. They may also be specified, for example, in the SET clause of the UPDATE statement:

```
  UPDATE    PLAYERS
  SET       LEAGUENO = :leagueno:null_leagueno
  WHERE     ...
```

Explanation: If the value of the indicator NULL_LEAGUENO equals zero, the LEAGUENO column gets the value of the host variable LEAGUENO; otherwise, it is set to NULL.

26.12 Cursors for Querying Multiple Rows

SELECT INTO statements return only one row with values. SELECT statements that *can* return more than one row require a different approach. For this, a new concept has been added, called the *cursor*, plus four new SQL statements are introduced: the DECLARE CURSOR, OPEN, FETCH, and CLOSE statements. If you declare a cursor with the DECLARE CURSOR statement, you link it to a table expression. SQL executes the SELECT statement of the cursor with the special OPEN statement, and, next, you can fetch the result into the program row by row with FETCH statements. At a certain moment in time, you can view only one row from the result, the current row. It is as if an arrow is always pointing to precisely one row from the result—hence, the name *cursor*. With the FETCH statement, you move the cursor to the next row. If all rows have been processed, you can remove the result with a CLOSE statement.

We give an example next and work through it in detail afterward. However, try to understand the program yourself before reading the explanation.

Example 26.12: Develop a program that displays an ordered list of all player numbers and surnames. For each row, print a row number alongside.

```
PROGRAM ALL_PLAYERS;
DECLARATIONS
    pno     : SMALLINT;
    name    : CHAR(15);
    rowno   : INTEGER;
BEGIN
DECLARE c_players CURSOR FOR
        SELECT    PLAYERNO, NAME
        FROM      PLAYERS
        ORDER BY PLAYERNO;
    # Print a report heading
    WRITE 'ROWNO  PLAYER NUMBER  SURNAME';
    WRITE '=====  =============  =========';
    # Start the SELECT statement
    OPEN c_players;
    # Look for the first player
    rowno := 0;
    FETCH c_players INTO :pno, :pname;
    WHILE sqlcode = 0 DO
        rowno := rowno + 1;
        WRITE rowno, pno, pname;
        # Look for the next player
        FETCH c_players INTO :pno, :pname;
    ENDWHILE;
    CLOSE c_players;
END
```

The result is:

```
ROWNO  PLAYER NUMBER  SURNAME
=====  =============  =========
    1              2  Everett
    2              6  Parmenter
    3              7  Wise
```

```
      4             8    Newcastle
      5            27    Collins
      6            28    Collins
      7            39    Bishop
      8            44    Baker
      9            57    Brown
     10            83    Hope
     11            95    Miller
     12           100    Parmenter
     13           104    Moorman
     14           112    Bailey
```

With the DECLARE CURSOR statement, a cursor is declared by linking it to a table expression. In some ways, this is comparable to declaring host variables. The DECLARE CURSOR statement is a nonexecutable SQL statement. In this example, we have given the cursor the name C_PLAYERS. Now, via the cursor name, we can refer to the table expression in other statements. Note that, even though the cursor has been declared, the table expression is not processed at this point.

```
<declare cursor statement> ::=
    DECLARE <cursor name> CURSOR FOR <table expression>
    [ <for clause> ]

<for clause> ::=
    FOR UPDATE [ OF <column name>
        [ { , <column name> }... ] ] |
    FOR READ ONLY
```

A cursor consists of a name and a table expression. The name of the cursor must satisfy the same rules as apply to table names; see Chapter 15. We explain the meaning of the FOR clause in Section 26.15. A DECLARE CURSOR statement itself, like normal declarations, does nothing. Only after an OPEN statement does the table expression in the cursor become active. In the OPEN, FETCH, and CLOSE statements, the cursor is referred to by the cursor name.

Multiple cursors can be declared in each program. That is why they get a name: to refer to the right one.

In the OPEN statement, a cursor name is specified. This must be the name of a declared cursor. In the previous example, the cursor with the name C_PLAYERS is opened.

The OPEN statement makes sure that SQL executes the table expression that is associated with the cursor. After the OPEN statement has been processed, the result of the table expression becomes available and SQL keeps this result somewhere. Where it is kept is not important to us. After the OPEN statement, the result of the table expression is still invisible to the program.

You can open a cursor more than once within a program. Each time, the result can consist of other rows because other users or the program itself updates the tables.

If the table expression contains host variables, they are assigned a value every time the cursor is opened. This means that the result of the cursor after each OPEN statement might be different, depending on whether the values of the host variables have been changed or whether the contents of the database has been changed.

```
<open statement> ::=
   OPEN <cursor name>
  [ USING <host variable> [ { , <host variable> }... ]]
```

The FETCH statement is used to step through and process the rows in the result of the table expression one by one. In other words, we use the FETCH statement to render the result visible. The first FETCH statement that is processed retrieves the first row, the second FETCH retrieves the second row, and so on. The values of the retrieved rows are assigned to the host variables. In our example, these are the PNO and SNAME host variables. Note that a FETCH statement can be used only after a cursor has been opened (with an OPEN statement). In the program, we step through all rows of the result with a WHILE-DO statement. After the FETCH statement has retrieved the last row, the next FETCH statement triggers setting the SQLCODE host variable to 100 (the code for "no row found" or end-of-file).

```
<fetch statement> ::=
    FETCH [ <direction> ] <cursor name>
    INTO  <host variable list>

<direction> ::=
   NEXT | PRIOR | FIRST | LAST |
   ABSOLUTE <whole number> | RELATIVE <whole number>

<host variable list> ::=
    <host variable element> [ { , <host variable element> }... ]

<host variable element> ::=
    <host variable> [ <null indicator> ]

<null indicator> ::= <host variable>
```

The FETCH statement has an INTO clause that has the same significance as the INTO clause in the SELECT INTO statement. The number of host variables in the INTO clause of a FETCH statement must match the number of expressions in the SELECT clause of the DECLARE CURSOR statement. Furthermore, the colon in front of a host variable name is mandatory. A SELECT statement within a DECLARE CURSOR statement may *not* contain an INTO clause because this function is taken over by the FETCH statement.

With the CLOSE statement, the cursor is closed again and the result of the table expression is no longer available. We do not necessarily have to fetch rows until the final row before we use the CLOSE statement. We advise you to close cursors as quickly as possible because the result of the cursor takes up space in the internal memory of the computer.

```
<close statement> ::= CLOSE <cursor name>
```

We have already mentioned that a cursor can be opened more than once in a program. However, before a cursor can be opened a second time, and before the program ends, the cursor *must* be closed.

Figure 26.2 shows the position of the cursor after certain SQL statements have been processed.

Figure 26.2   *The position of the cursor after specific SQL statements*

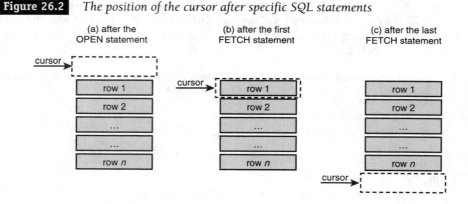

Example 26.13: Adjust the ALL_PLAYERS program so that it first asks for the town from which it should select its ordered list of players.

```
PROGRAM ALL_PLAYERS_2;
DECLARATIONS
    pno     : SMALLINT;
    name    : CHAR(15);
    town    : CHAR(10);
    ready   : CHAR(1);
    rowno   : INTEGER;
BEGIN
    # Cursor declaration
    DECLARE c_players CURSOR FOR
        SELECT   PLAYERNO, NAME
        FROM     PLAYERS
        WHERE    TOWN = :town
        ORDER BY PLAYERNO;
    # Initialize host variables
    ready := 'N';
    WHILE ready = 'N' DO
        WRITE 'From which town do you want to list
                the players';
        READ town;
        # Print a report heading
        WRITE 'ROWNO  PLAYERNO  SURNAME';
        WRITE '=====  ========  =======';
        # Start the SELECT statement
        OPEN c_players;
        # Look for the first player
        rowno := 0;
        FETCH c_players INTO :pno, :pname;
        WHILE sqlcode = 0 DO
            rowno := rowno + 1;
            WRITE rowno, pno, pname;
            # Look for the next player
            FETCH c_players INTO :pno, :pname;
        ENDWHILE;
        CLOSE c_players;
        WRITE 'Do you want to stop (Y/N)?';
        READ ready;
    ENDWHILE;
END
```

In Section 26.10, we noted that you should avoid the use of * in a SELECT clause in embedded SQL. This remark also applies to table expressions that make up cursors, for the same reasons.

Example 26.14: Find the three highest penalties that have been recorded.

```
PROGRAM HIGHEST_THREE;
DECLARATIONS
   rowno    : INTEGER;
   amount   : DECIMAL(7,2);
BEGIN
   DECLARE c_penalties CURSOR FOR
      SELECT    AMOUNT
      FROM      PENALTIES
      ORDER BY AMOUNT DESC;
   OPEN c_penalties;
   FETCH c_penalties INTO :amount;
   rowno := 1;
   WHILE sqlcode = 0 AND rowno <= 3 DO
      WRITE 'No', rowno, 'Amount, amount;
      rowno := rowno + 1;
      FETCH c_penalties INTO :amount;
   ENDWHILE;
   CLOSE c_penalties ;
END
```

The result is:

```
Nr 1 Amount   100.00
Nr 2 Amount   100.00
Nr 3 Amount    75.00
```

26.13 The Direction for Browsing Through a Cursor

You may also include a *direction* in a FETCH statement. If no direction is specified, as in the examples so far, the FETCH statement automatically retrieves the next row, but we can change that. For example, if FETCH PRIOR is specified, the previous row is retrieved. FETCH FIRST retrieves the first row, and FETCH LAST retrieves the last. For example, with FETCH ABSOLUTE 18, we jump directly to the eighteenth row. Finally, FETCH RELATIVE 7 is used to jump seven rows forward, and with FETCH RELATIVE -4, we jump four rows backward.

If a direction for stepping through the result of a cursor is specified in a FETCH statement, the term SCROLL must be included in the DECLARE CURSOR statement. This is the way to inform SQL that the cursor will be traversed in all directions. Such a cursor is sometimes called a *scroll* or a *scrollable cursor*.

```
<declare cursor statement> ::=
    DECLARE [ SCROLL ] <cursor name> CURSOR FOR
    <table expression>
    [ <for clause> ]

<for clause> ::=
    FOR UPDATE [ OF <column name>
        [ { , <column name> }... ] ] |
    FOR READ ONLY
```

26.14 Processing Cursors

In the previous section, we mentioned that when processing the OPEN statement, the result of the table expression is determined. However, that is not always the case because it could be very inefficient. Imagine that the result of a table expression consists of 50,000 rows and that this result is retrieved from hard disk. In most cases, this result is kept in internal memory, called the program buffer. Retrieving all this data from disk involves a lot of I/O, and keeping 50,000 rows takes up a big chunk of the program buffer. Now, imagine that the program closes the cursor after having browsed through the first ten rows. Much work will then have been performed unnecessarily behind the scenes. Because of this and other reasons, several methods have been invented to process the OPEN and FETCH statements internally in a more efficient way; see also Figure 26.3.

The first method is called the *row-by-row* method. It is a simple method, in which the OPEN statement does not determine the entire result of the table expression but only the first row. Only one row is read from disk and copied to the program buffer. Then, only one row is available if the first FETCH statement is executed. If the second FETCH statement is executed, the second row is retrieved from disk and transferred to the program buffer. The technical challenge is ensuring that the database server itself remembers what the next row should be. Fortunately, we are unconcerned with this aspect, but you probably can imagine that this is not a trivial exercise.

From a certain perspective, the row-by-row method is very efficient because only the rows required are retrieved from disk. However, three disadvantages exist. First, the method does not work if the result has to be ordered and an ordering has to be performed explicitly. Then, all rows must be retrieved from disk before one is transferred to the program buffer because the first row is known only after the rows have been ordered. Second, if the rows are retrieved one by one and fetching all rows takes several minutes, it could happen that rows are retrieved that did not exist when the user started to fetch the rows; you should not forget that you are not always the only user of the database. A comparable situation applies to removing rows, of course. The third disadvantage is applicable if the program runs in a client/server or Internet environment. In that case, the rows are sent across the network one by one, which is a very inefficient use of the network and has an adverse effect on the network capacity and the entire processing time of the program.

Figure 26.3   *Three methods to process a cursor*

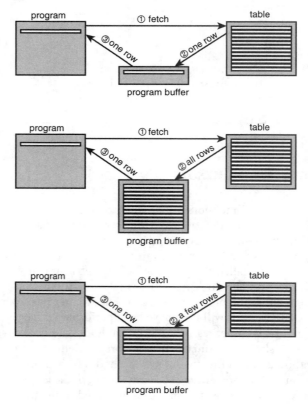

The second method is the *all-in-one* method. With this method, the full result of the cursor is determined when opening the cursor, and that result is kept in the program buffer or partly in the database buffer. This method does not have the same disadvantages as the row-by-row method, of course. However, the disadvantage is that if only some rows are used, unnecessary work has been done.

If SCROLL is specified in a DECLARE CURSOR statement, the all-in-one method is used automatically. This is because SQL does not know where the program begins: at the first or last rows, or somewhere in the middle. Also, when we jump forward or backward with the FETCH statement, it is guaranteed that the result will not change.

The third method tries to combine the advantages of the two other methods. Rows are retrieved in groups; therefore, we describe this as the *rows-in-groups* method. With the OPEN statement, for example, we retrieve ten rows at once and store them in the program buffer. Next, the first ten FETCH statements can be processed without the intervention of SQL. If the eleventh FETCH is executed next, the following ten rows are retrieved. The fact that rows are retrieved in groups and not one by one is invisible to the program itself. All this takes place behind the scenes. This is also a good solution in a client/server or Internet environment because rows can be sent over the network in packages.

For some programs, the row-by-row method is not acceptable; the result has to be determined at the time the first FETCH statement is executed. Changes made by other users cannot have an impact on the data that the user sees. This can be guaranteed by using the term INSENSITIVE. When an *insensitive cursor* is used, the entire result appears to be determined directly. In other words, the cursor does not respond to (that is, it is insensitive to) changes made by other users. If a *sensitive cursor* is declared, no guarantees are given.

```
<declare cursor statement> ::=
    DECLARE [ INSENSITIVE ] [ SCROLL ] <cursor name>
      CURSOR FOR <table expression>
    [ <for clause> ]
```

26.15 The FOR Clause

You can add a FOR clause to a DECLARE CURSOR statement. This FOR-clause has two forms. By using the first form, FOR UPDATE, you specify that you want to update or remove rows through cursors; use the second form to indicate explicitly that the rows of the cursor will be queried only, with no updates. Start with the first form.

```
<declare cursor statement> ::=
    DECLARE <cursor name> CURSOR FOR <table expression>
    [ <for clause> ]

<for clause> ::=
    FOR UPDATE [ OF <column name>
        [ { , <column name> }... ] ] |
    FOR READ ONLY
```

A special version of the UPDATE statement enables you to update the current row of a given cursor. Instead of a set-oriented change, we make changes in a specific row. For this reason, it is called a *positioned update*. The "normal" UPDATE statement is sometimes called a *searched update*.

Here is the extended definition of the UPDATE statement:

```
<update statement> ::=
   UPDATE <table reference>
   SET     <column assignment> [ { , <column assignment> }... ]
   [ WHERE  { <condition> | CURRENT OF <cursor name> } ]

<table reference> ::=
   <table specification> [ [ AS ] <pseudonym> ]

<column assignment> ::=
   <column name> = <scalar expression>
```

To use this positioned update, a FOR clause must be included in the DECLARE CUR-SOR statement of the cursor being updated. In this clause, you specify which of the columns will possibly be updated.

Example 26.15: The following program is based on the RAISE_WON_2 program from Section 26.6. We have made the following changes: The program shows the matches information for team 1, row by row, and asks, for each row, whether the number of sets won should be increased by one.

```
PROGRAM RAISE_WON_3;
DECLARATIONS
   pno    : SMALLINT;
   won    : INTEGER;
   choice : CHAR(1);
BEGIN
   # Cursor declaration
   DECLARE c_mat CURSOR FOR
      SELECT  PLAYERNO, WON
      FROM    MATCHES
      WHERE   TEAMNO = 1
      FOR     UPDATE OF WON;
   #
   OPEN c_mat;
   FETCH c_mat INTO :pno, :won;
   WHILE sqlcode = 0 DO
      WRITE 'Do you want the number of sets won for';
      WRITE 'player ', pno, ' to be increased by 1 (Y/N)?';
      READ choice;
```

```
        IF choice = 'Y' THEN
            UPDATE    MATCHES
            SET       WON = WON + 1
            WHERE     CURRENT OF c_mat;
        ENDIF;
        FETCH c_mat INTO :pno, :won;
    ENDWHILE;
    CLOSE c_mat;
    WRITE 'Ready';
END
```

Explanation: The only change in this program, compared to the original version, is that the DECLARE CURSOR statement has been expanded with a FOR clause. By doing this, we are making a provision for the values in the WON column to be updated at some point. In the UPDATE statement, we specify in the WHERE clause that in the row that is current for the C_MAT cursor, the WON column should be increased by one.

However, not all cursors can be updated. If the table expression of the cursor contains, for example, a GROUP BY clause, the cursor is read-only by definition. The rules that determine whether a cursor can be changed are the same as the rules that determine whether the virtual contents of a view can be changed. (These rules were described in Section 21.8, in Chapter 21, "Views.")

In addition, the rule applies that if the keywords INSENSITIVE or SCROLL, or an ORDER BY clause has been specified, the cursor cannot be updated.

It may be possible to update the table expression, but the program has no intention to change the result. SQL still assumes that a change is about to occur. This can be prevented by closing the cursor declaration with FOR READ ONLY. Then, the system knows that no change is going to be made.

26.16 Deleting Rows via Cursors

You can use cursors for deleting individual rows. The DELETE statement has a similar condition to the one we discussed in the previous section for the UPDATE statement. This is called a *positioned delete* or a *searched delete*.

```
<delete statement> ::=
    DELETE
    FROM    <table reference>
    [ WHERE { <condition> | CURRENT OF <cursor name> } ]

<table reference> ::=
    <table specification> [ [ AS ] <pseudonym> ]
```

Example 26.16: Develop a program that presents all the data from the PENALTIES table row by row and asks whether the row displayed should be deleted.

```
PROGRAM DELETE_PENALTIES;
DECLARATIONS
   pno           : SMALLINT;
   payno         : SMALLINT;
   payment_date  : DATE;
   amount        : DECIMAL(7,2);
   choice        : CHAR(1);
BEGIN
   # Cursor declaration
   DECLARE c_penalties CURSOR FOR
      SELECT   PAYMENTNO, PLAYERNO, PAYMENT_DATE, AMOUNT
      FROM     PENALTIES;
   #
   OPEN c_penalties;
   FETCH c_penalties INTO :payno, :pno, :payment_date,
                          :amount;
   WHILE sqlcode = 0 DO
      WRITE 'Do you want to delete this penalty?';
      WRITE 'Payment number  : ', payno;
      WRITE 'Player number   : ', pno;
      WRITE 'Payment date    : ', payment_date;
      WRITE 'Penalty amount  : ', amount;
      WRITE 'Answer Y or N ';
      READ choice;
      IF choice = 'Y' THEN
         DELETE
         FROM     PENALTIES
         WHERE    CURRENT OF c_penalties;
      ENDIF;
      FETCH c_penalties INTO :payno, :pno, :payment_date,
                             :amount;
   ENDWHILE;
   CLOSE c_penalties;
   WRITE 'Ready';
END
```

26.17 Dynamic SQL

Embedded SQL supports two forms: *static* and *dynamic*. So far, we have discussed static embedded SQL. With this form, the SQL statements are readable in the program code. They have been written out in the programs, so they will not change and are thus static. With dynamic embedded SQL, the (executable) SQL statements are created at runtime. If you read a program that contains dynamic SQL, it is impossible to determine what the program will do.

Since the arrival of Call-Level Interfaces (CLI) such as ODBC, the popularity of dynamic SQL has dropped. C. J. Date [DATE97] expresses this as follows:

> It is worth mentioning that the SQL Call-Level Interface feature provides an arguably better solution to the problem that dynamic SQL is intended to address than dynamic SQL itself does (in fact, dynamic SQL would probably never have been included in the standard if the Call-Level Interface had been defined first).

For the sake of completeness, we do not skip this subject entirely. We give two examples to give you an idea of what dynamic SQL looks like. For a detailed description, refer to [DATE97].

Example 26.17: Develop a program that reads in an SQL statement and subsequently executes it.

```
PROGRAM DYNAMIC_SQL;
DECLARATIONS
    sqlstat        : VARCHAR(200);
    payment_date   : DATE;
    amount         : DECIMAL(7,2);
    choice         : CHAR(1);
BEGIN
    WRITE 'Enter your SQL statement: ';
    READ sqlstat;
    EXECUTE IMMEDIATE :sqlstat;
    IF sqlcode = 0 THEN
        WRITE 'Your statement has processed correctly.';
    ELSE
        WRITE 'Your statement has not processed correctly.';
    ENDIF;
END
```

The result is:


```
Enter your SQL statement: DELETE FROM PENALTIES
Your statement has processed correctly.
```


Explanation: The READ statement is used to read in any SQL statement. This SQL statement is assigned to the SQLSTAT host variable. The SQL statement can be processed with the (new) SQL statement called EXECUTE IMMEDIATE. The task of this statement is to check, optimize, and process the statement that is in the host variable. Because EXECUTE IMMEDIATE is an executable statement, we can check with the help of SQL-CODE whether the statement was processed correctly.

Tools such as WinSQL pass every SQL statement that we enter to SQL. Of course, WinSQL does not know in advance which SQL statement you will enter. This problem can be solved by using dynamic SQL.

Example 26.18: Develop a program that executes a DELETE statement dynamically.


```
PROGRAM DYNAMIC_DELETE;
DECLARATIONS
    sqlstat    : VARCHAR(200);
    name       : CHAR(15);
    initials   : CHAR(3);
BEGIN
    sqlstat := 'DELETE FROM PLAYERS WHERE NAME = ?
                 AND INITIALS = ?';
    PREPARE STAT_PREPARED FROM :sqlstat;
    WRITE 'Enter a player name: ';
    READ name;
    WRITE 'Enter initials    : ';
    READ initials;
    EXECUTE STAT_PREPARED USING :name, :initials;
    IF sqlcode = 0 THEN
       WRITE 'Your statement has processed correctly.';
    ELSE
       WRITE 'Your statement has not processed correctly.';
    ENDIF;
END
```


Explanation: First, the DELETE statement is assigned to the host variable SQLSTAT. Obviously, there are two question marks in the two conditions. With dynamic SQL, we cannot specify host variables within SQL statements. Instead, we use question marks, called *placeholders*. Next, the SQL statement is prepared with an executable SQL statement that we have not discussed so far: the PREPARE statement. This statement examines the SQL statement that has been assigned to the variable SQLSTAT. The syntax of the statement is checked and, if it is correct, the optimizer is called for. However, it is still not possible to execute the statement because the DELETE statement does not know which players have to be deleted. A value is, therefore, given to the variables NAME and INITIALS; finally, the DELETE statement is executed with an EXECUTE statement. This statement differs somewhat from the one in the last example. In this example, a USING clause is used to specify the values of the two placeholders.

The PREPARE and EXECUTE statement together offer comparable functionality to the EXECUTE IMMEDIATE statement in the last example. There are at least two reasons to process an SQL statement in two steps. The first is that if a dynamic statement contains variables, it is always necessary to use two steps. Second, if the SQL statement is within a "loop," it is more efficient to place the PREPARE statement outside the "loop" and the EXECUTE statement within it. In this case, the statement is checked and optimized only once. This is shown in the next piece of code:

```
    :
BEGIN
    sqlstat := 'DELETE FROM PLAYERS WHERE NAME = ?
                AND INITIALS = ?';
    PREPARE STAT_PREPARED FROM :sqlstat;
    WHILE ... DO
        WRITE 'Enter a player number: ';
        READ name;
        WRITE 'Enter initials      : ';
        READ initials;
        EXECUTE STAT_PREPARED USING :name, :initials;
        IF sqlcode = 0 THEN
            WRITE 'Your statement has been processed
                    correctly.';
        ELSE
            WRITE 'Your statement has not been processed
                    correctly.';
        ENDIF;
    ENDWHILE;
END
```

There is one big restriction with the EXECUTE IMMEDIATE statement: SELECT statements cannot be processed this way. For this purpose, there are other SQL statements in dynamic embedded SQL.

We conclude the description of dynamic SQL by mentioning that the features of dynamic SQL are identical to those of static SQL.

26.18 Example of a C Program

In this chapter, we used a pseudo programming language for all the examples. In this section, we give two small examples of programs that have been written in the C programming language and, therefore, contain all the C details.

Example 26.19: Develop a C program that creates the TEAMS table.

```
#include <stdio.h>

EXEC SQL BEGIN DECLARE SECTION;
EXEC SQL END DECLARE SECTION;

EXEC SQL INCLUDE SQLCA;

main()
    {
    EXEC SQL CONNECT SPORTDB;
    if (sqlca.sqlcode = 0)
        {
        EXEC SQL CREATE TABLE TEAMS ( ... );
        printf("The TEAMS table has been created. \n");
        EXEC SQL COMMIT WORK;
        }

    exit(0);
    }
```

Here, you can see clearly the details that we omitted in all our previous examples, such as the statements BEGIN and END DECLARE SECTION, INCLUDE, and CONNECT.

Example 26.20: Develop a C program that adds a row to the TEAMS table.

```c
#include <stdio.h>

EXEC SQL BEGIN DECLARE SECTION;
     int      tno;
     int      pno;
     VARCHAR division[6];
EXEC SQL END DECLARE SECTION;

EXEC SQL INCLUDE SQLCA;

main()
    {
    EXEC SQL CONNECT SPORTDB;

    if (sqlca.sqlcode = 0)
       {
       printf("Enter a team number: ");
       scanf("%d",&tno);
       printf("Enter the number of the captain: ");
       scanf("%d",&pno);
       printf("Enter the division: ");
       scanf("%s",division.arr);
       division.len = strlen(division.arr);

       EXEC SQL INSERT INTO TEAMS
                       (TEAMNO, PLAYERNO, DIVISION)
               VALUES (:tno, :pno, :division);
       EXEC SQL COMMIT WORK;

       printf("The team has been added. \n");
       }
    exit(0);
    }
```

Transactions and Multi-User Usage

27.1 Introduction

So far in this book, we have assumed that you are the only user of the database. If you do the examples and exercises at home, that assumption is probably correct. But if you work with SQL in your company, for example, the odds are good that you share the database with many other users. We call this *multi-user* usage as opposed to *single-user* usage. Actually, in a multi-user environment, you should not be aware that other users are accessing the database concurrently because SQL hides this from you as much as possible. Still, the following question might occur to you: What will happen if I access a row that is already in use by someone else? In short, that question is the subject of this chapter. We start with the description of a concept that forms the basis of multi-user usage: the *transaction* (also called *unit of work*). The concepts *savepoint*, *lock*, *deadlock*, and *isolation level* also are discussed, and we consider the LOCK TABLE statement.

In this chapter, we look inside SQL. If that does not interest you, you can skip this chapter. For those who will develop real-life applications with SQL, we recommend studying this chapter carefully.

27.2 What Is a Transaction?

What exactly is a *transaction*? In this book, we define a transaction as a set of SQL statements that are entered by one user and that are ended by specifying whether all changes are to be made permanent or rolled back (or undone). By a "change," we mean each UPDATE, DELETE, and INSERT statement. SQL statements entered by different users cannot belong to the same transaction. At the end of this section, we explain why we might want to undo changes.

Many products for interactive SQL are set up in such a way that, first, each SQL statement is seen as a complete transaction and, second, each transaction (read: individual update) is automatically made permanent. This mode of working is called *autocommit*. Changes can be undone by the user only if he or she executes compensating changes. For example, if rows are added with an INSERT statement, this change can be undone only by executing one or more DELETE statements. However, we can turn off this automatic commitment of transactions.

If you use WinSQL as a product for interactive SQL, it works as follows. When a new connection is created, the check mark in the Autocommit Transactions box must be removed; see Figure 27.1. At the bottom of the screen, a little red ball appears (instead of a green one) to indicate that the user is now responsible for ending the transactions. In other products, the autocommit must be turned off in another way.

However, MySQL does not settle for that. When a session is started, the AUTOCOMMIT system parameter of MySQL likely is turned on. An SQL statement must be used to turn it off. So, after turning off autocommit for WinSQL, we have to do the same for MySQL. The statement to turn off autocommit is simple:

```
SET AUTOCOMMIT = 0
```

When autocommit must be turned on again, you issue this statement:

```
SET AUTOCOMMIT = 1
```

After the autocommit has been turned off, a transaction can consist of multiple SQL statements, and you must indicate the end of each transaction. Two separate SQL statements accomplish this. In the next example, we illustrate how all this works.

Figure 27.1 *Turning off autocommit*

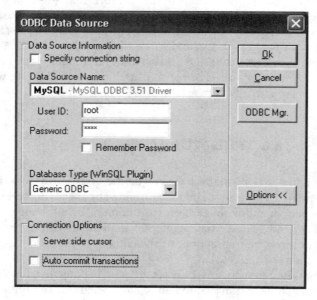

Example 27.1: Imagine that all penalties of player 44 are to be deleted.

```
DELETE
FROM      PENALTIES
WHERE     PLAYERNO = 44
```

The effect of this statement becomes apparent when you issue the following SELECT statement:

```
SELECT    *
FROM      PENALTIES
```

The result is:

```
PAYMENTNO   PLAYERNO   PAYMENT_DATE   AMOUNT
---------   --------   ------------   ------
        1          6   1980-12-08     100.00
        3         27   1983-09-10     100.00
        4        104   1984-12-08      50.00
        6          8   1980-12-08      25.00
        8         27   1984-11-12      75.00
```

Three rows have been deleted from the table. However, the change is not yet permanent (even though it looks that way) because autocommit has been turned off. The user (or application) has a choice now. The change can be undone with the SQL statement ROLLBACK or made permanent with the COMMIT statement.

```
<commit statement> ::=
   COMMIT [ WORK ]

<rollback statement> ::=
   ROLLBACK [ WORK ]
```

Let us take the first choice, and use the following statement:

```
ROLLBACK WORK
```

Explanation: If we repeat the SELECT statement used previously now, it returns the entire PENALTIES table. The three deleted rows appear in the result again. If we wanted to make the change permanent, we should have used the COMMIT statement:

```
COMMIT WORK
```

After this statement, the three rows would have been deleted from the table for good; the change would have been permanent.

We can omit the word WORK because it does not affect the processing.

COMMIT statements make the changes permanent and ROLLBACK statements undo them. Now the question is, which changes will be rolled back? Is it only the last change, or everything from the moment you started the application? To answer this, we return to the concept of a transaction. As we have already mentioned, a transaction is a set of SQL statements. For example, the earlier DELETE and SELECT statements form a (small) transaction. COMMIT and ROLLBACK statements always relate to the so-called *current* transaction. In other words, these statements relate to all SQL statements executed during the current transaction. Now the question is, how do we mark the beginning and end of a transaction? For now, we assume that the beginning of a transaction cannot be marked explicitly. (We return to this subject in Section 27.11.) The first SQL statement executed in an application is considered to be the beginning of the first transaction. The end of a transaction is marked by using a COMMIT or ROLLBACK statement. From this, you can conclude that an SQL statement that follows a COMMIT or ROLLBACK statement is the first statement of the new current transaction.

Example 27.2: To illustrate all this, here is a series of statements that are entered consecutively. It is not important whether these statements are entered interactively (with SQL, for example) or whether they have been embedded within a host language program:

```
INSERT ...
   DELETE ...
   ROLLBACK WORK
   UPDATE ...
   ROLLBACK WORK
   INSERT ...
   DELETE ...
   COMMIT WORK
   UPDATE ...
end of program
```

Explanation:

Lines 1–2: These two changes are not yet permanent.

Line 3: A ROLLBACK statement is executed. All changes of the current transaction are undone. These are the changes on lines 1 and 2.

Line 4: This change is not yet permanent. Because this statement follows a ROLLBACK statement, a new transaction is started.

Line 5: A ROLLBACK statement is executed. All changes of the current transaction are undone. This is the change on line 4.

Lines 6–7: These two changes are not yet permanent. Because the statement on line 6 follows a ROLLBACK statement, a new transaction is started.

Line 8: A COMMIT statement is executed. All changes of the current transaction become permanent. These are the changes on lines 6 and 7.

Line 9: This change is not yet permanent. Because this statement follows a COMMIT statement, a new transaction is started.

Line 10: Here the program is ended. All changes of the current transaction are undone—in this case, the change on line 9.

When a program stops without marking the end of a transaction, SQL automatically executes a ROLLBACK statement. We advise you, however, to make the last SQL statement executed by a program always a COMMIT or ROLLBACK statement.

Why would we want to undo transactions? This question can be formulated in another way: Why not always execute a COMMIT statement immediately after each change? There are two main reasons. The first deals with the fact that during the processing of SQL statements, something can go wrong, for whatever reason. For example, when you add new data, the database might become full, the computer might break down during the processing of an SQL statement, or a division by zero might occur during a calculation. Imagine that one of these problems occurs when you process one of the statements in the next example.

Example 27.3: Delete all data for player 6. We assume that no foreign keys have been defined.

```
DELETE FROM PLAYERS WHERE PLAYERNO = 6

DELETE FROM PENALTIES WHERE PLAYERNO = 6

DELETE FROM MATCHES WHERE PLAYERNO = 6

DELETE FROM COMMITTEE_MEMBERS WHERE PLAYERNO = 6

UPDATE TEAMS SET PLAYERNO = 83 WHERE PLAYERNO = 6
```

Five statements are required to remove all the information about a particular player: four DELETE statements and one UPDATE statement. In the last statement, player 6 is not removed from the TEAMS table, but replaced by player 83 because player 6 can no longer be captain (because he no longer occurs in the PLAYERS table). A new captain must be registered as well because the PLAYERNO column in the TEAMS table is defined as NOT NULL. If you use a DELETE statement instead of an UPDATE statement, data about the team captained by player 6 will also be deleted, and that is not what is intended. These five changes together form a unit and must be dealt with as one transaction. Imagine that the third DELETE statement goes wrong. At that moment, two changes of the transaction have been executed and three have not. The first two changes cannot be undone. In other words, the MATCHES and TEAMS tables contain data about a player who does not occur in the PLAYERS table, which is an unwanted situation. We conclude that either all five changes must be executed or none at all. Therefore, we must be able to undo the changes that have already been carried out.

The second reason concerns the user's own mistakes. Imagine that a user changes a large amount of data in different tables concerning a particular player and discovers later that he chose the wrong player. He must be able to roll back these changes. Here, the ROLLBACK statement can be useful.

In most SQL products, statements that change the catalog, such as CREATE TABLE, GRANT, and DROP INDEX, cannot be undone. Before and after the processing of such a statement, SQL automatically executes a COMMIT statement. This type of statement, therefore, ends any current transaction. Turning autocommit on or off has no effect.

Exercise 27.1: Determine for the following series of statements which will and which will not become permanent.

1. SELECT . . .
2. INSERT . . .
3. COMMIT WORK
4. ROLLBACK WORK
5. DELETE . . .
6. DELETE . . .
7. ROLLBACK WORK
8. INSERT . . .
9. COMMIT WORK
10. end of program

27.3 Starting Transactions

The first SQL statement of an application or the first SQL statement after a COMMIT or ROLLBACK starts a new transaction. This is called an implicit start of a transaction. However, it is possible to start a transaction explicitly with the START TRANSACTION statement.

```
<start transaction statement> ::=
   START TRANSACTION
```

Example 27.4: Rewrite Example 27.2 so that transactions are started explicitly.

```
START TRANSACTION
INSERT ...
DELETE ...
ROLLBACK WORK
START TRANSACTION
UPDATE ...
ROLLBACK WORK
START TRANSACTION
INSERT ...
DELETE ...
COMMIT WORK
START TRANSACTION
UPDATE ...
end of program
```

A START TRANSACTION statement automatically leads to a COMMIT of the changes that are not permanent yet. In addition, the autocommit is turned off. The SET AUTO-COMMIT statement is, therefore, not required. If the transaction is ended, the value of the AUTOCOMMIT variable is reset to the old value, regardless of what it was.

Instead of START TRANSACTION, you can also use the statement BEGIN WORK. However, the statement mentioned first is preferable because many other SQL products support it.

27.4 Embedded SQL and Transactions

As already mentioned, the concept of a transaction and the statements COMMIT and ROLLBACK also apply to SQL statements that are included in a host language: see Chapter 26, "Introduction to Embedded SQL."

Example 27.5: Extend the RAISE_WON_3 program from Section 26.15 with COMMIT and ROLLBACK statements.

```
PROGRAM RAISE_WON_4;
DECLARATIONS
    pno     : SMALLINT;
    won     : INTEGER;
    choice  : CHAR(1);
    stop    : CHAR(1);
BEGIN
    DECLARE c_mat CURSOR FOR
        SELECT  PLAYERNO, WON
        FROM    MATCHES
        WHERE   TEAMNO = 1
        FOR     UPDATE OF WON;
    #
    stop := 'N';
    OPEN c_mat;
    FETCH c_mat INTO :pno, :won;
    WHILE sqlcode = 0 AND stop = 'N' DO
        WRITE 'Do you want the number of sets won for ',
              player ';
        WRITE 'pno, ' to be increased by 1 (Y/N)?';
        READ choice;
        IF choice = 'Y' THEN
            UPDATE  MATCHES
            SET     WON = WON + 1
            WHERE   CURRENT OF c_mat;
            IF sqlcode < 0 THEN
                ROLLBACK WORK;
                stop := 'Y';
            ELSE
                FETCH c_mat INTO :pno, :won;
            ENDIF;
        ENDIF;
    ENDWHILE;
    CLOSE c_mat;
    COMMIT WORK;
    WRITE 'Ready';
END
```

Explanation: A COMMIT statement is added at the end of the program. So, after the last player has been processed, the cursor is closed and all changes become permanent. Within the WHILE-DO statement, a ROLLBACK statement is included. If the value of the SQLCODE host variable is negative after the UPDATE statement, something has gone wrong. In that case, all changes that have been executed so far are undone. Thus, even if a mistake occurs with the last player, all changes will still be undone.

27.5 Savepoints

In the previous sections, we discussed how complete transactions can be undone. It is also possible to undo only a part of a current transaction by using *savepoints*.

```
<savepoint statement> ::=
    SAVEPOINT <savepoint name>
```

To use savepoints, we must extend the definition of the ROLLBACK statement somewhat:

```
<rollback statement> ::=
    ROLLBACK [ WORK ]
    [ TO SAVEPOINT <savepoint name> ]
```

Here is another example to show how this works:

```
UPDATE ...
INSERT ...
SAVEPOINT S1
INSERT ...
SAVEPOINT S2
DELETE ...
ROLLBACK WORK TO SAVEPOINT S2
UPDATE ...
ROLLBACK WORK TO SAVEPOINT S1
UPDATE ...
DELETE ...
COMMIT WORK
```

Explanation:

Lines 1–2: These two changes are not yet permanent.

Line 3: A savepoint is defined with the name S1.

Line 4: This change is not yet permanent.

Line 5: A savepoint is defined with the name S2.

Line 6: This change is not yet permanent.

Line 7: A ROLLBACK is issued. However, not all changes are undone—only those performed *after* savepoint S2. This is the change on line 6. The changes on lines 1 and 2 are not yet permanent but are still present.

Line 8: This change is not yet permanent.

Line 9: A ROLLBACK to savepoint S1 is entered. All changes performed *after* savepoint S1 are undone. These are the changes on lines 4 and 8.

Lines 10–11: These two changes are not yet permanent.

Line 12: All nonpermanent changes are made permanent. These are the changes on lines 1, 2, 10, and 11.

When a change is undone to a certain savepoint, only the last changes of the current transaction can be undone.

Portability: *Not all SQL products support the use of savepoints.*

Exercise 27.2: Determine for the following series of statements which will and which will not become permanent.

1. SELECT ...
2. SAVEPOINT S1
3. INSERT ...
4. COMMIT WORK
5. INSERT ...
6. SAVEPOINT S1
7. DELETE ...
8. ROLLBACK WORK TO SAVEPOINT S1
9. DELETE ...
10. SAVEPOINT S2
11. DELETE ...
12. ROLLBACK WORK TO SAVEPOINT S1
13. COMMIT WORK
14. end of program

27.6 Problems with Multi-User Usage

Imagine that you have removed all rows from the PENALTIES table in a transaction, but you have not yet ended the transaction. What will the other users see if they query the PENALTIES table? Will they also see an empty table, or will they still see all the original rows? Are they allowed to see the changes that you have not yet made permanent? These problems are comparable to the problems of a policeman on a crossing. Whatever the policeman does and however he moves his arms, he must ensure that two cars do not use the crossing at the same time at the same place. SQL (the policeman) must ensure that two users (the cars) do not access the same data (the crossing) simultaneously in the wrong way.

The problem described here is just one of the possible problems due to the effects of multi-user usage, but there are more. In this section, we paint a picture of the four best-known problems by using a few examples. For more detailed descriptions and for other problems, we refer to [BERN97] and [GRAY93].

27.6.1 Dirty Read or Uncommitted Read

The problem when one SQL users sees data that has not been committed yet by another user is called a *dirty read* or *uncommitted read*.

Example 27.6: Assume the following series of events. These events are entered consecutively.

1. User U_1 wants to increase the amount of the penalty with payment number 4 by $25. For this, he uses the following UPDATE statement:

```
UPDATE    PENALTIES
SET       AMOUNT = AMOUNT + 25
WHERE     PAYMENTNO = 4
```

2. Before U_1 ends the transaction with a COMMIT statement, user U_2 accesses the same penalty with the following SELECT statement and sees the updated amount:

```
SELECT    *
FROM      PENALTIES
WHERE     PAYMENTNO = 4
```

3. U_1 rolls back the UPDATE statement with a ROLLBACK statement.

The result is that U_2 has seen data that was never "committed." In other words, he saw data that never even existed. The SELECT statement that U_2 executed is called a dirty read. User U_2 has seen "dirty" data.

27.6.2 Nonrepeatable Read or Nonreproducible Read

A special version of the dirty read is the *nonrepeatable read*, *nonreproducible read*, or *inconsistent read*. Here, a user reads partly dirty and partly clean data, and combines it. The same user is not aware that this result is based upon data that is only partly clean.

Example 27.7: The following events are entered consecutively.

1. With the following SELECT statement, user U_1 retrieves all players resident in Stratford and writes their player numbers on a piece of paper:

```
SELECT    PLAYERNO
FROM      PLAYERS
WHERE     TOWN = 'Stratford'
```

The result is: 6, 83, 2, 7, 57, 39, and 100. Then, U_1 starts a new transaction.

2. A few seconds later, user U_2 changes the address of player 7 (who lives in Stratford) with the following UPDATE statement:

```
UPDATE    PLAYERS
SET       TOWN = 'Eltham'
WHERE     PLAYERNO = 7
```

3. Next, user U_2 ends the transaction with a COMMIT statement.
4. Now U_1 queries one by one the addresses of the players that were written on the piece of paper, using the following SELECT statement, and prints them on labels:

```
SELECT    PLAYERNO, NAME, INITIALS,
          STREET, HOUSENO, POSTCODE, TOWN
FROM      PLAYERS
WHERE     PLAYERNO IN (6, 83, 2, 7, 57, 39, 100)
```

The result of these two changes is that U_1 also prints a label for player 7 because he assumed that player 7 still lived in Stratford. This means that the second SELECT statement in the same transaction does not give the same picture of the database. The result of the first SELECT statement cannot be reproduced, which, of course, is not desirable.

27.6.3 Phantom Read

The following problem is known as *phantom read*.

Example 27.8: The following events are again entered consecutively.

1. With the following SELECT statement, user U_1 is looking for all players resident in Stratford:

```
SELECT    PLAYERNO
FROM      PLAYERS
WHERE     TOWN = 'Stratford'
```

The result is: 6, 83, 2, 7, 57, 39, and 100. However, user U_1 does not end the transaction.

2. Some time later, user U_2 adds a new player who lives in Stratford and ends the transaction with a COMMIT statement.
3. User U_1 sees one more row when he executes the same SELECT statement: the row that was entered by user U_2.

This means that the second SELECT statement in the same transaction (just like the last example) does not present the same picture of the database. The difference between phantom read and nonrepeatable read is that, with the former, new data becomes available, and, with the latter, data is changed.

27.6.4 Lost Update

The final problem that we discuss is called *lost update* in the literature. The change of one user is overwritten by that of another.

Example 27.9: The following events are entered consecutively again.

1. User U_1 wants to increase the amount of the penalty with payment number 4 by $25. First, he queries the penalty amount with a SELECT statement (a transaction starts). The penalty appears to be $50.
2. A few seconds later, user U_2 wants to do the same. User U_2 wants to increase the amount of the penalty with payment number 4 by $30. He also queries the current value with a SELECT statement and sees $50. A second transaction begins here.
3. User U_1 executes the following UPDATE statement (notice the SET clause):

```
UPDATE    PENALTIES
SET       AMOUNT = AMOUNT + 25
WHERE     PAYMENTNO = 4
```

4. Next, user U_1 ends his transaction with a COMMIT statement.
5. User U_2 executes his UPDATE statement (notice the SET clause):

```
UPDATE    PENALTIES
SET       AMOUNT = AMOUNT + 30
WHERE     PAYMENTNO = 4
```

6. User U_2 also ends his transaction with a COMMIT statement.

The result of these two changes is that both users think that their change has been executed ("committed"). However, the change of user U_1 has disappeared. His change of $25 is overwritten by the change of user U_2. Losing changes, of course, is not desirable. SQL must take care that, after changes have been "committed," they actually are permanent.

All the problems we have described here can be solved easily by not allowing two users to run a transaction simultaneously. If the transaction of U_2 can start only if that of U_1 has ended, nothing will go wrong. In other words, the transactions are processed serially. However, imagine that you share the database with more than a hundred users. If you end a transaction, it will probably be a long time before it is your turn again. We then say that the level of *concurrency* is low: no two users can work simultaneously. Therefore, it is necessary to process transactions simultaneously, or in parallel. But to do this, SQL needs a mechanism to prevent the previously mentioned problems from occurring. This is the subject of the remaining of the chapter.

27.7 Locking

A number of different mechanisms exist to keep the level of concurrency high and still prevent problems. In this section, we discuss the mechanism that has been implemented in most SQL products: *locking*.

The basic principle of locking is simple. If a user accesses a certain piece of data, such as a row from the PLAYERS table, the row will be locked and other users will not be able to access that row. Only the user who has locked the row can access it. Locks are released when the transaction ends. In other words, the life of a lock is never longer than that of the transaction in which the lock is created.

Let us see what will happen with two of the problems discussed in the previous section. For the problem of the lost update (see Example 27.9), user U_1 accesses penalty number 4 first. SQL automatically places a lock on that row. Then user U_2 tries to do the same. This user, however, gets a message indicating that the row is not available. He must wait until U_1 has finished. This means that the final penalty amount will be $105 (work it out for yourself). In this case, the transactions of U_1 and U_2 are processed not in parallel, but *serially*. Other users who do not work with penalty number 4, but with another number, are processed concurrently.

For the problem of the nonrepeatable read (see Example 27.7), we now have a comparable situation. Only after U_1 has printed the labels can user U_2 change the address, which will no longer cause problems.

A locking mechanism works correctly if it meets the *serializability* criterion. This means that a mechanism works correctly if the contents of the database after (concurrently) processing a set of transactions are the same as the contents of the database after processing the same set of transactions serially (order is irrelevant). The state of the database after problem 1 is such that the penalty amount of penalty number 4 is $80. You will never manage to get the same amount by processing the two transactions of U_1 and U_2 serially. Whether you execute U_1's transaction first and then U_2's, or vice versa, the result will be $105, not $80.

Where does the database keep track of all those locks? This lock administration is kept in internal memory of the computer. Usually, a large part of the internal memory is reserved for this. This space is called the *buffer*. Therefore, locks are not stored in the database. We also mention, probably unnecessarily, that users do not see locks.

We stated that the transactions of users U_1 and U_2 are processed serially after locks have been placed. This is not ideal, of course. To increase the level of concurrency, most products support two types of locks: *share* and *exclusive*. (Sometimes, these locks are called *read* and *write*, respectively.) If a user has a share lock on a row, other users can read that row but cannot change it. The advantage is that users who only execute SELECT statements in their transactions do not hold each other up. If a user has an exclusive lock, other users cannot reach the row at all, even to read it. In the previous sections, we have assumed that each lock was an exclusive lock.

No separate SQL statement exists to indicate that you want to work with share locks, for example. SQL determines this itself. The type of lock is derived from the SQL statement. For example, if a SELECT statement is executed, a share lock is implemented. On the other hand, when you use an UPDATE statement, an exclusive lock is set.

27.8 Deadlocks

A well-known phenomenon that can occur if many users access the database simultaneously is what we call a *deadlock*. Simply put, a deadlock arises if two users wait for each other's data. Imagine that user U_1 has a lock on row R_1 and that he or she wants to place one on row R_2. Assume also that user U_2 is the "owner" of the lock on row R_2 and wants to place a lock on R_1. These two users are waiting for each other. If we go back to the analogy of a road crossing, have you ever been at a crossroads when four cars approach at the same time? Who can drive on first? This is also deadlock.

Some SQL products can discover that a deadlock has arisen. From time to time, such a product checks whether there are users waiting for each other. If they are found, SQL automatically aborts one of the transactions. It will feel as if SQL executed a ROLLBACK statement of its own accord. The transaction that is chosen differs for each product.

27.9 The Granularity of Locked Data

So far, we have described locking generally and in a rudimentary way. We have assumed that locks can be placed on individual rows. Some SQL products do not lock rows; they lock the entire physical *page* in which the row is stored (see also Section 20.2, in Chapter 20, "Using Indexes"). This means that if a row is changed, not only that single row, but also a set of rows, is locked. If the row is short, this number can be large. Some products lock even more data so that if a row is accessed, the entire table is locked.

The amount of data that is locked is called the *granularity*. The larger the granularity of a lock is, the lower the level of concurrency is and the simpler the internal administration is for SQL. In practice, we usually work with a granularity of one row or one physical page.

What does this mean for SQL? Not much because locking is hidden from the program and the user. For some SQL products, the granularity is fixed and the programmer cannot change it. With products that do support multiple levels of granularity, the granularity required must be specified. For example, with DB2, this can be specified per table with the ALTER TABLE statement. Here is an example.

Example 27.10: Define the granularity of locks for the PENALTIES table on row level.

```
ALTER TABLE PENALTIES LOCKSIZE ROW
```

Only a few products can indicate granularity at the beginning of a transaction. Still, this would be a very valuable feature.

27.10 The LOCK TABLE Statement

As we have already mentioned, during a transaction, all the data in use is locked against other users. To keep track of which data has been locked by which application, SQL must keep some internal administration. A user can execute many changes on a particular table within one transaction. For example, he might have a program that changes a column value of all rows of a table. These changes will be responsible for a huge amount of internal administrative work. To avoid this, you can lock the entire table in one process at the beginning of a transaction using the LOCK TABLE statement.

```
<lock table statement> ::=
   LOCK TABLE <table specification>
   IN <lock type> MODE

<lock type> ::= SHARE | EXCLUSIVE
```

Only base tables (tables that have been created with a CREATE TABLE statement) can be locked. At the end of a transaction, a lock is released automatically.

Example 27.11: Lock the entire PLAYERS table.

```
LOCK TABLE PLAYERS IN SHARE MODE
```

Explanation: In MySQL, a somewhat different syntax is used. The statement looks as follows:

```
LOCK TABLE PLAYERS READ
```

SQL supports the following lock types:

- **SHARE**—A lock of this type ensures that the application can read the table; other applications are also allowed to read the table, but they cannot change it.
- **EXCLUSIVE**—A lock of this type ensures that the application can change the table; other applications cannot gain access to the table and can neither read it nor change it.

Portability: *The LOCK TABLE statement is not supported by every SQL product.*

27.11   The Isolation Level

One further complication exists. When starting a transaction, you can set a so-called *isolation level*. This isolation level shows (the word says it already) to what extent the users are isolated from each other, or, in other words, to what extent they interfere with each other. So far, we have assumed only one isolation level. In SQL, we find the following levels:

- **Serializable**—If the isolation level is serializable, the users are the most separated from each other.
- **Repeatable read**—If the isolation level is repeatable read (read repeatability), share locks are set on all data that a user reads, and exclusive locks are placed on data that is changed. These locks exist as long as the transaction runs. This means that if a user executes the same SELECT statement several times within the same transaction, the result will always be the same. In previous sections, we assumed that this isolation level was desirable.
- **Cursor stability or read committed**—With cursor stability, the same locks are placed as for repeatable read. The difference is that share locks are released if the SELECT statement is processed. In other words, after the SELECT statement has been processed, but before the transaction ends, data becomes available for other users. This does not apply, of course, to changes. An exclusive lock is set on data that has been changed and remains there until the end of the transaction.
- **Dirty read or read uncommitted**—For reading data, dirty read is equal to cursor stability. However, with dirty read, a user can see the changes carried out by another user before that user has made his changes permanent with a COMMIT statement. In other words, the exclusive lock is released immediately after a change but before the transaction ends. This means that if you work with dirty read, the locking mechanism does not meet the serializability criterion.

In summary, with the isolation level called serializable, users have the greatest isolation from each other, but the level of concurrency is the lowest. This is the opposite of dirty read, in which users will definitely notice that they are not alone in using the system. They can read data that does not exist a few seconds later. However, the level of concurrency is the highest. It will rarely happen that a user will have to wait for another user. Table 27.1 indicates for each type of problem described in Section 27.6 whether this can occur for a specific isolation level.

Table 27.1   *Overview of Isolation Levels*

ISOLATION LEVEL	DIRTY READ	INCONSISTENT READ	NONREPEATABLE READ	PHANTOM READ	LOST UPDATE
Dirty read/read uncommitted	Yes	Yes	Yes	Yes	Yes
Cursor stability/ read committed	No	No	Yes	Yes	Yes
Repeatable read	No	No	No	No	Yes
Serializable	No	No	No	No	No

How the required isolation level is specified depends on the product. Some products support no SQL statement for specifying the isolation level. The level is set during precompilation for most products (see Section 26.4, in Chapter 26) and applies to all SQL statements in the precompiled program.

With other SQL products, the isolation level can be set using a specific SQL statement. This is the SET TRANSACTION statement:

```
<set transaction statement> ::=
    SET TRANSACTION ISOLATION LEVEL <isolation level>

<isolation level> ::=
    READ UNCOMMITTED |
    READ COMMITTED   |
    REPEATABLE READ  |
    SERIALIZABLE
```

In Section 27.2, we mentioned that the beginning of a transaction cannot be indicated explicitly. The first statement is the beginning of the transaction. However, it is possible to define the beginning of a transaction by using a SET TRANSACTION statement. In other words, when you enter a SET TRANSACTION statement, a new transaction starts automatically.

27.12   Answers

27.1

Line 1: A SELECT statement does not change the contents of tables but starts a transaction.

Line 2: This change is not yet permanent.

Line 3: A COMMIT statement is executed. All changes of the current transaction become permanent. This is the change of line 2.

Line 4: A ROLLBACK statement is executed. Because this is the first SQL statement following the previous COMMIT, a new transaction starts and ends here. No changes have been executed, so no changes have to be rolled back.

Lines 5–6: These two changes are not yet permanent.

Line 7: A ROLLBACK statement is executed. All changes of the actual transaction are undone. These are the changes of lines 5 and 6.

Line 8: This change is not yet permanent.

Line 9: A COMMIT statement is executed. All changes of the current transaction become permanent. This is the change of line 8.

Line 10: Here, the program is terminated. There is no current transaction, so the program can be terminated without problems.

27.2

Line 1: A SELECT statement does not change the contents of tables but starts a transaction.

Line 2: A savepoint is defined with the name S1.

Line 3: This change is not yet permanent.

Line 4: A COMMIT statement is executed. All changes of the current transaction become permanent. This is the change of line 3.

Line 5: This change is not yet permanent.

Line 6: A savepoint is defined with the name S1.

Line 7: This change is not yet permanent.

Line 8: A ROLLBACK statement is executed. Only the change of line 7 is undone. The change of line 5 is not yet permanent.

Line 9: This change is not yet permanent.

Line 10: A savepoint is defined with the name S2.

Line 11: This change is not yet permanent.

Line 12: A ROLLBACK statement is executed. Only the changes of lines 7, 9, and 11 are undone. The change of line 5 is (still) not yet permanent.

Line 13: A COMMIT statement is executed. All changes of the current transaction become permanent. This is the change of line 5.

Line 14: Here, the program is terminated. There is no current transaction, so the program can be terminated without problems.

28

Introduction to ODBC

28.1 Introduction

A disadvantage of embedded SQL is that only the programming languages for which a precompiler has been developed can be used. Without one, embedded SQL does not work. Usually precompilers are developed by the vendor of the SQL product. However, it is impossible for a vendor to develop a precompiler for every programming language and each development environment—there are just too many of them. This was one of the reasons another approach was considered for processing SQL statements, one that is less dependent on a host language.

The method found was based on the *Call-Level Interface* (CLI). A CLI is an application programming interface (API), which is a set of functions or routines with clearly defined interfaces that can be called from any programming language. APIs exist for all kinds of operations: to manipulate windows and buttons on the screen, to perform statistical calculations, and to access databases, for example. The latter of these is usually called a CLI.

When this method became known, each vendor began to develop a CLI for its own database server. Unfortunately, each vendor developed a different CLI. This changed with the introduction of Open DataBase Connectivity (ODBC), from Microsoft. It was the first commercially available CLI that was supported by many vendors.

This chapter explains the features of ODBC with the help of examples and the pseudo programming language with which you are now familiar. Of course, this is not a complete description of ODBC because that would require a complete book. For this, see the Microsoft Web site and [GEIG95].

28.2 The History of ODBC

The history of ODBC begins with the *SQL Access Group* (SAG). This consortium of companies was founded in August 1989. The first members included Apple, DEC, Gupta Software (which later became Centura Software), Hewlett-Packard, Informix (later taken over by IBM), Ingres (later taken over by Computer Associates), Microsoft, Novell, Oracle, Sybase, and Uniface (later merged with CompuWare). These companies realized that there was a need for a single standard CLI to access databases. At that time, each vendor had developed its own CLI. For example, Oracle supported OCI (Oracle Call Interface) and Sybase had DB-Library. All these CLIs had been developed for similar purposes but looked different. The SAG was set up to define a standard CLI with which applications could access databases in a way that was independent of the product and that could operate on several operating systems.

In 1991, the first version of a document describing the *SAG CLI* was published. Later that year, at a large exhibition in the United States, the first public demonstration was given of an application that accessed multiple databases concurrently with the SAG CLI. The standard CLI was born. It had been proven that it was possible to implement such a CLI.

Next, the following problem arose: How could vendors be convinced to implement this CLI as soon as possible? The solution was to transform the document into an official standard. To achieve that, the document was submitted as a proposal to ISO and X/Open. The latter accepted the document in 1993, and it became a part of the set of standards called the X/Open Portability Guide (XPG). It took ISO a little longer, but this organization accepted the proposal in 1995 and called it the ISO SQL/CLI standard. To this day, this is the standard that still exists.

In the end, the SAG became a workgroup within *The Open Group*, called The Open SQL Access Group; it is responsible for further development of this standard. The Open Group was a consortium formed by the merger of the *X/Open Group* and the *Open Software Foundation* (OSF). These two consortia merged in February 1996.

The tie between ODBC and ISO SQL/CLI is very tight. At the beginning of the 1990s, when Microsoft wanted to develop its own CLI for database access as part of *WOSA* (Windows Open Services Architecture), it was obvious that the SQL/CLI would serve as a starting point. It was decided to make ODBC compatible with this standardized CLI, to meet the standards. Currently, ODBC is a superset of the ISO SQL/CLI.

The first version, ODBC 1.0, was launched in 1992 and became the first commercial implementation of the SQL/CLI. It was a success from the beginning, even though the first version was only a developer's kit (SDK). At that time, many companies were trying to implement client/server applications, and ODBC played a very useful role. Later, in September 1993, the complete version was launched. In 1994, ODBC version 2.0 followed (again, first in SDK form), and this was considerably extended compared to its precursor. At the end of 1996, Version 3.0 became available; at the time of this writing, Version 3.5 is the current version. This is also the version that we discuss in this book.

28.3   How Does ODBC Work?

ODBC is much more than a document. On one hand, it is the definition of a CLI, a set of definitions and rules. On the other hand, it is software. First, we describe how ODBC, as implemented by Microsoft, works.

Logically, ODBC consists of two layers; see Figure 28.1. These two layers are between the application and a number of databases that the application can access. In ODBC, these are called *data sources*. A data source can be MySQL, DB2, Oracle, or Microsoft Access, for example.

Figure 28.1   *ODBC consists of two layers*

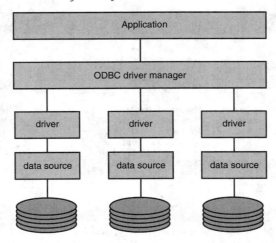

The application "talks" to the first layer of ODBC, called the *ODBC driver manager*. This module can be seen as a part of Windows itself. The job of the driver manager can be compared to that of the printer manager under Windows.

The working of ODBC resembles printing software. Therefore, let us first take a closer look at the job of the printer manager. If we want to print a document, we send it to the printer manager with an instruction that it should be printed by a specific printer. Because each printer is different—one might be a black-and-white printer, whereas another supports color; one might have a resolution of 600 dots per inch, and another 1200—a special driver has been developed for each printer. Although internally they differ considerably, the printer manager considers these drivers to be the same. Indeed, the printer manager has been set up to hide these differences from the users. In a sense, this module acts as a switchboard.

The ODBC driver manager has a comparable task. For example, if an application wants to access an MySQL database, the driver manager links to the appropriate *driver*; this is the second layer of ODBC. This driver has been developed specifically to access MySQL databases. If an application wants to access DB2, a driver is linked that has been developed specifically for DB2. The power of the drivers and whether the database is located at the other end of the world is transparent to the driver manager and, therefore, to the application. This kind of detail is hidden by drivers. Although each driver looks the same to the driver manager, the internal processing is different for each driver.

Via the Windows Control Panel, you can check which drivers have been installed on your own machine. Figure 28.2 shows a list with installed ODBC drivers. As an example, the first driver offers access to DB2, the second to dBASE files, and the fourth to Microsoft Access databases.

Drivers can be implemented in different ways. Figure 28.3 shows a number of possible implementations. In the first implementation, all software components run on the same machine. The application communicates with the ODBC driver manager, which, in turn, calls an ODBC driver. The latter communicates directly with a database server. In fact, the ODBC driver acts as an entry to the database server.

Figure 28.2   *List with installed ODBC drivers*

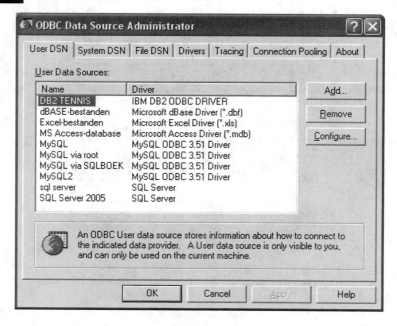

Figure 28.3   *Various implementations of ODBC*

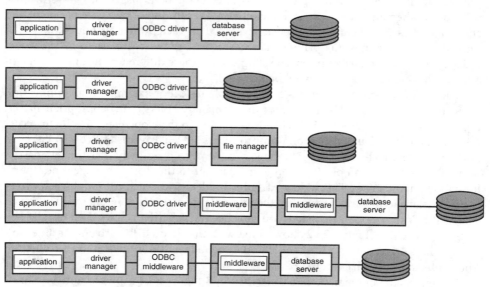

In the second implementation, the ODBC driver and the database server have been bundled together to form one layer of software that processes the calls of the ODBC API functions plus the SQL statements. Drivers that, for example, want to access data that is stored in spreadsheet files are built in this way because no available database server can be used. The third alternative is only a variation of the second. The difference is that the data is stored not locally, but on a remote file server.

The fourth implementation is important for client/server environments. The database server (together with the database) is located on a remote machine. To access that machine, *middleware* has been installed. These products have been optimized to send SQL statements through a local network. Most middleware products support their own CLI. The ODBC driver for this form of implementation translates the ODBC CLI to the product-dependent CLI. The driver itself does not know that a remote database server is accessed because it is completely shielded from this. For the fifth form, the ODBC driver and the middleware component on the client side have been brought together into one product.

However, no matter how the ODBC driver works, it is completely transparent to the ODBC driver manager and to all applications.

It is important to know that Microsoft is not the only company developing ODBC drivers; other companies are also doing this. There are even companies that supply drivers but not a database server product.

28.4   A Simple Example of ODBC

In this section, we show with a simple example what ODBC looks like to a programmer. The example deals with logging on to a database using ODBC.

Example 28.1: Develop a program that logs on to SQL using ODBC and reports back whether it succeeded.

```
PROGRAM LOGIN_VIA_ODBC;
DECLARATIONS
    user        : CHAR(30);
    password    : CHAR(30);
    h_env       : HENV;
    h_database  : HDBC;
    rc          : RETCODE;
BEGIN
    WRITE 'What is your name?';
    READ user;
    WRITE 'What is your password?';
    READ password;
```

```
  # Allocate host variables that ODBC needs
  SQLAllocHandle(SQL_HANDLE_ENV, SQL_NULL_HANDLE, &h_env);
  SQLSetEnvAttr(h_env, SQL_ATTR_ODBC_VERSION,
                SQL_OV_ODBC3, 0);
  SQLAllocHandle(SQL_HANDLE_DBC, h_env, &h_database);
  # Log on to the SQL database
  rc := SQLConnect(h_database, 'SQL', SQL_NTS, user,
                   SQL_NTS, password, SQL_NTS);
  # The value of rc is checked to
  # determine whether the login was a success
  IF rc = SQL_SUCCESS OR rc = SQL_SUCCESS_WITH_INFO THEN
     WRITE 'The logging on has succeeded!';
     # Log off
     SQLDisconnect(h_database);
  ELSE
     WRITE 'The logging on has not succeeded!';
  ENDIF;
  # Deallocate all ODBC host variables
  SQLFreeHandle(SQL_HANDLE_DBC, h_database);
  SQLFreeHandle(SQL_HANDLE_ENV, h_env);
END
```

We explain this program line by line. The program contains a number of function calls that are used by every ODBC program. The first ODBC function called is SQLAl-locHandle. With this call, an *environment handle* is created. The concept *handle* is often used in ODBC, which recognizes several kinds of handles, of which the environment handle is one. The others are discussed later in this chapter. Technically, a handle is a pointer to a specific area of internal memory that is reserved for this function; see Figure 28.4. The memory area to which a pointer refers holds general data on the environment. The size and location of the memory area are not important to the program. (Besides, this can be different for each new version of ODBC.)

Figure 28.4   *The black dot represents a handle that points to a certain area in internal memory; the handle is stored in a variable.*

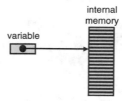

The SQLAllocHandle function must always be the first ODBC function invoked. With this function, a number of important internal variables are initialized and, as noted, internal memory is reserved. This indispensable memory area is used by ODBC as a scribbling pad. Calling SQLAllocHandle might be compared with starting up a car. The SQLAllocHandle function is one of the few functions that is processed entirely by the ODBC driver manager itself.

The SQLAllocHandle function has three parameters. We use the first one to indicate the type of handle to create. In this example, we indicate with the literal SQL_HANDLE_ENV that an environment handle must be created. SQL_HANDLE_ENV is one of the many *ODBC literals*. In this chapter, we introduce several of them. It is not necessary to assign these literals a value because their respective values have been predefined and, by simply linking a given file, the values are allocated automatically. The second parameter of the SQLAllocHandle function is not relevant for this call; therefore, SQL_NULL_HANDLE is specified. At the position of the third parameter, we specify the variable in which we will store the handle.

In previous versions of ODBC, the function SQLAllocEnv was called instead of the SQLAllocHandle function. In Version 3.0 of ODBC, it was announced that this function will be removed in future versions; it is called a *deprecated* function. So, although it is still possible to use deprecated functions, they will not be supported in the future. Therefore, it is recommended that they are not used any longer.

The opposite of the SQLAllocHandle function is SQLFreeHandle, with which the reserved memory area is released. The function has two parameters: the type of handle and the environment handle. After this function has been called, it is impossible to call another ODBC function. To the program, it looks as though ODBC has been switched off. If you want to work with ODBC after this statement has been processed, SQLAllocHandle must be called again. In previous versions, this function was called SQLFreeEnv.

After the environment handle has been created, you must indicate which behavior of ODBC you will be using. You specify this with the function SQLSetEnvAttr. This function must be called before you proceed to log on to a database. With the call in the example, you indicate that you would like to have the behavior of ODBC Version 3.0.

It is possible to work with multiple databases simultaneously within a program; this implies that you can log on to multiple databases. However, before you can log on to a database, it is necessary to create a handle for it. For this, you also use the SQL-AllocHandle function, but now with the ODBC literal SQL_HANDLE_DBC as the first parameter. (*DBC* stands for database connection.) Space in internal memory is reserved to store data about the database. In the example, the variable H_DATABASE is initialized. H_DATABASE is a *database handle* (sometimes called a connection handle). Within ODBC, you do not refer to a database by its name, but by a database handle. A database handle can be reused for multiple databases, if it is not used simultaneously. If you want to work with two databases simultaneously, it is necessary to create two database handles, so you have to call SQLAllocHandle twice with SQL_HANDLE_DBC as its first parameter. For ODBC Version 3.0, the creation of a database handle was performed with the deprecated function SQLAllocConnect.

A database handle must also be removed at the end of a program. In the previous example, we once again use the SQLFreeHandle function. After this function has been used, it is no longer possible to access the database. In previous versions of ODBC, this was done with the SQLFreeConnect function.

The important function call in this example is SQLConnect, which is used to actually log on to a database. It is comparable to the CONNECT statement of embedded SQL; see Section 26.9, in Chapter 26, "Introduction to Embedded SQL." This function has seven parameters. With the first one, we specify the handle of the database to which we want to log on. The second is the data source—in this case, that is SQL. For the driver manager, this parameter identifies the driver that has to be retrieved and linked. The fourth and sixth parameters are used to specify the user and password, respectively. The third, fifth, and seventh parameters are not that important here. The literal SQL_NTS stands for null-terminated string. In fact, the respective lengths of the parameters must be indicated here, unless the strings are closed in a specific way. However, we could have used the number 3 as the third parameter—the length of the word *SQL*.

Each ODBC function has a *return code* as a result. We did not evaluate the return after each call, but we have done so for the SQLConnect function. We do this because we want to know whether we have logged on successfully. For each possible return code, an ODBC literal has been defined to simplify working with return codes. The most common is SQL_SUCCESS. For embedded SQL, checking whether a return code is equal to SQL_SUCCESS can be compared with checking whether the SQLCODE variable is equal to zero. Another possible return code is SQL_SUCCESS_WITH_INFO. If the return code is equal to this value, the SQL statement has also been executed correctly. There is even information available that we can query. We return to this subject later. And, of course, the return code SQL_ERROR exists.

In principle, each call from an ODBC function can go wrong or, in other words, can return an error message. That is why a programmer should check the return code after each function call. However, we omit this in this chapter because it would make the examples too long and unnecessarily complex.

SQLDriverConnect can also be called instead of the SQLConnect function. This function performs the same task but allows more data to be specified. For example, it is possible to enter a complete login specification. When this function is called, a window is shown into which the user can enter more login information.

After we have logged on, we call an SQLDisconnect. The only parameter that this function requires is a database handle.

It will be obvious that each program that wants to access a database with ODBC should call the functions described in this section at least once. For the sake of convenience, we omit them in the following sections and examples.

In Section 26.4, in Chapter 26, we discussed the precompiling of programs for embedded SQL. When ODBC is used, this is not necessary. For example, if we used C as the programming language, the calls of the ODBC functions would follow the syntax of C, and we could call the C compiler directly. It is important, however, to indicate the location of all ODBC functions when linking the library; otherwise, it is not possible to create a load module.

28.5 Return Codes

In the program LOGIN_VIA_ODBC, the use of return codes has already been shown. However, ODBC offers some additional, rather more extended, features for handling error message. In older versions of ODBC, a special function called SQLError was used to request detailed information about the message:

```
IF rc = SQL_SUCCESS OR rc = SQL_SUCCESS_WITH_INFO THEN
    WRITE 'The logging on has succeeded!';
    # Log off
    SQLDisconnect(h_database);
ELSE
    WRITE 'The logging on has not succeeded!';
    SQLError(henv, h_database, SQL_NULL_STMT, sqlstate,
             native_error, error_text, &text_length,
             max_length);
    WRITE 'Reason: ', error_text;
ENDIF;
```

Explanation: SQLError has eight parameters. The first one is the environment handle, and the second is the database handle. The third is not used in this example; therefore, we specify the ODBC literal SQL_NULL_STMT. The fourth parameter contains the actual ODBC error. The fifth parameter contains the code for the error, but as it is known to the data source. The sixth parameter is a pointer to the internal memory area that holds the error message. The seventh parameter indicates the length of the error message. Finally, the eighth parameter indicates the maximum length of the error message.

In ODBC Version 3.0, the features have been extended. With the function SQLGet-DiagRec, a list of errors can be retrieved. Then, a WHILE-DO statement can be used to go through the list of errors.

28.6 Retrieving Data About SQL

When you are logged on, much information about the database can be retrieved, including, for example, the type of driver or the data types that are supported by the underlying database server. Here are a few examples:

- SQLDataSources—This function returns a list of data sources accessible by the program. The window shown in Figure 28.2 may have been created with this function.
- SQLDrivers—This function returns a list of drivers accessible by the program. This could be the same list as in Figure 28.2.

- SQLGetInfo—This function returns general information about the driver and the data source to which the database handle is linked.
- SQLGetFunctions—This function returns information about which ODBC functions are supported by a specific driver.
- SQLGetTypeInfo—This function returns information about which SQL data types are supported by the data source.

28.7 DDL Statements and ODBC

So far, we have shown only how to log on. Our programs have not accessed the data in the database yet. Let us begin by including DDL statements.

Example 28.2: Develop a program that, depending on the choice of the end user, creates or removes an index on the PLAYERS table; see also Example 26.1.

```
PROGRAM PLAYERS_INDEX;
DECLARATIONS
   choice        : CHAR(1);
   sql_stat      : CHAR(100);
   rc            : RETCODE;
   h_statement   : HSTMT;
   h_database    : HDBC;
BEGIN
   WRITE 'Do you want to create (C) or drop
           (D) the PLAY index?';
   READ choice;
   # Dependent on choice, create or drop the index
   IF choice = 'C' THEN
      SQLAllocHandle(SQL_HANDLE_STMT, h_database,
                     &h_statement);
      sql_stat := 'CREATE UNIQUE INDEX PLAY ON PLAYERS
                     (PLAYERNO)';
      rc := SQLExecDirect(h_statement, sql_stat, SQL_NTS);
      SQLEndTran(SQL_NULL_HENV, h_database, SQL_COMMIT);
      WRITE 'Index PLAY is created!';
      SQLFreeHandle(SQL_HANDLE_STMT, h_statement);
   ELSE IF choice = 'D' THEN
```

```
        SQLAllocHandle(SQL_HANDLE_STMT, h_database,
                        &h_statement);
        sql_stat := 'DROP INDEX PLAY';
        rc := SQLExecDirect(h_statement, sql_stat, SQL_NTS);
        SQLEndTran(SQL_NULL_HENV, h_database, SQL_COMMIT);
        WRITE 'Index PLAY is dropped!';
        SQLFreeHandle(SQL_HANDLE_STMT, h_statement);
    ELSE
        WRITE 'Unknown choice!';
    ENDIF;
END
```

Explanation: This program uses a number of new ODBC functions. The structure of the program is simple. Depending on what the user enters, a CREATE or DROP INDEX statement is processed. There are comparable function calls before and after these two statements. The first is the (now familiar) SQLAllocHandle function that reserves space in memory for an SQL statement. This function is called at least once if statements have to be processed. As the first parameter, we specify the ODBC literal SQL_HANDLE_STMT to indicate what type of handle should be created. The host variable H_STATEMENT is now a so-called *statement handle*. In previous versions of ODBC, statement handles were created with the deprecated function SQLAllocStmt.

Space is returned with the function SQLFreeHandle. After execution of this function, the H_STATEMENT can no longer be used. In previous versions of ODBC, statement handles were removed with the deprecated function SQLFreeStmt.

So far, we have seen three types of handles: environment, connection, and statement handles. A program can allocate only one environment handle, but multiple connection handles. For each connection handle, several statement handles can be created. This hierarchy of handles is represented in Figure 28.5.

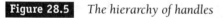

Figure 28.5   *The hierarchy of handles*

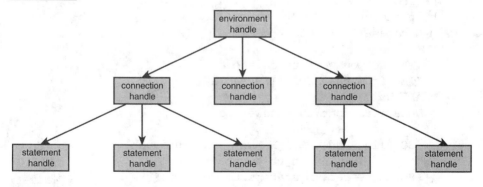

After the statement handle has been created, the SQL statement that must be executed is assigned to a host variable. In C, this usually is done with the strcpy function. Next the function SQLExecDirect is used to process the statement. The parameters are, successively, the statement handle that must be used, the host variable in which the SQL statement is located, and the length of this host variable. (We use SQL_NTS once again.) With this call, the statement is passed to the database server and processed. Whether the statement has been processed correctly can be derived from the return code. This function call looks very much like the EXECUTE IMMEDIATE statement of dynamic SQL.

The function that is called next is SQLEndTran. (This function used to be called SQLTransact.) With this function, a running transaction is ended with a COMMIT or ROLLBACK. This function has three parameters. The first parameter is not relevant to this example. The second indicates the database on which the COMMIT or ROLLBACK should be executed. The fact that a database must be specified here has to do with the fact that it is possible to log on to multiple database simultaneously. The third parameter indicates with the literal SQL_COMMIT or SQL_ROLLBACK what the action is supposed to be. Therefore, calling this function is similar to executing the COMMIT and ROLLBACK statements, respectively.

28.8 DML Statements and ODBC

As long as DELETE, INSERT, and UPDATE statements contain no host variables, including these statements in a program with ODBC is similar to the method used for DDL and DCL statements.

Example 28.3: Develop a program that removes all the rows from the PENALTIES table; see also Example 26.2.

```
PROGRAM DELETE_PENALTIES;
DECLARATIONS
    choice        : CHAR(1);
    h_statement   : HSTMT;
    h_database    : HDBC;
BEGIN
    WRITE 'Do you want to delete all rows';
    WRITE 'from the PENALTIES table (Y/N)?';
    READ choice;
    # Determine what the answer is.
    IF choice = 'Y' THEN
        SQLAllocHandle(SQL_HANDLE_STMT, h_database,
                    &h_statement);
        SQLExecDirect(h_statement, 'DELETE FROM PENALTIES',
                    SQL_NTS);
```

```
          SQLEndTran(SQL_NULL_HENV, h_database, SQL_COMMIT);
          SQLFreeHandle(SQL_HANDLE_STMT, h_statement);
          WRITE 'All rows are deleted!';
      ELSE
          WRITE 'The rows are not deleted!';
      ENDIF;
   END
```

Explanation: This program does not require much explanation because the function calls are similar to the one in Example 28.2. SQLAllocHandle is called to reserve memory space in which ODBC can keep data about the statement. Next, the DELETE statement is assigned to a host variable. The statement is processed with the SQLExecDirect function. SQLEndTran makes the change permanent. Finally, memory space is released with SQLFreeHandle.

ODBC supports a special function that can be used after processing an UPDATE, INSERT, or DELETE statement to request how many rows have been processed. In this example, we would like to know how many rows have actually been deleted. This is the SQLRowCount function. The next example can easily be extended with this function. The procedure is obvious:

```
   :
   IF choice = 'Y' THEN
      SQLAllocHandle(SQL_HANDLE_STMT, h_database,
                     &h_statement);
      SQLExecDirect(h_statement, 'DELETE FROM PENALTIES',
                    SQL_NTS);
      SQLRowCount(h_statement, &number_of_rows);
      SQLEndTran(SQL_NULL_HENV, h_database, SQL_COMMIT);
      SQLFreeHandle(SQL_HANDLE_STMT, h_statement);
      WRITE 'There are ', number_of_rows, ' deleted!';
   ELSE
      WRITE 'The rows are not deleted!';
   ENDIF;
   :
```

28.9   Using Host Variables in SQL Statements

In the example of the SQLExecDirect function, the SQL statement did *not* contain host variables. However, just as with embedded SQL, we are allowed to specify them. How does that work? As always, we illustrate this with an example.

Example 28.4: Develop a program that increases by one the number of sets won for a given match; see Example 26.3.

```
PROGRAM RAISE_WON;
DECLARATIONS
    mno            : SMALLINT;
    sql_stat       : CHAR(100);
    h_statement    : HSTMT;
    h_database     : HDBC;
BEGIN
    SQLAllocHandle(SQL_HANDLE_STMT, h_database,
                   &h_statement);
    sql_stat := 'UPDATE MATCHES SET WON = WON + 1
                WHERE MATCHNO = ?';
    # Increase the number of sets won
    SQLPrepare(h_statement, sql_stat, SQL_NTS);
    SQLBindParameter(h_statement, 1, SQL_PARAM_INPUT,
                     SQL_C_SLONG, SQL_SMALLINT, 0,
                     0, &mno, 0, NULL);
    WRITE 'Enter the match number: ';
    READ mno;
    SQLExecute(h_statement);
    SQLEndTran(SQL_NULL_HENV, h_database, SQL_COMMIT);
    SQLFreeHandle(SQL_HANDLE_STMT, h_statement);
    WRITE 'Ready!';
END
```

Explanation: New in this program is that the SQLExecDirect function has been replaced by three other functions: SQLPrepare, SQLBindParameter, and SQL-Execute. SQLPrepare verifies the syntax of the SQL statement (which is included as a parameter) but does not execute it. The function has the same parameters as SQL-ExecDirect but does less. Note that the SQL statement does not contain host variables, such as are used in embedded SQL, but uses question marks. A question mark stands for a value that is not be filled in. In fact, the use of SQLPrepare can be compared to the PREPARE statement of dynamic SQL, where question marks also indicate variables.

The SQLBindParameter function links the question marks to a certain host variable. A question mark, or parameter, can be used everywhere we otherwise could have placed a literal, column specification, or expression. Actually, the same rules apply here as for embedded SQL. In this example, we link the (only) question mark to the host variable MNO. The function has the following ten parameters:

- The statement handle.
- The number of the parameter. This is the sequence number of a question mark within the SQL statement.

- The type of parameter. Three types of parameters are supported: input, output, and in plus output. For these three types, the following three ODBC literals have been defined, respectively: SQL_PARAM_INPUT, SQL_PARAM_OUTPUT, and SQL_PARAM_INPUT_OUTPUT.

- The C data type of the parameter. For each C data type, a number of literals have been defined: SQL_C_BINARY, SQL_C_BIT, SQL_C_CHAR, SQL_C_DATE, SQL_C_DEFAULT, SQL_C_DOUBLE, SQL_C_FLOAT, SQL_C_SLONG, SQL_C_SSHORT, SQL_C_STINYINT, SQL_C_TIME, SQL_C_TIMESTAMP, SQL_C_ULONG, SQL_C_USHORT, and SQL_C_UTINYINT.

- The SQL data type of the parameter. For each data type, an ODBC literal has been defined, the name of which begins with SQL_ followed by the name of the data type.

- The precision of the column.

- The scale of the column.

- A pointer to the host variable itself.

- The maximum length of the host variable. If the host variable is numeric, it can be set to zero.

- A pointer to the address in which the length of the host variable is located.

The SQLBindParameter function was introduced in ODBC Version 2.0. This function replaces the function SQLSetParam used in ODBC Version 1.0. The latter function can no longer be used.

A host variable used within SQL statements must be specified according to strict rules. For example, the MNO host variable must have a data type that is comparable to the data type of the MATCHNO column because it is compared with that column. These rules are dependent on the column with which they are compared. Again, we refer to the manuals for these rules. As we said in the beginning of this chapter, we confine ourselves to the specification of the SQL data types.

After the parameter has been linked to a host variable, and when the host variable contains a value, the SQL statement can be executed. Because the statement has already been verified, the SQLExecute function can be executed immediately.

If we want to remove several matches by using the same statement, it is not necessary to link the host variable repeatedly. The program would look as follows:

```
PROGRAM RAISE_WON_N;
DECLARATIONS
    :
BEGIN
    SQLAllocHandle(SQL_HANDLE_STMT, h_database,
                   &h_statement);
    sql_stat := 'UPDATE MATCHES SET WON = WON + 1
                 WHERE MATCHNO = ?';
```

```
    SQLPrepare(h_statement, sql_stat, SQL_NTS);
    SQLBindParameter(h_statement, 1, SQL_PARAM_INPUT,
                     SQL_C_SLONG, SQL_SMALLINT, 0, 0,
                     &mno, 0, NULL);
    counter := 1;
    WHILE counter <= 100 DO
       WRITE 'Enter the match number: ';
       READ mno;
       SQLExecute(h_statement);
       counter := counter + 1;
    ENDWHILE;
    SQLEndTran(SQL_NULL_HENV, h_database, SQL_COMMIT);
    SQLFreeHandle(SQL_HANDLE_STMT, h_statement);
    WRITE 'Ready!';
END
```

The following example shows what a program would look like if a statement contains multiple parameters.

Example 28.5: Develop a program for entering penalty data.

```
PROGRAM ENTER_PENALTIES;
DECLARATIONS
    pno          : SMALLINT;
    payno        : SMALLINT;
    pay_date     : DATE;
    amount       : DECIMAL(7,2);
    sql_stat     : CHAR(100);
    h_statement  : HSTMT;
    h_database   : HDBC;
BEGIN
    WRITE 'Enter the payment number of the penalty: ';
    READ payno;
    WRITE 'Enter the player number of the penalty: ';
    READ pno;
    WRITE 'Enter the date on which the penalty is paid: ';
    READ pay_date;
    WRITE 'Enter the penalty amount: ';
```

```
      READ amount;
      # Prepare the INSERT statement
      SQLAllocHandle(SQL_HANDLE_STMT, h_database,
                     &h_statement);
      sql_stat := 'INSERT INTO PENALTIES
                    (PAYMENTNO, PLAYERNO, PAY_DATE, AMOUNT)
                    VALUES (?, ?, ?, ?)';
      SQLPrepare(h_statement, sql_stat, SQL_NTS);
      # Link the parameters to the host variables
      SQLBindParameter(h_statement, 1, SQL_PARAM_INPUT,
                       SQL_C_SLONG,SQL_SMALLINT, 0, 0,
                       &pno, 0, NULL);
      SQLBindParameter(h_statement, 2, SQL_PARAM_INPUT,
                       SQL_C_SLONG, SQL_SMALLINT, 0, 0,
                       &payno, 0, NULL);
      SQLBindParameter(h_statement, 3, SQL_PARAM_INPUT,
                       SQL_C_DATE, SQL_DATE, 0, 0, &pay_date,
                       0, NULL);
      SQLBindParameter(h_statement, 4, SQL_PARAM_INPUT,
                       SQL_C_FLOAT, SQL_DECIMAL, 7, 2,
                       &amount, 0, NULL);
      # Add the new data to the PENALTIES table
      SQLExecute(h_statement);
      SQLEndTran(SQL_NULL_HENV, h_database, SQL_COMMIT);
      SQLFreeHandle(SQL_HANDLE_STMT, h_statement);
      WRITE 'Ready!';
   END
```

Explanation: It is obvious that, for each question mark (which indicates a parameter), the SQLBindParameter function is called.

28.10   Settings for a Statement Handle

It is possible to assign certain settings to almost every statement handle. These settings have an impact on the way statements are processed, and they influence their results. These settings are assigned with the SQLSetStmtAttr function. This function used to be called SQLSetStmtOption. As an example, we indicate how the number of rows in the result of a SELECT statement can be limited.

Example 28.6: Get the addresses of the first ten players.

```
    :
SQLAllocHandle(SQL_HANDLE_STMT, h_database, &h_statement);
sql_stat := 'SELECT PLAYERNO, NAME, INITIALS,
              STREET, HOUSENO, TOWN, POSTCODE
              FROM PLAYERS';
SQLSetStmtAttr(h_statement, SQL_MAX_ROWS, 10, SQL_NTS);
SQLExecDirect(h_statement, sql_stat, SQL_NTS);
SQLFreeHandle(SQL_HANDLE_STMT, h_statement);
    :
```

Explanation: After the statement handle has been created and before the statement is processed, SQLSetStmtAttr is called. The value of the SQL_MAX_ROWS setting is set to 10. Regardless of the actual number of rows in the result of the SELECT statement, ten rows are returned, at most. If the maximum must be removed again, the same function with the same setting must be called, but with the maximum value now set to zero.

SQLSetStmtAttr has several settings. There are settings for, among other things, the type of cursor that must be created and the maximum processing time of an SQL statement. The next sections contain more examples.

28.11   SELECT Statements

If we want to retrieve the result of a SELECT statement in a program, the procedure is not much different from that for the examples of embedded SQL from Sections 26.10 and 26.12, in Chapter 26. In ODBC, we also use the cursor mechanism to fetch rows with values in the program. However, one important difference exists: In ODBC, there is no difference, as there is in embedded SQL, between SELECT statements that always return one row of data and those in which the number of rows in the result is undefined. There is another distinction as well: With ODBC, data can be retrieved value by value, row by row, or in groups of rows. We discuss each possibility in this section.

28.11.1 Retrieving Data Value by Value

The way values are retrieved one by one is easy to understand, so this is where we begin.

Example 28.7: Develop a program that prints the address data of player 27 row by row.

```
PROGRAM ADDRESS_VALUE_BY_VALUE;
DECLARATIONS
    pno          : SMALLINT;
    name         : CHAR(15);
    init         : CHAR(3);
    street       : CHAR(15);
    houseno      : CHAR(4);
    town         : CHAR(10);
    postcode     : CHAR(6);
    sql_stat     : CHAR(100);
    sqlcode      : RETCODE;
    h_statement  : HSTMT;
    h_database   : HDBC;
BEGIN
    SQLAllocHandle(SQL_HANDLE_STMT, h_database,
                   &h_statement);
    sql_stat := 'SELECT PLAYERNO, NAME,
                INITIALS, STREET, HOUSENO, TOWN, POSTCODE
                FROM PLAYERS WHERE PLAYERNO = 27';
    SQLExecDirect(h_statement, sql_stat, SQL_NTS);
    IF SQLFetch(h_statement) = SQL_SUCCESS THEN
        SQLGetData(h_statement, 1, SQL_C_SLONG, &pno, ...);
        SQLGetData(h_statement, 2, SQL_C_CHAR, &name, ...);
        SQLGetData(h_statement, 3, SQL_C_CHAR, &init, ...);
        SQLGetData(h_statement, 4, SQL_C_CHAR, &street, ...);
        SQLGetData(h_statement, 5, SQL_C_CHAR, &houseno,
                   ...);
        SQLGetData(h_statement, 6, SQL_C_CHAR, &town, ...);
        SQLGetData(h_statement, 7, SQL_C_CHAR, &postcode,
                   ...);
        # Present address data
        WRITE 'Player number :', pno;
        WRITE 'Surname       :', name;
        WRITE 'Initials      :', init;
        WRITE 'Street        :', street, ' ', houseno;
        WRITE 'Town          :', town;
        WRITE 'Postcode      :', postcode;
    ELSE
        WRITE 'There is no player number 27';
    ENDIF;
    SQLFreeHandle(SQL_HANDLE_STMT, h_statement);
END
```

Explanation: The first statements in this program were discussed in earlier sections. First, a statement handle is created with SQLAllocHandle; next, the SELECT statement is processed with SQLExecDirect. In this context, this function is comparable to the DECLARE and OPEN CURSOR statements together. Thus, a cursor is created.

Note that because the SELECT statement in this example contains no parameters, it is not necessary to execute an SQLPrepare first and then an SQLExecute, even though this would have been allowed.

With SQLExecDirect, the first (and only) row in the result of the SELECT statement is retrieved by a call of the SQLFetch function. As far as functionality goes, this function corresponds to the FETCH statement in embedded SQL. Only one fetch has to be executed in this program because the result of this SELECT statement always consists of only one row.

The values retrieved with the SQLFetch function are not yet known to the program. In the program, we can fetch those values one by one with the SQLGetData function. This function assigns one value of the row to a host variable.

SQLGetData has six parameters. The first parameter is the statement handle. The second parameter is the sequence number of the column value in the row. The previous program retrieves all column values, but this is not mandatory. If necessary, a certain column value can even be retrieved several times.

The C data type of the host variable is indicated by the third parameter. For each C data type, a number of literals have been defined, including SQL_C_BINARY, SQL_C_BIT, SQL_C_CHAR, SQL_C_DATE, SQL_C_DEFAULT, SQL_C_DOUBLE, SQL_C_FLOAT, SQL_C_SLONG, SQL_C_SSHORT, SQL_C_STINYINT, SQL_C_TIME, SQL_C_TIMESTAMP, SQL_C_ULONG, SQL_C_USHORT, and SQL_C_UTINYINT.

The fourth parameter is the host variable to which the value has to be assigned. The fifth parameter represents the length of the host variable. The sixth parameter is important. The result of a SELECT INTO statement in embedded SQL can contain a NULL value. This also applies to the SELECT statement in the previous example. That NULL value must be collected, if possible. This is not done in ODBC in the same way as in embedded SQL, with NULL indicators (see Section 26.11, in Chapter 26). However, if the value that is retrieved with SQLGetData is equal to the NULL value, the last parameter is set to SQL_NULL_DATA. Again, this is an ODBC literal.

The SQLFreeHandle function removes the statement handle. If the cursor belonging to this statement is still open, it will be closed automatically.

A disadvantage of this method of retrieving data has to do with efficiency. In a client/server environment, it could mean that each value is sent through the network separately. This will not cause problems if only a few values are retrieved, but when many rows are retrieved, the procedure will be very slow. Why, therefore, has this technique been developed? SQLGetData is useful when only a few values are retrieved or if one very large value is fetched, such as an image or a piece of music. The size of this type of values can be many megabytes large.

28.11.2　Retrieving Data Row by Row

If we want to retrieve data row by row, the expressions from the SELECT clause must be linked or "bound" to the host variables. For this, the SQLBindCol function is used.

After the SQLExecDirect function has been executed, for each expression in the SELECT clause, an SQLBindCol function must be executed. This is called *binding*. If then an SQLFetch function is used to retrieve a row, the value of each column is assigned directly to the corresponding host variable.

Example 28.8: Rewrite the previous program so that the data is retrieved row by row. The inner body of that program will look as follows:

```
BEGIN
    SQLAllocHandle(SQL_HANDLE_STMT, h_database,
                    &h_statement);
    sql_stat := 'SELECT PLAYERNO, NAME,
                    INITIALS, STREET, HOUSENO, TOWN, POSTCODE
                    FROM PLAYERS WHERE PLAYERNO = 27';
    SQLExecDirect(h_statement, sql_stat, SQL_NTS);
    SQLBindCol(h_statement, 1, SQL_C_SLONG, &pno, ...);
    SQLBindCol(h_statement, 2, SQL_C_CHAR, &name, ...);
    SQLBindCol(h_statement, 3, SQL_C_CHAR, &init, ...);
    SQLBindCol(h_statement, 4, SQL_C_CHAR, &street, ...);
    SQLBindCol(h_statement, 5, SQL_C_CHAR, &houseno, ...);
    SQLBindCol(h_statement, 6, SQL_C_CHAR, &town, ...);
    SQLBindCol(h_statement, 7, SQL_C_CHAR, &postcode, ...);
    IF SQLFetch(h_statement) = SQL_SUCCESS THEN
        # Present address data
        WRITE 'Player number :', pno;
        WRITE 'Name         :', name;
        :
    ELSE
        WRITE 'There is no player number 27';
    ENDIF;
    SQLFreeHandle(SQL_HANDLE_STMT, h_statement);
END
```

Explanation: The SQLBindCol function has six parameters. The first is the statement handle, and the second is a sequence number that indicates the expression from the SELECT clause. The third parameter represents the C data type of that expression, and the fourth parameter is the host variable to which the value has to be assigned. The other two parameters are irrelevant to us.

To make the difference between the SQLGetData and SQLBindCol functions clearer, we use another example in which the SELECT statement retrieves several rows from the PLAYERS table.

Example 28.9: Develop a program for printing all address data of all players.
With the SQLGetData function, the program looks like this:

```
PROGRAM ADDRESS_ALL_VALUE_BY_VALUE;
DECLARATIONS
     pno         : SMALLINT;
     name        : CHAR(15);
     init        : CHAR(3);
     street      : CHAR(15);
     houseno     : CHAR(4);
     town        : CHAR(10);
     postcode    : CHAR(6);
     sql_stat    : CHAR(100);
     h_statement : HSTMT;
     h_database  : HDBC;
BEGIN
     SQLAllocHandle(SQL_HANDLE_STMT, h_database,
                       &h_statement);
     sql_stat := 'SELECT PLAYERNO, NAME,
                  INITIALS, STREET, HOUSENO, TOWN, POSTCODE
                  FROM PLAYERS';
     SQLExecDirect(h_statement, sql_stat, SQL_NTS);
     WHILE SQLFetch(h_statement) = SQL_SUCCESS DO
        SQLGetData(h_statement, 1, SQL_C_SLONG, &pno, ...);
        SQLGetData(h_statement, 2, SQL_C_CHAR, &name, ...);
        SQLGetData(h_statement, 3, SQL_C_CHAR, &init, ...);
        SQLGetData(h_statement, 4, SQL_C_CHAR, &street, ...);
        SQLGetData(h_statement, 5, SQL_C_CHAR, &houseno,
                     ...);
        SQLGetData(h_statement, 6, SQL_C_CHAR, &town, ...);
        SQLGetData(h_statement, 7, SQL_C_CHAR, &postcode,
                     ...);
        # Present address data
        WRITE pno, name, init, street, houseno, town,
              postcode;
     ENDWHILE;
     SQLFreeHandle(SQL_HANDLE_STMT, h_statement);
END
```

With the SQLBindCol function, the program looks like this:

```
PROGRAM ADDRESS_ALL_ROW_BY_ROW;
DECLARATIONS
     pno            :  SMALLINT;
     name           :  CHAR(15);
     init           :  CHAR(3);
     street         :  CHAR(15);
     houseno        :  CHAR(4);
     town           :  CHAR(10);
     postcode       :  CHAR(6);
     sql_stat       :  CHAR(100);
     h_statement    :  HSTMT;
     h_database     :  HDBC;
BEGIN
   WRITE 'Enter the player number: ';
   SQLAllocHandle(SQL_HANDLE_STMT, h_database,
                  &h_statement);
   sql_stat := 'SELECT PLAYERNO, NAME,
                INITIALS, STREET, HOUSENO, TOWN, POSTCODE
                FROM PLAYERS';
   SQLExecDirect(h_statement, sql_stat, SQL_NTS);
   SQLBindCol(h_statement, 1, SQL_C_SLONG, &pno, ...);
   SQLBindCol(h_statement, 2, SQL_C_CHAR, &name, ...);
   SQLBindCol(h_statement, 3, SQL_C_CHAR, &init, ...);
   SQLBindCol(h_statement, 4, SQL_C_CHAR, &street, ...);
   SQLBindCol(h_statement, 5, SQL_C_CHAR, &houseno, ...);
   SQLBindCol(h_statement, 6, SQL_C_CHAR, &town, ...);
   SQLBindCol(h_statement, 7, SQL_C_CHAR, &postcode, ...);
   WHILE SQLFetch(h_statement) = SQL_SUCCESS DO
      # Present address data
      WRITE pno, name, init, street, houseno, town,
            postcode;
   ENDWHILE;
   SQLFreeHandle(SQL_HANDLE_STMT, h_statement);
END
```

It is obvious from the amount of code within the WHILE statement that the second solution is much "lighter."

We extend the last example by adding parameters to the SELECT statement.

Example 28.10: Develop a program for printing all the address data of only those players whose number is greater than a specific player number.

```
PROGRAM ADDRESS_SOME;
DECLARATIONS
    pno           : SMALLINT;
    name          : CHAR(15);
    init          : CHAR(3);
    street        : CHAR(15);
    houseno       : CHAR(4);
    town          : CHAR(10);
    postcode      : CHAR(6);
    sql_stat      : CHAR(100);
    h_statement   : HSTMT;
    h_database    : HDBC;
BEGIN
    WRITE 'Enter the player number: ';
    READ pno;
    SQLAllocHandle(SQL_HANDLE_STMT, h_database,
                   &h_statement);
    sql_stat := 'SELECT PLAYERNO, NAME,
                 INITIALS, STREET, HOUSENO, TOWN, POSTCODE
                 FROM PLAYERS WHERE PLAYERNO > ?';
    SQLPrepare(h_statement, sql_stat, SQL_NTS);
    # Link the parameters to the host variables
    SQLBindParameter(h_statement, 1, SQL_PARAM_INPUT,
                   SQL_C_SLONG, SQL_SMALLINT, 0, 0,
                   &pno, 0, NULL);
    SQLExecute(h_statement);
    SQLBindCol(h_statement, 1, SQL_C_SLONG, &pno, ...);
    SQLBindCol(h_statement, 2, SQL_C_CHAR, &name, ...);
    SQLBindCol(h_statement, 3, SQL_C_CHAR, &init, ...);
    SQLBindCol(h_statement, 4, SQL_C_CHAR, &street, ...);
    SQLBindCol(h_statement, 5, SQL_C_CHAR, &houseno, ...);
    SQLBindCol(h_statement, 6, SQL_C_CHAR, &town, ...);
    SQLBindCol(h_statement, 7, SQL_C_CHAR, &postcode, ...);
    WHILE SQLFetch(h_statement) = SQL_SUCCESS DO
        # Present address data
        WRITE pno, name, init, street, houseno, town,
              postcode;
    ENDWHILE;
    SQLFreeHandle(SQL_HANDLE_STMT, h_statement);
END
```

Explanation: With the SELECT statement, we fetch the data of the player whose player number is entered. Note the use of the question mark.

28.11.3 Retrieving Data in Groups of Rows

Rows can be retrieved in groups as well. The first thing that needs to be done is to define the host variables differently. In this case, we have to reserve space in the internal memory for a group of rows.

If we use the example from the previous section again, the declarations of host variables will look as follows. It is obvious that space is reserved here for ten player numbers, ten names, ten initials, and so on:

```
PROGRAM ADDRESS_GROUP_BY_GROUP;
DECLARATIONS
    pno           : ARRAY [10] OF SMALLINT;
    name          : ARRAY [10] OF CHAR(15);
    init          : ARRAY [10] OF CHAR(3);
    street        : ARRAY [10] OF CHAR(15);
    houseno       : ARRAY [10] OF CHAR(4);
    town          : ARRAY [10] OF CHAR(10);
    postcode      : ARRAY [10] OF CHAR(6);
    sql_stat      : CHAR(100);
    sqlcode       : RETCODE;
    h_statement   : HSTMT;
    h_database    : HDBC;
BEGIN
    :
```

The beginning of the program is identical. A statement handle is created, the SELECT statement is processed with SQLExecDirect, and, finally, with calls to SQL-BindCol, all columns are linked to the host variables, respectively:

```
WRITE 'Enter the player number: ';
READ pno;
SQLAllocHandle(SQL_HANDLE_STMT, h_database,
               &h_statement);
sql_stat := 'SELECT PLAYERNO, NAME,
            INITIALS, STREET, HOUSENO, TOWN, POSTCODE
            FROM PLAYERS';
SQLExecDirect(h_statement, sql_stat, SQL_NTS);
```

```
SQLBindCol(h_statement, 1, SQL_C_SLONG, &pno[1], ...);
SQLBindCol(h_statement, 2, SQL_C_CHAR, &name[1], ...);
SQLBindCol(h_statement, 3, SQL_C_CHAR, &init[1], ...);
SQLBindCol(h_statement, 4, SQL_C_CHAR, &street[1], ...);
SQLBindCol(h_statement, 5, SQL_C_CHAR, &houseno[1],
        ...);
SQLBindCol(h_statement, 6, SQL_C_CHAR, &town[1], ...);
SQLBindCol(h_statement, 7, SQL_C_CHAR, &postcode[1],
        ...);
```

Two aspects in this piece of code should be noted. First, we are not required to use a loop to bind the variables. One call per variable of the SQLBindCol function is sufficient. Second, we specify the first element of this array within the call of this function.

Next, we want to fetch the rows in groups of ten. SQLFetch cannot be used for this; we have to use SQLExtendedFetch:

```
SQLSetStmtAttr(h_statement, SQL_ROWSET_SIZE, 10);
WHILE SQLExtendedFetch(h_statement, SQL_FETCH_NEXT, 1,
        &number_of_rows, messages) = SQL_SUCCESS DO
    # Present address data
    counter : =1
    WHILE counter <= number_of_rows DO
        WRITE pno, name, init, street, houseno, town,
            postcode;
        counter := counter + 1;
    ENDWHILE;
ENDWHILE;
SQLFreeHandle(SQL_HANDLE_STMT, h_statement);
END
```

By calling the SQLExtendedFetch function, we try to retrieve the first ten rows. Whether that succeeded can be derived from the host variable NUMBER_OF_ROWS.

The maximum number of rows retrieved cannot be derived from the host variable itself. This is determined by assigning a value to the ODBC variable SQL_ROWSET_SIZE with the use of the SQLSetStmtAttr function. Had we given this variable a value of 8, the rows would have been retrieved in groups of eight. The effect would have been that not all elements of the arrays would have received a new value; only the first eight would have.

SQLExtendedFetch, therefore, allows us to retrieve several rows simultaneously. However, it also offers other features that SQLFetch does not have. These include features to navigate through the result of a SELECT statement. Instead of retrieving only the next group of rows, for example, we can also retrieve the previous group or a group with a specific sequence number. Instead of using the literal SQL_FETCH_NEXT, we can also use SQL_FETCH_FIRST, SQL_FETCH_LAST, SQL_FETCH_PRIOR, SQL_FETCH_ABSOLUTE, SQL_FETCH_RELATIVE, and SQL_FETCH_BOOKMARK. The names of these literals speak for themselves.

As we said before, because we use SQLBindCol here, the values are linked to the host variables. The form used here is called *column-wise binding*. Another form is *row-wise binding*. For column-wise binding, all host variables are independent of each other, forming stand-alone arrays. We could have defined these variables as follows:

```
DECLARATIONS
    TYPE address IS
        pno       : SMALLINT;
        name      : CHAR(15);
        init      : CHAR(3);
        street    : CHAR(15);
        houseno   : CHAR(4);
        town      : CHAR(10);
        postcode  : CHAR(6);
    ENDTYPE;
    addresses     : ARRAY [10] OF address;
```

There is only one array, ADDRESSES, consisting of eight elements. We must also adjust the call of the SQLBindCol function:

```
SQLBindCol(h_statement, 1, SQL_C_SLONG,
    &addresses[1].pno, ...);
```

This is an example of *row-wise binding*. An entire row with data is "bound" in one operation. Before you can use this function, the SQLSetStmtAttr function must be called with the parameter SQL_ATTR_PARAM_BIND_TYPE.

28.12 Asynchronous Processing of SQL Statements

All functions discussed so far are processed synchronously. Synchronous processing means that if a function is called, the application waits until it is ready. For example, Win-SQL waits until the database server is finished processing the SQL statements. The same applies to embedded SQL and ODBC: The application waits until the statement has been processed. The application and the database server work not simultaneously but serially.

ODBC allows functions to be processed *asynchronously*. When they are processed asynchronously, SQL statements are sent to the database server for processing; meanwhile, the application can do something else. At a certain moment, the application asks whether the function has been processed. In this form of processing, the database server and application are actually active simultaneously. Synchronous processing corresponds to serial processing, whereas asynchronous processing corresponds to parallel processing. The two processing forms are illustrated in Figure 28.6. The white arrows indicate that processing is occurring.

Figure 28.6   *Synchronous versus asynchronous processing of SQL statements*

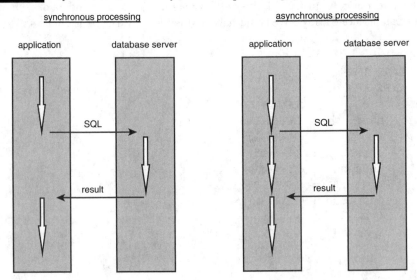

If it is possible to process a specific SQL statement asynchronously; we can specify this with the SQLSetStmtOption in ODBC. Here is an example.

Example 28.11: Develop a program that deletes all penalties.

```
PROGRAM HIGHEST_PENALTY_ASYNCHRONOUS;
DECLARATIONS
    busy : BOOLEAN;
BEGIN
    :
    SQLAllocHandle(SQL_HANDLE_STMT, h_database,
                   &h_statement);
    SQLSetStmtAttr(h_statement, SQL_ASYNC_ENABLE,
                   SQL_ASYNC_ENABLE_ON, 0);
    SQLExecDirect(h_statement, 'DELETE FROM PENALTIES',
                   SQL_NTS);
    :
    Do something else.
```

```
        :
    busy := true;
    WHILE busy DO
        busy := (SQLExecDirect(h_statement,
                    'DELETE FROM PENALTIES',
                    SQL_NTS) = SQL_STILL_EXECUTING);
    ENDWHILE;
    WRITE 'All penalties are deleted.';
    SQLFreeHandle(SQL_HANDLE_STMT, h_statement);
    SQLEndTran(SQL_NULL_HENV, h_database, SQL_COMMIT);
    :
END
```

Explanation: With the SQLSetStmtAttr function, the DELETE statement is defined as asynchronous. Next, the statement is executed. With synchronous processing, the program would wait until SQLExecDirect had finished, but here the program continues. By using a "loop," we then check whether the DELETE statement is ready. We can do this by repeatedly calling the same function. As long as the value of the function call is equal to the ODBC literal SQL_STILL_EXECUTING, it has not yet been processed.

For each individual statement, it is possible to say whether it must be processed asynchronously, but you may also define that the entire connection with all its statements is to be processed asynchronously with a single instruction. For this, we use the SQLSetConnectAttr function. After this, each statement for which this is possible is processed asynchronously.

The big advantage of asynchronous processing is that several processes can be executed simultaneously. We could even execute several SQL statements in parallel. We illustrate this with the following example.

Example 28.12: Develop a program that logs on to ten different databases and executes the same SQL statement on each database (assuming that those databases contain the same tables); processing must be done simultaneously.

```
PROGRAM TEN_DATABASES;
DECLARATIONS
    :
    counter        : INTEGER;
    h_env          : HENV;
    h_database     : ARRAY OF HDBC[10];
    h_statement    : ARRAY OF HSTMT[10];
    busy           : ARRAY OF BOOLEAN[10];
```

```
BEGIN
   SQLAllocHandle(SQL_HAND_ENV, SQL_NULL_HANDLE, &h_env);
   SQLSetEnvAttr(h_env, SQL_ATTR_ODBC_VERSION,
                 SQL_OV_ODBC3, 0);
   # Log on to ten databases
   counter := 1;
   WHILE counter <= 10 DO
      SQLAllocHandle(SQL_HANDLE_DBC ,h_env,
                     &h_database[counter]);
      server := 'SQL'+CONVERT_CHAR(counter);
      SQLConnect(h_database[counter], server, SQL_NTS,
                 'BOOKSQL', SQL_NTS, 'BOOKSQLPW' SQL_NTS);
      counter := counter + 1;
   ENDWHILE;
   # Execute ten DELETE statements in parallel
   counter := 1;
   WHILE counter <= 10 DO
      SQLAllocHandle(SQL_HANDLE_STMT, h_database[counter],
                     &h_statement [counter]);
      SQLSetStmtAttr(h_statement [counter],
                     SQL_ASYNC_ENABLE,
                     SQL_ASYNC_ENABLE_ON, 0);
      SQLExecDirect(h_statement [counter],
                    'DELETE FROM PENALTIES',
                    SQL_NTS);
      busy[counter] := true;
      counter := counter + 1;
   ENDWHILE;
   # Check if all ten statements are ready
   something_busy := true;
   WHILE something_busy DO
      counter := 1;
      WHILE counter <= 10 AND busy[counter] DO
         busy[counter] :=
            (SQLExecDirect(h_statement[counter],
                           'DELETE FROM PENALTIES',
                           SQL_NTS) <>
                           SQL_STILL_EXECUTING);
         counter := counter + 1;
      ENDWHILE;
      counter := 1;
      something_busy := false;
```

```
        WHILE counter <= 10 AND NOT something_busy DO
            IF busy[counter] THEN
                something_busy := TRUE;
            ENDIF;
            counter := counter + 1;
        ENDWHILE;
    ENDWHILE;
    # Log off on all databases
    counter := 1;
    WHILE counter <= 10 DO
        SQLEndTran(SQL_NULL_HENV, h_database[counter],
                    SQL_COMMIT);
        SQLFreeHandle(SQL_HANDLE_STMT, h_statement[counter]);
        SQLDisconnect(h_database[counter]);
        SQLFreeHandle(SQL_HANDLE_DBC, h_database[counter]);
        counter := counter + 1;
    ENDWHILE;
    SQLFreeHandle(SQL_HANDLE_ENV, h_env);
END
```

Explanation: The program consists of four "loops." The first one is used to log on to ten different databases as BOOKSQL. The second loop sends the same SQL statement to ten different databases. All these statements are processed asynchronously. The third loop verifies that they are all ready, and the fourth loop disconnects the ten databases.

The SQLCancel function cancels a SELECT statement that has been started asynchronously but prematurely. In the following piece of code, a statement is started asynchronously. The program waits ten seconds and determines whether the statement is ready. If not, the statement is cancelled.

```
SQLSetStmtAttr(h_statement, SQL_ASYNC_ENABLE,
                SQL_ASYNC_ENABLE_ON, 0);
SQLExecDirect(h_statement, sql_stat, SQL_NTS);
:
WAIT 10 seconds;
:
IF SQLExecDirect(h_statement, sql_stat, SQL_NTS) =
    SQL_STILL_EXECUTING THEN
    SQLCancel(h_statement);
ENDIF;
```

Programming for asynchronous processing of statements is, of course, more complex than serial processing of statements, but the performance advantages at runtime can be considerable.

28.13 The FOR Clause

Section 26.15, in Chapter 26, showed that the rows in the result of a cursor can be updated and deleted via special versions of the UPDATE and DELETE statements: the so-called *positioned update* and the *positioned delete*. For this purpose, the special condition CURRENT OF <cursor> was added to the WHERE component. In ODBC, an almost identical solution has been implemented in which this special condition is also used.

Example 28.13: Change the year in which all players joined the club, and use a cursor to do this.

```
PROGRAM UPDATE_JOINED;
DECLARATIONS
    pno              : SMALLINT;
    name             : CHAR(15);
    init             : CHAR(3);
    street           : CHAR(15);
    houseno          : CHAR(4);
    town             : CHAR(10);
    postcode         : CHAR(6);
    sql_stat         : CHAR(100);
    sql_upd          : CHAR(100);
    h_selstatement   : HSTMT;
    h_updstatement   : HSTMT;
    h_database       : HDBC;
BEGIN
    SQLAllocHandle(SQL_HANDLE_STMT, h_database,
                   &h_selstatement);
    SQLAllocHandle(SQL_HANDLE_STMT, h_database,
                   &h_updstatement);
    SQLSetCursorName(h_selstatement, 'C1', SQL_NTS);
    sql_stat := 'SELECT PLAYERNO, NAME,
                 INITIALS, STREET, HOUSENO, TOWN, POSTCODE
                 FROM PLAYERS';
    sql_upd := 'UPDATE PLAYERS SET JOINED = 2000 WHERE
                 CURRENT OF C1';
    SQLExecDirect(h_selstatement, sql_stat, SQL_NTS);
```

```
SQLBindCol(h_selstatement, 1, SQL_C_SLONG, &pno, ...);
SQLBindCol(h_selstatement, 2, SQL_C_CHAR, &name, ...);
SQLBindCol(h_selstatement, 3, SQL_C_CHAR, &init, ...);
SQLBindCol(h_selstatement, 4, SQL_C_CHAR, &street, ...);
SQLBindCol(h_selstatement, 5, SQL_C_CHAR, &houseno,
            ...);
SQLBindCol(h_selstatement, 6, SQL_C_CHAR, &town, ...);
SQLBindCol(h_selstatement, 7, SQL_C_CHAR, &postcode,
            ...);
WHILE SQLFetch(h_selstatement) = SQL_SUCCESS DO
    SQLExecDirect(h_updstatement, sql_upd, SQL_NTS);
ENDWHILE;
SQLEndTran(SQL_NULL_HENV, h_database, SQL_COMMIT);
SQLFreeHandle(SQL_HANDLE_STMT, h_selstatement);
SQLFreeHandle(SQL_HANDLE_STMT, h_updstatement);
END
```

Explanation: The first two SQLAllocHandle calls create two statement handles: one for the SELECT statement and one for the UPDATE statement. Because we use a cursor name in the UPDATE statement, we have to define it. This is done with the SQLSetCursorName function. The cursor name that we assign to the SELECT statement is C1. A cursor name must be assigned before the SELECT statement is executed, which means before the SQLExecDirect function is called. With the WHILE statement, we browse through the result of the SELECT statement, and for each row, we execute the UPDATE statement. It is obvious that the same method is used here as in embedded SQL.

ODBC offers an alternative function, SQLSetPos, for working with positioned update (and positioned delete). We do not cover this here.

Chapter 27, "Transactions and Multi-User Usage," dealt extensively with transactions, locking, and concurrency levels, but only with regard to embedded SQL. ODBC supports the four isolation levels specified in Section 27.11, in Chapter 27. With the SQLSetConnectAttr function, you can set the isolation level of a transaction. This function looks as follows:

```
SQLSetConnectAttr(h_database, SQL_ATTR_TXN_ISOLATION,
                  SQL_TXN_READ_UNCOMMITTED, 0)
```

Beyond the isolation level SQL_TXN_READ_UNCOMMITTED, you can use SQL_TXN_READ_COMMITTED, SQL_TXN_REPEATABLE_READ, and SQL_TXN_SERIALIZABLE.

28.14 Accessing Catalog Tables with ODBC

As already mentioned in this book, the structures of the catalog tables are not the same for the various SQL products. They differ in naming and structure. Obviously, this makes it difficult to write a program that accesses the catalog and remains independent of a particular SQL product. To solve this elegantly, several functions have been defined in ODBC with which catalog data can be retrieved in a product-independent way. These functions follow (their names are self-explanatory):

- SQLColumnPrivileges
- SQLColumns
- SQLForeignKeys
- SQLPrimaryKeys
- SQLProcedureColumns
- SQLProcedures
- SQLSpecialColumns
- SQLStatistics
- SQLTablePrivileges
- SQLTables

The parameters of all these functions are almost the same. The first parameter is a statement handle. Then, several parameters can indicate which database objects are sought. For example, we might want a list containing all columns of a specific table or all tables of a certain user. The last parameters contain the data we are looking for. With an example, we show you how this function works.

Example 28.14: Develop a program that lists all columns of the PLAYERS table (created by BOOKSQL).

```
PROGRAM COLUMNS_PLAYERS;
DECLARATIONS
    column_name      : CHAR(128);
    column_data_type : CHAR(128);
    nullable         : SMALLINT;
    sqlcode          : RETCODE;
    h_statement      : HSTMT;
BEGIN
    SQLAllocHandle(SQL_HANDLE_STMT, h_database,
                   &h_statement);
```

```
IF SQLColumns(h_statement, NULL, 0, ' BOOKSQL ',
              SQL_NTS, 'PLAYERS', SQL_NTS,
              NULL, 0) = SQL_SUCCESS THEN
   SQLBindCol(h_statement, 4, SQL_C_CHAR, column_name,
              128, &cbcolumn_name);
   SQLBindCol(h_statement, 6, SQL_C_CHAR,
              column_data_type, 128,
              &cbcolumn_data_type);
   SQLBindCol(h_statement, 11, SQL_C_SSHORT, nullable,
              0, &cbnullable);
   WHILE SQLFetch(h_statement) = SQL_SUCCESS DO
      WRITE 'Column name          : ', column_name;
      WRITE 'Data type of column : ', column_data_type;
      WRITE 'Yes or no NULL       : ', nullable;
   ENDWHILE;
ENDIF;
SQLFreeHandle(SQL_HANDLE_STMT, h_statement);
WRITE 'Ready';
END
```

Explanation: With the SQLColumns function, a SELECT statement is created behind the scenes that will access the underlying catalog tables. Now we can use the SQLFetch function to retrieve the data required. In this program, we use SQLBindCol to retrieve the values. The result of the SQLColumns contains 12 columns, of which we will use only 3. For each column, the precision, scale, length, and radix can be determined.

28.15 Levels and Support

Section 28.3 states that all ODBC drivers look the same on the "outside." However, this is not entirely true. ODBC drivers can differ from each other in three ways. The difference can be because they are based on different versions of ODBC. Even though ODBC Version 3.0 has been available since the end of 1996, at the time of this writing, there are still drivers available that support only Version 2.0. Additional functions exist in version 3.0. With the function SQLGetInfo and the parameter SQL_DRIVER_ODBC_VER, it is possible to ask for the version of an ODBC driver.

Second, ODBC drivers can differ in the functions supported. In a given ODBC driver, for example, the SQLForeignKeys function could be missing. The reasons for this can vary. The underlying data source might not support foreign keys, so there would be no point in implementing such a function. However, it also could be that the data source has these keys, but the function simply has not been implemented in the ODBC driver. In an ODBC environment, the functions supported are indicated with a *conformance level.* ODBC has three documented conformance levels, simply called core, level 1, and level 2. If an ODBC driver supports level 2, all functions have been implemented. If only the core level is supported, the set of functions is minimal. Level 1 is between the two other levels. With the function SQLGetInfo and the parameter SQL_ODBC_API_CONFORMANCE, it is possible to ask for the level supported by an ODBC driver.

Not all ODBC drivers support the same set of SQL statements, and this is the third reason why they can vary. To find out which SQL statements are supported and which are not, use the function SQLGetInfo and the parameter SQL_ODBC_SQL_CONFORMANCE. There are three possible answers: SQL_OSC_MINIMUM, SQL_OSC_CORE, and SQL_OSC_EXTENDED. We refer to the sources that we mentioned earlier for a precise specification of what these levels mean.

28.16 The Competitors of ODBC

At one time, ODBC held absolute sway in the world of CLIs with regard to accessing databases, but that changed in 1997 when Microsoft announced *OLE DB* and when *JDBC* was produced for the Java world. In between ODBC and OLE DB, Microsoft introduced DAO and RDO and, later, *ADO.NET*. In addition, all kinds of CLIs were invented for languages such as Perl, PHP, and Python. It is not within the scope of this book to describe these two CLIs in detail, but a short summary is appropriate.

The easiest way to describe OLE DB is by comparing it to ODBC, which is a CLI for accessing, via a single CLI, structured data that is stored in different data sources. By "structured data," we mean numbers, words, and codes. ODBC allows us to write one application that operates with, for example, an Oracle, Informix, and DB2 database.

OLE DB is a CLI for accessing, via a single API, all types of data stored in different data sources. OLE DB is not restricted to structured data alone. The CLI is designed to work with images, voice, and video. Data stored in text documents and e-mail messages can also be accessed. Data that is accessed with OLE DB does not have to be stored in a database.

Another difference between OLE DB and ODBC is that the latter can pass only SQL statements to the underlying data source. OLE DB has been developed in such a way that statements in other languages can also be passed. Therefore, by definition, OLE DB is not SQL-oriented.

However, OLE DB does not replace ODBC; it completes it. The most obvious indication of this is that OLE DB accesses ODBC if structured data is to be retrieved. In addition, OLE DB can use other CLIs to retrieve nonstructured data.

If you look at ODBC closely, you can see that it has strong links to the programming language C. Because of the growth of the Internet and the World Wide Web, another programming language has become popular: *Java.* In principle, Java and ODBC can work together, but Java is an object-oriented language, and ODBC is far from object-oriented. That is why there was a need for a database API that was developed especially for Java: JDBC (Java DataBase Connectivity).

ADO stands for ActiveX Data Object. With the introduction of the .NET platform, the Microsoft world got another CLI, called ADO.NET. This CLI, based upon XML, was especially developed to integrate with the .NET platform. All programming languages that use .NET, including C#, Visual Basic, and COBOL, can use ADO.NET.

With regard to functionality, JDBC is very similar to ODBC. A programmer who is familiar with ODBC will have little trouble learning JDBC. The CLI is different, of course, because it is an object-oriented CLI. JDBC will not replace ODBC because the two CLIs are aimed at different families of programming languages.

29

Optimization of Statements

Introduction

I n Chapter 20, "Using Indexes," we showed that the presence of an index can improve the execution time of certain statements. The question remains, though, whether the optimizer can always develop the best processing strategy for all statements. Unfortunately, the answer is that it cannot. Some statements are written in such a way that the optimizer is in no position to develop the fastest processing strategy. This occurs principally when WHERE clause conditions are too complex or when the optimizer is taken along a "false trail." In addition, even when indexes are available, the optimizer sometimes chooses a sequential processing strategy for those statements.

Practice has shown that a certain number of general forms of SQL statements are not easily optimized and give rise to long processing times. By reformulating such statements, you can give the optimizer a better chance of developing an optimal processing strategy. In this chapter, we provide a number of guidelines for formulating "faster" statements. In other words, we are giving the optimizer a "helping hand."

In view of the size of the tables in the sample database, almost every SQL statement is fast. The result is that the guidelines in this chapter will not improve the execution time of the statements. However, you can fill the PLAYERS table with many thousands of rows, and that way you can test whether the guidelines apply. For this purpose, you should execute the same two statements that we have used in Section 20.9.3, in Chapter 20, to show the impact of indexes.

> **Portability:** *All optimizers are not the same. Big differences in quality exist between the optimizers of the various products. One optimizer can devise a better processing strategy for a larger number of statements than another. The guidelines we present do not apply to all SQL statements and to all situations. We advise you to examine them in the context of your product. We also advise you to look for additional guidelines applicable to your product.*

29.2 Avoid the OR Operator

In most cases, SQL will not use an index if the condition in a WHERE clause contains the OR operator. These statements can be rewritten in two ways. In certain circumstances, we can replace the condition with one containing an IN operator, or we can replace the complete statement with two SELECT statements linked with UNION.

Example 29.1: Get the names and initials of players 6, 83, and 44.

```
SELECT    NAME, INITIALS
FROM      PLAYERS
WHERE     PLAYERNO = 6
OR        PLAYERNO = 83
OR        PLAYERNO = 44
```

SQL will not use the index on the PLAYERNO column, although we assume that such an index has been defined. However, we can replace the condition in the SELECT statement simply by an IN operator. Then, SQL will probably use the index.

```
SELECT    NAME, INITIALS
FROM      PLAYERS
WHERE     PLAYERNO IN (6, 83, 44)
```

For UPDATE and DELETE statements, the same applies.

Example 29.2: Get the players who joined the club in 1980, plus the players who live in Stratford.

```
SELECT    *
FROM      PLAYERS
WHERE     JOINED = 1980
OR        TOWN = 'Stratford'
```

In this situation, SQL will develop a sequential processing strategy regardless of the presence of indexes on the TOWN and JOINED columns. However, we cannot replace the condition with an IN operator as in the previous example. Instead, we can replace the entire statement with two SELECT statements combined with UNION:

```
SELECT      *
FROM        PLAYERS
WHERE       JOINED = 1980
UNION
SELECT      *
FROM        PLAYERS
WHERE       TOWN = 'Stratford'
```

In this situation, it is *not* possible to replace UPDATE and DELETE statements with a UNION. In such a case, two separate statements are required.

Example 29.3: Update the penalty amount to $150 for all penalties that are equal to $100 or that were incurred on December 1, 1980.

```
UPDATE      PENALTIES
SET         AMOUNT = 150
WHERE       AMOUNT = 100
OR          PAYMENT_DATE = '1980-12-01'
```

Another formulation is:

```
UPDATE      PENALTIES
SET         AMOUNT = 150
WHERE       AMOUNT = 100
```

and

```
UPDATE      PENALTIES
SET         AMOUNT = 150
WHERE       PAYMENT_DATE = '1980-12-01'
```

Let us return to the example with the SELECT statement. With UNION, SQL automatically executes a DISTINCT and all duplicate rows are removed. However, there are no duplicate rows in this example because the SELECT clause includes the primary key of the PLAYERS table.

If the original SELECT statement had looked like the following one (no primary key column in the SELECT clause), an alternative formulation with UNION would not have been possible. The reason is that the following statement could produce duplicate rows, whereas the version with the UNION operator removes duplicate rows from the result. The two formulations would give different results.

```
SELECT   NAME
FROM     PLAYERS
WHERE    JOINED = 1980
OR       TOWN = 'Stratford'
```

If the original statement had contained DISTINCT, the alternative would have been possible.

29.3   Avoid Unnecessary Use of the UNION Operator

In the previous section, we recommended using the UNION operator. We do not mean, however, that UNION should be used whether it is relevant or not. This operator must also be used with care.

Example 29.4: Get, for each match, the match number and the difference between the number of sets won and lost.

```
SELECT   MATCHNO, WON - LOST
FROM     MATCHES
WHERE    WON >= LOST
UNION
SELECT   MATCHNO, LOST - WON
FROM     MATCHES
WHERE    WON < LOST
```

Odds are, during the processing of this statement, SQL will browse the entire MATCHES table twice. This can be prevented by using an ABS function in the SELECT statement:

```
SELECT   MATCHNO, ABS(WON - LOST)
FROM     MATCHES
```

SQL will browse the MATCHES table only once and execute the calculation for each row. The expression in the SELECT statement is somewhat more complex than the one used in the previous statement, but the extra processing time caused by this is easily compensated for by the gain in processing time caused by browsing the table only once.

29.4 Avoid the NOT Operator

If the condition in a WHERE clause contains the NOT operator, SQL will generally not use an index. Replace a NOT operator, if possible, with a comparison operator.

Example 29.5: Get the players who did not join the club after 1980.

```
SELECT    *
FROM      PLAYERS
WHERE     NOT (JOINED > 1980)
```

The WHERE clause can be replaced by the following:

```
WHERE     JOINED <= 1980
```

Another solution is possible if you know the permitted set of values for a column.

Example 29.6: Get the players who are not men.

```
SELECT    *
FROM      PLAYERS
WHERE     NOT (SEX = 'M')
```

We know that the SEX column can contain only the values M and F. Therefore, we could also formulate the statements as follows:

```
SELECT    *
FROM      PLAYERS
WHERE     SEX = 'F'
```

29.5 Isolate Columns in Conditions

When an index is defined on a column that occurs in a calculation or scalar function, that index will not be used.

Example 29.7: Find the players who joined the club ten years before 1990.

```
SELECT     *
FROM       PLAYERS
WHERE      JOINED + 10 = 1990
```

On the left of the comparison equal to operator, there is an expression that contains both a column name and a literal. To the right of the same operator is another literal. The index on the JOINED column will not be used. A faster execution could be expected with the following formulation:

```
SELECT     *
FROM       PLAYERS
WHERE      JOINED = 1980
```

Now, the expression to the left of the comparison operator contains only one column name. In other words, the column has been isolated.

29.6 Use the BETWEEN Operator

If you look in the condition of a WHERE clause for values in a particular range using the AND operator, SQL will generally not use an index. We can replace such a condition with a BETWEEN operator.

Example 29.8: Find the player numbers of the players born in the period from January 1, 1962, to December 31, 1965.

```
SELECT     PLAYERNO
FROM       PLAYERS
WHERE      BIRTH_DATE >= '1962-01-01'
AND        BIRTH_DATE <= '1965-12-31'
```

An index on the BIRTH_DATE column will not be used here. The index will be used if we adjust the condition as follows:

```
SELECT    PLAYERNO
FROM      PLAYERS
WHERE     BIRTH_DATE BETWEEN '1962-01-01' AND '1965-12-31'
```

29.7 Avoid Particular Forms of the LIKE Operator

In some cases, when an index is defined on a column used with the LIKE operator in a WHERE clause condition, the index will not be considered. If the mask in the LIKE operator begins with a percentage sign or an underscore character, the index cannot be used.

Example 29.9: Find the players whose names end with the letter *n*.

```
SELECT    *
FROM      PLAYERS
WHERE     NAME LIKE '%n'
```

The index will not be used, and, unfortunately, there is no alternative solution for this example.

29.8 Add Redundant Conditions to Joins

Sometimes, joins can be accelerated easily by adding an extra condition to the WHERE clause, which does not change the end result.

Example 29.10: Get the payment number and name of the player for all penalties incurred for player 44.

```
SELECT    PAYMENTNO, NAME
FROM      PENALTIES AS PEN, PLAYERS AS P
WHERE     PEN.PLAYERNO = P.PLAYERNO
AND       PEN.PLAYERNO = 44
```

Sometimes, SQL can develop a more efficient processing strategy if the condition is extended with a redundant condition, as shown earlier. Obviously, the result of the statement does not change.

```
SELECT    PAYMENTNO, NAME
FROM      PENALTIES AS PEN, PLAYERS AS P
WHERE     PEN.PLAYERNO = P.PLAYERNO
AND       PEN.PLAYERNO = 44
AND       P.PLAYERNO = 44
```

29.9 Avoid the HAVING Clause

In a SELECT statement, conditions can be specified in two places, in the WHERE and the HAVING clauses. Always try to place as many conditions as possible in the WHERE clause and as few as possible in the HAVING clause. The main reason is that indexes are not used for conditions specified in the HAVING clause.

Example 29.11: Find, for each player with a number higher than 40, the player number and the number of penalties incurred.

```
SELECT     PLAYERNO, COUNT(*)
FROM       PENALTIES
GROUP BY   PLAYERNO
HAVING     PLAYERNO >= 40
```

The condition in the HAVING clause can also be specified in the WHERE clause. This makes the HAVING clause completely superfluous:

```
SELECT     PLAYERNO, COUNT(*)
FROM       PENALTIES
WHERE      PLAYERNO >= 40
GROUP BY   PLAYERNO
```

29.10 Make the SELECT Clause as Small as Possible

The SELECT clause of a main query formulates which data is to be presented. Avoid the use of unnecessary columns because it can affect the processing speed in a negative way.

You are allowed to specify multiple expressions in the SELECT clause of a subquery if that subquery is linked to the main query with the EXISTS operator. However, the end result of the SELECT statement is not affected by the expressions specified. Therefore, the advice is to formulate only one expression consisting of one literal in the SELECT clause.

Example 29.12: Get the player numbers and names of the players for whom at least one penalty has been paid.

```
SELECT    PLAYERNO, NAME
FROM      PLAYERS
WHERE     EXISTS
          (SELECT    '1'
           FROM      PENALTIES
           WHERE     PENALTIES.PLAYERNO = PLAYERS.PLAYERNO)
```

29.11 Avoid DISTINCT

Specifying DISTINCT in the SELECT clause leads to the removal of duplicate rows from a result. This can have a negative effect on the processing time. Therefore, avoid the use of DISTINCT when it is not required or even redundant. In Section 9.4, in Chapter 9, "SELECT Statement: SELECT Clause and Aggregation Functions," we described when DISTINCT is superfluous. DISTINCT is not necessary in subqueries.

Example 29.13: Find, for each match, the match number and the name of the player.

```
SELECT    DISTINCT MATCHNO, NAME
FROM      MATCHES, PLAYERS
WHERE     MATCHES.PLAYERNO = PLAYERS.PLAYERNO
```

DISTINCT is unnecessary here because the SELECT clause contains the primary key of the MATCHES table, as well as a condition on the primary key of the PLAYERS table.

29.12 Use the ALL Option with Set Operators

In Chapter 13, "Combining Table Expressions," we discussed the ALL option for the set operators UNION, INTERSECT, and EXCEPT. Adding ALL to these operators has the effect that duplicate rows are *not* removed from the result. The ALL option has a function that is comparable to ALL in the SELECT clause; see Section 9.4, in Chapter 9. If ALL is not specified, all rows have to be sorted to be able to remove duplicate rows (sorting takes places behind the scenes). In other words, the guidelines given in the previous section also apply to the ALL option: If possible, use ALL in conjunction with the set operators.

Example 29.14: Find the names and initials of the players who live in Stratford and Douglas.

```
SELECT    NAME, INITIALS
FROM      PLAYERS
WHERE     TOWN = 'Stratford'
UNION ALL
SELECT    NAME, INITIALS
FROM      PLAYERS
WHERE     TOWN = 'Douglas'
```

Explanation: Because of the presence of the keyword ALL, SQL will *not* perform a sort to remove possible duplicate rows. Luckily, this result will never return duplicate rows because each player lives in only one town. So, in this example, a sort would always be performed unnecessarily, thus wasting performance.

29.13 Prefer Outer Joins to UNION Operators

The outer join was a late addition to SQL. The result is that many statements still do not make use of it. The UNION operator is used many times to simulate an outer join. Here is an example.

Example 29.15: Find, for each player, the player number, name, and penalties incurred by him or her; order the result by player number.

This question used to be solved with the following construct:

```
SELECT    PLAYERS.PLAYERNO, NAME, AMOUNT
FROM      PLAYERS, PENALTIES
WHERE     PLAYERS.PLAYERNO = PENALTIES.PLAYERNO
UNION
SELECT    PLAYERNO, NAME, NULL
FROM      PLAYERS
WHERE     PLAYERNO NOT IN
          (SELECT    PLAYERNO
           FROM      PENALTIES)
ORDER BY 1
```

However, this is a complex statement for SQL. Such statements seldom have a fast processing time. For example, the PLAYERS table is accessed twice, once in each select block. Avoid this type of formulation and use the new formulation, in which the outer join is formulated explicitly:

```
SELECT    PLAYERNO, NAME, AMOUNT
FROM      PLAYERS LEFT OUTER JOIN PENALTIES
          USING (PLAYERNO)
ORDER BY 1
```

29.14 Avoid Data Type Conversions

SQL automatically performs data type conversions. The following condition, for example, is correct even if the numeric PLAYERNO column is compared with an alphanumeric literal:

```
WHERE PLAYERNO = '44'
```

Converting data types adversely affects the processing speed, obviously. If this type of conversion is not really required, try to avoid it.

29.15 The Largest Table Last

When you formulate joins, it is possible that the sequence of the tables in the FROM clause can affect the processing speed. The rule is: Specify the largest table last in the FROM clause. Thus, the following FROM clause:

```
FROM    PLAYERS, TEAMS
```

would be better if replaced by the following because the PLAYERS table is the larger table:

```
FROM    TEAMS, PLAYERS
```

29.16 Avoid the ANY and ALL Operators

Many optimizers will not use an index when processing conditions with the ALL operator. Replace an ALL operator, if possible, with one of the aggregation functions: MIN or MAX.

Example 29.16: Get the player numbers, names, and dates of birth of the oldest players. (We already used this example in Section 8.12.)

```
SELECT    PLAYERNO, NAME, BIRTH_DATE
FROM      PLAYERS
WHERE     BIRTH_DATE <= ALL
          (SELECT    BIRTH_DATE
           FROM      PLAYERS)
```

We can replace the ALL operator here with the MIN function.

```
SELECT    PLAYERNO, NAME, BIRTH_DATE
FROM      PLAYERS
WHERE     BIRTH_DATE =
          (SELECT    MIN(BIRTH_DATE)
           FROM      PLAYERS)
```

The same reasoning applies to the ANY operator.

Example 29.17: Find the player numbers, names, and dates of birth of the players who are not among the oldest players.

```
SELECT    PLAYERNO, NAME, BIRTH_DATE
FROM      PLAYERS
WHERE     BIRTH_DATE > ANY
          (SELECT    BIRTH_DATE
          FROM       PLAYERS)
```

We can also replace the ANY operator with the MIN function in this example.

```
SELECT    PLAYERNO, NAME, BIRTH_DATE
FROM      PLAYERS
WHERE     BIRTH_DATE >
          (SELECT    MIN(BIRTH_DATE)
          FROM       PLAYERS)
```

Exercise 29.1: Get alternative formulations for the following statements:
1.

```
SELECT    *
FROM      PLAYERS
WHERE     (TOWN = 'Stratford'
AND       STREET = 'Edgecombe Way')
OR        (NOT (BIRTH_DATE >= '1960-01-01'))
```

2.

```
SELECT    DISTINCT *
FROM      PLAYERS
```

3.

```
SELECT    *
FROM      TEAMS
WHERE     TEAMNO IN
          (SELECT    TEAMNO
           FROM      MATCHES
           WHERE     WON * LOST = WON * 4)
```

4.

```
SELECT    DISTINCT TEAMNO
FROM      MATCHES
WHERE     TEAMNO IN
          (SELECT    TEAMNO
           FROM      TEAMS
           WHERE     NOT (DIVISION <> 'second'))
```

5.

```
SELECT    DISTINCT P.PLAYERNO
FROM      PLAYERS AS P, MATCHES AS M
WHERE     P.PLAYERNO <> M.PLAYERNO
```

6.

```
SELECT    PLAYERNO, 'Male'
FROM      PLAYERS
WHERE     SEX = 'M'
UNION
SELECT    PLAYERNO, 'Female'
FROM      PLAYERS
WHERE     SEX = 'F'
```

7.

```
SELECT    BIRTH_DATE, COUNT(*)
FROM      PLAYERS
GROUP BY  BIRTH_DATE
HAVING    BIRTH_DATE >= '1970-01-01'
```

Exercise 29.2: The difference between a "fast" and a "slow" statement depends on the number of rows in the tables: the more rows, the bigger the difference. The number of rows in the sample database is small. However, in Section 20.8, in Chapter 20, the PLAYERS_XXL table has been created and that table contains many rows. Now, we extend this table by filling it with 500,000 rows. Enter the following SELECT statements and determine the processing time. (Some of these statements have been described in the previous exercise.) A watch is not required because in the window at the bottom of the screen, WinSQL reports the processing time of each SQL statement. Next, determine a faster formulation, get the processing time once again, and see whether you have indeed sped up the statement. You will see that some statements have been sped up considerably.

1.

```
SELECT    PLAYERNO, NAME, BIRTH_DATE
FROM      PLAYERS
WHERE     STREET <= ALL
          (SELECT   STREET
           FROM     PLAYERS)
```

2.

```
SELECT    DISTINCT *
FROM      PLAYERS
```

3.

```
SELECT     PLAYERNO, 'Male'
FROM       PLAYERS
WHERE      SEX = 'M'
UNION
SELECT     PLAYERNO, 'Female'
FROM       PLAYERS
WHERE      SEX = 'F'
```

4.

```
SELECT     POSTCODE, COUNT(*)
FROM       PLAYERS
GROUP BY   POSTCODE
HAVING     POSTCODE >= 'Y'
```

5.

```
SELECT     *
FROM       PLAYERS
WHERE      NOT (PLAYERNO > 10)
```

29.17 The Future of the Optimizer

This chapter clearly shows that the current optimizers are not optimal yet. In some cases, the optimizer cannot determine the most efficient processing strategy. This can lead to poor processing times. This applies not only to database servers with SQL as their database language, but also to any system that has to determine the processing strategy itself.

A lot of research is being carried out to improve optimizers. Experience shows that each new version of an SQL product is faster than its predecessor. This trend will continue in the years to come. One day, optimizers will always find better strategies than most human programmers. E. F. Codd, founder of the relational model, put it as follows [CODE82]:

> If suitable fast access paths are supported, there is no reason why a high-level language such as SQL . . . should result in less efficient runtime code . . . than a lower level language . . . .

29.18 Answers

29.1

1.

```
SELECT     *
FROM       PLAYERS
WHERE      TOWN = 'Stratford'
AND        STREET = 'Edgecombe Way'
UNION
SELECT     *
FROM       PLAYERS
WHERE      BIRTH_DATE < '1960-01-01'
```

2.

```
SELECT     *
FROM       PLAYERS
```

3. Condition WON * LOST = WON * 4 cannot be simplified to LOST = 4 because both sides of the equation are divided by WON to get a simplified condition. WON can be equal to 0, and that would mean that we divide by 0, which is not allowed:

```
SELECT     DISTINCT TEAMS.*
FROM       TEAMS, MATCHES
WHERE      TEAMS.TEAMNO = MATCHES.TEAMNO
AND        WON * LOST = WON * 4
```

4.

```
SELECT     DISTINCT T.TEAMNO
FROM       TEAMS AS T, MATCHES AS M
WHERE      T.TEAMNO = M.TEAMNO
AND        DIVISION = 'second'
```

5.

```
SELECT    PLAYERNO
FROM      PLAYERS
```

6.

```
SELECT    PLAYERNO,
          CASE SEX
              WHEN 'F' THEN 'Female'
              ELSE 'Male' END
FROM      PLAYERS
```

7.

```
SELECT    BIRTH_DATE, COUNT(*)
FROM      PLAYERS
WHERE     BIRTH_DATE >= '1970-01-01'
GROUP BY BIRTH_DATE
```

29.2
1.

```
SELECT    PLAYERNO, NAME, BIRTH_DATE
FROM      PLAYERS_XXL
WHERE     BIRTH_DATE =
          (SELECT   MIN(BIRTH_DATE)
           FROM     PLAYERS_XXL)
```

2.

```
SELECT    *
FROM      PLAYERS_XXL
```

3.

```
SELECT    PLAYERNO,
          CASE SEX
              WHEN 'F' THEN 'Female'
              ELSE 'Male' END
FROM      PLAYERS_XXL
```

4.

```
SELECT    POSTCODE, COUNT(*)
FROM      PLAYERS_XXL
WHERE     POSTCODE >= 'Y'
GROUP BY  POSTCODE
```

5.

```
SELECT    *
FROM      PLAYERS_XXL
WHERE     PLAYERNO <= 10
```

V | Procedural Database Objects

In Section 1.4, in Chapter 1, "Introduction to SQL," we stated that for a long time SQL was a purely declarative language, but this changed in 1986–1987 when Sybase came onto the market. With this product, the first commercial implementation of the *stored procedure* became a fact, and that changed the character of SQL. A stored procedure can informally be described as a piece of code that can be activated; this piece of code consists of well-known SQL statements, such as INSERT and SELECT, but also procedural statements, such as IF-THEN-ELSE. Because stored procedures offered many practical advantages, other vendors started to implement them, too. This meant the end of the pure declarative character of SQL. Since their inclusion in the SQL2 standard, stored procedures have formed a real part of the language.

Later, other nondeclarative database objects were added, such as stored functions and triggers. These are all database objects that we create with CREATE statements and store in the catalog. They differ, however, because they are based on procedural code. That is why we call them *procedural database objects*.

Because nowadays all important SQL products support these objects, we devote this entire section to this subject. We describe stored procedures, stored functions, and triggers.

Portability: *Procedural database objects were added to the SQL2 standard after the vendors had implemented them. The negative effect of this has been that not one product implements the standard precisely. Vendors had to select a language before the standardization committee had finished. It should also be noted that, unfortunately, the products do not use the same syntax. In some cases, the syntactical differences are enormous. Oracle, for example, uses the language PL/SQL, Sybase and Microsoft SQL Server use the language Transact-SQL, and other products allow stored procedures to be formulated in well-known languages such as C and Java. The features that the products support with respect to stored procedures and triggers also differ greatly. In this part, we selected the syntax of MySQL so that you can run the examples.*

30

Stored Procedures

30.1 Introduction

T his chapter is devoted to the procedural database object called the *stored procedure* or database procedure. We start by giving its definition:

> A stored procedure is a certain piece of code (the procedure) consisting of declarative and procedural SQL statements stored in the catalog of a database that can be activated by calling it from a program, a trigger, or another stored procedure.

Thus, a stored procedure is a piece of code. This code can consist of declarative SQL statements, such as CREATE, UPDATE, and SELECT, possibly complemented with procedural statements, such as IF-THEN-ELSE and WHILE-DO. The code from which a stored procedure has been built is, therefore, not a part of a program, but is stored in the catalog.

Calling a stored procedure is comparable to calling a "normal" procedure (otherwise called a function or routine) in procedural languages. For calling stored procedures, a new SQL statement has been introduced. When calling stored procedures, you can also specify input and output parameters. As the definition indicates, stored procedures can be called from other stored procedures, just as functions in C can call other functions. The definition states that stored procedures can also be activated from triggers; we return to this subject in Chapter 32, "Triggers."

The stored procedure offers the possibility of storing certain parts of a program centrally in the catalog of the database server. They can then be called from all programs. For this reason, a database server that supports stored procedures is sometimes also called a *programmable database server*.

We can best illustrate what a stored procedure is and show its possibilities with a number of examples. Therefore, this chapter describes several examples of increasing complexity.

30.2   An Example of a Stored Procedure

Before we begin with a simple example, to process stored procedures and other procedural objects, we must change a property in WinSQL (that is, if you use this product). The *terminator string* must be switched to a symbol other than the semicolon. The reason is that the semicolon is used within procedural database objects. Therefore, change it, for example, to the number sign (#); see Figure 30.1.

Example 30.1: Create a stored procedure that removes all matches played by a specific player.

```
CREATE PROCEDURE DELETE_MATCHES
    (IN P_PLAYERNO INTEGER)
BEGIN
    DELETE
    FROM    MATCHES
    WHERE   PLAYERNO = P_PLAYERNO;
END
```

Figure 30.1   *The terminator string in WinSQL*

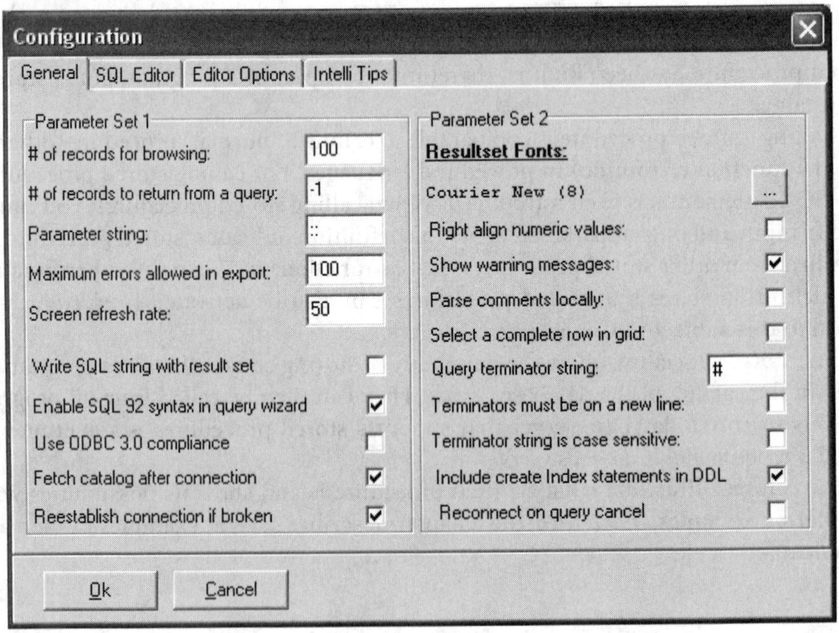

Explanation: The CREATE PROCEDURE statement is actually one SQL statement, just as CREATE TABLE and SELECT are. The statement is made up of several other SQL statements. We return to this subject and discuss it extensively later in this chapter. Each stored procedure consists of at least three parts: a list of parameters, a body, and a name.

The previous procedure has only one parameter, called P_PLAYERNO (the player number). The word IN indicates that this parameter is an input parameter. The value of this parameter can be used within the procedure, but after the execution of the procedure, the variable that is used at the call will stay unchanged.

Between the keywords BEGIN and END, the *procedure body* is specified. In this example, the body is very simple because it consists of only a single DELETE statement. New in this statement is the use of the parameter P_PLAYERNO. Here is the rule: Everywhere a scalar expression is allowed, a parameter may be used.

In most products, the names of the procedures within a database have to be unique, just as with the names of users. However, this requirement does not apply to all the products. In Oracle, for example, procedures may have the same name, but then the parameter lists have to be different. In that case, the number of parameters must be different, or, if the number of parameters is equal, the data types of the parameters must be different. If a procedure is called, one of the procedures is activated, depending on the parameter list.

The result of the previous CREATE PROCEDURE statement is not that the DELETE statement is executed. The only thing that happens is that the syntax of the statement is verified and, if it is correct, it is stored in the catalog. This is comparable to creating views.

To activate a stored procedure, a separate SQL statement must be used: the CALL statement.

Example 30.2: Remove all matches of player 8 by using the DELETE_MATCHES procedure.

```
CALL DELETE_MATCHES (8)
```

Explanation: This statement is straightforward. The value of the player number that is assigned to the parameter P_PLAYERNO is included between the brackets. If we compare this with classic programming languages, the CREATE PROCEDURE statement is comparable to the declaration of a procedure, and with CALL, the procedure is invoked.

Portability: *In some SQL products, the statement EXECUTE PROCEDURE is used instead of CALL. For other products, it is sufficient to enter the name of the procedure to activate a stored procedure.*

Figure 30.2 shows in a graphical way how a stored procedure is processed. The left block represents the program from which the procedure is called, the middle block represents the database server, and the right side represents the database and its catalog. The process begins when the procedure is called from the program (step 1). The database server receives this call and finds the matching procedure in the catalog (step 2). Next, the procedure is executed (step 3). This can result in inserting new rows or, in the situation of the DELETE_MATCHES procedure, removing rows. If the procedure is finished, a code is returned indicating that the procedure was processed correctly (step 4). No communication takes place between the database server and the program during the execution of the procedure.

Figure 30.2   *The processing steps of a stored procedure*

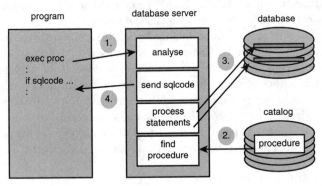

How the database server actually calls and processes the stored procedure is not important to the programmer or the program. The processing of a stored procedure can be seen as an extension of the processing of the program itself. Imagine that a program calling the stored procedure DELETE_MATCHES looks as follows:

```
Answer := 'Y';
WHILE answer = 'Y' DO
    PRINT 'Do you want to remove all matches of another
            player (Y/N)? '
    READ answer
    IF answer = 'Y' THEN
        PRINT 'Enter a player number: ';
        READ pno;
        CALL DELETE_MATCHES(pno);
    ENDIF;
ENDWHILE;
```

The final result of this program is the same as if we replaced the stored procedure call with the body of the procedure itself:

```
Answer := 'Y';
WHILE answer = 'Y' DO
    PRINT 'Do you want to remove all matches of another
            player (Y/N)? '
    READ answer
    IF answer = 'Y' THEN
        PRINT 'Enter a player number: ';
        READ pno;
        DELETE
        FROM    MATCHES
        WHERE   PLAYERNO = :pno;
    ENDIF;
ENDWHILE;
```

In the following sections, we describe the features and syntax of stored procedures step by step, along with the statements that can be used within the body of a stored procedure.

30.3 The Parameters of a Stored Procedure

A stored procedure has zero, one, or more parameters. Through these parameters, the procedure is capable of communicating with the outside world. Three types of parameters are supported. With input parameters, data can be passed to a stored procedure. The procedure in Example 30.1, for example, contained one input parameter: the player number of the matches that must be removed. The stored procedure uses output parameters when an answer or result must be returned. For example, we could create a stored procedure that finds the name of a player. That name is the output parameter then. The third type is the input/output parameter. As the name suggests, this parameter can act as input as well as an output parameter.

```
<create procedure statement> ::=
    CREATE PROCEDURE <procedure name> ( [ <parameter list> ] )
        <procedure body>

<parameter list> ::=
    <parameter specification>
        [ { , <parameter specification> }... ]

<parameter specification> ::=
    [ IN | OUT | INOUT ] <parameter> <data type>
```

Make sure that the names of parameters are not equal to the names of columns. If we want to change P_PLAYERNO in the previous example into PLAYERNO, SQL will not return an error message. The DELETE statement will consider the second PLAYERNO as the name of the column, not of the parameter. As a result, with every call, the stored procedure will remove all the players.

30.4 The Body of a Stored Procedure

The *body* of a stored procedure contains all the statements that must be executed when the procedure is called. The body always begins with the word BEGIN and ends with END. In between, all statement types can be specified. These can be the well-known SQL statements from the previous chapters—thus, all DDL, DCL, and DML statements, and also the procedural statements, are allowed as well. These are other versions of statements that we see in all procedural programming languages, such as IF–THEN–ELSE and WHILE DO. As with embedded SQL, there are statements to declare and update cursors. Local variables can be declared, and it is possible to assign values to them.

```
<create procedure statement> ::=
    CREATE PROCEDURE <procedure name> ( [ <parameter list> ] )
       <procedure body>

<procedure body> ::= <begin-end block>

<begin-end block> ::=
    [ <label> : ] BEGIN <statement list> END [ <label> ]

<statement list> ::= { <body statement> ; }...

<statement in body::=
    <declarative statement> |
    <procedural statement>

<declarative statement> ::=
    <call statement>                  |
    <close statement>                 |
    <commit statement>                |
    <delete statement>                |
    <execute immediate statement>     |
    <fetch statement>                 |
    <insert statement>                |
    <lock table statement>            |
```

(continued)

```
        <open statement>               |
        <rollback statement>           |
        <savepoint statement>          |
        <select statement>             |
        <select into statement>        |
        <set statement>                |
        <set transaction statement>    |
        <star -transaction statement>  |
        <update statement>

<procedural statement> ::=
        <begin-end block>              |
        <call statement>               |
        <close statement>              |
        <declare condition statement>  |
        <declare cursor statement>     |
        <declare handler statement>    |
        <declare variable statement>   |
        <fetch cursor statement>       |
        <flow control statement>       |
        <open cursor statement>        |
        <set statement>
```

With a begin-end block, statements can be grouped into one statement. Sometimes, such a block is called a *compound statement*. The body of a stored procedure is, in fact, a begin-end block. Blocks may be nested. In other words, you can define subblocks within begin-end blocks. So, this is a legal body of a stored procedure.

```
BEGIN
    BEGIN
        BEGIN
        END;
    END;
END
```

Note that each statement, including each begin-end block must end with a semi-colonbegin-end. However, this is not required for the begin-end block that indicates the end of the procedure body.

A *label* may be assigned to a begin-end block. In fact, the block is named with it:

```
BLOCK1 : BEGIN
    BLOCK2 : BEGIN
        BLOCK3 : BEGIN
        END BLOCK1;
    END BLOCK2;
END BLOCK3
```

Labeling blocks has two advantages. First, labeling makes it easier to determine which BEGIN belongs to which END, especially when many blocks are used within a stored procedure. Second, certain SQL statements, such as LEAVE and ITERATE, need these names. We return to this topic in Section 30.7.

A closing label behind END is not necessary. However, if it is used, it must refer to a label that stands in front of a BEGIN. The following code is not allowed, for example:

```
BLOCK1 : BEGIN
    SET VAR1 = 1;
END BLOCK2
```

The following statement is not correct, either. The name of the closing label BLOCK2 does exist, but it belongs to the wrong BEGIN:

```
BLOCK1 : BEGIN
    BLOCK2 : BEGIN
        SET VAR1 = 1;
    END
END BLOCK2
```

30.5 Local Variables

Within a stored procedure, *local variables* can be declared. They can be used to keep temporary intermediate results. If we need a local variable within a stored procedure, we must introduce it first with a DECLARE statement. So, SQL is different from similar languages such as PHP, in which a variable, if it is used, is declared implicitly.

With a declaration, the data type of the variable is determined and an initial value can be specified. The data types that are supported are the ones that may be used in CREATE TABLE statements; see Section 15.3, in Chapter 15, "Creating Tables."

```
<declare variable statement> ::=
   DECLARE <variable list> <data type> [
      DEFAULT <expression> ]

<variable list> ::=
   <variable> [ { , <variable> }... ]
```

Example 30.3: Declare a numeric and an alphanumeric variable.

```
DECLARE NUM1 DECIMAL(7,2);
DECLARE ALPHA1 VARCHAR(20);
```

Multiple variables carrying the same data type can be declared with one DECLARE statement.

Example 30.4: Declare two integer variables.

```
DECLARE NUMBER1, NUMBER2 INTEGER;
```

By adding a default expression, variables get an initial value.

Example 30.5: Create a stored procedure in which an initial value is assigned to a local variable. Next, call this stored procedure.

```
CREATE PROCEDURE TEST
   (OUT NUMBER1 INTEGER)
BEGIN
   DECLARE NUMBER2 INTEGER DEFAULT 100;
   SET NUMBER1 = NUMBER2;
END

CALL TEST (@NUMBER)

SELECT @NUMBER
```

The result is:


```
@NUMBER
-------
    100
```


Explanation: If DECLARE statements are used, they must be included as the first statements of a begin-end block. @NUMBER is a user variable.

The expression for the default value is not limited to literals but may consist of compound expressions, including scalar subqueries.

Example 30.6: Create a stored procedure in which a local variable is initiated with the
number of players in the PLAYERS table.


```
CREATE PROCEDURE TEST
    (OUT NUMBER1 INTEGER)
BEGIN
    DECLARE NUMBER2 INTEGER
        DEFAULT (SELECT COUNT(*) FROM PLAYERS);
    SET NUMBER1 = NUMBER2;
END
```


Local variables can be declared within each begin-end block. After the declaration,
the variables can be used in the relevant block, including all subblocks of that block.
Those variables are unknown in the other blocks. In the following construct, the variable V1 may be used in all blocks. V2, on the other hand, can be used only in the first
subblock, called B2. In the second subblock B3, this variable is unknown, so the SET
statement will not be accepted. The last SET statement will also not be accepted.


```
B1 : BEGIN
    DECLARE V1 INTEGER;
    B2 : BEGIN
        DECLARE V2 INTEGER;
        SET V2 = 1;
        SET V1 = V2;
    END B2;
    B3 : BEGIN
```

```
      SET V1 = V2;
   END B3;
      SET V2 = 100;
END B1
```

Do not confuse local variables with user variables. The first difference is that, in front of local variables, no @ symbol is placed. Another difference is that user variables exist during the entire session. Local variables disappear immediately after the processing of the begin-end block in which they have been declared is finished. User variables can be used within and outside a stored procedure, whereas local variables have no meaning outside a procedure.

For your information, SQL does not support arrays as local variables.

30.6 The SET Statement

The SET statement can be used to assign a value to local variables. The rule that any expression can be used applies here as well.

```
<set statement> ::=
   SET <local variable definition>
      [ {, <local variable definition> }... ]

<local variable definition> ::=
   <local variable> { = | := } <scalar expression>
```

In the previous sections, we showed several examples of the SET statement. The following examples are also correct:

```
SET VAR1 = 1;
SET VAR1 := 1;
SET VAR1 = 1, VAR2 = VAR1;
```

In the last example, a value is assigned to VAR1 first, and that value is assigned to VAR2 via VAR1 next.

30.7 Flow-Control Statements

Within the body of a stored procedure, the well-known procedural statements can be used. Their definitions are specified here:

```
<flow control statement> ::=
    <if statement>        |
    <case statement>      |
    <while statement>     |
    <repeat statement>    |
    <loop statement>      |
    <leave statement>     |
    <iterate statement>

<if statement> ::=
    IF <condition> THEN <statement list>
        [ ELSEIF <condition> THEN <statement list> ]...
        [ ELSE <statement list> ]
    END IF

<case statement> ::=
    { CASE <expression>
          WHEN <expression> THEN <statement list>
          [ WHEN <expression> THEN <statement list> ]...
          [ ELSE <statement list> ]
      END CASE } |
    { CASE
          WHEN <condition> THEN <statement list>
          [ WHEN <condition> THEN <statement list> ]...
          [ ELSE <statement list>
      END CASE }

<while statement> ::=
    [ <label> : WHILE <condition> DO <statement list>
    END WHILE [ <label> ]

<repeat statement> ::=
    [ <label> : ] REPEAT <statement list>
    UNTIL <condition>
    END REPEAT <label>
```

(continued)

```
<loop statement> ::=
   [ <label> : ] LOOP <statement list>
   END LOOP [ <label> ]

<leave statement> ::= LEAVE <label>

<iterate statement> ::= ITERATE <label>

<statement list> ::= { <statement in body> ; }...

<begin-end block> ::=
   [ <label> : ] BEGIN <statement list> END [ <label> ]

<label> ::= <name>
```

Let's begin with examples of the IF statement.

Example 30.7: Create a stored procedure that determines which of the two input parameters is highest.

```
CREATE PROCEDURE DIFFERENCE
    (IN P1 INTEGER,
     IN P2 INTEGER,
     OUT P3 INTEGER)
BEGIN
    IF P1 > P2 THEN
        SET P3 = 1;
    ELSEIF P1 = P2 THEN
        SET P3 = 2;
    ELSE
        SET P3 = 3;
    END IF;
END
```

Explanation: The ELSE clause is not mandatory, and you may specify many ELSEIF clauses.

Example 30.8: Create a stored procedure that generates numbers according to the Fibonnaci algorithm.

A Fibonnaci algorithm generates numbers as follows. You start with two numbers, such as 16 and 27. The first generated number is the sum of those two, which is 43. Then, the second generated number is the sum of the number that was generated last (43), plus the number in front of that: 27, result 70. The third number is 70 plus 43, giving 113. The fourth number is 113 plus 70, and so on. If the sum exceeds a specific maximum, that maximum is subtracted. In the following examples, we assume that the maximum equals 10,000. If this problem is to be solved with stored procedures, the calling program has to remember the two previous numbers because a stored procedure does not have a memory. For every call, these two numbers have to be included. The procedure itself looks as follows:

```
CREATE PROCEDURE FIBONNACI
    (INOUT NUMBER1 INTEGER,
     INOUT NUMBER2 INTEGER,
     INOUT NUMBER3 INTEGER)
BEGIN
    SET NUMBER3 = NUMBER1 + NUMBER2;
    IF NUMBER3 > 10000 THEN
        SET NUMBER3 = NUMBER3 - 10000;
    END IF;
    SET NUMBER1 = NUMBER2;
    SET NUMBER2 = NUMBER3;
END
```

Call this stored procedure three times, beginning with the values 16 and 27:

```
SET @A=16, @B=27

CALL FIBONNACI(@A,@B,@C)

SELECT @C

CALL FIBONNACI(@A,@B,@C)

SELECT @C

CALL FIBONNACI(@A,@B,@C)

SELECT @C
```

The results of the three SELECT statements are, respectively, 43, 70, and 113. Here, we indicate how this procedure can be called from a program (our pseudo language is used with this):

```
number1 := 16;
number2 := 27;

counter := 1;
while counter <= 10 do
    CALL FIBONNACI (:number1, :number2, :number3);
    print 'The number is ', number3;
    counter := counter + 1;
endwhile;
```

Example 30.9: Create a stored procedure that indicates which table, PLAYERS or PENALTIES, has the largest number of rows.

```
CREATE PROCEDURE LARGEST
    (OUT T CHAR(10))
BEGIN
    IF (SELECT COUNT(*) FROM PLAYERS) >
       (SELECT COUNT(*) FROM PENALTIES) THEN
        SET T = 'PLAYERS';
    ELSEIF (SELECT COUNT(*) FROM PLAYERS) =
           (SELECT COUNT(*) FROM PENALTIES) THEN
        SET T = 'EQUAL';
    ELSE
        SET T = 'PENALTIES';
    END IF;
END
```

Explanation: As this example shows, conditions are allowed to contain scalar subqueries. However, this stored procedure would be more efficient if the results of the subqueries were assigned to local variables first and, subsequently, if the values of the variables were compared in the condition. In the previous example, the subqueries are sometimes executed twice.

The CASE statement makes it possible to specify complex IF–THEN–ELSE constructs. The IF statement in Example 30.7, for example, can be rewritten as follows:

```
CASE
    WHEN P1 > P2 THEN SET P3 = 1;
    WHEN P1 = P2 THEN SET P3 = 2;
    ELSE SET P3 = 3;
END CASE;
```

SQL supports three statements to create loops: the WHILE, the REPEAT, and the LOOP statements.

Example 30.10: Create a stored procedure that calculates the number of years, months, and days between two dates.

```
CREATE PROCEDURE AGE
    (IN   START_DATE   DATE,
     IN   END_DATE     DATE,
     OUT  YEARS        INTEGER,
     OUT  MONTHS       INTEGER,
     OUT  DAYS         INTEGER)
BEGIN
    DECLARE NEXT_DATE, PREVIOUS_DATE DATE;

    SET YEARS = 0;
    SET PREVIOUS_DATE = START_DATE;
    SET NEXT_DATE = START_DATE + INTERVAL 1 YEAR;
    WHILE NEXT_DATE < END_DATE DO
        SET YEARS = YEARS + 1;
        SET PREVIOUS_DATE = NEXT_DATE;
        SET NEXT_DATE = NEXT_DATE + INTERVAL 1 YEAR;
    END WHILE;

    SET MONTHS = 0;
    SET NEXT_DATE = PREVIOUS_DATE + INTERVAL 1 MONTH;
    WHILE NEXT_DATE < END_DATE DO
        SET MONTHS = MONTHS + 1;
        SET PREVIOUS_DATE = NEXT_DATE;
        SET NEXT_DATE = NEXT_DATE + INTERVAL 1 MONTH;
    END WHILE;
```

```
    SET DAYS = 0;
    SET NEXT_DATE = PREVIOUS_DATE + INTERVAL 1 DAY;
    WHILE NEXT_DATE <= END_DATE DO
        SET DAYS = DAYS + 1;
        SET PREVIOUS_DATE = NEXT_DATE;
        SET NEXT_DATE = NEXT_DATE + INTERVAL 1 DAY;
    END WHILE;
END
```

This stored procedure works as follows:

```
SET @START = '1991-01-12'

SET @END = '1999-07-09'

CALL AGE (@START, @END, @YEAR, @MONTH, @DAY)

SELECT @START, @END, @YEAR, @MONTH, @DAY
```

Explanation: The first loop determines the number of intervening years, the second indicates the number of months, and the last indicates the number of days. Of course, scalar functions can be used to realize the same in a more simple way; this method is chosen only to illustrate the WHILE statement.

In a WHILE statement, a check is done first to see whether the specified condition is true; only if the condition is true is the statement executed. At the REPEAT statement, the statements are executed first; then, a check is done to see whether the condition is true. The first WHILE statement from Example 30.10 can be rewritten as follows:

```
SET YEARS = -1;
SET NEXT_DATE = START_DATE;
REPEAT
    SET PREVIOUS_DATE = NEXT_DATE;
    SET NEXT_DATE = PREVIOUS_DATE + INTERVAL 1 YEAR;
    SET YEARS = YEARS + 1;
UNTIL NEXT_DATE > END_DATE END REPEAT;
```

Before we explain the LOOP statement, we describe the LEAVE statement. The LEAVE statement can be used to stop the processing of a begin-end block early. However, the relevant block must have a label.

Example 30.11: Create a stored procedure in which a block is ended prematurely.

```
CREATE PROCEDURE SMALL_EXIT
    (OUT P1 INTEGER, OUT P2 INTEGER)
BEGIN
    SET P1 = 1;
    SET P2 = 1;
    BLOCK1 : BEGIN
        LEAVE BLOCK1;
        SET P2 = 3;
    END;
    SET P1 = 4;
END
```

If we call this stored procedure, the value of the second parameter will be equal to 1 and the value of P1 will be equal to 4. The SET statement that comes right after the LEAVE statement is not executed, contrary to the SET statement specified after BLOCK1 that is actually executed.

With the LOOP statement, we do not use a condition—we use a LEAVE statement to end the loop.

The first WHILE statement from Example 30.10 can be rewritten as follows:

```
SET YEARS = 0;
SET PREVIOUS_DATE = START_DATE;
SET NEXT_DATE = START_DATE + INTERVAL 1 YEAR;
YEARS_LOOP: LOOP
    IF NEXT_DATE > END_DATE THEN
        LEAVE YEARS_LOOP;
    END IF;
    SET YEARS = YEARS + 1;
    SET PREVIOUS_DATE = NEXT_DATE;
    SET NEXT_DATE = NEXT_DATE + INTERVAL 1 YEAR;
END LOOP YEARS_LOOP;
```

Example 30.12: Create a stored procedure that does not respond for a certain number of seconds.

```
CREATE PROCEDURE WAIT
   (IN WAIT_SECONDS INTEGER)
BEGIN
   DECLARE END_TIME INTEGER
      DEFAULT NOW() + INTERVAL WAIT_SECONDS SECOND;
   WAIT_LOOP: LOOP
      IF NOW() > END_TIME THEN
         LEAVE WAIT_LOOP;
      END IF;
   END LOOP WAIT_LOOP;
END
```

Explanation: If we call this stored procedure with CALL(5), SQL checks whether the 5 seconds have passed. If so, we leave the loop with the LEAVE statement.

The ITERATE statement is the counterpart of the LEAVE statement. The difference between the two is that, with the LEAVE statement, we leave a loop early, whereas we restart the loop with ITERATE.

Example 30.13: Create a stored procedure with an ITERATE statement.

```
CREATE PROCEDURE AGAIN
   (OUT RESULT INTEGER)
BEGIN
   DECLARE COUNTER INTEGER DEFAULT 1;
   SET RESULT = 0;
   LOOP1: WHILE COUNTER <= 1000 DO
      SET COUNTER = COUNTER + 1;
      IF COUNTER > 100 THEN
         LEAVE LOOP1;
      ELSE
         ITERATE LOOP1;
      END IF;
      SET RESULT = COUNTER * 10;
   END WHILE LOOP1;
END
```

Explanation: The value of the parameter RESULT will always be equal to 0. The stored procedure will never come at the statement SET RESULT = COUNTER * 10. The reason is that the IF statement leads to the processing of the LEAVE statement (and then we leave the loop) or to the processing of the ITERATE statement. In that case, the processing jumps again to the loop with the name LOOP1.

30.8   Calling Stored Procedures

A procedure can be called from a program, from interactive SQL, and from stored procedures. In all three cases, the CALL statement is used.

```
<call statement> ::=
    CALL [ <database name> . ] <stored procedure name>
        ( <expression list> )

<expression list> ::= <expression>  [ { , <expression> }... ]
```

Even though the statement is not complex, there are certain rules. The number of expressions in the expression list must always be equal to the number of parameters of the stored procedure. In front of the procedure name, the name of a database may be specified. SQL automatically places that same database name in all the DML statements in front of all table names. This does not apply when a database name is explicitly specified in front of a table name, of course.

Any scalar expression may be used as the input parameter of a stored procedure. SQL calculates the value of that expression before the value is passed on to the procedure.

Example 30.14: Call the stored procedure called WAIT from Example 30.12, and wait just as many seconds as there are rows in the PENALTIES table.

```
CALL WAIT ((SELECT COUNT(*) FROM PENALTIES))
```

Stored procedures can call themselves *recursively*. This use is illustrated next with an example in which a special version of the PLAYERS table, called the PLAYERS_WITH_PARENTS table, is used. Most columns from the original PLAYERS table have been removed, and two columns have been added instead: FATHER_PLAYERNO and MOTHER_PLAYERNO. These two columns contain player numbers and are filled if the father and/or mother of the player concerned also plays at the tennis club. See Figure 30.3 for a graphical overview of the family relationships between several players.

```
CREATE TABLE PLAYERS_WITH_PARENTS
       (PLAYERNO             INTEGER NOT NULL PRIMARY KEY,
        FATHER_PLAYERNO  INTEGER,
        MOTHER_PLAYERNO  INTEGER)

ALTER TABLE PLAYERS_WITH_PARENTS ADD
    FOREIGN KEY (FATHER_PLAYERNO)
        REFERENCES PLAYERS_WITH_PARENTS (PLAYERNO)

ALTER TABLE PLAYERS_WITH_PARENTS ADD
    FOREIGN KEY (MOTHER_PLAYERNO)
        REFERENCES PLAYERS_WITH_PARENTS (PLAYERNO)

INSERT INTO PLAYERS_WITH_PARENTS VALUES
    (9,NULL,NULL), (8,NULL,NULL), (7,NULL,NULL),
    (6,NULL,NULL), (5,NULL,NULL), (4,8,9), (3,6,7),
    (2,4,5), (1,2,3)
```

Figure 30.3   *The family relationships between several players*

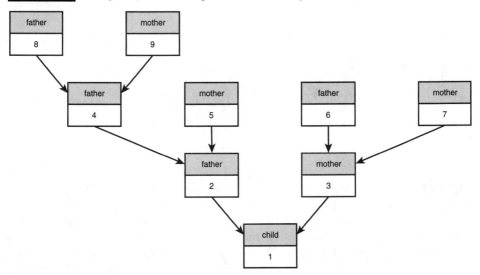

Example 30.15: Develop a stored procedure that calculates, for a specific player, the number of parents, grandparents, great-grandparents, and so on who also play for the club. After that, call the stored procedure for players.

```
CREATE PROCEDURE TOTAL_NUMBER_OF_PARENTS
    (IN P_PLAYERNO INTEGER,
     INOUT NUMBER INTEGER)
BEGIN
    DECLARE V_FATHER, V_MOTHER INTEGER;
    SET V_FATHER =
        (SELECT    FATHER_PLAYERNO
         FROM      PLAYERS_WITH_PARENTS
         WHERE     PLAYERNO = P_PLAYERNO);
    SET V_MOTHER =
        (SELECT    MOTHER_PLAYERNO
         FROM      PLAYERS_WITH_PARENTS
         WHERE     PLAYERNO = P_PLAYERNO);

    IF V_FATHER IS NOT NULL THEN
        CALL TOTAL_NUMBER_OF_PARENTS (V_FATHER, NUMBER);
        SET NUMBER = NUMBER + 1;
    END IF;

    IF V_MOTHER IS NOT NULL THEN
        CALL TOTAL_NUMBER_OF_PARENTS (V_MOTHER, NUMBER);
        SET NUMBER = NUMBER + 1;
    END IF;
END

SET @NUMBER = 0

CALL TOTAL_NUMBER_OF_PARENTS (1, @NUMBER)

SELECT @NUMBER
```

Explanation: The result of the last SELECT statement is 8. Apart from the way this procedure works, you can clearly see the recursive style of calling procedures. But how does
it work precisely? We assume that the procedure is called with the number of a player—
for example, 27—as the first parameter and a variable in which the number of ancestors
is recorded as the second parameter. However, this variable first must be initialized and
set to 0; otherwise, the procedure will not work correctly. The first SELECT statement
determines the player numbers of the father and mother. If the father is indeed a member of the club, the procedure TOTAL_NUMBER_OF_PARENTS is again called (recursively), this time with the player number of the father as the input parameter. When this
procedure has finished, the number of ancestors of the father is shown. Next, we add 1

because the father himself must also be counted as the ancestor of the child. Thus, it is possible that, for the father, TOTAL_NUMBER_OF_PARENTS is activated for the third time, because he, in turn, has a father or mother who is still a member of the club. After the number of ancestors has been determined for the father, the same is done for the mother.

In practice, the need to walk through a hierarchy from top to bottom, or vice versa, and perform calculations occurs often. A production company, for example, records which products are a part of other products. A car consists of, among other things, a chassis and an engine. The engine itself contains sparking plugs, a battery, and other parts, and this hierarchy goes on and on. Another example involves departments in large companies. Departments consist of smaller departments, which, in turn, consist of even smaller departments. And there are many more examples to think of.

30.9 Stored Procedures with SELECT INTO

Just as with embedded SQL, the results of SELECT statements within stored procedures can be retrieved in two ways. If the SELECT statement is guaranteed to return one row at the most, the SELECT INTO statement can be used.

Example 30.16: Create a stored procedure that calculates the total of the penalties of a certain player. After that, call the procedure for player 27.

```
CREATE PROCEDURE TOTAL_PENALTIES_PLAYER
    (IN P_PLAYERNO INTEGER,
     OUT TOTAL_PENALTIES DECIMAL(8,2))
BEGIN
    SELECT SUM(AMOUNT)
    INTO    TOTAL_PENALTIES
    FROM    PENALTIES
    WHERE   PLAYERNO = P_PLAYERNO;
END

CALL TOTAL_PENALTIES_PLAYER (27, @TOTAL)

SELECT @TOTAL
```

Explanation: The result of the SELECT INTO statement is immediately assigned to the output parameter TOTAL_PENALTIES.

Another example in which the SELECT INTO statement could be used well is Example 30.15. The first two SET statements with subqueries could be replaced by one SELECT INTO statement, to improve the processing speed:

```
SELECT   FATHER_PLAYERNO, MOTHER_PLAYERNO
INTO     V_FATHER, V_MOTHER
FROM     PLAYERS_WITH_PARENTS
WHERE    PLAYERNO = P_PLAYERNO
```

Example 30.17: Create a stored procedure that retrieves the address of a player.

```
CREATE PROCEDURE GIVE_ADDRESS
    (IN  P_PLAYERNO SMALLINT,
     OUT P_STREET    VARCHAR(30),
     OUT P_HOUSENO   CHAR(4),
     OUT P_TOWN      VARCHAR(30),
     OUT P_POSTCODE CHAR(6))
BEGIN
    SELECT TOWN, STREET, HOUSENO, POSTCODE
    INTO   P_TOWN, P_STREET, P_HOUSENO, P_POSTCODE
    FROM   PLAYERS
    WHERE  PLAYERNO = P_PLAYERNO;
END
```

Example 30.18: Example 30.8 shows how the next value of a Fibonnaci series can be calculated with a stored procedure. The disadvantage of this solution is that the stored procedure has three parameters, of which only one is relevant to the calling program: the third parameter. It would be better if we could remember the two first parameters within the stored procedure, but then the stored procedure would need a memory, which is kept between two calls. There is no such memory, but we could simulate it by storing the values of these variables in a table. For this, we use the following table:

```
CREATE TABLE FIBON
        (NUMBER1   INTEGER NOT NULL PRIMARY KEY,
         NUMBER2   INTEGER NOT NULL)
```

We need a stored procedure to assign an initial value to the two columns; see the next example. The DELETE statement is used to empty the table in case it contains remnants of a previous exercise. Next, we use an INSERT statement to give the columns an initial value:

```
CREATE PROCEDURE FIBONNACI_START()
BEGIN
    DELETE FROM FIBON;
    INSERT INTO FIBON (NUMBER, NUMBER2) VALUES (16, 27);
END
```

The original Fibonnaci procedure will now look as follows:

```
CREATE PROCEDURE FIBONNACI_GIVE
    (INOUT NUMBER INTEGER)
BEGIN
    DECLARE N1, N2 INTEGER;
    SELECT NUMBER1, NUMBER2
    INTO    N1, N2
    FROM    FIBON;
    SET NUMBER = N1 + N2;
    IF NUMBER > 10000 THEN
       SET NUMBER = NUMBER - 10000;
    END IF;
    SET N1 = N2;
    SET N2 = NUMBER;
    UPDATE FIBON
    SET     NUMBER1 = N1,
            NUMBER2 = N2;
END
```

The last two values are retrieved with a SELECT INTO statement. The procedure is probably obvious. The part of a program in which the procedures are called might look like this:

```
CALL FIBONNACI_START()

CALL FIBONNACI_GIVE(@C)

SELECT @C

CALL FIBONNACI_GIVE(@C)
```

```
SELECT @C

CALL FIBONNACI_GIVE(@C)

SELECT @C
```

The first advantage of the previous solution is that when a procedure is called, only one parameter has to be passed. The second advantage has to do with the way the Fibonnaci algorithm works: In the second solution, the internal workings are much more hidden from the calling program.

Example 30.19: Create a stored procedure that removes a player. Imagine that the following rule applies: A player can be removed only if he or she has incurred no penalty and only if he or she is not a captain of a team. It is also assumed that no foreign keys have been defined.

```
CREATE PROCEDURE DELETE_PLAYER
    (IN P_PLAYERNO INTEGER)
BEGIN
    DECLARE NUMBER_OF_ PENALTIES INTEGER;
    DECLARE NUMBER_OF_TEAMS   INTEGER;
    SELECT COUNT(*)
    INTO   NUMBER_OF_PENALTIES
    FROM   PENALTIES
    WHERE  PLAYERNO = P_PLAYERNO;

    SELECT COUNT(*)
    INTO   NUMBER_OF_TEAMS
    FROM   TEAMS
    WHERE  PLAYERNO = P_PLAYERNO_;

    IF NUMBER_OF_PENALTIES = 0 AND NUMBER_OF_TEAMS = 0 THEN
        CALL DELETE_MATCHES (P_PLAYERNO);
        DELETE FROM PLAYERS
        WHERE  PLAYERNO = P_PLAYERNO;
    END IF;
END
```

This stored procedure can be optimized by checking, after the first SELECT statement, whether the number of penalties is not equal to zero. If this is the case, the procedure can be interrupted because the second SELECT statement is no longer necessary.

30.10 Error Messages, Handlers, and Conditions

All the error messages supported by SQL have a unique code, called the *SQL error code*, a piece of describing text, and a code called SQLSTATE, which has been added to comply with the SQL standard. The SQLSTATE codes are not unique; several error codes can have the same SQLSTATE. For example, SQLSTATE 23000 belongs to, among other things, the following error codes:

Error 1022—Can't write; duplicate key in table
Error 1048—Column cannot be null
Error 1052—Column is ambiguous
Error 1062—Duplicate entry for key

The manuals of SQL list all the error messages and their respective codes.

Processing SQL statements in stored procedures can lead to error messages. For example, when a new row is added but the value in the primary key already exists, or an index is removed that does not exist, SQL stops the processing of the stored procedure. We illustrate this with an example.

Example 30.20: Create a stored procedure with which an existing team number is entered.

```
CREATE PROCEDURE DUPLICATE
    (OUT P_PROCESSED SMALLINT)
BEGIN
    SET P_PROCESSED = 1;
    INSERT INTO TEAMS VALUES (2,27,'third');
    SET P_PROCESSED = 2;
END

CALL DUPLICATE(PROCESSED)
```

Explanation: Because team 2 already exists, the INSERT statement results in an error message. SQL stops the processing of the stored procedure right away. The last SET statement is no longer processed, and the parameter PROCESSED is not set to 2.

With a special version of the DECLARE statement, the DECLARE HANDLER statement, we can prevent SQL from stopping the processing:

```
<declare handler statement> ::=
   DECLARE <handler type> HANDLER FOR <condition value list>
      <procedural statement>

<handler type> ::=
   CONTINUE |
   EXIT    |
   UNDO

<condition value list> ::=
   <condition value> [ { , <condition value> }... ]

<condition value> ::=
   SQLSTATE [ VALUE ] <sqlstate value> |
   <mysql error code>                  |
   SQLWARNING                          |
   NOT FOUND                           |
   SQLEXCEPTION                        |
   <condition name>
```

With the DECLARE HANDLER statement, a so-called *handler* is defined. A handler
indicates what should happen if the processing of an SQL statement leads to a certain
error message. The definition of a handler consists of three parts: the type of handler, the
condition, and the action.

Three types of handlers exist: CONTINUE, EXIT, and UNDO. When we specify a CON-
TINUE handler, SQL does not interrupt the processing of the stored procedure, whereas
the processing is indeed stopped with an EXIT handler.

Example 30.21: Create a stored procedure with which a team number is entered. If that
number already exists, the processing of the procedure should continue. When the processing has finished, the output parameter contains the SQLSTATE code of the possible error message.

```
CREATE PROCEDURE SMALL_MISTAKE1
    (OUT ERROR CHAR(5))
BEGIN
   DECLARE CONTINUE HANDLER FOR SQLSTATE '23000'
      SET ERROR = '23000';
   SET ERROR = '00000';
   INSERT INTO TEAMS VALUES (2,27,'third');
END
```

Explanation: After the call of this stored procedure, the ERROR parameter has the value 23000. But how does it work? Obviously, the INSERT statement leads to an error message of which the code is 23000. When an error occurs, SQL checks whether a handler has been defined for this code, which happens to be the case in this example. Next, SQL executes the additional statement belonging to the DECLARE statement (SET ERROR = '23000'). After that, SQL checks what kind of handler it is; in this case, it is a CONTINUE handler. Because of this, the processing of the stored procedure goes on where it was. If the INSERT statement could have been executed without mistakes, the ERROR parameter would have had the value 00000.

You are allowed to define several handlers within a stored procedure, provided that they apply to different error messages.

Example 30.22: Create a special version of the previous example.

```
CREATE PROCEDURE SMALL_MISTAKE2
   (OUT ERROR CHAR(5))
BEGIN
   DECLARE CONTINUE HANDLER FOR SQLSTATE '23000'
      SET ERROR = '23000';
   DECLARE CONTINUE HANDLER FOR SQLSTATE '21S01'
      SET ERROR = '21S01';
   SET ERROR = '00000';
   INSERT INTO TEAMS VALUES (2,27,'third',5);
END
```

Explanation: The error message with SQLSTATE code 21S01 is returned if the number of values in the INSERT statement does not comply with the number of columns in the table. In this example, the output parameter will have the value 21S01 when the procedure is processed.

Instead of an SQLSTATE code, you can also define an error code. The handlers in the previous example could have been defined as follows:

```
DECLARE CONTINUE HANDLER FOR 1062 SET ERROR = '23000';
DECLARE CONTINUE HANDLER FOR 1136 SET ERROR = '21S01';
```

The SQLWARNING handler is activated for all SQLSTATE codes beginning with 01, the NOT FOUND handler for all codes beginning with 02, and the SQLEXCEPTION handler for all codes that do not begin with 01 or 02. The three handlers can be used when we do not want to define a separate handler for every error message possible.

Example 30.23: Create a stored procedure with which a team number can be entered. If something goes wrong with the processing of the INSERT statement, the procedure has to continue.

```
CREATE PROCEDURE SMALL_MISTAKE3
    (OUT ERROR CHAR(5))
BEGIN
    DECLARE CONTINUE HANDLER FOR SQLWARNING, NOT FOUND,
        SQLEXCEPTION SET ERROR = 'XXXXX';
    SET ERROR = '00000';
    INSERT INTO TEAMS VALUES (2,27,'third');
END
```

To improve the readability, we can give certain SQLSTATE and error codes a name and use this name later with the declaration of a handler. Defining a condition is done with a DECLARE CONDITION statement.

```
<declare condition statement> ::=
    DECLARE <condition name> CONDITION FOR
    { SQLSTATE [ VALUE ] <sqlstate value> } |
        <mysql error code> }
```

Example 30.24: Change the stored procedure SMALL_MISTAKE1 and use conditions instead of handlers.

```
CREATE PROCEDURE SMALL_MISTAKE4
    (OUT ERROR CHAR(5))
BEGIN
    DECLARE NON_UNIQUE CONDITION FOR SQLSTATE '23000';
    DECLARE CONTINUE HANDLER FOR NON_UNIQUE
        SET ERROR = '23000';
    SET ERROR = '00000';
    INSERT INTO TEAMS VALUES (2,27,'third');
END
```

Explanation: The condition NON_UNIQUE can be used instead of the SQLSTATE code.
Handlers and conditions can be defined within each begin-end block. A handler is relevant for all SQL statements that belong to the same block, plus all its subblocks.

Example 30.25: Develop a stored procedure called SMALL_MISTAKE5.

```
CREATE PROCEDURE SMALL_MISTAKE5
   (OUT ERROR CHAR(5))
BEGIN
   DECLARE NON_UNIQUE CONDITION FOR SQLSTATE '23000';
   DECLARE CONTINUE HANDLER FOR NON_UNIQUE
      SET ERROR = '23000';
   BEGIN
      DECLARE CONTINUE HANDLER FOR NON_UNIQUE
         SET ERROR = '23000';
   END;
   BEGIN
      DECLARE CONTINUE HANDLER FOR NON_UNIQUE
         SET ERROR = '00000';
      INSERT INTO TEAMS VALUES (2,27,'third');
   END;
END
```

Explanation: In this procedure, the parameter ERROR will have the value 00000 when something goes wrong with the INSERT statement.

In fact, the rules for the range of handlers are equivalent to those of declared variables.

Two or more handlers cannot be defined for the same error message and within the same begin-end block. For example, the following two statements in the same stored procedure are not allowed:

```
DECLARE CONTINUE HANDLER FOR SQLSTATE '23000'
   SET ERROR = '23000';
DECLARE EXIT HANDLER FOR SQLSTATE '23000'
   SET ERROR = '24000';
```

However, the same handler can be defined in a subblock; see the following example:

```
CREATE PROCEDURE SMALL_MISTAKE6 ()
BEGIN
   DECLARE CONTINUE HANDLER FOR SQLSTATE '23000'
      SET @PROCESSED = 100;
   BEGIN
```

```
        DECLARE CONTINUE HANDLER FOR SQLSTATE '23000'
            SET @PROCESSED = 200;
        INSERT INTO TEAMS VALUES (2,27,'third');
    END;
END
```

If the processing of the INSERT statement goes wrong, SQL checks whether a relevant DECLARE statement occurs within that same begin-end block. If so, it is activated; otherwise, SQL tries to find a relevant handler in the surrounding begin-end block.

30.11 Stored Procedures with a Cursor

To process a SELECT statement of which the result possibly contains more than one row, cursors must be used, just as with embedded SQL.

```
<declare cursor statement> ::=
    DECLARE <cursor name> CURSOR FOR <table expression>

<open statement> ::=
    OPEN <cursor name>

<fetch statement> ::=
    FETCH <cursor name> INTO <variable> [ { , <variable> }... ]

<close statement> ::=
    CLOSE <cursor name>
```

Example 30.26: Create a stored procedure that counts the number of rows in the PLAY-ERS table.

```
CREATE PROCEDURE NUMBER_OF_PLAYERS
    (OUT NUMBER INTEGER)
BEGIN
    DECLARE A_PLAYERNO INTEGER;
    DECLARE FOUND BOOLEAN DEFAULT TRUE;
    DECLARE C_PLAYERS CURSOR FOR
        SELECT PLAYERNO FROM PLAYERS;
```

```
    DECLARE CONTINUE HANDLER FOR NOT FOUND
        SET FOUND = FALSE;
    SET NUMBER = 0;
    OPEN C_PLAYERS;
    FETCH C_PLAYERS INTO A_PLAYERNO;
    WHILE FOUND DO
        SET NUMBER = NUMBER + 1;
        FETCH C_PLAYERS INTO A_PLAYERNO;
    END WHILE;
    CLOSE C_PLAYERS;
END
```

Explanation: The WHILE statement can be used to browse the result of the cursor row by row while the variable FOUND is true. If a FETCH statement does not produce a result, the CONTINUE handler is activated and FOUND is set to false. This stops the WHILE statement.

Example 30.27: Create a stored procedure that removes all the penalties of the players who are older than 30 years.

```
CREATE PROCEDURE DELETE_OLDER_THAN_30()
BEGIN
    DECLARE V_AGE, V_PLAYERNO,V_YEARS,
        V_MONTHS, V_DAYS INTEGER;
    DECLARE V_BIRTH_DATE DATE;
    DECLARE FOUND BOOLEAN DEFAULT TRUE;
    DECLARE C_PLAYERS CURSOR FOR
        SELECT PLAYERNO, BIRTH_DATE
        FROM    PLAYERS;
    DECLARE CONTINUE HANDLER FOR NOT FOUND
        SET FOUND = FALSE;
    OPEN C_PLAYERS;
    FETCH C_PLAYERS INTO V_PLAYERNO, V_BIRTH_DATE;
    WHILE FOUND DO
        CALL AGE (V_BIRTH_DATE, NOW(), V_YEARS,
            V_MONTHS, V_DAYS);
        IF V_YEARS > 30 THEN
            DELETE FROM PENALTIES WHERE PLAYERNO = V_PLAYERNO;
        END IF;
        FETCH C_PLAYERS INTO V_PLAYERNO, V_BIRTH_DATE;
    END WHILE;
    CLOSE C_PLAYERS;
END
```

Explanation: With cursor C_PLAYERS, we walk through the PLAYERS table. If the age of a player concerned is greater than 30, we remove that player's penalties.

Example 30.28: Develop a stored procedure to determine whether a player belongs to the top three players of the club. In this example, "top three" is defined as the three players who have won the largest number of sets in total.

```
CREATE PROCEDURE TOP_THREE
    (IN P_PLAYERNO INTEGER,
     OUT OK BOOLEAN)
BEGIN
    DECLARE A_PLAYERNO, BALANCE, SEQNO INTEGER;
    DECLARE FOUND BOOLEAN;
    DECLARE BALANCE_PLAYERS CURSOR FOR
        SELECT   PLAYERNO, SUM(WON) - SUM(LOST)
        FROM     MATCHES
        GROUP BY PLAYERNO
        ORDER BY 2;
    DECLARE CONTINUE HANDLER FOR NOT FOUND
        SET FOUND = FALSE;
    SET SEQNO = 0;
    SET FOUND = TRUE;
    SET OK = FALSE;
    OPEN BALANCE_PLAYERS;
    FETCH BALANCE_PLAYERS INTO A_PLAYERNO, BALANCE;
    WHILE FOUND AND SEQNO < 3 AND OK = FALSE DO
        SET SEQNO = SEQNO + 1;
        IF A_PLAYERNO = P_PLAYERNO THEN
            SET OK = TRUE;
        END IF;
        FETCH BALANCE_PLAYERS INTO A_PLAYERNO, BALANCE;
    END WHILE;
    CLOSE BALANCE_PLAYERS;
END
```

Explanation: The stored procedure uses a cursor to determine for each player what the difference is between the total number of sets won and the total number of sets lost (the balance). These players are ordered by balance: the player with the largest difference first and the one with the smallest last. With the WHILE statement, we "browse" through the first three rows of this result. The parameter OK has the value true if the entered player number is equal to one of the first three players.

30.12 Stored Procedures and Transactions

Within stored procedures, all the well-known transaction-oriented statements can be used, such as COMMIT, ROLLBACK, and START TRANSACTION. A transaction does not begin with the start of a stored procedure, nor does it stop with the end of it. With regard to the transactions, SQL does not see the difference between SQL statements that are delivered by the applications and those that are delivered by the stored procedures. This means, for example, that when certain changes of an application are not permanent yet and a stored procedure is called that also executes some changes, all changes are part of the current transaction. It also means that if a stored procedure sends a COMMIT statement and there are still nonpermanent changes, they also are made permanent.

Example 30.29: Develop a stored procedure that adds a new team.

```
CREATE PROCEDURE NEW_TEAM ()
BEGIN
    INSERT INTO TEAMS VALUES (100,27,'first');
END
```

Imagine that the application executes the following statements:

```
SET AUTOCOMMIT = 1

START TRANSACTION

INSERT INTO TEAMS VALUES (200,27,'first')

CALL NEW_TEAM()

ROLLBACK WORK
```

The ROLLBACK statement is now responsible for removing the row that has been entered with the INSERT statement, and also for removing the row that has been added by the stored procedure.

30.13 Stored Procedures and the Catalog

We have not defined a catalog view for stored procedures; you must access the catalog of SQL directly. This catalog table is called ROUTINES.

Example 30.30: Get the columns of the ROUTINES table.

```
SELECT    COLUMN_NAME
FROM      INFORMATION_SCHEMA.COLUMNS
WHERE     TABLE_SCHEMA = 'INFORMATION_SCHEMA'
AND       TABLE_NAME = 'ROUTINES'
ORDER BY  ORDINAL_POSITION
```

The result is:

```
COLUMN_NAME
------------------
SPECIFIC_NAME
ROUTINE_CATALOG
ROUTINE_SCHEMA
ROUTINE_NAME
ROUTINE_TYPE
DTD_IDENTIFIER
ROUTINE_BODY
ROUTINE_DEFINITION
EXTERNAL_NAME
EXTERNAL_LANGUAGE
PARAMETER_STYLE
IS_DETERMINISTIC
SQL_DATA_ACCESS
SQL_PATH
SECURITY_TYPE
CREATED
LAST_ALTERED
SQL_MODE
ROUTINE_COMMENT
DEFINER
```

There is also a SHOW statement for the stored procedures for retrieving information from the catalog.

Example 30.31: Get the characteristics of the procedure called FIBONNACI.

```
SHOW PROCEDURE STATUS LIKE 'FIBONNACI'
```

Example 30.32: Get the CREATE PROCEDURE statement for the procedure called FIBONNACI.

```
SHOW CREATE PROCEDURE FIBONNACI
```

The result is:

```
PROCEDURE   SQL_MODE   CREATE PROCEDURE
---------   --------   ------------------------------------
FIBONNACI              CREATE PROCEDURE `tennis`.`FIBONNACI`
                          (INOUT NUMBER1 INTEGER,
                           INOUT NUMBER2 INTEGER,
                           INOUT NUMBER3 INTEGER)
                       BEGIN
                          SET NUMBER3 = NUMBER1 + NUMBER2;
                          IF NUMBER3 > 10000 THEN
                             SET NUMBER3 = NUMBER3 - 10000;
                          END IF;
                          SET NUMBER1 = NUMBER2;
                          SET NUMBER2 = NUMBER3;
                       END
```

30.14 Removing Stored Procedures

Just as for tables, views, and indexes, it is possible to remove stored procedures from the catalog. For this, SQL supports the DROP PROCEDURE statement.

```
<drop procedure statement> ::=
   DROP PROCEDURE [ <database name> . ] <procedure name>
```

Example 30.33: Remove the DELETE_PLAYER procedure.

```
DROP  PROCEDURE DELETE_PLAYER
```

> **Portability:** *Some SQL products also remove stored procedures indirectly. This happens when tables, views, or other database objects to which a stored procedure refers are removed. This indirect method can be compared to removing views if the underlying (base) tables are removed. The SQL products that do not remove the stored procedures in these situations send an error message if a program nevertheless tries to activate the stored procedure.*

30.15 Compiling and Recompiling

Most SQL products enable you to create multiple tables in one database with the same name, provided that they have different owners. If a table name is specified in a stored procedure without being qualified by the owner, which table is actually meant? The answer to this question is different for each product. For Oracle and Ingres, for example, the procedure is compiled the moment the stored procedure is created. This implies that during creation it is determined which tables should be accessed when the procedure is called. Imagine that two users—one named John—created a table with the name PLAYERS. If John's procedure is called, John's PLAYERS table will also be accessed, regardless of who called that procedure.

So, this holds for, among others, Oracle and Ingres, but not for all SQL products. Microsoft SQL Server and Sybase, for example, work in an opposite way. If in the procedure the PLAYERS table is mentioned and John executes that procedure, his PLAYERS table is used. If Diane calls the procedure, her table is accessed.

The moment of compiling is also different for each product. Some products perform their compilation when the procedure is created; others do so when the procedure is called for the first time, and still other products do it every time the procedure is called. With Microsoft SQL Server and Sybase, you can explicitly indicate in the CREATE PRO-CEDURE statement when compiling should take place.

Example 30.34: Define the DELETE_MATCHES_2 procedure in such a way that it is compiled every time it is called.

```
CREATE PROCEDURE DELETE_MATCHES_2
    (PLAYERNO_VAR IN  SMALLINT) AS
    WITH RECOMPILE
BEGIN
    :
    :
END
```

Explanation: The addition of WITH RECOMPILE guarantees that, for each call of the procedure, the compiler is called again. The advantage of this is that the processing strategy, or the processing plan, of the procedure repeatedly is adjusted to the current situation of the database. The disadvantage is that recompilation takes time and performance decreases. For each separate procedure, database managers should determine the best method.

Sybase enables you to include the option WITH RECOMPILE when you activate the procedure. The result is that the procedure is recompiled before it is executed. All calls occurring hereafter use the recompiled procedure.

Therefore, when it is necessary to recompile a procedure, you can do this with Sybase by executing the procedure. Oracle uses a separate ALTER PROCEDURE for this.

Example 30.35: Recompile the DELETE_MATCHES procedure.

```
ALTER PROCEDURE DELETE_MATCHES COMPILE
```

30.16 Security with Stored Procedures

Who is allowed to call a stored procedure? Every SQL user? No, to access tables and views, privileges are required. These are granted with the GRANT statement. There is a special privilege for this called EXECUTE. The definition of this form of the GRANT statement looks as follows:

```
<grant statement> ::=
   <grant execute statement>

<grant execute statement> ::=
   GRANT EXECUTE
   ON    <stored procedure name>
   TO    <grantees>
   [ WITH GRANT OPTION ]

<grantees> ::=
   PUBLIC                                         |
   <user name> [ { , <user name> }... ] |
   <role name> [ { , <role name> }... ]

<grantees> ::= <user> [ { , <user> }... ]
```

Example 30.36: Give John the privilege to call the DELETE_MATCHES procedure.

```
GRANT  EXECUTE
ON     DELETE_MATCHES
TO     JOHN
```

However, John does *not* need to have a privilege for the SQL statements that are executed within the procedure. With respect to the DELETE_MATCHES procedure, John does not need an explicit DELETE privilege for the MATCHES table.

The person who does need this privilege is the developer who created the procedure. In other words, if a user creates a stored procedure, he or she must have privileges for all SQL statements executed within the procedure.

For most products, it also holds that a procedure will not be executed if the owner of a stored procedure loses several privileges after the procedure has been created correctly. SQL will send an error message when the procedure is called.

30.17 Advantages of Stored Procedures

Several examples have shown the features of stored procedures. This section covers the advantages of the use of stored procedures. These advantages refer to several areas: maintenance, performance, security, and centralization.

The first advantage, maintenance, has to do with the way applications can be set up with the use of stored procedures. If a specific set of updates on the database logically forms a unit, and if this set of updates is used in multiple applications, it is better to put them in one procedure. Examples are: remove all data of a player (at least five statements) and calculate the number of ancestors of a player. The only thing that needs to be done is to activate the procedure in the programs. This improves the productivity, of course, and prevents a programmer from implementing the set of updates "incorrectly" in his or her program.

The second advantage of stored procedures has nothing to do with productivity or maintenance, but with performance. If an application activates a procedure and waits for completion, the amount of communication between the application and the database server is minimal. This is in contrast to the application sending each SQL statement separately to the database server. Especially now that more applications access the database server through a network, it is important to minimize the amount of communication. This reduces the chance that the network will get overloaded. Briefly, the use of stored procedures can minimize network traffic.

Another advantage has to do with compiling SQL statements. In some database servers, SQL statements are compiled at precompile time (called *binding* in DB2). In brief, compiling means that the syntax of the statements is verified, that the existence of the tables and columns used is checked, that privileges are verified, and that the optimizer is asked to determine the optimal processing strategy. The result, the compiled

SQL statement, is stored in the database. It is then no longer necessary to compile the SQL statements when the programs runs. However, not all database servers compile SQL statements. They compile the statements during the execution of the program, which, of course, reduces the speed. If SQL statements in these systems are stored in stored procedures, they are precompiled again. The advantage of stored procedures for this type of database server is an improved performance.

Stored procedures are not dependent on a particular host language; they can be called from different host languages. This means that if multiple languages are used for development, certain common code does not have to be duplicated (for each language). For example, a specific stored procedure can be called from an online Java application, from a batch application written in C, or from a PHP program operating in an Internet environment.

31

Stored Functions

31.1 Introduction

S tored functions show a strong resemblance to stored procedures. Stored functions are also pieces of code consisting of SQL and procedural statements that are stored in the catalog and can be called from applications and SQL statements. However, there are a few differences.

A stored function can have input parameters but does not have output parameters. The stored function itself is the output parameter. In the next sections, we use examples to illustrate this.

After stored functions have been created, they can be called within several expressions, just as the familiar scalar functions. Therefore, we do not call stored functions using a CALL statement.

Stored functions must contain a RETURN statement. This special SQL statement is not allowed in stored procedures.

The definition of the CREATE FUNCTION procedure looks very much like that of the stored procedure. The definition also starts with a name, followed by parameters, and it ends with a body, but there are a few small differences. Because a stored function can have only input parameters, IN, OUT, and INOUT cannot be specified. The RETURNS specification follows the parameters. This indicates the data type of the value that is returned by the stored function.

```
<create function statement> ::=
    CREATE FUNCTION <function name>
        ( [ <parameter list> ] )
        RETURNS <data type>
        <function body>
```

(continued)

```
<parameter list> ::=
   <parameter specification>
      [ { , <parameter specification> }... ]

<parameter specification> ::= <parameter> <data type>

<function body> ::= <begin-end block>

<begin-end block> ::=
   [ <label> : ] BEGIN <statement list> END [ <label> ]

<statement list> ::= { <statement in body> ; }...

<statement in body> ::=
   <declarative statement> |
   <procedural statement>  |
   <return statement>

<return statement> ::= RETURN <scalar expression>
```

31.2 Examples of Stored Functions

We begin with several examples.

Example 31.1: Create a stored function that returns the American dollar value of the penalty amounts. After that, get for each penalty the payment number and the euro and dollar value of each penalty amount.

```
CREATE FUNCTION DOLLARS(AMOUNT DECIMAL(7,2))
   RETURNS DECIMAL(7,2)
BEGIN
   RETURN AMOUNT * (1 / 0.8);
END

SELECT    PAYMENTNO, AMOUNT, DOLLARS(AMOUNT)
FROM      PENALTIES
```

The result is:

PAYMENTNO	AMOUNT	DOLLARS(AMOUNT)
1	100.00	125.00
2	75.00	93.75
3	100.00	125.00

Explanation: The fact that the result of the stored function has a decimal data type is specified after RETURNS. With the special RETURN statement, we give the stored function a value. Each stored function must contain at least one RETURN statement.

You can also see that this new stored function can be called as if it is a stored function that is supplied by SQL. There is no visible difference between calling a scalar function, such as SUBSTR and COS, and calling a stored function.

Example 31.2: Create a stored function that returns the number of players in the PLAYERS table as a result. After that, call this stored function.

```
CREATE FUNCTION NUMBER_OF_PLAYERS()
    RETURNS INTEGER
BEGIN
    RETURN (SELECT COUNT(*) FROM PLAYERS);
END

SELECT NUMBER_OF_PLAYERS()
```

Explanation: This example shows first that SQL statements are allowed within stored functions and, second, that the RETURN statement may contain complex compound expressions.

Example 31.3: Create two stored functions that determine, respectively, the number of penalties and the number of matches of a certain player. After that, get the numbers, names, and initials of those players whose number of penalties is greater than the number of matches.

```
CREATE FUNCTION NUMBER_OF_PENALTIES
    (P_PLAYERNO INTEGER)
    RETURNS INTEGER
BEGIN
    RETURN (SELECT    COUNT(*)
```

```
                FROM       PENALTIES
                WHERE      PLAYERNO = P_PLAYERNO);
    END

    CREATE FUNCTION NUMBER_OF_MATCHES
        (P_PLAYERNO INTEGER)
        RETURNS INTEGER
    BEGIN
        RETURN (SELECT    COUNT(*)
                FROM      MATCHES
                WHERE     PLAYERNO = P_PLAYERNO);
    END

    SELECT    PLAYERNO, NAME, INITIALS
    FROM      PLAYERS
    WHERE     NUMBER_OF_PENALTIES(PLAYERNO) >
              NUMBER_OF_MATCHES(PLAYERNO)
```

The result is:

```
PLAYERNO   NAME       INITIALS
--------   -------    --------
      27   Collins         DD
      44   Baker            E
```

Example 31.4: Create a stored function that calculates the number of days between two dates, using the same arithmetic method as in Example 30.10.

```
    CREATE FUNCTION NUMBER_OF_DAYS
        (START_DATE DATE,
         END_DATE DATE)
        RETURNS INTEGER
    BEGIN
        DECLARE DAYS INTEGER;
        DECLARE NEXT_DATE, PREVIOUS_DATE DATE;
        SET DAYS = 0;
        SET NEXT_DATE = START_DATE + INTERVAL 1 DAY;
        WHILE NEXT_DATE <= END_DATE DO
```

```
         SET DAYS = DAYS + 1;
         SET PREVIOUS_DATE = NEXT_DATE;
         SET NEXT_DATE = NEXT_DATE + INTERVAL 1 DAY;
      END WHILE;
      RETURN DAYS;
   END
```

Explanation: All statements, such as DECLARE, SET, and WHILE, may be used.

Example 31.5: Create a stored function with the same functionality as the stored procedure in Example 30.19, to remove a player. Imagine that the rule applies that a player can be removed only when he or she has not incurred a penalty and when he or she is not a captain. We also assume that no foreign keys have been defined.

```
CREATE FUNCTION DELETE_PLAYER
    (P_PLAYERNO INTEGER)
    RETURNS BOOLEAN
BEGIN
    DECLARE NUMBER_OF_PENALTIES INTEGER;
    DECLARE NUMBER_OF_TEAMS  INTEGER;
    DECLARE EXIT HANDLER FOR SQLWARNING RETURN FALSE;
    DECLARE EXIT HANDLER FOR SQLEXCEPTION RETURN FALSE;

    SELECT COUNT(*)
    INTO   NUMBER_OF_PENALTIES
    FROM   PENALTIES
    WHERE  PLAYERNO = P_PLAYERNO;

    SELECT COUNT(*)
    INTO   NUMBER_OF_TEAMS
    FROM   TEAMS
    WHERE  PLAYERNO = P_PLAYERNO;

    IF NUMBER_OF_PENALTIES = 0 AND NUMBER_OF_TEAMS = 0 THEN
        DELETE FROM MATCHES
        WHERE  PLAYERNO = P_PLAYERNO;
        DELETE FROM PLAYERS
        WHERE  PLAYERNO = P_PLAYERNO;
    END IF;
    RETURN TRUE;
END
```

Explanation: If the stored function is processed correctly, this function returns 0 as the result; otherwise, the value is 1.

Example 31.6: Create a stored function that does not do anything but call the stored procedure NUMBER_OF_PLAYERS that we created in Example 30.26.

```
CREATE FUNCTION NUMBER_OF_PLAYERS ()
    RETURNS INTEGER
BEGIN
    DECLARE NUMBER INTEGER;
    CALL NUMBER_OF_PLAYERS(NUMBER);
    RETURN NUMBER;
END
```

Explanation: This example shows that stored procedures and stored functions can have the same name. It is also allowed to call stored procedures from stored functions.

31.3 Removing Stored Functions

A DROP statement also exists for the stored function.

```
<drop function statement> ::=
    DROP FUNCTION [ <database name> . ] <function name>
```

Example 31.7: Remove the PLACE_IN_SET stored function.

```
DROP FUNCTION PLACE_IN_SET
```

32

Triggers

32.1 Introduction

A database server is passive by nature. It performs an action only if we explicitly ask for it with, for example, an SQL statement. In this chapter, we describe the database concept that turns a passive database server into an active one. This concept is called a *trigger*. Just as with stored procedures, we start by giving a definition:

> A trigger is a piece of code consisting of procedural and declarative statements stored in the catalog and activated by the database server if a specific operation is executed on the database, and only then when a certain condition holds.

A trigger shows many similarities to a stored procedure. First, the trigger is also a procedural database object stored in the catalog. Second, the code itself consists of declarative and procedural SQL statements. Therefore, UPDATE, SELECT, and CREATE, and also IF-THEN-ELSE and WHILE-DO statements, can occur within a trigger.

However, there is one important difference between the two concepts. The way in which triggers are called deviates from that of stored procedures. Triggers *cannot* be called explicitly, either from a program or from a stored procedures. There is no CALL or EXECUTE TRIGGER statement or similar statement available. Triggers are called by SQL itself, without the programs or users being aware of it. Calling triggers is *transparent* to them.

But how and when are triggers called? A trigger is called by SQL when a program, interactive user, or stored procedure executes a specific database operation, such as adding a new row to a table or removing all rows. So, triggers are executed automatically by SQL, and it is impossible to activate triggers from a program. It is also impossible to "switch off" triggers from a program.

Portability: *Even though triggers were added only to the SQL3 standard, many SQL products now support triggers. However, just as with stored procedures, not every product uses the same syntax. The implementation of MySQL is still somewhat limited. That is why we have decided to use a syntax that is supported by many products. Therefore, some of the examples will not work in MySQL.*

32.2 An Example of a Trigger

In most examples in this section and the next section, we use a new table in the database of the tennis club: the CHANGES table. Imagine that this table is used to record which users have updated the PLAYERS table and at what moment.

Example 32.1: Create the CHANGES table.

```
CREATE TABLE CHANGES
        (USER              CHAR(30) NOT NULL,
         CHA_TIME          TIMESTAMP NOT NULL,
         CHA_PLAYERNO      SMALLINT NOT NULL,
         CHA_TYPE          CHAR(1) NOT NULL,
         CHA_PLAYERNO_NEW  INTEGER,
         PRIMARY KEY       (USER, CHA_TIME,
                            CHA_PLAYERNO, CHA_TYPE))
```

Explanation: The meaning of the first two columns is obvious. In the third column, CHA_PLAYERNO, the player number of the player who was added or removed, or whose column value was changed, is recorded. If the player number of a player is changed, the new player number is recorded in the CHA_PLAYERNO_NEW column. This column is therefore used only when the player number is updated; otherwise, a NULL value is stored. In the CHA_TYPE column, the type of change is filled in: I(nsert), U(pdate), or D(elete). The primary key of this table is formed by the columns USER, CHA_TIME, CHA_PLAYERNO, and CHA_TYPE. In other words, if a user executes two changes of the same type on the same player at the same moment, it needs to be recorded only once.

The definition of the CREATE TRIGGER statement is given next. Triggers consist of four main elements: the *trigger moment*, the *trigger event*, the *trigger condition*, and the *trigger action*. These elements appear clearly in the following definition. For a description of the concept of begin-end blocks, refer to Section 30.4, in Chapter 30, "Stored Procedures."

```
<create trigger statement> ::=
    CREATE TRIGGER <trigger name>
    <trigger moment>
    <trigger event>
    [ <trigger condition> ]
    <trigger action>
```

(continued)

```
<trigger moment> ::=
    BEFORE | AFTER | INSTEAD OF

<trigger event> ::=
    { INSERT | DELETE | UPDATE [ OF <column list> ] }
    { ON | OF | FROM | INTO } <table specification>
    [ REFERENCING { OLD | NEW | OLD_TABLE | NEW_TABLE }
      AS <variable> ]
    FOR EACH { ROW | STATEMENT }

<trigger condition> ::= ( WHEN <condition> )

<trigger action> ::= <begin-end block>
```

Note that in the more academic literature, triggers are sometimes called *ECA rules* (for "Event, Condition, Action"). However, terms such as *production rules*, *forward-chaining rules*, *assertions*, and just *rules* are also used. See [WIDO96] for an extensive description of triggers.

We begin in a way that is now familiar, with a simple example in which a minimal set of specifications is used.

Example 32.2: Create the trigger that updates the CHANGES table automatically as new rows are added to the PLAYERS table.

```
CREATE TRIGGER INSERT_PLAYERS
    AFTER
    INSERT ON PLAYERS FOR EACH ROW
    BEGIN
        INSERT INTO CHANGES
            (USER, CHA_TIME, CHA_PLAYERNO,
             CHA_TYPE, CHA_PLAYERNO_NEW)
        VALUES (USER, CURDATE(), NEW.PLAYERNO, 'I', NULL);
    END
```

Explanation: Just like every SQL statement for creating a database object, the statement begins by assigning a name to the trigger: INSERT_PLAYER. Next, all the other specifications follow.

The second line contains the trigger moment (AFTER). This element specifies when the trigger must be started. In this case, it happens *after* the INSERT statement on the PLAYERS table has been processed.

The third line contains the trigger event. This element specifies the operations for which the trigger has to be activated. In this case, the trigger must be activated at an INSERT statement on the PLAYERS table. Sometimes, this is called the *triggering statement*, and the PLAYERS table is called the *triggering table*. If the triggering statement has taken place, the body of the trigger, or the *trigger action*, must be executed. The trigger action is, in fact, what the trigger is about to do. It is usually a number of statements that are executed. We focus on the trigger action in more detail later.

The words ON, OF, FROM, and INTO after the words INSERT have no special meaning. You can use them as you want.

The word AFTER as a trigger moment, however, is important. If we use a SELECT statement in the trigger action to query the number of rows of the PLAYERS table, the row added is actually counted. The reason for this is that the trigger action is started after the triggering statement has been processed. If we had specified BEFORE, the row would not have been included because the trigger action would have been executed first. AFTER is usually used if we want to execute several more changes after the triggering statement and BEFORE if we want to verify whether the new data is correct (meaning, satisfying the constraints applied).

A third possible trigger moment is INSTEAD OF. If this specification is used, the triggering statement is not executed at all—only the trigger action is. The trigger action is then executed instead of the triggering statement.

The trigger event contains the specification FOR EACH ROW. This is used to specify that, for each individual row that is inserted into the PLAYERS table, the trigger action has to be activated. So, if we add a set of rows to the PLAYERS table with one INSERT SELECT statement in one operation, the trigger will still be executed for each row. (See Section 14.3, in Chapter 14, "Updating Tables," for a description of this statement.) The counterpart of FOR EACH ROW is FOR EACH STATEMENT. If we had specified this, the trigger would have been activated only once for each triggering statement. This means that if we inserted a thousand rows with one INSERT SELECT statement, the trigger would still be executed only once. Alternatively, if we remove a million rows with one DELETE statement, and if the triggering statement is a DELETE, the trigger is still executed only once if FOR EACH STATEMENT is specified.

A trigger action can be just as simple or as complex as the body of a stored procedure. The trigger action in our example is very simple because it consists of only one INSERT statement. This additional INSERT statement inserts one row, consisting of four values, in the CHANGES table. These are, respectively, the value of the system variable USER, the system date and time, the player number of the new player, and the literal I to indicate that it is an INSERT.

NEW is specified in front of the column name PLAYERNO. This is an important specification. If a row is inserted, it looks as if there is a table called NEW. The column names of this NEW table are equal to those of the triggering table (those in which the new row appears). As a result of specifying NEW in front of PLAYERNO, the player number that is added to the PLAYERS table is used. Its use will be obvious when we change rows in the PLAYERS table. We come back to this issue later.

To conclude this section, we mention that triggers can also call stored procedures. Therefore, the previous CREATE TRIGGER statement can be divided into two parts. First, we create a stored procedure:

```
CREATE PROCEDURE INSERT_CHANGE
     (IN CPNO          INTEGER,
      IN CTYPE         CHAR(1),
      IN CPNO_NEW      INTEGER)
BEGIN
    INSERT INTO CHANGES (USER, CHA_TIME, CHA_PLAYERNO,
                         CHA_TYPE, CHA_PLAYERNO_NEW)
    VALUES (USER, CURDATE(), CPNO, CTYPE, CPNO_NEW);
END
```

Next, we create the trigger:

```
CREATE TRIGGER INSERT_PLAYER
    AFTER INSERT ON PLAYERS FOR EACH ROW
    BEGIN
        CALL INSERT_CHANGE(NEW.PLAYERNO, 'I', NULL);
    END
```

32.3   More Complex Examples

The previous section contained one example of a trigger. In this section, we give some other examples.

Example 32.3: Create the trigger that updates the CHANGES table automatically when rows from the PLAYERS table are removed.

```
CREATE TRIGGER DELETE_PLAYER
    AFTER DELETE ON PLAYERS FOR EACH ROW
    BEGIN
        CALL INSERT_CHANGE (OLD.PLAYERNO, 'D', NULL);
    END
```

Explanation: This trigger is almost the same as the one in Example 32.1. However, there are two differences. In the first place, the triggering statement is, of course, a DELETE. Second, and this is an important difference, the keyword OLD is now specified instead of NEW. After removing a row, there is a table called OLD with column names that are equal to those of the triggering table, the one in which the removed row occurs.

When you update rows, the NEW and the OLD tables both exist. The row with the old values appears in the OLD table, and the new row is in the NEW table.

Example 32.4: Create the trigger that updates the CHANGES table automatically when rows in the PLAYERS table are changed.

```
CREATE TRIGGER UPDATE_PLAYER
    AFTER UPDATE ON PLAYERS FOR EACH ROW
    BEGIN
        CALL INSERT_CHANGES
            (NEW.PLAYERNO, 'U', OLD.PLAYERNO);
    END
```

After the UPDATE specification, you can specify which update of which columns the trigger has to be activated for.

Example 32.5: Create the UPDATE_PLAYER2 trigger that updates the CHANGES table automatically if the LEAGUENO column is changed.

```
CREATE TRIGGER UPDATE_PLAYER2
    AFTER UPDATE(LEAGUENO) ON PLAYERS FOR EACH ROW
    BEGIN
        CALL INSERT_CHANGE
            (NEW.PLAYERNO, 'U', OLD.PLAYERNO);
    END
```

Explanation: Now the trigger is activated only if the LEAGUENO column is updated. In the previous UPDATE_PLAYER trigger, the trigger was still activated for each update.

These examples demonstrate one of the advantages of stored procedures again: Code that has already been developed can be reused. This is an advantage with respect to both productivity and maintenance.

So far, we have discussed only examples of triggers consisting of a trigger event and a trigger action. Let us give an example in which the *trigger condition* is used. To clarify the trigger condition, we rewrite the UPDATE_PLAYER2 trigger from the previous section.

Example 32.6: Rewrite the UPDATE_PLAYER2 trigger so that only the changes to the LEAGUENO table column in the CHANGES table are recorded.

```
CREATE TRIGGER UPDATE_PLAYER
    AFTER UPDATE OF PLAYERS FOR EACH ROW
    WHEN ( NEW.LEAGUENO <> OLD.LEAGUENO )
    BEGIN
        INSERT INTO CHANGES
        (USER, CHA_TIME, CHA_PLAYERNO, CHA_TYPE,
            CHA_PLAYERNO_OLD)
        VALUES (USER, SYSDATE, NEW.PLAYERNO, 'U',
            OLD.PLAYERNO);
    END
```

Explanation: A rule is added to the trigger, the WHEN clause of the trigger, or the trigger condition. This condition verifies whether the change made indeed answers our question: Has the LEAGUENO changed? This is done by comparing the new value to the old. In fact, with this condition, a kind of filter is obtained.

The condition does not always have to be related to columns of the tables. If we want to activate triggers between 09:00 a.m. and 07:00 p.m., we could specify the following WHEN clause:

```
WHEN ( CURRENT TIME BETWEEN
            CONVERT_TIME('09:00.00') AND
            CONVERT_TIME('19:00.00') )
```

Alternatively, when a trigger has to be activated for just a number of specific users, we use the following:

```
WHEN ( USER IN ('JOHN', 'PETER', 'MARK') )
```

Triggers can also be used efficiently to record redundant data.

For the following example, we use a new table called PLAYERS_MAT in which the player number and the number of matches for each player are stored.

Example 32.7: Create the PLAYERS_MAT table and fill it with relevant data from the PLAYERS and MATCHES table.

```
CREATE TABLE PLAYERS_MAT
       (PLAYERNO INTEGER NOT NULL PRIMARY KEY,
        NUMBER_OF_MATCHES INTEGER NOT NULL)

INSERT INTO PLAYERS_MAT (PLAYERNO, NUMBER_OF_MATCHES)
SELECT   PLAYERNO,
         (SELECT   COUNT(*)
          FROM     MATCHES AS M
          WHERE    P.PLAYERNO = M.PLAYERNO)
FROM     PLAYERS AS P
```

Example 32.8: Create a trigger on the PLAYERS table that makes sure that if a new player is added, he or she is also added to the PLAYERS_MAT table.

```
CREATE TRIGGER INSERT_PLAYERS
    AFTER INSERT ON PLAYERS FOR EACH ROW
    BEGIN
        INSERT INTO PLAYERS_MAT
        VALUES(NEW.PLAYERNO, 0);
    END
```

Explanation: A new player cannot have matches yet, which is why the number is set to 0.

Example 32.9: Create a trigger on the PLAYERS table that makes sure that if a new player is removed, he or she is also removed from the PLAYERS_MAT table.

```
CREATE TRIGGER DELETE_PLAYERS
    AFTER DELETE ON PLAYERS FOR EACH ROW
    BEGIN
        DELETE FROM PLAYERS_MAT
        WHERE PLAYERNO = OLD.PLAYERNO;
    END
```

Explanation: This could also be done with a foreign key.

Example 32.10: Create a trigger on the MATCHES table that makes sure that if a new match is added for a player, this information is also passed on to the PLAYERS_MAT table.

```
CREATE TRIGGER INSERT_MATCHES
    AFTER INSERT ON MATCHES FOR EACH ROW
    BEGIN
        UPDATE PLAYERS_MAT
        SET    NUMBER_OF_MATCHES = NUMBER_OF_MATCHES + 1
        WHERE  PLAYERNO = NEW.PLAYERNO;
    END
```

Example 32.11: Create a trigger on the MATCHES table that makes sure that if an existing match table for a player is removed, this information is also passed on to the PLAYERS_MAT table.

```
CREATE TRIGGER DELETE_MATCHES
    AFTER DELETE ON MATCHES FOR EACH ROW
    BEGIN
        UPDATE PLAYERS_MAT
        SET    NUMBER_OF_MATCHES = NUMBER_OF_MATCHES - 1
        WHERE  PLAYERNO = OLD.PLAYERNO;
    END
```

Several other triggers are needed, but these examples give an idea of what is required. The main advantage of all these triggers is that no program has to worry about the updating of the PLAYERS_MAT table. As long as the triggers exist, the contents of this table are equal to the contents of the PLAYERS and MATCHES tables.

Example 32.12: Imagine that the PLAYERS table contains a column called SUM_PENALTIES. This column contains for each player the sum of his or her penalties. Now, we would like to create triggers that automatically keep record of the values in this column. To this end, we have to create two triggers.

```
CREATE TRIGGER SUM_PENALTIES_INSERT
    AFTER INSERT ON PENALTIES FOR EACH ROW
    BEGIN
        DECLARE TOTAL DECIMAL(8,2);
```

```
        SELECT     SUM(AMOUNT)
        INTO       TOTAL
        FROM       PENALTIES
        WHERE      PLAYERNO = NEW.PLAYERNO;

        UPDATE     PLAYERS
        SET        SUM_PENALTIES = TOTAL
        WHERE      PLAYERNO = NEW.PLAYERNO
     END

CREATE TRIGGER SUM_PENALTIES_DELETE
   AFTER DELETE, UPDATE ON PENALTIES FOR EACH ROW
   BEGIN
      DECLARE TOTAL DECIMAL(8,2);

        SELECT     SUM(AMOUNT)
        INTO       TOTAL
        FROM       PENALTIES
        WHERE      PLAYERNO = OLD.PLAYERNO;

        UPDATE     PLAYERS
        SET        SUM_PENALTIES = TOTAL
        WHERE      PLAYERNO = OLD.PLAYERNO
     END
```

Explanation: The first trigger is activated when a new penalty is added, and the second is activated when a penalty is deleted or when a penalty amount changes. If a player is added, the new sum of the penalty amounts of that new player (NEW.PLAYERNO) is determined. Next, an UPDATE statement is used to update the PLAYERS table. We make use of the local variable called TOTAL.

The UPDATE and SELECT statements can also be combined, of course. Then, the trigger action would consist of only one statement:

```
UPDATE     PLAYERS
SET        SUM_PENALTIES = (SELECT   SUM(AMOUNT)
                            FROM     PENALTIES
                            WHERE    PLAYERNO = NEW.PLAYERNO)
WHERE      PLAYERNO = NEW.PLAYERNO
```

The structure of the second trigger is equal to that of the first. The only difference is that we have to specify OLD.PLAYERNO now.

Exercise 32.1: What is the most important difference between a stored procedure and a trigger?

Exercise 32.2: Create a trigger that guarantees that there is at any time only one treasurer, one secretary, and one chairman.

Exercise 32.3: Create a trigger that guarantees that the sum of all penalties of one player is not greater than $250.

Exercise 32.4: Imagine that the TEAMS table contains a column called NUMBER_OF_MATCHES. This column contains for each team the number of matches played by that team. Create the triggers required to update the values in this column automatically.

32.4 Triggers as Integrity Constraints

Triggers can be used for many purposes, including updating redundant data and securing the integrity of the data. In Chapter 16, "Specifying Integrity Constraints," we discussed what integrity constraints are and what the possibilities are. With triggers, a wide range of integrity constraints can be specified. To give more examples of triggers, we show how specific integrity constraints can be written as triggers.

All check integrity constraints (see Section 16.6, in Chapter 16) are easy to implement with triggers.

Example 32.13: Be sure that the year of birth of a player is at least smaller than the year he or she joined the club. (This integrity constraint is in line with Example 16.13.)

We show two solutions, one in which standard SQL is used and another in which the possibilities of MySQL are used.

According to standard SQL:

```
CREATE TRIGGER BORN_VS_JOINED
    BEFORE INSERT, UPDATE(BIRTH_DATE, JOINED) OF PLAYERS
        FOR EACH ROW
    WHEN (YEAR(NEW.BIRTH_DATE) >= NEW.JOINED)
    BEGIN
        ROLLBACK WORK;
    END
```

According to MySQL:

```
CREATE TRIGGER BORN_VS_JOINED
   BEFORE INSERT, UPDATE ON PLAYERS FOR EACH ROW
   BEGIN
      IF YEAR(NEW.BIRTH_DATE) >= NEW.JOINED) THEN
         ROLLBACK WORK;
      END IF;
   END
```

Explanation: The trigger is simple and needs to be activated only for INSERT and UPDATE statements, not for DELETE statements. If the new data is incorrect, the running transaction is rolled back.

Example 32.14: The PENALTIES.PLAYERNO column is a foreign key pointing to PLAYERS.PLAYERNO; redefine this foreign key as a trigger.

We need two triggers, one for changes in the PENALTIES table and one for changes in the PLAYERS table. Again, we show two solutions.

Trigger on the PENALTIES table, according to standard SQL:

```
CREATE TRIGGER FOREIGN_KEY1
   BEFORE INSERT, UPDATE(PLAYERNO) OF PENALTIES FOR EACH ROW
   BEGIN
      DECLARE NUMBER INTEGER;
      SELECT   COUNT(*)
      INTO     NUMBER
      FROM     PLAYERS
      WHERE    PLAYERNO = NEW.PLAYERNO;
      IF NUMBER = 0 THEN
         ROLLBACK WORK;
      END IF;
   END
```

According to MySQL:

```
CREATE TRIGGER FOREIGN_KEY1
   BEFORE INSERT, UPDATE ON PENALTIES FOR EACH ROW
   BEGIN
```

```
    IF (SELECT COUNT(*) FROM PLAYERS
        WHERE PLAYERNO = NEW.PLAYERNO) = 0 THEN
        ROLLBACK WORK;
    END IF;
END
```

Explanation: With the SELECT statement, we determine whether the player number of the newly inserted or updated player appears in the PLAYERS table. If not, the variable NUMBER has a value greater than zero, and the transaction is rolled back.

The trigger on the PLAYERS table with standard SQL:

```
CREATE TRIGGER FOREIGN_KEY2
    BEFORE DELETE, UPDATE(PLAYERNO) OF PLAYERS FOR EACH ROW
    BEGIN
        DELETE
        FROM      PENALTIES
        WHERE     PLAYERNO = OLD.PLAYERNO;
    END
```

The trigger on the PLAYERS table with MySQL:

```
CREATE TRIGGER FOREIGN_KEY2
    BEFORE DELETE, UPDATE ON PLAYERS FOR EACH ROW
    BEGIN
        DELETE
        FROM      PENALTIES
        WHERE     PLAYERNO = OLD.PLAYERNO;
    END
```

Explanation: The method chosen corresponds to the triggers: ON DELETE CASCADE and ON UPDATE CASCADE. If the player number is removed from the PLAYERS table, the related penalties are fully removed.

Of course, it is not the intention that you implement all integrity constraints with triggers from now on. Indeed, doing so would do no good to the performance. The rule is that if you can implement the integrity constraint with a CHECK or FOREIGN KEY, you should do so.

So, why do we keep on talking about the implementation of integrity constraints with the use of triggers? This is because the functionality of triggers goes further than what is possible with the integrity constraints discussed in Chapter 16. For example, it is not possible to use one of the keys or the check integrity constraint to specify that if the penalty amounts are changed, the new amount should always be greater than the last one. With triggers, this can be done.

32.5 Removing Triggers

Just like any other database object, there is a DROP statement for removing triggers from the catalog:

```
<drop trigger statement> ::=
   DROP TRIGGER [ <table name> . ] <trigger name>
```

Example 32.15: Remove the BORN_VS_JOINED trigger.

```
DROP TRIGGER BORN_VS_JOINED
```

Removing triggers has no further influence, except that, from that moment on, the trigger will no longer be activated.

32.6 Differences Between SQL Products

Besides the differences in syntax, the products differ with regard to the functionality offered. For each product, you can ask the following questions:

■ Can we specify several triggers for a combination of a specific table and a specific change? For example, if we can specify two or more INSERT triggers for one table, the order in which those triggers are activated should be absolutely clear because this could affect the end result. It should then be possible to specify an order, or we should determine the order by using an algorithm. (For example, the one that is created first must be executed first.) To prevent this type of problem, several products do not allow you to define two or more triggers on the same table.

■ Does processing a statement belonging to a trigger lead to activating another (or the same) trigger? If the action of a trigger contains update statements, one update on a table can lead to updates on other tables (or maybe even another row in the same table). Of course, these additional updates can activate other triggers again and, thus, even more updates. In other words, one update in an application can result in a waterfall of updates. Not every SQL product is capable of activating triggers indirectly.

- When exactly is a trigger action processed? Is the action processed immediately after the update, or is it delayed until the end of the current transaction? Ingres employs the first option, but this certainly does not apply to all products. Some products activate all triggers just before the COMMIT statement; the advantage of this method is, among other things, that when the transaction is ended with a ROLLBACK statement, the trigger action does not have to be executed and rolled back later.

- Which trigger events are supported? In this chapter, we discussed only the trigger events that are also supported by Ingres. The only events that can activate a trigger are an INSERT, an UPDATE, and a DELETE statement, or a combination of these three. Theoretically, it is also possible that other event forms are supported—every SQL statement should, in fact, be leading to the activation of a trigger. For example, if an ALTER TABLE statement is used to remove a column, or if a privilege is granted with a GRANT statement, that should also activate a trigger. In addition, it should be possible to specify triggers that are activated not with an SQL statement, but because a certain moment in time has been reached, such as at 5:00 in the evening.

- Can triggers be defined on catalog tables? Several products do not allow this feature, although the advantage of this is that DDL statements, such as CREATE TABLE and GRANT, can still activate triggers. These statements lead to updates of the catalog tables.

32.7 Answers

32.1 The most important difference between a stored procedure and a trigger is that triggers cannot be called directly from programs or other stored procedures.

32.2

```
CREATE TRIGGER MAX1
    AFTER INSERT, UPDATE(POSITION) OF COMMITTEE_MEMBERS
        FOR EACH ROW
    BEGIN
        SELECT   COUNT(*)
        INTO     NUMBER_MEMBERS
        FROM     COMMITTEE_MEMBERS
        WHERE    PLAYERNO IN
                 (SELECT   PLAYERNO
                  FROM     COMMITTEE_MEMBERS
                  WHERE    CURRENT DATE BETWEEN
                           BEGIN_DATE AND END_DATE
```

```
                    GROUP BY POSITION
                    HAVING    COUNT(*) > 1)
          IF NUMBER_MEMBERS > 0 THEN
              ROLLBACK WORK;
          ENDIF;
      END
```

32.3

```
CREATE TRIGGER SUM_PENALTIES_250
    AFTER INSERT, UPDATE(AMOUNT) OF PENALTIES
        FOR EACH ROW
    BEGIN
        SELECT   COUNT(*)
        INTO     NUMBER_PENALTIES
        FROM     PENALTIES
        WHERE    PLAYERNO IN
                 (SELECT   PLAYERNO
                  FROM     PENALTIES
                  GROUP BY PLAYERNO
                  HAVING   SUM(AMOUNT) > 250);
        IF NUMBER_PENALTIES > 0 THEN
            ROLLBACK WORK;
        ENDIF;
    END
```

32.4

```
CREATE TRIGGER NUMBER_MATCHES_INSERT
    AFTER INSERT OF MATCHES FOR EACH ROW
    BEGIN
        UPDATE    TEAMS
        SET       NUMBER_MATCHES =
                  (SELECT    COUNT(*)
                  FROM       MATCHES
                  WHERE      PLAYERNO = NEW.PLAYERNO)
        WHERE     PLAYERNO = NEW.PLAYERNO
END

CREATE TRIGGER NUMBER_MATCHES_DELETE
    AFTER DELETE, UPDATE OF MATCHES FOR EACH ROW
    BEGIN
        UPDATE    TEAMS
        SET       NUMBER_MATCHES =
                  (SELECT    COUNT(*)
                  FROM       MATCHES
                  WHERE      PLAYERNO = OLD.PLAYERNO)
        WHERE     PLAYERNO = OLD.PLAYERNO
END
```

VI | Object Relational Concepts

In the 1970s, a number of concepts were introduced that had a great influence on many areas of computing. These so-called *object-oriented concepts* (OO concepts) were adopted first by programming languages. They were added to languages such as C and Pascal, and later also to COBOL. For example, C++ was the object-oriented version of C. Languages such as Smalltalk, Java, and C# were object-oriented from the beginning. Later, analysis and design methods, operating systems, and CASE tools were also extended with these OO concepts.

At some stage, it was the databases' turn. An entire group of new databases was introduced, all of them completely based on the OO concepts (see [COOP97]). Initially, these products did not support SQL. If a company were interested in this technology, a heavy and expensive migration of the existing SQL database was required. However, the vendors of relational databases soon realized that there was a need for these OO concepts and decided to add them to their own SQL products. The marriage between OO and relational technology was a fact, and the name became *object relational database*, although you will find other names in the literature as well, such as *universal database*, *extensible database*, and *non-first normal form database*. For extensive descriptions of object relational databases, see [DELO95] and [STON99].

The important database vendors put the first implementations of their object relational products on the market around 1997. In 1998, the SQL3 standard appeared, in which many of these new concepts were included. Unfortunately, what the vendors did varied enormously.

In this section, we deal with what we currently consider object relational concepts, but we start with two remarks. First, within a few years, this term will probably no longer be used. These new concepts will be accepted by then and will no longer be seen as special or exclusive. Future users will not notice that these object relational concepts were added to SQL at a later stage. Second, there is still an ongoing discussion about whether all these concepts stem from the world of object orientation. For some of them, it must be said that they probably do not. However, we do not intend to act as a referee in this book; therefore, we qualify them all with this name.

The features that the SQL products and SQL3 offer differ extensively, and the syntax they use is not completely the same. That is why we have selected a syntax in this chapter that looks like the one supported by several products. However, we do not give syntax definitions because of all the differences between the products and because MySQL does not support these concepts. This part has been added primarily to give you a global idea of how those object relational concepts look within SQL and the effect they have on the SQL statements.

User-Defined Data Types, Functions, and Operators

33.1 Introduction

C hapter 5, "SELECT Statement: Common Elements," described data types as INTE-GER, CHAR, and DATE. These are the so-called base data types and are an integral part of SQL. They offer certain features, and we can apply predefined operations to them. For example, we can perform calculations on values with the INTEGER data type, and we can apply operators such as + and – to them. However, the base data types of SQL are very elementary. Some users need much more complex and specialized data types. In an environment in which geographical data is stored, a data type as a two-dimensional (2D) coordinate, for example, would be very useful. Similarly, the data type color could be useful in a paint factory. Of course, we also need to have the operators for such data type. For the data type 2D coordinate, we would like to have operators as "calculate the distance between two coordinates" and, for color, "mix two colors."

More SQL products allow users to define their own data types with related operators. To make the distinction clear, these are called *user-defined data types*. The SQL products and also the SQL3 standard support user-defined data types.

SQL supports several types of user-defined data types. In this chapter, we describe, among other things, the distinct, the opaque, and the named row types. For each data type, we explain the possibilities of the SQL products in this field and discuss what has been defined in the SQL3 standard. Creating user-defined functions and operators also is explained.

33.2 Creating User-Defined Data Types

User-defined data types must be created, of course. For this, a special CREATE statement exists, just as there exist statements for creating tables, views, and synonyms.

Example 33.1: Create the data types called PAYMENTNO, PLAYERNO, and MONEY-AMOUNT, and use them in the CREATE TABLE statement for the PENALTIES table.

```
CREATE TYPE PAYMENTNO AS INTEGER

CREATE TYPE PLAYERNO AS INTEGER

CREATE TYPE MONEYAMOUNT AS DECIMAL(7,2)

CREATE    TABLE PENALTIES
          (PAYMENTNO    PAYMENTNO NOT NULL PRIMARY KEY,
           PLAYERNO     PLAYERNO,
           PAY_DATE     DATE,
           AMOUNT       MONEYAMOUNT)
```

Explanation: The user-defined data types are used in positions where base data types usually occur. This is always allowed. Wherever a base data types can be used, a user-defined data type can also be used. The example also shows that column names and names of data types can be the same.

User-defined data types have many similarities with base data types. One is that a data type has no population or "contents" (a table does, on the other hand). For example, with INSERT statements, rows are added to a table and the contents are built up. However, INSERT and other statements cannot be executed on a data type. Data types cannot be manipulated in any way. Therefore, we cannot request all possible values of the INTEGER or a user-defined data type by using a SELECT statement. One could say that a data type has a static, virtual content. This virtual content consists of all values that might occur in the underlying data type. Therefore, all numeric values between -9,999,999.99 and 999,999.99 are allowed in the MONEYAMOUNT data type. An SQL data type is, in fact, comparable to a type in Pascal or a class in Java; the data type describes possible values.

From the previous CREATE TYPE statements, it is obvious that a user-defined data type depends upon a base data type. Moreover, user-defined data types can also refer to each other.

Example 33.2: Create the data type SMALL_MONEYAMOUNT.

```
CREATE TYPE SMALL_MONEYAMOUNT AS MONEYAMOUNT
```

Several types of user-defined data types exist. Those created earlier are called distinct data types. A *distinct data type* is directly or indirectly (through another distinct data type) defined upon an existing base data type. In the next sections, the other types are described.

One of the great advantages of working with user-defined data types is that apples cannot be compared to pears. The following SELECT statement was allowed with the original definition of the PENALTIES table, but not any longer:

```
SELECT    *
FROM      PENALTIES
WHERE     PAYMENTNO > AMOUNT
```

This was allowed because both columns were numeric. Now that the AMOUNT column is defined on the data type MONEYAMOUNT, it can be compared only to columns defined on that same data type. This might sound like a restriction but is actually an advantage. The condition in the SELECT statement was an odd question anyhow. In other words, the advantage of working with user-defined data types is that senseless statements are rejected. In the world of programming languages, this is called *strong typing*. Languages such as Algol, Pascal, and Java have supported this concept from the beginning. Note that it is possible to compare values of different data types, but then we have to indicate that clearly. We return to this topic later.

It is also easy to remove data types:

```
DROP TYPE MONEYAMOUNT
```

What happens if a data type is removed while columns are defined on it? The answer to this question is, again, that it depends on the product. Some products allow a data type to be removed only if there are no columns or other user-defined data types defined on it. Other products do allow the removal and replace the user-defined data type of the column with the underlying data type. In other words, the specification of the dropped data type is copied to all the columns with that data type.

In the literature on the relational model, instead of the term *data type*, the term *domain* is used regularly.

Exercise 33.1: Create the data type NUMBER_OF_SETS and use it for the columns WON and LOST of the MATCHES table.

33.3 Access to Data Types

Usually, data types have an owner. The person who creates them is the owner of that data type. Other users can use the data type in their own CREATE TABLE statements, but they must be granted permission explicitly. A special version of the GRANT statement is introduced for granting this privilege.

Example 33.3: Give JIM permission to use the MONEYAMOUNT data type.

```
GRANT    USAGE
ON       TYPE MONEYAMOUNT
TO       JIM
```

Explanation: USAGE is the new form. After this GRANT statement is executed, JIM can define tables with columns based on this new data type.

Note that some products do not use the word USAGE for this; they use the word EXECUTE, just as for stored procedures. The meaning and effect are identical.

Of course, this statement also has a counterpart:

```
REVOKE   USAGE
ON       TYPE MONEYAMOUNT
TO       JIM
```

But what happens when the privilege is revoked after JIM has used the data type in a CREATE TABLE statement? The effect of this statement also depends on the product, but most products employ the following rule: The right to use a data type can be revoked only if the user has not used the data type yet.

33.4　Casting of Values

In Section 33.2, we indicated that the use of user-defined data types involves strong typing, but what if we nevertheless want to compare apples to pears? To this end, we have to change the data type of the values. For this, we use an explicit form of casting, as discussed in Section 5.11, in Chapter 5.

For each new data type, SQL automatically creates two new scalar functions for casting. One function transforms values of the user-defined data type to values of the underlying base data type (this function carries the name of the base data type); the other works the other way around and carries the name of the user-defined data type. These functions are called *destructor* and *constructor*, respectively. For the data type MONEY-AMOUNT, the destructor is called DECIMAL and the constructor MONEYAMOUNT. Note that in object-oriented programming languages, these two terms are used to remove and create objects, respectively.

Example 33.4: Find the payment numbers of the penalties of which the penalty amount is greater than $50.

There are two equivalent formulations for this:

```
SELECT    PAYMENTNO
FROM      PENALTIES
WHERE     AMOUNT > MONEYAMOUNT(50)
```

and

```
SELECT    PAYMENTNO
FROM      PENALTIES
WHERE     DECIMAL(AMOUNT) > 50
```

Explanation: In the first SELECT statement, the value 50 (which is probably a "normal" number for the INTEGER data type) is transformed into a money amount. Then, it can be compared to comparable values in the AMOUNT column. Thus, the constructor MONEYAMOUNT constructs money amounts out of numeric values. The second statement shows that money amounts can be converted into "normal" numbers by using the destructor called DECIMAL. The result of both statements is, of course, the same.

Example 33.5: Find the payment numbers of the penalties of which the player number is greater than the penalty amount.

```
SELECT    PAYMENTNO
FROM      PENALTIES
WHERE     INTEGER(PLAYERNO) > INTEGER(PAYMENTNO)
```

Explanation: Because the PLAYERNO and the PAYMENTNO data types are created on the same base data type, which is INTEGER, they both have a destructor called INTEGER. In other words, now there are two functions with the same name, but they work on different data types. This does not cause any problems within SQL, which can keep the two functions apart because the parameters of the functions are different with respect to their data types. This concept, in which different functions carry the same name, is called *overloading*. The function name INTEGER is overloaded in this example.

Note that to change the data type of a value to compare it to values that have another data type is sometimes called *semantic override*.

Casting of values is also important when you enter new values with INSERT and UPDATE statements. Now that three columns in the PENALTIES table have a user-defined data type, we can no longer put simple numeric values in this column. We are forced to use casting with the INSERT statement now.

Example 33.6: Add a new penalty.

```
INSERT INTO PENALTIES (PAYMENTNO, PLAYERNO, PAY_DATE,
                       AMOUNT)
VALUES                (PAYMENTNO(12), PLAYERNO(6),
                       '1980-12-08', MONEYAMOUNT(100.00))
```

33.5 Creating User-Defined Operators

Just as in any programming language, SQL supports operators such as +, −, *, and /. We described them in Chapter 5. A few general remarks about these operators:

■ In theory, these operators are not required. For operators such as + and *, the functions ADD_UP and MULTIPLY could have been created. These operators have been added, however, to make things easier.

■ As stated, every base data type has a number of possible operations. For example, with the numeric data types, we can employ operations such as add, multiply, and subtract so that we can add a couple of months to the date data type and create a new date.

■ Overloading of functions is described in Section 33.4. Overloading of operators also exists: Whether we use the + for two numbers or for two alphanumeric values leads to completely different results. Depending on the data types of the values, the two numbers are added or the alphanumeric values are concatenated.

Some SQL products allow operators to be created for user-defined data types. In principle, these are the operations that apply to the underlying data type, but we can also define our own operations. SQL products enable you to do this only for scalar functions.

Let us continue with the discussion of the data type MONEYAMOUNT. Imagine that there are two columns, AMOUNT1 and AMOUNT2, that are both defined on this data type MONEYAMOUNT and that we want to add up. Because MONEYAMOUNT is not a normal numeric value, we cannot use the operators + and −. The following expression would no longer be allowed:

```
AMOUNT1 + AMOUNT2
```

This must now be done with the following expression:

```
DECIMAL(AMOUNT1) + DECIMAL(AMOUNT2)
```

We can solve this more elegantly by also defining the + symbol for values of the MONEYAMOUNT data type.

```
CREATE FUNCTION "+" (MONEYAMOUNT, MONEYAMOUNT)
    RETURNS MONEYAMOUNT
    SOURCE "+" (DECIMAL(), DECIMAL())
```

Explanation: The + operator is defined once again, and again it is overloaded. It makes the expression AMOUNT1 + AMOUNT2 legal.

Imagine that the data type COLOR and the function MIX (to mix two colors) have been defined. Next, the + operator can be created, for example, as an operator to mix two colors.

```
CREATE FUNCTION "+" (COLOR, COLOR)
    RETURNS COLOR
    SOURCE MIX (COLOR, COLOR)
```

The capability to define user-defined operators does not increase the functionality of SQL, but it makes it easier to formulate certain statements.

33.6 Opaque Data Type

A distinct data type is based on one base data type and inherits all the features of that base data type. In addition, some products enable you to define completely new data types that are not dependent on a base data type. These are called *opaque data types*. *Opaque* means "nontransparent." You could say that an opaque data type is a user-defined base data type.

Opaque data types are required when it is too complex to define them with the help of a base data type. For example, if we want to define the data type 2D coordinate, we must store two numbers somehow: the X and the Y coordinates. This does not work if we use only base data types. However, we can do it with opaque data types, as shown by the next example.

Example 33.7: Create the data type TWODIM to store two-dimensional coordinates.

```
CREATE TYPE TWODIM
       (INTERNALLENGTH = 4)
```

Explanation: What is clearly noticeable is that there is indeed *no* base data type used in the CREATE TYPE statement. The only thing that is registered is how much space one value of this type will occupy on disk—namely, 4 bytes, which has been selected because, for the sake of convenience, we assume that a coordinate consists of two whole numbers.

However, before this new data type can be used in a CREATE TABLE statement, we have to define a number of functions. We must create, for example, a function that converts a value, entered by the user, to something that is stored on hard disk and a function that works the other way around. This is not required for base data types. If we use the CHAR data type, we assume that these functions already exist. Now, we must create them ourselves. We do not go more deeply into this topic because it depends strongly on the product. We simply note that, in addition to the required functions, other functions can be defined to increase the functionality. In most cases, these are external functions.

33.7 Named Row Data Type

The third user-defined data type is the *named row data type*. With it, we can group values logically belonging to each other as one unit. For example, all values belonging to an address are grouped.

Example 33.8: Create the named row data type called ADDRESS and use it in a CREATE TABLE statement.

```
CREATE    TYPE ADDRESS AS
          (STREET      CHAR(15) NOT NULL,
           HOUSENO     CHAR(4),
           POSTCODE    CHAR(6),
           TOWN        CHAR(10) NOT NULL)

CREATE    TABLE PLAYERS
          (PLAYERNO    INTEGER PRIMARY KEY,
           NAME        CHAR(15),
           :           :
           RESIDENCE   ADDRESS,
           PHONENO     CHAR(13),
           LEAGUENO    CHAR(4))
```

Explanation: Instead of having to define four columns in the CREATE TABLE statement, only one will do: RESIDENCE. That means that in one row in the column RESIDENCE, not one value, but a row with four values, is stored. This row of four values has a name (or, in other words, is named) of ADDRESS, which explains the term named row. The column RESIDENCE is a *composite column*. For each column belonging to a named row data type, a NOT NULL specification can be included.

Of course, you can use a data type several times in the same CREATE TABLE statement, for example:

```
CREATE   TABLE PLAYERS
         (PLAYERNO            INTEGER PRIMARY KEY,
          :                   :
          RESIDENCE           ADDRESS,
          MAILING_ADDRESS     ADDRESS,
          HOLIDAY_ADDRESS     ADDRESS,
          PHONENO             CHAR(13),
          LEAGUENO            CHAR(4))
```

Working with composite columns affects the formulations of SELECT and other statements. We illustrate this with some examples.

Example 33.9: Get the numbers and complete addresses of the players resident in Stratford.

```
SELECT   PLAYERNO, RESIDENCE
FROM     PLAYERS
WHERE    RESIDENCE.TOWN = 'Stratford'
```

The result is:

PLAYERNO	STREET	HOUSENO	POSTCODE	TOWN
6	Haseltine Lane	80	1234KK	Stratford
83	Magdalene Road	16A	1812UP	Stratford
2	Stoney Road	43	3575NH	Stratford
7	Edgecombe Way	39	9758VB	Stratford
57	Edgecombe Way	16	4377CB	Stratford
39	Eaton Square	78	9629CD	Stratford
100	Haseltine Lane	80	1234KK	Stratford

<============== RESIDENCE ============>

Explanation: In the SELECT clause, only one column has to be specified instead of four. Obviously, the result consists of five columns. The notation RESIDENCE.TOWN is new. This *point notation* indicates that only a part of the address is requested.

Example 33.10: Get the numbers of the players living at the same address as player 6.

```
SELECT    OTHERS.PLAYERNO
FROM      PLAYERS AS P6,  PLAYERS AS OTHERS
WHERE     P6.RESIDENCE = OTHERS.RESIDENCE
AND       P6.PLAYERNO = 6
```

Explanation: Instead of a join condition on four columns (STREET, HOUSENO, TOWN, and POSTCODE), one simple join condition, in which the composite column is used, is sufficient.

Casting of values is also important with named row data types. We give you an example of a SELECT and an INSERT statement.

Example 33.11: Get the number and name of the player living at the address 39 Edgecombe Way, Stratford, with postcode 9758VB.

```
SELECT    PLAYERNO, NAME
FROM      PLAYERS
WHERE     RESIDENCE =
          ADDRESS('Edgecombe Way', 39, '9758VB',
                  'Stratford')
```

Explanation: In this example, we can see clearly how the four values are cast into one ADDRESS value so that they can be compared with the column RESIDENCE.

Example 33.12: Enter a new player.

```
INSERT INTO PLAYERS
        (PLAYERNO, NAME, ..., ADDRESS, PHONENO, LEAGUENO)
VALUES (6, 'Parmenter', ...,
        ADDRESS('Haseltine Lane', 80, '1234KK',
                'Stratford'), '070-476537', 8467)
```

Named row data types are usually defined on base and distinct data types, but they can also be "nested." An example is given next. First, the data type POSTCODE is defined, consisting of two components: a part of four digits and a part of two letters. Next, this new named row data type is used in the definition of the ADDRESS data type.

```
CREATE    TYPE POSTCODE AS
          (DIGITS      CHAR(4),
          LETTERS      CHAR(2))

CREATE    TYPE ADDRESS AS
          (STREET      CHAR(15) NOT NULL,
          HOUSENO      CHAR(4),
          POSTCODE     POSTCODE,
          TOWN         CHAR(10) NOT NULL)
```

Example 33.13: Get the numbers and the full addresses of the players resident in post-code area 2501.

```
SELECT    PLAYERNO, RESIDENCE
FROM      PLAYERS
WHERE     RESIDENCE.POSTCODE.DIGITS = '2501'
```

Example 33.14: Get the numbers and complete addresses of the players with postcode 1234KK.

```
SELECT    PLAYERNO, RESIDENCE
FROM      PLAYERS
WHERE     RESIDENCE.POSTCODE = POSTCODE('1234', 'KK')
```

Explanation: In the condition, two values are grouped into one value with a POSTCODE data type. A casting function is used for this.

In addition to the named row data type, some SQL products support the *unnamed row data type*. This data type also puts values together, but this group does not get a separate name.

```
CREATE     TABLE PLAYERS
           (PLAYERNO      INTEGER PRIMARY KEY,
           NAME           CHAR(15),
           :              :
           RESIDENCE      ROW (STREET      CHAR(15) NOT NULL,
                               HOUSENO     CHAR(4),
                               POSTCODE    CHAR(6),
                               TOWN        CHAR(10) NOT NULL),
           PHONENO        CHAR(13),
           LEAGUENO       CHAR(4))
```

Explanation: We can see that the four values are grouped together here. However, no data type is defined explicitly. The effect of an unnamed row data type on SELECT and other statements is the same as that of the named row data type. The difference, however, is that the specification cannot be reused in several places. If there is also a MAILING_ADDRESS column, we must define the four subcolumns once again.

For casting of values, the word ROW is used:

```
INSERT INTO PLAYERS
       (PLAYERNO, NAME, ..., ADDRESS, PHONENO, LEAGUENO)
VALUES (6, 'Parmenter', ...,
        ROW('Haseltine Lane', 80, '1234KK', 'Stratford'),
        '070-476537', 8467)
```

Exercise 33.2: What is wrong in the following SELECT statement? (We assume that the situation is the same as in Example 33.14.)

```
SELECT     RESIDENCE
FROM       PLAYERS
WHERE      RESIDENCE LIKE '12%'
```

Exercise 33.3: Create the data type RESULT, consisting of two columns called WON and LOST, and use this new data type at the MATCHES table.

33.8 The Typed Table

So far, we have used the named row data type only to specify columns, but this data type can also be used to assign a data type to a table. The result is that it is no longer necessary to specify the columns and their data types explicitly; instead, the columns of the named row data type must form the columns of the table.

Example 33.15: Create a type for the PLAYERS table.

```
CREATE    TYPE T_PLAYERS AS
          (PLAYERNO      INTEGER NOT NULL,
          NAME          CHAR(15) NOT NULL,
          INITIALS      CHAR(3) NOT NULL,
          BIRTH_DATE    DATE,
          SEX           CHAR(1) NOT NULL,
          JOINED        SMALLINT NOT NULL,
          STREET        CHAR(15) NOT NULL,
          HOUSENO       CHAR(4),
          POSTCODE      CHAR(6),
          TOWN          CHAR(10) NOT NULL,
          PHONENO       CHAR(13),
          LEAGUENO      CHAR(4))

CREATE    TABLE PLAYERS OF T_PLAYERS
          (PRIMARY KEY PLAYERNO)
```

Explanation: With the specification OF T_PLAYERS in the CREATE TABLE statement, we indicate that all the columns of the PLAYERS table are of that data type. Nevertheless, certain constraints must still be specified, and that explains the specification of the primary key. The NOT NULL integrity constraint is the only rule that can be included within the CREATE TYPE statement. A table that is defined in this way is called a *typed table*. Whether a table is typed or nontyped has no impact on SELECT and update statements.

The advantage of typed tables is that tables with the same structure can be defined in a very simple way. Imagine that there is another PLAYERS table consisting of players who used to be members of the tennis club. This table probably has the same columns, so it should now be easy to create the table:

```
CREATE    TABLE OLD_PLAYERS OF T_PLAYERS
          (PRIMARY KEY PLAYERNO)
```

33.9   Integrity Constraints on Data Types

Some SQL products enable you to specify integrity constraints on a data type. These integrity constraints restrict the permitted values of the data type and, thus, the populations of the columns defined on that data type.

Example 33.16: Define the data type NUMBER_OF_SETS and specify that only the values 1, 2, and 3 are legal.

```
CREATE    TYPE NUBER_OF_SETS AS SMALLINT
          CHECK (VALUE IN (0, 1, 2, 3))

CREATE    TABLE MATCHES
          (MATCHNO      INTEGER PRIMARY KEY,
           TEAMNO       INTEGER NOT NULL,
           PLAYERNO     INTEGER NOT NULL,
           WON          NUMBER_OF_SETS NOT NULL,
           LOST         NUMBER_OF_SETS NOT NULL)
```

Explanation: In the CREATE TYPE statement, a check integrity constraint is specified. This constraint indicates, with a condition, the legal values. Values are legal when they satisfy the condition. The reserved word VALUE stands for a possible value of that specific data type. Any simple condition can be used here, which means that comparison operators AND, OR, NOT, BETWEEN, IN, LIKE, and IS NULL all can be used. Subqueries are not allowed, however.

Now the advantage is that if the integrity constraint for NUMBER_OF_SETS changes, this has to be carried out only in one place.

Example 33.17: Change the data type NUMBER_OF_SETS so that the value 4 is also permitted.

```
ALTER    TYPE NUMBER_OF_SETS AS SMALLINT
         CHECK (VALUE BETWEEN 0 AND 4)
```

When a condition is changed, a problem could arise if we make the condition more restrictive. Imagine that NUMBER_OF_SETS is defined as only the values 0, 1, and 2. What happens if the columns defined on this data type already have a value that is beyond this range? Products solve this by not allowing such a change of the data type to occur. First, the columns must be adjusted.

33.10 Keys and Indexes

Primary keys, foreign keys, and indexes can be created on columns with user-defined data types. For the named row data types, they can be defined on the full value or on a part of it.

Example 33.18: Define an index on the column RESIDENCE in the PLAYERS table.

```
CREATE INDEX I_RESIDENCE
    ON PLAYERS(RESIDENCE)
```

Example 33.19: Define an index on only the POSTCODE part of the column RESIDENCE in the PLAYERS table.

```
CREATE INDEX I_RESIDENCE
    ON PLAYERS(RESIDENCE.POSTCODE)
```

The only exception is when indexes on opaque data types must be defined. Each product offers very different features here.

33.11 Answers

33.1

```
CREATE TYPE NUMBER_OF_SETS AS TINYINT

CREATE TABLE MATCHES
       ( MATCHNO      INTEGER NOT NULL PRIMARY KEY,
         TEAMNO       INTEGER NOT NULL,
         PLAYERNO     INTEGER NOT NULL,
         WON          NUMBER_OF_SETS NOT NULL,
         LOST         NUMBER_OF_SETS NOT NULL)
```

33.2 The FROM clause of the statement is correct, but the WHERE clause is not. The LIKE operator cannot be executed on the compound column just like that. A correct alternative is:

```
SELECT    RESIDENCE
FROM      PLAYERS
WHERE     RESIDENCE.POSTCODE LIKE '12%'
```

33.3

```
CREATE TYPE RESULT AS
     ( WON      NUMBER_OF_SETS,
       LOST     NUMBER_OF_SETS)

CREATE TABLE MATCHES
     ( MATCHNO     INTEGER NOT NULL PRIMARY KEY,
       TEAMNO      INTEGER NOT NULL,
       PLAYERNO    INTEGER NOT NULL,
       RESULT      RESULT NOT NULL)
```

Inheritance, References, and Collections

Inheritance of Data Types

I n the introduction of this part, we mentioned that not all object-relational concepts are considered to be object-oriented. The concepts that we discuss in this chapter are definitely object-oriented: inheritance, references or row identifications, and collections.

The most important OO concept is *inheritance*. Most specialists also find it the most appealing concept. With inheritance of data types, one data type inherits all the properties of another data type and can contain a few additional properties itself. By "properties," we mean, for example, the columns the data type consists of or the functions defined on that data type.

Example 34.1: Define the named row data types ADDRESS and FOREIGN_ADDRESS.

```
CREATE    TYPE ADDRESS AS
          (STREET      CHAR(15) NOT NULL,
           HOUSENO     CHAR(4),
           POSTCODE    POSTCODE,
           TOWN        CHAR(10) NOT NULL)

CREATE    TYPE FOREIGN_ADDRESS AS
          (COUNTRY     CHAR(20) NOT NULL) UNDER ADDRESS
```

Explanation: The data type ADDRESS contains four columns, and the data type FOR-EIGN_ADDRESS contains five. The data type FOREIGN_ADDRESS is now a so-called *sub*-type of ADDRESS, and ADDRESS is a *super*type of FOREIGN_ADDRESS. Actually, each foreign address is an address, but not all addresses are foreign addresses.

Next, we define a table for which we use the subtype:

```
CREATE    TABLE PLAYERS
          (PLAYERNO            INTEGER PRIMARY KEY,
          :                    :
          RESIDENCE            ADDRESS,
          HOLIDAY_ADDRESS      FOREIGN_ADDRESS,
          PHONENO              CHAR(13),
          LEAGUENO             CHAR(4))
```

The following example shows the effect of working with subtypes on the SELECT statement.

Example 34.2: Get the player number, the town, and the country of the holiday address of each player whose town begins with the capital letter *J* and for whom the digit part of the postcode of the holiday address is unknown.

```
SELECT    PLAYERNO, HOLIDAY_ADDRESS.TOWN,
          HOLIDAY_ADDRESS.COUNTRY
FROM      PLAYERS
WHERE     RESIDENCE.TOWN LIKE 'J%'
AND       HOLIDAY_ADDRESS.POSTCODE.DIGITS IS NULL
```

Explanation: In the SELECT clause, the TOWN column of the HOLIDAY_ADDRESS is requested. This column is not explicitly defined in the FOREIGN_ADDRESS data type. SQL realizes with such a query that if the column requested is not available, it must look for it in the supertype. In this case, that is ADDRESS, which does have a column called TOWN. The COUNTRY column is also requested. The WHERE clause contains two conditions. The first is a form that we have seen before. With the second condition, the POST-CODE value of the HOLIDAY_ADDRESS is requested first (inherited of the supertype ADDRESS), and then the digit part of the postcode is asked for.

Functions that have been defined for a specific data type can also be used to manipulate values of a subtype of that data type. Imagine that the function POPULATION has a whole number as the output parameter, representing the number of residents of that town. The input parameter is a value of the data type ADDRESS. Because FOREIGN_ADDRESS inherits everything from the data type ADDRESS, we can also use a foreign address as input.

Example 34.3: Get the player number of each player who is on holiday in a town with a population of more than a million.

```
SELECT    PLAYERNO
FROM      PLAYERS
WHERE     POPULATION(HOLIDAY_ADDRESS) > 1000000
```

34.2 Linking Tables via Row Identifications

In OO databases, all the rows (or their equivalents) have a unique identification. The user does not generate this identification with, for example, an INSERT statement, but it is instead generated by the system itself. These identifications are often called *row identifications*, *object identifiers*, or *surrogate keys*. These unique row identifications can be used to link rows and to have rows refer to each other.

SQL also has adopted this concept. Here, a unique identification is assigned to each row. The row identifications are of no value to the users, but only to the system itself. Although they can be requested and printed, they bear no information. If a row receives an identification, it belongs to that row forever. If the row is removed, the matching identification will never be reused. Note that unique row identifications are not the same as primary keys (even though they do show a resemblance). Later in this chapter, we explain the differences.

Row identifications are stored together with the row, but it is not necessary to define columns for them explicitly. These column values are generated automatically. One could say that each table has a hidden column in which the row identifications are stored.

The row identification (or the value of the hidden column) can be requested with the REF function.

Example 34.4: Get the Row Identification of the Player with number 6.

```
SELECT    REF(PLAYERS)
FROM      PLAYERS
WHERE     PLAYERNO = 6
```

The result is:

```
REF(PLAYERS)
--------------------------------------------------
000028020915A58C5FAEC1502EE034080009D0DADE15538856
```

Explanation: The REF function has the name of a table as its only parameter and returns the row identification. How row identifications actually look (on disk) depends on the product. As an example, a possible Oracle row identification is displayed.

As said, row identifications can be used to "link" rows. The identification of one row is stored within another row. In other words, one row refers or points to another.

Example 34.5: Define the tables of the tennis club again, but use row identifications this time.

```
CREATE    TABLE PLAYERS
          (PLAYERNO     INTEGER PRIMARY KEY,
          NAME          CHAR(15) NOT NULL,
          :             :
          LEAGUENO      CHAR(4))

CREATE    TABLE TEAMS
          (TEAMNO       INTEGER PRIMARY KEY,
          PLAYER        REF(PLAYERS) NOT NULL,
          DIVISION      CHAR(6) NOT NULL)

CREATE    TABLE MATCHES
          (MATCHNO      INTEGER PRIMARY KEY,
          TEAM          REF(TEAMS) NOT NULL,
          PLAYER        REF(PLAYERS) NOT NULL,
          WON           SMALLINT NOT NULL,
          LOST          SMALLINT NOT NULL)

CREATE    TABLE PENALTIES
          (PAYMENTNO    INTEGER PRIMARY KEY,
          PLAYER        REF(PLAYERS) NOT NULL,
          PAY_DATE      DATE NOT NULL,
          AMOUNT        DECIMAL(7,2) NOT NULL)

CREATE    TABLE COMMITTEE_MEMBERS
          (PLAYER       REF(PLAYERS) PRIMARY KEY,
          BEGIN_DATE    DATE NOT NULL,
          END_DATE      DATE,
          POSITION      CHAR(20))
```

Explanation: Wherever a foreign key occurred, a column is now specified that points to another table. These are called *reference columns*. The link that is created between, for example, the PLAYERS and TEAMS tables could now be represented as in Figure 34.1.

Figure 34.1 *Reference columns*

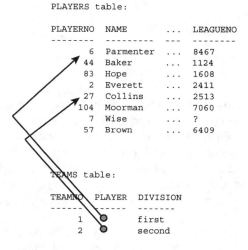

```
PLAYERS table:

PLAYERNO  NAME          ...   LEAGUENO
--------  ---------     ---   --------
       6  Parmenter     ...   8467
      44  Baker         ...   1124
      83  Hope          ...   1608
       2  Everett       ...   2411
      27  Collins       ...   2513
     104  Moorman       ...   7060
       7  Wise          ...   ?
      57  Brown         ...   6409


TEAMS table:

TEAMNO  PLAYER  DIVISION
------  ------  --------
     1          first
     2          second
```

Reference columns must be filled with row identifications. The INSERT and UPDATE statements have been extended for this purpose.

Example 34.6: Add a new team. The captain of this team is player 112.

```
INSERT   INTO TEAMS (TEAMNO, PLAYER, DIVISION)
VALUES   (3, (SELECT REF(PLAYERS)
             FROM   PLAYERS
             WHERE  PLAYERNO = 112), 'first')
```

Explanation: The SELECT statement retrieves the row identification of player 6 and then stores it in the PLAYER column.

Example 34.7: The captain of team 1 is no longer player 6, but player 44.

```
UPDATE   TEAMS
SET      PLAYER = (SELECT REF(PLAYERS)
                   FROM   PLAYERS
                   WHERE  PLAYERNO = 44)
WHERE    TEAMNO = 1
```

The linking of tables with row identifications has a great influence on the way in which joins can be formulated. It becomes much easier to formulate most joins.

Example 34.8: Find, for each team, the team number and the name of the captain.

```
SELECT    TEAMNO, PLAYER.NAME
FROM      TEAMS
```

Explanation: For each row in the TEAMS table, two values are printed: the value of the TEAMNO column and the value of the expression PLAYER.NAME. This is an expression that we have not discussed yet. Let us deal with it in more detail.

For the sake of convenience, we call this a *reference expression*. A reference expression always begins with a reference column. In this case, it is the column PLAYER. This column refers to the PLAYERS table. After the reference column is the NAME column from that table. The final result is that the name of the player, who is the captain of the team, is printed.

It looks as if this statement does not execute a join at all, but the join is hidden in the reference expression PLAYER.NAME. For each team, SQL finds the row identification of the player (the captain). This identification is stored in the column PLAYER. Next, SQL looks for the row with this identification in the hidden column of the PLAYERS table. If it is found, the value in the NAME column is retrieved. In other words, this statement does not specify a classical join indeed. Behind the scenes, the previous SELECT statement is converted to the following:

```
SELECT    TEAMS.TEAMNO, PLAYERS.NAME
FROM      TEAMS, PLAYERS
WHERE     TEAMS.PLAYER = REF(PLAYERS)
```

First, the table to which the PLAYER column refers is added to the FROM clause. Then, a join condition is added to the statement. In this join condition, TEAMS.PLAYER is compared to the REF of the table to which the column refers.

Two aspects should be taken into account. First, a reference column can contain a NULL value, of course. In that case, no join will be executed on the other table, and the value of the reference expression is then NULL. Second, the reference column can contain a row identification that does not occur in the other table. Imagine that the row identification in the PLAYER column of the TEAMS table does not occur in the PLAYERS table. In that case, that team would not occur in the result when an inner join is executed. However, for this type of expression, an outer join is always executed. So actually, the previous statement is not executed, but the following one is:

```
SELECT    TEAMS.TEAMNO, PLAYERS.NAME
FROM      TEAMS LEFT OUTER JOIN PLAYERS
          ON (TEAMS.PLAYER = REF(PLAYERS))
```

Example 34.9: For each match played by someone from Eltham and for a team from the first division, find the match number, the name of the player, and the name of the captain of the team.

```
SELECT   MATCHNO, PLAYER.NAME, TEAM.PLAYER.NAME
FROM     MATCHES
WHERE    PLAYER.TOWN = 'Eltham'
AND      TEAM.DIVISION = 'first'
```

Explanation: The statement contains three reference expressions: PLAYER.NAME, TEAM.PLAYER.NAME, and PLAYER.TOWN. The first and last have well-known forms, a reference column followed by a "normal" column. However, the second expression has a new form. Here, the reference column TEAM is followed by another reference column, PLAYER, which is followed by NAME. This expression must be read as: Get, for each row concerned, the NAME of the PLAYER who is captain of the TEAM. In fact, this reference expression replaces a join specification of the MATCHES table by that of TEAMS first and then that of PLAYERS.

No restriction governs the length of reference expressions. The only restriction is that the last column cannot be a reference column.

Example 34.10: Create two tables with employee and department data.

```
CREATE   TABLE EMPLOYEES
         (EMPLOYEENO   INTEGER PRIMARY KEY,
         NAME          CHAR(15) NOT NULL,
         DEPARTMENT    REF(DEPARTMENTS))

CREATE   TABLE DEPARTMENTS
         (DEPARTMENTNO INTEGER PRIMARY KEY,
         NAME          CHAR(15) NOT NULL,
         BOSS          REF(EMPLOYEES))
```

The following statement is now valid:

```
SELECT   DEPARTMENTNO, BOSS.DEPARTMENT.BOSS.NAME
FROM     DEPARTMENTS
```

Explanation: For each department, we want to know the name of the boss of the department and where the boss of each department works.

Reference columns can also refer to the table of which they are a part.

Example 34.11: Create the PLAYERS table with the new columns FATHER and MOTHER. These two columns are used if the father and mother are also members of the tennis club.

```
CREATE    TABLE PLAYERS
          (PLAYERNO     INTEGER PRIMARY KEY,
          NAME          CHAR(15) NOT NULL,
          FATHER        REF(PLAYERS),
          MOTHER        REF(PLAYERS),
          :             :
          LEAGUENO      CHAR(4))
```

Example 34.12: For each player whose mother also plays for the tennis club, get the player number and the name of the father.

```
SELECT    PLAYERNO, FATHER.NAME
FROM      PLAYERS
WHERE     MOTHER IS NOT NULL
```

Example 34.13: Get the player number of each player whose grandfather also plays for the tennis club.

```
SELECT    PLAYERNO
FROM      PLAYERS
WHERE     MOTHER.FATHER IS NOT NULL
OR        FATHER.FATHER IS NOT NULL
```

Using references has a number of advantages.

- **Advantage 1:** It is not possible to make mistakes when assigning a data type to a foreign key. The data type of a foreign key must always be equal to that of the primary key. This cannot go wrong because for a reference column, only the table name is specified.
- **Advantage 2:** Some primary keys are very wide with regard to the number of columns and the number of bytes. The effect is that the foreign keys (that refer to it) are also wide and take up a lot of storage space. When you work with reference columns, only the row identification is stored. This could be smaller and, thus, saves storage space.

- **Advantage 3:** Primary keys can be changed. If that happens, the foreign keys should also be adjusted; see Chapter 16, "Specifying Integrity Constraints." This slows the update, of course. However, this does not apply to references because, first, the row identifications (the hidden columns) cannot be changed. Second, there will never be additional changes in the other tables as a result of this. When you want to change one value in the primary key, you can change only that value.
- Certain SELECT statements become easier to formulate; see Examples 34.8 and 34.9.

However, the use of references also has a number of disadvantages:

- **Disadvantage 1:** Certain update statements become more difficult to formulate; see Examples 34.6 and 34.7.
- **Disadvantage 2:** With respect to linking tables, the reference offers only one-way traffic. It is now easy to retrieve data about players for each match, but not the other way round. We illustrate this with an example.

Example 34.14: For each player, find the number and the numbers of his or her matches.

```
SELECT    P.PLAYERNO, M.MATCHNO
FROM      PLAYERS AS P, MATCHES AS M
WHERE     REF(P) = M.PLAYER
```

- **Disadvantage 3:** Designing databases also becomes more difficult. Initially, there was only one method to define relationships between two tables, but now there are two. The question is, then, which of the two should you use, and when? And must you use the same method everywhere, or does it depend on the situation? If you do not use the same method everywhere, users will have to pay close attention when they formulate their SQL statements. The following always applies with respect to database design: The more choices, the more difficult database design becomes.
- **Disadvantage 4:** A reference column is not the same as a foreign key. The population of a foreign key is always a subset of that of a primary key, but this does not apply to reference columns. For example, if a player is removed from the PLAY-ERS table, the row identifications occurring in the other tables are not removed as well. The impact is that the MATCHES table will contain so-called *dangling references*. Therefore, reference columns cannot enforce the integrity of data in the way foreign keys can.

34.3   Collections

In this book, we have assumed that a column contains only one value for each row. In this section, we introduce a new concept, the *cell*. A cell is the intersection of a column and a row. So far, we have assumed that a cell can contain only one value. Of course, it is possible to store multiple values in a cell, such as a complete address consisting of a street name, house number, postcode, and so on, separated by commas. We interpret this value as if it consists of several values. SQL, on the other hand, still considers this value as one atomic value.

However, this changes with the adoption of OO concepts into SQL. Now, you can store sets of values in a cell, and SQL will truly regard this set as a set, not as one atomic value. Such a set is called a *collection*. With a collection, you could, for example, record for one player any number of phone numbers in the column PHONES.

Example 34.15: Define the PLAYERS table so that a set of phone numbers can be stored.

```
CREATE     TABLE PLAYERS
           (PLAYERNO     INTEGER PRIMARY KEY,
            :            :
            PHONES       SETOF(CHAR(13)),
            LEAGUENO     CHAR(4))
```

Explanation: The term SETOF indicates that a set of value can be stored within the column PHONES. The table itself could look as follows. (Just as in the set theory, brackets are used to indicate a set.) It is obvious that some players have two and some even have three phone numbers.

PLAYERNO	...	TOWN	PHONES	LEAGUENO
6	...	Stratford	{070-476537, 070-478888}	8467
44	...	Inglewood	{070-368753}	1124
83	...	Stratford	{070-353548, 070-235634, 079-344757}	1608
2	...	Stratford	{070-237893, 020-753756}	2411
27	...	Eltham	{079-234857}	2513
104	...	Eltham	{079-987571}	7060
7	...	Stratford	{070-347689}	?
57	...	Stratford	{070-473458}	6409
39	...	Stratford	{070-393435}	?
112	...	Plymouth	{010-548745, 010-256756, 015-357347}	1319

```
  8 ... Inglewood  {070-458458}                           2983
100 ... Stratford  {070-494593}                           6524
 28 ... Midhurst   {071-659599}                              ?
 95 ... Douglas    {070-867564, 055-358458}                  ?
```

Of course, the use of collections in tables affects the other SQL statements. Here are some examples of how data can be entered in this specific column and how it can be queried with the SELECT statement.

Example 34.16: Add a new player with two phone numbers.

```
INSERT   INTO PLAYERS (PLAYERNO, ... , PHONES, ...)
VALUES   (213, ..., {'071-475748', '071-198937'}, ...)
```

Explanation: The brackets specify the set of phone numbers. Within the brackets, you are allowed to include zero, one, or more values. Zero can be used when this player has no phone.

Example 34.17: Assign player 44 a new phone number.

```
UPDATE   PLAYERS
SET      PHONES = {'070-658347'}
WHERE    PLAYERNO = 44
```

Example 34.18: Get the numbers of the players who can be reached at the phone number 070-476537.

```
SELECT   PLAYERNO
FROM     PLAYERS
WHERE    '070-476537' IN (PHONES)
```

The result is:

```
PLAYERNO
--------
       6
```

Explanation: In this SELECT statement, a new form of the IN operator is used. Usually, a list of literals or expressions (see Section 8.6) or a subquery (see Section 8.7) is specified after the IN operator. What is given between brackets represents a set of values for both forms. The same applies to this new form because the column PHONES also represents a set of values. This form of the IN operator can be used only for collections, not for other columns.

Example 34.19: Get the numbers of the players who have more than two telephone numbers.

```
SELECT    PLAYERNO
FROM      PLAYERS
WHERE     CARDINALITY(PHONES) > 2
```

The result is:

```
PLAYERNO
--------
      83
     112
```

Explanation: To determine the number of values in a collection, the CARDINALITY function can be used. When the number of values is determined, the NULL values are not counted and duplicate values count as one.

The statement could have been defined as follows:

```
SELECT    PLAYERNO
FROM      PLAYERS
WHERE     2 < (SELECT COUNT(*) FROM TABLE(PLAYERS.PHONES))
```

Explanation: The statement looks like an ordinary statement, except that the FROM clause in the subquery contains a new construct: TABLE(PHONES). This construct transforms the set in a table (consisting of one column) into a number of rows. The number of rows is, of course, equal to the number of values in the collection. For each player, there will be another table.

The reason this more complex solution has been added is that it offers more features than that with the CARDINALITY function.

Example 34.20: Get the numbers of the players with the largest set of phone numbers.

```
SELECT    PLAYERNO
FROM      PLAYERS
WHERE     CARDINALITY(PHONES) >= ALL
          (SELECT   CARDINALITY(PHONES)
          FROM      PLAYERS)
```

The result is:

```
PLAYERNO
--------
      83
     112
```

Example 34.21: Find the numbers of the players who have the same set of phone numbers as player 6.

```
SELECT    PLAYERNO
FROM      PLAYERS
WHERE     PHONES =
          (SELECT   PHONES
          FROM      PLAYERS
          WHERE     PLAYERNO = 6)
```

Explanation: The statement is obvious. You can also use > and < instead of the comparison operator =. If we would use the comparison operator >, the statement would answer the question: Who has at least the same telephone numbers as player 6? However, this person can have multiple phone numbers. Less than means: Who has at least one phone number that player 6 also has?

Example 34.22: Get a list of all phone numbers from the PLAYERS table. The list should be presented in ascending order.

Unfortunately, this question is not as simple as it seems. The following statement, for example, is not correct. The column PHONES does not return one set of values that can be ordered but returns a set consisting of sets.

```
SELECT    PHONES
FROM      PLAYERS
ORDER BY  1
```

First, this column must be "flattened," as it is called.

```
SELECT    PS.PHONES
FROM      THE (SELECT PHONES
                 FROM    PLAYERS) AS PS
ORDER BY  1
```

Explanation: In Section 10.7, in Chapter 10, "SELECT Statement: The GROUP BY Clause," we stated that the FROM clause can contain a subquery. We will make use of that feature again, but now we put the word THE in front of it. The effect is that the result of the subquery, consisting of a set with sets, is transformed into one set consisting of atomic values. Thus, the set is flattened.

The result of the subquery itself can be represented as follows:

```
PHONES
------------------------------------
{070-476537, 070-478888}
{070-368753}
{070-353548, 070-235634, 079-344757}
{070-237893, 020-753756}
{079-234857}
{079-987571}
{070-347689}
{070-473458}
{070-393435}
{010-548745, 010-256756, 015-357347}
{070-458458}
{070-494593}
{071-659599}
{070-867564, 055-358458}
```

The result after THE operator has been used looks as follows:

```
PHONES
----------
070-476537
070-478888
070-368753
070-353548
070-235634
079-344757
070-237893
020-753756
079-234857
079-987571
070-347689
070-473458
070-393435
010-548745
010-256756
015-357347
070-458458
070-494593
071-659599
070-867564
055-358458
```

Now it is a "normal" table again, consisting of one column with a set of values. This result table is called PS in the FROM clause. We ask for this column in the SELECT statement, and the values are ordered in the ORDER BY clause.

Flattening of collections offers several possibilities, as illustrated in the following examples.

Example 34.23: Get the number of phone numbers of players 6 and 44 all together.

```
SELECT    COUNT(DISTINCT PS.PHONES)
FROM      THE (SELECT  PHONES
               FROM     PLAYERS
               WHERE    PLAYERNO IN (6, 44)) AS PS
```

Explanation: The subquery itself returns two sets of phone numbers: one for player 6 and one for player 44. The THE operator flattens the two sets to one set of rows, each consisting of one atomic value. With this operator, nonduplicate values are removed automatically. That is why we use DISTINCT in the COUNT function.

Example 34.24: Get the phone numbers that player 6 and 44 have in common.

```
SELECT    PS1.PHONES
FROM      THE (SELECT PHONES
               FROM    PLAYERS
               WHERE   PLAYERNO = 6) PS1
INTERSECT
SELECT    PS2.PHONES
FROM      THE (SELECT PHONES
               FROM    PLAYERS
               WHERE   PLAYERNO = 44) PS2
```

In the previous examples, the collection is defined on a column with a base data type. User-defined data types can be used as well. Likewise, user-defined data types can also make use of collections. The following are examples of both.

Example 34.25: Define the PLAYERS table so that a set of phone numbers can be stored; use the PHONE data type.

```
CREATE    TYPE PHONE AS
          (AREA_CODE          CHAR(3),
           SUBSCRIBER_NO      CHAR(6))

CREATE    TABLE PLAYERS
          (PLAYERNO           INTEGER PRIMARY KEY,
           :                  :
           PHONES             SETOF(PHONE),
           LEAGUENO           CHAR(4))
```

Example 34.26: Define the PLAYERS table so that a set of phone numbers can be stored, but define the table in such a way that the set of values is defined with the PHONES data type.

```
CREATE    TYPE PHONES AS
          (PHONE         SETOF(CHAR(13))

CREATE    TABLE PLAYERS
```

```
(PLAYERNO     INTEGER PRIMARY KEY,
  :           :
 PHONES       PHONES,
 LEAGUENO     CHAR(4))
```

34.4 Inheritance of Tables

In the first section of this chapter, we described inheritance of data types extensively. This section deals with *inheritance of tables*. Usually, inheritance of data types is regarded as very useful, but inheritance of tables is, on the other hand, a very controversial subject; see, among others, [DARW98].

To explain how this principle works, we introduce the following two named row data types. The second, OLD_PLAYERS, is a subtype of the first and has an additional column. This RESIGNED column uses a date to indicate when somebody left the club.

```
CREATE    TYPE T_PLAYERS AS
          (PLAYERNO      INTEGER NOT NULL,
           NAME          CHAR(15) NOT NULL,
           INITIALS      CHAR(3) NOT NULL,
           BIRTH_DATE    DATE,
           SEX           CHAR(1) NOT NULL,
           JOINED        SMALLINT NOT NULL,
           STREET        CHAR(15) NOT NULL,
           HOUSENO       CHAR(4),
           POSTCODE      CHAR(6),
           TOWN          CHAR(10) NOT NULL,
           PHONENO       CHAR(13),
           LEAGUENO      CHAR(4))

CREATE    TYPE T_OLD_PLAYERS AS
          (RESIGNED      DATE NOT NULL) UNDER T_PLAYERS
```

After these two data types have been created, we can define the following two tables:

```
CREATE    TABLE PLAYERS OF T_PLAYERS
          (PRIMARY KEY PLAYERNO)

CREATE    TABLE OLD_PLAYERS OF T_OLD_PLAYERS UNDER PLAYERS
```

Explanation: In Section 33.8, in Chapter 33, "User-Defined Data Types, Functions, and Operators," you saw how typed tables are created. New to the previous construct is that the OLD_PLAYERS table is defined as UNDER PLAYERS, which makes it a *subtable* of PLAYERS; in other words, PLAYERS becomes a *supertable* of OLD_PLAYERS. Because it is defined in this way, OLD_PLAYERS inherits all properties of the PLAYERS table, including the primary key.

Supertables can have several subtables, and subtables are allowed to have subtables themselves. A set of tables linked as subtables and supertables is called a *table hierarchy*. SQL has a few restrictions regarding a table hierarchy:

A table cannot be a subtable or a supertable of itself, directly or indirectly. Imagine that OLD_PLAYERS has a subtable called ANCIENT_PLAYERS. Then, we cannot define PLAYERS as a subtable of ANCIENT_PLAYERS. A cyclic structure would then appear in the table hierarchy, and that is not allowed.

A subtable can have only one direct supertable; this is called single inheritance. Multiple inheritance is not allowed.

The SQL products that currently support inheritance of tables allow only typed tables in the table hierarchy.

The table hierarchy must correspond to the type hierarchy. This means that if the type T_OLD_PLAYERS had not been defined as a subtype of T_PLAYERS, we would not have been allowed to enter the two earlier CREATE TABLE statements.

The use of table inheritance affects the SELECT statement. We illustrate this with examples in which we assume that the PLAYERS table contains just four rows (player 6, 44, 83, and 2) and that the OLD_PLAYERS table has three additional players (players 211, 260, and 280).

Example 34.27: Show the entire PLAYERS table.

```
SELECT    *
FROM      PLAYERS
```

Explanation: This statement returns all players from the PLAYERS table and from all the underlying subtables. Therefore, the result contains players 6, 44, 83, 2, 211, 260, and 280. However, only the columns of the PLAYERS table are shown.

Example 34.28: Get all the old players.

```
SELECT    *
FROM      OLD_PLAYERS
```

Explanation: This statement returns all old players from the OLD_PLAYERS table, who are players 211, 260, and 280. Of course, this is a subset of the result of the previous statement because not all the players are old. For each old player, all the columns of the OLD_PLAYERS table are shown, which means that the RESIGNED column is included as well.

Example 34.29: Get all columns of all players, except those appearing in the OLD_PLAYERS table. Therefore, give only the young players.

We can solve this question by using the EXCEPT operator:

```
SELECT    *
FROM      PLAYERS
EXCEPT
SELECT    *
FROM      OLD_PLAYERS
```

However, this query can also be formulated with a special construct added specifically for this purpose:

```
SELECT    *
FROM      ONLY(PLAYERS)
```

Explanation: This statement returns *only* players from the PLAYERS table who do not appear in the subtables: players 6, 44, 83, and 2.

In Figure 34.2, we present in a graphical way the differences among these three FROM clauses.

For INSERT statements, no special rules hold with regard to the use of super- and subtables. However, many of the remarks and rules that apply to the SELECT statement also hold for the UPDATE and DELETE statements.

Figure 34.2   *Which FROM clause gives which result?*

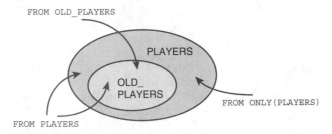

Example 34.30: Change the year in which a player joined the club to 1980 for all players born before 1980.

```
UPDATE    PLAYERS
SET       JOINED = 1980
WHERE     BIRTH_DATE < '1980-01-01'
```

Explanation: This update changes the year in which a player joined the club for all players, including the old players, born before 1980. If we want to update only the young players, we must use ONLY again:

```
UPDATE    ONLY(PLAYERS)
SET       JOINED = 1980
WHERE     BIRTH_DATE < '1980-01-01'
```

Example 34.31: Remove all players born before 1980.

```
DELETE
FROM      PLAYERS
WHERE     BIRTH_DATE < '1980-01-01'
```

Explanation: This DELETE statement also removes the old players who were born before 1980. If we want to update only the young players, then once again, ONLY must be specified in the FROM clause.

The Future of SQL

"SQL was, is, and will stay for the foreseeable future the database language for relational database servers." That is how we started this book. We know exactly what SQL used to look like and how it looks today. It is beyond doubt that the language will still be the dominant database language for many more years; there is no real competitor yet. But what will SQL look like in the future? We discuss this issue briefly in this chapter.

The integration of SQL and another popular language, Java, has begun and will continue in the coming years. Several SQL products already use Java to specify user-defined data types. A Java class can be used as a new data type in, for example, a CREATE TABLE statement. Another form of integration is that stored procedures will be written in Java; currently, many vendors use their own proprietary language for this. However, other and more powerful forms of integration can easily be invented and will definitely appear on the market.

The most common form of preprogrammed SQL used to be embedded SQL. However, the advent of first client/server technology and later Internet technology decreased the importance of this form. The use of CLIs is increasing. This all started with ODBC, but because of the increasing interest in OLE DB and JDBC, CLIs will eventually become the standard form for programming SQL. Embedded SQL will not disappear but will be pushed to the background.

At the beginning of Chapter 34, "Inheritance, References, and Collections," we mentioned that object-relational concepts are relatively new at the time of this writing. In fact, the major database vendors began to implement them seriously only in 1997. Many things are still liable to change, and many new object-relational concepts will be added to SQL. Most important is that the merging of OO concepts and SQL has started, and, because of this, the face of SQL will change dramatically over the years.

SQL was born in an era in which databases were mainly used to manage operational data and to create reports. Data warehouses, OLAP, and data mining tools are changing the use of SQL drastically. We have already seen that vendors such as IBM, Microsoft, and Oracle have extended their SQL dialect with facilities that are very useful to OLAP vendors and that increase the speed of SQL. It is to be expected that other vendors will follow their lead and that more concepts, specifically developed for the technologies mentioned, will be added to SQL.

XML has become the language for data exchange. If XML documents are stored in SQL databases, the need arises to manipulate and query those documents. Classic SQL is not suitable for this. XML documents could be regarded as hierarchical objects, and SQL is not capable of handling this kind of objects. That is why vendors have developed extensions to SQL to make it possible to manipulate SQL. An extension called *SQL/XML* is an example of this. Also, a new database language called *XQuery* has been developed specifically to store, update, and query XML documents. To what extent XQuery will take the place of SQL, that's for the future to show.

The performance of SQL products is also improving, and several reasons can be found for this. The products are becoming faster, primarily as the result of the continuous research work done by the vendors. However, development in the field of hardware also leads to faster SQL products. Hard disks and CPUs are becoming faster, and more internal memory is becoming available. All these aspects have a positive impact on the performance of SQL products. And we can say with confidence that those performance improvements will continue for some time. In ten years' time, we will be laughing at the performance levels that we are very pleased with now.

A less positive expectation is that the portability of SQL will decrease. If we look back at the first edition of this book and compare it with the current version now 20 years later, and look at the number of differences in the SQL dialects of the various products, this number has increased. In the beginning, all products supported almost the same dialect. The differences were minimal, and many differences were dictated by the operating system on which the products ran. Nowadays, the number of differences is much higher and the differences are greater as well. This applies particularly to new areas, such as user-defined data types and object-relational concepts. In short, products are diverging; they are growing apart. It is obvious that the influence of standardization committees such as ISO and ANSI is declining. However, representatives of many of the vendors have representatives on the committees responsible for the SQL standards, which makes the situation very strange.

In spite of these reservations, we expect that SQL will exist for at least another ten years, and its position in the database world is fairly safe. As mentioned in the preface, SQL is *intergalactic dataspeak*, and there is no competitor on the horizon.

A | **Syntax of SQL**

A.1 Introduction

In this appendix, we explain the notation method we have used to define the statements, we present the definitions of the SQL statements we have discussed in this book, and we show the list of reserved words.

The definitions in this appendix can differ from those in the previous chapters. The main reason for this is that, in the chapters, we explained the statements and concepts step by step. To avoid too much detail, we sometimes used simple versions of the definitions. This appendix contains the complete definitions.

A.2 The BNF Notation

In this appendix and throughout the book, we have used a formal notation method to describe the syntax of all SQL statements and the common elements. This notation is a derivative of the so-called *Backus Naur Form* (BNF), which is named after John Backus and Peter Naur. The meaning of the metasymbols that we use is based on that of the metasymbols in the SQL standard.

BNF adopts a language of *substitution rules* or *production rules*, consisting of a series of symbols. Each production rule defines one *symbol*. A symbol could be, for example, an SQL statement, a table name, or a colon. A *terminal symbol* is a special type of symbol. All symbols, apart from the terminal symbols, are defined in terms of other symbols in a production rule. Examples of terminal symbols are the word CLOSE and the semicolon.

You could compare a production rule with the definition of an element, in which the definition of that element uses elements defined elsewhere. In this case, an element equates to a symbol.

The following *metasymbols* do not form part of the SQL language but belong to the notation technique:

```
< >
::=
|
[ ]
...
{ }
;
"
```

We now explain each of these symbols.

The Symbols < and >

Nonterminal symbols are presented in brackets (< and >). A production rule exists for every nonterminal symbol. We show the names of the nonterminal symbols in lowercase letters. Two examples of nonterminal symbols are <select statement> and <table reference>.

The : : = Symbol

The ::= symbol is used in a production rule to separate the nonterminal symbol that is defined (left) from its definition (right). The ::= symbol should be read as "is defined as." See the following example of the production rule for the CLOSE statement:

```
<close statement> ::= CLOSE <cursor name>
```

Explanation: The CLOSE statement consists of the terminal symbol CLOSE followed by the nonterminal symbol cursor name. There should also be a production rule for <cursor name>.

The | Symbol

Alternatives are represented by the | symbol. Here, we give an example of the production rule for the element <character>:

```
<character> ::= <digit> | <letter> | <special symbol> | ''
```

Explanation: We should conclude from this that a character is a digit, a letter, a special symbol, or two quotation marks; it must be one of the four.

The Symbols [and]

Whatever is placed between square brackets ([and]) *may* be used. Here is the production rule for the ROLLBACK statement:

```
<rollback statement> ::= ROLLBACK [ WORK ]
```

Explanation: A ROLLBACK statement always consists of the word ROLLBACK and can optionally be followed by the word WORK.

The . . . Symbol

The three dots indicate what may be repeated one or more times. Here, our example is the production rule for an integer:

```
<whole number> ::= <digit>...
```

Explanation: An integer consists of a series of digits (with a minimum of one).

The Symbols { and }

All symbols between braces ({ and }) form a group. For example, braces used with the | symbol show precisely what the alternatives are. The following example is a part of the production rule for the FROM clause:

```
<from clause> ::=
    FROM <table reference> [ { , <table reference> }... ]
```

Explanation: A FROM clause begins with the terminal symbol FROM and is followed by at least one table reference. It is possible to follow this table reference with a list of elements, with each element consisting of a comma followed by a table reference. Do not forget that the comma is part of SQL and not part of the notation.

The ; Symbol

Some symbols have the same definition. Instead of repeating them, the semicolon (;) can be used to shorten the definitions. The following definition

```
<character literal>      ;
<varchar literal>        ;
<long varchar literal> ::= <character string>
```

is equivalent to these three definitions:

```
<character literal>      ::= <character string>
<varchar literal>        ::= <character string>
<long varchar literal> ::= <character string>
```

The " Symbol

A small number of metasymbols, such as the " symbol, are part of particular SQL statements themselves. To avoid misunderstanding, these symbols are enclosed by double quotation marks. Among other things, this means that the symbol " that is used within SQL is represented in the production rules as " " ".

Additional Remarks

■ Whatever is presented in uppercase letters, as well as the symbols that are not part of the notation method, must be adopted unaltered.

■ The sequence of the symbols in the right part of the production rule is fixed.

■ Blanks in production rules have no significance. Generally, they have been added to make the rules more readable. Therefore, the two following production rules mean the same:

```
<alphanumeric literal> ::= ' [ <character>... ] '
```

and

```
<alphanumeric literal> ::= '[<character>...]'
```

A.3 Reserved Words in SQL3

Each programming language and database language (and this includes SQL) supports so-called *reserved words* or *keywords*. Examples in SQL are SELECT and CREATE. In most SQL products, these reserved words may not be used as names for database objects such as tables, columns, views, and users. Each product has its own set of reserved words (although two SQL products will have many reserved words in common, of course). You should refer to the product documentation to find out which these are. The following list contains reserved words as defined in the SQL3 standard.

ABSOLUTE, ACTION, ADD, ALL, ALLOCATE, ALTER, AND, ANY, ARE, AS, ASC, ASSERTION, AT, AUTHORIZATION, AVG

BEGIN, BETWEEN, BIT, BIT_LENGTH, BOTH, BY

CASCADE, CASCADED, CASE, CAST, CATALOG, CHAR, CHARACTER,

CHAR_LENGTH, CHARACTER_LENGTH, CHECK, CLOSE, COALESCE, COLLATE, COLLATION, COLUMN, COMMIT, CONNECT, CONNECTION, CONSTRAINT, CONSTRAINTS, CONTINUE, CONVERT, CORRESPONDING, COUNT, CREATE, CROSS, CURRENT, CURRENT_DATE, CURRENT_TIME, CURRENT_TIMESTAMP, CURRENT_USER, CURSOR

DATE, DAY, DEALLOCATE, DEC, DECIMAL, DECLARE, DEFAULT, DEFERRABLE, DEFERRED, DELETE, DESC, DESCRIBE, DESCRIPTOR, DIAGNOSTICS, DISCONNECT, DISTINCT, DOMAIN, DOUBLE, DROP

ELSE, END, END-EXEC, ESCAPE, EXCEPT, EXCEPTION, EXEC, EXECUTE, EXISTS, EXTERNAL, EXTRACT

FALSE, FETCH, FIRST, FLOAT, FOR, FOREIGN, FOUND, FROM, FULL

GET, GLOBAL, GO, GOTO, GRANT, GROUP

HAVING, HOUR

IDENTITY, IMMEDIATE, IN, INDICATOR, INITIALLY, INNER, INPUT, INSENSITIVE, INSERT, INT, INTEGER, INTERSECT, INTERVAL, INTO, IS, ISOLATION

JOIN

KEY

LANGUAGE, LAST, LEADING, LEFT, LEVEL, LIKE, LOCAL, LOWER

MATCH, MAX, MIN, MINUTE, MODULE, MONTH

NAMES, NATIONAL, NATURAL, NCHAR, NEXT, NO, NOT, NULL, NULLIF, NUMERIC

OCTET_LENGTH OF, ON, ONLY, OPEN, OPTION, OR, ORDER, OUTER, OUTPUT, OVERLAPS

PARTIAL, POSITION, PRECISION, PREPARE, PRESERVE, PRIMARY, PRIOR, PRIVILEGES, PROCEDURE, PUBLIC

READ, REAL, REFERENCES, RELATIVE, RESTRICT, REVOKE, RIGHT, ROLLBACK, ROWS

SCHEMA, SCROLL, SECOND, SECTION, SELECT, SESSION, SESSION_USER, SET, SIZE, SMALLINT, SOME, SQL, SQLCODE, SQLERROR, SQLSTATE, SUBSTRING, SUM, SYSTEM_USER

TABLE, TEMPORARY, THEN, TIME, TIMESTAMP, TIMEZONE_HOUR, TIMEZONE_MINUTE, TO, TRAILING, TRANSACTION, TRANSLATE, TRANSLATION, TRIM, TRUE

UNION, UNIQUE, UNKNOWN, UPDATE, UPPER, USAGE, USER, USING

VALUE, VALUES, VARCHAR, VARYING, VIEW

WHEN, WHENEVER, WHERE, WITH, WORK, WRITE

YEAR

ZONE

This is the list of reserved words of MySQL. The words that already appear in the previous list have been left out.

ANALYZE, ASENSITIVE

BEFORE, BIGINT, BINARY, BLOB

CALL, CHANGE, CONDITION

DATABASE, DATABASES, DAY_HOUR, DAY_MICROSECOND, DAY_MINUTE, DAY_SECOND, DELAYED, DETERMINISTIC, DISTINCTROW, DIV, DUAL

EACH, ELSEIF, ENCLOSED, ESCAPED, EXIT, EXPLAIN

FLOAT4, FLOAT8, FORCE, FULLTEXT

HIGH_PRIORITY, HOUR_MICROSECOND, HOUR_MINUTE, HOUR_SECOND

IF, IGNORE, INDEX, INFILE, INOUT, INT1, INT2, INT3, INT4, INT8, ITERATE

KEYS, KILL

LABEL, LEAVE, LIMIT, LINES, LOAD, LOCALTIME, LOCALTIMESTAMP, LOCK, LONG, LONGBLOB, LONGTEXT, LOOP, LOW_PRIORITY

MEDIUMBLOB, MEDIUMINT, MEDIUMTEXT, MIDDLEINT, MINUTE_MICROSECOND, MINUTE_SECOND, MOD, MODIFIES

NO_WRITE_TO_BINLOG

OPTIMIZE, OPTIONALLY, OUT, OUTFILE

PURGE

RAID0, READS, REGEXP, RELEASE, RENAME, REPEAT, REPLACE, REQUIRE, RETURN, RLIKE

SCHEMAS, SECOND_MICROSECOND, SENSITIVE, SEPARATOR, SHOW, SONAME, SPATIAL, SPECIFIC, SQLEXCEPTION, SQLWARNING, SQL_BIG_RESULT, SQL_CALC_FOUND_ROWS, SQL_SMALL_RESULT, SSL, STARTING, STRAIGHT_JOIN

TERMINATED, TINYBLOB, TINYINT, TINYTEXT, TRIGGER

UNDO, UNLOCK, UNSIGNED, USE, UTC_DATE, UTC_TIME, UTC_TIMESTAMP

VARBINARY, VARCHARACTER

WHILE

X509, XOR

YEAR_MONTH

ZEROFILL

We strongly advise that you follow these recommendations when choosing the names of database objects:

- Avoid one-letter words, even if they do not occur in the list.
- Avoid words that could be seen as abbreviations of words in the list; for example, do not use DATA because the word DATABASE appears in the list.
- Avoid derivations of words in the list, such as plural and verbal forms. Therefore, do not use CURSORS (plural of CURSOR) or ORDERING (present participle of the verb ORDER).

A.4 Syntax Definitions of SQL Statements

This section contains the definitions of all the SQL statements as they are described in this book. Certain common elements, such as condition and column list, are "used" by several statements. If an element belongs to only one statement, it is included in Section A.4.2 together with its statement. All others are explained in Section A.4.3. We begin with the different groups of SQL statements.

A.4.1 Groups of SQL Statements

In Section 4.16, in Chapter 4, "SQL in a Nutshell," we indicated that the set of SQL statements can be divided into groups, such as DDL, DML, and DCL statements. Furthermore, in Chapter 26, "Introduction to Embedded SQL," we made a distinction between executable and nonexecutable SQL statements. In this section, we indicate precisely which group each statement belongs to.

SQL statement:

```
<sql statement> ::=
    <executable statement>        |
    <non-executable statement>
```

Executable statement:

```
<executable statement> ::=
    <declarative statement> |
    <procedural statement>
```

Declarative statement:

```
<declarative statement> ::=
   <ddl statement> |
   <dml statement> |
   <dcl statement>
```

DDL statement:

```
<ddl statement> ::=
   <alter database statement>    |
   <alter sequence statement>    |
   <alter table statement>       |
   <create database statement>   |
   <create function statement>   |
   <create index statement>      |
   <create procedure statement>  |
   <create sequence statement>   |
   <create table statement>      |
   <create trigger statement>    |
   <create view statement>       |
   <drop database statement>     |
   <drop function statement>     |
   <drop index statement>        |
   <drop procedure statement>    |
   <drop sequence statement>     |
   <drop table statement>        |
   <drop trigger statement>      |
   <drop view statement>         |
   <rename table statement>
```

DML statement:

```
<dml statement> ::=
   <call statement>      |
   <close statement>     |
   <commit statement>    |
```

(continued)

```
    <delete statement>                  |
    <execute immediate statement>       |
    <fetch statement>                   |
    <insert statement>                  |
    <lock table statement>              |
    <open statement>                    |
    <rollback statement>                |
    <savepoint statement>               |
    <select statement>                  |
    <select into statement>             |
    <set statement>                     |
    <set transaction statement>         |
    <start transaction statement>       |
    <update statement>
```

DCL statement:

```
<dcl statement> ::=
    <alter user statement>      |
    <create role statement>     |
    <create user statement>     |
    <drop role statement>       |
    <drop user statement>       |
    <grant statement>           |
    <revoke statement>
```

Nonexecutable statement:

```
<non-executable statement> ::=
    <begin declare statement>   |
    <declare cursor statement>  |
    <end declare statement>     |
    <include statement>         |
    <whenever statement>
```

Procedural statement:

```
<procedural statement> ::=
    <begin-end block>            |
    <call statement>             |
    <close statement>            |
    <declare condition statement> |
    <declare cursor statement>   |
    <declare handler statement>  |
    <declare variable statement> |
    <fetch cursor statement>     |
    <flow control statement>     |
    <open cursor statement>      |
    <set statement>              |
    <return statement>
```

Flow-control statement:

```
<flow control statement> ::=
    <if statement>        |
    <case statement>      |
    <while statement>     |
    <repeat statement>    |
    <loop statement>      |
    <leave statement>     |
    <iterate statement>
```

A.4.2 Definitions of SQL Statements

Alter database statement:

```
<alter database statement> ::=
    ALTER DATABASE [ <database name> ]
        [ <database option>... ]
```

Alter sequence statement:

```
<alter sequence statement> ::=
    ALTER SEQUENCE [ <user name>. ] <sequence name>
        [ <sequence option>... ]

<sequence option> ::=
    RESTART [ WITH <integer literal> ]                   |
    INCREMENT BY <integer literal>                       |
    { MAXVALUE <integer literal> | NOMAXVALUE }          |
    { MINVALUE <integer literal> | NOMINVALUE }          |
    { CYCLE | NOCYCLE }                                  |
    { ORDER | NOORDER }                                  |
    { CACHE <integer literal> | NOCACHE }
```

Alter table statement:

```
<alter table statement> ::=
    ALTER TABLE <table specification> <table structure change>

<table structure change> ::=
    <table change>                   |
    <column change>                  |
    <integrity constraint change> |
    <index change>

<table change> ::=
    RENAME [ TO | AS ] <table name>                                          |
    CONVERT TO CHARACTER SET { <character set name> | DEFAULT }
        [ COLLATE <collating sequence name> ]

<column change> ::=
    ADD [ COLUMN ] <column definition>
        [ FIRST | AFTER <column name> ]                          |
    ADD [ COLUMN ] <table schema>                                |
    DROP [ COLUMN ] <column name> [ RESTRICT | CASCADE ] |
    CHANGE [ COLUMN ] <column name> <column definition>
        [ FIRST | AFTER <column name> ]                          |
    MODIFY [ COLUMN ] <column definition>
        [ FIRST | AFTER <column name> ]                          |
```

(continued)

```
    ALTER [ COLUMN ] { SET DEFAULT <expression> | DROP DEFAULT }

<integrity constraint change> ::=
    ADD <table integrity constraint>   |
    DROP PRIMARY KEY                   |
    DROP CONSTRAINT <constraint name>

<index change> ::=
    ADD <index type> INDEX <index name>
    ( <column in index> [ { , <column in index> }... ] )
```

Alter user statement:

```
<alter user statement> ::=
    ALTER USER <user name> IDENTIFIED BY <password>
```

Begin declare statement:

```
<begin declare statement> ::=
    BEGIN DECLARE SECTION
```

Call statement:

```
<call statement> ::=
    CALL [ <database name> . ] <procedure name>
        ( <expression list> )
```

Case statement:

```
<case statement> ::=
    { CASE <expression>
        WHEN <expression> THEN <statement list>
        [ WHEN <expression> THEN <statement list> ]...
        [ ELSE <statement list> ]
      END CASE } |
    { CASE
        WHEN <condition> THEN <statement list>
        [ WHEN <condition> THEN <statement list> ]...
        [ ELSE <statement list>
      END CASE }
```

Close statement:

```
<close statement> ::=
    CLOSE <cursor name>
```

Commit statement:

```
<commit statement> ::=
    COMMIT [ WORK ]
```

Create database statement:

```
<create database statement> ::=
    CREATE DATABASE <database name> [ <database option>... ]
```

Create function statement:

```
<create function statement> ::=
   CREATE FUNCTION <function name>
      ( [ <parameter list for function> ] )
      RETURNS <data type>
      <function body>

<parameter list for function> ::=
   <parameter specification for function>
      [ { , <parameter specification for function> }... ]

<parameter specification for function> ::=
   <parameter> <data type>

<function body> ::= <begin-end block>
```

Create index statement:

```
<create index statement> ::=
   CREATE <index type> INDEX <index name>
      ON <table specification>
      ( <column in index> [ { , <column in index> }... ] )
```

Create procedure statement:

```
<create procedure statement> ::=
   CREATE PROCEDURE <procedure name>
      ( [ <parameter list for procedure> ] )
      <procedure body>

<parameter list for procedure> ::=
   <parameter specification for procedure>
      [ { , <parameter specification for procedure> }... ]

<parameter specification for procedure> ::=
   [ IN | OUT | INOUT ] <parameter> <data type>

<procedure body> ::= <begin-end block>
```

Create role statement:

```
<create role statement> ::=
   CREATE ROLE <role name>
```

Create sequence statement:

```
<create sequence statement> ::=
   CREATE SEQUENCE [ <user name>. ] <sequence name>
      [ <sequence option>... ]

<sequence option> ::=
   START WITH <integer literal>                         |
   INCREMENT BY <integer literal>                       |
   { MAXVALUE <integer literal> | NOMAXVALUE } |
   { MINVALUE <integer literal> | NOMINVALUE } |
   { CYCLE | NOCYCLE }                                  |
   { ORDER | NOORDER }                                  |
   { CACHE <integer literal> | NOCACHE }
```

Create table statement:

```
<create table statement> ::=
   CREATE [ TEMPORARY ] TABLE
      <table specification> <table structure>

<table structure> ::=
   LIKE <table specification>              |
   ( LIKE <table specification> )          |
   <table contents>                        |
   <table schema> [ <table contents> ]
```

Create trigger statement:

```
<create trigger statement> ::=
   CREATE TRIGGER <trigger name>
   <trigger moment>
   <trigger event>
   [ <trigger condition> ]
   <trigger action>

<trigger moment> ::=
   BEFORE | AFTER | INSTEAD OF

<trigger event> ::=
   { INSERT | DELETE | UPDATE [ OF <column list> ] }
   { ON | OF | FROM | INTO } <table specification>
   [ REFERENCING { OLD | NEW | OLD_TABLE | NEW_TABLE }
     AS <variable> ]
   FOR EACH { ROW | STATEMENT }

<trigger condition> ::= ( WHEN <condition> )

<trigger actie> ::= <begin-end block>
```

Create user statement:

```
<create user statement> ::=
   CREATE USER <user name> IDENTIFIED BY <password>
```

Create view statement:

```
<create view statement> ::=
   CREATE [ OR REPLACE ] VIEW <view name> [ <column list> ] AS
      <table expression>
      [ WITH [ CASCADED | LOCAL ] CHECK OPTION ]
```

Declare condition statement:

```
<declare condition statement> ::=
   DECLARE <condition name> CONDITION FOR
   { SQLSTATE [ VALUE ] <sqlstate value> } |
      <mysql error code> }
```

Declare cursor statement:

```
<declare cursor statement> ::=
   DECLARE [ INSENSITIVE ] [ SCROLL ] <cursor name>
      CURSOR FOR
   <table expression>
   [ <for clause> ]
```

Declare handler statement:

```
<declare handler statement> ::=
   DECLARE <handler type> HANDLER FOR <condition value list>
      <procedural statement>

<handler type> ::=
   CONTINUE |
   EXIT    |
   UNDO

<condition value list> ::=
   <condition value> [ { , <condition value> }... ]

<condition value> ::=
   SQLSTATE [ VALUE ] <sqlstate value> |
   <mysql error code>                  |
   SQLWARNING                          |
   NOT FOUND                           |
   SQLEXCEPTION                        |
   <condition name>
```

Declare variable statement:

```
<declare variable statement> ::=
    DECLARE <local variable list> <data type>
        [ DEFAULT <expression> ]
```

Delete statement:

```
<delete statement> ::=
    DELETE
    FROM <table reference>
    [ WHERE { <condition> | CURRENT OF <cursor name> } ]
```

Drop database statement:

```
<drop database statement> ::=
    DROP DATABASE <database name>
```

Drop function statement:

```
<drop function statement> ::=
    DROP FUNCTION [ <database name> . ] <function name>
```

Drop index statement:

```
<drop index statement> ::=
    DROP INDEX <index name>
```

Drop procedure statement:

```
<drop procedure statement> ::=
    DROP PROCEDURE [ <database name> . ] <procedure name>
```

Drop role statement:

```
<drop role statement> ::=
    DROP ROLE <role name>
```

Drop sequence statement:

```
<drop sequence statement> ::=
    DROP SEQUENCE [ <user name>. ] <sequence name>
```

Drop table statement:

```
<drop table statement> ::=
    DROP TABLE <table specification>
```

Drop trigger statement:

```
<drop trigger statement> ::=
    DROP TRIGGER [ <table name> . ] <trigger name>
```

Drop user statement:

```
<drop user statement> ::=
   DROP USER <user name>
```

Drop view statement:

```
<drop view statement> ::=
   DROP VIEW <table specification>
```

End declare statement:

```
<end declare statement> ::=
   END DECLARE SECTION
```

Execute immediate statement:

```
<execute immediate statement> ::=
   EXECUTE IMMEDIATE <host variables>
```

Fetch statement:

```
<fetch statement> ::=
   FETCH [ <direction> ] <cursor name>
   INTO  <host variable list>

<direction> ::=
   NEXT | PRIOR | FIRST | LAST |
   ABSOLUTE <whole number> | RELATIVE <whole number>
```

Grant statement:

```
<grant statement> ::=
    <grant table privilege statement>       |
    <grant database privilege statement>    |
    <grant user privilege statement>        |
    <grant role statement>                  |
    <grant execute statement>               |
    <grant sequence privilege statement>

<grant table privilege statement> ::=
    GRANT   <table privileges>
    ON      <table specification>
    TO      <grantees>
    [ WITH GRANT OPTION ]

<grant database privilege statement> ::=
    GRANT <database privileges>
    ON    [ <database name> . ] *
    TO    <grantees>
    [ WITH GRANT OPTION ]

<grant user privilege statement> ::=
    GRANT <user privileges>
    ON    *.*
    TO    <grantees>
    [ WITH GRANT OPTION ]

<grant execute statement> ::=
    GRANT   EXECUTE
    ON      { <procedure name> | FUNCTION <function name> }
    TO      <grantees>
    [ WITH GRANT OPTION ]

<grant role statement> ::=
    GRANT   <role name> [ { , <role name> }... ]
    TO      <grantees>

<grant sequence privilege statement> ::=
    GRANT <sequence privileges>
    ON    SEQUENCE <sequence name>
    TO    <grantees>
    [ WITH GRANT OPTION ]
```

If statement:

```
<if statement> ::=
    IF <condition> THEN <statement list>
        [ ELSEIF <condition> THEN <statement list> ]...
        [ ELSE <statement list> ]
    END IF
```

Include statement:

```
<include statement> ::=
    INCLUDE <file>
```

Insert statement:

```
<insert statement> ::=
    INSERT INTO <table specification> <insert specification>

<insert specification> ::=
    [ <column list> ] <values clause>        |
    [ <column list> ] <table expression>
```

Iterate statement:

```
<iterate statement> ::=
    ITERATE <label>
```

Leave statement:

```
<leave statement> ::=
    LEAVE <label>
```

Lock table statement:

```
<lock table statement> ::=
    LOCK TABLE <table specification> IN <lock type> MODE

<lock type> ::= SHARE | EXCLUSIVE
```

Loop statement:

```
<loop statement> ::=
    [ <label> : ] LOOP <statement list> END LOOP [ <label> ]
```

Open statement:

```
<open statement> ::=
    OPEN <cursor name>
    [ USING <host variable> [ { , <host variable> }... ]]
```

Rename table statement:

```
<rename table statement> ::=
    RENAME TABLE <table name change>

<table name change> ::= <table name> TO <table name>
```

Repeat statement:

```
<repeat statement> ::=
    [ <label> : ] REPEAT <statement list>
    UNTIL <condition>
    END REPEAT <label>
```

Return statement:

```
<return statement> ::=
   RETURN <scalar expression>
```

Revoke statement:

```
<revoke statement> ::=
   <revoke table privilege statement>    |
   <revoke database privilege statement> |
   <revoke user privilege statement>     |
   <revoke role statement>               |
   <revoke execute statement>            |
   <revoke sequence privilege statement>

<revoke table privilege statement> ::=
   REVOKE  <table privileges>
   ON      <table specification>
   FROM    <grantees>

<revoke database privilege statement> ::=
   REVOKE  <database privileges>
   ON      [ <database name> . ] *
   FROM    <grantees>

<revoke user privilege statement> ::=
   REVOKE  <user privileges>
   ON      *.*
   FROM    <grantees>

<revoke role statement> ::=
   REVOKE  <role name> [ { , <role name> }... ]
   FROM    <grantees>

<revoke execute statement> ::=
   REVOKE  EXECUTE
   ON      { <procedure name> | FUNCTION <function name> }
   FROM    <grantees>

<revoke sequence privilege statement> ::=
   REVOKE <sequence privileges>
   ON      SEQUENCE <sequence name>
   FROM    <grantees>
```

Rollback statement:

```
<rollback statement> ::=
    ROLLBACK [ WORK ] [ TO [ SAVEPOINT ] <savepoint name> ]
```

Savepoint statement:

```
<savepoint statement> ::=
    SAVEPOINT <savepoint name>
```

Select statement:

```
<select statement> ::=
    <table expression>
    [ <for clause> ]
```

Select into statement:

```
<select into statement> ::=
    <select clause>
    <into clause>
  [ <from clause>
  [ <where clause> ]
  [ <group by clause>
  [ <having clause> ] ] ]
```

Set statement:

```
<set statement> ::=
    SET <local variable definition>
        [ {, <local variable definition> }... ]

<local variable definition> ::=
    <local variable> { = | := } <scalar expression>
```

Set transaction statement:

```
<set transaction statement> ::=
   SET TRANSACTION ISOLATION LEVEL <isolation level>

<isolation level> ::=
   READ UNCOMMITTED |
   READ COMMITTED   |
   REPEATABLE READ  |
   SERIALIZABLE
```

Start transaction statement:

```
<start transaction statement> ::=
   START TRANSACTION
```

Update statement:

```
<update statement> ::=
   UPDATE <table reference>
   SET    <column assignment> [ { , <column assignment> }... ]
   [ WHERE { <condition> | CURRENT OF <cursor name> } ]

<column assignment> ::=
   <column name> = <scalar expression>
```

Whenever statement:

```
<whenever statement> ::=
   WHENEVER <whenever condition> <whenever action>

<whenever condition> ::= SQLWARNING | SQLERROR | NOT FOUND

<whenever action> ::= CONTINUE | GOTO <label>
```

While statement:

```
<while statement> ::=
   [ <label> : WHILE <condition> DO <statement list>
   END WHILE [ <label> ]
```

A.4.3 Common Elements

This section contains the general common elements used in various SQL statements. The elements that are defined as a name are all grouped at the end of this section.

```
<aggregation function> ::=
   COUNT    ( [ DISTINCT | ALL ] { * | <scalar expression> } ) |
   MIN      ( [ DISTINCT | ALL ] <scalar expression> )        |
   MAX      ( [ DISTINCT | ALL ] <scalar expression> )        |
   SUM      ( [ DISTINCT | ALL ] <scalar expression> )        |
   AVG      ( [ DISTINCT | ALL ] <scalar expression> )        |
   STDDEV   ( [ DISTINCT | ALL ] <scalar expression> )        |
   VARIANCE ( [ DISTINCT | ALL ] <scalar expression> )

<alphanumeric data type> ::=
   CHAR [ ( <length> ) ]               |
   CHARACTER [ ( <length> ) ]          |
   VARCHAR ( <length> )                |
   CHAR VARYING ( <length> )           |
   CHARACTER VARYING ( <length> ) |
   LONG VARCHAR

<alphanumeric expression> ::=
   <alphanumeric scalar expression> |
   <alphanumeric row expression>    |
   <alphanumeric table expression>

<alphanumeric literal> ::= <character string>

<alphanumeric scalar expression> ::=
   <singular scalar expression> COLLATE <name> |
   <compound scalar expression>

<alternate key> ::= UNIQUE <column list>
```

(continued)

```
<any all operator> ::=
   <comparison operator> { ALL | ANY | SOME }

<begin-end block> ::=
   [ <label> : ] BEGIN <statement list> END [ <label> ]

<blob data type> ::= BLOB

<boolean data type> ::= BOOLEAN

<boolean literal> ::= TRUE | FALSE

<case expression> ::=
   CASE <when definition> [ ELSE <scalar expression> ] END

<character> ::= <digit> | <letter> | <special symbol> | ''

<character string> ::= ' [ <character>... ] '

<check integrity constraint> ::= CHECK ( <condition> )

<column definition> ::=
   <column name> <data type> [ <null specification> ]
   [ <column integrity constraint> ] [ <column  option>... ]

<column in index> ::= <column name> [ ASC | DESC ]

<column integrity constraint> ::=
   PRIMARY KEY                          |
   UNIQUE                               |
   <check integrity constraint>

<column list> ::=
   ( <column name> [ { , <column name> }... ] )

<column name> ::= <name>

<column option> ::=
   DEFAULT <literal>                    |
   COMMENT <alphanumeric literal>

<column specification> ::=
   [ <table specification> . ] <column name>
```

(continued)

```
<column subquery> ::= ( <table expression> )

<comparison operator> ::=
   = | < | > | <= | >= | <>

<compound alphanumeric expression> ::=
   <scalar alphanumeric expression> "||"
      <scalar alphanumeric expression>

<compound date expression> ::=
   <scalar date expression> [ + | - ] <date interval>

<compound numeric expression> ::=
   [ + | - ] <scalar numeric expression>                        |
   ( <scalar numeric expression> )                              |
   <scalar numeric expression>
      <mathematical operator> <scalar numeric expression>

<compound scalar expression> ::=
   <compound numeric expression>         |
   <compound alphanumeric expression>    |
   <compound date expression>            |
   <compound time expression>            |
   <compound timestamp expression>       |
   <compound hexadecimal expression>

<compound table expression> ::=
   <table expression> <set operator> <table expression>

<compound time expression> ::=
   ADDTIME( <scalar time expression> , <time interval> )

<compound timestamp expression> ::=
   <scalar timestamp expression> [ + | - ] <timestamp interval>

<condition> ::=
   <predicate>                      |
   <predicate> OR <predicate>       |
   <predicate> AND <predicate>      |
   ( <condition> )                  |
   NOT <condition>
```

(continued)

```
<database privilege> ::=
   SELECT                        |
   INSERT                        |
   DELETE                        |
   UPDATE                        |
   REFERENCES                    |
   CREATE                        |
   ALTER                         |
   DROP                          |
   INDEX                         |
   CREATE TEMPORARY TABLES       |
   CREATE VIEW                   |
   CREATE ROUTINE                |
   ALTER ROUTINE                 |
   EXECUTE ROUTINE               |
   LOCK TABLES

<database option> ::=
   [ DEFAULT ] CHARACTER SET <character set name> |
   [ DEFAULT ] COLLATE <collating sequence name>

<data type> ::=
   <numeric data type>      |
   <alphanumeric data type> |
   <temporal data type>     |
   <boolean data type>      |
   <blob data type>

<date interval> ::=
   INTERVAL <interval length> <date interval unit>

<date interval unit> ::=
   DAY | WEEK | MONTH | QUARTER | YEAR

<date literal> ::= ' <years> - <months> - <days> '

<days> ::= <digit> [ <digit> ]

<decimal data type> ::=
   DECIMAL [ ( <precision> [ ,<scale> ] ) ] |
   DEC     [ ( <precision> [ ,<scale> ] ) ] |
   NUMERIC [ ( <precision> [ ,<scale> ] ) ] |
   NUM     [ ( <precision> [ ,<scale> ] ) ]
```

(continued)

```
<decimal literal> ::=
   [ + | - ] <whole number> [ .<whole number> ] |
   [ + | - ] <whole number>.                     |
   [ + | - ] .<whole number>

<digit> ::= 0 | 1 | 2 | 3 | 4 | 5 | 6 | 7 | 8 | 9

<exponent> ::= <integer literal>

<expression> ::=
   <scalar expression> |
   <row expression>    |
   <table expression>

<expression list> ::= <expression> [ { , <expression> }... ]

<float data type> ::=
   FLOAT [ ( <length> ) ] |
   REAL                   |
   DOUBLE [ PRECISION ]

<float literal> ::= <mantissa> { E | e } <exponent>

<for clause> ::=
   FOR UPDATE [ OF <column name> [ { , <column name> }... ] ] |
   FOR READ ONLY

<foreign key> ::=
   FOREIGN KEY <column list> <referencing specification>

<from clause> ::=
   FROM <table reference> [ { , <table reference> }... ]

<grantees> ::=
   <user name> [ { , <user name> }... ] |
   <role name> [ { , <role name> }... ] |
   PUBLIC

<group by clause> ::=
   GROUP BY <group by specification list>
      [ WITH { ROLLUP | CUBE } ]

<group by expression> ::= <scalar expression>
```

(continued)

```
<group by specification> ::=
    <group by expression>          |
    <grouping sets specification>  |
    <rollup specification>

<group by specification list> ::=
    <group by specification> [ { , <group by specification> }... ]

<grouping sets specification> ::=
    GROUPING SETS ( <grouping sets specification list> )

<grouping sets specification> ::=
    <group by expression>                       |
    <rollup specification>                       |
    ( <grouping sets specification list> )

<grouping sets specification list> ::=
    <grouping sets specification>
    [ { , <grouping sets specification> }... ]

<having clause> ::= HAVING <condition>

<hexadecimal literal> ::= X <character string>

<host variable> ::= ":" <host variable name>

<host variable element> ::=
    <host variable> [ <null indicator> ]

<host variable list> ::=
    <host variable element> [ { , <host variable element> }... ]

<hours> ::= <digit> [ <digit> ]

<index type> ::= UNIQUE | CLUSTERED

<integer data type> ::=
    SMALLINT |
    INTEGER  |
    INT      |
    BIGINT

<integer literal> ::= [ + | - ] <whole number>
```

(continued)

```
<interval length> ::= <scalar expression>

<into clause> ::=
   INTO <host variable> [ { , <host variable> }... ]

<join condition> ::=
    ON <condition> | USING <column list>

<join specification> ::=
   <table reference> <join type> <table reference>
      <join condition>

<join type> ::=
   [ INNER ] JOIN          |
   LEFT  [ OUTER ] JOIN |
   RIGHT [ OUTER ] JOIN |
   FULL  [ OUTER ] JOIN |
   UNION JOIN              |
   CROSS JOIN

<length> ::= <whole number>

<letter> ::=
   a | b | c | d | e | f | g | h | i | j | k | l | m |
   n | o | p | q | r | s | t | u | v | w | x | y | z |
   A | B | C | D | E | F | G | H | I | J | K | L | M |
   M | O | P | Q | R | S | T | U | V | W | X | Y | Z

<like pattern> ::= <scalar alphanumeric expression>

<literal> ::=
   <numeric literal>       |
   <alphanumeric literal>  |
   <temporal literal>      |
   <boolean literal>       |
   <hexadecimal literal>

<local variable> ::= <variable name>

<local variable list> ::=
   <local variable> [ { , <local variable> }... ]

<mantissa> ::= <decimal literal>
```

(continued)

```
<mathematical operator> ::= * | / | + | -

<micro seconds> ::= <whole number>

<minutes>  ::= <digit> [ <digit> ]

<months>  ::= <digit> [ <digit> ]

<mysql error code> ::= <whole number>

<null indicator> ::= <host variable>

<null specification> ::= NOT NULL

<numeric data type> ::=
   <integer data type> |
   <decimal data type> |
   <float data type>

<numeric literal> ::=
   <integer literal> |
   <decimal literal> |
   <float literal>

<order by clause> ::=
   ORDER BY <sorting> [ { , <sorting> }... ]

<password> ::= '< name>'

<precision> ::= <whole number>

<predicate> ::=
   <predicate with comparison > |
   <predicate with in>          |
   <predicate with between>     |
   <predicate with like>        |
   <predicate with null>        |
   <predicate with exists>      |
   <predicate with any all>

<predicate with any all> ::=
   <scalar expression> <any all operator> <column subquery>
```

(*continued*)

```
<predicate with between> ::=
   <scalar expression> [ NOT ] BETWEEN <scalar expression>
      AND <scalar expression>

<predicate with exists> ::= EXISTS <table subquery>

<predicate with in> ::=
   <scalar expression> [ NOT ] IN <scalar expression list> |
   <scalar expression> [ NOT ] IN <column subquery>        |
   <row expression> [ NOT ] IN <row expression list>       |
   <row expression> [ NOT ] IN <table subquery>

<predicate with like> ::=
   <scalar expression> [ NOT ] LIKE <like pattern>
      [ ESCAPE <character> ]

<predicate with null> ::=
   <scalar expression> IS [ NOT ] NULL

<predicate with comparison> ::=
   <scalar expression> <comparison operator>
      <scalar expression> |
   <row expression> <comparison operator> <row expression>

<primary key> ::= PRIMARY KEY <column list>

<pseudonym> ::= <name>

<referencing action> ::=
   ON UPDATE { CASCADE | RESTRICT | SET NULL } |
   ON DELETE { CASCADE | RESTRICT | SET NULL }

<referencing specification> ::=
   REFERENCES <table specification> [ <column list> ]
   [ <referencing action>... ]

<rollup specification> ::=
   ROLLUP ( <group by expression list> ) |
   CUBE ( <group by expression list> )   |
   ( )

<row expression> ::= <singular row expression>
```

(continued)

```
<row expression list> ::=
   ( <scalar expression list>
      [ { , <scalar expression list> }... ] )

<row subquery> ::= <subquery>

<scalar alphanumeric expression> ::=
   <singular alphanumeric expression> |
   <compound alphanumeric expression>

<scalar date expression> ::=
   <singular date expression> |
   <compound date expression>

<scalar expression> ::=
   <singular scalar expression> |
   <compound scalar expression>

<scalar expression list> ::=
   ( <scalar expression> [ { , <scalar expression> }... ] )

<scalar hexadecimal expression> ::=
   <singular hexadecimal expression> |
   <compound hexadecimal expression>

<scalar numeric expression> ::=
   <singular numeric expression> |
   <compound numeric expression>

<scalar subquery> ::= <subquery>

<scalar time expression> ::=
   <singular time expression> |
   <compound time expression>

<scalar timestamp expression> ::=
   <singular timestamp expression> |
   <compound timestamp expression>

<scale> ::= <whole number>

<seconds> ::= <digit> [ <digit> ]
```

(continued)

```
<select block head> ::=
    <select clause>
  [ <from clause>
  [ <where clause> ]
  [ <group by clause>
  [ <having clause> ] ] ]

<select block tail> ::=
  [ <order by clause> ]

<select clause> ::=
    SELECT [ DISTINCT | ALL ] <select element list>

<select element> ::=
    <scalar expression> [[ AS ] <column name> ] |
    <table specification>.*                       |
    <pseudonym>.*

<select element list> ::=
    <select element> [ { , <select element> }... ] |
    *

<sequence privilege> ::= ALTER | USAGE

<sequence privileges> ::=
    <sequence privilege> [ { , <sequence privilege> }... ]

<sequence reference> ::=
    { NEXT | PREVIOUS ] VALUE FOR [ <user name> . ] <sequence name>

<set operator> ::=
    UNION | INTERSECT | EXCEPT |
    UNION ALL | INTERSECT ALL | EXCEPT ALL

<singular row expression> ::=
    ( <scalar expression> [ { , <scalar expression> }... ] ) |
    <row subquery>

<singular scalar expression> ::=
    <singular numeric expression>        |
    <singular alphanumeric expression>   |
    <singular date expression>           |
    <singular time expression>           |
    <singular timestamp expression>      |
    <singular hexadecimal expression>
```

Each of the previous singular scalar expressions has the following different forms:

```
<singular scalar expression> ::=
   <literal>                 |
   <column specification>    |
   <system variable>         |
   <cast expression>         |
   <case expression>         |
   NULL                      |
   ( <scalar expression> )   |
   <scalar function>         |
   <aggregation function>    |
   <scalar subquery>         |
   <local variable>          |
   <host variable>           |
   <system parameter>        |
   <sequence reference>

<singular table expression> ::= <select block head>

<sort direction> ::= ASC | DESC

<sorting> ::=
   <scalar expression> [ <sort direction> ] |
   <sequence number> [<sort direction> ]    |
   <column heading> [ <sort direction> ]

<special symbol> ::= all special characters, such as !, # and *

<sqlstate value> ::= <alphanumeric literal>

<statement in body> ::=
   <declarative statement> |
   <procedural statement>

<statement list> ::= { <statement in body> ; }...

<subquery> ::= ( <table expression> )

<system parameter> ::= @@ <variable name>

<table contents> ::= [ AS ] <table expression>
```

(continued)

```
<table element> ::=
   <column definition>            |
   <table integrity constraint>

<table expression> ::=
   { <singular table expression>  |
     <compound table expression> }
   [ <select block tail> ]

<table integrity constraint> ::=
   [ CONSTRAINT <constraint name> ]
   { <primary key>                |
     <alternate key>              |
     <foreign key>                |
     <check integrity constraint> }

<table privilege> ::=
   SELECT                         |
   INSERT                         |
   DELETE                         |
   UPDATE [ <column list> ]       |
   REFERENCES [ <column list> ]   |
   ALTER                          |
   INDEX

<table privileges> ::=
   ALL [ PRIVILEGES ] |
   <table privilege> [ { , <table privilege> }... ]

<table reference> ::=
   { <table specification> |
     <join specification>  |
     <table subquery>       }
   [ [ AS ] <pseudonym> ]

<table schema> ::=
   ( <table element> [ { , <table element> }... ] )

<table specification> ::=
   [ <database name> . | <user> . ] <table name>

<table subquery> ::= ( <table expression> )
```

(continued)

```
<temporal literal> ::=
   <date literal>      |
   <time literal>      |
   <timestamp literal>

<temporal data type> ::=
   DATE      |
   TIME      |
   TIMESTAMP

<time interval> ::= <scalar time expression>

<time literal> ::= ' <hours> : <minutes> [ : <seconds> ] '

<timestamp interval> ::=
   INTERVAL <interval length> <timestamp interval unit>

<timestamp interval unit> ::=
   MICROSECOND | SECOND | MINUTE | HOUR |
   DAY | WEEK | MONTH | QUARTER | YEAR

<timestamp literal> ::=
   ' <years> - <months> - <days> <space>
     <hours> : <minutes> [ : <seconds> [ . <micro seconds> ] ] '

<values clause> ::=
   VALUES <row expression> [ { , <row expression> } ... ]

<user privilege> ::=
   SELECT                  |
   INSERT                  |
   DELETE                  |
   UPDATE                  |
   REFERENCES              |
   CREATE                  |
   ALTER                   |
   DROP                    |
   INDEX                   |
   CREATE TEMPORARY TABLES |
   CREATE VIEW             |
   CREATE ROUTINE          |
   ALTER ROUTINE           |
   EXECUTE ROUTINE         |
```

(continued)

```
      LOCK TABLES                    |
      CREATE USER

<user variable> ::= @ <variable name>

<when definition> ::= <when definition-1> | <when definition-2>

<when definition-1> ::=
   <scalar expression>
   WHEN <scalar expression> THEN <scalar expression>
   [ { WHEN <scalar expression> THEN <scalar expression> } ]...

<when definition-2> ::=
   WHEN <condition> THEN <scalar expression>
   [ { WHEN <condition> THEN <scalar expression> } ]...

<where clause> ::= WHERE <condition>

<whole number> ::= <digit>...

<years> ::= <whole number>

<collating sequence name>  ;
<condition name>           ;
<constraint name>          ;
<cursor name>              ;
<database name>            ;
<function name>            ;
<host name>                ;
<host variable name>       ;
<index name>               ;
<character set name>       ;
<column name>              ;
<label>                    ;
<procedure name>           ;
<role name>                ;
<savepoint name>           ;
<table name>               ;
<trigger name>             ;
<user name>                ;
<variable name>            ;
<view name>                ::=
   <letter> { <letter> | <digit> | _ }...
```

B Scalar Functions

S QL supports a large number of scalar functions. In this appendix, we present the following for the functions supported by many SQL products: the name, a description, the data type of the result of the function, and a few examples. The functions are sorted by name.

Some functions have more than one name. To make the search easier, we have included them all, but we refer to the functions with the same name.

ABS(*par1*)

Description: This function returns the absolute value of a numeric expression.

Data type: Numeric

```
ABS(-25)      ⇨  25
ABS(-25.89)   ⇨  25.89
```

ACOS(*par1*)

Description: This function returns, in radians, the angle size for any given arc cosine value. The value of the parameter must lie between -1 and 1 inclusive.

Data type: Numeric

```
ACOS(0)            ⇨  1.5707963267949
ACOS(-1) - PI()    ⇨  0
ACOS(1)            ⇨  0
ACOS(2)            ⇨  NULL
```

ADDDATE(*par1, par2*)

Description: This function adds an interval (the second parameter) to a datestamp or timestamp expression (the first parameter). See Section 5.13.3, in Chapter 5, "SELECT Statement: Common Elements," for specifying intervals. If the second parameter is not an interval but is a numeric value, SQL assumes that this value represents a number of days.

Date type: Date or timestamp

```
ADDDATE('2004-01-01', INTERVAL 5 MONTH) ⇨ '2004-06-01'
ADDDATE(TIMESTAMP('2004-01-01'), INTERVAL 5 MONTH)
    ⇨ '2004-06-01 00:00:00'
ADDDATE('2004-01-01 12:00:00', INTERVAL 5 DAY)
    ⇨ '2004-01-06 12:00:00'
ADDDATE('2004-01-01', 5) ⇨ '2004-01-06'
```

ADDTIME(*par1, par2*)

Description: This function adds two time expressions. The result is an interval consisting of a number of hours, minutes, and seconds. Therefore, the number of hours can be greater than 24.

Data type: Time

```
ADDTIME('12:59:00', '0:59:00')      ⇨ '13:58:00'
ADDTIME('12:00:00', '0:00:00.001') ⇨ '12:00:00.001000'
ADDTIME('100:00:00', '900:00:00')  ⇨ '1000:00:00'
```

ASCII(*par1*)

Description: This function returns the ASCII value of the first character of an alphanumeric expression.

Data type: Numeric

```
ASCII('Database') ⇨ 68
ASCII('database') ⇨ 100
ASCII('')         ⇨ 0
ASCII(NULL)       ⇨ NULL
```

ASIN(*par1*)

Description: This function returns, in radians, the angle size for any given arc sine value. The value of the parameter must lie between −1 and 1 inclusive; otherwise, the result is equal to the NULL value.

Data type: Numeric

```
ASIN(1)      ⇨  1.5707963267949
ASIN(0)      ⇨  0
ASIN(NULL)   ⇨  NULL
```

ATAN(*par1*)

Description: This function returns, in radians, the angle size for any given arc tangent value.

Data type: Numeric

```
ATAN(0)    ⇨  0
ATAN(100)  ⇨  1.56079666010823
ATAN(1)    ⇨  0.78539816339745
```

ATAN2(*par1, par2*)

Description: This function returns, in radians, the angle size for any given arc tangent value.

Data type: Numeric

```
ATAN2(30,30)  ⇨  0.78539816339745
ATAN2(-1,-1)  ⇨  -2.3561944901923
```

ATANH(*par1*)

Description: This function returns the hyperbolic arc tangent value of the parameter that must be specified in radians.

Data type: Numeric

```
ATANH(0.4)  ⇨  0.255412811882995
```

BIN(*par1*)

Description: This function transforms the numeric value of the parameter into a binary value. This binary value consists of ones and zeroes, and has the alphanumeric data type.

Data type: Alphanumeric

```
BIN(7)          ⇨ '111'
BIN(1000000)  ⇨ '11110100001001000000'
```

BIT_COUNT(*par1*)

Description: This function shows the number of bits needed to present the value of the parameter. Here, 64-bit integers are used.

Data type: Numeric

```
BIT_COUNT(3)   ⇨ 2
BIT_COUNT(-1)  ⇨ 64
```

BIT_LENGTH(*par1*)

Description: This function returns the length in bits of an alphanumeric value.

Data type: Numeric

```
BIT_LENGTH('database')   ⇨ 64
BIT_LENGTH(BIN(2))       ⇨ 16
```

CEILING(*par1*)

Description: This function returns the highest whole number that is greater than or equal to the value of the parameter.

Data type: Numeric

```
CEILING(13.43)    ⇨ 14
CEILING(-13.43)  ⇨ -13
CEILING(13)       ⇨ 13
```

CHAR(*par1*)

Description: This function returns the alphanumeric character of the numeric parameter. See the CHR function.

Data type: Alphanumeric

```
CHAR(80)                                          ⇨ 'P'
CHAR(82) + CHAR(105) + CHAR(99) + CHAR(107) ⇨ 'Rick'
```

CHARACTER_LENGTH(*par1*)

Description: This function returns the length of an alphanumeric expression.

Data type: Numeric

```
CHARACTER_LENGTH('database')                          ⇨ 8
CHARACTER_LENGTH((SELECT MAX(NAME) FROM PLAYERS)) ⇨ 6
CHARACTER_LENGTH('')                                  ⇨ 0
CHARACTER_LENGTH(NULL)                                ⇨ NULL
CHARACTER_LENGTH(BIN(8))                              ⇨ 4
```

CHARSET(*par1*)

Description: This function returns the name of the character set of the alphanumeric parameter.

Data type: Alphanumeric

```
CHARSET('database')                          ⇨ 'latin1'
CHARSET((SELECT MAX(NAME) FROM PLAYERS))     ⇨ 'latin1'
CHARSET((SELECT MAX(TABLE_NAME)
         FROM   INFORMATION_SCHEMA.TABLES))  ⇨ 'utf8'
```

CHAR_LENGTH(*par1*)

Description: This function returns the length of an alphanumeric expression. See the CHARACTER_LENGTH function.

Data type: Numeric

```
CHAR_LENGTH('database')                         ⇨ 8
CHAR_LENGTH((SELECT MAX(NAME) FROM PLAYERS))    ⇨ 6
CHAR_LENGTH('')                                 ⇨ 0
CHAR_LENGTH(NULL)                               ⇨ NULL
CHAR_LENGTH(BIN(8))                             ⇨ 4
```

CHR(*par1*)

Description: This function returns the alphanumeric character belonging to the numeric parameter. See the CHAR function.

Data type: Alphanumeric

```
CHR(80)                                          ⇨ 'P'
CHR(82) + CHR(105) + CHR(99) + CHR(107) ⇨ 'Rick'
```

COALESCE(*par1, par2, par3, ...*)

Description: This function can have a variable number of parameters. The value of the function is equal to the value of the first parameter that is not equal to NULL.

If E_1, E_2, and E_3 are three expressions, the specification:

```
COALESCE(E_1, E_2, E_3)
```

is equivalent to the following case expression:

```
CASE
    WHEN E_1 IS NOT NULL THEN E_1
    WHEN E_2 IS NOT NULL THEN E_2
    WHEN E_3 IS NOT NULL THEN E_3
    ELSE NULL
END
```

Data type: Depends on parameters

```
COALESCE('John', 'Jim', NULL)                   ⇨ 'John'
COALESCE(NULL, NULL, NULL, 'John', 'Jim') ⇨ 'John'
```

COERCIBILITY(*par1*)

Description: This function determines the coercibility value of an expression.

Data type: Numeric

```
COERCIBILITY(NULL)        ⇨ 5
COERCIBILITY('Database')  ⇨ 4
```

COLLATION (*par1*)

Description: This function gets the name of the collating sequence of the alphanumeric parameter.

Data type: Alphanumeric

```
COLLATION('database')
    ⇨ 'latin1_swedish_ci'
COLLATION((SELECT MAX(NAME) FROM PLAYERS))
    ⇨ 'latin1_swedish_ci'
COLLATION((SELECT MAX(TABLE_NAME)
          FROM   INFORMATION_SCHEMA.TABLES))
    ⇨ 'utf8_general_ci'
```

CONCAT(*par1, part2*)

Description: This function combines two alphanumeric values. The same effect can be obtained with the || operator.

Data type: Alphanumeric

```
CONCAT('Data','base')  ⇨ 'Database'
```

CONNECTION_ID()

Description: This function returns the numeric identifier of the connection.

Data type: Numeric

```
CONNECTION_ID()  ⇨ 4
```

CONV(par1, part2, par3)

Description: This function converts the value (first parameter) of one number base (second parameter) to another (third parameter). The value of the two last parameters must be between 2 and 36; otherwise, the result is equal to NULL. Furthermore, the value of the first parameter should fit into the number base of the first parameter; otherwise, the result is 0.

Data type: Alphanumeric

```
CONV(1110, 2, 10)    ⇨  '14'
CONV(1110, 10, 2)    ⇨  '10001010110'
CONV(1110, 10, 8)    ⇨  '2126'
CONV(1110, 10, 16)   ⇨  '456'
CONV(35, 10, 36)     ⇨  'Z'
CONV(35, 10, 37)     ⇨  NULL
CONV(8, 2, 10)       ⇨  '0'
```

CONVERT(*par1, par2*)

Description: This function converts the data type of the first parameter. The second parameter must be equal to one of the well-known data types, including BINARY, CHAR, DATE, DATETIME, TIME, SIGNED, SIGNED INTEGER, UNSIGNED, UNSIGNED INTEGER, or VARCHAR. This specification:

```
CONVERT(par1, type1)
```

is equal to:

```
CAST(par1 AS type1)
```

The following formulations may also be used:

```
CONVERT(par1 USING type1)
```

Data type: Depends on the second parameter

```
CONVERT(45, CHAR(2))                 ⇨  '45'
CONVERT('2000-01-42', DATE)          ⇨  '2000-01-01'
CONVERT(12.56, UNSIGNED INTEGER)     ⇨  13
CONVERT(-12.56, UNSIGNED INTEGER)    ⇨  18446744073709551603
```

CONVERT_TZ(*par1, part2, par3*)

Description: This function determines what the timestamp value of a timestamp expression (first parameter) is when the time zone is changed. The second parameter indicates the current time zone, and the third parameter indicates the new time zone.

Date type: Timestamp

```
CONVERT_TZ('2005-05-20 09:30:40', '+00:00', '+9:00')
   ⇨ 2005-05-20 18:30:40
```

COS(*par1*)

Description: This function returns, in radians, the cosine value for any angle size.

Data type: Numeric

```
COS(0)        ⇨ 1
COS(PI()/2)   ⇨ 0
COS(PI())     ⇨ -1
```

COT(*par1*)

Description: This function returns, in radians, the cotangent value for any angle size.

Data type: Numeric

```
COT(10)       ⇨ 1.54235
COT(PI()/2)   ⇨ 0
COT(NULL)     ⇨ NULL
```

CURDATE()

Description: This function returns the system date. In some SQL products, to get the system date, the system variable SYSDATE should be used.

Data type: date

```
CURDATE()  ⇨ '2005-02-20'
```

CURRENT_DATE()

Description: This function returns the system date with the format YYYY-MM-DD. If the function is regarded as a numeric expression, the system date is presented as a numeric value with the format YYYYMMDD. If the brackets are left out, the function changes into the system variable CURRENT_DATE. See the CURDATE function.

Data type: Date or double

```
CURRENT_DATE()        ⇨  '2005-02-20'
CURRENT_DATE() + 0 ⇨  20050220
CURRENT_DATE          ⇨  '2005-02-20'
```

CURRENT_TIME()

Description: This function returns the system time with the format HH:MM:SS. The abbreviation HH stands for the hours, MM for minutes, and SS for seconds. If the function is regarded as a numeric expression, the system time is presented as a numeric value with the format HHMMSS. If the brackets are left out, the function changes into the system variable CURRENT_TIME. See the CURTIME function.

Data type: Time or double

```
CURRENT_TIME()        ⇨  '16:42:24'
CURRENT_TIME() + 0 ⇨  164224
CURRENT_TIME          ⇨  '16:42:24'
```

CURRENT_TIMESTAMP()

Description: This function returns the system date and time with the format YYYY-MM-DD HH:MM:SS. The abbreviation YYYY stands for years, the first MM for months, DD for days, HH for hours, the second MM for minutes, and SS for seconds. If the function is regarded as a numeric expression, the system date and time are presented as a numeric value with the format YYYYMMDDHHMMSS. If the brackets are left out, the function changes into the system variable CURRENT_TIMESTAMP.

Data type: Timestamp or double

```
CURRENT_TIMESTAMP()        ⇨  '2005-10-16 20:53:45'
CURRENT_TIMESTAMP() + 0 ⇨  20051016205345
CURRENT_TIMESTAMP          ⇨  '2005-10-16 20:53:45'
```

CURRENT_USER()

Description: This function returns the name of the SQL user.

Data type: Alphanumeric

```
CURRENT_USER()  ⇨  'root@localhost'
```

CURTIME()

Description: This function returns the system time with the format HH:MM:SS. The abbreviation HH stands for hours, MM for minutes, and SS for seconds. In some products, this function is briefly called TIME.

Data type: Alphanumeric

```
CURTIME()  ⇨  '16:42:24'
```

DATABASE()

Description: This function shows the name of the current database.

Data type: Alphanumeric

```
DATABASE()  ⇨  'TENNIS'
```

DATE(*par1*)

Description: This function transforms the parameter into a date value. The parameter should have the format of a correct date or timestamp.

Data type: Date

```
DATE('2005-12-01')            ⇨  '2005-12-01'
DATE('2005-12-01 12:13:14')   ⇨  '2005-12-01'
```

DATE_ADD(*par1, par2*)

Description: This function adds an interval (the second parameter) to a date or timestamp expression (the first parameter). See Section 5.13.3, in Chapter 5, for specifying intervals. See the ADDDATE function.

Date type: Date or timestamp

```
DATE_ADD('2004-01-01', INTERVAL 5 MONTH)  ⇨  '2004-06-01'
DATE_ADD('2004-01-01 12:00:00', INTERVAL 5 DAY)
   ⇨  '2004-01-06 12:00:00'
```

DATEDIFF(*par1, par2*)

Description: This function calculates the number of days between two date or time-stamp expressions.

Date type: Numeric

```
DATEDIFF('2004-01-12', '2004-01-01')                      ⇨ 11
DATEDIFF('2004-01-01', '2004-01-12')                      ⇨ -11
DATEDIFF('2004-01-12 19:00:00', '2004-01-01') )          ⇨ 11
DATEDIFF('2004-01-12 19:00:00', '2004-01-01 01:00:00')   ⇨ 11
DATEDIFF('2004-01-12', CURDATE())                        ⇨ -643
```

DATE_FORMAT(*par1, par2*)

Description: This function transforms a date or timestamp expression (the first parameter) to an alphanumeric value. The second parameter describes the format of that alphanumeric value. Several special format strings can be used; see the following table.

FORMAT STRING	EXPLANATION
%a	Three-letter English abbreviation of the weekday (for example, Sun, Mon, or Sat)
%b	Three-letter English abbreviation of the month (for example, Jan, Feb, or Mar)
%c	Numeric code for the month (0 up to and including 12)
%D	Day of the month with an English suffix, such as 0th, 1st, and 2nd
%d	Two-digit numeric code for the day of the month (00 up to and including 31)
%e	One- or two-digit numeric code for the day of the month (0 up to and including 31)
%f	Six-digit numeric code for the number of microseconds (000000 up to and including 999999)
%H	Two-digit numeric code for the hour (00 up to and including 23)
%h	Two-digit numeric code for the hour (01 up to and including 12)
%I	Two-digit numeric code for the hour (01 up to and including 12)
%i	Two-digit numeric code for the number of minutes (00 up to and including 59)
%j	Three-digit numeric code for the day of the year (001 up to and including 366)
%k	One or two-digit numeric code for the hour (0 up to and including 23)

FORMAT STRING	EXPLANATION
%l	One or two-digit numeric code for the hour (1 up to and including 12)
%M	English indication of the month (for example, January, February, or December)
%m	Two-digit, numeric code for the month (00 up to and including 12)
%p	Indication of AM or PM
%r	Indication of the time (in 12 hours) with the format HH:MM:SS, followed by AM or PM
%S	Two-digit numeric code for the number of seconds (00 up to and including 59)
%s	Two-digit numeric code for the number of seconds (00 up to and including 59)
%T	Indication of the time (in 24 hours) with the format HH:MM:SS followed by AM or PM
%U	Two-digit numeric code for the week in the year (00 up to and including 53), for which Sunday is considered to be the first day of the week
%u	Two-digit numeric code for the week in the year (00 up to and including 53), for which Monday is considered to be the first day of the week
%V	Two-digit numeric code for the week in the year (01 up to and including 53), for which Sunday is considered to be the first day of the week
%v	Two-digit numeric code for the week in the year (01 up to and including 53), for which Monday is considered to be the first day of the week
%W	English indication of the day in the week (for example, Sunday, Monday, or Saturday)
%w	One-digit code for the day in the week (0 up to and including 6), for which Sunday is considered to be the first day of the week
%X	Four-digit numeric code that indicates the year in which the week starts belonging to the specified date, for which Sunday is the first day of the week
%x	Four-digit, numeric code that indicates the year in which the week starts belonging to the specified date, for which Monday is the first day of the week
%Y	Four-digit numeric code for the year
%y	Two-digit numeric code for the year
%%	Returns the percentage sign

Data type: Alphanumeric

```
DATE_FORMAT('2005-10-16', '%a %c %b')      ⇨ 'Sun 10 Oct'
DATE_FORMAT('2005-10-06', '%d %e %D')      ⇨ '06 6 6th'
DATE_FORMAT('2005-01-16', '%j %M %m')      ⇨ '016 January 01'
DATE_FORMAT('2005-01-09', '%U %u %V %v')   ⇨ '02 01 02 01'
DATE_FORMAT('2005-12-31', '%U %u %V %v')   ⇨ '52 52 52 52'
DATE_FORMAT('2005-01-09', '%W %w')         ⇨ 'Sunday 0'
DATE_FORMAT('2005-01-02', '%X %x')         ⇨ '2005 2004'
DATE_FORMAT('2005-01-09', '%Y %y')         ⇨ '2005 05'
DATE_FORMAT('2005-01-01 12:13:14.012345', '%f') ⇨ '012345'
DATE_FORMAT('2005-01-01 12:13:14', '%H %h %I %i')
   ⇨ '13 01 01 14'
DATE_FORMAT('2005-01-01 12:13:14', '%k %l %p') ⇨ '12 12 PM'
DATE_FORMAT('2005-01-01 12:13:14', '%S %s %T')
   ⇨ '14 12 12:13:14'
DATE_FORMAT('2005-01-09', 'Database')      ⇨ 'Database'
DATE_FORMAT('2005-01-09', 'It is this day %W')
   ⇨ 'This day is Sunday'
```

DATE_SUB(*par1, par2*)

Description: This function subtracts an interval (the second parameter) from a date or timestamp expression (the first parameter). See Section 5.13.3, in Chapter 5, for specifying intervals. See the SUBDATE function.

Data type: Date or timestamp

```
DATE_SUB('2004-01-01', INTERVAL 5 MONTH) ⇨ '2003-08-01'
DATE_SUB('2004-01-01 12:00:00', INTERVAL 5 DAY)
   ⇨ '2003-12-27 12:00:00'
```

DAY(*par1*)

Description: This function returns the number of the day of the month from a date or timestamp expression. The value of the result is always a whole number between 1 and 31 inclusive. See the DAYOFMONTH function.

Date type: Numeric

```
DAY('2004-01-01')              ⇨  1
DAY('2004-01-01 09:11:11')     ⇨  1
DAY(CURRENT_DATE())            ⇨  17
DAY(CURRENT_TIMESTAMP())       ⇨  17
```

DAYNAME(par1)

Description: This function returns the name of the day of the week from a date or time-stamp expression.

Data type: Alphanumeric

```
DAYNAME('2005-01-01') ⇨ 'Saturday'
```

DAYOFMONTH(par1)

Description: This function returns the number of the day of the month from a date or timestamp expression. The value of the result is always a whole number between 1 and 31 inclusive. See the DAY function.

Data type: Numeric

```
DAYOFMONTH('2004-01-01')              ⇨  1
DAYOFMONTH('2004-01-01 09:11:11')     ⇨  1
DAYOFMONTH(CURRENT_DATE())            ⇨  17
DAYOFMONTH(CURRENT_TIMESTAMP())       ⇨  17
```

DAYOFWEEK(par1)

Description: This function returns the number of the day of the week from a date or timestamp expression. The value of the result is always a whole number between 1 and 7 inclusive.

Data type: Numeric

```
DAYOFWEEK('1005-07-29')            ⇨  2
DAYOFWEEK(CURRENT_TIMESTAMP())     ⇨  3
```

DAYOFYEAR(*par1*)

Description: This function returns the number of the day of the year from a date or time-stamp expression. The value of the result is always a whole number between 1 and 366 inclusive.

Data type: Numeric

```
DAYOFYEAR('2005-07-29')            ⇨ 210
DAYOFYEAR('2005-07-29 12:00:00')   ⇨ 210
DAYOFYEAR(CURDATE())               ⇨ 291
```

DEFAULT()

Description: This function returns the default value of a certain column. See also Example 15.13, in Chapter 15, "Creating Tables."

Data type: Depends on the column

```
DEFAULT(DATE)     ⇨ '1990-01-01'
DEFAULT(AMOUNT)   ⇨ 50.00
```

DEGREES(*par1*)

Description: This function converts a number of degrees to a value in radians.

Data type: Numeric

```
DEGREES(1.570796)  ⇨ 90
DEGREES(PI())      ⇨ 180
```

EXP(*par1*)

Description: This function returns the result of the number e to the power of x, where x is the value of the parameter and e the basis of natural logarithms.

Data type: Numeric

```
EXP(1)  ⇨ 2.718281828459
EXP(2)  ⇨ 7.3890560989307
```

FLOOR(*par1*)

Description: This function returns the smallest whole number that is less than or equal to the value of the parameter.

Data type: Numeric

```
FLOOR(13.9)    ⇨ 13
FLOOR(-13.9)   ⇨ -14
```

FORMAT(*par1, par2*)

Description: This function formats a numeric value to the pattern nn,nnn,nnn.nnn. The second parameter represents the number of decimals behind the comma and must be greater than or equal to zero.

Data type: Alphanumeric

```
FORMAT(123456789.123, 2)  ⇨  '123,456,789.12'
FORMAT(123456789.123, 0)  ⇨  '123,456,789'
```

FOUND_ROWS()

Description: This function returns the number of rows in the result of the previous SELECT statement.

Data type: Numeric

```
FOUND_ROWS()  ⇨  14
```

FROM_DAYS(*par1*)

Description: This function determines the date belonging to a number of days that have elapsed since the year 0. The parameter forms the number of days and must be between 366 and 3,652,424.

Data type: Date

```
FROM_DAYS(366)                         ⇨  '0001-01-01'
FROM_DAYS(366*2000)                    ⇨  '2004-02-24'
FROM_DAYS(3652424)                     ⇨  '9999-12-31'
FROM_DAYS(3652500)                     ⇨  '0000-00-00'
FROM_DAYS(3652424) - INTERVAL 5 DAY    ⇨  '9999-12-26'
```

GET_FORMAT(*par1, par2*)

Description: This function returns a format that can be used in other functions, such as DATE_FORMAT, TIME_FORMAT, and STR_TO_DATE. The first parameter represents the data type. This must be equal to DATE, TIME, or DATETIME. The second parameter represents the format type. Possible values are EUR, INTERNAL, ISO, JIS, and USA. The following examples reflect all the possibilities.

Data type: Alphanumeric

```
GET_FORMAT(DATE,  'EUR')             ⇨  '%d.%m.%Y'
GET_FORMAT(DATE,  'INTERNAL')        ⇨  '%Y%m%d'
GET_FORMAT(DATE,  'ISO')             ⇨  '%Y-%m-%d'
GET_FORMAT(DATE,  'JIS')             ⇨  '%Y-%m-%d'
GET_FORMAT(DATE,  'USA')             ⇨  '%m.%d.%Y'
GET_FORMAT(TIME,  'EUR')             ⇨  '%H.%i.%s'
GET_FORMAT(TIME,  'INTERNAL')        ⇨  '%H%i%s'
GET_FORMAT(TIME,  'ISO')             ⇨  '%H:%i:%s'
GET_FORMAT(TIME,  'JIS')             ⇨  '%H:%i:%s'
GET_FORMAT(TIME,  'USA')             ⇨  '%h:%i:%s %p'
GET_FORMAT(DATETIME,  'EUR')         ⇨  '%Y-%m-%d %H.%i.%s'
GET_FORMAT(DATETIME,  'INTERNAL')    ⇨  '%Y%m%d%H%i%s'
GET_FORMAT(DATETIME,  'ISO')         ⇨  '%Y-%m-%d %H:%i:%s'
GET_FORMAT(DATETIME,  'JIS')         ⇨  '%Y-%m-%d %H:%i:%s'
GET_FORMAT(DATETIME,  'USA')         ⇨  '%Y-%m-%d %H.%i.%s'

DATE_FORMAT('2005-01-01', GET_FORMAT(DATE,  'EUR'))
     ⇨  '01.01.2005'
DATE_FORMAT('2005-01-01', GET_FORMAT(DATE,  'ISO'))
     ⇨  '2005-01-01'
```

GREATEST(*par1, par2, ...*)

Description: This function returns the greatest value from a series of parameters.

Data type: Depends on parameters

```
GREATEST(100, 4, 80)                                    ⇨  100
GREATEST(DATE('2005-01-01'), DATE('2005-06-12'))
     ⇨  '2005-06-12'
```

HEX(*par1*)

Description: If the parameter is numeric, this function returns the hexadecimal representation of the parameter. If the parameter is alphanumeric, this function returns a two-digit code for each character.

Data type: Alphanumeric

```
HEX(11)      ⇨ 'B'
HEX(16)      ⇨ '10'
HEX(100)     ⇨ '64'
HEX(1000)    ⇨ '3E8'
HEX('3E8')   ⇨ '334538'
HEX('ç')     ⇨ 'E7'
```

HOUR(*par1*)

Description: This function returns the number of the hour from a time or timestamp expression. The value of the result is always a whole number between 0 and 23 inclusive.

Data type: Numeric

```
HOUR('2005-01-01 12:13:14')  ⇨ 12
HOUR('12:13:14')             ⇨ 12
HOUR(CURTIME())              ⇨ 19
```

IF(par1, par2, par3)

Description: If the value of the first parameter is true, the result of the function is equal to the value of the second parameter; otherwise, it is equal to the value of the third parameter. The specification

```
IF(E₁, E₂, E₃)
```

in which E_1, E_2, and E_3 are expressions, is equal to the following case expression:

```
CASE
    WHEN E₁ = TRUE THEN E₂
    ELSE E₃
END
```

Data type: Depends on the two last parameters

```
IF((5>8), 'Jim', 'John') ⇨ 'John'
IF((SELECT COUNT(*) FROM PLAYERS) =
    (SELECT COUNT(*) FROM PENALTIES), TRUE, FALSE) ⇨ 0
```

IFNULL(*par1, par2*)

Description: If the value of the first parameter is equal to the NULL value, the result of the function is equal to the value of the second parameter; otherwise, it is equal to the value of the first parameter. The specification

```
IFNULL(E₁, E₂)
```

in which E_1, and E_2 are expressions, is equal to the following case expression:

```
CASE E₁
    WHEN NULL THEN E₂
    ELSE E₁
END
```

Data type: Depends on the parameters

```
IFNULL(NULL, 'John') ⇨ 'John'
IFNULL('John', 'Jim') ⇨ 'John'
```

INSERT(par1, par2, par3, par4)

Description: The value of the fourth parameter is placed on the part of the first parameter that starts with the position indicated with the second parameter, and that is a number of characters long (and that is the third parameter).

Data type: Alphanumeric

```
INSERT('abcdefgh',4,3,'zzz') ⇨ 'abczzzgh'
INSERT('abcdefgh',4,2,'zzz') ⇨ 'abczzzfgh'
INSERT('abcdefgh',4,0,'zzz') ⇨ 'abczzzdefgh'
INSERT('abcdefgh',4,-1,'zzz') ⇨ 'abczzz'
INSERT('abcdefgh',1,5,'zzz') ⇨ 'zzzfgh'
```

INSTR(*par1, par2*)

Description: This function returns the starting position of the second alphanumeric value within the first alphanumeric value. The INSTR function has the value zero if the second alphanumeric value does not appear within the first.

Data type: Numeric

```
INSTR('database','bas') ⇨ 5
INSTR('system','bas')   ⇨ 0
```

INTERVAL(*par, par2, par3, ...*)

Description: This function determines between which two values in a list the first parameter appears. After the first parameter, the values must be specified in ascending order.

Data type: Depends on the two last parameters

```
INTERVAL(3,0,1,2,3,4,5,6,7) ⇨ 4
INTERVAL(7,0,6,11,16,21)    ⇨ 2
```

ISNULL(*par1*)

Description: The value of this function is equal to 1 if the first parameter is equal to the NULL value; otherwise, it is equal to 0. The specification

```
ISNULL(E₁)
```

in which E_1 is an expression, is equal to the following case expression:

```
CASE E₁
    WHEN NULL THEN 1
    ELSE 0
END
```

Data type: Depends on parameters

```
ISNULL((SELECT LEAGUENO FROM PLAYERS WHERE PLAYERNO=27)) ⇨ 0
ISNULL((SELECT LEAGUENO FROM PLAYERS WHERE PLAYERNO=7))  ⇨ 1
```

LAST_DAY(*par1*)

Description: This function returns the last day of the month belonging to a date or time-stamp expression.

Data type: Date

```
LAST_DAY('2004-02-01')  ⇨  '2005-02-29'
LAST_DAY('2005-02-01')  ⇨  '2005-02-28'
```

LCASE(*par1*)

Description: This function converts all uppercase letters of the value of the parameter to lowercase letters.

Data type: Alphanumeric

```
LCASE('RICK')  ⇨  'rick'
```

LEAST(*par1, par2, ...*)

Description: This function returns the smallest value from a series of parameters.

Data type: Depends on parameters

```
LEAST(100, 4, 80)                                    ⇨  4
LEAST(DATE('2005-01-01'), DATE('2005-06-12'))  ⇨  2005-01-01
```

LEFT(*par1, par2*)

Description: This function returns the left part of an alphanumeric value (the first parameter). The length of the part that is used is indicated with the second parameter.

Data type: Alphanumeric

```
LEFT('database', 4)              ⇨  'data'
LEFT('database', 0)              ⇨  ''
LEFT('database', 10)             ⇨  'database'
LEFT('database', NULL)           ⇨  ''
LENGTH(LEFT('database', 0))      ⇨  0
LENGTH(LEFT('database', 10))     ⇨  8
LENGTH(LEFT('database', NULL))   ⇨  0
```

LENGTH(*par1*)

Description: This function returns the length in bytes of an alphanumeric value.

Data type: Numeric

```
LENGTH('database')          ⇨ 8
LENGTH('data     ')         ⇨ 8
LENGTH(RTRIM('abcd    '))   ⇨ 4
LENGTH('')                  ⇨ 0
LENGTH(NULL)                ⇨ NULL
```

LN(*par1*)

Description: This function returns the logarithm to the base value e of the parameter. See the LOG function.

Data type: Numeric

```
LN(50)       ⇨ 3.9120230054281
LN(EXP(3))   ⇨ 3
LN(0)        ⇨ NULL
LN(1)        ⇨ 0
```

LOCALTIME()

Description: This function returns the system date and system time. If the function is used within a numeric expression, the result is numeric. The brackets may be left out. See the NOW and LOCALTIMESTAMP functions.

Data type: Timestamp or double

```
LOCALTIME()       ⇨ '2005-02-20 12:26:52'
LOCALTIME() + 0   ⇨ 20050220122652
```

LOCALTIMESTAMP()

Description: This function returns the system date and system time. If the function is used within a numeric expression, the result is numeric. The brackets may be left out. See the NOW and LOCALTIME functions.

Data type: Timestamp or double

```
LOCALTIMESTAMP()        ⇨  '2005-02-20 12:26:52'
LOCALTIMESTAMP() + 0 ⇨ 20050220122652
```

LOCATE(*par1, par2, par3*)

Description: This function returns the starting position of the first alphanumeric value within the second alphanumeric value. The LOCATE function has the value zero if the first alphanumeric value does not occur within the second. A third parameter may be included to indicate a position from which the search may be started.

Data type: Numeric

```
LOCATE('bas','database')      ⇨  5
LOCATE('bas','database',6) ⇨ 0
LOCATE('bas','system')        ⇨  0
```

LOG(*par1*)

Description: This function returns the logarithm to the base value e of the parameter.

Data type: Numeric

```
LOG(50)        ⇨  3.9120230054281
LOG(EXP(3)) ⇨ 3
LOG(0)          ⇨  NULL
LOG(1)          ⇨  0
```

LOG(par1, par2)

Description: This function returns the logarithm of the second parameter where the first parameter forms the base value.

Data type: Numeric

```
LOG(10,1000) ⇨ 3
LOG(2,64)      ⇨  6
```

LOG2(*par1*)

Description: This function returns the logarithm to the base value 2 of the parameter.

Data type: Numeric

```
LOG2(2)              ⇨ 1
LOG2(64)             ⇨ 6
LOG2(POWER(2,10))    ⇨ 10
```

LOG10(*par1*)

Description: This function returns the logarithm to the base value 10 of the parameter.

Data type: Numeric

```
LOG10(1000)          ⇨ 3
LOG10(POWER(10,5))   ⇨ 5
```

LOWER(*par1*)

Description: This function converts all uppercase letters of the value of the parameter to lowercase letters. See the LCASE function.

Data type: Alphanumeric

```
LOWER('RICK')  ⇨ 'rick'
```

LPAD(par1, par2, par3)

Description: The value of the first parameter is filled in the front (the left side) with the value of the third parameter just until the total length of the value is equal to that of the second parameter. If the maximum length is smaller than that of the first parameter, the first parameter is shortened on the left side.

Data type: Alphanumeric

```
LPAD('data', 16, 'base')  ⇨ 'basebasebasedata'
LPAD('data', 6, 'base')   ⇨ 'badata'
LPAD('data', 2, 'base')   ⇨ 'da'
```

LTRIM(*par1*)

Description: This function removes all blanks that appear at the beginning of the parameter.

Data type: Alphanumeric

```
LTRIM('   database')  ⇨  'database'
```

MAKEDATE(*par1, par2*)

Description: The second parameter represents a number of days, and those are added to the second parameter. This second parameter must be a numeric, date, or timestamp expression.

Data type: Date

```
MAKEDATE(2005, 1)                        ⇨  '2005-01-01'
MAKEDATE(2005, 10)                       ⇨  '2005-01-10'
MAKEDATE('2005-01-01', 1)                ⇨  '2005-01-01'
MAKEDATE('2005-01-01 12:26:52', 1)  ⇨  '2005-01-01'
```

MAKETIME(*par1, par2, par3*)

Description: This function creates a time from a number of hours (the first parameter), a number of minutes (the second parameter), and a number of seconds (the third parameter). The number of minutes and the number of seconds must be between 0 and 59 inclusive; otherwise, the function returns the NULL value as result.

Data type: Time

```
MAKETIME(12,13,14)    ⇨  '12:13:14'
MAKETIME(12,90,14)    ⇨  NULL
MAKETIME(120,13,14)  ⇨  '120:13:14'
```

MICROSECOND(*par1*)

Description: This function returns the number of microseconds from a time or time-stamp expression. The value of the result is always a whole number between 0 and 999999 inclusive.

Data type: Numeric

```
MICROSECOND('2005-01-01 12:13:14.123456')  ⇨ 123456
MICROSECOND('12:13:14.1')                   ⇨ 100000
```

MID(par1, par2, par3)

Description: This function extracts part of the alphanumeric value of the first parameter. The second parameter identifies the start position, and the third parameter identifies the number of characters. See the SUBSTRING function.

Data type: Alphanumeric

```
MID('database',5)     ⇨ 'base'
MID('database',10)    ⇨ ''
MID('database',5,2)   ⇨ 'ba'
MID('database',5,10)  ⇨ 'base'
MID('database',-6)    ⇨ 'tabase'
```

MINUTE(*par1*)

Description: This function returns the number of minutes from a time or timestamp expression. The value of the result is always a whole number between 0 and 59 inclusive.

Data type: Numeric

```
MINUTE(CURTIME())    ⇨ 52
MINUTE('12:40:33')   ⇨ 40
```

MOD(*par1*)

Description: This function returns the remainder from the division of two parameters.

Data type: Numeric

```
MOD(15,4)       ⇨ 3
MOD(15.4, 4.4)  ⇨ 2.2
```

MONTH(*par1*)

Description: This function returns the number of the month from a date or timestamp expression. The value of the result is always a whole number between 1 and 12 inclusive.

Data type: Numeric

```
MONTH('1988-07-29')  ⇨  7
```

MONTHNAME

Description: This function returns the name of the month from a date or timestamp expression.

Data type: Alphanumeric

```
MONTHNAME('1988-05-20')  ⇨  'May'
MONTHNAME('1988-06-20')  ⇨  'June'
```

NOW()

Description: This function returns the system date and system time.

Data type: Timestamp

```
NOW()  ⇨  '2005-12-20 12:26:52'
```

NULLIF(*par1, par2*)

Description: If the value of the first parameter is not equal to that of the second parameter, the result of the function is equal to the NULL value; otherwise, it is equal to the first parameter. The specification

```
NULLIF(E₁, E₂)
```

in which E_1 and E_2 are two expressions, is equal to the following case expression:

```
CASE
    WHEN E₁ = E₂ THEN NULL
    ELSE E₁
END
```

Data type: Depends on parameters

```
NULLIF(NULL, 'John')    ⇨ NULL
NULLIF('John', 'Jim')   ⇨ 'John'
NULLIF('John', 'John')  ⇨ NULL
```

OCT(*par1*)

Description: This function returns the decimal of the first parameter. This parameter has an octal value.

Data type: Alphanumeric

```
OCT(8)    ⇨ '10'
OCT(64)   ⇨ '100'
OCT(100)  ⇨ '144'
```

OCTET_LENGTH(*par1*)

Description: This function returns the length in bytes of an octal value.

Data type: Numeric

```
OCTET_LENGTH('100')     ⇨ 3
OCTET_LENGTH(OCT(64))   ⇨ 3
```

ORD(*par1*)

Description: This function returns the (ordinal) character set position of the first character of an alphanumeric expression.

Data type: Numeric

```
ORD('Database')  ⇨ 68
ORD('database')  ⇨ 100
ORD('')          ⇨ 0
ORD(NULL)        ⇨ NULL
```

PERIOD_ADD(*par1, par2*)

Description: This function adds a number of months to a specific date. The date must have the format YYYYMM or YYMM. The format of the result is YYYYMM. Therefore, this function does not work with traditional dates.

Data type: Alphanumeric

```
PERIOD_ADD('200508', 2)   ⇨ '200510'
PERIOD_ADD('200508', -2)  ⇨ '200506'
PERIOD_ADD('200508', 12)  ⇨ '200608'
```

PERIOD_DIFF(*par1, par2*)

Description: This function determines the number of months between two dates. Both dates must have the format YYYYMM or YYMM. Therefore, this function does not work with values with the date data type.

Data type: Numeric

```
PERIOD_DIFF('200508', '200510')  ⇨ -2
PERIOD_DIFF('200508', '200506')  ⇨ 2
PERIOD_DIFF('200508', '200608')  ⇨ -12
```

PI()

Description: This function returns the well-known number *pi*.

Data type: Numeric

```
PI()          ⇨ 3.141593
PI()*100000   ⇨ 314159.265359
```

POWER(*par1, par2*)

Description: The value of the first expression is raised to a specific power. The second parameter indicates the power.

Data type: Numeric

```
POWER(4,3)       ⇨ 64
POWER(2.5,3)     ⇨ 15.625
POWER(4, 0.3)    ⇨ 1.5157165665104
POWER(4, -2)     ⇨ 0.0625
```

QUARTER

Description: This function returns the quarter from a date or timestamp expression. The value of the result is always a whole number between 1 and 4 inclusive.

Data type: Numeric

```
QUARTER('1988-07-29')   ⇨ 3
QUARTER(CURDATE())      ⇨ 1
```

RADIANS(*par1*)

Description: This function converts a number in degrees to a value in radians.

Data type: Numeric

```
RADIANS(90)           ⇨ 1.5707963267949
RADIANS(180) - PI()   ⇨ 0
RADIANS(-360)         ⇨ -6.2831853071796
```

RAND(*par1*)

Description: This function returns a random number (with a float data type) between 0.0 and 1.0. The parameter indicates the starting point for the calculation of the next random value. The result is the same when this function is called repeatedly with the same parameter value. If no parameter has been specified, the next random value is calculated.

Data type: Numeric

```
RAND()                                    ⇨ 0.42908766346899
RAND(5)                                   ⇨ 0.40613597483014
CAST(RAND() * 10000 AS UNSIGNED INTEGER)  ⇨ 8057
```

REPEAT(*par1, par2*)

Description: This function repeats an alphanumeric value (the first parameter) a specified number of times. The second parameter indicates the number of times.

Data type: Alphanumeric

```
REPEAT('bla',4)   ⇨  'blablablabla'
REPEAT('X',10)    ⇨  'XXXXXXXXXX'
```

REPLACE(*par1, par2, par3*)

Description: This function replaces parts of the value of an alphanumeric expression with another value.

Data type: Alphanumeric

```
REPLACE('database','a','e')            ⇨  'detebese'
REPLACE('database','ba','warehou')     ⇨  'datawarehouse'
REPLACE('data base',' ','')            ⇨  'database'
```

REVERSE(*par1*)

Description: This function reverses the characters in an alphanumeric value.

Data type: Alphanumeric

```
REVERSE('database')  ⇨  'esabatad'
```

RIGHT(*par1, par2*)

Description: This function returns the right part of an alphanumeric value (the first parameter). The length of the part that is used is indicated with the second parameter.

Data type: Alphanumeric

```
RIGHT('database', 4)             ⇨  'base'
RIGHT('database', 0)             ⇨  ''
RIGHT('database', 10)            ⇨  'database'
RIGHT('database', NULL)          ⇨  ''
LENGTH(RIGHT('database', 0))     ⇨  0
LENGTH(RIGHT('database', 10))    ⇨  8
LENGTH(RIGHT('database', NULL))  ⇨  0
```

ROUND(*par1*, *par2*)

Description: This function rounds numbers to a specified number of decimal places. If the second parameter has not been specified, it is equal to the specification of 0.

Data type: Numeric

```
ROUND(123.456,2)   ⇨ 123.46
ROUND(123.456,1)   ⇨ 123.5
ROUND(123.456,0)   ⇨ 123
ROUND(123.456,-1)  ⇨ 120
ROUND(123.456,-2)  ⇨ 100
ROUND(123.456)     ⇨ 123
```

RPAD(par1, par2, par3)

Description: The value of the first parameter is filled in the front (the right side) with the value of the third parameter just until the total length of the value is equal to that of the second parameter. If the maximum length is smaller than that of the first parameter, the first parameter is shortened on the right side.

Data type: Alphanumeric

```
RPAD('data', 16, 'base')  ⇨ 'databasebasebase'
RPAD('data', 6, 'base')   ⇨ 'databa'
RPAD('data', 2, 'base')   ⇨ 'da'
```

RTRIM(*par1*)

Description: This function removes all blanks from the end of the value of the parameter.

Data type: Alphanumeric

```
RTRIM('database     ')                ⇨ 'database'
CONCAT(RTRIM('data     '), 'base')  ⇨ 'database'
```

SECOND(*par1*)

Description: This function returns the number of seconds from a time or timestamp expression. The value of the result is always a whole number between 0 and 59 inclusive.

Data type: Numeric

```
SECOND(CURTIME())    ⇨ 6
SECOND('12:40:33')   ⇨ 33
```

SEC_TO_TIME(*par1*)

Description: This function transforms a number of seconds in a time.

Data type: Time

```
SEC_TO_TIME(1)              ⇨ '00:00:01'
SEC_TO_TIME(1000)           ⇨ '00:16:40'
SEC_TO_TIME((24*60*60)-1)   ⇨ '23:59:59'
SEC_TO_TIME(24*60*60*2)     ⇨ '48:00:00'
```

SESSION_USER()

Description: This function returns the name of the SQL user.

Data type: Alphanumeric

```
SESSION_USER() ⇨ 'root@localhost'
```

SIGN(*par1*)

Description: This function returns the character of a numeric value.

Data type: Numeric

```
SIGN(50)   ⇨ 1
SIGN(0)    ⇨ 0
SIGN(-50)  ⇨ -1
```

SIN(*par1*)

Description: This function returns, in radians, the sine value of any angle size.

Data type: Numeric

```
SIN(0)          ⇨ 0
SIN(PI()/2) ⇨ 1
SIN(PI())       ⇨ 0
```

SOUNDEX(*par1*)

Description: This function returns the SOUNDEX code of the alphanumeric parameter. A SOUNDEX code consists of four characters. Alphanumeric values that sound roughly the same are converted to identical SOUNDEX codes. The SOUNDEX code is specified according to the following rules:

■ All blanks at the beginning of the parameter are removed.
■ All the following letters are removed from the parameter, provided that they do not appear on the first position: a e h i o u w y.
■ The following values are assigned to the remaining letters:

```
b f p v           = 1
c g j k q s x z   = 2
d t               = 3
l                 = 4
m n               = 5
r                 = 6
```

■ If two linked letters have the same value, the second is removed.
■ The code is broken after the fourth character.
■ If the remaining code consists of less than four characters, it is filled with zeroes.
■ Characters appearing behind a blank are skipped.
■ If the value of the parameter does not begin with a letter, the result is equal to 0000.

Data type: Alphanumeric

```
SOUNDEX('Smith')     ⇨ 'S530'
SOUNDEX('Smythe')    ⇨ 'S530'
SOUNDEX('Bill')      ⇨ 'B400'
SOUNDEX(' Bill')     ⇨ 'B400'
SOUNDEX('Billy')     ⇨ 'B400'
```

SPACE(*par1*)

Description: This function generates a row with blanks. The number of blanks is equal to the value of the numeric parameter.

Data type: Alphanumeric

```
SPACE(1)              ⇨  ' '
SPACE(5)              ⇨  '     '
LENGTH(SPACE(8))  ⇨  8
```

SQRT(*par1*)

Description: This function returns the square root of the value of the parameter.

Data type: Numeric

```
SQRT(225)  ⇨  15
SQRT(200)  ⇨  14.14
SQRT(-5)   ⇨  NULL
```

STRCMP(*par1, par2*)

Description: This function compares the values of two alphanumeric expressions. The result is 0 if the values of the parameters are equal, –1 if the value of the first parameter is smaller, and 1 if the value of the right one is smaller.

Data type: Numeric

```
STRCMP(1,1)  ⇨  0
STRCMP(1,2)  ⇨  -1
STRCMP(2,1)  ⇨  1
```

STR_TO_DATE(*par1, par2*)

Description: This function is the opposite of the DATE_FORMAT function. A certain alphanumeric value is converted to a date or timestamp value through a number of format strings. If the format strings do not fit in the first parameter, the function returns a NULL value as result.

Data type: Date or timestamp

```
STR_TO_DATE('2005 Sun Oct 1st', '%Y %a %b %D')⇨ '2005-10-01'
STR_TO_DATE('2005/11/10', '%Y/%c/%d')           ⇨ '2005-11-10'
```

SUBDATE(*par1, par2*)

Description: This function subtracts an interval (the second parameter) from a date or timestamp expression (the first parameter). See Section 5.13.3, in Chapter 5, for the specification of intervals. If the second parameter is not an interval but a numeric number, SQL assumes that this value represents a number of days.

Data type: Date or timestamp

```
SUBDATE('2004-01-01', INTERVAL 5 MONTH) ⇨ '2003-08-01'
SUBDATE('2004-01-01 12:00:00', INTERVAL 5 DAY)
    ⇨ '2003-12-27 12:00:00'
SUBDATE('2004-01-01', 5) ⇨ '2003-12-27'
```

SUBSTRING(*par1, par2, par3*)

Description: This function extracts part of the alphanumeric value of the first parameter. The second parameter identifies the starting position, and the third one identifies its number of characters. If the third parameter has not been specified, up to the last character is included.

Data type: Alphanumeric

```
SUBSTRING('database',5)      ⇨ 'base'
SUBSTRING('database',10)     ⇨ ''
SUBSTRING('database',5,2)    ⇨ 'ba'
SUBSTRING('database',5,10)   ⇨ 'base'
SUBSTRING('database',-6)     ⇨ 'tabase'
```

SUBSTRING(*par1* FROM *par2* FOR *par3*)

Description: This function extracts part of the alphanumeric value of the first parameter. The second parameter identifies the starting position, and the third one identifies its number of characters. If the third parameter has not been specified, up to the last character is included.

Data type: Alphanumeric

```
SUBSTRING('database' FROM 5)              ⇨ 'base'
SUBSTRING('database' FROM 10)             ⇨ ''
SUBSTRING('database' FROM 5 FOR 2)        ⇨ 'ba'
SUBSTRING('database' FROM 5 FOR 10)       ⇨ 'base'
SUBSTRING('database' FROM -6)             ⇨ 'tabase'
```

SUBSTRING_INDEX(*par1, par2, par3*)

Description: This function looks for the *n*th appearance of an alphanumeric value in the value of the first parameter. The second parameter shows which value must be looked for, and the third parameter returns the number *n*. If the third parameter is positive, the function looks for the *n*th appearance from the left side and returns everything that is found left from that appearance. If the third parameter is negative, the function looks for the *n*th appearance from the right and returns everything that is found right from that appearance.

Data type: Alphanumeric

```
SUBSTRING_INDEX('database', 'a', 3)        ⇨ 'datab'
SUBSTRING_INDEX('database', 'a', -3)       ⇨ 'tabase'
SUBSTRING_INDEX('database', 'data', 1)     ⇨ ''
SUBSTRING_INDEX('database', 'data', -1)    ⇨ 'base'
```

SUBTIME(*par1, par2*)

Description: This function subtracts two time expressions and returns a new time.

Data type: Time

```
SUBTIME('12:59:00', '0:59:00')        ⇨ '12:00:00'
SUBTIME('12:00:00', '0:00:00.001')    ⇨ '11:59:59.999000'
SUBTIME('100:00:00', '900:00:00')     ⇨ '-800:00:00'
```

SYSDATE()

Description: This function returns the system date and system time. If the function is used within a numeric expression, the result is numeric. See the LOCALTIME and LOCALTIMESTAMP functions.

Data type: Timestamp or numeric

```
SYSDATE()        ⇨ '2005-02-20 12:26:52'
SYSDATE() + 0 ⇨ 20050220122652
```

SYSTEM_USER()

Description: This function returns the name of the SQL user.

Data type: Alphanumeric

```
SYSTEM_USER() ⇨ 'root@localhost'
```

TAN(*par1*)

Description: This function returns, in radians, the tangent value of any angle size.

Data type: Numeric

```
TAN(0)        ⇨ 0
TAN(PI())    ⇨ 0
TAN(PI()/4 ⇨ 1
TAN(1)        ⇨ 1.5574077246549
```

TIME()

Description: This function returns the time part of a time or timestamp expression.

Data type: Time

```
TIME('2005-12-08 12:00:00') ⇨ '12:00:00'
TIME('12:13')                    ⇨ '12:13:00'
```

TIMEDIFF(*par1, par2*)

Description: This function returns the amount of time that has elapsed between two time expressions.

Data type: Time

```
TIMEDIFF('12:00:01','12:00:00') ⇨ '00:00:01'
TIMEDIFF('12:00:00','12:00:01') ⇨ '-00:00:01'
TIMEDIFF('23:01:01','22:00:59') ⇨ '01:00:02'
```

TIME_FORMAT(*par1, par2*)

Description: This function transforms a time, date, or timestamp expression (the first parameter) to an alphanumeric value. The second parameter indicates the format of that alphanumeric value, and several special format strings can be used here; see the following table. This function looks like the DATE_FORMAT function; however, all time-related format strings may be used now.

FORMAT STRING	EXPLANATION
%f	Six-digit numeric code for the number of microseconds (000000 up to and including 999999)
%H	Two-digit numeric code for the hour (00 up to and including 23)
%h	Two-digit numeric code for the hour (01 up to and including 12)
%I	Two-digit numeric code for the hour (01 up to and including 12)
%i	Two-digit numeric code for the number of minutes (00 up to and including 59)
%k	One- or two-digit numeric code for the hour (0 up to and including 23)
%l	One- or two-digit numeric code for the hour (1 up to and including 12)
%p	Indication of AM or PM
%r	Indication of the time (in 12 hours) with the format HH:MM:SS followed by AM or PM
%S	Two-digit numeric code for the number of seconds (00 up to and including 59)
%s	Two-digit numeric code for the number of seconds (00 up to and including 59)
%T	Indication of the time (in 24 hours) in the format hh:mm:ss followed by AM or PM
%%	Returns the percentage sign

Data type: Alphanumeric

```
TIME_FORMAT('11:12:13','%h') ⇨ '11'
TIME_FORMAT('11:12:13','%f') ⇨ '000000'
TIME_FORMAT('12:00:00', 'It is now %h o''clock')
   ⇨ 'It is now 12 o'clock'
```

TIMESTAMP(*par1, par2*)

Description: This function transforms the first parameter into a timestamp value. If a second parameter is specified, it should be a time expression, and that is added to the value of the first parameter.

Data type: Timestamp

```
TIMESTAMP('2005-12-08')              ⇨ '2005-12-08 00:00:00'
TIMESTAMP('2005-12-08 12:00:00')     ⇨ '2005-12-08 12:00:00'
TIMESTAMP('2005-12-08 12:00:00', '11:12:13')
                                     ⇨ '2005-12-08 23:12:13'
TIMESTAMP('2005-12-08 12:00:00', '-11:12:00')
                                     ⇨ '2005-12-08 00:48:00'
TIMESTAMP('2005-12-08 12:00:00', '-48:00')
                                     ⇨ '2005-12-06 12:00:00'
```

TIMESTAMPADD(*par1, par2, par3*)

Description: This function adds a certain interval to a date or timestamp expression. The first parameter indicates the unit of the interval, such as days, months, or years, and the second parameter indicates the number of days or months. The third parameter is the expression to which the interval is added. Supported interval units are YEAR, QUARTER, MONTH, WEEK, DAY, HOUR, MINUTE, SECOND, and FRAC_SECOND.

Data type: Date or timestamp

```
TIMESTAMPADD(DAY, 2, '2005-12-08')    ⇨ '2005-12-10'
TIMESTAMPADD(MONTH, 2, '2005-12-08')  ⇨ '2006-02-08'
TIMESTAMPADD(YEAR, -2, '2005-12-08')  ⇨ '2003-12-08'
TIMESTAMPADD(MINUTE, 3, '2005-12-08 12:00:00')
    ⇨ '2005-12-08 12:03:00'
TIMESTAMPADD(FRAC_SECOND, 3, '2005-12-08 12:00:00')
    ⇨ '2005-12-08 12:00:00.000003'
```

TIMESTAMPDIFF(*par1, par2, par3*)

Description: This function calculates the time between two date or timestamp expressions. The first parameter indicates the unit of the interval, such as days, months, or years; the second and third parameters form the two expressions. Supported interval units are YEAR, QUARTER, MONTH, WEEK, DAY, HOUR, MINUTE, SECOND, and FRAC_SECOND.

Data type: Numeric

```
TIMESTAMPDIFF(DAY, '2005-12-04', '2005-12-08') ⇨ 4
TIMESTAMPDIFF(DAY, '2005-12-08', '2005-12-04') ⇨ -4
TIMESTAMPDIFF(YEAR, '1960-12-08', NOW())        ⇨ 45
TIMESTAMPDIFF(MINUTE, '2005-12-08 12:00:00',
    '2005-12-08 12:03:00') ⇨ 3
TIMESTAMPDIFF(FRAC_SECOND, '2005-12-08',
    '2005-12-08 12:00:00.000003') ⇨ 43200000003
```

TIME_TO_SEC(*par1*)

Description: This function transforms a time into a number of seconds.

Data type: Numeric

```
TIME_TO_SEC('00:00:01') ⇨ 1
TIME_TO_SEC('00:16:40') ⇨ 1000
TIME_TO_SEC('23:59:59') ⇨ 83399
TIME_TO_SEC('48:00:00') ⇨ 172800
```

TO_DAYS(*par1*)

Description: This function determines how many days have elapsed between the specified date (the parameter) and the year 0.

Data type: Numeric

```
TO_DAYS('2005-12-08') ⇨ 732653
```

TRIM(*par1*)

Description: This function removes all blanks from the start and from the end of an alphanumeric value (the parameter). Blanks in the middle are not removed.

Data type: Alphanumeric

```
TRIM('database    ') ⇨ 'database'
TRIM('    da ta  ') ⇨ 'da ta'
```

TRUNCATE(*par1, par2*)

Description: This function truncates numbers to a specified number of decimal places.

Data type: Numeric

```
TRUNCATE(123.567, -1)  ⇨  120
TRUNCATE(123.567, 1)   ⇨  123.5
TRUNCATE(123.567, 5)   ⇨  123.56700
```

UCASE(*par1*)

Description: This function converts all lowercase letters of the value of the parameter to uppercase letters. See the UPPER function.

Data type: Alphanumeric

```
UCASE('Database')  ⇨  'DATABASE'
```

UNHEX(*par1*)

Description: This function returns the hexadecimal representation of the parameter. Each pair of characters is converted to the corresponding character.

Data type: Alphanumeric

```
UNHEX('334538')      ⇨  '3E8'
UNHEX('E7')          ⇨  'ç'
UNHEX(HEX('SQL'))    ⇨  'SQL'
```

UPPER(*par1*)

Description: This function converts all lowercase letters of the value of the parameter to uppercase letters.

Data type: Alphanumeric

```
SQL, UPPER('Database')  ⇨  'DATABASE'
```

USER()

Description: This function returns the name of the SQL user.

Data type: Alphanumeric

```
USER()  ⇨  'root@localhost'
```

UTC_DATE()

Description: This function returns the actual UTC date. *UTC* stands for *Coordinated Universal Time*, or Zulu time, or *Greenwich mean time* (GMT). If the function is part of a numeric expression, the result of the function will also be numeric.

Data type: Date or numeric

```
UTC_DATE()        ⇨  '2005-01-01'
UTC_DATE() + 0  ⇨  20050101
```

UTC_TIME()

Description: This function returns the actual UTC date; see the UTC_DATE function. If the function is part of a numeric expression, the result of the function will also be numeric.

Data type: Date or numeric

```
UTC_TIME()                                      ⇨  '2005-01-01'
HOUR(TIMEDIFF(UTC_TIME(), TIME(NOW())))  ⇨  1
```

UTC_TIMESTAMP()

Description: This function returns the actual UTC date and time; see the UTC_DATE function. If the function is part of a numeric expression, the result of the function will also be numeric.

Data type: Date or numeric

```
UTC_TIMESTAMP()  ⇨  '2005-01-01 13:56:12'
```

UUID()

Description: This function generates an 18-byte wide unique code. The abbreviation *UUID* stands for *Universal Unique Identifier*. The first three parts of this code are derived from the system time. The fourth part must make sure that the codes are unique, in case duplicate values can arise because of time zones. The fifth part identifies the server in a certain way. Generating unique values is not guaranteed, but it is most likely that it happens.

Data type: Alphanumeric

```
UUID()  ⇨  '2bf2aaec-bc90-1028-b6bf-cc62846e9cc5'
UUID()  ⇨  '390341e3-bc90-1028-b6bf-cc62846e9cc5'
```

VERSION()

Description: This function returns an identification of the version number of MySQL.

Data type: Alphanumeric

```
VERSION()  ⇨  '5.0.7-beta-nt'
VERSION()  ⇨  '5.0.3-alpha-log'
```

WEEK(*par1*)

Description: This function returns the week from a date or timestamp expression. The value of the result is always a whole number between 1 and 53 inclusive.

Data type: Numeric

```
WEEK('1988-07-29')  ⇨  30
WEEK('1997-01-01')  ⇨  1
WEEK('2000-12-31')  ⇨  53
WEEK(CURDATE())     ⇨  7
```

WEEKDAY(*par1*)

Description: This function returns the number of the day in the week. The result is a number between 0 (Monday) and 6 (Sunday).

Data type: Numeric

```
WEEKDAY('2005-01-01')  ⇨  5
```

WEEKOFYEAR(*par1*)

Description: This function returns the week number belonging to a certain date expression. The result is a number between 1 and 53.

Data type: Numeric

```
WEEKOFYEAR('2005-01-01')  ⇨  53
WEEKOFYEAR('2005-01-03')  ⇨  1
```

YEAR(par1)

Description: This function returns the number of the year from a date or timestamp expression. The result is always a number greater than 1.

Data type: Numeric

```
YEAR(NOW())  ⇨  1998
```

YEARWEEK(par1, par2)

Description: If only one parameter is specified, this function returns the year followed by the week number in the format YYYYWW from a date or timestamp expression. The week number goes from 01 to 53 inclusive. It is assumed that a week starts on Sunday. If a second parameter is specified, it must be the same code as the one used in the WEEK function.

Data type: Numeric

```
YEARWEEK('2005-12-03')    ⇨  200548
YEARWEEK('2005-12-03',0)  ⇨  200548
YEARWEEK('2005-01-02',0)  ⇨  200501
YEARWEEK('2005-01-02',1)  ⇨  200453
```

C | Bibliography

[ASTR80]   Astrahan, M. M., et al. "A History and Evaluation of System R." *IBM RJ 2843*, June 1980.

[BERN97]   Bernstein, P. A., and E. Newcomer. *Principles of Transaction Processing.* (Morgan Kaufmann Publishers, 1997).

[BOYC73a]   Boyce, R. F., et al. "Specifying Queries as Relational Expressions: SQUARE." *IBM RJ 1291*, October 1973.

[BOYC73b]   Boyce, R. F., and D. D. Chamberlin. "Using a Structured English Query Language as a Data Definition Facility." *IBM RJ 1318*, December 1973.

[CATT97]   Cattell, R. G. G., et al. *The Object Database Standard: ODMG 2.0.* (Morgan Kaufmann Publishers, 1997).

[CHAM76]   Chamberlin, D. D., et al. "SEQUEL 2: A unified approach to Data Definition, Manipulation, and Control." *IBM R&D*, November 1976.

[CHAM80]   Chamberlin, D. D. "A Summary of User Experience with the SQL Data Sublanguage." *IBM RJ 2767*, March 1980.

[CODD70]   Codd, E. F. "A Relational Model of Data for Large Shared Data Banks." *Communications of the ACM* 13, no. 6 (June 1970).

[CODD79]   Codd, E. F. "Extending the Database Relational Model to Capture More Meaning." *ACM Transactions on Database Systems* 4, no. 4 (December 1979).

[CODD82]   Codd, E. F. "Relational Database: A Practical Foundation for Productivity." Turing Award Lecture in *Communications of the ACM* 25, no. 2 (February 1982).

[CODD90]   Codd, E. F. *The Relational Model for Database Management, Version 2.* (Addison-Wesley, 1990).

[COOP97]   Cooper, R. *Object Databases: An ODMG Approach.* (International Thomson Computer Press, 1997).

[DARW98]   Darwen, H., and C. J. Date. *The Third Manifesto: Foundation for Object/Relational Databases.* (Addison-Wesley, 1998).

[DATE95]   Date, C. J. *An Introduction to Database Systems Volume I*, Sixth Edition. (Addison-Wesley, 1995).

[DATE97]   Date, C. J., and H. Darwen. *A Guide to the SQL Standard*, Fourth Edition. (Addison-Wesley, 1997).

[DELO95]   Delobel, C., C. Lécluse, and P. Richard. *Databases: From Relational to Object-Oriented Systems.* (International Thomson Publishing, 1995).

[ELMA03]   Elmasri, R., and S. B. Navathe. *Fundamentals of Database Systems*, Fourth Edition. (Addison-Wesley, 2003).

[GEIG95]   Geiger, K. *Inside ODBC.* (Microsoft Press, 1995).

[GILL96]   Gill, H. S., and P. C. Rao. *The Official Client/Server Computing Guide to Data Warehousing.* (Que, 1996).

[GRAY93]   Gray, J., and A. Reuter. *Transaction Processing: Concepts and Techniques.* (Morgan Kaufmann Publishers, 1993).

[GULU99]   Gulutzan, P., and T. Pelzer. *SQL-99 Complete, Really.* (Miller Freeman, 1999).

[ISO87]   ISO TC97/SC21/WG3 and ANSI X3H2. *ISO 9075 Database Language SQL.* (International Organization for Standardization, 1987).

[ISO92]   ISO/IEC JTC1/SC21. *ISO 9075:1992 (E) Database Language SQL.* (International Organization for Standardization, 1992).

[KIM85]   Kim, W., D. S. Reiner, and D. S. Batory (eds.). *Query Processing in Database Systems.* (Springer-Verlag, 1985).

[LANS92]   van der Lans, R. F. *The SQL Guide to Oracle.* (Addison-Wesley, 1992).

[LARO04]   Larose, D. T. *Discovering Knowledge in Data: An Introduction to Data Mining.* (Wiley-Interscience, 2004.)

[MELT01]   Melton, J., and A. R. Simon. *SQL:1999 Understanding Relational Language Components.* (Morgan Kaufmann Publishers, 2001).

[MELT03]   Melton, J., and A. R. Simon. *SQL:1999 Understanding Object-Relational and Other Advanced Features.* (Morgan Kaufmann Publishers, 2003).

[SIMS04]   Simsion, G. C., and G. C. Witt. *Data Modeling Essentials, Third Edition*. (Morgan Kaufmann Publishers, 2004).

[STON86]   Stonebraker, M. *The INGRES Papers: Anatomy of a Relational Database System*. (Addison-Wesley, 1986).

[STON99]   Stonebraker, M., D. Moore, and P. Brown. *Object-Relational Database Servers, the Next Great Wave*. (Morgan Kaufmann Publishers, 1999).

[THOM02]   Thomsen, E. *OLAP Solutions: Building Multidimensional Information Systems*, Second Edition. (John Wiley & Sons, 2002).

[WIDO96]   Widom, J., and S. Ceri. *Active Database Systems, Triggers and Rules for Advanced Database Processing*. (Morgan Kaufmann Publishers, 1996).

[ZLOO77]   Zloof, M. M. *Query By Example*. Proceedings NCC 44. Anaheim, Calif., May 1975 (AFIPS Press, 1977).

Index

Register
Your Book

at www.awprofessional.com/register

You may be eligible to receive:

- Advance notice of forthcoming editions of the book
- Related book recommendations
- Chapter excerpts and supplements of forthcoming titles
- Information about special contests and promotions throughout the year
- Notices and reminders about author appearances, tradeshows, and online chats with special guests

Contact us

If you are interested in writing a book or reviewing manuscripts prior to publication, please write to us at:

Editorial Department
Addison-Wesley Professional
75 Arlington Street, Suite 300
Boston, MA 02116 USA
Email: AWPro@aw.com

Visit us on the Web: http://www.awprofessional.com

About the CD-ROM

System Requirements

The following are the minimum and recommended system requirements for using this book's companion CD-ROM.

Operating Systems

The supplied version of MySQL can be installed on the following 32-bit Windows operating systems: 9x, Me, 2000, XP, or Windows Server 2003. Installing on 2000, XP, or Server 2003 permits you to run the MySQL server as a service. Running the MySQL server as a service is strongly recommended. Generally, you should install MySQL on Windows using an account that has administrator rights.

Contents

The companion CD-ROM contains the following:

- The MySQL database server. The version included is Version 5.0.7 for Windows. You can also download this product free of charge for many other platforms, including Linux, Sun Solaris, FreeBSD, MAC OS, HP-UX, IBM AIX, and Novell NetWare from the Web site www.mysql.com.
- The WinSQL query tool.

Not included on the CD are the SQL examples. They can be downloaded from the Web site www.r20.nl.

Installation and Use

For directions on how to install the products MySQL and WinSQL, and how to install the example tables, see Chapter 3. Also visit the Web site www.r20.nl for additional instructions.

Technical Support

The contents of the companion CD-ROM are provided *as-is* and do not include technical support. For updates, corrections, and discussions on the SQL examples, visit www.r20.nl. For technical support on MySQL or WinSQL, please contact the vendors of those applications.